 ‍ **Fred Leong**
Department of Psychology
Southern Illinois University
Carbondale, Illinois 62901

D0948430

Career Choice
and Development

Duane Brown
Linda Brooks
and Associates

Career Choice and Development

Applying Contemporary Theories to Practice

Second Edition

 Jossey-Bass Publishers

San Francisco • Oxford • 1990

CAREER CHOICE AND DEVELOPMENT
Applying Contemporary Theories to Practice
  by Duane Brown, Linda Brooks, and Associates

Copyright © 1990 by: Jossey-Bass Inc., Publishers
                      350 Sansome Street
                      San Francisco, California 94104
                                &
                      Jossey-Bass Limited
                      Headington Hill Hall
                      Oxford OX3 0BW

Library of Congress Cataloging-in-Publication Data

Career choice and development : applying contemporary theories to
    practice / Duane Brown, Linda Brooks, and associates. — 2nd ed.
        p.   cm. — (The Jossey-Bass management series) (The Jossey-
    Bass social and behavioral science series)
      Includes bibliographical refrences.
      ISBN 1-55542-196-2
      1. Career development.   2. Vocational guidance.   I. Brown, Duane.
    II. Brooks, Linda, date.   III. Series.   IV. Series: The Jossey-
    Bass social and behavioral science series.
    HF5381.C265143   1990
    331.7'02 — dc20   89-28868
                                                                      CIP

Manufactured in the United States of America

The paper in this book meets the guidelines for
permanence and durability of the Committee on
Production Guidelines for Book Longevity of
the Council on Library Resources.

JACKET DESIGN BY WILLI BAUM

SECOND EDITION

Code 9006

A joint publication in
The Jossey–Bass
Management Series
and
The Jossey–Bass
Social and Behavioral Science Series

Contents

ix

Contents

Preface to the Second Edition

The goals of this second edition of *Career Choice and Development* remain the same as those of the first: to promote a fuller understanding of the process of career development and to explore ways it can be facilitated. Similarly, the approach to this task is relatively unchanged: leading authorities present the latest statements on major theories of career development and discuss the practical implications of these theoretical positions. Despite these similarities, some important changes have been made.

First, in an effort to make this edition more comprehensive in its coverage of current theory, we have added three theoretical chapters and deleted one. Thus, in Chapter Eleven, Linda Brooks provides an overview of recent developments in theory. Duane Brown reviews decision-making models in Chapter Twelve, and Douglas T. Hall contributes a chapter on career development theory in organizations (Chapter Thirteen). The chapter by Ginzberg in the first edition has been eliminated, partially to make room for the additions but, more important, because it has had little impact on current career development research or practice. Ginzberg, Ginzburg, Axelrad, and Herma's original statement (1951) had a significant impact on the development of theory and a lesser impact on research; it never had a significant influence on practice. A brief overview of this theory is provided in Chapter One, and readers interested in the history

xiii

of career development theory may consult the original source or the 1984 edition of the present volume.

Second, to further encourage the application of theory to practice, we have added a chapter in which the major contributors discuss their approaches to individual career counseling with the same client, K (Chapter Fifteen). These discussions provide more concrete illustrations of the application of theory to practice. To provide space for this additional chapter, as well as for the three theory chapters already noted, we have eliminated three chapters in the first edition that focused on practice with special populations: the chapters on women and minorities, midlife, and career planning in the workplace.

Nevertheless, because one of our major goals is to expand thinking about the career development of women and ethnic minorities, three new directions in career development theorizing (Chapter Eleven) focus on theories developed to explain the career development of women. Sadly, no similar efforts have been advanced regarding the career development of ethnic minorities. We asked all the contributors to discuss the application of their theories to women and ethnic minorities, but not all complied. As a result, this volume presents advances in our thinking about the career development of women, but no similar advances have been made regarding the career development of ethnic minorities since the publication of the 1984 edition.

In summary, the second edition of *Career Choice and Development* reflects two important changes. First, there is an increased emphasis on theory, with the addition of chapters on decision-making models, recent developments in career development theorizing, and career development theory in organizations. Second, the emphasis on practice has been retained but with a greater focus on the applications of the major theories represented in this book. The result, we hope, is a more comprehensive coverage of theory and better integration of these theories into practical application.

Acknowledgments

We want to begin by thanking those persons who read and reacted so constructively to the first edition. For about five years, we have received from our students and colleagues a continuous flow of suggestions to be considered if we ever developed a second edition. These informal comments and the many formal reviews of the first edition were instrumental in shaping this volume. Nevertheless, the contributions of our distinguished colleagues, who have given decades of their lives to advancing career development, are what have made both the first edition and this one unique. We extend our appreciation to them, both for their direct contributions to this volume and for their enduring contributions to the field.

We also want to thank Susan Cochran, Rebecca Frank, Annette Perot, Karen Thigpen, and Jane Trexler for their invaluable assistance on this project. Karen handled all correspondence with accuracy and good humor, while Jane processed the mountains of material that eventually became this book. Susan, Becky, and Annette assisted with the unenviable task of sorting and compiling the huge reference list that we accumulated from the various contributors. To Karen, Jane, Susan, Becky, and Annette, we can only say that without your efforts, this project might never have come to fruition.

Chapel Hill, North Carolina   Duane Brown
January 1990   Linda Brooks

Preface to the First Edition

≉≉≉≉≉≉≉≉≉≉≉≉≉≉≉≉≉≉≉≉≉≉≉≉≉≉

Career development is, for most people, a lifelong process of getting ready to choose, choosing, and, typically, continuing to make choices from among the many occupations available in our society. Each person undertaking this process is influenced by a great number of factors, including family, personal values and aptitudes, and societal context. Because of the centrality of work in most people's lives, it is important that we strive to understand the career development process and how it can be influenced to benefit individuals as well as the greater society.

The goals of the book are to promote a fuller understanding of the process of career development and to explore ways it can be facilitated. Our primary approach to achieving these goals has been to ask leading authorities in the field to present the latest versions of their theories and then to take the next step — write about the translation of their ideas into practice. The authenticity of the positions set forth in this book and the systematic application of major theories to various aspects of career development are, to our knowledge, unmatched in the literature. Our own chapters, which address important current issues in the field, also emphasize the translation of theory into practice.

One of the unique aspects of this book is that it presents major theorists' most up-to-date ideas side by side in a similar format so that they can be directly compared. Many of the theories discussed in this book have been updated elsewhere as new research and thinking have challenged their authors' original propositions, but those updates are scattered among a variety of sources. This book is designed to function as a primary reference, bringing together in one place the most current ideas of recognized authorities in the field of career development.

Another important aspect of this volume is its emphasis on the practical aspects of career development theory. Authors of the theoretical presentations explicitly discuss the practical implications of their theoretical positions. Moreover, since the volume also contains separate chapters on career counseling with special populations — women and ethnic minorities, midlife career changers, and adults in the workplace — the career practitioner should find a wealth of ideas for new theoretically and empirically based ways to work with these clients.

Each theoretical presentation also includes a section on needed research that will interest those involved in studying career development. These statements can serve as points of departure for future empirical investigations.

Acknowledgments

A volume such as this one obviously involves the cooperation and support of many persons. Without the contributors, the goals of this volume could not have been accomplished. It has been a gratifying and enriching experience to work with this distinguished group of colleagues. Their good humor and continued support, encouragement, and patience are gratefully acknowledged. Our appreciation is also extended to Mary Boston, Lyda Beemer, and Patricia Maynor for their work in producing the manuscript. The counseling psychology students at University of North Carolina, Chapel Hill, and colleagues too numerous to mention who provided informal consultation and support deserve special recognition. We also wish to thank our friends and relatives, who cheerfully bore with us through the development of the manuscript.

Chapel Hill, North Carolina   Duane Brown
April 1984   Linda Brooks

The Authors

Duane Brown is professor of counseling psychology in the School of Education at the University of North Carolina, Chapel Hill. He received his B.S. degree (1959) in education and his M.S. (1962) and Ph.D. (1965) degrees in counseling, all from Purdue University.

Brown, who is a nationally certified career counselor, has focused his scholarly interests primarily on career counseling and career development, but he has also made numerous contributions in other areas, particularly consultation. His scholarly contributions consist of more than sixty articles and book chapters and fourteen books and monographs.

Brown held academic appointments at Iowa State (1965 to 1968) and West Virginia University (1968 to 1973) before joining the faculty at the University of North Carolina, Chapel Hill.

Linda Brooks is associate professor of counseling psychology and coordinator of the counseling psychology program in the School of Education at the University of North Carolina, Chapel Hill. She received her B.S. degree (1962) in journalism from Southern Illinois University, her M.A. degree (1964) in college student personnel administration from Ohio University, and her Ph.D. degree (1973) in counseling psychology from the University of Texas.

        Brook's research and academic interests are in the areas of career development and professional training of counseling psychologists. Brooks has worked as a counseling psychologist in university counseling centers in Colorado, Maryland, and South Carolina. For three years she was director of a career counseling center at Converse College, Spartanburg, South Carolina.

Edward S. Bordin is professor of psychology (retired), University of Michigan, Ann Arbor.

Henry Borow is professor emeritus of social and behavior sciences and counseling psychology, University of Minnesota, Minneapolis.

Douglas T. Hall is professor of organizational behavior in the School of Management, Boston University.

Lawrence Hotchkiss is a research associate at the Decision Resources Corporation, Washington, D.C.

John D. Krumboltz is professor of education and psychology at Stanford University.

Patricia W. Lunneborg is professor of psychology (retired), University of Washington, Seattle.

Anna Miller-Tiedeman is president of the Lifecareer Foundation, Vista, California.

Lynda K. Mitchell is associate professor, Department of Administration and Counseling, California State University, Los Angeles.

Anne Roe is secretary-treasurer of the Simroe Foundation, Tucson, Arizona.

David J. Srebalus is professor of counseling psychology and rehabilitation counseling at West Virginia University.

Donald E. Super is professor emeritus of psychology and education, Teachers College, Columbia University.

David V. Tiedeman is provost of William Lyon University, San Diego.

Stephen G. Weinrach is professor of counseling and human relations, Villanova University.

Career Choice
and Development

Duane Brown

Linda Brooks

1

Introduction to Career Development: Origins, Evolution, and Current Approaches

In the wise choice of a vocation there are three broad factors: (1) a clear understanding of yourself, your aptitudes, abilities, interests, ambitions, resources, limitations and their causes; (2) a knowledge of the requirements and conditions of success, advantages and disadvantages, compensation, opportunities, and prospects in different lines of work; (3) true reasoning on the relations of these two groups of facts.

Parsons, 1909, p. 5

Historical Perspective and Current Challenges

The roots of career development theory and practice can be traced to Frank Parsons, who started the Vocation Bureau in 1908 in Boston. Although Parsons's three-step schema cannot be called a formal theory in the strict sense, his statement does summarize the first conceptual framework for career decision making and thus the first guide for career counselors.

Parsons believed that if a person chose a vocation, rather than merely hunting for a job, the worker's satisfaction and success would increase and the employer's costs and inefficiency would decrease. He developed techniques to help individuals identify their resources, abilities, and interests and match these traits to the "conditions of success in different industries" (Parsons, 1909, p. 8). This emphasis on increasing the success and satisfaction of the individual remains central to career development theory and practice today, but the emphasis on increasing productivity has been of little concern to most theorists.

The historical context of Parsons's approach was the emergence of America as an industrial nation with a concern about how to distribute workers, especially immigrants, across occupations and how to better prepare youth for the adult world of work. Two developments that grew out of this concern were vocational guidance and vocational education programs. Vocational education was developed in response to criticism that public education was too "bookish" and unrelated to the realities of life. Preparing youth for work through vocational education was only part of the picture, however. Vocational guidance programs were developed at the same time to help youth make rational, informed decisions about suitable occupations. Thus, vocational guidance and vocational education became partners in the effort to effectively distribute workers across the occupational structure (Herr and Cramer, 1979).

Because the needs of the marketplace were the predominant concern of the times, the primary emphasis of vocational guidance and education became the study of occupations, rather than the study of the psychological aspects of individual preferences, interests, and values. It was believed that occupational information provided an adequate basis for vocational choice. This occupational model, representing step 2 of Parsons's approach to matching individuals and jobs, dominated the vocational guidance scene until the 1940s.

From 1930 to 1950, various complex economic and social factors emerged that shifted the emphasis from step 2 (occupational information) to step 1 (identification of individual traits) of the Parsonian approach. For example, the Depression produced a need to help retrain dislocated workers and find new jobs for them. World War II resulted in a need to select and train persons for the armed forces. The relatively new technique of factor analysis allowed a psychometrically sophisticated approach to identifying individual aptitudes and traits. From these and other developments came the Minnesota aptitude tests (for spatial relations, clerical aptitude, and so on) and the Army General Classification Tests, as well as occupational-interest inventories, such as those developed by Kuder and Strong (Crites, 1969, 1978b).

These dual emphases on the study of occupations (which resulted in the U.S. Employment Service's publication in 1939 of the *Dictionary of Occupational Titles*) and the study of the individual (which produced the various psychometric assessment instruments) converged in the trait and factor theory of vocational guidance. As will be seen in the next chapter, the trait and factor approach is a more scientific version of Parsons's matching individuals and jobs.

Some contemporary theories of occupational choice and career development have clear roots in the structural tradition begun by Parsons and popularized by such trait and factor adherents as E. G. Williamson. Other psychological theories were also influencing those concerned about occupational choice. The impact of Freud's psychoanalytical theory, the neoanalytical thinking of Erikson, Maslow's needs theory, phenomenology, and behavioral theorizing can be seen in contemporary theories of career choice and development.

In 1951, Ginzberg, Ginzburg, Axelrad, and Herma (an economist, a psychiatrist, a sociologist, and a psychologist, respectively) set forth a radical new psychologically based theory of career development that broke with the static trait and factor theory of occupational choice. They posited occupational choice as a developmental process that occurs over a number of years, a largely irreversible process characterized by compromise because people must balance interests, aptitudes, and opportunity. In their original formulations, they assumed that occupational choice occurred over a number of years but was completed in early adulthood.

Ginzberg (1972) later reformulated this earlier theorizing. In his reformulation, he held that occupational choice continues throughout the life span. He changed his position on the irreversibility of the career development process, and he revised the proposition that occupational choice is necessarily characterized by compromise. In a second revision of the theory, he made the following statement: *"Occupational choice is a lifelong process of decision making for those who seek major satisfactions from their work. This leads them to reassess repeatedly how they can improve the fit between their changing career goals and the realities of the world of work"* (Ginzberg, 1984, p. 180; italics in original).

Ginzberg and his colleagues' (1951) statement provided a revolutionary, albeit psychological, perspective on the career development process. Their introduction of the idea that career choice occurs developmentally stands as a landmark contribution.

The theory developed by Ginzberg and his colleagues had a significant initial impact on our thinking about career development, as was substantiated in Ginzberg's later reformulation (1984). That influence now has ceased, and the theory is primarily of historical interest, but the psychological tradition from which the theory grew still commands center stage in theorizing about career choice and development.

While psychological theories have had a predominant influence on theories of career development, such sociologists as Hollingshead (1949), Reissman (1953) and Sewell, Haller, and Strauss (1957) have studied sociological variables related to occupational choice and status attainment, and some, such as Musgrave (1967), have offered sociologically based theories of occupational choice. Because of lack of reconciliation between these two major approaches, however, theories have tended to be either primarily psychological, focusing on the individual, or primarily sociological, focusing on social variables that influence initial choices and eventual career status. Neither approach to theorizing is very satisfying. One result is that counselors are left without specific theoretical guidelines for helping individuals from the various socioeconomic strata, since most psychologically oriented theories appear to assume that all people

function in the same manner in making career decisions, regardless of social class. Despite this problem and others, theories
and practices of career development have proliferated.

During the 1920s and 1930s, the primary concern of
career counseling was facilitating the occupational choice of white
males. With the civil rights and women's movements of the 1960s
and 1970s and the assertion of national concern for the poor,
the objectives of career development practitioners have shifted
to include not only facilitating occupational choice for these
groups but also helping them deal with the unique circumstances
of their entry into the world of work. Moreover, today's practitioners are challenging organizations to develop new concerns
for the career development of their workers. As greater numbers
of workers change careers at midlife, it becomes evident that
career development services and programs are needed throughout the life cycle. To respond effectively to the diverse career
development needs of individuals in our society, we need, at
the minimum, sound theoretical and conceptual frameworks with
demonstrated practical application.

One goal of this book is to present updated theoretical
statements on the most common approaches to explaining career
development. Another is to translate these theoretical formulations into practical applications for career counseling. Other
goals are to help the reader assess empirical support for the
theories and to identify needed research directions.

We used two criteria in selecting theories for extended
discussion: their current influence on research and practice, and
their implications for building future theory. Of the theories
given extended treatment here, Bordin's (Chapter Five) and
Miller-Tiedeman and Tiedeman's (Chapter Nine) do not meet
the first criterion, but they do have implications for future theory.
Krumboltz's theory (Chapter Six) has numerous implications
for both research and practice, but it seems to be influencing
practice alone. Trait and factor theory (Chapter Two), Holland's
typologies (Chapter Three), Super's formulations (Chapter
Seven), Roe's model (Chapter Four), and the sociological/eco-
nomic perspective (Chapter Eight) are having the greatest influence on research and practice at this time. A number of

theories that may be influential in the future or that are having a limited current impact are also summarized.

To facilitate direct comparison of the theories, each contributor was asked to follow a standard outline. Therefore, the chapters on theory provide an overview, including historical antecedents and philosophical underpinnings; present the major propositions, including (in certain chapters) applications to women and ethnic minorities; review research on the theories' empirical validity; and discuss the practical applications for career counseling (including diagnosis, process, expected outcomes, and use of occupational information). If some contributors elected to omit some of these sections, it was either because they felt that their perspectives on particular issues were obvious or because they believed they had nothing to contribute to given areas.

Organizing a book of this type is difficult at best. In this edition, the task was more difficult because we chose to include, along with the historically important theories of occupational choice and career decision making, some new approaches to theorizing and an overview of models of career decision making. To give the reader a preview of the theories presented in this book, we devised a system that identifies the salient features of groups of theories. Since no one system allows for mutually exclusive categories, the one we use here is arbitrary and risks both oversimplification and misinterpretation. Nevertheless, we hope it will be useful.

Theories of Why Occupations Are Chosen

The theories presented in Chapters Two through Five seek to explain why, but not how, people choose particular occupations. In one way or another, each theory views career choice or attainment as the result of a match between the person and the occupation. Trait and factor theory (Chapter Two), for example, asserts that people seek out jobs with requirements that are consistent with their personality traits. Traits of particular importance are interests and aptitudes. In a variation of this theme, Holland's theory (Chapter Three) sees people as choosing work environments that are congruent with their personality types. Both models place emphasis on observable personality characteristics. In contrast, the theories of Roe (Chapter Four) and Bordin (Chapter Five) stress intrinsic personality needs as the primary determinants of choice. Thus, people select occupations that satisfy important psychological needs.

The Miller-Tiedeman and Tiedeman (Chapter Nine) position represents a major departure from the theories of Holland, Roe, and Bordin in that Miller-Tiedeman and Tiedeman attempt to explain how "careerists" experience their environment and redefine themselves and their environments in the process. It is important that Chapter Nine makes no attempt to set forth causal laws or to define theoretical constructs, in sharp contrast to the other positions presented in this volume.

These approaches (except that of Miller-Tiedeman and Tiedeman, who focus on the continuing interaction) focus on the "person" side of the person-situation equation. The sociological perspective (Chapter Eight), by contrast, stresses the cultural and social determinants of career choice. Social-class boundaries may either facilitate or truncate choice; in any case, they act as a critical filter of the kinds of information, encouragement, and opportunities available to the individual. Thus, the person is steered by socioeconomic factors toward an occupational role that matches his or her social status.

A Theory of Occupational Decision Making

Krumboltz (Chapter Six) has developed a theory of career decision making that is uniquely and primarily based on social learning theory. Moreover, Krumboltz attempts to explain how such factors as gender, ethnicity, and socioeconomic status influence career decision making. Krumboltz, unlike Holland, Roe, Bordin, or the trait and factor theorists, attempts to provide some insight into the decision-making process, as well as into the factors that influence choice.

Theories of Career and Life Development

One of the theories included in this volume is less interested in explaining career choice than in describing the process or evolution of choice. The focuses of this theory are on life stages and the career-related issues and concerns that occur at different developmental stages. Super (Chapter Seven) is concerned about the developmental stages that occur throughout the lifespan. He identifies, in career terms, the developmental tasks of each stage and highlights the importance of self-concept in the selection and implementation of career choice. He also emphasizes the interrelationship of life roles.

Recent Developments in Theory Building

In the first edition, we elected to highlight all theories of occupational decision making and career development that had historical significance. In this edition, some of those theories (for example, Ginzberg, Ginzburg, Axelrad, and Herma, 1951) have been deleted because of their lack of influence or their stage of development, but we have included some emerging theories (Chapter Eleven) that explain various aspects of the occupational decision-making/career development process. In some instances, emerging theories are having considerable impact on research; in others, this is not the case. None is having a significant impact on practice, even though the formulations in the theoretical statements do contain some implications for practitioners. Nevertheless, since one of our purposes in revising this volume was to stimulate research, practice, and theorizing, we have included emerging theories.

Models of Career Decision Making

As already noted, Krumboltz's social learning theory of career decision making focuses both on the factors that shape career choices and on the process of how career decisions are reached. In Chapter Twelve, six models of career decision making are presented that either attempt to describe the process engaged in by the decision maker or suggest ways to improve the process. For the most part, these six models are less complete (hence the use of the term *model*) than Krumboltz's formulations, but the models go into greater detail about the nature of the decision-making process and should therefore be of interest.

Organizational Career Development

Vocational psychologists, career counselors, industrial psychologists, and others have long recognized that the term *career development* is used differently by people who facilitate the careers of those in organizations than it is by people who work in other settings. Not surprisingly, theories have evolved to explain organizational career development. Hall (Chapter Thirteen) differentiates between these two perspectives and discusses the major theories of organizational career development. This chapter was included to give the reader a perspective on how organizational psychologists view career development, as well as to stimulate the development of models that can be used either within or outside organizations.

Applications of Theory to Practice

This volume has a dual thrust—theory and practice—that will be most obvious in the extended treatments of the major theories of occupational choice and career development (Chapters Two through Nine), in the chapter on models of career decision making (Chapter Twelve), and in the chapter on career counseling methods and practice (Chapter Fourteen). In each of these chapters, either the theory presentation is followed by a section on implications for practice or (as in the chapter on career counseling methods and practice) the entire chapter is devoted to practice. In Chapter Fourteen, Brooks attempts to synthesize the implications of the major theories of career development and occupational choice for career counseling. Her chapter addresses such questions as "How do the theories differ in their views of the diagnostic component of career counseling?"

A second totally practice-oriented chapter in this book deals with the case of K, a young woman caught in a career-planning dilemma (Chapter Fifteen). In that chapter, many of the contributors to this volume discuss the case of K from their own theoretical perspectives. In effect, Chapter Fifteen is an extension of the sections on applications to practice found in many of the other chapters.

Chapter Sixteen will be of interest to practitioners, not because it provides practical solutions to concrete problems, but because it examines certain trends and issues related to career development. Should we have separate theories and approaches for minorities? How will occupational displacement affect career counseling? Of course, there are no answers to these questions, but an attempt has been made to identify and delineate facets of central problems.

Over 50 percent of this book is devoted, directly or indirectly, to practical matters, but no encyclopedic attempt has been made in this area; rather, key issues confronting career counselors and career development programmers have been addressed. The result is a series of timely discussions that should be interesting and enlightening.

Philosophical Assumptions and Career Development Theory

Nearly a dozen theories of career development, occupational choice, organizational career development, and career decision making are contained in the chapters that follow. For the most part, the philosophical underpinning of these theories is logical positivism, a position that has dominated the philosophy of science for several hundred years.

The assumptions of logical positivism are relatively straightforward and can be summarized as follows (Collin and Young, 1986; Hoshmand, 1989; Passmore, 1967; Wilber, 1989):

1. People can be separated from their environments for study, and they can be further subdivided for study.
2. Human behavior can be objectively observed and measured and operates in a lawful, linear fashion; cause and effect can be inferred.
3. The traditional scientific method is the accepted paradigm for identifying facts about human behavior.
4. The contexts (environments) in which people operate are considered as neutral or relatively unimportant; thus, the focus of inquiry should be observable actions of human beings.

Increasingly, social scientists are rejecting logical positivism, both on philosophical and scientific grounds. As Wilber (1989) states, logical positivism requires that knowledge be verifiable and thus exclude such areas as art, music, philosophy, and history from the realm of knowledge because they are not, in the strictest sense, verifiable. Wilber goes on to state, *"If they wish to be consistent* logical positivists have to exclude purpose, value, and meaning [from the realm of knowledge] since these also are nonempirical" (p. 332; emphasis in original). Wilber goes on to attack logical positivism, citing Passmore (1967), who states that logical positivism is considered as dead as a philosophical movement can be. Nevertheless, logical positivism is not dead in career development.

In place of logical positivism, a number of social scientists, such as Collin and Young (1986), Hoshmand (1989), and Wilber (1989), suggest the adoption of a phenomenological position. The assumptions of this position are as follows:

1. All aspects of the universe are interconnected; it is impossible to separate figure from ground and subject from object.
2. There are no absolutes; thus, human functioning cannot be reduced to laws or principles, and cause and effect cannot be inferred.
3. Human behavior can be understood only in the context in which it occurs.
4. The subjective frame of reference of human beings is the only legitimate source of knowledge. Events occur outside human beings. As individuals understand their environment and participate in these events, they define themselves and their environment.

Implications for the Reader

Two types of theories are presented in this volume, most of which come from the logical-positivism position. Only one, the theory presented by Miller-Tiedeman and Tiedeman in Chapter Nine, is clearly based on the phenomenological position. Not unexpectedly, theories growing out of logical positivism attempt to establish principles that can explain, predict, and be used as the basis of controlling career development behavior. As such, they are both descriptive and prescriptive. Descriptive theories tend to provide a normative perspective; that is, they attempt to explain the normal course of development. Prescriptive theories offer solutions for remediating career development or dealing with problems of occupational choice.

The phenomenological approach to theory building is neither predictive nor control-oriented; rather, it "uncover[s] the pattern and tendencies of career action as they are commonly understood" (Collin and Young, 1986, p. 848). Collin and Young go on to suggest that there is no single meaning in a career and that the meanings attached to careers cannot be neatly categorized. Meaning can be derived by the person and by someone else, such as a career counselor, in conversation with this person, discussing perceptions about his or her environment and subjective reactions to events.

In studying theories from the logical-positivism and phenomenological positions, the problem for the reader is to shift philosophical gears. This is particularly important in reading Miller-Tiedeman and Tiedeman's chapter because they describe an evolution in their perspective, from logical positivism to phenomenology. It would be a mistake to approach their work, or the work of any other theoretician whose thinking is based on the phenomenological perspective, with the intention of evaluating it by means of logical-positivism criteria, since the two kinds of theorists have different objectives. If one reads each type of theories from the philosophical position of the author, the result will be much more satisfying.

2

Duane Brown

Trait and Factor Theory

Historical Background

In his book *Social Reforms and the Origins of Vocational Guidance,* Stephens (1970) described the industrial, social, and economic climate in this country at the turn of the twentieth century. Most notable among the forces of the time was a growing humanitarianism that had as its focus the Amerian worker. Out of this movement were to come vast reforms in labor legislation, vocational education, and vocational guidance.

Frank Parsons — engineer, lawyer, teacher, and social reformer — is credited with spearheading the vocational guidance movement, although, as Stephens (1970) aptly notes, he did not work alone. Like other humanitarians, Parsons was concerned about the exploitation of workers by the industrial monopolists. This concern led him to propose reforms in business, to prevent exploitation of workers, and in education and other social institutions, to help workers choose jobs that matched their abilities and interests.

Parsons and his colleagues were also concerned about youth. One manifestation of this concern was their study of dropouts in Washington, D.C., and Boston. Another result was the establishment of the Vocation Bureau as an agency with the Boston settlement house (Civic Service House), which was intended to help individuals identify their strengths and determine how these might be used in various jobs (Brewer, 1942). Parsons believed that high schools should provide assistance to all boys and girls to ease the transition from school to work, and he worked until his death, in 1908, to persuade Boston educators to provide this service.

Parsons (1909) outlined a three-part model of career guidance that served as a cornerstone for trait and factor theory, which emerged more fully in the decades that followed. Parsons advocated personal analysis, job analysis, and matching through scientific advising as the basis of occupational choice making. More specifically, he advocated that individuals gain a full understanding of their personal attributes, including both strengths and weaknesses; that they gain a thorough understanding of the conditions for success in given occupations, as well as information about compensation and mobility; and that they apply "true reasoning," based on the information at hand, to the choice-making process.

A number of counselors, educators, and psychologists advocated and expanded Parsons's ideas after his death. The rise of differential psychology, with its emphasis on the identification of traits through scientific measurement, also provided great impetus to his ideas. D. G. Paterson, in particular, developed tests and other psychometric instruments that provided career counselors with tools to conduct the personal analysis necessary for wise choice making. His work and that of others, such as J. G. Darley at the Minnesota Employment Stability Research Institute, became known as the Minnesota point of view, a term often used synonymously with trait and factor theory. One of the Minnesota group — E. G. Williamson — emerged as the major spokesperson for trait and factor theory, although he did not restrict his writings to occupational choice.

Vocational psychologists at the University of Minnesota provided the basis of trait and factor theory by developing numerous special-aptitude tests, personality inventories, and other devices (Paterson and others, 1941). Their work was aimed at helping career counselors get Americans back to work during the Great Depression. These tests were also used by job analysts of the time to replace observational procedures and interviews with workers (Williamson, 1965) in analyzing job demands. One result of their work was the publication by the U.S. Employment Service (1977) of the *Dictionary of Occupational Titles.* The Minnesota group also produced numerous books that provided information about counseling techniques, assessment and diagnostic strategies, and job placement.

Miller (1964), Williamson (1964, 1965), and others have described a movement related to Parsons's work in industrial psychology, work that became a part of the trait and factor tradition. During the early 1900s, industrial psychologists in Europe and in this country used tests as placement tools, validated them, based job analysis on job performance, and explored the relationship between attention and job performance in the Western Electric plant in Chicago. One of the more systematic approaches used by industrial psychologists was the individual psychographic method. Viteles (1932) describes the process by which psychologists used tests, interview data, and observations as the basis of constructing individual psychographs (psychological profiles). The psychograph was used in some businesses as the basis of hiring and job placement.

The Theory

Before we can understand trait and factor theory, we must address several issues: What is a trait? Are traits stable and enduring enough to be useful to those interested in predicting occupational behavior? Can we measure traits effectively?

During the first third of this century (and perhaps even later), traits were assumed to be "enduring psychic and neurological structures located somewhere in the mind or nervous system" (Hogan, DeSoto, and Solano, 1977, p. 255). Because of this assumption, psychologists believed that instruments could be developed to measure the intrinsic qualities of the individual. (It appears that when factor-analytical techniques were used in the study of such traits as intellect, the word *factor* began to be used interchangeably with *trait,* but a factor is actually a form of statistical evidence that a trait exists.) These assumptions are now widely viewed as the *test-trait fallacy* (Mischel, 1968; Tryon,

1979). Psychologists from Thurstone to Jensen have spoken of such traits as intellect as though test scores reflected inner properties of the individual, but the position taken by Tryon (1979) and Anastasi (1983) is that traits are learned entities that have validity only with regard to a specific task or situation. Anastasi (1983, p. 177) states unequivocally that traits "are not underlying entities or causal factors but descriptive categories."

Because traits are learned, they are obviously subject to change as new learning occurs. This has raised questions about the stability and endurance of traits, and the controversy is far from resolved. Nevertheless, the traits of greatest interest to career counselors and vocational psychologists—interests, special aptitudes, and scholastic aptitude—do seem relatively stable (Hogan, DeSoto, and Solano, 1977).

Can traits be measured precisely enough to make their study and use worthwhile? Herr and Cramer (1979, p. 72) obviously think not, for "despite all the trait-and-factor approach has to offer—its statistical sophistication, testing refinement, and technologies application—the resulting prediction of individual success in specific occupations has been discouragingly imprecise." Ghiselli (1973, p. 465) reviewed the literature regarding the predictive power of tests and inventories and concluded that "a coefficient on the order of .30 describes the general validity of tests for training criteria, and one on the order of .20 gives the value of proficiency criteria." Taken alone, these coefficients would tend to support Herr and Cramer's (1979) statement, but Ghiselli goes on to say that these average coefficients do not indicate the true value of tests for the prediction of training and proficiency criteria. The best question to ask is which test maximizes prediction. If this question is asked, tests can be shown to predict training ($r = .47$) and proficiency criteria ($r = .33$) at a substantially higher rate. Hogan, DeSoto, and Solano (1977), echoing Ghiselli's view that average validity coefficients are of little use in evaluating the utility of trait-oriented measures, also cite evidence that validity coefficients exceed .60 in some cases.

Prediction of success is not the only concern of trait and factor adherents. During the last twenty-five years, the focus of thinking has shifted to include construct validity, or the extent to which inference can be drawn about the test taker on the basis of a test score or a battery of scores (Hogan and Nicholson, 1988). For example, when a career counselor administers an interest inventory to a client, the counselor is interested to some degree in how well the inventory predicts job choice and subsequent satisfaction (predictive validity). The counselor is at least equally interested in how that same score can help the client identify his or her own values, preferences for work activities, decision-making style, and way of being perceived by others.

How interested one is in predictive rather than construct validity is likely to depend on the use to which test results will be put. Industrial psychologists involved in designing a personnel selection and placement program will probably be most concerned with predictive validity, while people attempting to facilitate self-awareness will focus more on construct validity.

The researchers who have reviewed trait and factor theory have reached various conclusions about its underlying assumptions and propositions. Some, such as Miller (1964), seem to caricature the ideas; others (Crites, 1981; Klein and Wiener, 1977) are highly sensitive to current thinking. Klein and Weiner's conclusions can be paraphrased as follows:

1. Each individual has a unique set of traits that can be measured reliably and validly.
2. Occupations require that workers possess certain very specific traits for success, although a worker with a rather wide range of characteristics can still be successful in a given job.
3. The choice of an occupation is a rather straightforward process, and matching is possible.
4. The closer the match between personal characteristics and job requirements, the greater the likelihood of success (productivity and satisfaction).

The first two assumptions are relatively clear, and this chapter will not discuss them in greater detail except to point out that other researchers, including Super and Holland, have founded their theories on the ideas that each person has a unique set of traits and that workers must possess certain identifiable characteristics to be successful in particular jobs. Most career development theorists appear to believe that matching of worker to occupation is both possible and desirable.

Trait and factor career counselors have always viewed career choice as a relatively straightforward cognitive process. Williamson (1939), however, recognizes emotional instability as a probable cause of uncertainty in occupational choice. In this situation, Williamson's advice is to help the individual clarify his or own thinking. Williamson's model has little else to offer, beyond this advice, for working with such a client; instruction in problem-solving skills could prove helpful.

Empirical Support

Trait and factor theory is one of the most (if not the most) heuristic of the theories presented in this volume. The technical manuals of the General Aptitude Test Battery (U.S. Employment Service, 1970), the Differential Aptitude Test Technical Manual (Bennett, Seashore, and Wesman, 1974), the Armed Services Vocational Aptitude Battery (U.S. Department of Defense, 1976), and numerous aptitude tests designed to predict clerical facility or mechanical reasoning contain hundreds of studies designed to test trait-oriented ideas. There are hundreds of other studies regarding the use of interest inventories to predict job success and job satisfaction. Some of these studies are relatively insignificant; others, like Strong's (1955) follow-up study, are classics. Such research continues, sometimes with limited results (for example, Johnson's and Hogan's attempt in 1981 to relate interests to effective police performance). One recent study, however, provides results that are more supportive of trait-oriented thinking: Lopez, Kesselman, and Lopez's (1981) trait-oriented approach to job analysis. (This study will be discussed in more detail in the section on practical applications.)

Generally, trait measures have been positively related to job success and job satisfaction. When our best available (not our average) validity coefficients are considered, these measures have been not only positive but also relatively strong. As the situation now stands, trait measures cannot account for more than 36 percent of the variance associated with various criteria, and usually the proportion is less. Nevertheless, as Hogan, DeSoto, and Solano (1977) suggest, a substantial percentage of the remaining variance can probably be attributed to person-by-situation interaction; this position needs further research.

Trait and factor thinking has produced a rich, empirically based literature, but a number of authors have incorrectly concluded that these ideas are no longer viable. Osipow (1983), for example, has suggested that most trait and factor ideas have been absorbed into other theories and that few adherents to the approach remain. Weinrach and Crites have also commented on the decline of trait-oriented ideas. Weinrach (1979b) attributes this decline to rigidity inherent in the idea of matching individuals to occupations and to the rise of Carl Rogers's non-directive philosophy. Crites (1981, p. 49) comments that because many practitioners have not updated themselves, "this approach has gone into incipient decline. It has dissolved into what has been caricatured as three interviews and a cloud of dust."

Counselors who have followed the "three interviews and a cloud of dust" approach never really understood trait and factor theory, for Williamson (1939, p. 55) never advocated a "test and tell" approach: "These clinicians [clinical counselors] are not mere mental testers; they provide professional counseling for complex and difficult problems of . . . adjustment." Of the importance of taking the point of view of students, Williamson writes (1939, p. 45), "There can be no effective personnel program unless administrators and teachers have become enthusiastic advocates of the pupil point of view," and with respect to the techniques used to help students, including tests, Williamson emphasizes that unless such techniques evolve from the pupil's point of view, they will not help the student.

Despite disparaging comments by Crites, Weinrach, and Osipow, the fact is that trait and factor theory occupies center stage in the occupational choice-making literature, partially because of Holland's work, which will be discussed in the next chapter. The theory's continuing relevance is also due in no small part to Bolles (1988), whose best-selling *What Color Is Your Parachute?* is widely used by professionals and laypersons alike. Both Holland and Bolles basically use the trait and factor approach.

No theory or approach yet developed has satisfactorily replaced trait-oriented thinking, whether the concern is work adjustment, career counseling, or personnel selection. There are, of course, competing ideas in all of these areas, and some ideas are more elegant and eloquent than others. Many trait and factor adherents are working in business, industry, research, and career counseling, as will be seen in the following section.

Practical Applications

Career Counseling. For Williamson (1939), counseling is a six-step process of analysis, synthesis, diagnosis, prognosis, counseling, and follow-up. These steps remain essentially intact in all of his later writings (Williamson, 1964, 1965, 1972; Williamson and Hahn, 1940).

Analysis is essentially a data-collection phase and involves gathering information from all appropriate sources, including student files, tests, inventories, interviews, biographies, and so forth. Once data are collected, the counselor must synthesize or summarize the data in a manner that will allow determination of the client's strengths and weaknesses. When this is done, the counselor is ready to complete the diagnosis, a process begun at the outset of analysis.

Crites (1981) has pointed out that the major task of the trait and factor career counselor is diagnosis. For Williamson, diagnosis is a process of analyzing the data and drawing inferences on the basis of judgments about students' strengths and weaknesses. Williamson stresses (1939, p. 47) that both statistical/actuarial and clinical approaches should be used in the diagnostic process but that clinical "hunches" are more likely to be correct "if they grow out of, and follow, a thorough measurement analysis superimposed upon the background of the student's case history."

Diagnosis has two steps: identifying the problem and discovering its causes. Counselors look at the presenting problem and its recurring themes, along with more objective data. Using the same data, they then seek to determine why the client is experiencing the problem. According to Williamson, certain types of problems occur with great regularity, and diagnosis can be enhanced if the counselor anticipated them. Williamson posits four common types of career-choice problems: those that involve no choice, uncertain choice, unwise choice, and discrepancy between interests and aptitudes. Crites (1969) sees diagnostic systems as largely unreliable because independent judges place clients in different categories. He also points out that categories are not mutually exclusive and are rarely exhaustive. Williamson's work shows awareness of these difficulties, and his work also shows that these categories are associated with subtypes of problems and other (personnel) problems. Whatever the difficulties, Williamson's four categories of problems can be viewed as points of departure for the diagnostic process.

Initially, one can diagnose uncertainty about career choice by asking students how certain their choices are or by asking them to estimate their chances of success in their chosen fields. Scales and questionnaires that focus on definitions of choice or on the future may also be helpful. There are now over a dozen scales for career decision making that can also be employed. Reasons for uncertainty may include premature choice, lack of educational adjustment, lack of self-understanding, poor understanding of the world of work, fear of failure, worries about pleasing friends or family members, insecurity about one's aptitude, and a host of other factors.

Students who have made no vocational choice usually present themselves as undecided (and without options) or as having no idea about future careers. The causes of no choice are similar to those of uncertain choice (lack of opportunity to observe jobs and inability to make decisions may be factors in both cases). Students who have made no choice may also have dominant interests in things other than careers, interests that divert them from choosing.

Discrepancy between interests and aptitudes is also a common concern presented to career counselors. This discrepancy is sometimes between stated interests and aptitudes; at other times, it is between measured interests and aptitudes. The causal factors related to this career-choice problem are nearly identical to those already named, although lack of opportunities to develop interests, test aptitudes, and test reality is also significant in this situation.

People have made unwise career choices if there is little evidence to support the likelihood of their success. Williamson (1939) identifies several factors related to unwise choices, including the following:

- Aptitudes that are inappropriate to goals
- Goals that are unrelated to interests
- Personality traits that would make job adjustment difficult
- Choice of an occupation that offers little opportunity for entry
- Choices that are made on the basis of promises of employment from friends or relatives, or because of pressure from parents and others
- Lack of occupational information
- Desire for prestige
- Misconceptions about careers

These are common causes of unwise career choice, as is the lack of opportunity to try jobs out directly.

Once a diagnosis is made, the counselor is ready for prognosis, which Williamson characterizes as quite different from diagnosis. Prognosis is the process by which the counselor forecasts the "future outcome of probable adjustment" (Williamson, 1939, p. 112) of the client, on the basis of the available data and the diagnosis. The question is how successful the student will be in his or her efforts to achieve the established goals. The answer to this question determines the counselor's course of action. If it is determined that the client cannot be successful, counseling follows.

Despite the stereotype of trait and factor counseling as "three interviews and a cloud of dust," Williamson stresses that many interviews may be needed to help students in the choice-making process. He also stresses the need for rapport as the basis of counseling and warns that some of the techniques he proposed may undermine rapport and should be used cautiously. Williamson offers no single rule of thumb for counselors to establish rapport with all clients, but he does emphasize that the counselor needs a good reputation, respect for the client, and kindliness. Throughout Williamson's writings, he characterizes the counseling relationship as one between equals and has referred to the counselor as a friendly authority figure (1972), a position he sees as inescapable, regardless of the counselor's philosophy.

Williamson (1939) outlined numerous counseling techniques to be used with clients who are experiencing the four general types of occupational choice-making problems. For the person who has made an unwise occupational choice, he suggests such direct approaches as recommending against the choice and proposing alternatives. He also suggests that individuals be taught about the decision-making process and that interest inventories and occupational information be employed to broaden clients' horizons. For the student who has made no occupational choice, he recommends vocal free association in addition to direct advising and the use of interest inventories and occupational information. Vocal free association consists of determining possible choices on the basis of objective data and soliciting reactions to job roles by asking, for example, "How would you like to be an engineer?" Whenever a discrepancy between interests and aptitudes occurs, the counselor may want to propose related fields that would be more satisfactory. Williamson also suggests cooperative review of the pros and cons of each occupation being considered. Direct experiences are recommended for clients who have made unwise occupational choices. Tours, tryout experiences, and conferences with successful workers are techniques that may be helpful with this group.

To summarize, Williamson (1939, 1965) recommends a number of counseling techniques designed to help clients explore their personal attributes (tests and inventories, probing questions), discover more about jobs (occupational information, tours, interviews with workers), learn about decision making (explanations, direct teaching), relate jobs to themselves (pros and cons of jobs, occupational information, vocal free association), and take action (direct suggestions, persuasion). Two of these — the use of tests and occupational information in counseling — will be discussed in more detail because of their importance.

Information about oneself has always been viewed by trait and factor advocates as a prerequisite of good choice making. Clarke, Gelatt, and Levine (1965) and Prediger (1974) have reiterated this position. Prediger concludes that there are few alternatives to tests in providing this type of information. Prediger also stresses that the determining factor regarding the value of tests in self-exploration is the skill and humanity of the counselor.

Tests and inventories can serve a number of functions in career counseling. They can allow individuals to compare themselves to a normative group within an educational organization or an occupational group and make estimates of their overall chances of success. This process can be enhanced by the use of expectancy tables built on local data or, in some instances, predictive equations based on regression analyses. Tests can provide new insights not readily available, such as comparing one's interests to successful workers or corroborating the existence of an interest that has been only vaguely stated. Tests can motivate people by exposing previously unconsidered career options. But tests can limit, as well, by discouraging minorities from pursuing academic areas that "appear" out of their reach or by indicating that women are best suited for traditional careers. Interpretation of test results requires that the counselor possess a thorough knowledge of the test, including its psychometric properties; the clinical background to understand the testee; the ability to communicate test results in a straightforward, understandable fashion; and, as Williamson and Hahn (1940) note, a knowledge of the educational and occupational structure that the individual is considering.

Lister and McKenzie (1966) and Biggs and Keller (1982) have provided a number of guidelines for interpreting tests. The client's readiness to accept the information is a primary concern and can be developed by the counselor's demonstrating that the test results will help the client solve his or her problem. If the client clearly has no career choice, a link between resolving this concern and test results needs to be established. Biggs and Keller also suggest that the client be apprised that tests do not measure intrinsic qualities but rather qualities that are learned and that may vary from situation to situation. Biggs and Keller go on to suggest that when clients are provided with test results that they believe can be influenced, they are motivated to change. Tittle (1973) has pointed out that extreme care needs to be taken in interpreting tests to women and minorities. Biggs and Keller's suggestions seem particularly relevant for these groups.

As we have seen, Williamson (1939) advocates a great deal of direct advice based on both statistical data and clinical judgment. This approach suggests a rather passive role for the client. Biggs and Keller (1982) suggest a more active role for the client, to ensure that the information received from tests is being properly evaluated. Evaluation is particularly important because, as Prediger (1974) points out, test results may help clients explore and modify their personal constructs and thus the subjective probabilities that are used in the decision-making process. Meehl's (1954) research, and research that has followed, has dampened enthusiasm for clinical judgment, although the practice is still widespread. Prediger (1974), however, has made a number of pertinent points in this regard. First, he suggests that clients use subjective outcome probabilities in their decision making. Second, he says that tests may help students explore and perhaps modify their value systems and thus the subjective probabilities used in decision making. Third, he states that the client must be the ultimate predictor, on the basis of what are more or less continually shifting perceptions, because of the client's experience, of which tests are a part.

Trait and factor approaches to test interpretation have traditionally focused on actuarial approaches — that is, predicting the likelihood of success on the basis of similarities between the testee and occupational incumbents. Prediger (1971, 1974) suggests a second approach: the discriminant-centaur model (Tiedeman, Rulon, and Bryan, 1951). As Prediger (1974) indicates, this approach to test interpretation makes no attempt to predict success but attempts to identify jobs that are occupied by people similar to the client. The Strong Vocational Interest Blank uses this approach. Prediger's (1974) point is that the regression approach indicates high probability of success in occupational groups that include few people similar to the client. This is particularly problematic when one considers the relationship of job satisfaction to job tenure. Prediger suggests that one solution is to identify occupations that include people similar to the client and then use the regression approach to consider the likelihood of the client's success.

Williamson (1939, 1965) recognizes certain basic uses of occupational information: informing clients about occupations; providing reality-testing experiences; motivating clients to conduct continued exploration, pursue continued education, or alter inappropriate career choices. Most career counselors now recognize the importance of using occupational information, but, as Magoon (1964) cynically observes, a visitor from another planet might conclude that occupational information is classified: our clients have to go through some rather unusual rituals to get to the material, and many consider it unreadable when they do manage to obtain it. We have also placed more emphasis on getting clients to seek information that on teaching them what to do with the information once they have found it. Like Williamson, counselors seem to assume that the intrinsic value of the occupational information is so evident as to require no explanation of its use.

The most common way of providing occupational information is through the printed word, although it is often uninteresting to clients. Magoon (1964) and Laramore (1968, 1971) have demonstrated that brief tape recordings and films can enhance the interest of people seeking occupational information. Williamson advocates direct contact with workers or job tryout, if possible, as a means of gaining firsthand occupational information, a position echoed by Bergland (1974). In the absence of direct tryout opportunities, simulation experiences are also possible in some instances (Herr and Cramer, 1979).

The actual selection and use of occupational information depends on many factors. According to Pritchard (1962), the needs of clients and the availability of such resources as occupational files, film strips, and work settings are major determinants of the materials that will be used. The type of problem being addressed will also be a major determining factor (for example, a monograph or filmstrip may be sufficient for the junior high schooler just beginning to explore automechanics). For undecided clients, direct experience with the worker and the workplace may be needed to provide reality testing. Direct experience may also be needed to confirm choices or to dissuade students who have made what appear to be unwise choices. Therefore, the decision of what materials to use, when to use them, and how to use them represents a complex problem.

With regard to materials to be used, the criteria of effectiveness and efficiency must be considered. Efficiency is defined here in terms of the time clients must spend getting the necessary information. Obviously, studying materials that are already available from the counselor is more efficient than undergoing a six-week internship. Efficiency must be considered in the light of effectiveness, however: to what extent will the information provide the necessary data for decision making? Only the student can answer this question.

The choice of when to use occupational materials quite obviously depends on the stage of the counseling session and the readiness of the client. The clinical judgment of the career counselor must be the guide in this area.

How to use materials is also a rather complex matter. Trait and factor theory emphasizes that the basic use of occupational information is in allowing clients to find occupations that match their abilities and needs. Parsons (1909) has also stressed that the individual should get information about working conditions and mobility. To this, Prediger (1974) would add that the information should also focus on the type of person in the occupation, so that comparisons can be drawn between the client's personal characteristics and those of occupational incumbents. Either material that contains this information must be presented or counselors must teach clients how to secure it from existing sources (because few single types of occupational material contain the full range of information that clients need, the latter approach appears to hold more promise).

Williamson (1939, 1965) recognizes that, regardless of the techniques employed, the outcome of counseling will not always be positive. The client may make a tentative occupational choice, or the problem may persist, either because diagnosis is inaccurate or incomplete or because counseling has been ineffective. In either case, the appropriate course is referral. In Williamson's view, the effective career counselor has a number of backup resources (other career counselors, persons who are knowledgeable about certain occupations, a special collection of printed matter that discusses problems of career adjustment, and so forth) that can be used as referral resources. In some instances, the outcome of the referral will be termination; in others, it will be interruption of the process.

If the client develops a tentative occupational choice, then the counselor often functions quite directly to help him or her implement that choice. The counselor may find a suitable preparation experience, identify employment opportunities, or teach the skills needed to secure the job and hold it.

Follow-up is the final step of the counseling process. Essentially, it involves determining whether the course of action established as a result of counseling is the correct one, in the student's view. If the results have been satisfactory, then no further steps are necessary. If desirable results have not been obtained, the process may have to be reinitiated.

Work Adjustment. Career counselors have long been criticized for placing too much emphasis on the choice maker and not enough on the object of the decision-making process: the job. The theory of work adjustment, first published twenty-five years ago (Dawis, England, and Lofquist, 1964) and elaborated and commented on in a number of subsequent publications (Dawis, Lofquist, and Weiss, 1968a, 1968b ; Dawis and Lofquist, 1976; Lofquist and Dawis, 1969, 1972), addresses this issue by means of a trait-oriented approach.

The originators of the theory of work adjustment posit that "each individual seeks to achieve and maintain correspondence with his (her) environment" (Dawis, Lofquist, and Weiss, 1968b, p. 3). While recognizing that each individual exists in a number of environments, they have focused on work because it is a major environment of virtually every life. Correspondence occurs when the individual and the environment are "co-responsive" — that is, work meets the needs of the individual, and the individual meets the demands of the work environment. Correspondence is not the result of a one-time match; rather, it is a dynamic process because both the needs of the individual and the demands of the job change. If correspondence is maintained, the result is job tenure.

Each individual possesses certain needs that he or she expects to have fulfilled on the job. Individuals also have abilities that can be used to perform job duties. These needs and abilities collectively make up the "work personality." The workplace can be described in terms of its ability requirements and its potential to meet needs (Dawis, Lofquist, and Weiss, 1968a; Lofquist and Dawis, 1969). When the worker meets the demands of the situation, there is reinforcement. The result is satisfaction for the worker and satisfactory ratings from the employer. If an individual's needs change and are not satisfied, there is dissatisfaction. Similarly, if the demands of the job change so that the individual no longer possesses the ability to perform adequately, the result is likely to be termination. The entire work-adjustment process is depicted in Figure 2.1.

Vocational psychologists at the University of Minnesota have produced a number of instruments that permit vocational counselors to use work-adjustment theory. The Minnesota Satisfaction Questionnaire (MSQ) was developed to measure individual needs that could be met through work (Weiss, England, Dawis, and Lofquist, 1967). The inventories contain twenty scales, including the following:

1. Activity—being able to keep busy all the time.
2. Compensation—my pay and the amount of work I do.
3. Creativity—the choice to try my own methods of doing the job.
4. Security—the way my job provides for steady employment.
5. Supervision—technical—the way my boss handles workers [Weiss, England, Dawis, and Lofquist, 1967, pp. 1–2].

The MSQ directs workers to indicate how satisfied they are with various aspects of their jobs. Scores are then converted to percentiles and compared with normative data to provide a measure of job satisfaction.

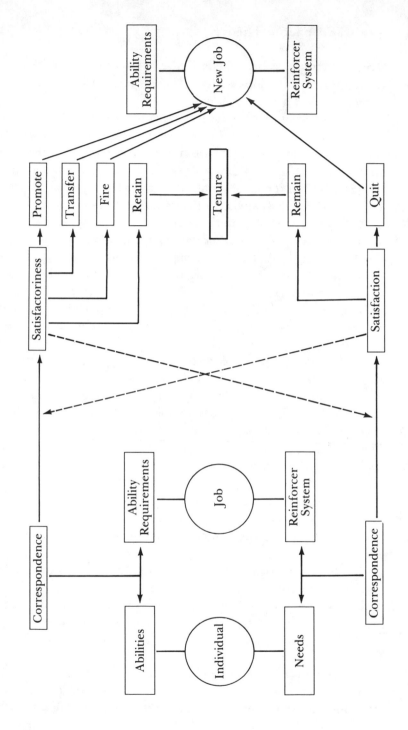

Figure 2.1. Lofquist and Dawis's Conceptualization of the Work-Adjustment Process.

Job satisfactoriness is measured by the Minnesota Satisfactoriness Scales (MSS) (Gibson, Weiss, Dawis, and Lofquist, 1970), developed to measure job performance. This measure consists of ratings on job performance, conformance, dependability, and personal adjustment, as rated by supervisors. Along with the MSQ, the MSS can provide an indication of correspondence.

Other tests and inventories are also important. Abilities are measured by the General Aptitude Test Battery (U.S. Department of Labor, 1979b) and vocational needs by the Minnesota Importance Questionnaire (Weiss, England, Dawis, and Lofquist, 1967). Theoretically, at least, these two together are indicators of the work personality. Similarly, two measures — the Occupational Aptitude Pattern-Structure (U.S. Department of Labor, 1979a) and the Occupational Reinforced Patterns (Rosen and others, 1972) — are used to measure work environment. The first is a list of aptitudes (abilities required by a number of jobs), and the second asks employees and supervisors to rate the reinforcement patterns associated with particular jobs. The interrelationships of these measures are shown in Figure 2.2.

Lofquist and Dawis (1972) report use of the work-adjustment theory in the selection and placement of vocational-technical students, in the vocational assessment and counseling of disadvantaged University of Minnesota employees, and, most extensively, in the Minnesota Division of Rehabilitation's Vocational Assessment Program (they also report that a follow-up study of participants in the latter effort has yielded positive data regarding the value of the approach). They include an annotated bibliography of forty-seven research reports and twenty-nine monographs on work adjustment, and they list forty dissertations stimulated by the theory of work adjustment (these works all appeared during or before 1972).

Also of practical concern is a test, used in a self-directed counseling program, that is based on the theory of work adjustment (Vandergoot and Engelkes, 1977). Although Vandergoot and Engelkes found that people assigned to the self-directed program generally fared no better than those assigned to career

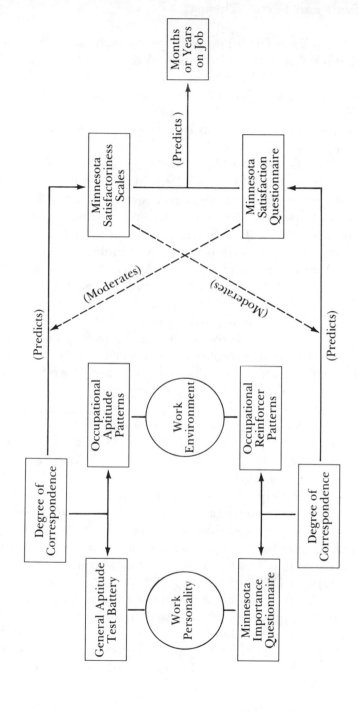

Figure 2.2. The Theory of Work Adjustment in Operational Terms.

counselors, they conclude that their self-directed approach may be a more efficient way of providing counseling services.

Research and writing have also continued to refine both the theory and the instruments developed to operationalize its constructs. Shubsachs, Rounds, Dawis, and Lofquist (1978) conducted a factor-analytical study of the variables related to reinforcement in the work setting. They conclude that self-reinforcement, reinforcement from the workplace and the organization, and reinforcement by means of altruism account for most instances of reinforcement. In another factor-analytical study, Lofquist and Dawis (1978) conclude that the twenty-one needs listed in the Minnesota Importance Questionnaire can be reduced to six value dimensions: safety, comfort, aggrandizement, altruism, achievement, and autonomy.

The theory of work adjustment continues to be defined by two of its originators (Dawis and Lofquist, 1976). They posit that certain aspects of individual personality result in greater or lesser ability to develop "co-responsiveness." Certain individuals possess a personality-style dimension called *activeness*. People with this style dimension act on their work environments to increase correspondence. Others possess a style dimension — *reactiveness* — that is characterized by changes in "the expression or manifestation of the work personality to increase correspondence" (Dawis and Lofquist, 1976, p. 57). Two other personality-style dimensions that influence correspondence are *celerity* and *flexibility*. Celerity refers to the speed with which the individual acts to increase correspondence, and flexibility involves tolerance for "discorrespondence." Dawis and Lofquist conclude that these ideas need more testing before conclusions about their utility can be reached.

Minorities and Women. Trait and factor theory is as applicable to women and minorities as it is to white males, but the instruments selected to measure traits must be carefully chosen to avoid invalid discriminatory information. It has been established, for example, that intelligence tests discriminate against blacks, bilingual groups, and others whose cultures do not approximate that of middle-class white America (see

Anastasi, 1982, for a fuller discussion of this issue). Therefore, these tests must be used carefully, if at all. The now famous *Griggs* v. *Duke Power Company* Supreme Court decision makes it unlawful to use tests for job screening unless there is clear evidence that they are related to job performance.

Interest inventories have also been criticized because of the possibility that they are constructed to relate women's scores to traditionally female careers and men's scores to traditionally male careers. One result of this controversy is the National Institute of Education's guidelines to help users determine whether interest inventories are sex-biased (the guidelines appear in most basic measurement books and can be obtained from the U.S. Department of Education). For a fuller discussion of these issues, see Tittle and Zytowski (1978).

Ethical, moral, and legal considerations demand that tests be selected carefully and used judiciously. They can provide valuable information if used by skilled professionals. Some would have us discard tests altogether; in doing so, however, we would eliminate one important source of information that can be used to help clients (Anastasi, 1982).

Employers have been under increasing pressure by government agencies to demonstrate that their selection procedures provide equal opportunity for employment. Lopez, Kesselman, and Lopez (1981) believe that their threshold traits analysis (TTA), based on trait-oriented ideas, can serve as a basis of equitable personnel decisions. The first step in the development of the TTA was task analysis, which involved administering questionnaires asking job incumbents to weight the importance of frequency of occurrence of factors that indicate whether a task is related to a certain job. Each questionnaire statement is assigned to a task that is linked to a trait. Then, workers and supervisors are asked to rate the relevance and level of preference needed for job performance of each task identified.

In the TTA approach, traits are presumed to fall into one of five domains: social, motivational, learned, mental, and physical. Problem solving is seen as a trait in the mental domain that is related to the job function of information processing. Problem solving is also divided conceptually into four increasingly complex levels, which can be observed and verified through job analysis. Paper-and-pencil tests have been developed to predict the criterion. Although the predictive validity coefficients in TTA have not been strong (none exceeded .45), the authors nevertheless believe that TTA shows promise for selecting personnel.

Career Guidance Programs in Schools. For about fifteen years, the Hawaiian Department of Education, in collaboration with Ashiya University (Japan), has been administering a career development program based on trait and factor theory (Inaba, 1982). The program aims to improve students' ability to understand themselves, increase their understanding of job requirements, help them relate self-knowledge to occupational requirements in making job choices, and provide work experiences as one source of occupational information. Each year, students are given the Fukuyama Profile (F Test), and their progress is monitored in these areas. Feedback is provided to students, and curricular and guidance efforts are mounted to correct deficiencies uncovered by assessment. This model rests squarely on trait and factor theory and points to the continuing influence of the theory in a variety of settings.

At the Fifth International Conference on Vocational Guidance, numerous speakers (Inaba, 1987; Nishida, 1987; Rangel, 1987; Weingart, 1987; Zenke, 1987) reported on the application of trait and factor theory to career exploration programs for junior and senior high school students. They also described F Test–based measurement of students' progress toward such goals as ability to choose methodically from among occupations. Inaba (1987) reported on programs in Hawaii. Rangel (1987) focused on a Birmingham, Alabama, pilot program. Weingart (1987) described a similar effort in New York City. Zenke (1987) reported on the results of a pilot program in East Germany, and Nishida (1987) examined development in Japanese junior high school students of the ability to select occupations. Trait and factor approaches are alive and well in schools, as well as in other settings.

Computerized Career-Guidance Systems

Computerized counseling and career-guidance systems are increasingly popular. Some, like DISCOVER (published by the American College Testing Corporation), incorporate ideas external to trait and factor thinking but ultimately fall back on the model of matching individuals to the characteristics of occupations. Others (for example, SIGI, CHOICES, GIS, and CVIS) are squarely based on traditional trait and factor thinking. In SIGI (Student Interactive Guidance and Information System, published by Educational Testing Service), the user identifies work values and calls up a data base about jobs related to those values. In CHOICES, the user either estimates his or her traits or takes actual tests and inventories. Once these data are complete, the user selects one of four routes to occupational information.

It is also noteworthy that many of what were formerly paper-and-pencil interest and personality inventories are now available in computer-administered versions. People who want rapid results can simply take the tests on their computer and get their scores. In some instances, they can get detailed interpretations as well.

Stephen G. Weinrach
David J. Srebalus

Holland's Theory of Careers

Background of the Theory

John L. Holland traces his interest in the theory of careers back to his military experience as an induction interviewer between 1942 and 1946. He hypothesized at the time that people could be classified into a relatively small number of types. His subsequent experience as a counselor to students at Case Western Reserve University (1950 to 1953) and to physically disabled and psychiatric patients at the Perry Point, Maryland, Veterans Administration Hospital (1953 to 1956) only reinforced this then unpopular belief. His recollections of this period are of frustration with the tentative nature of the relationship between in-

Note: The authors wish to express their appreciation to John L. Holland for his assistance in the preparation of this chapter. Portions of this chapter have been adapted and reprinted from Stephen G. Weinrach (ed.), *Career Counseling: Theoretical and Practical Perspectives,* copyright 1979, McGraw-Hill, Inc., and are used with the permission of McGraw-Hill Publishing Company. Portions of this chapter have been quoted, adapted, and reprinted from John L. Holland, *Making Vocational Choices: A Theory of Vocational Personalities* and *Work Environments,* 2e, © 1985, pp. 1–33. Adapted/reprinted by permission of Prentice Hall, Inc., Englewood Cliffs, New Jersey.

terest measurement and occupations, on the one hand, and with the proliferation of cumbersome occupational classification systems, on the other (Weinrach, 1980a).

Holland, like most practitioners at the time, used the popular Strong Vocational Interest Blank (SVIB), which required machine scoring, and the Kuder Vocational Preference Record, which required the counting of pinholes. He became impatient with these scoring practices and so, as a lark, he started interpreting a set of hand-scoring keys for the SVIB. The formulations for his Vocational Preference Inventory (VPI) (Holland, 1985b) evolved from his review of the more than thirty SVIB scales (Weinrach, 1980a). He developed the notion of an environmental component from reading the work of Murray (1938) and Linton (1945) while a graduate student at the University of Minnesota.

When Holland was at the University of Minnesota, during the late 1940s and early 1950s, pioneering work in vocational psychology was being conducted by John Darley, Ralph Berdie, and Donald G. Paterson. The Minnesota point of view is synonymous with trait and factor counseling. Although the trait and factor approach and Holland's theory are in some respects similar, Holland's work represents a digression from the work of his teachers.

Holland's original theory (1959) was to undergo a series of major and minor revisions, its most recent statement completed in 1985 (Holland, 1985a). The theory's basic reliance on a typology for personalities and work environments remained constant while new concepts and reformulations of the relationships among concepts clarified and expanded the theory. Over his long career, Holland has credited numerous individuals for their contributions to his work. In fact, trademarks of his career have been expansive collaboration with others, the welcoming of criticism, and the sponsorship of colleagues as they have tested his theory through research.

Holland and others have carefully operationalized the theory's important constructs through the development of devices that have practical as well as theoretical value. They include the Vocational Preference Inventory (VPI) (Holland, 1985b), the Self-Directed Search (SDS) (Holland, 1985c), My Vocational Situation (MVS) (Holland, Daiger, and Power, 1980), and the Vocational Exploration and Insight Kit (VEIK) (Holland and others, 1980a). A major achievement has been the translation of the *Dictionary of Occupational Titles* (U.S. Employment Service, 1939) into the *Dictionary of Holland Occupational Codes* (Gottfredson, Holland, and Ogawa, 1982).

Holland intends his theory to explain the everyday questions people ask about their careers, especially regarding the career decisions they must make. He is interested in finding explanations for the personal and environmental characteristics related to stability and career change. Intimately tied to these questions is a strong commitment to finding effective methods for assisting people with career problems. Holland has preferred to limit his theory by basing it on "simple, inexpensive, practical definitions and measures" (Holland, 1985a, p. 7). While more elegant and complex theorizing may increase explanatory power, Holland thinks it results in too cumbersome a tool for actual career assistance. Instead, symmetry added to simplicity results in a theory with the greatest appeal and application. Thus, we will see parallel sets of ideas applied both to people and to environments. The theory is evaluated not only according to the results of empirical research but also according to the extent of its acceptance by practitioners and the public.

Holland's theory of careers (1973a, 1985a) is based on the assumption that, since vocational interests are one aspect of what is commonly called personality, the description of an individual's vocational interests is also a description of the individual's personality. Data obtained from interest inventories have traditionally been used in research on interest measurement and vocational counseling, and such data have been viewed as rather restricted in their application. Nevertheless, they do tell us much about an individual's self-concept (Bordin, 1943; Super, 1972), life goals (Baird, 1970), and originality (Holland, 1963a). Personality traits are identified by preferences for school subjects, recreational activities, hobbies, and work; and vocational interests can be viewed as an expression of personality.

Holland's theory is structural-interactive because it provides explicit links among various personality characteristics and corresponding job titles and because it organizes the massive number of data about people and jobs. Holland (1982a, p. 2) describes what the different structural-interactive approaches have in common: "(1) The choice of an occupation is an expression of personality and not a random event, although chance plays a role. (2) The members of an occupational group have similar personalities and similar histories of personal development. (3) Because people in an occupational group have similar personalities, they will respond to many situations and problems in similar ways. (4) Occupational achievement, stability, and satisfaction depend on congruence between one's personality and the job environment."

The Theory

Holland's work on personality focuses on the study of types (typology). He contends that each individual, to some extent, resembles one of six basic personality types. The more one resembles any given type, the more likely one is to manifest some of the behaviors and traits associated with that type. Just as there are six types of personalities, there are six types of environments, which, like personalities, can be described according to certain attributes or characteristics. *Environments are characterized by the people who occupy them.* For example, the personality type of those who work in a school (teachers) differs from that of people who work in an office (say, file clerks). Environmental type is assessed by a survey of its occupants.

Assumptions. Four basic assumptions underlie Holland's (1985a) theory:

1. *"In our culture, most persons can be categorized as one of six types: realistic, investigative, artistic, social, enterprising, or conventional"* (p. 2). The acronym RIASEC is helpful for remembering the names and order of the six types. The use of types represents an ideal to which each individual can be compared. The manner

in which an individual chooses to relate to the environment indicates his or her type.

2. *"There are six kinds of environments: realistic, investigative, artistic, social, enterprising, or conventional"* (p. 3). For the most part, each environment is populated by individuals of the corresponding personality type. For example, more realistic individuals than social individuals are found in realistic environments. As people congregate, they create environments in which individuals of certain types dominate, and the environments thus created can be identified in the same manner as the individuals who dominate them.

3. *"People search for environments that will let them exercise their skills and abilities, express their attitudes and values, and take on agreeable problems and roles"* (p. 4). This assumption is well expressed in the saying "Birds of a feather flock together."

4. *"Behavior is determined by an interaction between personality and environment"* (p. 4). Knowledge of a person's personality and of his or her work environment can predict such important outcomes as career choice, job changes, vocational achievement, and so forth. Holland's theory attempts to describe people as well as environments.

Six Types. Holland (1966) originally believed that the individual could be characterized as belonging to a single one of the six types. In his revisions of the theory, however, Holland (1973a, 1985a) suggests that while one of the six types usually predominates in people, there are also *subtypes,* or *personality* patterns, that provide more complete descriptions. Such patterns profile individuals according to the typology. A person's complete profile would include characteristics of all six types, but subtypes are developed on the basis of the three most prevalent types found in the individual. Thus, a subtype called SAE would describe a person who has social, artistic, and enterprising traits, in that order. The Holland profiles are called three-letter codes and have become a kind of shorthand for characterizing people as well as occupations.

The three-letter code is useful because individuals use a wide range of strategies for coping with their environments, and those many coping strategies fall within the boundaries of two or more types. Artistic and realistic types, for example, cope differently. Heredity and a variety of cultural and personal forces contribute to the development of elements from each of the six personality types.

Characteristics associated with each type and subtype include likes as well as dislikes. Members of each typological group tend to approach certain kinds of activities and avoid others. According to one's values, the characteristics used to define each type and subtype (conforming versus nonconforming, rational versus emotional, practical versus impractical, attention-getting versus shy) may or may not seem flattering. A complete description and explanation of the types can be found in Holland (1985a); a brief description of the six types follows.

The *realistic* individual prefers activities that involve the systematic manipulation of machinery, tools, or animals. Such an individual may lack social skills. A typical realistic occupation is that of machinist.

Investigative people tend to be analytical, curious, methodical, and precise. Investigative individuals often lack leadership skills. A typical investigative occupation is that of biologist.

Artistic individuals tend to be expressive, nonconforming, original, and introspective. Artistic individuals may lack clerical skills. Decorators and musicians are artistic types.

Social individuals enjoy working with and helping others but avoid ordered, systematic activities that involve tools and machinery. Social types tend to lack mechanical and scientific ability. Bartenders, funeral directors, and counselors are all social types.

Enterprising individuals enjoy activities that entail manipulating others to attain organizational goals or economic gain, but they tend to avoid symbolic and systematic activities. Enterprising individuals often lack scientific ability. Salespeople, office managers, and lawyers are enterprising types.

Conventional types enjoy systematically manipulating data, filing records, or reproducing materials. They tend to avoid artistic activities. Secretaries, file clerks, and financial experts are conventional types.

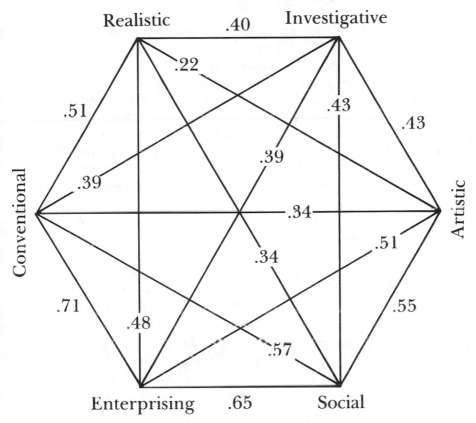

Figure 3.1. A Hexagonal Model for Interpreting
Interclass and Intraclass Relationships.

Source: Crabtree, P. D. "A Test of Holland's Hexagonal Model of Occupational
Classification Using a Rural High School Population." Unpublished doctoral
dissertation, Ohio University, 1971.

The Hexagon. Figure 3.1 graphically represents the relationships among the constructs in Holland's theory. Its use is
essential to understanding the theory, instruments, and classification system. Each of the six types, in the order just presented,
appears on one point of the hexagon. One of the uses of the
hexagon is to show psychological similarity across types. If the
six-sided figure were drawn to scale according to the strength

of the correlations (degree of similarity across types), it would be a misshapen polygon, not a hexagon.

Five Key Concepts. In addition to the four basic assumptions, Holland (1973a) introduces five key concepts:

1. *Consistency:* This concept applies to personality as well as to environmental types. Some pairs of types have more in common than other pairs do; for example, artistic and social types have more in common than investigative and enterprising types. One of the main functions of the hexagon is to define the degree of personality consistency. The closer the types that figure in an individual's personality appear on the hexagon, the more consistent the individual is said to be. For example, the realistic individual who expresses interest in investigative and conventional activities (RIC) is considered to be more consistent than the realistic individual who expresses a preference for enterprising and social activities (RES). The simplest way to operationalize consistency is to use the first two letters of a person's Holland code (Holland, 1985a). High consistency is seen when the first two letters are adjacent on the hexagon (for example, RI or SE). Medium consistency is seen when another letter on the hexagon stands between the first two letters of the person's code (for example, RA or SC). Low consistency is seen when the first two letters of the code are separated by two intervening letters on the hexagon (for example, RS or AC).

2. *Differentiation:* Some people or environments are very pure; that is, they show great resemblance to a single type and less resemblance to other types. Other people or environments show relatively equal resemblance to several types. An individual or an environment that showed equal resemblance to all types would be considered undifferentiated, or poorly defined. Differentiation for people is determined by their SDS (Holland, 1985c) or VPI (Holland, 1985b) profiles. Scores for all six types are used to operationalize the most simple definition of differentiation: one subtracts the lowest score from the highest score for an index (Holland, 1985a).

3. *Identity:* This is the concept most recently added to Holland's theory, and it is considered a secondary construct to

support both the formulations for the types and those for the environments (Holland, 1984). For people, identity is defined as the possession of a clear and stable picture of one's goals, interests, and talents. For environments, identity is defined as the organization's clarity, stability, and integration of goals, tasks, and rewards. The Vocational Identity scale of MVS (Holland, Daiger, and Power, 1980) is used to measure this construct for people. For example, people with low scores on this instrument have many, as opposed to few, occupational goals. Environmental identity is inversely related to the number of different occupations in a setting; for example, an elementary school may comprise five occupations, and so that setting would have an identity of 1/5, or 20.

4. *Congruence:* "Different types require different environments" (Holland, 1985a, p. 5). There is congruence when individuals work or live in an environment whose type is identical or similar to their own types. When an artistic individual, however, works or lives in a conventional environment, there is incongruence. Individuals tend to flourish in environments that provide the kinds of rewards that are important to them; for example, social types prefer the rewards that social environments offer. The hexagon can be used to determine the degree of congruence between an individual's type and environment. A perfect fit would be a realistic type in a realistic environment. The next-best fit, or the next-highest degree of congruence, would be a personality type that is adjacent to an environment type—say, a realistic person working in an investigative environment. The least degree of congruence between person and environment appears when the types are at opposite points on the hexagon. Holland (1987a) endorses several ways of operationalizing the construct of congruence. Using summary codes, as already described, a counselor can make a clinical judgment.

A simple six-point index for comparing three-letter codes between persons and environments was developed by Zener and Schnuelle (1972) and is described in the SDS Manual (Holland, 1985c). Iachan (1984) has developed the most sophisticated method of measuring congruence that is endorsed by Holland

(1987a). Other approaches also exist (Kwak and Pulvino, 1982; Wiggins and Moody, 1981).

5. *Calculus:* According to Holland (1985a, p. 5), "the relationships within and between types or environments can be ordered according to a hexagonal model in which the distances between the types or environments are inversely proportional to the theoretical relationships between them." The hexagon provides a graphic representation of the degree of consistency within or between a person or an environment; it also explains the internal relationships of the theory. It has several practical uses. Besides helping counselors understand the theory, it can also be used by clients. *You and Your Career* (Holland, 1985e) offers a succinct description of the hexagon in language that most clients with a seventh-grade reading level should be able to comprehend.

Other Influential Variables. Holland (1985a) identifies intelligence, gender, and social class as important influences on how stability and change occur in career pathways. They affect the development of personality—the actual type that one becomes. For example, gender stereotypes in American culture seem to encourage different expressed interests on the part of males and females. As American culture has changed over the past forty years, however, so have interest profiles changed according to gender. Thus, personality is seemingly affected by gender, which may in turn be affected by culture.

Social influences work to ensure stability more than change in a person's career. For example, a client working with a counselor to make a career change may find the execution of the change thwarted by corporate policies common in our culture. Holland recognizes these cultural realities and cautions us to consider them in combination with the ideas generated by his theory. Within Holland's framework, data gathered about careers do demonstrate how age, gender, social class, and required effort tend to limit career options (Gottfredson, 1981). Thus, Holland (1985a) emphasizes that predictions based on his theoretical constructs work better when the variables just described are taken into consideration.

Current Status. To date, Holland has provided five major accounts of his theory (Holland, 1959, 1966, 1973a, 1985a; Holland and Gottfredson, 1976). In one of his prefaces (Holland, 1985a, p. x), he says, "I hope this fifth statement is my last revision. I am 65 and entitled to a different career or at least some rest." In the same preface, he expresses indebtedness to the ideas and criticisms of ten giants in career development as part of his last effort to revise the theory. Acknowledgments for lifelong help are also extended by name to twenty-one others. We see Holland's theory spanning over thirty years and encompassing the ideas of many other experts in career development and career counseling. Few theoretical approaches come from such a broad foundation, and few have influenced so many, nor are many used today as much as Holland's is.

The reader will recall that Holland wanted to develop a theory that would have sufficient explanatory power but remain simple and practical. He and his associates seem to have achieved those goals. The criteria commonly used to assess the popularity of a given theory include the number of published journal articles on the topic, sales of instruments based on the theory, the number of convention programs devoted to the topic, and the number of doctoral dissertations devoted to aspects of the theory and the instruments. By all these criteria, Holland's seems to be the most popular career theory of the past decade.

In this popular and evolving theory, to date, we can note the following important changes over its history:

1. The theory has expanded its constructs, becoming more comprehensive and explicit.
2. Throughout its evolution, new concepts (for example, identity) have been added to prop up others; weak-performing constructs (for example, consistency) have been demoted in significance. The theory's limitations are more explicit.
3. The theory remains in the tradition of differential psychology, with special ties to interest measurement and personality typologies.
4. It has moved away from all-or-none distinctions among

environmental and personality types and toward statements of degree and patterning.

5. All major constructs have operational definitions, and these
    enable careful empirical verification of the theory.

6. A two-dimensional scientific model (the hexagon) has been
    added.

7. Empirical evidence, pro and con, has been generated in
    more than 450 noteworthy studies. Subjects across these
    studies have been people of diverse characteristics, and
    this diversity has aided in the generalization of the theory
    to people of many subcultures.

8. Application of the theory to career planning and counsel-
    ing has been exhaustively encouraged through the develop-
    ment and refinement of practitioner and self-help tools.

9. Precise procedures have been developed to teach the theory
    and evaluate mastery of it (see Holland, 1985c).

10. While continually open to revision based on empirical
    evidence, Holland's theory has successfully resisted the
    kinds of modification intended to satisfy prescriptive cul-
    tural and political pressures (more about this will be said
    later).

These factors have placed Holland's theory in the forefront of
career development literature. Super (1985) favorably reviews
Holland's most recent revision. Brown (1987) calls it the best
current theory of vocational choice.

Empirical Support

As mentioned earlier, more than 450 noteworthy studies have
tested Holland's theoretical constructs between 1959 and early
1988. Early in this period, research was concerned with the
definition of personality types. It led to the development of the
VPI and the SDS and to revision of the theory to include subtypes, or patterns. Research followed on the psychometric characteristics of these two instruments. More recent research has
been concerned with testing the constructs of congruence, consistency, and differentiation and how they are related to choice

stability, satisfaction, certainty of choice, career maturity, and occupational achievement. Other studies have investigated special groups according to race, sex, social class, age, and so forth. Generally speaking, research supports the theory.

Holland's goal was to devise a simple theory with a symmetrical structure that would encourage practitioners to use it because of its ease of application. Gati (1984) believes that a more complex, multidimensional theory would be better able to predict vocational phenomena than Holland's can, but Holland has been unwilling to sacrifice utility for increased explanatory power. Let us now examine some of the evidence in favor of the theory (Holland, 1985a, provides a much more comprehensive review of empirical evidence).

Personality Types. Large-scale investigations by Holland and his colleagues, using a variety of methods and dependent variables, were the early sources for the framing of the six personality types. Holland's (1962) monograph on a longitudinal study of over two thousand National Merit finalists was followed by six additional studies that used large samples of high school and college students, in addition to National Merit finalists (Holland, 1963a,b,c,d, 1963–64, 1964, 1968; Holland and Nichols, 1964; Abe and Holland, 1965). In all, over thirty thousand subjects were studied across these investigations. The results showed that the types (and, later, the subtypes) were representative of the populations studied. With each successive effort, the results became more explicit and substantial.

Holland (1963b,c,d, 1963–64) studied male and female students who used an adjective checklist, among other things, to describe themselves (and, eventually, the six different personality types). Holland refined this use of adjectives to describe the six types and later published a revised checklist (Holland, 1973a). Since then, numerous studies have tested the type descriptions by correlating Holland codes with different scales on personality inventories, to determine whether the descriptions corresponded to profiles on the personality inventories. This work has produced extensive evidence in favor of Holland's type descriptions. Examples of such studies (along with the personality measures they used) are the 16 PF (Bachtold, 1976; Bolton, 1985; Cattell, Eber, and Tatsuoka, 1970; Peraino and Willerman, 1983; Ward, Cunningham, and Wakefield, 1976; Williams, 1972); Edwards Personal Preference Schedule (Wakefield and Cunningham, 1975); Myers-Briggs Type Indicator (Nord, 1976); Neuroticism-Extraversion-Openness Inventory (NEO) (Costa, McCrae, and Holland, 1984); and Rokeach's list of terminal values (Lokan and Taylor, 1986). Perhaps the most definitive evidence for the distinctive qualities of the six personality types is provided by Gottfredson, Holland, and Ogawa (1982) in the *Dictionary of Holland Occupational Codes*.

Congruence. There is considerable evidence that congruence is a good predictor of career stability, satisfaction, and adjustment (Spokane, 1985). In general, personality type, as measured by interest inventories, will predict either the training or the work that one selects (Gottfredson and Holland, 1975; McGowan, 1982). In the counseling profession, congruence predicts the counselor's competence through its relationship to ratings by clients and supervisors (Wiggins and Moody, 1983). Training and work choices congruent with personality type are also associated with increased satisfaction (Meir, Keinan, and Segal, 1986; Smart, Elton, and McLaughlin, 1986; Wiggins, 1984; Wiggins and Moody, 1983). Congruence is also related to vocational maturity, as measured by the Attitude Scale of the Career Maturity Inventory (Guthrie and Herman, 1982); to stability of choice (Rose and Elton, 1982); and to achievement among accountants (Schwartz, Andiappan, and Nelson, 1986).

Differentiation and Consistency. Holland calls the research on both differentiation and consistency "checkered" in that there is a balance between positive and negative results (Holland, 1985a). Several studies show a relationship between differentiation and stability of choice (Holland, 1968; Taylor, Kelso, Longthorp, and Pattison, 1980). Relationships have been demonstrated between differentiation and effective decision making (Holland, Gottfredson, and Nafziger, 1975) and job satisfaction (Wiggins, 1984). Monahan (1987) proposes an improved method of determining differentiation, which may improve differentiation's predictive power in future investigations.

As mentioned earlier in this chapter, Holland (1985a) has demoted the construct of consistency because of the research evidence. Some positive evidence from well-designed studies shows a relationship between consistency and persistence in a college major (Barak and Rabbi, 1982; Wiley and Magoon, 1982), occupational stability (Gottfredson, 1977), and grade-point average (Wiley and Magoon, 1982). Wiggington (1983) showed that vocational clients, as compared to nonclients, show less differentiation and consistency in their interest profiles. Strahan (1987) discusses different approaches to measuring consistency.

Identity. As an added construct to Holland's theory, identity has just begun to be studied empirically. It has been associated with occupational commitment (Grotevant and Thorbecke, 1982), life satisfaction among homemakers and displaced home-makers (Olson, 1985), and level of career decision (Slaney and Dickson, 1985). Use of the MVS to measure identity has been viewed favorably by a diverse sample to whom it was administered (Pallas, Dahmann, Gucer, and Holland, 1983).

Special Groups. Several recent studies show the usefulness of Holland's theory with racial minorities (Gade, Fuqua, and Hurlburt, 1988; Greeniee, Damarin, and Walsh, 1988; Sheffey, Bingham, and Walsh, 1986; Walsh, Hildebrand, Ward, and Matthews, 1983; Walsh, Woods, and Ward, 1986). Holland himself (1985c) effectively summarizes age, gender, and racial differences. Revisions of both the VPI and the SDS have corrected items that may have exaggerated the differences commonly found between male and female interest profiles. His theory has generated considerable research on bias-free career counseling (Holland, 1973a, 1973b, 1975, 1982b; Zener and Schnuelle, 1972).

Holland's theory has been applied to a variety of concerns, such as the assessment of marital and family interactions (Bruch and Gilligan, 1980) and marital compatibility (Wiggins and

Weslander, 1979). A mathematical model for comparing environmental codes with personality types is another recent development (Kwak and Pulvino, 1982; Iachan, 1984).

Areas of Needed Research. The preceding discussion of Holland's theory has not discussed any of the criticisms leveled against it. Nevertheless, many refinements of his theory have come about over the years in response to objections. Holland (1985a, p. 119) lists the following weaknesses of his typology:

1. The hypotheses about the person-environment interactions have received support, but they also require more testing;
2. The formulations about personal development and change have received some support but they need a more comprehensive examination;
3. The classification of occupations may differ slightly for the different devices used to assess the types; and
4. Many important personal and environmental contingencies still lie outside the scope of the theory, although an attempt has been made to include the role of education, sex, intelligence, social class, and other major variables.

In addition, Holland (interviewed by Weinrach, 1980a) has indicated that the biggest weaknesses of his theory are its formulations about stability and change.

Practical Applications

Instrumentation. Holland has developed four instruments: the Vocational Preference Inventory (VPI) in 1953 (most recently revised in 1985), the Self-Directed Search (SDS) in 1971 (most recently revised in 1985), the Vocational Exploration and Insight Kit (VEIK) (Holland and others, 1980a), and My Vocational Situation (MVS) (Holland, Daiger, and Power, 1980). Publication of the VPI preceded the publication of Holland's theoretical papers. The VPI requires clients to indicate their interest or lack of interest in 160 occupational titles. The instrument evolved from Holland's belief that many individuals' vocational choices can be estimated by their thoughts and feelings, as evoked by the stimulus of occupational titles. Most people appear able to indicate their like or dislike of such occupations as building wrecker, physician, author, flight attendant, jockey, FBI agent, and bank examiner.

Holland (1985b) lists four uses for the VPI. It can be a brief personality inventory for students and adults, an addition to a battery of personality inventories, an interest inventory, and an assessment technique for the investigation of career theory and behavior. The VPI has gone through eight revisions intended to ensure its reliability and gender fairness. It has the advantage of being inexpensive, interesting, and closely related to the comprehensive occupational classification system (Gottfredson, Holland, and Ogawa, 1982) and to thirty years of theory-testing research. Both hand- and computer-scored versions are available, and they correlate closely with each other (Hodgkinson, 1986).

In addition to yielding scores on Holland's six personality types, the VPI provides data about the individual's personality and personal characteristics. Scales include Self-Control, Masculinity, Status, Infrequency (of response), and Acquiescence. The VPI and the SDS are similar in that both report results in terms of the six personality types, but they differ as well. The VPI is intended for use by vocational counselors with their clients, whereas the SDS can be self-administered. Both the VPI and the SDS contain dimensions not measured by the other (the VPI is less comprehensive). The VPI elicits like-dislike responses to occupational titles, whereas the SDS measures self-reported competencies, activities, and so on. The VPI is less expensive and less time-consuming than the SDS. The VPI and the SDS may be used at any time in a person's life when career decisions must be made.

The SDS was first published in 1971. It was revised in 1977 and again in 1985. The SDS consists of an assessment workbook for one-time use, to be scored by the client, and a reusable booklet (Holland, 1985d). The workbook begins with a section on occupational daydreams. The sections that follow deal with activities, competencies, attitudes toward specific occupations, and self-estimates of abilities. The raw scores are converted into a three-letter summary code, which reflects a preferred style. The order of the three letters in the summary code is hierarchical, the first letter representing the strongest preference for a particular type.

According to Holland (1985c, p. 13), when counselors interpret the summary code, they should remember the "rule of 8":

> Counselors need a rule of thumb to decide when a difference between two summary scale scores is large enough to be meaningful. Both clients and counselors are prone to interpret trivial differences between scales. Based upon the standard error of differences of scores, scale differences less than 8 should be regarded as trivial because they are within the limits of measurement error. In looking at the SDS profile, assume that scores are the same unless they differ by at least 8. For example, a person whose three highest scores were R = 30, I = 25, and E = 23 should regard the scores as about equal and search the Occupations Finder [Holland, 1985d] for all permutations of R, I, and E, rather than focussing only on RIE occupations.

Exploring the various permutations is particularly appropriate when the code is undifferentiated. When the code is clearly differentiated, however, to explore the various permutations would negate the strongest characteristics. If the occupations under the categories identified by the client's summary code do not interest the client, then the code can be expanded easily to encompass other permutations of the letters. For example, ESC can be expanded to include SEC, SCE, ECS, CSE, and CES.

With the SDS, the summary code provides the link between the workbook and the reusable booklet (Holland, 1985d). The latter is intentionally organized according to the three-letter summary codes, rather than alphabetically, to force the client to browse through and explore (at least momentarily) the full range of occupations. The SDS manual (Holland, 1987a) provides an alphabetical listing of the occupations that appear in the booklet. The booklet itself lists the 1,156 most common occupations in the United States. Each entry includes a six-digit number based on the *Dictionary of Occupational Titles* (U.S. Employment Service, 1977), which facilitates further exploration, and a separate single-digit number, which gives an index of the educational level that the occupation requires.

A computerized version — SDS-CV — has also been developed (Reardon, Psychological Assessment Resources, and Holland, 1985; Reardon, 1987; Reardon and Loughead, 1988). It has several advantages over the self-scoring form. The SDS-CV scores the section on occupational daydreams separately, and so the client and the counselor can determine whether there is a discrepancy between that score and the summary code for the remainder of the instrument (discrepancy identification is an important concept in the interpretation of psychometric instruments; see Weinrach, 1980b). The level of vocational identity (as measured by MVS), the level of congruence, and the degree of consistency and differentiation are also included, and an Interpretation Report (for the client) and a Professional Summary (for the counselor) can be printed.

The SDS-CV, an interactive system, eliminates the possibility of arithmetical errors and reduces administration and scoring time. The counselor sacrifices the advantage of having the client search through the *Occupations Finder* booklet for occupations that correspond to each summary code, but the counselor gains the efficiency and accuracy of a computer-generated list. The SDS-CV matches occupations with summary codes (and all their permutations) from the pool of occupations found in the booklet. Users' reactions to the SDS-CV have been very positive (Reardon and Loughead, 1988).

Both the hand-scored and computer-scored versions of the SDS are available from Psychological Assessment Resources, Inc. (P.O. Box 998, Odessa, FL 33556; 800/331-8378). Form E (for "easy") of the SDS can be used by people who read at the fourth-grade level, and evidence supports its use with reading-deficient high school students (Maddux and Cummings, 1986; Winer, Wilson, and Pierce, 1983). Krieshok (1987) favorably reviews the 1985 version of the SDS and recommends its use under the supervision of a counselor. New versions of the instrument have reduced computational errors committed by clients (Elliott and Byrd, 1985). Users' satisfaction with the SDS is high (Gault and Meyers, 1987; Pallas, Dahmann, Gucer, and Holland, 1983). The SDS has been subjected to vigorous evaluation and review by Holland and other researchers (Cutts, 1977; Holland, 1972, 1979; Pallas and others, n.d.; Seligman, 1974; Weinrach, 1979b), and it is frequently used as the basis for research in doctoral dissertations. Touchton and Magoon (1977) have investigated Holland's use of occupational daydreams.

In 1980, Holland developed the Vocational Exploration and Insight Kit (VEIK), intended for clients "who are somewhat or very stressed about their vocational future" (Holland and others, 1980a, p. 1). The VEIK requires clients to sort eighty-four cards, generate additional occupations that interest them but are not included among the cards, and analyze what it is about some occupations that interests them and what it is about other occupations that does not interest them. The VEIK's workbook format requires clients to record their responses to a series of questions on the basis of how they have sorted the cards. The VEIK's four goals are (in language addressed to the client) to "(1) help you increase the number of occupations you are considering as future careers, (2) help you understand what you want out of a job and career, (3) help you see how your past experience and present vocational goals are related, and (4) help you clarify where you are now and what some next steps might be" (Holland and others, 1980a, p. 1).

Because the VEIK's fifteen steps can take up to five hours to complete, the client needs considerable perseverance and tolerance for ambiguity. In several places, the client is directed to take a break or put the VEIK aside for another day, to minimize the effects of fatigue. The materials include (besides the eighty-four occupations printed on separate cards) three cards inscribed "would not choose," "in question," or "might choose"; the SDS and a booklet called *Understanding Yourself and Your Career,* which is part of the SDS; a card sort; and an action plan. The VEIK can be administered to individuals and to small groups. Although it requires a minimum of the counselor's time, some clients may require encouragement and clarification throughout, and many clients could probably benefit from consultation with a counselor at the end.

My Vocational Situation (MVS) (Holland, Daiger, and Power, 1980) is a brief, self-administered, easily scored instrument. There are only twenty questions, and scoring takes about ten seconds. It has scales to measure vocational identity, need for occupational information, and barriers to a chosen occupational goal. Used mostly to measure identity, MVS does show decent reliabilities for that scale, ranging from .86 to .89. The occupational information and barriers scales have reliabilities that range from .23 to .79. Reliabilities are better for college students than for high school students.

The VPI and the SDS are not the only instruments used for assessing types. The Kuder DD (Kuder, 1985) provides a computer printout of the individual's interests according to job titles, and job titles can be converted to Holland codes. The Strong-Campbell Interest Inventory (SCII) (Campbell, 1985) also provides Holland codes. The *Professional Manual* of the SDS (Holland, 1985c) and the *Dictionary of Holland Occupational Codes* (Gottfredson, Holland, and Ogawa, 1982) list occupations and their corresponding Holland codes alphabetically.

Holland's Occupational Classification. Holland's theory loosely organizes people and environments. A logical outgrowth of this approach is the development of a classification system. Holland's Occupational Classification classifies occupations according to the psychological similarities of its workers. Holland's theory is structural-interactive; thus, by its very nature, it provides a link between the individual and the world of work. Holland's Occupational Classification is that link.

Organizing occupational information around the coding system used in the theory and in the assessment instruments has the advantage of providing an integrated, coordinated, and systematic approach to the delivery of career counseling. Furthermore, it affords counselors and clients an opportunity to work together from a common frame of reference. There are two primary advantages of the system. First, it is easy for counselors and clients alike to understand; it is relatively simple, straightforward, and clear. Second, the output of the instrumentation — that is, the scores from the VPI and the SDS — serves as *input* to the system. Once clients have a summary code and have a modest understanding of it, they are ready to use the system, since it is organized according to the various permutations of the summary codes.

According to Helms (1973), there are three ways to use the Holland Occupational Classification: for organizing occupational information, analyzing work histories, and developing occupational exploration plans for clients. Each of these functions has a widely different application and can be used independently of the other two. Holland's system organizes occupations "into homogeneous groups based on . . . psychological similarities" (Helms, 1973, p. 69). There are many ways to organize occupational information. Libraries invariably use either the Dewey Decimal System or the Library of Congress classification system; counselors often file materials alphabetically. None of these schemes capitalizes on the inherent psychological similarities and differences among the materials being filed. To file occupational information according to the Holland Occupational Classification, follow these steps:

1. Obtain an alphabetical list of occupations and their corresponding summary codes. The manual of the SDS contains a partial list (Holland, 1985c). For a complete list of 12,099 occupations, consult Gottfredson, Holland, and Ogawa (1982).
2. Assign the proper Holland code to each piece of occupational information.
3. Decide how many separate files or boxes are desirable. Six will be needed if all materials are filed according to only the first letter of clients' summary codes. In this case, there would be one box each for R, I, A, S, E, and C. If the materials are filed according to a two-letter summary code,

thirty boxes will be needed. In this case, there would be a separate box for RI, RA, RS, RE, RC, and so forth. Those who have extensive materials and the space to store them can use a file for each of the seventy-two possible permutations of the three-letter summary codes. For those using either two- or three-letter summary codes, a separate box labeled with the first letter of each code should be set aside for filing materials that contain several occupations or materials that are general. For example, a brochure on careers in science could be filed under I.

A number of commmercially prepared guidance materials have already been assigned Holland codes, and the use of this classification system need not be limited to filing occupational information. For example, lists of schools that offer specialized training programs could also be filed in appropriate boxes, and students' reports of field trips could be filed according to appropriate summary codes.

Filing occupational information according to the Holland Occupational Classification provides easy access to information based on the results of both the VPI and the SDS. Once a client completes either one, he or she can be easily directed to the appropriate file. This system has a decided advantage over the alphabetical organization of materials. The structure of the classification system itself encourages clients to peruse occupational information relevant to their summary codes. When occupational information is stored in a library as part of a large collection, there are some obstacles. The use of two different classification systems — one for occupational information, and the other for the rest of the collection — may present problems in terms of cataloguing and shelving materials.

Another use of the Holland Occupational Classification is in the analysis of work histories. Through this process, experienced workers can be shown similarities among various jobs. According to Helms (1973, p. 70), "each letter of an occupational code provides a clue to understanding the nature of a work environment." As an example, Helms cites occupations coded SEC. S-type environments require their occupants to have good social, interpersonal, and communication skills. S-type people are called on to understand and help others. The occupants of E-type environments are called on to be enterprising in terms of selling to or leading others. E-type people value status, money, and power; they tend to be self-confident, responsible, popular, and aggressive. The C portion of the summary code is the least important hierarchically. A C-type environment rewards individuals for manipulating data (for example, operating business and data-processing equipment). C-type people are typically conventional, conforming, orderly, and practical.

The summary code provides information both about the various work environments and about the people who occupy them. Counselors can query clients about the desirable and undesirable aspects of their previous work environments. Counselors can also make suggestions about alternative environments that may suit clients better. To extend this use of the Holland Occupational Classification, the counselor could compute a cumulative summary based on at least three of a client's previous occupations. This computation should be done separately for occupations that the client liked and did not like; combining the two computations into one cumulative summary code would make it impossible to isolate undesirable aspects of previous jobs from desirable aspects. To prepare a cumulative summary code, follow these steps:

1. Ask the client to list a minimum of three occupations that he or she liked (or disliked).
2. Determine the summary code for each occupation by consulting the alphabetical index to occupational classifications and codes (Holland, 1985c).
3. Each time a letter appears in the first position of the summary code, give it three points; each time a letter appears in the second position, give it two points; each time a letter appears in the third position, give it one point.
4. Add the points that each letter receives.
5. Rank-order them from highest to lowest.

The top three letters constitute the cumulative summary code.

Suppose a client reports having been unhappy as a gas station manager (RES), a crane operator (RCE), and a postmaster (ERC). The cumulative summary code would be computed as follows: R = 8; I = 0; A = 0; S = 1; E = 6; C = 3. The cumulative summary code would be REC. In discussing compatible work environments for this individual according to his expressed dissatisfaction with these three jobs, it would be logical to suggest that his future occupations not be characterized by any of these letters, particularly the first two (RE). Similarly, if a client names three jobs that were enjoyable but not sufficiently stimulating or challenging, the counselor can suggest that the client consider occupations that have similar cumulative summary codes but require more skills and education. This process is particularly important in vocational rehabilitation.

Suppose a client who has suffered a serious physical disability seeks career guidance. From a list of several previous jobs that were satisfactory, a cumulative summary code is computed. The counselor helps the client identify similar occupations according to the cumulative summary code, but these would be jobs that the client could perform in spite of the disability. If the cause of the disability is emotional rather than physical, the counselor can help the client identify jobs that have similar summary codes but are less stressful. Use of the cumulative summary code in this fashion gives the counselor the resources to be prescriptive — that is, to analyze, identify, and help the client choose an occupation consistent with his or her cumulative summary code.

Developing a plan for occupational exploration is another use of the Holland Occupational Classification. Used in this fashion, it is both a tool and a framework for the systematic exploration of careers. The following procedures can be used with clients individually or in small groups:

1. The counselor computes a cumulative summary code based on SDS scores, results of other interest inventories, college majors, leisure activities, career aspirations, and previous satisfactory work experiences. A college major can be converted into a Holland code if the college major is projected into one of its logical occupational titles. For example, "biology" becomes "biologist"; "English" becomes "English teacher" or "writer." (See Rosen, Holmberg, and Holland,

1987; this work permits clients to convert their summary codes into college majors, and vice versa.) Leisure activities frequently have vocational equivalents. For example, "woodworking" may become "carpenter," and "sewing" may become "sewing-machine operator," "dressmaker," or "fashion artist," according to the client's preference. Converting any occupational title into its corresponding Holland code is easy; consult either Holland (1987a) or Gottfredson, Holland, and Ogawa (1982). Vocational aspirations and previous successful work experiences can also be easily converted into Holland codes through consultation of Holland's alphabetical index.

2. The client is assigned a cumulative summary code and encouraged to explore at least six different occupations systematically by obtaining information, interviewing current jobholders, and assessing the relative advantages and disadvantages of each occupation.

3. Once the previous step is completed, the client discusses the results of the explorations and either makes a tentative decision or reports that none of the occupations is of any particular interest (for whatever reason). The counselor then encourages the client to identify additional occupations after the cumulative summary code is revised (the first and second letters are reversed).

4. If the client's second exploration proves unsatisfactory, the counselor may encourage the client to explore still other occupations after another recombination of the three-letter cumulative summary code (the last letter of the code is placed first).

If none of these steps proves useful, the client may have either an undifferentiated or an inconsistent profile.

An undifferentiated profile is flat: the client's interest in one type of occupation is no greater than his or her interest in most others. Depressed people often display undifferentiated profiles. Such clients may benefit from additional counseling. Simulated work experiences can also effectively assist clients who have undifferentiated profiles. Clients can be systematically exposed to all six basic types of work environments and be interviewed after completing each simulation. The client's preference for one set of activities over another can provide the foundation for creating a new summary code, this one based on personal experience. With the new summary code in hand, the counselor can assist the client in exploring the wide range of occupations that can be found with the new code.

An inconsistent profile is easier to deal with than an undifferentiated one. Clients with inconsistent profiles have summary codes whose first two letters appear on opposite corners of the hexagon — for example, A (artistic) and C (conventional). In terms of the people they attract, the A and C fields tend to be opposites. The same holds true for realistic-social and investigative-enterprising combinations.

Clients who have inconsistent profiles should be provided with simulated or real work experiences in the two opposing areas indicated by their summary codes. Such experiences may help them understand which environments make them most and least comfortable. Sometimes inconsistency can be resolved if the client is asked to distinguish between vocational and avocational interests. For example, consider a college professor of social sciences who scores very high on realistic activities because his hobby is welding and carpentry. Such an individual may thoroughly enjoy his hobbies but have little interest in making a career of them.

Differential treatment and differential diagnosis are basic to good counseling, regardless of a counselor's theoretical orientation. There is no single best way to help all clients. Holland and Gottfredson (1976, p. 26) speculate that a client's code may help indicate what kinds of attention may be useful: "Still unexplored is the possibility of using the typology to assign or suggest treatment according to type. For instance, I's may profit more from reading, S's from group activities, C's from structured workbooks." Intervention strategies should be adjusted to the needs and expectations of the client.

There will always be people who experience reading problems, indecisiveness, lack of interest, and frustration. The solutions are much the same, whether counselors are working from

Holland's perspective or from some other perspectives. Individuals with problems need specific types of interventions. Flat profiles are not uncommon. When they appear, counselors need to determine some of the contributing factors. Reading problems or errors in computation of the summary code should be checked first. Individuals with flat profiles are often as indecisive about career questions as they are about life in general. Vocationally related problems often have their counterparts in situations outside work. Vocational counseling cannot take place apart from educational and personal counseling. Vocational theories (and Holland's is no exception) apply best to individuals whose general development is normal. Individuals with severe personal or educational problems generally need to deal with them before career counseling can be successful.

Critique

Any popular theory, including Holland's, will attract criticism. It is a credit to the theory's popularity that so many of its aspects have been subjected to close scrutiny, not only by Holland but also by others (Brown, 1987; Holland, 1987b; Osipow, 1983). Issues raised about the theory include the following:

1. *The SDS in particular, and Holland's model in general, are sexist.* Critics use Holland's own data — which indicate that women score higher than men on the SDS conventional scale and that men score higher than women on the SDS realistic scale — as proof that the instrument is sexist. According to Holland (1973b, p. 5), "it is important to remember that, at the time of any vocational assessment of fitness for an occupation, everyone's performance (women, men, blacks, psychiatric or physically handicapped) depends upon one's past experience as well as one's innate potential. And, no matter what, everyone has to live for a while with his current level of proficiency. The SDS is one example of a device to help a person make decisions in terms of current assets or liabilities."

Reliable and valid interest inventories accurately reflect the interests of the individual when the inventory is administered.

That many women and men respond in traditional ways is not an indictment of the instruments; rather, it is a reflection of the cultural influences on their development. Good career counseling requires counselors to help their clients expand their vocational options (Holland, 1974a).

The SDS, aside from helping clients explore, serves other purposes. Gottfredson and Holland (1978) suggest that another valid use of the SDS would be to provide the client (in this case, a female) with feedback on her current vocational status. For an instrument to have construct validity, it would have to provide different scores for females and males because the personality constructs being measured are theoretically related to experience. As Gottfredson and Holland (1978, p. 44) write, "At the present time this experience is usually different for men and women. The removal of sex-related variance in the scores appears akin to the efforts in an earlier decade to remove social desirability from measures of personal adjustment. Social desirability seems to be a component of adjustment, and devices that eliminate it appear less valid than those that do not."

Holland (1982b, pp. 195–196) says, "It is unethical to reduce the predictive validity of an inventory to achieve an admirable social goal without first telling a person beforehand what your goal is and asking, is this acceptable? The assumption that . . . others make when they tear into a female's traditional options is not sanctioned by everyone. In addition, like many interventions, when you help people with nontraditional potentials, you simultaneously denigrate the traditional options of others. I know of no easy way out of this dilemma." Holland (1982b, p. 196) reports that in eighteen experimental designs, females and males benefited "equally according to several criteria: more options, self-understanding, reassurance."

More comment on reassurance may be appropriate; it is one of the important outcomes sought by people who are deciding on career directions. Many individuals enter career counseling with some idea of what they want. They seek reassurance that their occupational daydreams are related to their measured interests. This goal appears to be reasonable for both genders and achievable with the aid of the SDS and Holland's theory in general. Reassurance can do more than encourage good feeling; it can also stimulate thinking, clear understanding, and action. Use of Holland's theory can accomplish these goals equally well for males and females.

2. *The theory does not sufficiently explain how people become the types that they are.* According to Osipow (1983, p. 112) and Brown (1987, p. 17), Holland is vague on this topic. This is probably a fair criticism of Holland's earlier work. He has made some effort in this direction, however. Holland (1985a, p. 15) proposes that "types produce types." This effect is due to more than heredity. The personality type of a parent helps to create a large variety of environmental opportunities for a child, which strongly influence personality development. Access to activities, possessions, materials, and friendships are influenced by parents. These variables affect interests (which in turn affect competencies) that result in personality traits. All these factors mutually affect one another. The child in turn makes demands that change the parents and continue to influence the personality development of the child.

3. *Holland understates the need for vocational counseling.* Counseling, in the traditional sense, has been a dyadic relationship between a highly skilled counselor and a client in need of assistance. Even with the emergence of group counseling, the emphasis has been on establishing closer relationships. As a discipline, counseling tends to attract individuals who themselves prefer personal, close, intimate relationships as opposed to detached, impersonal ones. (Counselors are social types.) As a result, many counselors believe that all their clients need the same kinds of intense, personal relationships. According to Holland (1973c, p. 5), "These beliefs have prevented any major revision of the delivery system for vocational services. Some experience and recent experiments strongly imply that most people want help, not love."

4. *Matching models are static and outdated.* Holland's model is far removed from Parsons's (1909) strict approach to traits and factors. Furthermore, there is nothing to prevent counselors from repeating the matching process whenever clients need career counseling. Only the structural-interacive theories provide an

explicit link between the individual and the world of work. This feature permits the client to translate personal characteristics, interests, and abilities into an appropriate occupational title. It is pragmatic.

Some critics believe that Holland's system is simplistic and that career counseling, by implication, must be a highly complex procedure in every case. Holland disagrees. There appears to be ample evidence for the legitimacy of a typology like his. Holland would agree with his critics, however, that the process of assessing types is not always easy. A skilled counselor is often needed to assist a client who has an inconsistent or undifferentiated profile. Professionals are often needed to help students explore various permutations of their codes and locate appropriate occupational information.

Conclusions

Holland's theory and its instrumentation are among the most widely used, if not the most widely used today, by researchers and counselors alike. The hexagonal model and the Holland Occupational Classification are widely respected. Precisely because the model is so widely used, ongoing research is warranted and certain to continue. We can depend on Holland to lead the way in identifying areas for future study. As a scientist, he has already demonstrated his commitment to searching out the truth, without regard to its effect on his theory or its instrumentation.

Anne Roe

Patricia W. Lunneborg

4

Personality Development and Career Choice

Background of the Theory

My theoretical concerns have focused on two apparently disparate areas and their subsequent integration — personality theory and occupational classification. My purpose has been to view the whole range of occupations in terms of their relationship to individual differences in backgrounds, physical and psychological variables, and experiences. Although much of my work on occupations has focused on possible relationships between occupational behavior (not just choice) and personality, I have never considered personality to be the only or even the most important variable. My early experience and most of my early research were in clinical psychology (unusually, often with normal adults), and I became interested in occupational psychology as an extension of clinical studies of well-known artists and research scientists. As a result, my first approach to the psychology of occupations was not related to career development. In-

Note: The first portion of this chapter, concerning theory, was written by Anne Roe. The second portion, treating applications of the theory, was written by Patricia W. Lunneborg.

deed, I knew almost nothing of such studies until I agreed to a request that I write a book on the psychology of occupations (Roe, 1956), and I have no experience in career counseling. Hence, the theory was formulated without concern for its practical applications.

I found Maslow's (1954) concept of basic needs, arranged in a hierarchy of prepotency, to be the most useful approach from personality theory, since it offered the most effective way of discussing the relevance of the occupation to the satisfaction of basic needs. Maslow's list of basic needs follows in the order of their potency, from most to least potent:

1. The physiological needs
2. The safety needs
3. The need for belongingness and love
4. The need for importance, respect, self-esteem, independence
5. The need for information
6. The need for understanding
7. The need for beauty
8. The need for self-actualization

Maslow considers these needs innate and instinctive but, except for the physiological needs, modifiable. Generally, the lower the potency of the need in the hierarchy, the more suppressible it is. I differ with Maslow, however, in the position of the need for self-actualization, which I would consider to follow the need for importance, respect, self-esteem, and independence.

In our society, no single situation is potentially so capable of giving some satisfaction, at all levels of basic needs, as the occupation. This observation is immediately obvious for the physiological and safety needs. It is also clear that working with a congenial group is an important aspect of a satisfying occupation, and to be accepted by one's peers in it can only promote self-esteem. I would contend that, in our culture, social and economic status depend more on the occupation (of the individual, the father, or less frequently now, the husband) than on any other one thing—even wealth.

The Theory

To survey the whole range of occupations, one must have some way of ordering or classifying them. I found none of the available classification systems of any use to me, and therefore I had to construct one. None of the available classifications of occupations seemed to follow any logical principle of classification. In some, level was confused with type; in others, many occupations were not considered. Although the *Dictionary of Occupational Titles* (DOT) had an elaborate coding system, its major groupings were inconsistent, and I found its thousands of titles to be more than a little disconcerting. Furthermore, with the exception of the Minnesota Occupational Rating Scales (MORS), none of the existing classification systems had any psychological basis, and when occupations were grouped by similarity of ability patterns on the MORS, 214 different groups emerged, obviously too many to handle efficiently.

I turned to various factor analyses of interests, suggested to me probably by the MORS scales (Darley, 1941; Guilford and others, 1954; Kuder, 1946; Strong, 1943; Thurstone, 1931; Vernon, 1949). From a consideration of these, I selected eight groups that seemed to have referents in most of the interest studies and that would indicate the primary focus of the activity. On separate sheets, I listed occupations that seemed to fit under these headings, and I literally shuffled them around until I saw that they could be arranged along a continuum based on the intensity and nature of the interpersonal relationships involved in the occupational activities and in an order that would have contiguous groups more alike in this respect than noncontiguous ones. I thought of this system as a circle, with group 8 between group 1 and group 7.

I then considered the level of difficulty and responsibility involved in each occupation. Originally, I constructed 8 levels, so that I had an 8 by 8 classification. I presented this at a meeting in New York, which turned out to be very helpful because Super and a seminar group of his worked on the consistency of assignment of occupations to these categories and, as a result of difficulties, I dropped two levels from further consideration, leaving an 8 by 6 scheme. I thought of this arrangement as cylindrical, but I now consider a cone a more appropriate diagrammatical representation (see the figures that appear later in this chapter).

A description of each of the eight occupational groups follows:

1. *Service:* These occupations are primarily concerned with serving and attending to the personal tastes, needs, and welfare of other persons. Included are such occupations as social work, guidance, and domestic and protective services. The essential element is a situation in which one person is doing something for another.

2. *Business Contact:* These occupations are primarily concerned with the face-to-face sale of commodities, investments, real estate, and services. The person-to-person relation is again important, but it is focused on persuasion to a course of action, rather than on helping. The persuader will profit if his or her advice is followed; the advisee is supposed to.

3. *Organization:* These are the managerial and white-collar jobs in business, industry, and government — the occupations concerned primarily with the organization and efficient functioning of commercial enterprises and of government activities. The quality of person-to-person relations is largely formalized.

4. *Technology:* This group includes occupations concerned with the production, maintenance, and transportation of commodities and utilities. Here are occupations in engineering, crafts, and the machine trades, as well as in transportation and communication. Interpersonal relations are of relatively little importance, and the focus is on dealing with things.

5. *Outdoor:* This group includes the occupations primarily concerned with the cultivation, preservation, and gathering of crops, marine or inland water resources, mineral resources, forest products and other natural resources, and with animal husbandry. Because of the

increasing mechanization of some of these occupations, perhaps particularly those concerned with the petroleum industry, a number of jobs previously classified in this group have been moved to group 4. There still remain a great many persons, however, whose work is most appropriately classified here. Interpersonal relations are largely irrelevant.

6. *Science:* These are the occupations primarily concerned with scientific theory and its application under specified circumstances other than technology. Even in scientific research (as in physics) that is not at all person-oriented, as well as in such fields as psychology and anthropology, it is clear that there is a relationship to the occupations in group 7, with some return to more specific personal relations (for example, in the medical occupations that belong here).

7. *General Culture:* These occupations are primarily concerned with the preservation and transmission of the general cultural heritage. Interest is in human activities, rather than in individual persons. This group includes occupations in education, journalism, jurisprudence, the ministry, linguistics, and the subjects usually called the humanities. Most elementary and high school teachers are placed in this group. At higher levels, teachers are placed in groups by subject matter — for example, teachers of science in 6, or of art in 8, or of humanities in 7.

8. *Arts and Entertainment:* These occupations include those primarily concerned with the use of special skills in the creative arts and in entertainment. For the most part, the focus is on a relationship between one person (or an organized group) and a more general public. The interpersonal relation is important but neither so direct nor of the same nature as that in group 1 [adapted from Roe and Klos, 1972, pp. 202–203].

There are six levels in each group. The levels are based on degree of responsibility, capacity, and skill. These criteria are not exactly correlated, but whenever there are marked differences, level of responsibility is decisive. Responsibility includes not only the number and difficulty of the decisions to be made but also how many different kinds of problems must be coped with. This dimension is essentially a continuum, and each level includes a range of responsibilities.

1. *Professional and managerial 1 (independent responsibility):* This level includes the innovators and creators and top managerial and administrative people, as well as professionals who have independent responsibility in important respects. For occupations at this level, there is generally no higher authority than the social group. Several criteria are suggested: (1) important, independent, and varied responsibilities, (2) policymaking, and (3) education. (When a high level of education is relevant, it is at the doctoral or equivalent level.)

2. *Professional and managerial 2:* The distinction between this level and the previous one is primarily one of degree. Genuine autonomy may be present but with narrower or less significant responsibilities than in level 1. Suggested criteria are (1) medium-level responsibilities for self and others, with regard to both importance and variety, (2) policy interpretation, and (3) education at or above the bachelor's-degree level but below the doctoral level or its equivalent.

3. *Semiprofessional and small business:* The criteria suggested here are (1) low level of responsibility for others, (2) application of policy or determination for self only (as in managing a small business), and (3) education at the level of high school or technical school or the equivalent.

4. *Skilled:* This level and the following levels are classic subdivisions. Skilled occupations require apprenticeships or other special training or experience.

5. *Semiskilled:* These occupations require some training and experience, but markedly less than the occupations in level 4. In addition, much less autonomy and initiative are permitted in these occupations.

6.   *Unskilled:* These occupations require no special train-
     ing or education and not much more ability than is
     needed to follow simple directions and to engage in
     simple repetitive actions. At this level, group differen-
     tiation depends primarily on the occupational setting
     [adapted from Roe and Klos, 1972, pp. 208–209].

It is probable that level 6 will become increasingly irrelevant
and may be dropped.

Table 4.1 shows the classification by group and level and
includes examples for most categories. There are a few occupations at levels 5 and 6 for which no examples seem appropriate.

Even though agreement on classification of different occupations has been good (Lunneborg and Lunneborg, 1968),
I have classified all the occupations listed in the U.S. Department of Labor's *1965 Occupational Outlook Handbook* (Roe, 1966).

The theory contains five propositions on the origin of interests and needs:

1.   Genetic inheritance sets limits on the potential development
     of all characteristics, but the specificity of the genetic con-
     trol and the extent and nature of the limitation are different
     for different characteristics. It is probable that the genetic
     element is more specific and stronger in what we call in-
     tellectual abilities and temperament than it is in such other
     variables as interests and attitudes.
2.   The degrees and avenues of development of inherited char-
     acteristics are affected not only by experience unique to the
     individual but also by all aspects of the general cultural
     background and the socioeconomic position of the family.
     This proposition takes account not only of the fact that in-
     dividual experiences affect which and how far various in-
     herited characteristics may be developed but also of the fact
     that such factors as race, sex, and the social and economic
     position of the family are importantly involved. (This prop-
     osition is exemplified in the formula presented later.)
3.   The pattern of development of interests, attitudes, and other
     personality variables with relatively little or nonspecific

genetic control is primarily determined by individual experiences, through which involuntary attention becomes channeled in particular directions. The important word here is *involuntary*. The elements of any situation to which one gives automatic or effortless attention are keys to the dynamics of behavior. This proposition is clearly related to hypotheses concerning the relations between personality and perception.

a. These directions are first determined by the patterning of early satisfactions and frustrations. This patterning is affected by the relative strengths of various needs and the forms and relative degrees of satisfaction they receive. The two latter aspects are environmental variables.

b. The modes and degrees of need satisfaction determine which needs will become the strongest motivators. The nature of the motivation may be quite unconscious. The following are possible variations: (1) Needs that are satisfied routinely as they appear do not become unconscious motivators. (2) Needs for which even minimum satisfaction is rarely achieved will, if of a higher order (as used by Maslow, 1954), become expunged or will, if of a lower order, prevent the appearance of higher-order needs and will become dominant and restricting motivators. (3) Needs for which satisfaction is delayed but eventually accomplished will become (unconscious) motivators, largely according to the degree of satisfaction felt. Behavior that has received irregular reinforcement is notably difficult to extinguish (Ferster and Skinner, 1957). The degree of satisfaction felt will depend, among other things, on the strength of the basic need in the given individual, the length of time between arousal and satisfaction, and the values ascribed to the satisfaction of this need in the immediate environment.

4. The eventual pattern of psychic energies, in terms of attention-directedness, is the major determinant of interests.

5. The intensity of these needs and of their satisfaction (perhaps particularly as they have remained unconscious) and their

Table 4.1. Two-Way Classification of Occupations.

		Group						
Level	I Service	II Business Contact	III Organization	IV Technology	V Outdoor	VI Science	VII General Cultural	VIII Arts and Entertainment
1	Personal therapists. Social work supervisors. Counselors.	Promoters.	U.S. president and cabinet officer. Industrial tycoon. International bankers.	Inventive geniuses. Consulting or chief engineers. Ships' commanders.	Consulting specialists.	Research scientists. University, college faculties. Medical specialists. Museum curators.	Supreme Court justices. University, college faculties. Prophets. Scholars.	Creative artists, performers (great). Teachers (university equivalent). Museum curators.
2	Social workers. Occupational therapists. Probation, truant officers (with training).	Promoters. Public relations counselors.	Certified public accountants. Business and government executives. Union officials. Brokers (average).	Applied scientists. Factory managers. Ships' officers. Engineers.	Applied scientists. Landowners and operators (large). Landscape architects.	Scientists, semiindependent. Nurses. Pharmacists. Veterinarians.	Editors. Teachers (high school and elementary).	Athletes. Art critics. Designers. Music arrangers.
3	YWCA officials. Detectives, police sergeants. Welfare workers. City inspectors.	Salesmen: auto, bond, insurance. Dealers, retail and wholesale. Confidence men.	Accountants (average). Employment managers. Owners, catering, drycleaning, and so on.	Aviators. Contractors. Foremen (DOT I). Radio operators.	County agents. Farm owners. Forest rangers. Fish, game wardens.	Technicians, medical, X-ray, museum. Weather observers. Chiropractors.	Justices of the peace. Radio announcers. Reporters. Librarians.	Ad writers. Designers. Interior decorators. Showmen.

4	Barbers. Chefs. Practical nurses. Police officers.	Auctioneers. Buyers (DOT I). House canvassers. Interviewers, poll.	Cashiers. Clerks, credit, express, and so on. Foremen, warehouse. Salesclerks.	Blacksmiths. Electricians. Foremen (DOT II). Mechanics (average).	Laboratory testers, dairy products, and so on. Miners. Oil well drillers.	Technical assistants.	Law clerks.	Advertising artists. Decorators, window, and so on. Photographers. Racing car drivers.
5	Taxi drivers. General house workers. Waiters. City firemen.	Peddlers.	Clerks, file, stock, and so on. Notaries. Runners. Typists.	Bulldozer operators. Delivery people. Smelter workers. Truck drivers.	Gardeners. Farm tenants. Teamsters, cowpunchers. Miners' helpers.	Veterinary hospital attendants.		Illustrators, greeting cards. Showcard writers. Stagehands.
6	Chambermaids. Hospital attendants. Elevator operators. Watchmen.	Messenger boys.		Helpers. Laborers. Wrappers. Yardmen.	Dairy hands. Farm laborers. Lumberjacks.	Nontechnical helpers in scientific organizations.		

Source: Roe, A., and Klos, D. "Classification of Occupations." In J. M. Whiteley and A. Resnikoff (eds.), *Perspectives on Vocational Development.* Washington, D.C.: American Association for Counseling and Development, 1972, pp. 200–201. Copyright © 1972, American Association for Counseling and Development. Reprinted with permission.

organization are the major determinants of the degree of
motivation that reaches expression in accomplishment.

My subsequent research concentrated on proposition 3a.
Since early experience is usually dominated by the family situation, and particularly by relations with the parents, some description of parental behaviors was necessary, and I suggested that
these could be conceptualized as (1) emotional concentration
on the child, which could be either overprotective or overdemand-
ing, (2) avoidance of the child, expressed either as emotional
rejection or neglect, and (3) acceptance of the child, either casu-
ally or lovingly.

I then hypothesized that there are two basic orientations,
either toward or not toward persons; that these orientations are
related to early childhood experiences; and that they can be
related in turn to occupational choice. These alternatives are
illustrated in Figure 4.1.

In my attempt to investigate these possible relationships,
it soon became evident that no measure of parent-child relations
was adequate for this purpose. It was necessary to construct a
Parent-Child Relations Questionnaire (PCR I) based on the
classification reported here. This was done by Roe and Siegelman
(1963). Analysis of questionnaire results gave three factors.
Two — Loving-Rejecting (LR) and Casual-Demanding (CD) —
were bipolar, and one — Overt Attention (O) — was unipolar.
Only factors LR and O were assumed to affect person orientation.

Applicability to Women and Minorities. As I have noted
elsewhere, the occupational classification system falls short of
adequacy where women are concerned, except for the women
who enter careers and continue without interruption. This in-
adequacy is even more now than it was when the classification
was developed in 1954. There was no category for housewives,
for example. The actual activities of a housewife and mother
can be classified in all the categories, although I suppose if one
had to pick one, it would be group 7, preservation of the culture.
Now that so many women are not only housewives but also
working outside the home, it seems insufficient to categorize

Figure 4.1. Hypothesized Relations Between Major Orientation,
Occupational Choice, and Parent-Child Relations.

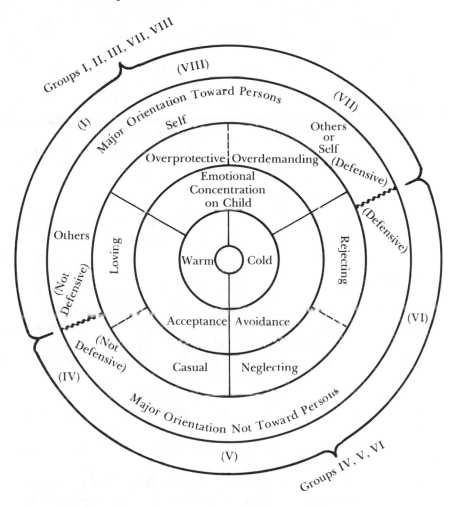

Source: Roe, A. "Early Determinants of Vocational Choice." *Journal of Counseling Psychology,* 1957, *4,* 216.

them only by their paid (or volunteer) jobs, and unless one
follows the frequent moving into and out of the workplace, it
becomes even clearer that something else is needed for them.
Ginzberg and others (1966) found that the questionnaire they

used to study well-educated men was just not applicable to equally well-educated women. I have discussed the problems of working women at some length (see Berg, 1972). There, although I did not discuss the problems of minority women, I specifically pointed out that their situation was in all respects worse.

The classification itself does not address minority issues, but they are considered in the formula developed later.

The Parent-Child Relations Questionnaire II has different forms for same-sex and cross-sex parent and child. Differences have been found between black and white subjects, data for which are given in the questionnaire's manual (Siegelman and Roe, 1979).

Current Status. An extensive consideration of the whole theory just presented here has appeared in a long, detailed, highly critical, but oddly ambivalent chapter by Osipow (1983). Rather than attempt to discuss that chapter in detail, I recommend it to the reader. Osipow's major objection throughout seems to be that the theory is not specifically adapted to or drawn up for the counseling situation. I can only remark that it was not devised to be. Osipow is careless in attributing to me generalizations I have not made—for example, that all scientists come from homes without parental warmth. Among his objections to our use of the Parent-Child Relations Questionnaire is that the attitude of one parent is frequently unlike that of the other. True enough, but the PCR I had different forms for the two parents. Perhaps the best study of PCR I is by Cox (1970). Cox does note that parents may react differently to sons and daughters, and Osipow also points out that parents' attitudes change with age. We have attempted to control this to some extent by stating that the questionnaire should be taken to apply to the situation when the child was about twelve. Certainly, there are drawbacks to retrospective studies, but I think that with due caution they can be extremely useful. Osipow considers only studies that relate the PCR to occupational choice, but the PCR has proved its usefulness in many other kinds of questions.

PCR I has been revised on the basis of a number of studies and is now available in a much improved and shorter version

(PCR II), which has four slightly different forms for same-sex and cross-sex parent and child and provides immediate factor scores for LR, CD, and O (Siegelman and Roe, 1979).

It seems clear that there is no direct link between parent-child relations and occupational choice. This finding does not invalidate the propositions that concern needs and interests without reference to occupations.

There was belated recognition that my two-dimensional classification was in reality a three-dimensional one, in which only two dimensions were explicit from the start: Level and Things-Versus-Persons. A third dimension is technically required by the circular arrangement of the groups. The nature of the other dimension is not entirely clear, although it has been suggested to be a theoretical versus economic continuum or one contrasting purposeful communication with resourceful utilization (Roe and Klos, 1972). Figure 4.2, which shows a truncated cone, and Figure 4.3, a diagram in two dimensions of a projection of the cone onto a plane surface, seem to be the most appropriate representations of these relationships.

A study by Borgen and Weiss (1968), showing that greater occupational rewards are available at higher levels of occupation, supports the idea that higher-level jobs have greater differentiation than lower-level jobs. Klos (Roe and Klos, 1972) has suggested a further classification to indicate the nature of the employer and the context in which the occupation is carried on, a potentially useful addition.

Empirical Support

Occupational Classification. Jones (1965), using students as subjects and their preferences as data, found that occupations can be ordered along a person-to-person continuum, with the ordering in terms of Roe groups 1, 8, 2, 3, 4, 5, 6, and 7. A factor analysis of his data found that about half of the total variance was explained in terms of two factors, the first of which he interpreted as being along a person-oriented, nonperson-oriented dimension, and the second as representing other-directed versus inner-directed occupations. Klos (Roe and Klos,

Figure 4.2. Three-Dimensional Conceptual Model
of Occupational Classification.

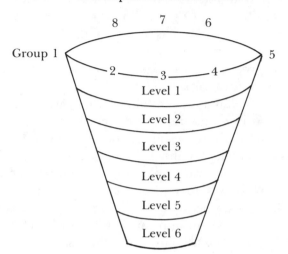

Source: Roe, A., and Klos, D. "Classification of Occupations." In J. M. Whiteley and A. Resnikoff (eds.), *Perspectives on Vocational Development*. Washington, D.C.: American Association for Counseling and Development, 1972, p. 213. Copyright © 1972, American Association for Counseling and Development. Reprinted with permission.

1972) defines the two dimensions in terms of interpersonal relations versus natural phenomena and purposeful communication versus resourceful utilization, as shown in Figure 4.4.

A study by Cole and Hanson (1971) supported the general idea of a circular configuration of interests in Holland's classification (and, more or less incidentally, in mine as well), but Lunneborg and Lunneborg (1977) found that more than two dimensions are needed to account for the structure of vocational interests. Meir (1970, 1973, 1978) has made extensive statistical analyses, but the overall results are somewhat confusing. He does point out that there is a large difference in numbers of occupations in different groups and levels, with some categories vacant. This is probably one of the problems with reconciling conflicting results. I have reviewed my classifications of the occupations listed in the *Occupational Outlook Handbook* for 1965, and I find the distributions for groups noted as follows, with mean-level rating:

Figure 4.3. Projection of Figure 4.2 onto a Plane Surface.

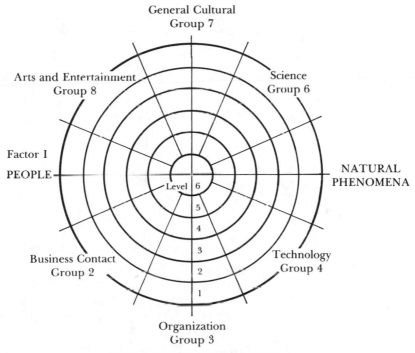

Factor II
PURPOSEFUL COMMUNICATION

General Cultural
Group 7

Arts and Entertainment
Group 8

Science
Group 6

Factor I
PEOPLE

NATURAL
PHENOMENA

Level 6
5
4
3
2
1

Business Contact
Group 2

Technology
Group 4

Organization
Group 3

RESOURCEFUL UTILIZATION

Source: Roe, A., and Klos, D. "Classification of Occupations." In J. M. Whiteley and A. Resnikoff (eds.), *Perspectives on Vocational Development.* Washington, D.C.: American Association for Counseling and Development, 1972, p. 213. Copyright © 1972, American Association for Counseling and Development. Reprinted with permission.

Group	1	2	3	4	5	6	7	8
Number of occupations	53	9	83	330	40	81	24	25
Mean-level rating	3.8	3.0	3.9	4.7	4.2	1.6	1.6	2.5

Several studies have demonstrated that job changes (or choices) occur within the same group about two-thirds of the time (Doyle, 1965; Holland and Whitney, 1968; Osipow, 1966; Roe and others, 1966). Contiguous categories were most often

Figure 4.4. Occupational Groups Ordered by Role Performers' Orientations to People, Key Data, and Natural Phenomena.

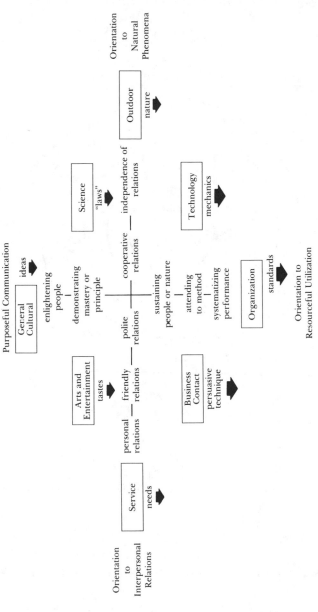

Note: Hypothesized key data are listed near each occupational group.
Source: Roe, A.,, and Klos, D. "Classification of Occupations." In J. M. Whiteley and A. Resnikoff (eds.), *Perspectives on Vocational Development.* Washington, D.C.: American Association for Counseling and Development, 1972, p. 206. Copyright © 1972, American Association for Counseling and Development. Reprinted with permission.

selected after that, although in Holland and Whitney's study this measure was higher for their categories than for mine. A study by Knapp and Knapp (1977) of secondary students in successive years demonstrated that among those for whom major area of interest changed, the likelihood of falling into any other group varied inversely with the distance of that group from the original one.

Gati and Meir (1982) compared circular and hierarchical models for the structure of interests and found them to be of similar efficiency in predicting occupational choice and satisfaction by congruency and consistency. They pointed out that each model has unique and distinctive predictions; hence, the models seem to complement each other rather than compete with each other.

Borgen and Weiss (1968) studied the validity of the level classification, and their conclusions "provide empirical confirmation for several of the dimensions which Roe postulates as underlying her classification of occupations level." They also point out that there are more reinforcers in higher-level occupations, which suggests that higher-level occupations provide more satisfactions for needs that are less potent in Maslow's hierarchy than lower-level occupations do. Knapp's (1967) investigation of five occupational levels within the eight Roe groups resulted in fourteen factors that, in general, were distributed in the upper and lower levels of the classification system.

Parent-Child Relations. Factor analyses of a number of different groups for the PCR I and II have all shown two bipolar factors and one unipolar factor. The bipolar variables are similar to variables that have been reported by investigators who used diverse methods for assessing parental behavior structure (for example, Goldin, 1969; Roe and Siegelman, 1963; Schaefer, 1961, 1965). Similar categories have been developed from direct observations of parent-child interactions, interviewing, and giving questionnaires to parents (Goldin, 1969; Roe and Siegelman, 1963). Content validity of the PCR I was supported by unanimous agreement of four judges on the assignment of items to the various scales; concurrent validity was supported by the work of Cox (1970). Tiboni (1976) found high correlation between PCR II scores for mothers and sons, which gives additional support to the validity of the PCR II. Both forms have been used effectively in studies of a wide variety of problems.

Parker and others (1967) have suggested changes in the PCR and offer a substitute questionnaire, which appears not to have been further tested. I feel that the PCR II answers their objections and that its four forms are much more adequate.

Parent-Child Relations and Occupational Choice. A number of studies have attempted to find a direct link between parent-child relations and occupational choice, as originally hypothesized (Brunkan, 1965; Grigg, 1959; Hagen, 1960; Green and Parker, 1965; Switzger and others, 1962; Utton, 1960). The results have been consistently negative. There is, however, some evidence that, within highly narrow fields of interest, the primary work activities chosen by individuals do reflect an attitude (toward versus not toward other people) related to experiences of early childhood.

Roe and Siegelman (1964) hypothesized that the degree of person orientation in later life is generally positively related to the amount of love and attention received in childhood, but that the degree of casualness or demandingness is irrelevant to later person orientation. We studied 142 male college seniors and 94 adults in four subsamples of men and women engineers and men and women social workers (the occupations were selected as extremes of person orientation). For the students, and for the men in general, the more love and attention in childhood, the greater the degree of person orientation in later life. Fewer significant relationships were found for the group of women. The factor casual-demanding had no effect on the degree of person orientation.

Using a family relations inventory, Byers, Forrest, and Zaccaria (1968) found several significant associations among early family relations, adult needs, and occupational choice among ministers and ministerial students. With the same instrument, Medvene (1969) found the theoretically expected relationships with person or data orientation among graduate psychology students.

Similarly, among male engineering students, Medvene and Shueman (1978) found that those who chose people-oriented sales and technical-services jobs more often described the dominant parent as accepting, whereas students who chose thing-oriented engineering jobs more often perceived the dominant parent as avoiding. Among women college seniors in mathematics, Handley and Hickson (1978) found that those who had been influenced primarily by people were going to become teachers. In contrast, women who had been influenced primarily by the ideas of mathematics were going to become scientists.

Hill (1974) found that MBA students who were going into accounting and systems analysis had significantly lower needs for interpersonal activity than did students who intended to do administrative work. Hill (1980), in a study of female business students, also found person orientation (using a measure of parent-child interactions with factors similar to the PCR) related to preference for specialization. Those who preferred finance also preferred less close interpersonal relations, in contrast to personnel majors, who needed more vigorous, active interpersonal lives. Accounting and marketing majors fell between these two groups in their need for interpersonal contact. Hill (1980) concludes that orientation toward or away from people may be a distinguishing factor in a person's choice of a business specialty.

A Formula for Occupational Choice. To express as succinctly as possible my present position on the variables that enter into vocational behavior, their relative importance, how they interact, and how these interactions may change with time, I have devised a formula that I have found useful as a teaching and mnemonic device. It is algebraic in form, but specific values cannot be assigned. It is taken to apply to one individual at a given time. The formula includes four groups of factors, each of which is designated by a letter in both upper and lower case. The lower-case letters represent coefficients indicating the weight to be attached to the factor; they may vary with time and circumstances. Such weights cannot be assigned with precision, but their usefulness lies in the fact that they can be changed to indicate changes in circumstances, which alter the relative importance of the different factors. For certain purposes, hypothetical weights can be given. The formula is:

$$S[(eE + bB + cC) + (fF, mM) + (lL + aA) + (pP \times gG \times tT \times iI)]$$

where S = sex; E = the general state of the economy; B = family background; L = learning and education; A = special acquired skills; P = physical; C = chance; F = friends, peer group; M = marital situation; G = cognitive (g); T = temperament and personality; and I = interests and values.

Sex is used as a general modifier, and it alone has no coefficient. Race presented similar problems but is now included in B, where it usually increases the value of b. Separation of the factors into groups indicated by parentheses is chiefly based on the degree of control the individual has over them.

Factors over which the individual has no personal control are joined by the first set of parentheses. Since they are not highly (if at all) interrelated, they are joined with a plus sign. E, the overall state of the economy, has been generally ignored in discussions of occupations, but it can be of prime importance — not only the national situation, war or peace, depression, inflation, or boom but also the immediate local labor situation. During war or periods of general expansion, opportunities may be opened to groups that had been excluded from them. In depressed periods, joblessness occurs more frequently in some groups than in others.

B, background, refers to the family of origin, and its position in the social group may dictate amount and kind of education, childrearing practices, and the aspirations of and for the children. Here, belonging to a minority group may be a heavily weighting aspect. Here also, as elsewhere, a crucial point is the extent to which the family differs from the majority in its location.

C, chance occurrences, have also been largely disregarded in studies of occupational selection, and yet they may be of crucial importance. In a study of occupational changes in midlife, Baruch and I (Roe and Baruch, 1967) were surprised that the specific changes made were so often attributed to a purely for-tuitous incident, such as meeting an old friend unexpectedly.

The second set of parentheses includes situations partially under the individual's control; usually only F or M is relevant. Especially with the young, the choices and activities of a peer group may be of great importance. For the married, such mat-ters as willingness or unwillingness of a spouse to move, or the need for a special environment or special medical care for some member of the family, may play a decisive role. Although such situations may be beyond the control of the individual, the mar-riage itself and the selection of friends are at least in part a matter of choice.

Factors covered in the third group are also partly under the individual's control and partly not, and, as with a peer group, the influence may decrease with time. L refers to general educa-tion and experience, and A refers to any special skills and tech-niques, such as are usually acquired through organized training methods.

In the last group, the usual categories of personal charac-teristics are combined as mutual multipliers (to express their intricate interactions). It is assumed that both genetic inheritance and experience are involved in all of these, but the relative im-portance of inheritance and experience is not known for any of them. The uniqueness of the individual, and what is usually referred to as personality, is expressed here, and the various factors named are those commonly considered to be involved in defining the personality.

P, physical, refers not only to appearance but also to special sensory and perceptual capacities. For most occupations, it is largely irrelevant, unless there is some extreme variation, as in height or weight, but any serious impairment, particularly if a sudden handicap occurs, may outweigh other factors. G is intended to cover cognitive abilities in general, such as g and any others, including special abilities of all sorts. The factor T covers temperament and such characteristics as are measured by personality tests. I, interests and values, are entered sepa-rately from T, in part because most investigators have dealt with them separately.

The crucial element in the factors in the last group (as well as in factor B) is not a level or a score, but rather the extent to which the individual deviates from the mean of the relevant group. For example, very high and very low intelligence are both differentiating. Weights can be assigned in terms of the extent of deviation from the mean — for example, a weight of 1 for a deviation between .0 and .5 sigma, a weight of 2 for a deviation between .5 and 1.0 sigma, and so on. This practice assumes a normal curve, of course, but it is based on an important assumption: For those who fall in the middle ranges of the population in all or most characteristics, occupational choice will depend on the relevant sex stereotypes and the immediate, perhaps chance, opportunities available.

Weights can also be assigned on a comparative basis, and this calculation can show probable age-related differences, which would be expected in Super's stages of vocational development in all but the last group (in which age changes are not likely) (Super and others, 1957). Beginning with the realistic phase of the state of exploration, the changes would be as follows:

Exploration	$(1E + 8B + 2C) + (7F) + (4L + 0A)$
Establishment	
Trial	$(7E + 6B + 2C) + (5F \text{ or } 1M) + (5L + 3A)$
Stable	$(6E + 4B + 2C) + (2M) + (6L + 5A)$
Maintenance	$(5E + 2B + 2C) + (2M) + (5L + 6A)$
Decline	$(5E + 1B + 4C) + (1M) + (4L + 5A)$

Although this formula was developed with the occupational life history in mind, it has further applicability. In the absence of a generally accepted theory encompassing normal development from the cradle to the grave, insights developed from studies of lifelong occupational histories have a good deal to contribute to such a theory.

Directions for Further Research. My classification of occupations seems to be highly satisfactory for men, but, as noted earlier, it is not adequate for women, largely because there is no place in it for the homemaker-mother role. There is also no system for accounting for part-time activities outside the home if the homemaker has them, or for measuring change from home to workforce. And what does one do about women who stay at home but assist their husbands in their work, such as the wife of the small contractor who takes his phone calls and sends out his bills, or the wife of the researcher who does a good deal of the record keeping? These shortcomings will need to be addressed as the classification system evolves.

More studies of the need satisfactions to be found in different occupations and in different occupational settings would be extremely helpful. There are few studies of the variability of different needs from person to person, whether in Maslow's or McClelland's systems, except for McClelland's "need for achievement" (McClelland and others, 1953). Few studies of the interactions between the occupation and other aspects of living have investigated the relative contributions of each to self-actualization.

Implications for Career Counseling. Without personal experience in counseling, there is not a great deal I can contribute that does not follow obviously from this research and speculation. I would repeat, however, the suggestion that the most important thing about most of the factors relevant to career choice is their closeness to the average of the appropriate group. It seems to me that failure to consider this statistic may well be a reason for the lack of success in early or adequate prediction of vocational choice.

The formula presented here can be useful not only in discussing the capacities of an individual but also in describing the requirements of any occupation. Beyond the issue of occupational choice, the formula can be used to understand the reasons for any choice among alternatives in any field.

Practical Applications of Roe's Theory of Career Development

The aspect of Anne Roe's theory that has found both the greatest support and the most applications in career counseling is her two-way occupational classification system (Roe, 1956). Many of these applications have a basis in career exploration and career-choice measures constructed with her occupational framework. Thus, they could logically be treated under any of the following headings. For the sake of brevity, however, each will be discussed only once.

Interest Assessment. The Career Occupational Preference System (COPS) Interest Inventory, also known as the California Occupational Preference Inventory (Knapp and Knapp, 1984, 1985), is based on Roe's interest framework. It provides fourteen scores, eight of which represent two levels of Science, Organization, Arts and Entertainment, and Service. Three additional scores correspond to three levels of Technology. Another three scores correspond to the Outdoor, Business Contact, and General Culture groups. COPS scores thus incorporate both dimensions of Roe's two-way classification system. The COPS system, keyed to the *Dictionary of Occupational Titles* (DOT) and the *Occupational Outlook Handbook* (OOH), includes a Career Briefs Kit, Career Cluster Booklets, Occupational Cluster Charts, Visuals (transparencies), and an Administration-Interpretation Device. The Interest Inventory, which may be scored by hand or by machine, can be used by high school, college, and adult clients. It consists of 168 job-activity items ("cook food for a hotel," "repair shoes or sandals"). COPS was included in Kapes and Mastie's (1982) guide to the most commonly used vocational guidance instruments.

The purpose of the COPS system is to foster greater career awareness through clustered occupational exploration — that is, to obtain information on a wide range of occupations within a specific cluster. It has good predictive validity for career choice or college major after graduation from high school. Knapp, Knapp, and Knapp-Lee (1985) found that 60 percent of a sample of 1,091 students tested in high school were, one to seven years after graduation, in jobs or majors that reflected one of their three highest-interest COPS scores. A standard-score method of determining predictability gave COPS a 74 percent hit rate. Science was the most predictable job area, and professional arts and nonprofessional business contact were the least predictable areas.

In addition to administration in schools (for which the COPS II at the fourth-grade reading level was also devised), the COPS system is intended for employment settings. It can be used for employees' self-awareness and personal development, as well as for selection and placement. Results can give both employee and employer a broader picture of the many jobs available within a specific cluster group.

The Vocational Interest Inventory (VII) (Lunneborg, 1981) consists of 112 forced-choice items, half of them occupational items and half of them activities items. The forced-choice format pulls interests apart and is especially useful for young adults who have not yet crystallized their interests. Developed over a fifteen-year period of research and field testing, and standardized on more than twenty-six thousand high school juniors and seniors, the VII is designed for high school and college career counseling. The VII is one of the first vocational interest instruments to have attempted to control for sex bias at the item level. The Test Report produced by Western Psychological Services (WPS) includes percentiles and T scores for each scale, an analysis and discussion of all scores at or above the 75th percentile, and a college-majors profile that shows how the individual's scores compare to the mean scores of graduating college majors who took the VII when they were high school juniors. The Guide to Interpretation provides brief descriptions of the people typical of each of Roe's eight interest groups, as well as examples of typical jobs for each interest area at five levels of education and training. The VII has been used since 1970 as part of the statewide precollege testing program in Washington State. Through WPS, the VII can be administered by microcomputer. It can be scored on one's own computer or computer-scored by WPS.

Another interest inventory that uses Roe's scheme is a fifty-six-item forced-choice inventory designed for women college graduates, which uses activities drawn from the fourth edition of the DOT (Lunneborg and Wilson, 1982). In the paperback guidebook that contains this inventory, Roe's framework is also used throughout one chapter. Here, for example, we find that over 60 percent of bachelor's degrees awarded to women were in general cultural majors, while minuscule numbers of women earned business, technical, and outdoor degrees.

In one of the major applications of Roe's framework, Meir (1975) constructed two interest inventories: *Ramak* (meaning "list of occupations" in Hebrew) consists of seventy-two occupational titles, and *Courses* is a list of sixty-four names of courses in higher education to which respondents indicate *yes, no,* or *undecided.* *Ramak* incorporates three levels — Professional, Semiprofessional, and Skilled — but only the Professional-Managerial level is represented in *Courses.* The extensive list of publications that Meir has generated using *Ramak* and *Courses* leaves little doubt that these inventories play a crucial role in vocational guidance throughout Israel. Secondary school teachers also use an occupational cylinder containing six hundred job titles to teach students about the hierarchical arrangement of levels and the circular configuration of Roe's fields (Meir and Shiran, 1979).

Vocational Counseling. Career development as a lifelong process is a key concept underlying Loughary and Ripley's (1978) attempts to teach career-planning skills to college students. As a part of their twenty-five-hour set of materials, knowledge about occupations is imparted through Roe's classification system. First, students read a list of eight occupational definitions and identify the correct work focus — Service, Business Contact, and so on. Then they put each of forty-two occupations into the appropriate eight columns (under Organization were placed messenger, CPA, typist, and U.S. president). Loughary and Ripley's workbook is one process for learning decision-making skills and implementing decisions in one's career and leisure choices.

Roe's framework is also a part of the comprehensive counseling procedure used at New Mexico State University for veterans attempting to have their educational benefits reinstated (Lynch, 1979). Crucial to this process is the client's exploration of at least three careers derived from Roe's classification system. A do-it-yourself career lab facilitates such exploration in clients who are described as having very unrealistic vocational expectations and inadequate knowledge of the world of work.

Miller (1986) has developed a four-step approach to working with clients who seek vocational guidance. It uses the hierarchical model of Roe's interests developed by Gati (1979) and is particularly useful for clients who want a straightforward, logical guidance procedure. The four steps are collecting self-information, sorting that information, collecting occupational information, and making a decision. Miller uses a vocational card sort that has clients organize cards according to Roe's eight interest groups. The first decision that clients make is between two major groups in the hierarchy: occupations oriented toward people (Service, Business Contact, Organization, General Culture) versus occupations oriented away from people (Technology, Outdoor, Science). The hierarchy is thus rooted in what Roe considered the crucial outcome of parental childrearing style: orientation in offspring toward or away from other people.

Another novel application of Roe's ideas regarding experiences in early childhood is a model of a career development pyramid (Stewart and Nejedlo, 1980); Roe is credited with inspiring the pyramid face labeled "Career-Choice Factors." Counselors can introduce the counseling process to clients by explaining that choices result from four components—self-concept, specific jobs, life-style, and such factors as the warmth or distance of parents.

The emphasis in Miller-Tiedeman's (1976a) Individual Career Exploration (ICE) inventory is the active involvement of eighth- to twelfth-grade students in investigating tentative occupational choices. This self-administered and self-scored inventory contains six self-assessments—interests, past experiences, appealing occupations, best skills, abilities (course grades), and values—all based on Roe's groups. The ICE also contains a six-item measure of Roe's decision levels, based on students' willingness to work hard and finish unpleasant tasks. After completing the ICE, students focus on their two highest occupational groups and decision levels. They consult Roe's (1976) booklet and select three or more specific occupations from among six hundred and gather detailed information about them. At this point, they consult the DOT, the OOH, or the Computerized Vocational Information System (CVIS). They fill in Job Information Checklists, supplied by Scholastic Testing Service, for each occupation. These checklists include the education and training costs required. At this last stage in the ICE self-counseling process, Roe's ideas also prevail. The Job Information Checklist first looks at occupations in terms of providing opportunities for eight prototypical Roe activities (for example, "opportunities for applying scientific and mathematical knowledge").

Teaching and Decision Making. Roe's framework is also used in CVIS, one of the first computerized systems in high schools in this country (Harris, 1968). The purpose of CVIS is to facilitate the retrieval of information about jobs for students, who can also use personal data in their career exploration (for example, class rank, composite test battery score, and Kuder Preference Record scores). One benefit of this system to counselors is a daily computer printout of students who have received "discrepancy messages" regarding the levels of the occupations they desire and their academic records. CVIS has been described as an automated library and filing system, not as a replacement for counselors, and it clearly includes both of the primary uses to which Roe's system has been put: teaching and personal decision making.

Teaching is the object of Miller-Tiedeman's (1977b) Individual Career Exploration (ICE) Inventory, Picture Form, for elementary and junior high school students. Students complete five exercises based on Roe's groups (for example, "tools you would like to use"). On the ICE record sheet, they total their scores to identify their highest and second-highest groups. They then use Roe's (1976) booklet to look up jobs that fall into these groups and proceed with a variety of information-gathering activities. Teachers emphasize that a career is a developmental process that lasts a lifetime and that one's interests change with new experiences and attitudes. It is important for students to understand stereotyping, life-styles that accompany particular jobs, and the education necessary for various decision levels in jobs—professional, skilled and semiprofessional, and semiskilled. The ICE Picture Form is primarily a teaching device in which Roe's system is used to present the world of work to young people making their very first career choices.

Teaching is also the motivation behind the *Hall Occupational Orientation Inventory* (HOOI) (Hall and Tarrier, 1976), devised for grades 3–7 and 8–16 and for adults and low-literate adults. Among its twenty-two scales are ten values-and-needs scales, which are underpinned by Roe's ideas as well as by Maslow's. Despite its testlike format, the goal of the HOOI is group instruction about job characteristics, workers' traits, and values and needs, with needs considered the primary organizing principle in everyone's life. Working with a counselor in a group, clients are expected to make improved occupational choices through clarification of values and needs.

Educational and vocational decisions after high school are the focus of the Washington Precollege Program's (WPC) (1988) student guide. The guide is intended to assist students in interpreting feedback from the WPC test battery, which includes the VII (Lunneborg, 1981). The student guidance report, which presents aptitude test scores, high school grades, and VII scores, also presents predictions for grades in college courses (the courses are organized according to Roe's framework). For example, in the Outdoor area, grade predictions are made for courses in agriculture, animal science, botany, environmental studies, forestry, geology, and horticulture. Using the guide, students consider their grade predictions, interests, career values, special skills, ability test scores, and earned grades to select the Roe fields from which to make tentative educational and career choices. All college programs offered in Washington State are presented within Roe's framework. To illustrate, a student attracted to the Organization area would find fifteen four-year college programs and forty-six community college programs devoted to organizational occupations. The guide even uses Roe's framework to project employment opportunities five years hence in Washington, Idaho, Montana, Oregon, and Alaska. For example, under General Culture one finds that the demand for broadcast news analysts will be very slight, whereas from three to six thousand new jobs for secondary teachers are expected.

Career Development Research. Countless career development research studies have successfully used Roe's system of groups and levels to classify subjects' occupations. Just a few will be cited here, to illustrate the wide utility and established validity of Roe's two-way scheme.

In his study of the predictive accuracy of measured versus expressed interests over a twenty-one-year period, Cairo (1982) uses Roe's fields and levels to classify his subjects' target occupations at age thirty-six, as well as their expressed occupational preferences at ages fifteen, eighteen, and thirty-five. Hughes (1972) uses Roe's levels of men's occupations as "actual" job levels, which he then predicts from measures of intelligence and self-concept. Hughes feels that his findings strongly support the hypothesis that people work at levels predictable from intelligence and self-concept. Working just with the groups to which the occupations of high school seniors' fathers belonged, Belz and Geary (1984) found that students with fathers in General Culture and Science occupations had higher SAT verbal and quantitative scores, while students with fathers in Service occupations were lowest on both SAT scores.

In the area of occupational change, Kleinberg (1976) looked at the vocational fields of men at ages twenty-five and thirty-five in Super's career-pattern study and found, as Roe would have predicted, that more change occurred between adjacent fields than between those farther apart in her circular configuration. Similarly, Kanchier and Unruh (1987) used Roe's classification system and found that 58 percent of men and women in Organization jobs did not change occupational category when they voluntarily left the same corporation. Another 21 percent of these job changers were one-step movers; most gravitated next door into Business Contact. Roe's levels are one of Betz's (1984) chief variables in a study of the job mobility of women ten years out of college. Consistent with a traditional female career, traditional women were less likely to change careers across the ten-year period and were more likely to stay at the same job level or go down a level. In contrast, pioneers in nontraditional careers more often moved up in job level.

Will students who have a positive attitude toward women in science (as measured by WiSS scores) themselves be attracted to Science jobs? Erb and Smith (1984) correlated the scales of a forty-nine-item career-interest test based on Roe's eight fields. They found the expected positive correlation of WiSS scores with Science interest and zero correlation of WiSS scores with Business Contact and Service interest.

Do occupations possess age stereotypes, just as they possess sex stereotypes? To find out, Gordon and Arvey (1986) used Roe classifications of fifty-nine occupations, both by eight interest areas and four levels of responsibility. They found that people do indeed perceive that different jobs are held by people of different ages. File clerks, for example, are thought to be about twenty-four years old, while mayors are thought to be in their late forties. Gordon and Arvey's subjects' stereotypes were remarkably accurate when compared to actual median ages in these two occupations. Subjects were least accurate at the lowest job levels. For example, such jobs as hospital attendant, heavy-equipment operator, and receptionist were seen to be held by young workers, when in fact they are not.

Are the occupations being considered by junior high school students related to their parents' occupational groups or levels? Campbell and Parsons (1972) had disadvantaged and advantaged seventh- and ninth-grade students indicate which jobs they were considering, which they preferred, and which they planned to enter. These occupations and those of their parents were coded according to Roe's groups and levels. Campbell and Parsons found little evidence for identification with the same-sex parent's field or level in either group. All students were considering jobs skewed toward the professional end of the scale, and the advantaged students aspired to greater heights than the disadvantaged students did. The strong correlations among the considered, preferred, and planned fields suggest an unrealistic degree of confidence in reaching professional goals.

For Project TALENT males, how would career plans in the last year of high school (1960), and at one, five, and eleven years thereafter, compare on the Flanagan, Holland, and Roe models? McLaughlin and Tiedeman (1974) found that career stability was about the same for all three frameworks. The three systems are thus equally useful to researchers and counselors who are interested in job change over the life span. (Within each framework, incidentally, the men moved away from scientific jobs and toward business and sales jobs.)

Further Evidence. In searching out these applications of Roe's classification system, I could not help gaining a powerful impression, which cannot be conveyed by a simple list of references. I lost count of the times I tracked down an article, only to discover that there was no concrete practical application I could cite; there was simply indebtedness to Roe for her ideas. How many counselors' daily practices are influenced by Roe's thinking on the early familial determinants of vocational choice? How many of us owe our emphasis on needs satisfaction to her? I will give but two recent examples.

Levinson (1987) found a special-education student with a WAIS-R IQ of 85, a Block Design score of 13, an Object Assembly score of 12, and automotive interest at the 90th percentile. The student was referred to a program in auto mechanics, which he successfully completed. It was not these test scores that most determined Levinson's recommendation, however; rather, it was his having noted the extreme degree of rejection and neglect this boy experienced from his parents and his peers. As a consequence, the boy stayed away from both school and home, and he developed a strong vocational orientation away from people and toward inanimate objects (this orientation, however, was used for a highly satisfactory diagnosis and referral).

Similarly, Moss and Bradley (1988) analyzed the case of a publican with a strong orientation toward people and vocational interests in Service, General Culture, and Arts and Entertainment. The publican's orientation toward people was attributed to his dominant parent, his mother, who was overprotective and demanded that he excel in school. Her irregular reinforcement of her son's need for love and belongingness was tied to his seeking of jobs that had strong social rewards (the most recent example had been a job as a substance-abuse counselor).

In conclusion, the applications presented here—interest assessment, vocational counseling, teaching and decision making, career development research, and the daily practice of career counseling — are testimony to the clinical wisdom and validity of Anne Roe's notions of career choice, developed over thirty years ago. As a clinician and personality researcher, intuiting and theorizing about career choice, she has always been outside the mainstream of counseling psychology, but the overwhelming evidence is that, as Zytowski (1986) put it, "Diverse ways of knowing may be equally valid."

5 *Edward S. Bordin*

Psychodynamic Model of Career Choice and Satisfaction

Background of the Theory

Almost from the beginning of my interest in vocational choice, I was looking at it from a dynamic point of view. In one of my early papers (Bordin, 1943), I was suggesting that, in responding to the Strong Vocational Interest Blank, the individual was giving expression to a concept of self in occupational terms. To the degree that interest inventories are valid, I proposed that the correspondence of an individual's professed and inventoried interest would be a partial function of the amount of occupational information possessed. Another direction of inference was that, to the degree that occupational self-concepts incorporated personality, that degree of correspondence was to be expected between interest and personality inventories. This early paper included a small demonstration that individuals can manipulate their scores by consciously adopting an alternative occupationally defined self-concept. Others (for example, Kelso, 1948; Longstaff, 1948) have subsequently confirmed that assumption. Finally, that paper asserted that if or when a person changes his or her concept in ways that can be expected to have impact on the vocational self, then corresponding changes in inventoried interests will occur, a prediction that was confirmed (Bordin and Wilson, 1953). It was only a short step beyond this idea to assume that vicissitudes in the development of self and self-concept will be reflected in inventoried interest patterns, and then to take the broader step, as Super did, relating self-concept to career development (Super and others, 1963).

Initially, I was thinking from the perspective of the counselor seeking to be helpful to students looking at the vocational implications of the curricular decisions they faced. For example, I reconciled trait and factor theories prevalent at the University of Minnesota with self-concept ideas stemming from Rogers and his associates at Ohio State and later at Chicago, in a set of diagnostic conceptions to be applied to the difficulties students had in making decisions (Bordin, 1946). Soon, however, my outlook broadened to a more general interest in personality development and in the ways that it can contribute to personal difficulties in general, including difficulties in vocational decision making. At about the same time, because of my move to the University of Michigan, I entered into a rich source of awareness and understandings regarding psychoanalytical theory. Graduate students and colleagues stimulated me and, I trust, were in turn stimulated to bring together the perspectives of normal and pathological development. The older analytical stance looked at the potential for converting pathological "fixations" into socially acceptable "sublimations." The sadistic destructive impulses of the would-be murderer were transformed into the socially useful activities of the butcher or surgeon. Sometimes the implication of psychodynamic theory was that the destructive impulses were the true ones and that only their diversion kept them in check. This interpretation of psychoanalytical theory remains. But let me get to the details of theory later.

My present theoretical position owes most to my collaboration with Stanley Segal and Barbara Nachmann, although they may wish to disassociate themselves from the present version. From their work and that of other students, we developed the now widely reproduced framework for mapping occupations from the point of view that their intrinsic work requirements give the individual a way of being that is consonant with the dynamics and structure of his or her personality. As will become apparent, the present point of view retains much of the earlier emphasis on the fate and transformation of basic motivations (libidinal and others) but gives greater prominence to ego development (for example, Erikson, 1959; Hartmann, 1964), including, of course, ego identity.

The Theory

I have chosen the tree as a metaphor for the structure of the theory to reflect the fact that there is a root set of assumptions, which then are developed into more specific propositions. Before getting to propositions, I want to be specific about the limits of our claims. These ideas are directed toward the participation of personality in career development and the series of choices that comprise it. They do not replace but are in addition to economic, cultural or ethnic, geographical or climatic, biological, and accidental factors. Of course, all these factors are in constant interaction. The economic pressures to gain a livelihood reflect geographical and climatic conditions; the scientific and technological aspects of culture influence the opportunities offered to various social classes and ethnic subgroups. At the same time, every one of these factors exerts its influence on personality and on motivational dynamics.

The theory proposes that the participation of personality in work and career is rooted in the role of play in human life. The all but unquenchable need for play stimulates its fusion with the necessities of work in the search for a self-satisfying vocation. The world of work provides a home for diverse persons with widely varying personalities. The theory will speak to both the decision processes through which this search for vocation is pursued and to the ways of construing the occupational world that are the targets of the search. Finally, the theory will address the question of the developmental sources of individual differences in the kinds and styles of satisfactions sought.

Although there is an effort to formalize the theory by stating propositions, there will be no effort to force or pretend more formalism than has actually been achieved. Thus, the reader will encounter efforts to state propositions whenever sufficient evidence has been found to support them.

The Spirit of Play as the Root. The spirit of play is caught in the term *spontaneity,* which is used to refer to the elements of self-expression and self-realization in our responses to situations. Spontaneity is a major key to differentiating work from play. What marks the essence of play is its intrinsically satisfying nature. Although we may engage in play for extrinsic reasons — for example, status, achievement, admiration, even money, in the case of the professional player (but then is it work or play?) — what distinguishes play from work is the satisfaction gained from simply engaging in the activity. Jogging for the purpose of slimming down or improving one's circulatory system is not play. Jogging because one enjoys a feeling of wholeness by losing self-consciousness in the rhythmic motion and the changing surroundings is play.

> *Proposition 1: This sense of wholeness, this experience of joy, is sought by all persons, preferably in all aspects of life, including work.*

The unquenchability of this urge toward spontaneity is illustrated under the most adverse conditions of external stress. A case in point is the stories of pranks by men in battle, such as the appearance of "Kilroy was here" signs in unexpected times or places (on enemy tanks) in World War II. Comparable observations have been made of individuals working on the assembly line, that place of alienated toil featured in Charlie Chaplin's film *Modern Times.* Observations have shown that workers seek free time, sometimes through sabotaging the machine, sometimes by prodigious feats of ingenuity that permitted them to get ahead of the conveyer belt (Blauner, 1964).

This ubiquitous urge, the first proposition states, can be expected to be expressed in the work area of the individual's life as in other areas. Every vocational counselor is familiar with the stereotypical comment "I am looking for something that would give me a (good or secure, according to how scared the person or economically risky the times are) living and something I will be happy doing." Even while a person must struggle with the necessity of finding a means of livelihood, he or she seeks personal meaning and some form of creative expression. This proposition, then, is one of the two assumptions in the model of the participation of personality in career. It is rarely if ever fully articulated or clearly perceived and may remain unarticulated or unconscious. The individual's organizing wishes and desires more or less silently operate as a guidance mechanism, steering him as he picks his way in the course of making training, job-entry, and job-change decisions, ever seeking to increase the congruence between the intrinsic satisfaction that work provides and his personal style. As is implied by the term *unconscious,* we cannot expect to find evidence of such a process by simply asking a person what wishes or desires have governed the series of decisions that have marked her career. It should, however, be possible to infer these enduring orientations from a careful examination of the individual's life history, especially by examining feelings, fantasies, dreams, and other imaginative responses directed to past, present, or future.

If the spontaneity of the spirit of play is so pervasive and so imperative, how can one account for the prevalent distinctions between work and play in adult life? Observers of children have noted that the fluid, spontaneous play of the very young child soon gives way to formalization of rules that introduce restraining boundaries to the areas of spontaneity. One can assume that this development partly reflects the demand of the maturing capacities of the child for more complex, directed expressions. The other factor in greater formalization and effort is the fact that work and play are naturally fused for the child, as they tend to be for adults in primitive societies. As the 1930 White House Conference stated, "With the young child, his work is his play and his play is his work" (quoted by Stone, 1971, p. 8). Thus, as the child matures, effort toward mastery is introduced. The words of Huizinga, in his influential analysis of play in adult life, capture very well this growing connection between spontaneity and effort. Speaking of the formal characteristics of play, Huizinga (1955, p. 13) characterizes it as "a free activity standing quite consciously outside 'ordinary' life as being 'not serious,' but at the same time absorbing the player intensely and utterly." The growing intensity, directedness, and complexity define the trend toward increasing effort.

Compulsion, as used in psychoanalytical theory, refers to the internalization of external pressures. In the child, these external pressures mainly come from parents or caretakers through the threats of withdrawal of love and the tangible accompaniments of rewards and punishments and deprivations. Gradually, and with an adequate base of love, these external pressures are internalized as conscience, duty, expectations, and other concepts of modes of behavior required by society before one can be rewarded by a livelihood. Research, such as that by Hoffman (1975) and Aronfreed (1968), does not provide specification of how much love represents an adequate base.

Compulsion and effort are intimately related. The greater the effort and the longer it endures, the stronger the physical and perhaps psychological pressure toward cessation and rest becomes. What sustains effort against this accumulating counterpressure is either inner interest and involvement or external threats of deprivation, punishment, or, in the extreme, annihilation, which in the adult can be internalized and experienced as a part of an inner compulsion — that is, to stay alive. Thus, there is a relationship between effort and compulsion, in which the need to rest under intense effort interacts with the degree to which originally externalized motives have been fully internalized as part of ego and self (Kegan, 1979).

As already suggested, maturation carries with it a pressure toward increasingly complex play, the satisfactions of which can be attained only through intense efforts of mastery. The kind of freely given effort required to satisfy one's interest in achieving the joy of playing Bach or Beethoven can easily become transformed, especially for a person of limited talent, into the drudgery of toiling over exercises. Even unsystematic observation suggests that individuals differ very greatly in their ability to sustain effort without their inner investments slipping away. When that happens, an activity that has had intrinsic value is transformed into a self-alienated compulsion. There seem to be persons so highly sensitized to external compulsion that instead of fusing work and play, they seek to keep them apart.

Proposition 2: The degree of fusion of work and play is a function of an individual's developmental history regarding compulsion and effort.

I have conjectured that the sources of this ability or inability to fuse work and play are likely to be found in formative experiences that influence the psychic chemistry of spontaneity, effort, and compulsion (Bordin, 1979). As a starting point, I have already pointed to intrinsic reasons why effort, pushed far enough, converts spontaneity into compulsion. How can one take account of individual differences in threshold for that conversion? My conjecture is that at least part of the answer will be found in another process factor, involving the deployment of attention. Several observations have led me to this idea. From clinical observations, I note how an overemphasis on awareness and precision can induce obsessive-compulsive states, where the individual is sapped of spontaneity and isolated from feelings. Zen philosophy, expressed through archery or flower arranging, alerts us to how self-conscious ambition inherently saps creativity and interest. In both athletics and the performing arts, failures to fuse technical skill with self-expression are noted as shortcomings of otherwise talented performers. Thus, overemphasis on analysis, activation of self-consciousness, and overambition may be intimately tied to failures to fuse work and play.

Developmental explanations must account for differences in the vulnerability of these intrinsic motivations to such distracting factors. Surely, one developmental factor proposed by Leiberman (1977) is the modeling of playfulness by parents, teachers, and other caretakers in introducing playfulness into work-oriented activities and in creating an atmosphere in which play flourishes. Yet I am not satisfied that modeling alone is sufficient to account for the compatibilities between spontaneity and effort. Apart from physiological factors, external compulsion is an inescapable part of social organization and social relations. The ideal life is not the unattainable life free of external compulsions but the life in which there is room for the external compulsions to be shaped to fit inner needs. Personal relationships being central to the quality of life, the individual needs to learn to come to terms with the pressures from others that are reflections of *their* needs and wishes. Therefore, the individual chemistry of spontaneity and effort is formed around the external compulsions encountered in early experiences with parents' (or other caretakers') authority.

Where there is a strong alliance between child and parent, formed out of a leadership that combines authority with mutuality and bonds of affection and respect, the child acquires a greater readiness to fuse effort and spontaneity, free of feelings of external compulsion. I think it is not accidental that at a time of loss of mutuality between the young and their elders — during our involvement in Vietnam — work and career were with greater frequency reacted to as "the rat race," to be escaped through dropping out or submitting passively. This was also the period of rebellion in education, when sensitivity to compulsion made all requirements, whether of curriculum or standards of performance, too painful to bear. It was during this period that I encountered the phenomenon of clients in vocational counseling protesting that transforming their hobbies into vocations would "take the fun out of it."

Decision Theory. Having defined and described the taproot of the chemistry of spontaneity, effort, and compulsion, we are prepared to move forward (upward, in our metaphor) to the series of branchings that grow from it.

> *Proposition 3: A person's life can be seen as a string of career decisions reflecting the individual's groping for an ideal fit between self and work.*

It is this fit that transforms the imperative to work (in order to survive) into a vocation. This fit is the means through which necessity is converted into self-fulfillment. In Gardner's (1968, p. 32) words, "what can be more satisfying than to be engaged in work in which every capacity or talent one may have is needed, every lesson one may have learned is used, every value one cares about is furthered?" Gardner goes on to poke fun at those who would treat such self-engrossment in work as an object of pity or even disease (the current fad is to speak of the "workaholic"). He says it is amusing that persons who can come close to achieving this ideal of fusing work and play get sympathy along with their pleasure, whereas those seeking their fun in formal play, to "scratch the dry soil in calculated diversions," are envied or criticized.

Earlier, I referred to the metaphor of the guidance mechanism, which, in silence and unnoticed, steers the individual through the string of decisions that represent a career. That "mechanism" is not best understood in mechanical terms but rather in the dynamic terms of the evolution of personality. Since occupations and persons evolve, the steering process of seeking an optimum fit involves the two changing factors of self and occupation. The younger the person, the more rapid and the more likely the change in personality. The "mechanism" influences the cognitive processes through which an individual assesses alternatives at each choice point, whether that choice point arises from external structure (for example, the next step in education or the next step in professional progress or job movement) or from internal structure (for example, feelings of deprivation or positive feelings of wishing to enlarge cne's satisfactions). The person seeks continually to encompass the facets of self through work. People with multiple talents and interests are attracted to occupations that permit maximum molding to fit self. For example, entry into the professions of law, medicine, and psychology permits much greater self-differentiation and fulfillment. Just as occupants at the same level of training and skill may differ in the range of needs they can accommodate—for example, medicine and psychology versus accounting or dentistry— there may be even greater differences among levels of the same occupation. Even at lower levels of the same occupation, there may be important differences, as Blauner (1964) found in comparing four machine-tending occupations (for example, the differences of amount and kind of control over one's time and effort that machine tending requires in the automobile industry versus the chemical industries). Unlike auto assembly-line workers, machine tenders in chemical industries have long periods of free time.

Closely related to consideration of lower-level jobs are two questions: whether opportunities for satisfaction in the work itself are confined to only a small number of elite jobs, and whether the nature of modern technological society creates a large mass underclass doomed to alienated toil devoid of intrinsic satisfaction. Answers to such questions must circumvent the bias of occupational ethnocentrism (for example, the intellectual's assumption that anyone blocked from her kinds of pursuits cannot possibly be engaged in anything intrinsically satisfying). Although there are not systematic data to provide a definitive answer, a reading of Terkel's (1972) interviews with people about their work shows that many can find satisfaction in relatively menial blue-collar jobs.

Mapping Motives and Occupations. One of the keys to understanding what is taking place at each turning point in a career path is understanding the particularization of the continuing search for self-fulfillment represented at each point. Most of the mathematical models of decision making include terms to represent the states of nature that define the opportunities and the base-rate probabilities, as well as terms to represent the utilities or payoffs associated with the alternative choices. Moreover, there are states of nature that define the opportunities and the base-rate probabilities. There are the enduring characteristics of the individual that forecast probabilities of success. The personality of the individual enters not only into assessment of the utilities but also into the subjective assessment of self and, through that, of the probabilities of success.

Remember that in this context, in speaking of utilities, I am referring to kinds of intrinsic satisfaction rather than to pay, status, or other kinds of extrinsic returns. Both kinds are incorporated into formal decision models. It is no wonder that most experiments on decision making are directed toward an equation in which the utility term is the unknown!

Apart from identifying the technicalities of decision models, the task is to identify some pivotal set of motives into which occupations or jobs can be mapped. An adequate set of coordinates will permit not only the mapping of the overarching occupational group but also the subspecialties and even an idiosyncratically organized special job. One major problem in accomplishing this, not yet fully solved, is to choose what level of casting motives is most appropriate. At one extreme, we have the bedrock, physiologically based motives founded on needs for survival and the Freudian drives for sex and aggression. At the other extreme are the presumed derivatives of these basic drives, named to fit specific situations, either unique to individuals or dictated by societal or cultural norms, which can balloon into lists numbering in the hundreds. Clearly, motives founded on such general drives as the need or wish to stay alive, sex, aggression, mastery, or competence are too general to provide a basis for differentiating jobs and occupations in terms of their intrinsic satisfactions. Some intermediate level of classification or conceptualization is needed, general enough to provide for basic grouping yet specific enough to permit needed differentiations. Along with these formal characteristics, the coordinates must carry explanatory power.

The starting place must, of course, be observation of people at work. Job analysis has a long-established tradition, but we must choose our perspectives carefully and be aware of the selective character of each. There is no single correct perspective. Each must be justified by how well it serves its purpose, not only theoretically but also in empirical terms. Looking at a job with the purpose of forecasting how quickly a person will learn it and the level of mastery attained inevitably focuses attention on the prior knowledge and skills that are required. It may include noting those personal elements that contribute to quality of learning and performance. Looking at jobs for the purpose of identifying the intrinsic satisfaction that a person could derive from working at it involves us in the personality area, which is marked by much less consensus. From a purely descriptive, trait-oriented view, one could make a list of characteristics — for example, social introversion-extraversion, intellectual–physically active, and so on. For others (I include myself), this is not enough. We seek a set of concepts and terms that integrates these traits conveying both their inner meaning and their continuities of past and present.

The solution that Nachmann, Segal, and I chose almost three decades ago (Bordin, Nachmann, and Segal, 1963) was to stay very close to the Freudian concepts of psychosexual development, which, it could be argued, represent basic physiological and socially based sources of satisfaction that are part of the universal biographies of individuals, regardless of sex or culture. Thus, we included being nurtured, fed, and fostered, as well as turning to aggressive acts, such as biting, cutting, and devouring. We sought to capture transformations of simple and primitive responses to more complex responses of the maturing individual. We saw the satisfactions of being informed and taught as extensions of those of being physically fed by mother or caretaker. Most important, we assumed that some individuals have shaping experiences that lead to their finding great satisfactions in feeding and fostering. Other characteristics of the individual — probably combinations of innate characteristics, the nature of individual early experiences, technological factors of the era and culture, and accidents of time, place, and geography — play a part in the particular form that this nurturance takes (for example, as teacher, cook, pediatrician). As a first approximation, we are prepared to include metaphorical or partial representations of nurturance — for example, a financial consultant who fosters her clients' financial well-being, or a gardener concerned with feeding and fostering plants.

Following this plan, we made a list of such satisfactions, to include the manipulative, both physical and interpersonal; the sensual, involving sight, sound, and touch; the anal, to include acquiring, time-ordering, hoarding, and smearing; the genital, to include erection, penetration, impregnation, and producing; the exploratory, again to include sight, sound, and touch; and, finally, flowing-quenching, exhibiting, and rhythmic movement. This formed one axis of our map. The other axis was composed of such judgments as the degree of involvement that a particular job offers; the instrumental mode of action (for example, feeding financial advice or using a cutting word); the objects or parts of objects toward which the action was directed; whether the action could be differentiated with regard to sexual mode (that is, masculine or feminine); and whether the effect was directly experienced or modified.

Although this way of looking at the intrinsic motives that can be satisfied by the variety of occupations continues to be useful, I find myself mixing it with a more integrative, perhaps ego-analytical, level. This level has me turning to curiosity, precision, power, expressiveness, and concern with right and wrong and justice, as well as to nurturance, in my efforts to understand the personality style incorporated into the individual's productive activities.

From my point of view, each of these parameters represents a complex aspect of personality. The term *curiosity,* in addition to referring to the epistemic and the interpersonal, includes the idea of curiosity directed toward the insides of bodies, human and subhuman. It reflects the differential expressions to be found in law, psychiatry, and clinical psychology as one kind of group, medicine and dentistry as another group, and in the most abstract versions of all the sciences as a third group. Similarly, the term *precision* is further subdivided into the emphasis on neatness and control, the concern with detail, and the involvement in building logical structures (such as those involved in organized thinking). The range of occupations incorporating one or more of these features includes law, accounting, and engineering, as well as being a machinist, clerk, or academician-scholar. The term *power* refers to physical power and its augmentation through mechanical means, as well as to the power of personality and intellect. Thus, the tractor operator, the engineer, the athlete, the lawyer, the writer, and the manager all represent some form of the expression of power. The term *expressiveness* is intended to cover the various self-displaying, performing satisfactions through rhythmic, sensual, and imaginative action, which are highly evident in the actor, the artist, and the musician but also enter into some elements of the work of the teacher, the lawyer, and the minister. The concern with right and wrong and justice is prominent in the ministry and in law but certainly also plays a part in the policeman's work. The preceding discussion of nurturance has brought out its range of expression except for calling attention to the differential importance of intimacy; the nurturant occupations can also be arranged in terms of the degree to which they require intimate and close involvement with the persons being nurtured.

As the reader will see, this level of conceptualization is most provocative of ideas about the striving toward inner meaning and wholeness that marks individual development, in which one's productive life figures importantly.

There is considerable overlap between this more integrative set of concepts and terms and those that Darley (Darley, 1941; Darley and Hagenah, 1955) and Holland (1959) developed as a backdrop for their interpretations of vocational interest tests. There are also elements of similarity to the system of classification proposed in the *Dictionary of Occupational Titles* (DOT) (U.S. Department of Labor, 1977), when it turns to the personal demands of jobs. The DOT divides all activities into three classes: those dealing with data, with people, and with things. Each class is then subdivided, from simple to complex. The subdivisions for data are synthesizing, coordinating, analyzing, compiling, computing, copying, and comparing. Those for people are mentoring, negotiating, instructing, supervising, diverting, persuading, speaking-signaling, serving, and taking instruction-helping. Those for things are setting up, precision working, operating-controlling, driving-operating, manipulating, tending, feeding-offbearing, and handling.

All of this leads me to my fourth proposition, which takes a metatheoretical form, as compared to the purely theoretical form of the preceding ones.

Proposition 4: The most useful system of mapping occupations for intrinsic motives will be one that captures life-styles or character styles and stimulates or is receptive to developmental conceptions.

Developmental Theory. The major question that the developmental aspect of our theory must address is how to account for the individual's reaching a state of readiness to seek and find satisfactions of a particular form. As the preceding discussion has indicated, this effort means trying to account for the development of particular character styles. Furthermore, it is in this sense that we can expect to find the roots of the personal elements of career choice in early experiences, some of them undergone before formal schooling begins. I now offer all of this as a formal proposition.

> *Proposition 5: The roots of the personal aspects of career development are to be found throughout the early development of the individual, sometimes in the earliest years.*

The more we can understand how best to define and measure enduring personal characteristics and how to account for their formation, the more specific we will be able to get about the kinds of shaping experiences that go into the formation of the kind of person who would seek the satisfaction of engineering, law, or social work or the satisfaction of being a machinist, a miner, or a bank clerk. One of the most important implications of this proposition is that it has us looking beyond the experiences of formal schooling in trying to account for career development.

Most personality theorists have looked to the constructs of self and identity as sources of understanding how personality is expressed through vocational choice. Inventories that assess interests, values, and life-style mainly reflect self-perceptions. Thus, the evolution of self and identity plays an important part in propositions about the developmental aspects of personality and vocational choice. The work of the object-relations theorists — for example, Kernberg, Kohut, and Mahler — has tended to concentrate on the most primitive aspects in self-other differentiations. My concern is with the later, continuing self-other issues. It is here that important factors in the evolution of vocational choices are to be found.

> *Proposition 6: Each individual seeks to build a personal identity that incorporates aspects of father and mother yet retains elements unique to the self.*

As Erikson (1959) has stipulated, the development of ego identity, while marked by significant events during the adolescent years, goes on as a continual process. It is important not to trivialize or oversimplify this idea by assuming that it is solely a rational decision process. Instead, the ego is embedded in the loving attachments of the growing infant and child coping with the stimulating challenges of expanding experience, which are accompanied by inevitable fears and anxieties. The individual draws to himself both the strengths and the weaknesses of those he loves, and he seeks to overcome those weaknesses and to build an independent, self-founded base for existence. This process is largely silent and unselfconscious. Not only are important parts away from the center of awareness, they are also often intertwined with anxieties, which in turn erect formidable barriers to undistorted awareness. It is important to emphasize that while mother and father are at the core of the identity-building process, the search for continuity is influenced by the extended family ethnic, cultural, and even national connections.

It should be evident that all this is larger than one's work role but does include it. The foregoing discussions have underlined how fully expressive of self our productive lives can be.

Apart from the major anomalies of development that neurosis represents, we can expect that normal development is not a smooth, continual process. Accumulating dissatisfactions and doubts are likely to culminate in particular decision points, whether these decision points are the normative ones set up by the educational system and the world of work, special conditions created by economic slumps or technological developments, or the outcome of an individual's incurring an enduring disability. Because such situations represent pressures to reexamine personal resolutions, they also represent opportunities to rework those resolutions in the direction of fuller self-realization and satisfaction.

Proposition 7: One source of perplexity and paralysis at career decision points will be found in doubts in and dissatisfactions with current resolutions of self.

Empirical Support

A half-century after the development of vocational interest testing and the heavy accumulation of evidence of close interaction between personality measures and vocational interests (see, for example, Osipow, 1973, chap. 6), there can be little doubt that personality plays a part in the work aspects of an individual's life. The challenge is to articulate and validate a much more specific set of propositions about the particular ways in which specified personal characteristics distinguish given occupations and are marked by certain developmental events. I must acknowledge that the foregoing set of propositions is merely the scaffold of the theoretical structure that is required. It will take a far greater cycle of empirical observations, and finer-grained theory construction than now exists, to reach that objective. In this section, I will review my sense (by no means comprehensive) of the current empirical base for this model of the personal factors in vocational choice, and I will fill in the theoretical structure. This review will be organized to follow the order of topics in the preceding section.

Fusing Work and Play. This is the area in which there is the least direct empirical evidence to test the tenability of ideas about the pervasiveness of the human search for spontaneity of expression (proposition 1) and the vicissitudes of expression in relation to effort and compulsion (proposition 2). The researcher's tendencies toward the segregation of observations may be a retarding factor. For example, there is the tendency to separate observations of work, play, and leisure (the latter a time use–linked concept). A second tendency is to direct observation toward the play activities of the young and the work of the adults. A third tendency is to concentrate observations of animals' play activities on juveniles.

This last tendency can be accounted for by reports that play is rare in adult animals (Aldis, 1975). On the other side is Eibl-Eibesfeldt's (1967) conviction that animals are capable of spontaneous (centrally activated) behavior. Whether or not there is an important qualitative distinction between humans and other animals in needs and capacity for play, Centers and Bugental (1966) provide evidence that intrinic interest in one's work is not a phenomenon narrowly restricted to the occupants of a relatively small group of elite jobs. In querying samples of the working population, they found that even though there was a positive correlation between job level and the importance of intrinsic motivation, substantial numbers of people who were engaged in semiskilled or unskilled jobs gave evidence of intrinsic satisfactions. Fully half reported that their work was interesting, and 35 percent cited opportunities for self-expression.

At present, there still has been no direct effort to put questions about the interaction of spontaneity, effort, and compulsion to empirical test. As an example of indirect or tangential evidence, Millar (1968) summarizes studies as showing that children of permissive parents were social, outgoing (in an aggressive as well as a friendly way), inquisitive, original, and constructive in their play. Autocratic parents produced children who were quiet, unaggressive, conforming, and restricted in curiosity, originality, and fancifulness. In education, philosophers and educators have gone through cycles of replacing emphasis on preserving spontaneity in learning to the other extreme of stressing the need for compulsive effort directed toward mastery of basic skills. An area of further research is the literature on teaching and learning methods, which may well yield studies that have a bearing on our questions. For the industrial setting, Notz (1975) has raised the question of the negative effects of extrinsic rewards on intrinsic motivations. In a series of laboratory studies of second-grade pupils, Pittman, Emery, and Boggiano (1982) demonstrated that, under conditions of extrinsic motivations (contingent reward), subjects showed the strongest preference for simple versions of a game. Under conditions of intrinsic motivations (noncontingent reward), subjects showed a preference for the most complex versions of a game. This study suggests to me that conditions of intrinsic motivation are associated with committing oneself more completely and more effortfully to an activity.

Clearly, the establishing of a solid evidential base for thinking about work and play and their separation or fusion lies in the future. Such research must concentrate on the work of children and the play of adults and the dynamics involved. It must be concerned with how childhood experiences with extrinsic and intrinsic motivating conditions relate to the role of work and play in adult life. What adults do with work and play in their later years, when retirement is possible or mandatory, would be a particularly important arena for study, both theoretically and practically. In addition, sex differences in attitudes toward work and play may prove of particular significance. My curbstone observation is that, during the past decade or two, women more than men have looked toward work as a means of self-fulfillment. It is the men who are more likely to view work in terms of "the rat race," in contrast to women, who are more likely to see it as a reprieve from the drudgery of homemaking. Probably the most important underlying aspect of these sex-linked attitudes is that women see homemaking and men see paid work as a forced choice by virtue of rigid sex-role requirements.

Personality and Vocational Decision Making. The immense conceptual-empirical tasks of this area can only be briefly sketched within my time and space limits. Compiling and validating an intrinsic motivational map of the world of work (proposition 4) can be greatly advanced by choosing for comparison occupations that from preliminary observation would appear to be very far apart in their involvements with one or more intrinsic motivational dimensions. Thus, Segal (1961) and Segal and Szabo (1964) chose accountants and creative writers because of observations about the differences both in identity formation and in the fate of expressiveness in the two occupations. Because of his interest in differential expressions of curiosity, Galinsky (1962) chose to contrast clinical psychologists and physicists. (Since this latter investigation was more concerned with shaping experiences than demonstrating existing personality differences, the results will be discussed in the next section.)

Another strategic consideration is where in the career cycle it is most appropriate to concentrate attention. The educational system is organized around a series of branching decisions, which make changes in career direction increasingly cumbersome and costly; in some cases, they approach irreversibility. If we assume that, with time, the search process leads to small discrepancies between personal needs and work, then there will be less experimental error in research directed at the later stages of the career cycle. For example, those who have spent at least several years of work on their careers are more likely to fit the needs that such work satisfies than are persons who are entering courses of study leading to such work. Given the increasingly larger error variance to be contended with earlier in the decision cycle, it becomes a test of the power and precision of our understanding to be able to find differences between two differently oriented career groups at the point of entry into training.

In reviewing the complexly accumulated data, I will move from the more general to the more specific. The most general level of empirical support would address the evidence that personality factors participate at all in vocational choice (proposition 3). Putting it another way, is there any evidence at all that incumbents of various occupational niches, whether students, apprentices, or actual workers, differ in personality by more than chance?

Using factor analysis in a series of studies of college men and women, Elton and Rose (Elton, 1967; Elton and Rose, 1967; Elton and Rose, 1970; Rose and Elton, 1971) found evidence that personality, as measured by the Omnibus Personality Inventory, participates in curricular choice more than aptitude does. In a further analysis that classified curricula according to Holland's categories, they found an important interaction factor of personality related to curricular type, according to sex. This finding suggests that personality factors, as related to work, will distribute themselves differently according to sex, and this hypothesis appears very reasonable. For example, I expect to find that along with the increasing appearance of women in engineering will come a tendency for them to be disproportionately represented in certain specialty areas, such as industrial and production engineering, which are concerned most with human factors in production. Most other studies conform to the general findings of Elton and Rose: that personality factors do participate in curricular choices, whether the measure is the

MMPI (Goldschmidt, 1967; Norman and Redlo, 1952), CPI (Goldschmidt, 1967; Korn, 1962; Whitlock, 1962), need (EPPS) (Byers, Forrest, and Zaccaria, 1968; Merwin and DiVesta, 1959), or miscellaneous other indices (Englander, 1960; Healy, 1968; Osipow, 1969; Weller and Nadler, 1975). With the MMPI, rarely (as in the case of Harder, 1959) have completely negative results been reported. Even in this case, sets of items empirically selected (but with no cross-validation) distinguished among business, education, and engineering students.

These data provide a largely undefinitive backdrop for our much more specific ideas of how personality participates in vocation. To get more definitive, we must center attention either on a particular set of motivations or on a particular class of occupations. Segal's (1961) interest in accountants and creative writers provides an illustration. Relying principally on Rorschach data and on his ideas about the differences in expressiveness, conformity versus nonconformity, and state of identification, Segal found predicted differences. A follow-up study (Segal and Szabo, 1964), which used a new sample and a sentence-completion test, produced confirmation of both the opposition and the other identity differences between the two groups. In general, the accountants exhibited evidence of a firm identification with their fathers, whereas the creative writers gave the appearance of being persons in search of an identity. This finding makes sense in that one of the characteristics of really great creative writers is displayed in fictional character development, in which writers provide us with highly meaningful portrayals of particular persons. Presumably, the creative writer in his or her continuing search for identity has great sensitivity to others and to their inner experiences.

The fascinating study by Fisher and Fisher (1981) of clowns, comedians, and actors, which included TAT and Rorschach data as well as life-history interviews, provides both amplifying and modifying information. Their clowns and comedians, more than the actors, were also observers of and commentators on people and life. The projective data show that the comedians and clowns, much more than the actors, reacted judgmentally toward others, as well as to themselves. The comedians' sensitivity to their own vulnerabilities seemed to increase their acuity in picking out the vulnerabilities in all of us. Even though the work of an actor would seem to facilitate the search for an identity, the data did not suggest that this was the case. I think, however, that the researchers were relying too heavily on their respondents' reports of very early decisions to follow their professions. Instead of constituting evidence of an early, firm formation of ego identity, the data may indicate that successful actors must early give up the aim of establishing a psychologically based identity and settle for the series of synthetic experiences of an identity that acting can provide. Support for this alternative interpretation can be found in Fisher and Fisher's (1981) report that "a number of actors spontaneously remarked that they could never do what the comic does, that is, expose oneself to an audience in one's own image, without disguise" (p. 156). One might expect psychotherapists to display similar qualities, given that their work requires similar sensitivity to others. As we shall see, Galinsky (1962) did find developmental factors characteristic of clinical psychologists that would be thought to be associated with such characteristics. Similarly, Henry, Sims, and Spray (1971) found that psychotherapists, whether psychiatrists, clinical psychologists, or social workers, display a distinctly "outgroup" or marginal status, whether it be in cultural, ethnic, religious, or class mobility.

In the case of the Fishers' (1981) research, it is noteworthy that two closely related groups of professionals, stand-up comedians and actors, were being differentiated from each other by means of projective tests and life-history material. What emerged from data was the picture of the comedian as a person very much concerned with good and evil, feeling inferior and small, turning to comedy as a priestly, healing (for himself as well as others?) function. The actors were more concerned with time preservation and continuity, perhaps reflecting a less severe, less critical mother but a more distant father.

Three other studies provide corroboration for the accounting side of Segal's (1961) findings. Schlesinger (1963) developed through factor analysis an inventory directed toward twelve anal character traits—for example, responsibility, regularity, and meticulous retentiveness as a style of life. When the inventory was given to senior accounting students and graduate students in chemical engineering and educational psychology, significant differences were found in four factor scores. The accountants and engineers were similar to each other and different from the psychologists in their great concern for responsibility (conformity and self-control), orderliness, and retentiveness and for exhibiting more hostility and competitiveness. White (1963) asked an established group of bank clerical personnel and a more heterogeneous group of applicants the following questions: (1) What would you most like to be if you were not a human being? Why? (2) What would you least like to be? Why? For the group most closely related to accountants, 30 of 49 chose as objects of dislike involvement with things that were dirty, sloppy, repulsive, slimy, infectious, or filthy; only 7 of the unselected group of 102 gave this response pattern. Miller's (1962) report, although not as directly related, provided support with evidence of the needs that differentiated YMCA boys' workers and business secretaries from comptrollers in general business. Both YMCA groups were different from the comptrollers in their nurturance and affiliative needs, but both business groups were different from the boys' workers in greater need for order.

Juni's (1981) investigation was of more general significance in turning attention back to our earlier, more physiologically and genetically based conception of motivational dimensions. Juni chose chefs and dentists as representing occupations with heavily loaded oral factors. These two, included in a list of twenty-two occupations, were presented to freshman and sophomore men and women for preference ranking. At the same time, the same subjects were asked to respond with their percepts when exposed to slides containing Rorschach cards. When these percepts were scored blind for oral-nonoral, those scores correlated with ranking of the oral occupation 0.24 ($p < 0.02$) for women and 0.17 ($p < 0.13$) for men, an encouraging but not clear-cut result. As we shall see in discussing Nachmann's (1960) study of lawyers, dentists, and social workers, one could assume that the role of orality in dentists is quite different from orality in chefs. Juni's report gives us no clue to this interaction of sex and the two oral occupations as a possible source of the difference for the two sex groups.

The analysis of engineers by Beall and Bordin (1964) is another good example of the specificity this model can achieve and of its level of empirical support. They saw the engineer as using the intangible and the abstract (physical laws) to produce concrete products. Typically, the engineer is concerned with augmenting human physical power with tools, machines, and the release of chemical or electrical energy. Typical sex-role cultural conditioning has made this more of a preoccupation of men than of women. The cognitive style of the engineer, "orderly, dispassionate, and planful," is similarly sex-linked. Given its work with mathematics, engineering provides an excellent outlet for the person who prefers to work with well-defined concepts and who is irritated or disturbed by open-ended or ambiguously specified terms. The engineer was seen as a person who identifies well with authority, especially male authority, but in an easy way that permits the engineer to be equally good as a follower or leader.

Beall and Bordin (1964) reviewed a good deal of empirical evidence that gives at least general support to their view of engineering. Later research has either supported or amplified their assumptions about engineering. For example, Ziegler (1973) reports that students who expressed a preference for science and research chose the following distinctive self-descriptive adjectives: cautious, curious, determined, methodical, persistent, precise, and thorough. Goldschmidt (1967) compared scores on five personality tests administered to freshmen for groups classified at graduation with regard to science or humanities. He interprets his results for those in science as reflecting a preference for logical, precise analyses, and he sees his subjects as relatively free of self-doubt, tending toward strict control of impulses, denying of emotions, prudent, conventional, energetic, preferring overt action, evaluating ideas on the basis of practicality and immediate application, not assertive or dominant, reserved, retiring, socially introverted, and not spontaneous. Except with regard to socially oriented behavior, these results fit expectations remarkably well. Kipnis, Lane, and Berger

(1969), distinguishing between freshmen and sophomores who enrolled in arts and science and those who enrolled in engineering, found that those who scored high on both impulsiveness and intelligence were more likely to enroll in arts and sciences and that, within engineering, those who scored higher on impulsiveness earned lower grades. In another sample of juniors and seniors, they found a negative correlation between impulsiveness and satisfaction for engineers but a zero relation for business majors. When Scott and Sedlacek (1975) compared male juniors in physical science with those in engineering on the California Personality Inventory, the physical-science group was marked by greater achievement, by independence, psychological-mindedness, femininity, and flexibility. The same instrument was used by Brown, Grant, and Patton (1981) to compare engineers, engineer managers, and nonengineer managers in high-technology industries. Dominance, reflecting social poise, was the major discriminator among the three groups.

Not so successful in attracting further tests, and less strongly supported by the few further studies available, is Barry and Bordin's (1967) analysis of the ministry. Their analysis features the introspective, idealistic role, concern with right and wrong, a service role in a mixed masculine-feminine mode, and public self-display. Reviewing previous research, they found support for these conclusions, as well as for assumptions that the minister's father will be absent or weak, that the mother will be the dominant influence but will speak in the name of an ideal of the father, and that a minister will be a strong influence in adolescence. Nauss (1968) reviewed some of this evidence and added more, toward the conclusion that ministers are more extraverted (not necessarily contradictory) but also are not more intuitive than general groups. Moreover, he points out differences in various denominational groups. Nachmann (1970), on the basis of interviews with clergymen practicing in Alaska, found similar lack of support for the introspective view. She did, however, find support for the important role of the mother, who was described as a strong woman and the person in the family who was most devoutly religious. Nachmann reports frequent spontaneous mention of the importance of the mother's satisfaction with her son's choice of the ministry. Support was also found for boyhood acquaintance with a minister who served as an ego ideal. Supporting Barry and Bordin's (1967) prediction of the importance of self-display, Nachmann characterizes the group as obviously enjoying an audience and as enjoying telling stories. She did not find the posited masculine-feminine mode but did find a masculine style. She speculates that the self-selective factor involved in choosing the Alaskan frontier may account for this result. In another investigation, Byers, Forrest, and Zaccaria (1968) found that clergymen had a significantly greater need for affiliation, introception, and change than the norm group did, and less need for order and endurance. Moreover, the clergymen reported their fathers as significantly more avoidant than fathers of the norm group. This was the only area in which recall of parents was different.

Research Support for the Developmental Aspects of the Model. Our model embraces two levels of developmental theory. Having examined an occupation, and having developed a theory about the motives intrinsic to its activities, we can turn to theories about how such motives develop, as a basis for empirical investigations of how developmental experiences shape vocational development (proposition 5). Thus, research on vocational development and more basic research on personality development are in a closely interacting relationship in which progress in one can further progress in the other.

Nachmann's (1960) study of lawyers, dentists, and social workers blazed the basic strategic trail. Starting with an examination of the work of lawyers, Nachmann identified three general characteristics: the prominence of verbal aggression, a concern with human justice, and the exercise of privileged curiosity about the lives of others. From these three characteristics, she sought to choose comparison occupations that had different characteristics. She identified dentistry and social work as well designed to serve her search for meaningful contrasts. In dentistry, words and verbal aggression do not have the importance they have in law; manual rather than verbal skill is required. The lawyer uses words aggressively in fighting his client's battle, whereas the dentist must inflict pain on her patient, for the patient's own good, in such intrinsically aggressive actions as grinding and drilling. The privileged curiosity of the dentist is confined to the insides of people's mouths, and human justice is of no professional concern. Social workers, however, participate in a similar way to lawyers in their privileged access to people's secrets. Whereas the lawyer's attachment to human justice involves reasoned concentration on the letter of the law ("the rule of law rather than men"), the social worker is more concerned with the spirit of the law and with how that is expressed in specific effects on the development of the client. Implicit in this difference are differences in the approach to authority. The lawyer is usually comfortable with testing the authority of the law and in fighting his client's battle within and against the authority of the judge. The social worker is often in the position of being both an agent of society and a critic of the adverse effects of society and social arrangements on the welfare of his or her clients. Casework demands empathy and acceptance, which are antipathetic to critical, aggressive reactions. Thus, unlike the lawyer's work, the social worker's job involves inhibiting aggression while using words and verbal skills.

Using a careful reading of theories of personality development (principally psychoanalytical) combined with common sense, Nachmann formulated a series of expectations for how students close to the point of entry into these three professions would differ in their childhood experiences. These experiences were to be explored through interviews. Her findings provide very strong support for her expectation that the fathers of both lawyers and dentists would be seen as the more decisive parents in home decisions. They would be seen as more successful, as people to be proud of, and as more likely to be engaged in typically male occupations than the fathers of social workers. Lawyers, more frequently than social workers, reported that their fathers were absent from the home during some significant time during the first eight years. Lawyers, more often than either of the other two groups, spontaneously mentioned adult males other than father as admired, influential figures in childhood; often, this figure was a maternal uncle or grandfather. The social workers' mothers, more often than in the other two groups, were reported as having worked outside the home during the subjects' childhoods. Dentists more frequently reported parental care as having emphasized physical well-being, cleanliness, or concern about injury, rather than intellectual nurturance. These illustrations are enough to give the flavor of Nachmann's findings, which, although not universally of statistical significance, were remarkably supportive of the idea that parents are influential in career choice.

One of the weaknesses of studies that depend on retrospective data is their vulnerability to retrospective falsification to fit current perceptions of the self. Thus, such data may reflect currently prevailing personal differences without shedding light on differences in actual past experience. Although Nachmann's results do not eliminate these reservations, her results are reassuring in that many of the obtained differences are for items much more resistant to such distortion, including predictions about fathers' absence, admiration for adult males other than the fathers, being taught reading skills at an early age by mothers (predicted for lawyers), mothers' working outside the home, and the death or separation of parents before the child was eight (predicted for social workers).

Because of his interest in the differing expressions of curiosity intrinsic to the occupations of clinical psychologist and physicist, Galinsky (1962) chose to compare the childhood experiences of groups of graduate students about to enter these two occupations. In addition to finding differences in their expression of curiosity, he saw the work of physicists as not concerned with other people or necessarily requiring work with them. Moreover, work in physics stresses objective thinking and dispassionate, unemotional analysis, yet it includes receptivity to new ideas and the ability to break away from conventional, commonsense views of the physical world. Galinsky saw clinical psychologists as differing from physicists in all these ways. Following Nachmann's interview methodology, he obtained equally strong supporting data. After establishing eleven general hypotheses about expected differences — for example, physicists will more frequently report having experienced home discipline that was rigid and that stressed obedience (strongly supported); the home environments of physicists will be reported as less conventional (unsupported) — he generated thirty-six specific items distributed among those hypotheses. All thirty-six of these items, regardless of statistical significance, were combined to form a physicist–clinical psychologist differentiation that was scored according to the direction predicted by the hypotheses, not according to the observed direction. When all forty of his sample of graduate students were arrayed according to this index, there were only four overlaps between the two groups.

Methodological objection to these two investigations is that the same investigator who generated the hypotheses also conducted the interviews. Some would go so far as to completely discount the findings. The weakness of the methodology is unquestionable, but the latter view seems to be an overreaction, although it is understandable for an already skeptical observer. Mitigating (although not removing) the defect is the fact that both investigators followed carefully developed, basically similar interview schedules (even though somewhat different sets of expectations were involved) and used independent coders for drawing the specific items.

A similar investigation by Greenwald (1963) shows that the expectations of the investigator cannot be an all-powerful determinant of the results. Greenwald compared the developmental experiences of psychotherapists, educational administrators, and historians, with clearly negative results. Greenwald's negative results may be partly attributable to his failure to carefully winnow his sample by checking vocational interest tests and by using interview questions to make certain that choice of occupation was not ruled by factors extraneous to the intrinsic ones under study — for example, pay and social status, rather than interest. Another factor, which he pointed to himself, was that since administrators and historians either pass through teaching on their way to their chosen professions or often include it as part of their jobs, nurturing others was a feature shared by all three groups. Since this study was directed particularly at presumed differences in modes of interpersonal relations represented by the three groups, these commonalities probably attenuated differences. Moreover, as Greenwald also suggests, this degree of discrimination was too exacting to be obtained from interviews alone.

The comparisons by Fisher and Fisher (1981) of developmental experiences of comedians (including some clowns) and actors, and some with such performers as musicians, dancers, and others, show that fine distinctions are possible. In the case of this latter study, life-history data could be further supplemented by relevant projective data from Rorschach and TAT. The comics and clowns, more than the actors, depicted their fathers as admirable, and they displayed a greater readiness to see figures in TAT cards as paternal. Similarly, comics and clowns more frequently saw their mothers as severe, punishing, and critical. They saw their mothers as communicating messages of unworthiness and their fathers as being unattainable idealized figures. In TAT responses, this group was less likely to see motherlike figures as possessing mothering qualities and more likely to see motherlike figures as demanding responsibility. Just as the interviews conveyed the comics' greater concern with concealment, both Rorschach and TAT percepts carried concealment themes more frequently. The performers, although less fully differentiated, did provide interview evidence that they were more like the actors in their lesser concern with distinctions of good and bad and in less frequently being asked to assume early, perhaps premature, responsibilities. Although the performers were also more similar to the actors in their attitudes toward and perceptions of their mothers, they were more similar to the comics and clowns in their perceptions of their fathers.

This review of developmental studies related to the model, along with the review of evidence that personality participates in the decision process, reveals a solid core of support, despite the crudities of our theoretical and methodological base. We cannot expect greater progress to be made in knowledge of personality in vocation than is being made in the field of personality in general. One promising direction would be the pulling together of basic developmental research on such personality characteristics as curiosity, with research on their expression in work. Let me illustrate the possibilities by using nurturance as an ex-

ample. Occupational studies, such as those by Merwin and
DiVesta (1959) and Miller (1962), give support to my clinical
observation of the importance of affiliative and nurturant needs
in the choice of social service work. It would be interesting to
pursue, through developmental studies, the origins of such
closely related traits as empathy, nurturance, and altruistic
behavior. We could build on the work of social psychologists
(Krebs, 1970; Macaulay and Berkowitz, 1970; Stotland and
others, 1978). Illustrative of potential insights to be gained is
Krebs's (1970) report of a study by an honors student, which
found that girls judged to be altruistic by roommates rated
themselves as higher on both nurturance and succorance. Another example is Krebs's (1970) summary of studies of various
populations, demonstrating that temporary states of dependency
of the recipient increased the probability of an altruistic act.
Equally provocative are London's (1970) hypotheses about personality traits, which he formulated after studying Christians
who saved Jews from the Nazis. He thought that the following
three characteristics would prove to be related to this altruistic
behavior: a spirit of adventurousness, an intense identification
with parental modes of moral conduct, and a sense of being
socially marginal. I am certain that similar inspiration can be
obtained through pursuing the somewhat more fragmentary
work on curiosity and power.

Finally, we turn to the specific developmental ideas in our
model that are concerned with the role of identity development
(proposition 6). This potentially rich area is surrounded by ambiguity, some of which is illustrated in my proposition. Some
of this ambiguity is attributable to changing ideas about sex roles
and the tendency to confuse sex role with identity. Indisputable
biological differences associated with sex differentiation surely
play a relatively undeviating role in identity formation, but
cultural conditioning, which is subject to change over time, is
certainly equally if not more important. Thus, the male or female
is influenced by obvious biological differences between males
and females in reacting to same-sex parents. Clearly, parents
will also be important mediators of the prevailing level of sex-
role differentiation in their culture. (We must not commit the

error of treating cultures, especially in multiethnic and multiclass societies, as more homogeneous than they are.)

While important, sex roles, both biologically and culturally determined, are not the only important elements of ego identity. There are two other factors of equal significance. One is the developing individual's use of parental love and care in meeting and enjoying the challenges and joys of living, which leads to continuities in his or her patterns of both coping with and enjoying those of one, the other, or both parents. No doubt, differing divisions of responsibilities between father and mother that are specific to a particular family influence which parent's personality style is influential and for what purposes. The other factor is the need for balancing continuity with discontinuity: the basic need for individuation pushes a search for a creative synthesis of these two and, while preserving a need for continuity, can provide us with a sense of being our own person, rather than a replica of parents, peer group, ethnic group, or representatives of another conforming pressure. While being human carries with it great pressures to feel joined to others, it also carries an equally strong pressure to preserve a sense of uniqueness. Most identities incorporate the effects and the individual's responses to these pressures and influences.

From the vantage point of the foregoing analysis, it should be clear that identity development and its expression through occupational choice cannot be reduced to simple associations with the occupations of parents or to associations with one parent rather than with the other. Yet the cultural characteristics of a given era may lead to just such findings. At the same time, because of variations in methodology and research design, findings are extremely difficult to integrate. Take two important studies as examples. One of them (Crites, 1962) concentrated on college males. Crites used the sons' ratings of themselves and their parents on the Semantic Differential Technique as a basis for judging identification and then related that identification to vocational interests as a surrogate for vocational choice. The other (Birnbaum, 1971) followed up honor female college graduates of the 1950s fifteen years later and added, for further comparison, a group of single women professors. The honor graduates were further subdivided into those who followed the traditional homemaker career and those who combined homemaker and work careers. These women gave reports on the attitudes and activities of their fathers and mothers.

Crites's data yielded results indicating that men were most strongly influenced by identification with their fathers, but there were effects of identification with mothers for those showing verbal interest and a mixed identification, particularly for those showing social service interests. Birnbaum's findings spoke to the then obvious fact that women face the prior choice of whether to adhere to the tradition of the homemaker role before making choices among other possible careers. Her results seemed to indicate that both groups of gifted women used their mothers as models in that the women who combined career and marriage were more likely to have had mothers who had done the same. The single professors, while showing attachments to fathers, also saw themselves as less attractive (perhaps to their fathers). In an investigation that partially replicated Crites (1962), Brunkan (1965) failed to find identification related to vocational interest pattern and found only that men were more clearly identified with their fathers.

Heilbrun (1969) studied both men and women but used perceptions of self, mother, and father in terms of the Adjective Checklist. By classifying Strong Vocational Interest Blank (SVIB) interest patterns in terms of primary or rejection patterns, he found that women's more frequent primary patterning was associated with a masculine mother or feminine father identification and that a rejection pattern was more probable for a feminine model (father or mother). These results are somewhat consistent with Stewart's (1959) earlier finding in studying high school boys. Using Q sorts obtained from the boys and their mothers and SVIB patterns from the boys, he found that the closer a boy's identification with his mother, the greater the likelihood of his rejection of masculine (according to the prevailing stereotype) interest patterns. White (1959) was another who used the Q-sort methodology, this time for college women, but White obtained Q sorts from both fathers and mothers. She found that her sample's sorts were closer to their mother's than their father's.

In another investigation that related parental identification to SVIB, Steimal and Suziedelis (1963) used a self-report inventory to derive an index of parental influence, the items of which touched on perceived similarity and attachment to father and mother. From a sample of 198 male first- and second-year college students, they selected two extreme groups, one predominantly father-influenced (N = 39) and the other predominantly mother-influenced (N = 45). When compared on interest scores, these two groups differed significantly on a number of scales, with the father-influenced group higher on engineer, chemist, production manager, math teacher, public administrator, senior CPA, and accountant and the mother-influenced group higher on real-estate salesman, advertising man, and lawyer. A minor part of the data, involving a further comparison of their early college majors, revealed a related tendency for the father-influenced group to select majors connected to the exact sciences and for the mother-influenced group to select the liberal arts.

Gysbers, Johnston, and Gust (1968) contribute data that suggest that career-oriented women are more likely than homemakers to prefer that their daughters engage in a career or a career–homemaker combination, which seems complementary to Birnbaum's (1971) results. Finally, we have some tangential findings in Helson's (1970) comparison of creative women mathematicians with other female mathematicians. She concludes that the creatives were more characterized by primary identifications with their professional fathers.

Although the data reviewed here form a complex, confusing pattern, there is an underlying theme that suggests that the patterns of identity formation are complex interreactions of the influence of both the same- and opposite-sex parent and reflect changing times and subcultural differences. Verification and clarification of such effects will continue to be difficult, especially if investigators use simplified research designs. Perhaps we ought to return to a more extensive series of clinically oriented and more holistic studies. Case studies of the sort reported by Galinsky and Fast (1966), illustrating the thesis that vocational choice can be a meaningful arena for examining conflicts in the search for identity (as addressed in proposition 7), can also be useful for examining the process of identity formation and the role of both parents in it. Two of the cases they describe show clear parental effects. In one of them, a young man's unwillingness to commit himself to a truly gratifying vocational goal was shown to be related to the model of a father who was anxious about his own competence, who devoted himself to his work to the exclusion of all else, and who translated his own anxiety into an impatient, critical reaction to his son's efforts at using tools in work activity. The result, as Galinsky and Fast saw it, was that the young man developed the unconscious formulation that it was dangerous to compete with his father by being in love with his work. In the other case, a young man seemed to have been blocked from forming a firm identity, by being raised only by his mother. The young man learned in high school that he was an illegitimate child. His fear of being able only to be like his mother — that is, like a woman — was apparent in his fear of being able only to be a teacher, his mother's occupation. He also feared not being able to be more masculine, such as he might have been if he had followed his family doctor's suggestion that he consider medicine as a career. Of course, both of these cases are very briefly presented. We know nothing of what the first young man's mother was like or of his relation to her or of what, if anything, the second young man might have learned about his father. Both kinds of information would be relevant to identity formation.

Practical Applications

A major application of the model will be to individual vocational counseling. It will also be useful in general developmental programs designed to aid individuals in identity formation and to lead to the development of vocational choice. A second area of application is the modification of work to permit more expression of self and thereby contribute to the quality of work life. The third area of potential application is in connection with the closely related phenomena of aging and retirement.

Vocational Counseling. An important feature of vocational counselors' work has been their effort to have their clients face the realities of the world of work. What is it that a given occupation requires? What knowledge and skills are you expected to bring? What are the abilities and aptitudes you should have to succeed? What can you expect to earn in entry positions, and what are the average earnings?

These are, of course, relevant questions, and any experienced vocational counselor has seen clients obsessed by their search for glamour, prestige, financial return, security of employment, and neglectful of the realities of their qualifications and prospects for particular jobs or occupations. My model implies that emphasis on such realities risks undermining the individual's push for self-realization through work. Emphasizing the realities of work may overemphasize work as a means of meeting the imperatives of earning a living or of searching for purely material satisfactions (propositions 1 and 2). Thus, from the beginning of a vocational counseling effort, one of the messages I am trying to convey is "What of yourself are you seeking to realize through work?" (proposition 3). This question is closely related to two other questions: "What is making the decision difficult? and "Just how are you thinking about yourself and your decision?" (proposition 7).

A female engineering student is wondering whether she wants to stay in the school of engineering or shift to some other school. I ask what wishes or views of herself prompted her to choose engineering in the first place. An arts college student talks of needing to make a choice of major by the end of the year and of being very uncertain. I ask about what seems to be making it difficult to decide. As students respond by talking about themselves and their thinking, I am listening for cues to conflicting senses of themselves. "My course would be clear if it were not for my doubt about whether I can think objectively and dispassionately, the way a lawyer must" (proposition 4). Soon we are discussing the person's sense of herself in this regard and what experiences have given rise to the doubt. Usually I have preliminary information about the student — education and occupation of parents, and number, sex, and age of siblings, and their educational and occupational status. If this student's parent is an engineer, lawyer, or accountant, I may refer to that in the context of asking whether she is seeing herself as different from that parent in that regard (proposition 6).

One common reaction to this model is to imagine that the usual client in vocational counseling will feel an assault on his or her privacy, and that the counselor is trying to turn vocational counseling into psychotherapy. My experience has been that bringing up such questions in the context I have illustrated is experienced as very natural and relevant. To the extent that it represents a different approach from what the client expects, it may be reacted to with pleasure: "I thought vocational counseling was going to be a mechanical process of my taking tests and your telling me what I am best suited for. I like this better. After reading Nader, I was skeptical about how much you can trust tests." Some clients, wary of such broader examination of themselves, while conceding the relevance of the question, may not be certain that they wish to take this broader approach. For this reason, I am alert to what expectations the client has and, even when the client is actively collaborating with me, am likely to stop reasonably early in the process to comment on my sense that our process may be different from what was expected and to ask whether that is an issue requiring negotiation. More frequently than not, the difference is responded to gratefully, without reason for negotiation and with eagerness to go ahead. The person feels excited by the beginnings of a new way of looking at life experiences and by indications of my interest in him or her as a person.

One of the consequences of the push to be realistic is that individual vocational counseling often falls into a two- or three-interview routine — a first, exploratory interview, followed by testing and one or two interviews around test interpretation and planning. My pattern seems to result in a significant number of single-interview contacts. Let me try to give a few illustrations. A slim, blonde, twenty-five-year-old married woman states on her information sheet that she needs vocational direction and that she hopes we can help her by administering an interest "test" and providing counseling. She completed undergraduate work in marketing and is currently enrolled as a special student. Her father, a college graduate, works for a finance company. Her mother is listed as a housewife, with one year of college. She has an elder sister, age twenty-eight, who is a teacher, and she has a thirteen-year-old younger sister still in school. She speaks of having taken business courses because of her father's pressure and of wanting to find something satisfying. I ask about teaching and mention her elder sister. She mentions her dream of teaching shop courses in a penal institution for women. Such a specific dream cries to be taken seriously, and so we explore it. It all hangs together. During her childhood, she gave up getting her mother's attention because her elder sister was the favored one. So she became a "son" to her father (propositions 5 and 6). She and he engaged in many projects in his home shop. Her husband, a financial analyst, is not as handy around the house as she is. Although she shows some concern about the reversal of roles in her marriage, she also feels strongly about sexist bias in work roles and is receptive to the alternative of being a junior high school shop teacher. We go on to discuss combinations of social work and vocational educational training. We touch on her lack of confidence in herself, but this is not something she wants to tackle at this time. We leave unexplored the personal significance of correctional work with women because time has run out, she feels resolved about her plans, and I sense that this is as far as she wants to go in this personal exploration, and so counseling ends.

As another illustration, a single-interview vocational counseling session was actually preceded by a twenty-minute intake meeting. In that meeting, a slim, blonde, tense, and slightly belligerent eighteen-year-old sophomore had provided little information about himself beyond what was on the preliminary information sheet. All he wanted was to take an SVIB; there was no career decision problem. Later he was willing to concede that he had to decide on a field of concentration and was uncertain "because I have too many interests." We discussed his interests (economics and German). I asked about enthusiasm other than courses (proposition 1), and he mentioned going into the wilderness with a couple of friends and traveling in order to observe people from other cultures. With our time running out, I was able to establish that helping him would involve more than an interest test and would require more time than we had available. He willingly agreed to another full-hour meeting four days later. At that time, he responded very readily to my question about further thoughts. He reported a new understanding that he could use his enthusiasms in deciding on an occupation. When we talked of anthropology as one version of his enthusiasms, he wondered whether he could make a living at it. It turned out that his father was a top executive in a multinational corporation (proposition 6). Although the young man did not need to duplicate that standard of living, he was concerned about occupational applications of his interests. Further exploration revealed that he had in fact done a great deal of thinking and was reasonably well informed. It seemed that either economics or anthropology would serve his purpose. Through economics, he could be working with the government or other organizations dealing with underdeveloped nations. The major questions became how much satisfaction he could derive from the more humanistic approach of anthropology versus the organizational approach of economics (proposition 2). He admitted that he had both interests. I wondered whether he had difficulties in making commitments, and we looked at the fact that these choices involve long-term commitments. He wondered how certain he could be about what would satisfy him so far in the future. I commented that such a long-term forecast was inevitably fallible; all we could ask is whether it would be consistent with the way he was now and currently wanted to be in the future. All this discussion led to a brief examination of the role of planning and precision in his way of being; he acknowledged them as important characteristics (propositions 4 and 5). With this, he felt finished and that testing was no longer necessary, and so we said good-bye.

A somewhat lengthier, more complex illustration is represented by the following case. A twenty-one-year-old senior in architecture was functioning well in his program but wrote: "Would like to take vocational testing to help in deciding what the hell I should do for a living." His expectations were expressed in a terse request that I "give the tests and tell [him] the results." During a brief intake interview, I was impressed by his blandness, which was consistent with his complaint that he lacked the interest and enthusiasm that he found in his fellow students.

Preliminary information showed his father to be a college graduate, whom he listed as a kitchen designer. Later I learned there
was also a family lumber yard. His mother was a housewife with
a master's degree. He was the third of four siblings; the eldest
was a sister; the next, a brother two years younger than she;
next was my client, seven years younger than his brother; and
last, a sister, two years younger than my client. Elder sister was
a housewife with a master's degree; elder brother, a college
graduate, was listed as a kitchen salesman; and younger sister
was a college student. Following his report of lack of enthusiasm,
I asked what prompted him to choose architecture as a major.
He replied that he had simply taken it for granted and, after
choosing it, discovered that his father was "a frustrated architect."
Moreover, he was convinced that his brother would probably
end up as an architect. Somehow the discussion surrounding
all this raised my suspicion that his father and brother, by their
avid interest, had given him the feeling that his choice of architecture was not his own (proposition 6). Subsequent tests and
other information provided some support for this supposition,
but it was far from the complete answer. With so little intake
time, and because he was very test-oriented and not very receptive to exploring, I arranged for him to take interest and personality tests.

His test results revealed a number of trends (propositions
4 and 5), and while his SVIB showed no marked pattern, there
was some support for the artistic side of his interest in architecture. His needs profile on the Edwards Personal Preference
Schedule featured achievement but also exhibition and aggression, with additional trends in abasement and heterosexuality.
There was avoidance of affiliation, introception, and dominance.
The Myers-Briggs emphasized thinking, impersonal analysis,
and logic. His responses to a sentence-completion test featured
what we came to speak of as "his dreams of glory"; for example, he completed the stem "my greatest ambition" with "is to
be great." Much of this concentrated on athletics.

When he returned after completing testing, he had already
transferred out of architecture. He felt liberated, he was not feeling serious about his courses, and he had a general feeling that

he was playing. With this as a starter and test results as a backdrop, we began to pay attention to certain patterns. Whenever he established a high aspiration, as he inevitably did, it was as though he heard a voice telling him that he had a fatal deficit that doomed him to failure. For example, early in this interview he spoke of thinking about journalism, simultaneously mentioning that he had been told that he could not write. I remarked that he would not be able to commit himself fully until he had dealt with these conflicting feelings (propositions 2 and 7) because the conflict seemed to turn things he really enjoyed into hard work devoid of satisfaction. Although he could see the conflict and even elaborate on it, he was reluctant to commit himself to working on it. His wish to stand alone seemed to be a source of reluctance to accept help. Beyond that, we came to his fear of psychology and psychiatry, founded in his mother's having had a breakdown and been hospitalized early in his life. He agreed to one more session to discuss whether he could accept help. Other than letting us reiterate and further clarify the problem we had uncovered, this additional session was of no avail. The clarification took the form of agreement that although he could put great effort into play, he was unable to approach work in a playful spirit. His feeling that playing means being dependent formed part of the barrier toward going into therapy. He saw himself as not likely to take therapy seriously, but likely only to play at it because he saw being in therapy as being dependent. The assurance that the therapist's job is to work with those very issues was not enough. He left to try to work on it on his own, assuring me that he would return if he failed. He has not yet returned.

This model not only has applications for individual vocational counseling; it can also be used in the workshop format adapted to the needs of youth, for developmentally oriented interventions designed to further their movement toward a fully integrated identity around work. A good example is Kelly's (1972) set of exercises in guided fantasy, which have been incorporated into workshops on vocational choice at both the high school and college levels (Warner and Jepsen, 1979). Just as projective methods, such as the sentence-completion technique, are ways of setting the individual's inner life free of an overly constricting devotion to reality, guided fantasy exercises are well adapted to maximum usefulness in the group process of a workshop. I might add that clinical psychologists and psychotherapists could make good use of our model to increase the sensitivity and comprehensiveness of their understanding of their clients. How personality is expressed in work can represent a vital source of understanding. Moreover, knowing the chosen occupations of parents and siblings can provide important clues to family dynamics. Knowing that a young man's father is a dentist or an accountant can alert the counselor to the possibility that this father had a fearful identification with *his* father, which has been repeated in the son.

Job Modification. As social and industrial psychologists have become increasingly concerned with the quality of life (for example, Campbell, Converse, and Rogers, 1976), attention has been turned to the quality of working life (Davis and Cherns, 1975). If the necessity of work is to be transformed from the drudgery of alienated toil into something incorporating a modicum of self-expression, jobs and work processes must be reexamined for ways of introducing elements of spontaneous choice. Industrialists have too easily assumed that the rationalization of production requires not only the use of machines, but also the reduction of humans to machinelike functions. Blauner (1964) has shown that machine tending need not reduce the worker to the same level of automaton as the machine he is taking care of. Ford (1969) has demonstrated through experiments conducted at AT&T that tasks can be modified to enlarge the workers' areas for choice and provide opportunities for the exercise of ingenuity or other forms of self-expression, with better morale and satisfaction. Industrialists need to be disabused of any convictions that playfulness and productivity are incompatible.

Aging and Retirement. In addressing applications to this area, I speak more of future hopes than of present accomplishments. A great deal of attention has been devoted, and rightly so, to the health and economic problems associated with this period of life, but there is a danger that we as a society may make the error of confusing playfulness with irresponsibility and dependence. Yes, aging and retirement do offer the hope of freeing the person from tyrannous imperatives, but we must not become concerned only with the realistic sources of such disappointments. Those who do research on aging or, more important, design support and intervention programs must give attention to the issues of fusing work and play and to the effect of aging on the decline of personal resources and their use. They must examine the role of redirection of effort and spontaneity in what happens and can happen. What part does the chemistry of compulsion, effort, and spontaneity play in whether a person displays enrichment or decline in aging and retirement? These are questions not only important for theory but also rich in applications.

Lynda K. Mitchell
John D. Krumboltz

6

❧❧❧❧❧❧❧❧❧❧❧❧❧❧❧❧❧❧❧❧❧❧❧❧

Social Learning Approach to Career Decision Making: Krumboltz's Theory

Background of the Theory

The social learning theory of career decision making (Krumboltz, 1979; Krumboltz, Mitchell, and Jones, 1976) is an outgrowth of the general social learning theory of behavior, which is most often associated with the work of Bandura (1977b). The social learning theory of behavior has its roots in reinforcement theory and classical behaviorism. It assumes that the individual personalities and behavioral repertoires that persons possess arise primarily from their unique learning experiences, rather than from innate developmental or psychic processes. These learning experiences consist of contact with and cognitive analysis of positively and negatively reinforcing events. However, to say that our current personalities and skills are a result of our learning experiences does not imply that humans are passive organisms that are controlled by environmental conditioning events. Social learning theory recognizes that humans are intelligent, problem-solving individuals who strive at all times to understand the reinforcement contingencies that surround them and who in turn control their environments to suit their own purposes and needs.

Social learning theory posits three major types of learning experiences that result in individual behavioral and cognitive skills and preferences that allow one to function effectively in one's environment. The first is *instrumental learning experiences,* which occur when the individual is positively reinforced or punished for the exercise of some behavior and its associated cognitive skills. Individuals tend to repeat behaviors for which they are positively reinforced (for example, studying hard for a history exam and getting an A) so that they can acquire more of the reinforcer. In the process of repeating the behavior, they often become more and more adept at the skills involved, and the behavior itself may become intrinsically interesting, so that external reinforcement is no longer required to maintain the behavior. Similarly, individuals tend to avoid behaviors for which they are punished, and they often learn to dislike performing these behaviors.

The second type of learning experience posited by social learning theory is *associative learning experiences,* which occur when individuals associate some previously affectively neutral event or stimulus with an emotionally laden event or stimulus. For example, a person might associate the hospital setting with the death of a beloved relative and thus become extremely reluctant to engage in any activities that are associated with hospitals, such as entering the field of medicine as a career. Or a person may associate the hospital setting with the performance of vital surgery that saved his or her life and may come to like medicine. In each case, the person has ascribed a positive or negative emotional aspect to the hospital, which is derived from events the person associates with it. Instrumental and associative learning experiences occur through *direct* experience with reinforcing or punishing events.

A third way in which persons learn a large part of their behavioral and cognitive skills and preferences has to do with *vicarious* experience. Humans, being intelligent creatures and excellent information processors, can learn new behaviors and skills very easily, simply by observing the behaviors of others or by gaining new information and ideas through such media as books, movies, and television. Whether or not they choose to exercise the cognitive and behavioral skills they acquire through observation depends to a large extent on their analyses of the reinforcement contingencies that are available for exercising those skills in the environment and their decisions about whether it is worth their while to attempt to collect the positive contingencies and avoid the punishing ones. Frequently, when individuals or groups perceive the reinforcement contingencies that exist in their environment as unreasonable or unfair, they set about influencing the environment to change those contingencies. Change can be accomplished individually or in groups.

Many books (for example, Bandura, 1969, 1973, 1977b) have been devoted to discussing empirical investigations that support the basic tenets of social learning theory. It is beyond the scope of this chapter to discuss the voluminous evidence in support of the general theory, although we will discuss the empirical evidence in support of the social learning theory of career decision making. The general theory considers economic and sociological conditions to be reinforcers, and it considers the psychology of the individual in examining learning experiences that lead to the acquisition of cognitive and behavioral skills and preferences. As has been noted elsewhere (Unruh, 1979), many current theories of career decision making, although scholarly and thoughtful, rely too heavily either on the role of sociological and economic factors in career decision making or on the role of intrapersonal psychological events. With its foundation in social learning theory, the social learning theory of career decision making must consider the impact of both sets of factors and their interaction.

The social learning theory of career decision making is associated with John Krumboltz and his colleagues. Two prior statements of the theory have appeared in the literature (Krumboltz, 1979; Krumboltz, Mitchell, and Jones, 1976). The following section summarizes these two prior statements and suggests further refinements and new directions.

The Theory

The social learning theory of career decision making is designed to address the question of why people enter particular educational programs or occupations, why they may change educational programs or occupations at selected points in their lives, and why they may express various preferences for different occupational activities at selected points in their lives. In addressing these questions, the theory examines the impact on the career decision-making process of such factors as genetic predisposition, environmental conditions and events, learning experiences, and cognitive, emotional, and performance responses and skills. It is posited that each of these factors plays a part in all career decisions that are made, but the different combinations of interactions of the factors produce the multitude of different career choices that different individuals make. Four categories of factors influence the career decision-making path for any individual.

1. Genetic Endowment and Special Abilities. Genetic endowment and special abilities are inherited qualities that may set limits on educational and occupational preferences and skills. Included are race, sex, and physical appearance and characteristics, including irreversible physical handicaps. The debate about the relative contribution of genetic and environmental factors to human behavior, although important, need not be resolved for us to posit, for the purposes of the social learning theory of career decision making, that certain individuals are born with greater or lesser ability to profit from environmental learning experiences or are offered different experiences altogether because of their inherited qualities (for example, differing environmental experiences offered to male and female children). It is a reasonable assumption that special abilities, such as intelligence, musical ability, artistic ability, and muscular coordination, result from the interaction of inherited predispositions and exposure to selected environmental events.

2. Environmental Conditions and Events. Environmental conditions and events that affect the career decision making of individuals include social, cultural, political, and economic forces as well as natural forces, such as natural disasters and the location of natural resources. These factors are generally outside the control of any one individual; their influence may be planned or unplanned. They include the following.

Number and nature of job opportunities. Cultural and historical forces may result in job opportunities being available in some settings but not being available in others. For example, opportunities to work as a deep-sea fisherman exist in coastal areas in Washington, Oregon, and California, but not in Nebraska. Similarly, one would have an easier time securing employment as a department store Santa in the United States than in Israel.

Number and nature of training opportunities. In the United States, one can receive occupational training through a variety of social institutions, such as public and private schools, military service, apprenticeship programs in business and industry, and even correspondence courses. In other cultures, other training routes may be available. Within and between cultures there is wide variation in the accessibility of these various training routes.

Social policies and procedures for selecting trainees and workers. The entry path to some jobs may be restricted unless certain requirements are met. For example, some jobs may require a high school diploma or a college degree. New legislation and judicial decisions may cause these requirements to be modified (for example, by outlawing the use of certain aptitude or intelligence tests as screening devices), and the requirements may or may not be related to job performance (a college diploma is frequently required for jobs that can be done perfectly well by persons who do not possess that degree). Nevertheless, the existence of these policies and procedures may influence people to modify their career paths to meet the requirements (for example, by obtaining a college degree when there is little intrinsic interest in the educational experience).

Rate of return for various occupations. The monetary and social rewards offered for preparing for various occupations vary widely according to the occupation. Similarly, different cultures value and reward some occupations and not others, and trends in what is rewarded may be affected by institutional and governmental action. Individuals tend to be influenced by what they perceive to be the current and probable future trends.

Labor laws and union rules. Labor unions may limit or increase the number of persons who enter them by the imposition of certain rules for membership. These rules may also affect the number of job opportunities and benefits available.

Physical events. Natural disasters, such as earthquakes, droughts, floods, and hurricanes, may destroy a region's economy, making it impossible for some people to continue in their occupations. Alternatively, some people may profit from the increased demand for materials and resources needed to rebuild the economy.

Availability of and demand for natural resources. It has frequently happened in our society that owners of land on which valuable natural resources, such as oil or gold, were found have suddenly changed their occupational activities (for example, dropping cattle ranching to be an oil producer).

Technological developments. In industrialized societies, new technological developments, such as computerization and robotics, may produce dramatic changes in the patterns of occupational opportunities available.

Changes in social organization. The creation of such social institutions as Social Security, Aid to Families with Dependent Children, and unemployment compensation affects the career paths of people who are entitled to benefits and produces a large number of jobs for people who are needed to manage and staff the organizations.

Family training experiences and resources. The family in which an individual is raised will communicate to each child certain values, demands, and expectations for achievement. The family's values and demands and the social and financial resources it is able to provide affect the individual's educational preferences, skill development, and occupational selections.

Educational system. The degree to which individuals strive to achieve and succeed educationally is affected by schools' organization and administrative policies and by the interests and personalities of teachers to whom students are exposed.

Neighborhood and community influences. Communities differ in the kinds of occupational role models and cultural and social stimulation available to the people who live in them.

3. Learning Experiences. The development of career preferences and skills and the selection of a particular career are influenced by the individual's past learning experiences. The specific character and sequence of these learning experiences are often not retrievable because the possibilities for the nature and scheduling of the patterns of stimuli and reinforcement are extremely complex and nearly infinite in their variety. Nevertheless, it is posited that each individual has a unique history of learning experiences that results in the chosen career path.

In an *instrumental learning experience,* the individual acts on the environment in such a way as to produce certain consequences. Figure 6.1 indicates the three major components of an instrumental learning experience in the general model. Each such experience is composed of antecedents, behavioral responses (both covert and overt), and consequences. An H-shaped figure is used to represent an instrumental learning experience. Ante-

Figure 6.1. Instrumental Learning Experience, General Model.

Antecedents	Behaviors	Consequences
Genetic endowment Special abilities and skills		Directly observable results of action
Planned and unplanned environmental conditions or events	Covert and overt actions	Covert reactions to consequences (cognitive and emotional responses)
Task or problem		Impact on significant others

cedents to instrumental learning experiences include the genetic endowments, special abilities, and environmental conditions and events previously mentioned. Also included as antecedents are the characteristics of the particular task or problem. The behavioral responses of instrumental learning experiences include both cognitive and emotional responses, as well as observable behaviors. The consequences include immediate and delayed effects produced by the behavior, as well as immediate or delayed impact on other persons. Also included are the cognitive and emotional responses individuals experience when they are the recipients of these consequences as the result of their behavior.

Figure 6.2 diagrams a specific example of an instrumental learning experience for a fictitious person, Dwight. Additional examples of instrumental learning experiences could include writing a term paper, preparing a meal, making conversation with a stranger at a party, or kissing someone of the opposite sex. As the fictitious example of Dwight indicates, the consequences that accrue to individuals because of their behavioral responses may not be uniformly positive. Whether or not the behavior is performed again will depend on the relative importance to the individual of the positive and negative consequences that occur.

In an *associative learning experience,* the individual perceives a connection between stimuli in the environment. Learning by observation of real or fictitious models is also considered an associative learning experience.

Some stimuli in the environment are seen as having positive or negative emotional associations — for example, being rich, being a criminal, or being incompetent. When previously neutral stimuli are paired with the emotionally positive or negative stimuli, the neutral stimuli will also take on the positive or negative characteristics in the mind of the observer. Thus, persons can come to view certain occupations as having positive or negative characteristics by hearing or reading such statements as "All doctors think they are God," "Television repairmen are out to rip you off," "All plumbers are rich," "All lawyers are crooked," or "Those who can, do; those who can't, teach; those who can't teach, teach teachers." Through observation, reading,

Figure 6.2. Instrumental Learning
Experience, Specific Example: Dwight.

Antecedents	Behaviors	Consequences
Dwight, age twenty, white, male, good muscular coordination, slender build.		Dwight takes first place in singles match. Coach and other players congratulate him heartily.
Medium size university where being on football team is primary basis of prestige for male students.	Dwight accepts coach's invitation. Plays in tournament against opposing team and puts forth best effort.	Dwight thinks, "I'm glad I played hard. I'll bet I could play even better in the future."
Tennis coach approaches Dwight after seeing him hit balls with friend and asks him to play on team. First tournament coming up in two weeks.		Girl on whom Dwight has crush turns down date with him in order to go out with Dwight's roommate, who is a football player.

and hearing about occupational members, people form occupational stereotypes. These stereotypes may last a lifetime and have a significant effect on career decision making. Such stereotypes may be formed from only one example.

The classical conditioning paradigm referred to in the introduction to this chapter, in which positive and negative events that occur to the person are generalized to whole categories of experiences, is also included here as an associative learning experience. For example, a person who associates the stimuli associated with hospitals with the death of a beloved relative may generalize that association to all stimuli associated with the profession of medicine. However, subsequent learning experiences, either planned or occurring naturally, may help one to change previously formed associations. Thus, through deliberate pairing of hospitals and doctors with pleasant events, or through exposure of the individual to new information about the medical profession, a dislike of these stimuli may be overcome.

Figure 6.3 presents the general model for associative learning experiences in the form of a circle. The upper part of the circle specifies the circumstances through which the individual is exposed to the paired stimuli. The lower left area of the circle represents the formerly neutral stimulus, or model, and the

Figure 6.3. Associative Learning Experience, General Model.

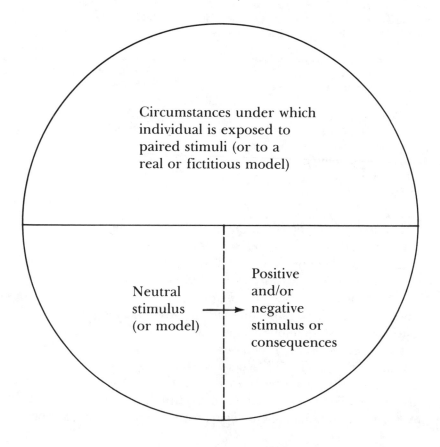

lower right area represents the positive or negative stimulus, or consequences. An arrow connects the two lower quadrants, to signify that the formerly neutral stimulus, or model, acquires the affective characteristics of the positive or negative stimulus through the process of stimulus pairing.

Figure 6.4 presents an example of an associative learning experience. In this hypothetical example, Dwight learns that newspaper reporters can inform the public of illegal activities of government officials and thereby achieve personal fame and glory.

4. Task Approach Skills. Interactions among learning experiences, genetic characteristics, special abilities, and environmental influences result in task approach skills. These skills include performance standards and values, work habits, perceptual and cognitive processes (for example, symbolic rehearsal, attention, and retention), mental sets, and emotional responses. The exact nature of the interactions among factors that result in task approach skills is not yet fully understood, but the previously learned task approach skills that are brought to each new task or problem affect the outcome of that task or problem. Furthermore, those task approach skills themselves may become modified. For example, as a member of a college tennis team, Dwight's tennis skills and workout habits may be sufficient for him to defeat most college opponents easily. If he were to decide to play on the professional circuit, however, he might quickly begin to lose matches. As the result of his losses, he might invest considerable effort in improving his task approach skills for tennis competition. Task approach skills are therefore factors that influence outcomes, and they are outcomes themselves as well.

Resulting Cognitions, Beliefs, Skills, and Actions

The complex interaction of the four types of influencing factors can be interpreted by individuals in an infinite variety of ways. While it is not possible to specify which combination of factors will produce which set of beliefs, it is clear that the

Figure 6.4. Associative Learning
Experience, Specific Example: Dwight.

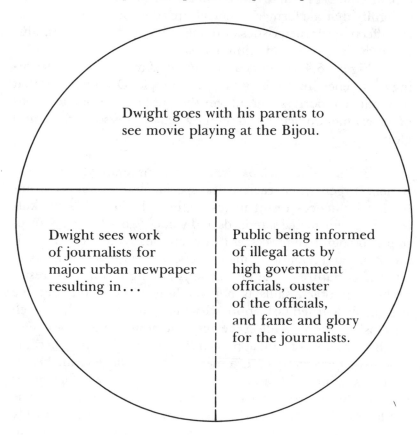

individual does formulate generalizations in an attempt to represent his or her own reality (Krumboltz, 1983). Some individuals can articulate these beliefs readily. When given a list, almost anyone can recognize the degree to which each stated belief represents his or her own point of view. Beliefs about oneself and about the world of work influence one's approach to learning new skills and ultimately affect one's aspirations and actions.

Self-Observation Generalizations. Individuals are constantly observing themselves and assessing their own performances according to their standards or with regard to the attitudes and skills of others. As a result of learning experiences, persons make generalizations about the nature of their attitudes and the extent of their skills. These self-observation generalizations may be covert or expressed overtly, and, like task approach skills, they influence the outcomes of new learning experiences and result from prior learning experiences. Therefore, although self-observation generalizations are discussed primarily in terms of outcomes of learning experiences, their reciprocal nature should be kept in mind. Self-observation generalizations may be divided into three major categories — self-observation generalizations about task efficacy, self-observation generalizations about interests, and self-observation generalizations about personal values.

Self-observation generalizations about task efficacy are persons' estimations about whether they possess the requisite skills to perform some task adequately. In making a self-observation generalization, one evaluates one's actual or vicarious performance in comparison to learned standards. Such statements as "I may not be able to make the debating team, but I can hold my own in a conversation" or "I'm good in math but lousy in English" or "It's hard for me to concentrate when I study" are representative of self-observation generalizations about task efficacy.

These observations are only as accurate as the standards to which they are compared. Thus, a straight-A student who receives a B in a course may consider herself a failure in that subject area, whereas a C student who receives a B may be jubilant. Furthermore, the settings in which self-observation generalizations about task efficacy are made may heavily influence their content. A student may describe to her fellow students her ability to write short stories very differently from the way she would describe it to her English teacher.

As a result of learning experiences, persons draw conclusions and make generalizations about which activities they do or do not enjoy. Psychologists and educators have invested considerable effort in determining the content of these self-observation generalizations about interests, primarily through the development of interest inventories. Many such inventories ask the individual to express the degree to which he likes, dislikes, or is indifferent to various activities. The resulting "interests" are based on self-observation generalizations derived from prior learning experiences. Some psychologists refer to these interests as if they were the original causes of occupational selections, but in the social learning theory of career decision making, interests are seen as an intermediate step linking the original causal learning experiences with subsequent choices and actions. There is no doubt, however, that interests are important in career decision making because they provide a relatively concise and accurate summary of individuals' reactions to their previous learning expriences and thus serve as useful predictors of future activity.

Self-observation generalizations about personal values are assessments persons make about their attitudes toward the desirability or worth of certain behaviors, events, or outcomes. Personal values result from both associative and instrumental learning experiences. As with interests, many psychometric instruments have been constructed to determine individuals' particular values. Such statements as "Prestige is important to me" and "I couldn't care less about the kind of people with whom I work" represent self-observation generalizations about values.

The general model for self-observation generalizations is presented in Figure 6.5, and Figure 6.6 presents a specific example of a self-observation generalization about task efficacy for Dwight.

World-View Generalizations. As a result of their learning experiences, persons make observations about the environment in which they live, and they use these generalizations to predict what will occur in the future and in other environments. For example, persons may make generalizations about the nature of various occupations ("To succeed in show business, you have to know the right people" or "The human service professions are suitable only for people who are naturally warm and intuitive about others"). World-view generalizations, like self-observation generalizations, may be more or less accurate. Their accuracy will depend on the numbers of experiences on which they are based and the representativeness of those experiences.

Figure 6.5. Self-Observation Generalizations, General Model.

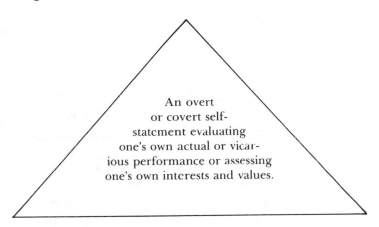

An overt
or covert self-
statement evaluating
one's own actual or vicarious performance or assessing
one's own interests and values.

Task Approach Skills and Career Decision Making. Task approach skills are learned cognitive and performance abilities that are used in the process of career decision making. They include work habits, mental sets (including emotional responses), perceptual and thought processes, and problem orientation. Task approach skills are used to cope with the environment, to interpret it in relation to self-observations and world-view generalizations, and to make overt and covert predictions about future events.

Figure 6.6. Self-Observation Generalizations
About Task Efficacy, Specific Example: Dwight.

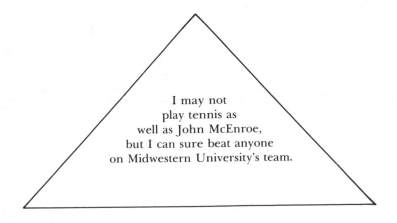

I may not
play tennis as
well as John McEnroe,
but I can sure beat anyone
on Midwestern University's team.

Krumboltz and Baker (1973) suggest the following task approach skills as important in career decision making. They are the abilities of (1) recognizing an important decision situation, (2) defining the decision or task manageably and realistically, (3) examining and accurately assessing self-observations and world-view generalizations, (4) generating a wide variety of alternatives, (5) gathering needed information about the alternatives, (6) determining which information sources are most reliable, accurate, and relevant, and (7) planning and carrying out this six-step sequence of decision-making behaviors.

The extent to which persons develop and use the task approach skills of career decision making depends on the sequence and consequences of relevant learning experiences. A systematic attempt to apply one or several of the skills may result in negative consequences (for example, a carefully researched decision to become an aerospace engineer may be reached just before unforeseen budget cuts in the space program). Such negative consequences, which depend more on uncontrollable and unpredictable environmental events than on the use of task approach skills, may convince persons that decision making is not worth the investment of time and effort. As a result, many persons may develop alternative strategies for decision making—for example, relying solely on intuition, or leaving the decision in the hands of fate. Figure 6.7 presents the general model for a task approach skill in the form of a parallelogram, and Figure 6.8

Figure 6.7. Task Approach Skill, General Model.

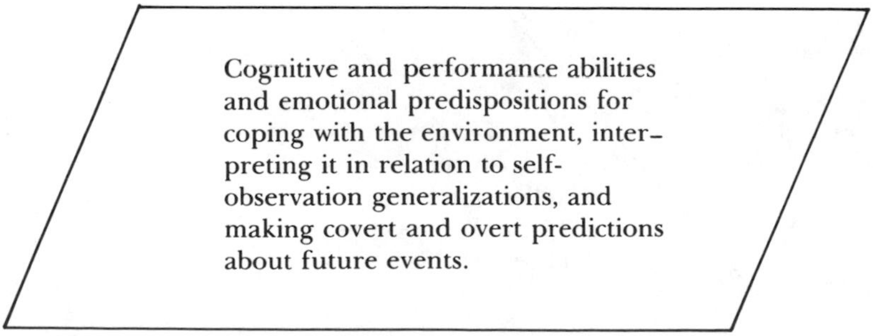

Cognitive and performance abilities and emotional predispositions for coping with the environment, interpreting it in relation to self-observation generalizations, and making covert and overt predictions about future events.

Figure 6.8. Task Approach Skill, Specific Example: Dwight.

"I'm pretty good at tennis, and I also get A's in my English classes. Journalism seems like a really interesting occupation, but so does playing professional tennis. I wonder how I could find out which occupation would suit me best?"

presents a specific example for Dwight. In the specific example, Dwight is demonstrating the task approach skills of recognizing an important situation, assessing his self-observation and world-view generalizations, and considering how best to gather reliable and relevant information about decision alternatives.

As a result of learning experiences and the generalizations and skills that develop from them, individuals engage in various behaviors that lead to entry into a career. These behaviors include applying for jobs or to schools or training programs, seeking promotions, and changing jobs or majors. Behaviors and decisions that are relevant to the career-planning process occur throughout one's lifetime.

An Example. Genetic factors, environmental conditions and events, instrumental and associative learning experiences and their consequences (task approach skills, self-observation and world-view generalizations, and actions) interact to produce a particular career path for each individual. Figure 6.9 presents, in an oversimplified manner, an illustrative career path for a hypothetical individual, Diane. As in the previous examples, H-shaped figures represent instrumental learning experiences, circles represent associative learning experiences, triangles represent self-observation generalizations, and parallelograms represent task approach skills. The genetic factors that influence Diane's development are represented in the square at the begin-

Figure 6.9. Career Path Sequence of Factors
Affecting Occupational Selection, Specific Example: Diane.

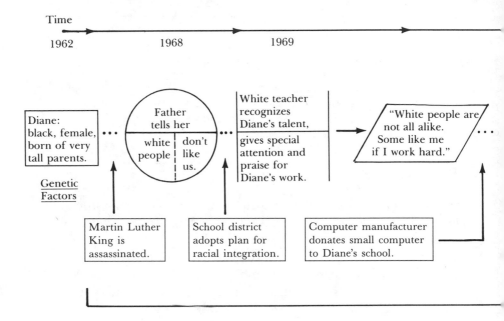

ning of the diagram, and the environmental conditions and events that influence her decision are represented in squares along the bottom of the diagram. Time proceeds from left to right. The triple arrows after certain events indicate that many options could have been chosen — the path is not deterministic. Persons can make choices; other alternatives always exist and could have been selected.

Diane's career path illustrates the influence on her of Martin Luther King's assassination, racial integration, the computer revolution, certain educational programs and policies, and some philanthropic actions. Also illustrated are a few of the major learning experiences that affected her selection of educational programs and an occupation. Obviously, only a few selected events were included in the diagram. Each individual is affected by innumerable environmental events and learning experiences.

Figure 6.9. Career Path Sequence of Factors
Affecting Occupational Selection, Specific Example: Diane, Cont'd.

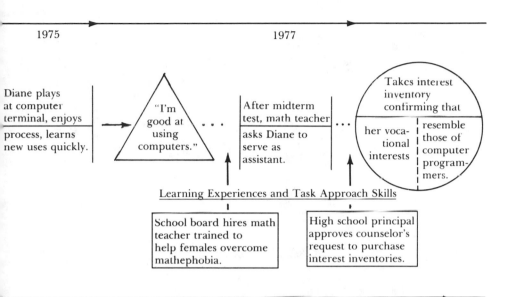

Applicability to Males, Females, and Minorities. According to the social learning theory of career decision making, all
individuals are born with certain inherited characteristics into
certain environments and are exposed to various learning experiences. They cannot control their heredity, but they can exert some influence on their environments and on the nature of
some of their learning experiences. The interactions of all these
factors result in self-observation and world-view generalizations
and task approach skills, which in turn lead to a sequence of
new learning experiences and decision behaviors throughout life.
These general processes operate regardless of the individual's
race, gender, or ethnic background. However, the specific nature
of the learning experiences to which one is exposed and the environmental conditions and events that influence career choice
are heavily influenced by such factors as race, gender, and cul-

Figure 6.9. Career Path Sequence of Factors
Affecting Occupational Selection, Specific Example: Diane, Cont'd.

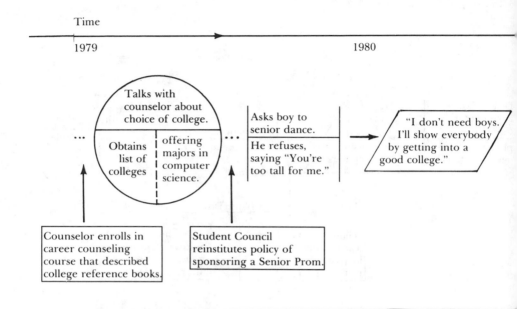

tural background. As the illustrative example of Diane indicates, the career choices of women have been and continue to be influenced by cultural norms regarding the acceptability of women's entering certain career paths. These kinds of environmental influences have a tremendous effect on whether women will be allowed the opportunity for various learning experiences that lead to nontraditional career choices.

Similarly, physical characteristics, in addition to gender, will have an effect on what learning experiences are offered to individuals. An adolescent male who is six feet, ten inches tall is more likely to be actively reinforced for prowess in basketball than one who is five feet, six inches. Certain physical characteristics are also required to enter such professions as the military, police and firefighting work, and high-fashion modeling.

Figure 6.9. Career Path Sequence of Factors
Affecting Occupational Selection, Specific Example: Diane, Cont'd.

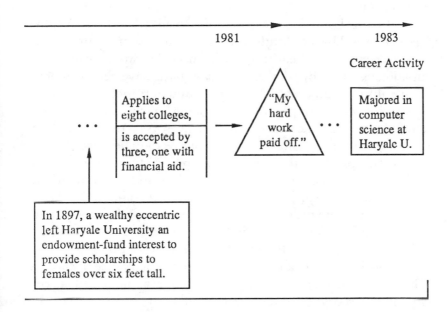

The cultural environment into which one is born has an effect on the kinds of role models with which one can come in contact. Furthermore, some cultures glamorize one occupation; others, another. Different cultures emphasize particular occupational values over others (for example, income versus religious service, or dedication to family versus dedication to occupational success). However, interventions can be designed to change normal cultural influences on career choice. For example, Obleton (1984) describes a "model-mentor" workshop in which black female students were paired with black professional women to encourage career exploration over an eight-week period. Anecdotal reports and a questionnaire survey showed that the participants felt the workshop had a beneficial effect on their career development. Although the theory emphasizes the impact of role models on career choice, it does not distinguish between naturally occurring and deliberately planned role-model encounters. Clearly, role models could alter normal cultural expectations if a deliberately structured mentoring program like Obleton's were effective.

In the United States, persons from other than Anglo-Saxon cultural backgrounds have frequently been victims of active discrimination. Learning experiences that would lead to occupational success by conventional standards have been withheld from culturally different individuals, and entrance into certain occupations has been prohibited for some, even if they managed to obtain the requisite learning experiences. As a result, children born into culturally different backgrounds may be raised in environments in which they are unable to learn the task approach skills necessary to break the cycle of poverty and discrimination.

The social learning theory of career decision making can be used to recognize and predict environmental conditions and events that are likely to provide learning experiences that will either foster or inhibit the career planning of individuals. The theory does not advocate any one particular sequence of career-relevant activities, as do many developmental models of career choice. It is recognized that there are many routes to successful career planning, where *successful* is defined as describing the route that leads to satisfaction for the individual. However, when individuals or groups perceive the learning experiences or opportunities that exist in their environment as unfair or discriminatory, they may undertake to change those factors in their environment, through either individual or collective action. Such action in the United States has resulted in, among other things, affirmative action legislation and some shifts in conventional values regarding occupations (for example, emphasis on low-stress work environments to promote physical and mental well-being).

Societal influences can be seen in the change in occupational preferences over time. Gerstein, Lichtman, and Barokas (1988) reanalyzed data from surveys of representative high school seniors in 1972 and 1980. They found that, by the end of these eight years, females were much more likely to choose professional occupations and less likely to choose the clerical/sales and teaching categories.

Values may be changing, too. Pirnot and Dustin (1986) used the Allport Study of Values to compare homemakers and career women of 1983 with those of 1966. Although the samples may not have been representative of the two populations at those two times, esthetic and economic values were dominant in 1983, while religious and social values characterized the 1966 sample.

Women who enter nontraditional (historically male-dominated) occupations have received much attention in the research literature. Although generalizations are dangerous, a review of that literature by Chusmir (1983) reports that women in nontraditional occupations tend to be active, androgynous, autonomous, dominant, expressive, individualistic, responsible, self-confident, and sociable. Chusmir reviewed research on special awareness workshops and mentoring programs designed to increase nontraditional career selection.

Foss and Slaney (1986) evaluated another strategy for increasing nontraditional choices among women. They used a thirty-minute videotape designed by Dege, Perreault, Mills-Novoa, and Hansen (1980). A pre-post analysis showed that the eighty college women chose more nontraditional careers for themselves and their hypothetical daughters after seeing the videotape.

It is important to distinguish between career-choice intentions, which are easy to change, and career-choice actions, which may be much more difficult to change. Indeed, the Foss and Slaney (1986) study reports that even women with liberal ideals were more likely to choose nontraditional careers for their daughters (a hypothetical choice) than for themselves (a real choice). Mohney and Anderson (1988) interviewed forty-seven female first-time enrollees in a college evening program, to identify factors that had influenced their enrollment. The real-life factors most often cited as having enabled enrollment were that their children were old enough, their finances were good enough, they had support from peers and partners, and they had adequate child care. Clearly, new learning experience and positive career actions require solid environmental support.

The social learning theory of career decision making suggests that maximum career development of all individuals requires each individual to have the opportunity to be exposed to the widest possible array of learning experiences, regardless of race, gender, or ethnic origin.

Empirical Support

The social learning theory of career decision making suggests many testable hypotheses, some of which will be discussed here. The hypotheses selected for discussion were chosen because some evidence bearing on their validity exists, although the theory is composed of many additional hypotheses that have yet to be directly or indirectly studied. Thus, the following hypotheses are not meant to be complete or comprehensive. As with other theories, research supporting or disconfirming various hypotheses suggested by the social learning theory of career decision making will lead to new or modified hypotheses and then to the evolution of the theory.

Educational and Occupational Preferences. The social learning theory suggests that educational and occupational preferences represent self-observation generalizations about interests, values, and task approach skills that have arisen as a result of various learning experiences. On the basis of the suggested structure of instrumental and associative learning experience, it is hypothesized that educational and occupational preferences develop when an individual (1) is positively reinforced for engaging in activities associated with certain occupations or activities relevant to training for certain occupations, (2) observes a valued model being reinforced for these activities, and (3) is positively reinforced by a valued person who advocates engaging in these activities.

Reviews by Mitchell (1979b) and Krumboltz and Rude (1981) cite studies that lend support to these hypotheses. Some of the studies cited in these reviews were not conducted for the purpose of testing hypotheses relevant to the social learning theory of career decision making. Some were sociological surveys, some involved research in sex-role identity, and others were an attempt to test interventions relevant to improving career decision making. However, all studies included appeared to be relevant to hypotheses of the social learning theory and are cited for that reason.

A thoughtful college-level intervention was proposed by Brooks and Haigler (1984). Students were taught that it was normal to be undecided and that counselors would provide structure for the process of deciding but could not dispense career prescriptions. Unobtrusive outcome measures were most encouraging, but no summative statistical analyses were reported.

At the high school level, a one-day career workshop for gifted students had a remarkable impact in a study reported by Kerr and Ghrist-Priebe (1988), where 31 percent of the participants claimed to have changed career or educational plans as a result of the experience.

Concerning the effect of direct positive reinforcement on the individual, Krumboltz and others (1967) and Krumboltz, Baker, and Johnson (1968) developed job experience kits and studied their effects on high school students. The kits were constructed to provide the students with an opportunity to achieve success experiences in job tasks that are typically encountered by members of some occupation. Mastery was ensured by careful graduating of the difficulty of the tasks involved. The studies indicated that students working with the kits expressed significantly more interest in the occupation involved than did a control group of students provided with information about the occupation in standard formats (pamphlets and films). A study of over 2,500 junior college students by Baird (1971) suggested that students in junior college who raise their level of aspiration for more education do so because of their high grades (reinforcement for academic effort). In addition to earning high grades, men tended to raise their level of aspiration on the basis of success in leadership, social science, and clubs; women based their higher aspirations on success in humanistic activities. Osipow (1972) found that subjects who were reinforced with bogus success feedback for either verbal (nonsense syllables) or visual (geometric forms) tasks increased their stated preference for the reinforced task over the nonreinforced (no feedback) task. Mansfield (1973) found that students expressed preference for and aspired toward occupations that emphasized tasks at which they perceived themselves as most competent. Oliver (1975) found that verbal reinforcement from counselors could modify the expressed career choices of high school students. These findings all lend support to the hypothesis that self-observation generalizations about vocational preferences are more likely to be expressed after individuals have been positively reinforced for activities relevant to those occupations.

The work of Hackett and Betz (1981) extended Bandura's self-efficacy theory to career decision making. In the social learning theory of career decision making, a self-efficacy expectation is one specific example of a self-observation generalization. For example, a student who scored 100 percent on her mathematics examination might say, "I'm good at math" (a self-observation generalization). The self-efficacy statement "I will do well at math" is a logical extension from present to future tense but is not essentially different.

Much of the research on self-efficacy treats expectancy beliefs as independent variables, without considering their origin as observations of the self in past learning situations. For example, a study by Lent, Brown, and Larkin (1986) concluded that self-efficacy contributed unique variance to the prediction of college grades, persistence, and range of perceived career options in technical and scientific fields. The high self-efficacy freshmen and sophomores achieved higher grades a year later, remained in the college of technology longer, and had given serious consideration to entering a wider range of science and technology options than had the low self-efficiency group. Where did these self-efficacy expectations originate? No mention of origins is included in the report, but a reasonable guess is that the highest self-efficacy expectations (and the most positive self-observation generalizations) were developed by those students who had received the best grades in the past. Unfortunately, the regression equations do not include prior college grades as predictors. They do include high school rank and PSAT scores, but, as the authors point out, the restriction in range in this high-ability sample makes these poor predictors. Thus, self-efficacy may have added unique variance because the other predictors were so weak and because the most relevant predictor — the events causing the self-efficacy expectations, namely, prior college grades in technology courses — was not included.

In the social learning theory of career decision making, self-efficacy expectations are dependent variables — the outcome of numerous learning experiences — not independent variables. They may also become useful predictors (like interest measures are) when they are easier to obtain than evidence of the events that cause them. If subsequent research shows that they can be modified by counseling or other techniques and that such modifications affect subsequent outcomes, then their psychological value will be enhanced considerably.

Concerning the hypothesis that educational and occupational preferences may develop from observation of a valued model who is positively reinforced for engaging in an occupational activity, Astin (1965) studied over 3,500 students in seventy-three colleges and universities. He found that students in a particular college tend to select careers for which a relatively high proportion of other students in that college are preparing. A study of 379 high school students, both black and white, conducted by Pallone, Rickard, and Hurley (1970) was designed to determine the effect of significant others on the vocational development of black and white youths. Both black and white students rated parents of the same sex and an appropriate occupational role model as the two most influential figures in their vocational development. All students except black females rated the occupational role model as the most influential. A study conducted with 110 female college seniors by Almquist (1974) indicated that women who selected traditionally male-oriented occupations were much more likely to cite female role models as influencing their choice than were those women who selected traditionally female-oriented occupations. A study conducted by Little and Roach (1974) indicated that women who observed a videotape in which models demonstrated and were reinforced for making nontraditional career choices subsequently made more career choices of a nontraditional nature than did women who did not view such a videotape. These findings all lend support to the hypothesis that self-observation generalizations about vocational preferences are more likely to be expressed for occupations in which an individual has observed a valued role model being reinforced for engaging in activities relevant to those occupations.

Concerning the hypothesis that individuals will express preference for occupational activities if they have been positively reinforced by a valued person who advocated engaging in these activities, studies by Trent and Medsker (1968) and Hawley (1972) are relevant. Trent and Medsker examined the effect of parental influence on over 4,600 high school graduates in the western and midwestern United States. They found that the decision to attend college was influenced by many factors (for example, ability and socioeconomic background), but a major determinant was students' perception of their parents as interested in their academic progress and supportive of higher education. Similarly, Hawley (1972) found in a study with 136 women college students that women who chose nontraditional careers listed the support and encouragement of significant men in their lives as crucial to their choice. These findings thus add support to the hypothesis that individuals will express a preference for occupational activities for which they have been positively reinforced by valued others.

The foregoing hypotheses are concerned with the effect of positive reinforcement on individuals' selection of occupational activities. The social learning theory of career decision making also delineates the effect of punishing consequences on the development of task approach skills and self-observation generalizations. It is posited that persons will learn to avoid and dislike those occupational activities for which they experience negative consequences. The converse of these three hypotheses concerning the effect of positive reinforcement on the development of self-observation generalizations that involve preferences can thus be constructed. It is hypothesized that an individual will reject certain educational and occupational choices when that individual (1) experiences negative consequences for engaging in activities associated with certain occupations, (2) observes a valued model experiencing negative consequences for these activities, or (3) has been positively reinforced by a valued person who does not advocate or actively discourages engaging in these activities.

The evidence in support of the hypotheses regarding the effects of negative consequences is not as extensive as that in support of the hypotheses regarding positive reinforcement. Two studies are relevant, however. Hind and Wirth (1969), in a study with 920 male college students, found that these students changed their majors if they received low grades in those majors during their academic careers, even if the students were of high ability. This finding lends some support to the hypothesis that experiencing punishing consequences (for example, low grades) will cause persons to reject former occupational preferences. A study by Rehberg and Sinclair (1970) with 1,455 adolescent males indicated that adolescents with lower occupational aspirations reported lack of parental encouragement to strive for success. This finding lends some support to the hypothesis that persons who have been positively reinforced by a valued person who does not advocate or discourages engaging in certain occupational activities will also reject those activities.

As Mitchell (1979b) has noted, secondary analysis of data from studies concerned with the effects of positive reinforcement reveals additional data relevant to the effects of punishing consequences on the development of aversion to occupational activities. However, without this reanalysis, it cannot automatically be assumed that in studies in which positive reinforcement increased the likelihood of a preference, negative consequences would have decreased that likelihood.

Development of Task Approach Skills. The social learning theory of career decision making posits that task approach skills relevant to career decision making are learned through both instrumental and associative learning experiences. Those task approach skills that seem important include skills in value clarifying, goal setting, predicting future events, generating alternatives, seeking information, and planning and generalizing (Krumboltz and Baker, 1973). If the relationship between task approach skills and learning experiences posited by the social learning theory is accurate, it can be hypothesized that persons will be more likely to learn these task approach skills if they (1) have been positively reinforced for demonstrating or attempting these skills or (2) have observed models being positively reinforced for demonstrating these skills.

A review by Krumboltz and Rude (1981) indicates that the task approach skill on which the most research has focused is information seeking. Concerning the hypothesis that persons who have been positively reinforced for engaging in task approach skills are more likely to learn these skills, Krumboltz and Schroeder (1965) and Krumboltz and Thoresen (1964) found that verbal reinforcement of statements indicating the intent to acquire more job information resulted in more overt information-seeking activities. A series of studies conducted with the job experience kits (Krumboltz, Baker, and Johnson, 1968; Krumboltz and others, 1967) indicate that positive reinforcing experiences with the kits (that is, successful mastery experiences) resulted in more overt occupational information seeking than did the mere presentation of occupational information. These findings thus lend support to the hypothesis that the development of task approach skills, at least the skill of information seeking, can be encouraged through the application of positive reinforcement for these skills.

Concerning the hypothesis that persons are more likely to develop and demonstrate task approach skills if they have observed models being reinforced for these skills, Krumboltz and Thoresen (1964) found that clients who listened to tape-recorded models who were praised for using or planning to use various information sources increased their information-seeking behavior. Similar results were reported with videotaped models in studies by Fisher, Reardon, and Burck (1976), Krumboltz, Varenhorst, and Thoresen (1967), and Thoresen and Krumboltz (1968).

However, what specific kind of information is actually read? When a sample of noncollege-bound high school–age youth was asked to rate the importance of different types of career information and then was unobtrusively observed reading it, correlations averaged near zero between importance ratings and amount of actual reading of different types (Sharf, 1984). Since some students may not necessarily be seeking the type of information they say is most important, future investigators could study whether a counselor's positive reinforcement of either the student or a model can increase the probability that a student will seek the type of information that the student deems most important.

Actions. The social learning theory of career decision making posits that the generalizations and skills that develop as the result of one's learning experiences lead to such career-relevant behaviors or actions as applying for specific jobs or training, accepting job offers and promotions, and changing jobs. It is hypothesized that preferences that develop as a result of learning experiences will be reflected in the actions taken by those persons who express them. To state this hypothesis another way, an individual is more likely to take actions that lead to enrollment in a given course or employment in a given occupation if that individual has recently expressed a preference for that course or occupation. Several large-sample studies lend support to this hypothesized relationship between expressed preference and actions. Astin (1965) found, in a study with 3,530 male college students, that the most significant factor determining final vocational choice at graduation was the student's initial choice at college entry. A review of eleven large-sample longitudinal studies by Whitney (1969) indicated that individuals' expressed choices predict their future employment about as well as do interest inventories or combinations of background characteristics and personality inventories. Data from Project TALENT (Flanagan, 1971) showed that expressed choice was as predictive of college major as were test scores for 35,000 students five years after high school. Astin and Bisconti (1973) found that men tended to select work settings consistent with their stated choices. These findings all lend support to the hypothesis that expressed preference is a valid predictor of actual occupational entry.

The social learning theory of career decision making also posits that persons will be more likely to take actions that lead to employment in a given occupation if they have been exposed to learning or employment opportunities in that occupation. A review by Horner, Buterbaugh, and Carefoot (1967) lends support to the hypothesis. They examined studies that investigated the educational, sociological, psychological, and economic factors influencing the career decision making of rural youth. Conclusions relevant to the hypothesis just stated were that (1) the occupation of farming tends to be transmitted from father to son and (2) on-the-job experience is an important influence in occupational choice.

A sample of 1,200 high school juniors was asked to rate how helpful various factors were in making decisions about future occupations (Noeth, Engen, and Noeth, 1984). The highest rating went to "interesting classes," with 51 percent labeling that factor as very helpful. The "family" (39 percent), "work experience" (32 percent), and "grades" (31 percent) came in next. The fact that work experience would be considered helpful is consistent with the theory's proposition that exposure to employment opportunities influence career choices and actions. The high rating of interesting classes and grades supports the theory's proposition that positive reinforcement of relevant activities is important in career choice.

Career exploration programs continue to be popular and to receive favorable ratings from participants in middle school (Rubinton, 1985), high school (Wiggins, 1987), and college (Heitzmann, Schmidt, and Hurley, 1986) settings. Lent, Larkin, and Hasegawa (1986) tested a career course focused on college students interested only in science and technology. Self-report and test-score indices showed general improvement, but the comparison group consisted of ten enrollees who dropped out before the class started. The task of determining whether these exposures to career opportunities actually affect subsequent career actions has understandably been too difficult for these researchers to tackle and remains a challenging assignment for an ambitious future researcher.

A central thesis of the theory concerns the impact of environmental factors on career decisions and actions. A study dramatically documenting this thesis was reported by Crabbs and Black (1984). Victims of a Texas flood were interviewed to assess the career consequences. A disproportionate number of job changes followed the flood, especially among those whose employers were perceived as insensitive to the flood damage and offered little tangible help.

Another hypothesis that can be derived from the processes posited in the social learning theory of career decision making is that individuals are more likely to take actions that lead to entry in a given occupation if their learned skills match the educational or occupational requirements. Mansfield's (1973) study, which compared the level of self-confidence of 206 Oxford University students with their estimates of their ability to succeed in their chosen occupations, indicated that students of high and low self-confidence alike claimed to have more abilities relevant to the occupations they had chosen than to occupations they had not chosen. Mansfield thus concluded that persons aspire to occupations for which they feel qualified, rather than to occupations for which they perceive a lack of skills.

The foregoing review of empirical evidence related to the social learning theory of career decision making suggests that there is considerable evidence to support the processes posited by the theory in regard to (1) the nature of learning experiences that lead to the development of educational and occupational preferences and (2) the nature of learning experiences that lead to the development of task approach skills, but there is somewhat less conclusive evidence for (3) the factors that lead to actions relevant to entry in selected occupations. It was stated previously that the hypotheses discussed here are only a small sample of those that could be derived from the theory. Much remains to be learned.

Needed Research Directions. Research was reviewed that indicated that some of the task approach skills that seem important in decision making (for example, information seeking) can be positively reinforced in individuals. Many other task approach skills would seem to be relevant to career decision making, and these skills have been identified elsewhere as needing more research. They include the ability to recognize an important decision situation (Tiedeman and Miller-Tiedeman, 1979), the ability to define the decision realistically so that it is manageable, the ability to examine and realistically assess personal values, interests, and skills (Katz, 1963, 1966), the ability to discriminate among information sources on the basis of their accuracy, reliability, and relevance (Mitchell and Krumboltz, 1987), and the ability to organize and initiate the necessary sequence of decision-making behaviors (Dinklage, 1968; Janis and Mann, 1977; Krumboltz and Baker, 1973). Research is lacking, both in the area of interventions to promote these skills and, perhaps more important, in attempts to determine whether these skills are in fact the essential career-relevant task approach skills.

Another critical area for future research would be investigating ways of helping people identify their troublesome, inaccurate self-observation and world-view generalizations. Krumboltz (1988a) has developed the Career Beliefs Inventory for just such a purpose, but research is needed on effective ways of using the results to help clients challenge their own assumptions. Related problems that deserve attention include (1) the processes by which people develop particular inaccurate generalizations from particular learning experiences, (2) the extent to which these generalizations may affect the process and content of decisions, and (3) intervention methods for helping people to examine and change inaccurate generalizations.

Some preliminary work has been done concerning a useful intervention for helping persons to change inaccurate generalizations once they are identified. Mendonca and Siess (1976) found that a cognitive restructuring approach was helpful in assisting persons with excessive anxiety about the career decision-making process to overcome their inhibitions and engage in appropriate career decision-making behavior. Similar results were obtained by Mitchell and Krumboltz (1987), who used a cognitive restructuring intervention with a sample of career-indecisive university students. A method of identifying whether anxiety is an antecedent cause of a client's indecisiveness or an unimportant consequence has been suggested by Kaplan and Brown (1987). Additional research studies need to be conducted to verify the usefulness of these and other interventions as a means of helping persons to change dysfunctional or inaccurate self-observation and world-view generalizations.

Practical Applications

Career Counseling. Career counseling is perceived to be generally effective. In a review of the research evidence in college settings since 1975, Pickering and Vacc (1984) identified forty-seven investigations, most of which produced positive results: "Short-term interventions, designed to facilitate career maturity and the development of decision-making skills through a behavioral orientation, have been most widely used, and their effectiveness has been supported" (Pickering and Vacc, 1984, p. 156).

Since counselors clearly can make a substantial impact on the career planning of students, one may well inquire about the procedures they use. O'Hare (1987) has pointed out that most career decision-making theories have few implications for practice; counselors who profess a particular model may not be able to apply it. However, the influence of cognitive models in psychology can be observed in career counseling now that cognitions, beliefs, generalizations, and thoughts are supplementing skills and behaviors, and there are some practical implications that follow.

The social learning theory of career decision making delineates four outcomes of learning experiences that determine the career decision-making behavior of individuals: self-observation generalizations, world-view generalizations, task approach skills, and actions (entry behaviors). The client who requests assistance with the career decision-making process may be experiencing difficulty in one or a combination of these four areas. In assessing and diagnosing the client's problem, the career counselor must first determine which of these areas is problematic.

Krumboltz (1983) has identified several types of problems that may arise because of dysfunctional or inaccurate world-view and self-observation generalizations.

1. *Persons may fail to recognize that a remediable problem exists.* For example, if one believes that "we must learn to accept things the way they are" or that "bosses always act that way," one may assume that one's problems and suffering are a normal

part of life, rather than a set of circumstances that might be altered.

2. *Persons may fail to exert the effort needed to make a decision or solve a problem.* For example, if one believes that "it is easier to avoid than to face decisions" or that "it is best to do whatever is familiar and easily available," one may fail to take constructive action on a problem, explore alternatives, or seek information.

3. *Persons may eliminate a potentially satisfying alternative for inappropriate reasons.* For example, if one believes that "living on the East Coast is bad; life is more casual and less judgmental in the West" or says, "I'd like to be a teacher but I'd have to teach in an inner-city urban area," one may fail to take advantage of potentially worthwhile alternatives because of beliefs based on misinformation, overgeneralizations, or false assumptions.

4. *Persons may choose poor alternatives for inappropriate reasons.* For example, if one says, "I'd rather succeed in a low-level job than risk failure in a more responsible position" or "Becoming a minister will give me the desirable qualities that religious people have," one may foreclose desirable alternatives and choose alternatives that result in years of regret and unhappiness.

5. *Persons may suffer anguish and anxiety over perceived inability to achieve goals.* For example, if one's goals are unrealistic ("If I can't have the best, I don't want anything at all") or in conflict with other goals ("I don't want a job where I'm supervised, but I don't have the courage to set up a business of my own"), one may again eliminate potentially desirable alternatives or accept less desirable ones because of these perceptions.

Krumboltz (1983) goes on to suggest that several processes may underlie the development of such problematic self-observation and world-view generalizations, including (1) drawing faulty generalizations ("I'm the only person in my class who is afraid of public speaking"), (2) making self-comparisons with a single standard ("I'm not as warm as Carl Rogers, so I could never be a counselor"), (3) exaggerating the estimate of the emotional impact of an outcome ("If I didn't succeed in business school, I just couldn't stand it"), (4) drawing false causal relationships ("To get ahead, you just have to be in the right place at the right time"), (5) being ignorant of relevant facts ("High school English teachers spend their day helping eager students to appreciate the finer points of literature"), and (6) giving undue weight to low-probability events ("I won't accept a job in California because it's going to fall into the ocean during the next earthquake").

Assessment. Counselors who suspect that a client's career decision-making problem is related to inaccurate or dysfunctional self-observation and world-view generalizations need to focus on four major assessment areas: (1) the content of the client's self-observation and world-view generalizations, (2) the processes by which they arose, (3) whether these beliefs and generalizations are truly problematic, and (4) whether stated beliefs disguise more fundamental but as yet unarticulated beliefs.

Several techniques may be useful in assessing the content of beliefs and generalizations and the processes by which they arise. The Career Beliefs Inventory (Krumboltz, 1988a) identifies presuppositions that may block people from achieving their career goals. Structured interviews were used by Mitchell and Krumboltz (1987). Clients were tape-recorded as they discussed their career decision-making problems. Counselor and client together then listened to the tapes and identified examples of dysfunctional beliefs and distorted thinking processes. Glass (1980) cites a study by Cacioppo, Glass, and Merluzzi (1979) in which the technique of thought listing was used. High and low socially anxious college men were informed that they would be interacting with an unfamiliar woman and were asked to identify the thoughts that occurred to them at the moment they were informed. A similar procedure could be used with career decision-making clients. They could be informed that they will be having an interview to discuss their career plans and then asked to list reasons for dreading or anticipating the interview. Hollon and Kendall (1981) reviewed studies in which the technique of "in vivo" self-monitoring was used. Career decision-making clients could record their thoughts in the social setting where problem behaviors occurred (for example, in discussing the choice of a major with other students). Beck and others (1979) developed a dysfunctional thoughts record (DTR) for the treatment of depression. Clients recorded a specific problem situation, the emotions that accompanied it, and the thoughts that seemed to be associated with the emotion. The intensity of emotional responses was recorded on a one-hundred-point self-rating scale. Similar DTR procedures could be developed for career decision-making clients. Thinking aloud during in vivo tasks is cited as a technique by Glass (1980) for discovering dysfunctional thoughts during problem-solving tasks. Simulated career decision-making tasks could be devised, and clients could be asked to think aloud while completing those tasks. Asking clients to think aloud during imagery could also be a useful means of discovering generalizations and beliefs. Counselors commonly ask their clients to fantasize about ideal jobs and work environments. Such fantasy could be directed toward a specific analysis of the thoughts that seem to block a client from achieving the fantasized ideal.

Counselors can also draw inferences from a client's verbal or overt behavior and present those inferences to the client. Psychometric instruments are another means by which clients' cognitions and beliefs can be assessed. The Inventory of Anxiety in Decision Making (Mendonca, 1974) asks respondents to write specific instances of current decision problems and rate their difficulty. Clients then respond on a five-point scale to descriptions of possible emotional reactions to the process of making a vocational decision. My Vocational Situation (Holland, Gottfredson, and Power, 1980) derives three subscores—the identity scale ("I don't know what my major strengths and weaknesses are"), the information scale ("I need the following information: how to find a job in my chosen field"), and the barriers scale ("I lack the special talents to follow my first choice"). The Career Decision Scale (Osipow and others, 1976) is designed to identify the specific reasons why people might be undecided about a career choice (for example, lack of information, or need to satisfy others).

Once such techniques as those just mentioned have been used to identify the content of and the process by which certain beliefs and generalizations have arisen, it is necessary for the counselor to determine whether these beliefs are truly central to the client's problem. Many beliefs may be inaccurate but relatively unimportant. The following guidelines are suggested for determining problematic beliefs and generalizations.

1. *Examine the assumptions and presuppositions of the expressed belief.* For example, the belief that "success is a result of hard work" or "success depends on one's choice of friends" provides many more alternatives for behavior and actions than the belief that "success is based on inherited talents."

2. *Look for inconsistencies between words and actions.* For example, clients who use many hours of a counselor's time in acquiring suggestions and advice about their career decision making, but who fail to take action on those suggestions, may have an underlying belief that enough time spent with a counselor will magically result in a decision.

3. *Test simplistic answers for inadequacies.* The client who presents a career decision-making problem in a simple statement, such as "I just have to find a job where I'll be the best at what I do," may not have examined the wealth of other factors related to job satisfaction.

4. *Confront attempts to build an illogical consistency.* Clients may tend to reject potentially viable alternatives simply because they are inconsistent with alternatives they have previously considered (for example, only alternatives that will please parents or spouses). Consistent refusal to examine other alternatives may indicate an unfounded belief that the consequences of displeasing one's parents will be disastrous.

5. *Identify barriers to the goal.* Such beliefs as "I can't major in premedicine because I'm no good at math" may be based on arbitrary or inaccurate evidence.

6. *Challenge the validity of key beliefs.* Many beliefs are of such a nature that they prohibit persons from exploring alternative possibilities. Persons who believe that someone who programs computers sits alone in front of a computer terminal all day will not begin to explore positions in com-

puter programming if they do not like to be alone. Counselors can use three crucial questions in challenging the validity of key beliefs: How do you know this is true? What steps could you take to find out if this is true? What evidence would convince you that the opposite is true? The client's resistance to answering or taking steps to answer these questions may provide useful insight into whether the belief is problematic.

These techniques for determining problematic self-observation and world-view generalizations should not be used until a climate of trust and rapport exists between client and counselor. The elicitation of the client's innermost thoughts and the process of challenging and confronting the basis for those thoughts cannot be accomplished until the client and counselor together agree on the objectives for counseling and the means by which those objectives can be realized. It is mandatory for the counselor to present a rationale for uncovering these beliefs and generalizations, explain the methods that will be used to uncover them, and enlist the full cooperation of the client in this mutual endeavor. Challenges to fervently held beliefs inevitably produce defensive reactions. Clients should be helped to see that examining their own beliefs is a task that can produce benefits for them. The counselor should teach the belief-testing process by modeling and reinforcing it and encouraging clients to get involved in the process themselves.

The task approach skills that seem important in decision making include the ability to determine when an important decision situation exists; define the problem in a manageable way; assess personal values, interests, and skills; generate a wide variety of alternatives; seek information about these alternatives; and organize and initiate the necessary sequence of decision-making behaviors. An early advocate of teaching rational decision-making skills, Gelatt (1987), has now reversed his position and espouses a more intuitive approach. However, a definitive line between rational and intuitive methods is hard to draw.

Assessing whether clients possess deficits in rational decision-making skills can be accomplished by several means.

Many psychometric instruments, such as the Career Maturity Inventory (Crites, 1978c) and the Cognitive Vocational Maturity Test (Westbrook and Parry-Hill, 1973), yield scores for knowledge about occupations, skills in information seeking, and skills in evaluating information. Various interest inventories (see Holland, 1977; Hansen and Campbell, 1985) can be used to determine whether clients are aware of their interest patterns. Similarly, values inventories, such as the Study of Values (Allport, Vernon, and Lindzey, 1970) and Work Values Inventory (Super, 1970), can be used to determine whether clients have assessed their values.

It is not always sufficient to use standardized paper-and-pencil measures to assess career decision-making competency, however. There is no guarantee that because persons can report knowledge of task approach skills on paper, they can actually use them in the environment. As a result of this discrepancy, Jones and Krumboltz (1970) developed an instrument to evaluate the task approach skills actually used to arrive at a decision: the Vocational Exploratory Behavior Inventory. Using this structured instrument, clients recorded the task approach skills they used in career decision making as they used them (for example, talking to counselors, visiting career centers, acquiring occupational information, and visiting job sites), as well as verifying data (names and addresses of persons and sites visited). By using an instrument of this sort, a counselor can determine whether clients have actually used various task approach skills.

Career decision-making simulations are another useful means by which counselors can assess the extent of a client's task approach skills. For example, the Life Career Game (Boocock, 1967) asks players to make decisions about time management, college, jobs, and marital and family planning for a fictitious individual. Such simulations may be especially useful with school-age clients as a means of assessing task approach skills in an enjoyable and entertaining way.

Intervention. In the section on needed research directions, it was noted that there is preliminary evidence that the cognitive restructuring therapies can be useful in helping persons to change dysfunctional or inaccurate beliefs and generalizations in the area of career decision making. Three major approaches have been taken in the development of cognitive restructuring interventions. Ellis (1970) has produced a list of "irrational beliefs" that he believes are at the root of most psychological distress (for example, "It is easier to avoid facing life's responsibilities than to face them," "It is terrible, horrible, and catastrophic when things are not the way one would like them"). Modification of these beliefs is accomplished through their rationalistic evaluation and direct confrontation with the client about their irrational components. More rational beliefs are then generated, and clients practice substituting them in problematic situations. A second approach is taken by Beck (1976), who has categorized the thought processes that underlie inaccurate or dysfunctional beliefs as distortions of reality, illogical thinking, use of inaccurate premises, dichotomous reasoning, magnification, and arbitrary inference. Therapy consists of explaining these processes to the client and encouraging the client to engage in a series of hypothesis-testing personal experiments to test the validity of the beliefs that have resulted from these processes. A third approach has been taken by Meichenbaum (1977), who has focused on how clients can modify behavioral deficits caused by stress- and anxiety-producing beliefs by developing a set of "self-statements," which allow one to prepare for a stressor, confront and handle a stressor, cope with feelings of being overwhelmed, and reinforce progress.

Keller, Biggs, and Gysbers (1982) discuss how each of these three approaches could be used in counseling clients with career decision-making problems. The use of rational emotive therapy in career counseling could be effective in helping clients become aware of irrational career beliefs, substitute more rational beliefs, and apply these beliefs to their career situations. Techniques derived from Beck's work could be used to help clients see how dysfunctional cognitive processes, such as overgeneralization, may contribute to their career problems. For example, Keller, Biggs, and Gysbers (1982) point out that some minority employees may be reluctant to apply for promotion because they believe minorities have no opportunity for advancement. Such a belief may prove to be unfounded, however, if actual data on the advancement rates of minorities in the company are gathered. Meichenbaum's self-instruction techniques could be used to help clients manage problematic career tasks. Counselors can verbally model for their clients covert self-instruction processes that promote successful completion of tasks. Such self-instructions could include "thoughts about the career task, planning for the next career steps, self-instructions, and self-praise" (Keller, Biggs, and Gysbers, 1982, p. 369). Techniques based on Meichenbaum's self-instruction training were used by Mendonca and Siess (1976) in a study with career-anxious college students. Students who were taught these techniques subsequently engaged in more appropriate career decision-making behavior than those who were not.

Mahoney and Arnhoff (1978) have pointed out that combining these three models for cognitive restructuring therapy suggests a counseling process consisting of (1) direct instruction about the role of cognitions in subjective stress and behavioral deficits, (2) monitoring of one's personal thought patterns, (3) modeling of a rationalistic evaluation and modification of personal thought patterns, (4) feedback on reported changes in thinking patterns and behavior, and (5) performance assignments and rehearsal tasks to improve discrimination and evaluation of performance-relevant cognitions. Mitchell and Krumboltz (1987) used this composite approach in a study with forty-eight career-indecisive college students and found that students who received cognitive restructuring combined with task approach skills intervention engaged in more appropriate career decision-making behaviors than those who received only a task approach skills intervention or those who received no intervention. Furthermore, students who received the combined cognitive restructuring intervention significantly reduced their anxiety about career decision making from pretreatment to posttreatment as compared with students who received the other two treatments.

In assisting clients to change dysfunctional or inaccurate beliefs and generalizations, it will be useful for the counselor to be sensitive to why clients may be resistant to altering, changing, or even revealing them, even if alternative beliefs may be more adaptive. There are two primary reasons. First, society reinforces individuals who give socially acceptable reasons for their behavior, and society punishes persons who engage in the same behaviors for unacceptable reasons. For example, a socially acceptable rationale for believing that one *must* work in San Francisco and nowhere else might be that one can be close to one's aging parents. The real but socially unacceptable reason may be the availability of homosexual contacts in that area. The second reason for resistance to revealing or examining beliefs has to do with extreme fears about the consequences of examining important beliefs. If one desperately wants to succeed in an occupation but suspects that failure is possible, one may assiduously avoid finding out whether failure is indeed likely. The reasoning process is something like "I want to go to college so much, but I could never live with myself if I flunked out, so I'm not even going to apply." The result is that the individual never goes to college and misses out on a potentially crucial success experience. What persons often fail to realize is that they produce the same objective consequences for themselves by avoiding activities that they fear as they would if they actually failed. For counseling unemployed clients, Young (1986) advocates that a counselor point out the distinction between the causes of unemployment (social forces that clients cannot control) and responsibility for its solution (specific actions they can take to obtain employment).

The social learning theory posits that persons will be more likely to learn and use the task approach skills of career decision making if they are positively reinforced for learning and using the skills or if they observe a model being positively reinforced for using the skills. Several studies have demonstrated support for these hypotheses (as mentioned in the section on empirical support) and exemplified how the processes of modeling and reinforcement can be used in counseling.

Simple positive reinforcement in the form of verbal praise (contingent on the client's expressing the intent to learn or use task approach skills) can be a very valuable tool (Krumboltz and Schroeder, 1965; Krumboltz and Thoresen, 1964). Success and mastery experiences are also very powerful reinforcers, and counselors can be instrumental in providing these to clients. The Job Experience Kits (Krumboltz, 1970) were based on research by Krumboltz and others (1967) and Krumboltz, Baker, and Johnson (1968). The kits were carefully designed to provide clients with the opportunity to work successfully at simulated job tasks; their use resulted in more information seeking and consideration of alternatives. Counselors who suggest career decision-making tasks to clients (for example, interviewing at job sites) should keep in mind the likelihood of clients' success in initial efforts, so that successes can lead to eagerness to continue the process. Even if failures occur later in the process, early successes will tend to maintain effort.

Providing appropriate role models for clients is also an extremely useful counseling technique. Models can both demonstrate the task approach skills of decision making and cause persons to consider occupations they would previously have rejected (Almquist, 1974; Fisher, Reardon, and Burck, 1976; Thoresen, Hosford, and Krumboltz, 1970). For example, counselors who conduct reentry women's groups often ask successful women in nontraditional professions to share their experiences with their groups.

Because of the unique learning history and previous environment of each client, the counselor may need to invest considerable effort in individualizing counseling methods. For example, Krumboltz and others (1967) found that giving subjects their free choice of Job Experience Kits was more effective than making required assignments of identical kits. Counselors can provide more opportunities for positively reinforcing experiences if they individualize those experiences to the previous learning experiences and interests of clients.

The interventions suggested in this chapter focus heavily on skills that can be used to examine and assess the self-observation and world-view generalizations that relate to one's values. The suggested interventions also focus on task approach skills that can be used to discover occupations that will satisfy one's values. A career decision that is consistent with one's values could be expected to result in longer adherence to the decision, as measured by job or occupational field tenure and increased reports of job satisfaction. However, career decision making is a lifelong process, especially in these times, when persons can be expected to change occupations several times during their lives. Therefore, one of the most important outcomes that should result from counseling interventions is a set of skills that can be used at all the career decision-making points of one's life, rather than just at the particular one for which the individual has sought counseling.

The social learning theory suggests that persons will be more likely to use occupational information if they experience positively reinforcing events associated with that use. In the past, much occupational information has been presented in a way that is unlikely to result in reinforcing outcomes (for example, being required to read informative but rather dull descriptions of occupations for a career guidance class). Two studies suggest means by which occupational information can be presented in a more interesting and reinforcing format. Jones and Krumboltz (1970) found that interest in various career areas was stimulated more by films that included problem-solving tasks for viewers than by standard films or printed information. Maola and Kane (1976) found that disadvantaged students learned more about occupations through the use of a computerized vocational instruction system than when they were presented the same information by a counselor. Such computerized systems as SIGI (System of Interactive Guidance and Information) (Katz, 1975) use both problem-solving tasks and computerization. It would seem logical that the more means that could be devised to introduce these reinforcing features into occupational information, the more likely clients would be to use and benefit from them.

What components of a career counseling program make it cost-effective? Pickering (1986) compared the use of career counselors, peer tutors, and a directed self-study program at two liberal arts colleges. With a maximum of fourteen subjects per cell, he found no significant differences among the three methods on the criteria he selected. Since the directed self-study was the least labor-intensive, it was labeled the most cost-effective. If Pickering had included a control group, and if the differences still had remained statistically insignificant, he would, by that same logic, have had to conclude that doing nothing is the most cost-effective way to help college students with their career problems. The inability to find significant differences is not the same as an assertion that no differences exist. Pickering used criterion measures that were relatively insensitive to any intervention, and so his small sample virtually guaranteed no significant differences. Counselors still need to use common sense in deciding how best to intervene.

In the study by Noeth, Engen, and Noeth (1984), cited earlier, only 12 percent of the sample rated the "counselor" factor as "very helpful" in occupational planning, a fact that the authors pointed to with some dismay, since 39 percent of the sample gave the same rating to "family." Let us look at that comparison more closely. Each student has a large, undefined number of people in his or her "family"—mother, father, siblings, cousins, uncles, aunts, and grandparents—some of whom the student encounters every day. When one counselor must serve some five hundred students, each student has 1/500th of a counselor—hardly a fair comparison. The fact that 12 percent of the sample rated the "counselor" factor as "very helpful" is a tribute to counselors—not grounds for questioning their role in the process. Furthermore, much of an effective counselor's work is behind the scenes, consulting with teachers and administrators about teaching methods and policy decisions that affect students' welfare (Krumboltz, 1988b). Some of those "interesting classes" that were so influential may have been inspired by a teacher-counselor conference, although the counselor's role remains invisible to students. Each student may be in contact with six teachers a day, five days a week; thus, there are thirty hours per week for some teacher to produce an "interesting class." The categorical comparison of "factors" ignores the number of contact hours and grossly underestimates the counselor's contribution.

Career Development Programs in Business and Industry. Organizations are becoming increasingly concerned with the effectiveness of their "human resource development." Dorn

(1986) has reviewed two examples of that concern: a process model suggested by Mihal, Sorce, and Comte (1984), and a study of how individuals join and leave organizations (Stumpf and Hartman, 1984). Schein (1982) suggests that this greater human sensitivity is due to the use of increasingly complex technologies, which require organizations to have the right kinds of human resources (employees) to manage them. It is thus becoming necessary for organizations to give more thought to how they will recruit, train, promote the career development of, and retain valuable employees. Changing social values have also contributed to organizations' concern in these areas. The entrance of women and minorities into positions traditionally reserved for white males has contributed to the need to reexamine career development and staffing patterns.

Schein (1982) mentions several factors that are crucial to the staffing process of organizations. They include (1) job analysis, (2) recruitment and selection, and (3) job design and job assignment.

The social learning theory of career decision making points out that both genetic characteristics and environmental conditions have a considerable effect on the career decision making of individuals. Persons have been denied access to certain organizations that provide employment because of their genetic characteristics (for example, race or sex) or physical handicaps. Even when organizations do not wish to deny employment because of race, sex, or physical handicaps, they may inadvertently do so. One way they may inadvertently deny access is by using recruitment literature or practices that emphasize role models with whom women or minorities cannot identify. Another way is by not considering modifications of jobs to accommodate handicapped employees. The social learning theory thus suggests that for organizations to promote optimal staff development, they need to examine both recruitment and job-analysis strategies carefully.

Organizations may also unwillingly discriminate against persons who have not been exposed to certain environmental conditions and events by using arbitrary and unnecessary selection criteria. For example, a certain profile on a personality test may be required for selection; persons from other cultures may not demonstrate this profile, but it may not be relevant to actual performance on the job. Organizations need to examine their selection criteria carefully for actual job relevance, to ensure proper staff development.

Schein (1982) points out several features regarding job design and job assignment that are also relevant to the social learning theory of career decision making. He notes that managers must be concerned with how to provide "optimal challenge" to their employees. *Optimal challenge* is defined as a set of activities that are neither too hard nor too easy for the employee and neither too meaningless nor too risky from the point of view of the organization. As the social learning theory suggests, if a job is too easy or too meaningless, it is unlikely to provide reinforcing consequences for the individual to maintain maximum performance. If the job is too difficult, employees will be unable to experience reinforcing consequences and will cease performing. If the job involves too much responsibility or risk from the point of view of the organization, employees may become too anxious or worried about their ability to perform the task. Self-observation generalizations may then develop, inhibiting future performance and constructive learning.

If organizations are to assist persons in planning for productive and satisfying careers, both the need of the organization to fill positions as they open and the need of the employees to have optimally challenging and productive work must be considered (Schein, 1982). Schein suggests several areas in which the career-planning process can be enhanced or inhibited: supervision and coaching, performance appraisal and judgment of potential, organizational rewards, promotions and other job changes, and career counseling. The social learning theory of career decision making suggests several means by which desired outcomes in each of these areas can be achieved.

Schein cites evidence from Bray, Campbell, and Grant (1974) and Hall (1976) that indicates that the first supervisor is often the most crucial in enhancing the career development of the employee and that training of supervisors in how to handle new employees is vital. The social learning theory would suggest that such training emphasize the roles supervisors can perform as modelers of competent behavior and as reinforcing agents for the development of requisite skills. Supervisors who emphasize a punishment orientation (for example, constantly pointing out employees' mistakes, rather than their successes), and who are afraid to allow an employee access to learning experiences because of fear of having their authority usurped, are unlikely to enhance the career development of employees.

Schein points out that, in many organizations, little day-to-day feedback is given to employees about their performance, and only formal evaluations (for example, yearly progress reports) are given. Consistent with the social learning theory, Schein notes that employees need feedback to identify potentially valuable learning experiences. Individuals who are not provided with feedback about their performance may become complacent and uninterested in improvement.

Organizational rewards include pay, benefits, perquisites, promotion, and recognition. Schein (1982, p. 15) notes that often organizational rewards are not contingent on the employee's actual performance and potential but are more responsive to criteria of "elegance, consistency, and what other organizations are doing." The social learning theory would suggest that rewards that are not contingent on performance will not improve performance.

For many employees, jobs that provide optimal challenge are most satisfying (Dalton and Thompson, 1976; Katz, 1977). Such challenge may involve promotion to positions of higher responsibility. However, most organizations have a pyramidal structure, which allows only a very few employees access to the upper ranks. Organizations must therefore look to other means of providing challenging learning experiences and reinforcement to enhance the career planning of their employees. Schein (1982) recommends the development of alternative career-planning paths, such as systems of job rotation, changing assignments, temporary assignments, and other lateral job moves. Potter (1987) has prepared a useful guide for employees who are experiencing few emotional satisfactions on the job and are "burning out."

The social learning theory of career decision making suggests that maximal career planning occurs when people have accurately assessed their own self-observation generalizations about interests, values, and skills, have assessed their worldview generalizations about the nature of occupations, and have the decision-making skills necessary to carry out plans and goals effectively. The Career Beliefs Inventory (Krumboltz, 1988a), described earlier, serves some of these purposes. Schein (1982) suggests that those responsible for the career counseling of an organization's employees have a responsibility to provide employees with the information they will need to determine how their own needs, talents, values, and plans coincide with opportunities within the organization. In this way, organizations can help to ensure maximal career planning.

Part of a career development program may involve designing work environments. One definition of what constitutes a well-designed work environment might be that it is a work environment that maximizes the quality of work life. Lawler (1982) points out that the ideal quality of work life may differ for different individuals, however. Some may equate it with such organizational practices and conditions as job enrichment, democratic supervision, employee involvement, and safe working conditions. Others may equate a good quality of work life with the demonstrated effects that working conditions have on employees' happiness, such as expressed satisfaction, growth and development as human beings, and safety. Lawler notes that the differences between these definitions are minimal, in most circumstances, since organizational practices and conditions that are equated with a good quality of work life frequently have beneficial effects on individuals. Salomone and Daughton (1984) advocate that career counselors systematically review preferred environmental domains with clients.

From the viewpoint of the social learning theory of career decision making, many of the procedures that were discussed in terms of career planning (for example, providing modeling and positive reinforcement, structuring job tasks to provide success experiences, and providing ongoing feedback) are likely to provide work environments that will result in the maximum quality of work life. The major thrust of Lawler's (1982) article, however, is that many organizations are reluctant to adopt these procedures. Evidence has accumulated that organizations are not providing adequate work environments for their employees. Quinn and Staines (1979) conducted a survey indicating that people's job satisfaction has decreased relative to the 1973 survey. Kahn (1981) reviews evidence indicating that work-related stress and dissatisfaction are related to many kinds of illness.

Why are organizations failing to provide a good quality of work environment for their employees? Lawler (1982) suggests that it is because there are few governmental incentives that encourage organizations to experiment with new work designs, and when the profit incentives to experiment with such designs are unavailable, experimentation is unlikely.

Social learning theory is concerned not only with how the environment affects individuals but also with how individuals can affect their environment. Just as large social-change efforts have been successful in modifying the behavior of organizations with regard to the recruitment, selection, and promotion of employees, so may they be effective in improving the quality of work environments.

7

Donald E. Super

꿈꿈꿈꿈꿈꿈꿈꿈꿈꿈꿈꿈꿈꿈꿈꿈꿈꿈꿈꿈꿈꿈꿈꿈

A Life-Span,
Life-Space Approach
to Career Development

Background of the Theory

It has always seemed important to maintain three time perspectives: the past, from which one has come; the present, in which one currently functions; and the future, toward which one is moving. All three are of indisputable importance, for the past shapes the present and the present is the basis for the future. But if I were forced to declare a preference in orientation to time, it would be for the future — even after more than fifty years of work experience.

Despite this preference for a future orientation, this is not the first time that I have talked or written about my antecedents, my philosophical base, and my formative influences (Pappas and Crites, 1978; Super, 1969, 1981a, 1981b). These works provide a fuller discussion of the antecedents of the theory.

The pioneers of career development are people from four disciplines. They are differential psychologists interested in work and occupations, developmental psychologists concerned with "the life course," sociologists focusing on occupational mobility as a function of social class, and personality theorists who view individuals as organizers of experience.

197

The primary contributions of differential psychology to career development have included the development and use of intelligence and aptitude tests during World War I and the early 1920s (Super, 1983b), the practical applications of the Minnesota Employment Stabilization Institute under Paterson during the Great Depression, and Strong's work on vocational interests.

Developmental psychology promised to help answer the question of how people come to have the abilities and interests that facilitate or impede behavior. Buehler (1933) studied life histories by focusing on experiences leading up to, associated with, and following occupational careers. The concept of life stages — in particular, the developmental tasks with which people were observed to cope — provided insights into the development of abilities, interests, and values and the interaction between individual and environment. It anticipated Havighurst's (1953) work on the same topic.

Occupational sociology, at first merely one form of social-class sociology, provided another kind of impetus. Davidson and Anderson's (1937) study of occupational mobility, followed by Miller and Form's (1951) use of longitudinal data on career changes, helped to point out the importance of studying environmental influences on occupations. The work of Hollingshead (1949) and of Warner, Meeker, and Eells (1949) was less directly career-oriented, but it helped to provide insights into the environment's impact on career development.

Personality theory, particularly the self-concept and personal-construct theories of Rogers (1951) and Snygg and Combs (1949), had a good deal to say about how people become what they are, how they change, and how they make decisions. Social learning theory (Bandura, 1977b) later built on the earlier work of E. L. Thorndike, Clark Hull, and Kenneth Spence to enrich our understanding of personality development.

My earlier studies of work, occupations, and psychometrics (Super, 1939, 1940), as well as my reading of Buehler (1933) and Davidson and Anderson (1937), stimulated an effort to synthesize what was known about career development (or, in the terminology of the time, *vocational adjustment*). The first result was two books (Super, 1942, 1949). The former was developmental; the latter dealt with psychometrics applied to vocational counseling. The second result was the refinement of my formulation of my 1942 theory of career development. This further development of my thinking occurred more or less concurrently with a similar effort by Ginzberg, Ginzburg, Axelrad, and Herma (1951). While we began and concluded our efforts independently, there was brief interaction during the process.

The Theory

As Crites (1969), Borow (1982), and I have pointed out, what I have contributed is not an integrated, comprehensive, and testable theory, but rather a "segmental theory" (Super, 1969, pp. 8–9), a loosely unified set of theories dealing with specific aspects of career development, taken from developmental, differential, social, personality, and phenomenological psychology and held together by self-concept and learning theory. Each of these segments provides testable hypotheses, and in due course I expect the tested and refined segments to yield an integrated theory.

Synthesizing Theories and Models. We all have a tendency to think of theories as mutually exclusive, despite what the writers just cited have said about segmental theories. In one important sense, there is no "Super's theory"; there is just the assemblage of theories that I have sought to synthesize. In another sense, the synthesis is (or aims to lead to) a theory. The Life-Career Rainbow (Figure 7.2) does some of this synthesizing work by bringing the life span and the life space into one model (maturing and playing a changing diversity of roles) and by noting the biological, psychological, and socioeconomic determinants of career development. But this multifaceted conceptualization of career development has not succeeded in making these various facets as clear as it should. As a result, in seminars and workshops during the late 1980s, I have developed another model of career development, a model designed to bring out the segmented but unified and developmental nature of career development, to highlight the segments, and to make their origin

Figure 7.1. A Segmental Model of Career Development.

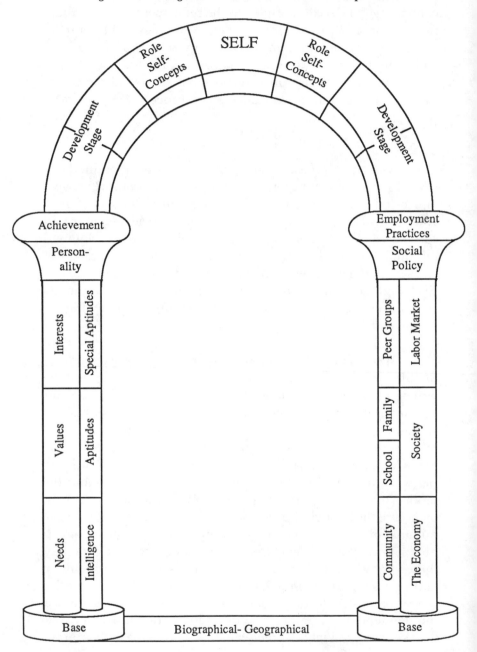

clear. The model might be called the Archway Model, because it uses stones (segments) and cement to make clear its complexity and its many contributors. It tells the same story as the Rainbow (Figure 7.2), but tells it in a different way.

The Archway Model is shown in Figure 7.1 and is deliberately presented and discussed before any of the other models in order to emphasize its synthetic, synthesizing nature. The Career Archway happens to use a Norman arch (a favorite church door in Cambridgeshire) for graphic purposes; it could also use a Gothic, Renaissance, or even Roman arch. Its base consists of three large stones, with the biological-geographical foundations of human development as the doorstep, and with a large stone at either end supporting (on the left) the person (psychological characteristics) and (on the right) the society (economic resources, economic structure, social institutions, and so on) that acts on the person and on which the person acts in growing up and functioning as a unit in society, in which the individual pursues his or her educational, familial, occupational, civic, and leisure careers.

Here, a brief digression into definitions of some often loosely used key terms seems called for, if confusion is to be avoided in important material that follows. This confusion arises in the use of the terms *personality* and *self-concepts*.

The *Wiley Encyclopedia of Psychology* (Corsini, 1984, 1987) cites Allport as having defined personality in terms of some four thousand traits uniquely combined in each person but fails to provide help in dealing with the divergent views it reports.

The old American classic among dictionaries of psychology (English and English, 1958) cites Allport as having identified fifty meanings of the term *personality* and its parent terms, and, according to Burnham (in Borgatta and Lambert, 1968), preferred the second of the *Oxford English Dictionary's* six more parsimonious definitions: "That quality or assemblage of qualities which makes a person what he is, as distinct from other persons. . . ." Drever (1952) is rather more explicit, calling personality "the integrated and dynamic organization of the physical, mental, moral, and social qualities of the individual that manifests itself to other people in the give and take of social life . . . the impulses and habits, interests, and complexes, the sentiments and ideals, the opinions and beliefs, as manifested in his social milieu . . . " (p. 203). Rather than reinvent the wheel, I would build on what Allport and Drever have done and attempt to refine the model of personality and its main constructs as follows.

Personality is the global construct used to include all of the qualities that constitute a person. Graphically, it is represented in the Archway Model by the left-hand column, with its *biological* base, the *needs* and *intelligence* that develop from it in interaction with the environment, and the *values* that derive from needs as objectives that are sought in activities found likely to lead to the attainment of those values, activities that are synthesized as *interests*. The parallel shaft in the complex column of personality shows *aptitudes* (for example, verbal, numerical, spatial) as derivatives of general intelligence, and *special aptitudes* (for example, clerical, mechanical) as further refinements. Even more refined combinations of aptitudes and personality need to be accommodated in the schema (artistic, musical, literary, athletic, social, and so on) but are not fitted into what becomes a very complex model.

The synthesis of all of these components of personality into something unitary is symbolized by the capital of the column, the *personality,* with the top of the capital representing the *achievements* that result from the use, misuse, or disuse of personal resources. *Traits,* such as sociability–solitariness, introversion–extraversion, and honesty–dishonesty, not listed in the Archway, are modes or styles of behavior in the interaction of the person and the environment; if represented graphically, they might best appear on the arrows that, in a complete figure, would show this interaction between the left-hand column and the right-hand column. *Attitudes,* more transitory than interests and traits, might also be shown on the interactive arrows, if drawn in. *Self-concepts,* such as self-efficacy, self-esteem, and role self-concepts, being combinations of traits ascribed to oneself, are included in personality as unshown combinations of the unshown traits (Super and others, 1963). In writing this, I am disposing of a very complex topic much too briefly. Dealt with equally briefly once before (Super and Bohn, 1970) and neglected by most theorists, it was recently addressed by an international consortium in psychology's convention programs at Sydney in 1988, and it will be dealt with again, in research reports, at the International Congress of Applied Psychology in Kyoto in 1990.

The fact must be stressed that these two columns interact, for in order not to clutter the diagram, the vectors between the columns have been left out. Lines should be drawn, with arrowheads at each end, representing the dynamic interaction of individual and society. Natural resources, the economy, and the family influence the development of aptitudes, values, and interest, as does their use in school and at work. The individual, using his or her abilities and seeking outlets for interests, acts on society in visible ways (for example, as a leader, as a protagonist in enacting equal rights legislation) and in ways that escape notice (for example, by quietly fitting into and helping a new and innovative organization to function). Of course, analogies should not be pushed too far, and this model is indeed an analogy, using an arch to represent a career. But there is interaction between the columns, for they tend both to push each other apart and to pull themselves closer to each other; that is why buttresses were invented.

The capitals of the columns represent the culmination, the integration of each of the aspects of the individual and of society. The arch itself is the career; like the columns, it is made up of a number of stones, or conceptual components, but they are derived from the columns. At each end of the arch are the developmental stages: at the left, childhood and adolescence; at the right, young adulthood and maturity. These stages each confront the individual with developmental tasks arising from chronological age and social expectations. During these stages, the individual occupies certain positions, such as those of child, student, worker, spouse, and so on, and develops concepts of himself or herself in each of these life roles. The keystone of the Archway is the person, the decision maker in whom all of the personal and social forces are brought together, organized in terms of concepts of self and of roles in society. These forces are weighed and used in the making of career decisions. The keystone, the person, is thus indeed the central component of the Archway, of the career.

But the separate stones of the Archway, the superimposed segments of a complex theory, are not enough, not even with the keystone, the person, and its concepts of self and roles. The stones need cement to hold them together, no matter how good the dry masonry in such a structure; the segmental theories need a logic to bind them together more firmly than can the interaction of psychological and socioeconomic forces. This cement, together with the vectors (shown in Figure 7.1 only by single lines between stones), is *learning theory*. As used in this way (Strong, 1943, pp. 682–683), the term is defined thus: "An interest is an expression of one's reaction to his environment. The reaction of liking–disliking is a resultant of satisfactory or unsatisfactory dealing with the object (add: activity, person, idea). Different people react differently to the same object. The different reactions, we suspect, arise because the individuals are different to start with. We suspect that people who have the kind of brain that handles mathematics easily will like such activities and vice versa. In other words, interests are related to abilities, and abilities, it is easy to see, can be inherited. There is, however, a pathetic lack of data to substantiate all this." In a previous text (Super, 1949), I attempted to extend Strong's rather limited theorizing to take into account more research and more theorizing; but the important point here is that, for a variety of reasons, interests are learned. Today we would say that interactive learning is the theory that explains the relationships of the segments of the Career Archway: social learning (as explicated most recently by Bandura) but also learning in encounters with objects, facts, and ideas. In counseling theory and practice, Krumboltz, Mitchell, and Jones (1976) have done the most to point up these applications. Bordin (1943) had already pointed out that expressions of interest are manifestations of self-concepts. Interactive experiential learning, self-concept, and occupations–concept formation take place through the interaction of the individual and the environment. This is what the Career Archway is designed to bring out.

It may be worth going one step farther in documenting the idea that mine is a segmental theory, one in which I have not striven to highlight and document a new theory based on one set of observations, or on one perspective. This is what Thorndike, Hull, and Bandura, in learning theory; Freud, Jung, Adler, Rank, Murray, Maslow, Allport, Rogers, and many others, in personality theory; Paterson, Darley, and others, in the field of aptitudes; and Strong, Darley, Bordin, and others, dealing with interests, have done. Instead, my goal has been to bring together contributions from them and others in order to construct a theory and a model of career development that takes these and other contributions to knowledge into account.

Such documentation would inscribe the names of Freud, Murray, and Maslow (to name just a few) on the segment of the left-hand column labeled Needs. It would chisel the names of Allport, Rosenberg, and others into the Values segment (above the Needs stone) and the names of Strong, Carter, Darley, Kuder, Holland, Campbell, Hansen, and others into the Interests segment. Intelligence and Aptitudes involve such names as Alfred Binet, L. L. Thurstone, Donald Paterson, Beatrice Dvorak, George Bennett, and J. P. Guilford. Learning theory would be the cement binding them together, cement mixed by Bandura and Krumboltz, although they have dealt only with social (omitting ideational and object) interaction. My name might appear on the Developmental Stage stones, following that of Charlotte Buehler and accompanied by those of Anne Roe and Eli Ginzberg. It might appear also on the three Self and Person stones, preceded by many names, beginning with George Meade and including Prescott Lecky, Carl Rogers, George Kelly, and Edward Bordin. On the stones of the right-hand column would appear such names as Howard Odum, Orville Brim, William Sewell, Peter Blau, Herbert Parnes, Delbert Miller, William Form, and Kenneth Roberts. In the middle of the Archway, relating the two columns, would be the names of aspiring integrators of theory, such as myself, Blau and others (1956), and Vondracek, Lerner, and Schulenberg (1986). The names are really too numerous to be listed here; they can only be suggested.

In their study of and treatise on occupational choice, Ginzberg, Ginzburg, Axelrad, and Herma (1951) focused on "the" choice — entry into the labor force — at a time when career-development theory was beginning to take form with a focus on the life span. They had stated that vocational counseling operated without a theory, and although I have shared that notion from reading its literature, vocational counseling *was* based on theory: on theories of differential psychology and of education as a method of fostering development.

Propositions Updated. An early contribution was a set of ten propositions (Super, 1953), later expanded to twelve (Super and Bachrach, 1957) and expanded again to take into account the results of career-development research (Fisher, 1989; Gribbons and Lohnes, 1968, 1982; Jordaan and Heyde, 1979; Kleinberg, 1976; Super, Kowalski, and Gotkin, 1967; Super and Overstreet, 1960). Slightly modified for clarity, and with occasional parenthetical updating, they follow:

1. People differ in their abilities and personalities, needs, values, interests, traits, and self-concepts.
2. People are qualified, by virtue of these characteristics, each for a number of occupations.
3. Each occupation requires a characteristic pattern of abilities and personality traits, with tolerances wide enough to allow both some variety of occupations for each individual and some variety of individuals in each occupation.
4. Vocational preferences and competencies, the situations in which people live and work, and, hence, their self-concepts change with time and experience, although self-concepts, as products of social learning, are increasingly stable from late adolescence until late maturity, providing some continuity in choice and adjustment.
5. This process of change may be summed up in a series of life stages (a "maxicycle") characterized as a sequence of growth, exploration, establishment, maintenance, and decline, and these stages may in turn be subdivided into (a) the fantasy, tentative, and realistic phases of the exploratory stage and (b) the trial and stable phases of the establishment stage. A small (mini) cycle takes place in transitions from one stage to the next or each time an individual is destabilized by a reduction in force, changes

in type of manpower needs, illness or injury, or other socioeconomic or personal events. Such unstable or multiple-trial careers involve new growth, reexploration, and reestablishment (recycling).

6. The nature of the career pattern — that is, the occupational level attained and the sequence, frequency, and duration of trial and stable jobs — is determined by the individual's parental socioeconomic level, mental ability, education, skills, personality characteristics (needs, values, interests traits, and self-concepts), and career maturity and by the opportunities to which he or she is exposed.

7. Success in coping with the demands of the environment and of the organism in that context at any given life-career stage depends on the readiness of the individual to cope with these demands (that is, on his or her career maturity). *Career maturity* is a constellation of physical, psychological, and social characteristics; psychologically, it is both cognitive and affective. It includes the degree of success in coping with the demands of earlier stages and substages of career development, and especially with the most recent.

8. Career maturity is a hypothetical construct. Its operational definition is perhaps as difficult to formulate as is that of intelligence, but its history is much briefer and its achievements even less definitive. Contrary to the impressions created by some writers, it does not increase monotonically, and it is not a unitary trait.

9. Development through the life stages can be guided, partly by facilitating the maturing of abilities and interests and partly by aiding in reality testing and in the development of self-concepts.

10. The process of career development is essentially that of developing and implementing occupational self-concepts. It is a synthesizing and compromising process in which the self-concept is a product of the interaction of inherited aptitudes, physical makeup, opportunity to observe and play various roles, and evaluations of the extent to which the results of role playing meet with the approval of superiors and fellows (interactive learning).

11. The process of synthesis of or compromise between in-

dividual and social factors, between self-concepts and reality, is one of role playing and of learning from feedback, whether the role is played in fantasy, in the counseling interview, or in such real-life activities as classes, clubs, part-time work, and entry jobs.

12.   Work satisfactions and life satisfactions depend on the extent to which the individual finds adequate outlets for abilities, needs, values, interests, personality traits, and self-concepts. They depend on establishment in a type of work, a work situation, and a way of life in which one can play the kind of role that growth and exploratory experiences have led one to consider congenial and appropriate.

13.   The degree of satisfaction people attain from work is proportional to the degree to which they have been able to implement self-concepts.

14.   Work and occupation provide a focus for personality organization for most men and women, although for some persons this focus is peripheral, incidental, or even nonexistent. Then other foci, such as leisure activities and homemaking, may be central. (Social traditions, such as sex-role stereotyping and modeling, racial and ethnic biases, and the opportunity structure, as well as individual differences, are important determinants of preferences for such roles as worker, student, leisurite, homemaker, and citizen.)

The social and economic determinants of career choice and other social, economic, and psychological aspects of work, such as life stages and developmental tasks and stable, unstable, conventional, and multiple-trial career patterns, are discussed in Super (1957). This extensive treatment of political, social, and economic factors in career development was ahead of its time and was disregarded by most readers (for example, Osipow, 1973). Such methods as multivariate analysis have more recently been used (for example, Card, 1978; Gribbons and Lohnes, 1982) to combine social, economic, and psychological determinants, making it possible to move beyond description to the prediction of career development.

Self-concept theory, as applied in my paper (Super, 1951) viewing occupational choice as an attempt to implement a self-concept, was a simple formulation, but the notion of translating one's idea of oneself into occupational terms, and then seeking to prepare for and pursue an occupation, had and still has widespread appeal. However, it needed a method that would enable counselors to put it to use. David Tiedeman, then at Harvard, with Robert O'Hara as one of his students, obtained funding from the College Entrance Examination Board to make it possible for those two from Harvard, Henry Borow from Minnesota, and Jean Pierre Jordaan and myself at Columbia to meet regularly for a series of working seminars. We prepared papers and met to discuss these in some depth. The result was two monographs (Super and others, 1963; Tiedeman and O'Hara, 1963).

One chapter in the Columbia volume sought to synthesize the results of research up to that time; another chapter examined ways of comparing self- and occupational concepts and developed a model for the translation process. In still another chapter, two students, Starishevsky and Matlin, developed this model further and called it the incorporation model and process. In yet another chapter, Jordaan picked up my suggestion that Berlyne's (1960) synthesis of work on curiosity was basic to career exploration, and he reviewed research and theory on exploratory behavior as the prime method of developing personal and situational concepts. He wrote a seminal essay that has only recently begun to command the attention that it should have had in career education and career guidance (see Blustein and Strohmer, 1987). In the final chapter, I sought to bring life-stage theory up to date. This monograph was part of the refinement and application that were needed for the improvement of my synthesizing approach. It seems to have had little impact other than to add stimulus to the carrying out of studies of the translation or implementation model (Helbing, 1987; Kidd, 1984; Super, 1982a, 1984).

The focus on career or vocational maturity did have a number of important products. Developed first in a journal article (Super, 1955b), and then further refined in my text (Super, 1957) and in the Career Pattern Study (CPS) monograph (Super and others, 1957), the concept of vocational maturity sought to devise a basis for describing and assessing the stage of career development reached by students of differing ages and grades, the types of career development tasks they were confronting and how they confronted them, and their readiness for career decisions. The concept was closely tied, not to that of biological development, but rather to that of developmental tasks, as used by Buehler (1933) and as conceived by Havighurst (1953). Developmental tasks are those with which society confronts individuals when they reach certain levels of biological, educational, and vocational attainment. The 1963 chapter updated my thinking on career maturity by describing the tasks of development in more detail, along with their attributes and behaviors, in adolescence and adulthood. Empirical data on which to build were provided by the second CPS monograph (Super and Overstreet, 1960) on the construct and the assessment of career development.

Launching the first issue of *The Counseling Psychologist,* John Whiteley published a pair of my papers first presented at a symposium on vocational development at Washington University in 1968 (Super, 1969), along with it a set of commentaries by Holland, Osipow, Campbell, Westbrook, Resnikoff, O'Hara, and Bingham. Concern was expressed that the term *career model* might mean that there is or should be just one model of a career, but it should have been made clear (and it was at least implicit) that the existence of a variety of career patterns (Miller and Form, 1951; Super, 1957) provides several models — stable and unstable, conventional, and multiple-trial. The career model, as contrasted with the occupational model, was intended to denote a longitudinal, developmental approach, rather than a single-choice, matching approach, such as that of differential psychology and of congruence theory, as now used by Holland.

My use of theory has occasionally been viewed (for example, by Lo Cascio, 1967) as a "middle-class theory." Indeed, there is a middle-class bias in a society in which most people seek security and high living standards in employment. In such a society, anticipatory socialization for stable and conventional careers appears desirable. So does recognition of the fact that people, occupations, and opportunities change, with resulting destabilization and a need for reexploration and reestablishment. But it is relevant that my segmental theory was refined in a long-term project with a good sample of youth, who were in fact from predominantly semiskilled families (Super and Overstreet, 1960).

Some writers have been critical of the wide scope of my formulations, recognizing the complexities of career development but preferring to disregard them so as to work on one approach (for example, Holland, 1973a). Pursuing more limited goals can have great impact on the field but neglects too many determinants, as Holland (1985a) has recognized in his revised book.

The CPS multifactorial approach and longitudinal view have turned attention to career development tasks and stages, career maturity, exploratory behavior, career transitions, career as contrasted with occupational success, and self-concept implementation. The insights may soon be greater, and with them may come methods and tools of greater validity because of better theoretical bases and greater comprehensiveness (Super, 1983a).

Although the follow-up studies of the CPS subjects at the ages of twenty-five (Super, Kowalski, and Gotkin, 1967), thirty-six (Kleinberg, 1976), and fifty (Fisher, 1989) are still not integrated into the literature, and although a monograph of selected longitudinal case studies is only partly written, I have made several recent attempts to bring my views up to date in print. My original intention had been to rewrite my basic text on career development once the CPS monographs were done, thus building on a better data base. However, the increasing and widespread interest in career development has made it seem wise to publish some ideas earlier, including this revised chapter.

"A Life-Span, Life-Space Approach to Career Development" was first written in 1974 (Super, 1980). It sought to bring life-stage and role theory together to convey a comprehensive picture of multiple-role careers, together with their determinants and interactions. The Life-Career Rainbow (Figure 7.2) is a graphic device for portraying life-span, life-space career development. All the elements used in the figure had been treated in earlier work; it was the graphic representation of a career that was novel. It has proved its value in workshops with counselors, with general adults in a high school course (Super and Bowlsbey, 1979), and in Bowlsbey's computerized DISCOVER system (Bowlsbey, 1984).

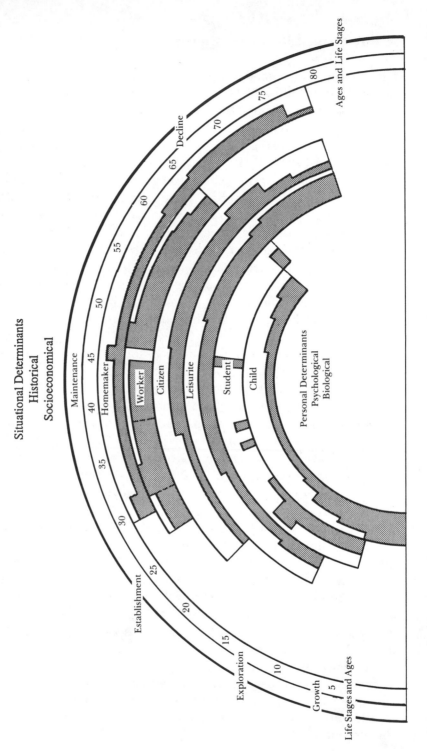

Figure 7.2. The Life-Career Rainbow: Six Life Roles in Schematic Life Space.

Career maturity is the first dimension depicted by the Life-Career Rainbow. It is longitudinal; it is the life span, the course of life, the maxicycle. (The second dimension, life space, is discussed later.) The outer band of the Rainbow shows the major life stages, their normal but not invariable sequence, and their approximate ages: Growth, or childhood; Exploration, or adolescence; Establishment, or young adulthood; Maintenance, or middle adulthood; and Decline, or old age. Some writers on career development prefer to call this last stage Disengagement, a term that does have the advantage of making all the terms descriptive of the nature of the principal developmental tasks of each stage.

Career maturity is defined as the individual's readiness to cope with the developmental tasks with which he or she is confronted because of his or her biological and social developments and because of society's expectations of people who have reached that stage of development. This readiness is both affective and cognitive, as shown in the CPS work (Super and Overstreet, 1960) and by research with the Career Development Inventory, or CDI (Thompson and others, 1981, 1982, 1984). The CDI assesses two affective variables: career planning, or planfulness; and career exploration, or curiosity. It also assesses three cognitive characteristics: knowledge of the principles of career decision making and ability to apply them to actual choices; knowledge of the nature of careers, occupations, and the world of work; and knowledge of the field of work in which one's occupational preference falls.

A component of career or vocational maturity identified in the CPS model and in Crites's (1978c) adaptation is realism. This is a mixed affective and cognitive entity best assessed by combining personal, self-report, and objective data, as in comparing the aptitudes of the individual with the aptitudes typical of people in the occupation to which he or she aspires. Realism is thus a "trait" not well measured by any one instrument, such as the CDI or Crites's Career Maturity Inventory. No single measure can be called *maturity;* any test or inventory score is at best an assessment of one or more aspects of a complex whole.

Another way of describing the life stages is shown in Figure 7.3. It identifies the substages that tend to be seen in each stage, although, as the broken lines indicate, the stages

Figure 7.3. Life Stages and Substages Based on the Typical Development Tasks, with Focus on the Maxicycle.

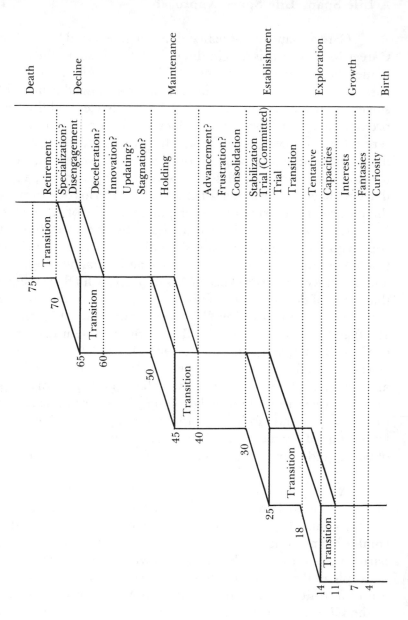

Note: Each transition, whether psychogenic, sociogenic, econogenic, or all of these, has its own minicycle of growth, exploration, establishment, maintenance, and decline: its recycling.

tend to overlap and are not clearly defined by age limits. It is here that this conceptual scheme differs radically from Levinson and others' (1978) formulation. Although that scheme resembles this one when it is put in comparable graphic form, these researchers view the stages as essentially biologically determined and as progressing in a well-ordered sequence. My formulation has sought to make it clear not only that the ages of transitions are very flexible but also that each transition involves a recycling through one or more of the stages—a minicycle. Thus, the high school graduate entering his or her first job usually goes through a period of growth in the new role, of exploration of the nature and expectations of that role. He or she becomes established (and perhaps disestablished) in it, maintains the role if successful, and then experiences decline or disengagement, if with further growth he or she becomes ready to make a job or occupational change. Similarly, the established worker, frustrated or advancing, may experience new growth and explore new roles and seek to get established in one of them. Implicit in my formulation of the life-stage model, and explicit in the variations in the age limits of the stages, are the terms *trial* and *transition* to denote recycling. The concepts need to be spelled out in more detail. Table 7.1 illustrates the notion of recycling. It shows the sample tasks, most typical of other life stages, being appropriately encountered at atypical life stages. As Havighurst (1953) points out, and as some CPS cases show, skipping a stage in the normal cycle can result in difficulties at a later stage (for example, failure to explore often leads to a poor choice of occupation or job).

The Life-Career Rainbow has been turned from a model and a heuristic device into a subjective assessment and counseling device by printing it as an exercise form for use in career courses and workshops (Super and Bowlsbey, 1979). Each person fills in the arcs of the Rainbow (the life-career roles) so as to show how he or she currently invests his or her time and affect in each role, and how he or she would like to make these investments at some important time in the future (for students in high school or college, at about age twenty-five; for adults, ideally). Seeing themselves thus helps alert students to the possible importance

Table 7.1. The Cycling and Recycling of Developmental Tasks Through the Life Span.

Life Stage	Age			
	Adolescence 14–25	Early Adulthood 25–45	Middle Adulthood 45–65	Late Adulthood over 65
Decline	Giving less time to hobbies	Reducing sports participation	Focusing on essential activities	Reducing working hours
Maintenance	Verifying current occupational choice	Making occupational position secure	Holding own against competition	Keeping up what is still enjoyed
Establishment	Getting started in a chosen field	Settling down in a permanent position	Developing new skills	Doing things one has always wanted to do
Exploration	Learning more about more opportunities	Finding opportunity to do desired work	Identifying new problems to work on	Finding a good retirement spot
Growth	Developing a realistic self-concept	Learning to relate to others	Accepting one's limitations	Developing nonoccupational roles

Source: Adapted from Super and Thompson, 1981.

of future roles and helps them want to plan for them, and it frequently provides adults with important insights into what they are and into how what they would like to be differs from the actual.

The life-span, or longitudinal, dimension of the Rainbow has been turned into psychometric devices yielding profiles of traits, first identified and provisionally assessed in the Career Pattern Study, by three inventories (Crites, 1978c; Super and others, 1981, 1985). The Career Maturity Inventory (Crites, 1978c) and the Career Development Inventory (Super and others, 1981), usually referred to as the CMI and the CDI, were developed for use at the high school (CMI and CDI) and college (CDI) levels. They are both multidimensional, seeking to measure several kinds of attitudes and knowledge that were found in the CPS to be among the constituents of readiness to make career decisions. Evaluations of those instruments are found in Kapes and Mastie (1982, 1988).

Super and Kidd (1979) consider the possibilities and problems of assessing these same variables in adults. They conclude that multidimensional inventories and tests of career maturity or adaptability cannot be developed for general adult populations as they can for general student populations because the latter group has a general culture in common (that of the secondary schools or colleges of the country in which they live and study), but adults in various occupations or other adult roles (such as full-time homemaker, civic volunteer, or leisurite) live in universes of attitudes and information that are too diverse to be assessed by the same instruments. One has only to compare the world of a coal miner in an isolated mountain valley with that of an aerospace engineer in a metropolitan area, or the life of a farmer on the Great Plains with that of a fashion designer in New York, Chicago, Atlanta, or San Francisco to recognize this fact. For this reason, Crites (1982) developed his Career Adjustment and Development Inventory (CADI), and Super, Thompson, and Lindeman (1988) published their Adult Career Concerns Inventory (ACCI). In a study involving both of them, Savickas, Passen, and Jarjoura (1988) showed what they assess: the CADI, developmental task coping and mastery;

the ACCI, developmental task concerns. The CADI has internal consistency coefficients of 0.82 for the total score but only 0.49 to 0.65 (median 0.535) for the part scores; the ACCI, 0.97 for the total score and from 0.77 to 0.93, with a median of 0.89, for its substage scales. Specifications for multidimensional career adaptability tests and inventories have been developed for targeted adult populations, such as young semiskilled blue-collar workers and electronics engineers, but no attempt to develop such instruments has been funded (Super and Knasel, 1979). The use of such measures in career assessment and counseling is dealt with later in this chapter.

Role salience is the second dimension depicted by the Rainbow. It is latitudinal. It is the life space, the constellation of positions occupied and roles played by a person. The individual here portrayed (not a "model," in the sense of an ideal or even an average) occupied the position of child from birth until entering school and, like most children, played no other major role until then. As he or she got older, he or she added more roles. Six major roles were played from about age twenty-nine until the parents died and retirement came at age sixty-five, after which three major roles were played until death at the age of seventy-nine. Lowenthal and others (1975) have brought out, in an analysis of life stages that examines changes in roles and in values, the role diffusion that characterizes late adolescence and young adulthood and the role focusing that comes with maintenance and decline. As pointed out in Super (1980), the various roles interact. The addition of a new role reduces the participation (the shaded or colored space in the arc of the role) of one or more others and sometimes affects the affective commitment (which might be shown by the depth of the shading or coloring of the role space). These various roles can be extensive (supportive or supplementary), compensatory, or neutral (Champoux, 1981; Super, 1940). They can also be conflicting if they make inroads into time and energy needed elsewhere. They can enrich life or overburden it.

The Life-Career Rainbow helps us focus on the concept and measurement of role salience (Nevill and Super, 1986, 1988; Super and Nevill, 1984). Since 1978, role salience has played a major part in the Work Importance Study (WIS), a twelve-country project reviewing national literatures, specifying sample items for a comprehensive, cross–national values inventory, and providing each participating country with a national role-salience inventory. A version of the Rainbow, as used with the Salience Inventory, appears in Figure 7.2. It portrays the changing importance of each of the major life roles of one individual, from late adolescence until death, with earlier roles sketched in but not treated for importance. With its two major instruments ready for use in twelve countries and ten languages, the WIS has obtained normative data and examines the degree to which people in whom certain roles are salient seek various values in these roles. From this work, we expect to get a clearer picture of the meanings of work, homemaking, leisure, study, and community service; a better understanding of the impact that a change in occupation has on self-actualization; and an understanding of the degree to which, when work is not rewarding or is not available, other roles replace it as outlets for abilities, interests, and values.

A symposium volume of encyclopedic size and scope on career development in Great Britain (Watts, Super, and Kidd, 1981) was the occasion for a comprehensive synthesis of approaches to career development. In another volume published the same year (Montross and Shinkman, 1981), I contributed a chapter dealing specifically with my developmental self-concept approach, in which I made the point that self-concept theory, as I have used it, is both very similar to and very different from congruence theory, as Holland has used it. It is similar in that occupational choice is viewed as the choice by the individual of a role and of a setting in which he or she will fit comfortably and find satisfaction — as the implementation of an occupational self-concept. It is different in that Holland's interest has been primarily in the single choice and in the assessment of people and occupations for more effective matching, whereas mine has been in the nature, sequence, and determinants of the choices that constitute a career over the life span. A general summary statement (Super, 1981a, pp. 38–39) reads as follows:

> Choice, matching, and selection theories range from those which focus on aptitudes and interests that make for differential choice of and success in occupations, through personality theories which view infant and child develop-

as the key determinants, to situational or social-structural theories which tend to treat social class and the opportunity structure as the principal or even sufficient determinants of occupational choice or assignment. These approaches merge, in varying degrees, in what might be called "socialized-individual" approaches which themselves vary from treating the individual as the organizer of his experiences to viewing him as one who, willy nilly, is socialized to become what society wants him to be. This last type of theory tends to become a manpower-selection rather than an occupational-choice or career-development.

Also basically differential theories, but different in that the emphasis is put on the individual as the organizer of his experience, are the personal-situational theories such as personal construct or self-concept and congruence theory, the last an elaborated version of the second. As Holland and I have formulated them they have dominated the theoretical approaches of the past twenty-five years and merge, in practice, with differential theories stressing objective data on aptitudes, interests and opportunities, to produce a broad-gauged and pragmatic set of practices.

Developmental theories, while not rejecting the matching approaches, treat them as an insufficient basis for career guidance. This is because studies of the life span and life space have made it clear that occupational choice or assignment is not something that happens once in a lifetime, on leaving school or university. These theories hold that people and situations develop, and that a career decision tends to be a series of mini-decisions of varying degrees of importance. They hold that these mini-decisions add up to a series of occupational choices each of which only seems to be one maxi-decision. Career education and guidance should therefore take into account the sequential nature of decision-making and equip youths and adults to anticipate and cope with these mini-decisions and to make them add up to flexible maxi-decisions — hence the life-stage and developmental-task emphasis of the developmental theories, exemplified in JoAnn Bowlsbey's and my

(Super and Bowlsbey, 1979) published course in *Guided Career Exploration*. The developmental theories, like the differential, have tended to neglect the processes by means of which mini- and maxi-decisions are made.

Theorists and practitioners alike have now come to see that decision-making is also central to career development (Super, 1980). This latest trend has not been at the expense of earlier theories, but, like each of the major approaches which have attracted and held attention over the years, has aimed at their enrichment. Just as career development theory embraces occupational-matching theories, so does it now embrace decision-making theory. Construed at first as a theory of determinants, and then as a theory of stages at which the determinants must be considered, career decision-making theory has, as it became explicit, broadened to include decision processes, both descriptive and prescriptive (Jepsen and Dilley, 1974). Types of decisions have now been identified (Jepsen, 1974b), and this has now led to a focus on decision-making styles (Harren, 1979a). Styles are viewed as traits which manifest themselves in varying combinations and degrees in varying situations (Arroba, 1978). Here lies a new research frontier.

Theorists still tend to focus, perhaps legitimately in view of the size of their problem, on segmental theories. Each is thus generally considered to neglect other aspects of theory, other aspects of career development and career behavior. Those who do seek to encompass more suffer from the appearance of superficiality. But someday global theories of career development will be made up of refined, validated and well-assembled segments, cemented together by some synthesizing theory to constitute a whole which will be more powerful than the sum of its parts. It has been my view that self-concept theory, treating the individual as the socialized organizer of his or her experience, might be this cement. [I now see it more as the keystone, with social-learning theory as the cement.] This may be true, as some claim, only for the abler and more advantaged, but not for the less able and less advantaged; Salomone and Slaney's (1978) research, however, suggests that it may also be true for many people at all social levels. If so, we now need to know how to identify those for whom this self-concept or personal-constructs model is valid, and those to whom other theories apply. [It should be added that Kidd's (1982, 1984) research in my Cambridge laboratory also showed that self-concept theory works at most socioeconomic levels, even in England.]

Self-concept theory might better be called *personal construct theory,* to show the individual's dual focus on self and on situation. It and interactive or experiential learning theory are viewed here as central to a global segmental theory. It has thus seemed important to pay more attention to them than any one person can do as a researcher. The part played by self-concepts in career decisions was therefore made a part of my Leverhume Fund–supported research grant at the National Institute for Careers Education and Counseling (NICEC) and of my fellowship at Wolfson College, Cambridge, during the years that I spent there to help launch a program of research in career development in Britain. Jennifer Kidd, research assistant at NICEC, was challenged by the theory and, like many other British psychologists and counselors who were influenced by their sociologist colleagues' obsession with social class, she doubted its applicability to the bulk of British students. Like Roberts (1977, 1981), she believed that the opportunity structure, with its social class–determined access system, was so powerful a determinant that self-concepts and other psychological characteristics could not play an important role in career development. Unlike many of her compatriots, she wanted to ascertain empirically what part self-concepts actually do play. Her doctoral dissertation (Kidd, 1982) was a study of these issues. It found evidence that self-concepts do indeed play a role in England.

Occupational self-concept theory (*congruence theory,* in Holland, 1985a) in vocational psychology is essentially a matching theory, in which individuals consider their own attributes and the attributes required by occupations. It also involves consideration of the self in the opportunity structure. Individuals match attributes, formulate preferences, make choices, and seek to implement these choices by obtaining needed training and finding suitable employment. The theory can be *static,* with the focus on the first occupational choice, as in Blau and others (1956) and in Holland's (1973a) early work, which implies that a good match once made remains a good match. It can be *developmental,* with a series of changing preferences for changing situations being expressed in successive approximations that lead to better matches. It is essentially a personal or *psychological* theory, in which the focus is on individuals who choose and adapt, but it is also a *social* theory in that it views individuals as persons who choose on the basis of personal assessments of the changing socioeconomic situation and of the social structure in which they live and function. For the latter reason, it was perhaps an error to adopt the term *self-concepts,* rather than *personal constructs,* since Kelly's (1955) formulation later provided better for the personal perception and construction of the environment. Calling the approach a *self-concept theory* led readers to miss things, such as several chapters in *The Psychology of Careers* that dealt with the social, economic, and political determinants of careers, as well as with the family from a psychological and a sociological perspective.

A collection of collaborative essays (Super and others, 1963), in which my colleagues and I sought to make more precise and operational the overly mystical language of phenomenology, was inspired by recognition of the fact that people have not just one self-concept but rather constellations of self-concepts, a fact that was in due course established by Garfinkle (1958) and various others. Garfinkle showed that high school students' concepts of themselves as students are empirically differentiated from their general self-concepts and, by inference, from their concepts of themselves in other roles, such as athlete and child in a family. Role theory, of course, had recognized this fact long before, but role theory had not affected self-concept theory, as evidenced by the title of Wylie's (1974, 1979) book, *The Self-Concept.*

Developing a more scientific lexicon for self-concept theory also involved identifying the different aspects of self-concepts that had been considered by theorists and researchers, as well as completing a needed taxonomy. One outcome of this taxonomical work was the important distinction between, on the one hand, concepts of personality traits, or attributes of the self (for example, gregariousness and dogmatism), referred to as the *dimensions* of self-concepts, and, on the other hand, the characteristics of these dimensions (for example, clarity, stability, and self-esteem), called *metadimensions*. The usage typical of writers on these subjects is open to criticism on the grounds that it confuses dimensions and metadimensions, a confusion that has resulted in use of the term *self-concept* as a synonym for (and even instead of) the term *self-esteem*.

Another outcome of the classification system was the distinction between *self-concepts* and *self-concept systems*. The former denote the qualities of single traits; the latter denote the qualities of sets or constellation of traits. The metadimension of *clarity*, for example, can apply to any one trait, for a person may see himself or herself as very clearly gregarious or may have only a vague idea of that dimension of the self. The metadimension of *structure* can apply, however, only to a constellation of dimensions or traits, for one or more of these must be significantly higher than the others before the profile of dimensions can be clearly structured.

Despite the fact that such writers as Snygg and Combs (1949) have occasionally noted the distinction between what Super (1963) calls *dimensions* and *metadimensions* of self-concepts, the distinction has elsewhere gone unnoted and has been neglected by virtually all the mainstream writers on self-concepts. Snygg and Combs, Wylie, and others focus largely on self-esteem, even while noting the existence of a few other metadimensions, such as clarity and structure. Some of Kelly's followers have focused on scope, or cognitive complexity, without placing either it or self-esteem in any kind of taxonomy. Only Horrocks and Jackson (1972) seem to have recognized the need to categorize the qualities of self-concepts and to develop a taxonomy. It is difficult to understand how those who are critical of the lack of good theorizing on self-concept assessment can have failed to take advantage of these fundamental notions.

Table 7.2. The Metadimensions of Self-Concepts.

Dimensions	Super and others, 1963		Horrocks and Jackson, 1972	
	Metadimensions of Concepts	Metadimensions of Systems	Content	Other Aspects
Examples: Gregariousness, intelligence			Example: Gregariousness	
	Self-esteem			Positive-negative
	Stability			Stability
	Clarity			Clarity
	Abstraction			
	Refinement			
	Certainty	Regnancy		Intensity
	Realism	Harmony		Consistency
		Structure		
		Scope		
		Flexibility		Salience
		Idiosyncrasy		(focus on self)
				Importance
				(relation
				to environment)

Table 7.2 juxtaposes the two schemata. It is noteworthy that six of Horrocks and Jackson's (1972) eight and six of my fourteen self-attitudes are identical, that four of my earlier categories are not included in theirs, and that two of theirs do not appear in mine.

The discussion of terminology, structure, and measurement makes the use of self-concept theory in career development appear static — as a matching rather than a developmental approach — because of the historical need to concentrate first on terminology and on conceptual matters and then on the operationalization of constructs in measurement and only then on testing of the matching hypothesis. Only then can matching be treated as a series of successive approximations and as a sequence of matches made, sometimes gradually and sometimes abruptly, as people and situations change. As Holland (1969, 1985a) points out, the task of developing, refining, and validating global theories is too large and complex for any one person to expect to complete. The task must nevertheless be started. Super (1957) depicts a career as the life course of a person encountering a series of developmental tasks and attempting to handle them in such a way as to become the kind of person he or she wants to be. With a changing self and changing situations, the matching process is never really completed. Matching occurs only temporarily, when major decisions are made; and even then, minor decisions continue to be made. Thus, a major match is made when a person decides to accept a certain job, but minor matches involving changes in the individual and in the job continue as the worker acquires new skills and adapts behavior to new situational requirements, and as the job situation changes in keeping with the personality of the worker and with the changing workplace. In Super (1963), I sought to refine the constructs and provide for the development of the instruments for self-concept research, and the focus was on matching, on any match; only after that could the sequential nature of matching be treated. This may also be said of Holland (1969, 1985a) and of Lofquist and Dawis (1969). Helbing (1987) has carried both self-concept theory and measurement considerably farther in significant respects.

Applicability to Women and Minorities. Applicability, at all socioeconomic levels, to males, females, and minority groups, as well as to majority groups defined as white and middle class, has been a frequently raised question during the past decade or two. In career development theory, it was addressed at the inception of the Career Pattern Study (Super and others, 1957). The project staff was divided at first on hypotheses concerning the relationship between socioeconomic status and vocational maturity; later empirical results (Super and Overstreet, 1960) showed correlations of parental occupational level and various indices of career maturity, ranging from -0.06 to 0.26, or 0.27, with an index made up of the best single maturity measures. Such a relationship is of theoretical importance and has some implications for career education but is much too low to be of practical importance in individual counseling. Vocational maturity is, of course, just one aspect of career development theory, but it assesses some important determinants and outcomes of development. It does not seek to describe the processes of development or other types of outcomes, such as career attainments and satisfactions.

The same relationships were looked into when the CPS subjects reached the twelfth grade (Jordaan and Heyde, 1979). By that time, the ninth-grade data had been reworked to ensure comparability at both grade levels and to yield factor scores, rather than purified a priori scales, but the results were essentially the same: there was virtually no occupational level–career maturity correlation in ninth grade, and in twelfth grade the uncontaminated correlations ranged from 0.19 to 0.34. The impact of socioeconomic status is thus real in the last years of school, especially in the cognitive domain of occupational information, but it is not great.

Jordaan and Heyde (1979) summarized such studies as the one by Gribbons and Lohnes (1968), which also yielded correlations between socioeconomic status and career maturity, as measured by their interview-based scales, that were no higher than 0.33 in eighth grade (median = 0.12); in tenth grade, they were only 0.17 (median = 0.05). Crites's Career Maturity Inventory, as well as CDI research, which included inner-city blacks in Flint, Michigan, also showed no significant social-class or ethnic differences. Ansell's results agreed. In a study using the Gribbons and Lohnes (1968) scales, Ansell (1970) pooled data from grades eight through twelve. When he treated the data by grade, he found differences between middle- and lower-class youths in grades ten through twelve, although not in grades eight and nine. This result seems to confirm what Jordaan and Heyde (1979) found: that socioeconomic status has some effect on career maturity in the last years of high school but not in the earlier years. Jordaan and Heyde (1979, pp. 159–160) conclude: "In summary, socioeconomic status appears to be a relatively insignificant determinant of vocational maturity among young adolescents. Its role in the later years of high school is more marked, but even here, according to the CPS findings and Ansell's data, it accounts for only a small proportion of the observed variance in vocational maturity."

In recent studies (Nevill and Super, 1988; Super and Nevill, 1984), the relation between socioeconomic status and career maturity, as assessed by the Career Development Inventory (Super and others, 1981), was examined in high school sophomores and juniors and in university students, and it was again found to be negligible. Although it is still possible for severe poverty to affect vocational maturity, its negative effects appear to be limited to a very small proportion of the poor who in inner cities get as far as the tenth and eleventh grades. Socioeconomic status may well affect self-concepts, but its effects on career maturity appear to be minimal.

That career patterns are affected by socioeconomic status and academic ability has, of course, been frequently and well documented (Hollingshead, 1949; Miller and Form, 1951). The very poor and the very wealthy find that occupations near the end of the socioeconomic scale that is farthest from them are virtually closed (unless the poor, despite barriers that are both psychological and material, do well in high school and go on to college). The sons and daughters of the poor are more likely than others to have unstable or multiple-trial careers; the sons and daughters of the more economically favored are more likely to have conventional or stable careers, and the latter are more likely to find satisfaction in their work (Centers, 1949), a finding that is regularly reconfirmed by opinions surveys.

That the life stages and developmental tasks are affected by socioeconomic status is a hypothesis that has not often been directly investigated, although some critics of career development theory have at least implied that they are so affected. Exploration may well be limited by socioeconomic status, but in the Career Pattern Study (Super and Overstreet, 1960) the correlation of status with the use of community resources for exploration was found to be virtually nil. The establishment process may well be different: the prevalence of unstable and multiple-trial career patterns in blue-collar workers, and of conventional and stable patterns in white-collar workers, supports this hypothesis; similarly, the maintenance stage, at the lower statuses, may be more difficult. More research on these issues is clearly needed.

Those who are particularly concerned with the disadvantaged have assumed that the role self-concepts play in careers is very much affected by socioeconomic status. Two studies bear directly on this issue, one by Salomone and Slaney (1978) in the United States and one by Kidd (1982, 1984) in the United Kingdom. As noted earlier, both studies found, despite expectations to the contrary — particularly in class-conscious Britain, where social class and the opportunity structure are generally viewed as assigning children and young people to occupational levels (Roberts, 1981) — that self-concept theory, as used by Holland and myself, appears to apply as well to youth and adults in the lower classes as to youth and adults in the middle classes. Along with other factors, such as intelligence, interest, and social status, how a person sees himself or herself is thus empirically established as an important determinant of career development. The fact that self-concepts are learned by experiences with people, objects, and ideas makes it seem very likely that socioeconomic status functions as a career determinant in at least two ways: it tends to open up or close opportunities, and it helps to shape occupational concepts and self-concepts.

Social learning theory (Bandura, 1977b) can be looked to for an understanding of how self-concepts develop, Bandura having formulated the basic theory. He surely drew on the work of George Meade, Freud, Edward L. Thorndike, Clark Hull, and others, since role models and key figures originated as constructs in the writings not only of psychologists but also of sociologists and psychoanalysts. Krumboltz, Mitchell, and Jones (1976) first applied social learning theory to career decision making, but vocational psychologists, such as Strong (1943), had already drawn on early work on learning (from objects and ideas, as well as from people) to explain the development of vocational interests and preferences, viewing aptitude as leading to achievement, achievement to acclaim and satisfaction, and satisfaction to interest and preference.

In the next section of this chapter, on the development of career maturity in childhood and in that section's Figure 7.4, it will be seen again that what might best be called *experiential* or *interactive learning*, rather than social learning, throws light on how a variety of determinants operate in career development. The term *interactive learning* includes not only social (interpersonal) learning but also learning from interaction with complex situations, ideas, and objects. Thus, one learns about one's physical prowess by lifting a heavy load or hitting the bull's eye, about linguistic ability by picking up or studying a language, and about the satisfactions of beauty by its contemplation.

Krumboltz (in Brown and Lent, 1984, pp. 243–245) describes the decision process in the choice of an occupation as being "determined by four categories of influences: (1) genetic endowment and special abilities, (2) environmental conditions and events [at the top of the Rainbow and in the right-hand column of the Archway], (3) learning experiences [interaction between the two columns in the Archway, which is stressed in the work of Vondracek, Lerner, and Schulenberg, 1986], and (4) task approach skills" (not made clear in either the Rainbow or the Archway, although my model of career maturity includes attitudes, knowledge, and skills that Krumboltz calls "skills, performance standards and values, work habits, perceptual and cognitive processes, mental sets, and emotional responses an individual brings to new situations and tasks"). These are Havighurst's and my "readiness to cope with developmental tasks."

It may be protested that the variables just named are determinants, not processes, as Krumboltz labels them. The process, of course, is the interaction between the determinants. Krumboltz and his colleagues go on to describe how the interactions between the individual and society result in "self-observation generalizations." These are self-percepts, such as "I'm a good baseball player, but I'd never make it in the major leagues." In self-concept theory, these percepts are viewed as organized into generalized self-observations, or self-concepts (Super and others, 1963). Social learning, experiential learning, and interactive learning are therefore the processes of self-concept and occupational-concept formation. They are the outcomes of assimilating feedback and of organizing it in ways compatible with existing self-concepts. Thus is acquired the repertoire of behaviors used to respond to new situations and to cope with career development tasks; thus do career maturity and career adaptability develop. Krumboltz's contribution has been to turn the spotlight back to learning as the basic process of career development—learning that is both affective and cognitive.

Career development in childhood has been too little studied because those who have been concerned with development in childhood have not been concerned with career development, and those who have been concerned with career education (that is, helping to foster career development) have, for lack of theories and models of the elementary years, simply imported adolescent models. They have focused on the dissemination of occupational information at an age when such knowledge has no rational personal meaning. Such efforts have been redeemed, to some extent, by the recognition that adult role models are important to children and that, through admiration, identification, and emulation, occupational information can be personalized, even though a given model may not be realistically appropriate for the child in question.

Dissatisfaction with this situation has led some school officials to seek theories of career development more appropriate to the elementary school years. In the public schools of Charles County, Maryland, Carolyn Graham approached JoAnn Bowlsbey and me with the problem. After searching reviews of the literature and drawing a blank, we drew up a theoretical model of career development in childhood. An interview schedule for testing it was devised, and a corps of elementary school counselors was trained to use it to collect data. The data were analyzed to refine the model, which was drawn from the only helpful literature: that on child development. The result is shown in Figure 7.4, also a person-environment interaction model. (This work has been written up only as a report to the Board of Education of Charles County, Maryland, because of other preoccupations and reluctance to become involved in so many diverse types of endeavor as to interfere with the quality of work.)

Figure 7.4, building on Berlyne's (1960) review of research on curiosity and exploration and on Jordaan's (1963) landmark essay, begins at the bottom with *curiosity* and shows how it leads to exploratory behavior. (In Berlyne, this was observed only in animals and in infants, for the topics have been virtually unstudied in older children, adolescents, and adults, despite the stress on career exploration in the schools.) *Exploratory behavior,* if rewarded either internally or by others, leads to *information* and to *further exploration;* if unrewarded, it leads to *conflict* and

Figure 7.4. A Person-Environment Interactive
Model of the Bases of Career Maturity.

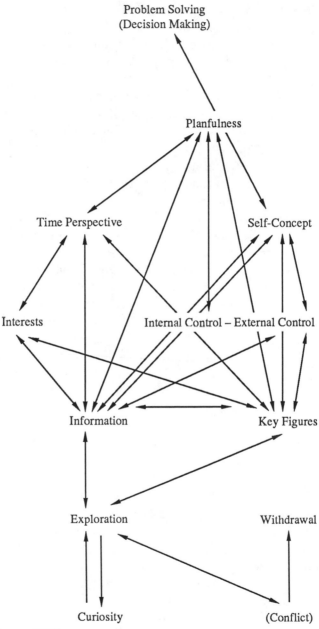

Source: Super, 1981b.

withdrawal. Some school psychologists have observed the latter in what has been called the "fourth-grade slump," a loss of interest in school and a decline in school achievement, attributed to increasing demands for the achievement of school-imposed learning goals that may not coincide with the goal of satisfying curiosity. Some observers now believe that the current emphasis on mastery of basic skills has pushed the slump down into the lower grades. Satisfying exploration leads to the identification of *key figures,* people who have been helpful or interesting and who serve in some ways as role models. Success leads to feelings of *autonomy,* of being somewhat in control of one's present and even of one's future; it also leads to the development of *interest* in the things in which one has been successful. Finding that one can to some extent control one's activities helps in the development of *self-esteem* and at the same time leads to an *understanding of time* and of the notion that one can plan for future events and have some success in their shaping. Thus develops *planfulness* and with it the ability to identify and *solve problems,* to make decisions. At this point, information becomes more than something that is interesting because of its attention-getting qualities and drama (or boring, for lack of the same); it becomes something that is helpful for attaining personal goals and controlling the future. Educational and occupational information now acquire meaning.

The importance of information for career development in the elementary years lies in its potential to arouse interest in the future and—incidentally, and even perhaps accidentally—provide information that may be drawn on in later years (although the odds seem to be against this). Of prime importance would seem to be the stimulation and cultivation of curiosity in ways that lead to the development of interests, to the discovery of role models or key figures, and to feelings of internal control that are realistic for one's age and stage, combined with acceptance and constructive use of external controls (helped by having good role models), self-esteem, time perspective, and planfulness. In this way, career and occupational information, as we now define them, become meaningful and helpful in elementary and middle schools. They are means, not ends in themselves—means for developing the attitudes and skills of career readiness.

Gender and Sex. Sex has been studied in relation to career development. It had been hypothesized (Richardson, 1974) that girls and women, being by tradition less involved in work and careers than boys and men are, would tend to score lower on vocational maturity measures than males would. Crites (1978c) reports norms for males and females combined, for the sex differences with his CMI were found to be slight. The authors of the CDI also found slight sex differences; those that were observed tended to favor girls, especially on the cognitive scales (Super and others, 1981). Most recently, other CDI studies (Nevill and Super, 1988; Super and Nevill, 1984) at both the college and high school levels have found slight *cognitive* sex differences, which again favor females. Particularly important is the finding that the salience of the work role, rather than sex or socioeconomic status, is what determines career maturity.

The hypothesis that the careers of males and females differ in some important respects has been generally assumed because of women's role as childbearers. Super (1957) notes the fact that (some thirty years ago) available data on career patterns were for males only, and that study suggests modifications that appeared to be needed. These were examined empirically by Mulvey (1963) and by Vetter (1973) and found support. Observation, which needs scientific confirmation, suggests that what was true twenty years ago may no longer be true. We need current data. But these patterns in women were described as follows: stable homemaking; conventional or traditional (working, followed by marriage and full-time homemaking); stable working, double-track (working while homemaking); interrupted (perhaps now the common or conventional pattern of working, homemaking, and again working, either while homemaking or after having given up homemaking); unstable (recycling); and multiple-trial. In men, the patterns have been found to be stable, conventional, unstable, and multiple-trial only, because homemaking has traditionally been an incidental rather than a major role for men, but we now know from scientific studies that it plays an important part in the careers of college-educated men, although less noticeably in other men. The theory therefore appears to be essentially applicable to both sexes, if modified to take childbearing into account.

Is life-stage theory — the concept of developmental tasks — as valid for females as for males? The original formulation by Buehler (1933) was derived from data obtained for both sexes. The task formulation later made by Havighurst (1953, 1964) also viewed stages and tasks as essentially similar. The material on career patterns tends to support this position. Recent research by Lowenthal and others (1975) confirms it. The differences are differences of degree, not of kind, and are associated with childbearing and childrearing and with sex-role stereotyping based thereon.

Finally, on sex differences, there is the question of the part that self-concepts play in the career development of males and females. In theory, there is no difference. Empirically, both sexes (Kidd, 1982) appear to make decisions on the basis of their self-concepts and their concepts of the circumstances in which they live.

Blacks. The applicability of current data on career maturity to ethnic minorities has been looked into but is still in need of further study. LoCascio (1974), as already seen, has contended, on the basis of limited data from inner-city New York, that the available measures are not appropriate for disadvantaged blacks, but Emery (1978) found that the CDI was acceptable to and had construct validity with inner-city blacks in a middle-class school in Baltimore, and Myers and others (1972) report no differences between large heterogeneous samples of blacks and whites in the city of Flint, Michigan, and its surrounding county. In its norming study, in a predominantly poor black high school in New Brunswick, New Jersey, the CDI was found acceptable to students, and the results, when reviewed for a number of students with the black director of guidance, were found meaningful and illuminating. In a study that used the New Brunswick data, data from a rural New Jersey area, and data from a heterogeneous Trenton suburb, Super and Nevill (1984) found that commitment to work or a career was an important determinant of career maturity, whereas sex and socioeconomic status played only a small role. Work salience, discussed earlier, thus emerges as a construct of major importance. Such data are now undergoing further analysis elsewhere to isolate economically disadvantaged blacks for comparisons with their advantaged peers and with whites.

Adults. The applicability of the term *career maturity* to adults has also been an important question in recent years because of increased awareness of recycling and of the minicycles, which suggest that chronological maturity and career maturity are different. The linkage between age and developmental tasks faced is not as close in adulthood as it is in adolescence. For this reason, I have restudied the construct in young adults (Super and Kidd, 1979; Super and Knasel, 1979) and drawn from such studies as Morrison's (1977) on the adaptivity of managers. The result has been a change in terminology, designed to describe better the nature of career development status in adulthood. Readiness for career decision making in adulthood should be called *career adaptability,* rather than *career maturity* (Super and others, 1988). It is recognizing the developmental tasks that one faces or should (normatively speaking) face in one's current and next career stage, as well as preparing or acting to cope with them.

Current Status

During the past decades, this career development model has been refined and extended. Differential psychology has made technical, but not substantive, advances. Operational definitions of career maturity have been modified, and the model has been modified with them. Our understanding of recycling through stages in a minicycle has been refined, but the basic construct is essentially the same as when it was first formulated, years ago. Ideas about how to assess self-concepts have evolved as research has thrown light on their measurement, and knowledge of how applicable self-concept theory is to various subpopulations has been extended, but this segment of the model has not greatly changed. Life-stage theory has been refined but mostly confirmed by several major studies during the past decade. The role of learning theory has been highlighted by the work on social learning, but to the neglect of other kinds of interactive learning. The career model is perhaps now in the maintenance stage, but health maintenance does not mean stasis but rather updating and innovating as midcareer changes are better recognized and studied.

The concept of life stages has been modified in recent years, from envisioning mainly a maxicycle to involving mini-cycles of growth, exploration, establishment, maintenance, and decline, linked in a series within the maxicycle. Reexploration and reestablishment have thus attracted a great deal of attention, and the term *transition* has come to denote these processes. Transitions are generally considered to be likely several times during a career (Levinson and others, 1978; London and Stumpf, 1982; Schlossberg, Troll, and Leibowitz, 1978). Interest in adult development, as well as a more rapidly changing technology and economy, have helped to highlight the need for and the problems of transition. Schneidman (1989) developed the concept of a spiral model of careers, drawing on prior theory and on his own data on septuagenarians. The notion is helpful in graphing minicycles but has careers spiraling downward, and if determinants were added, it could become very confusing.

Important, too, is the greater emphasis on the fact that the typical impetus for any specific transition is not necessarily age itself, for the timing of transitions (stage) is a function of the individual's personality and abilities, as well as of his or her situation. My use of stage theory thus differs from that of Levinson and others (1978) and Piaget (Piaget and Inhelder, 1969). Furthermore, the popular career-education concept of exploration as something completed in midadolescence has been shown to be invalid (Fisher, 1989; Super, Kowalski, and Gotkin, 1967). Instead, it carries on, in many cases, into the middle and late twenties, sometimes into the early thirties, and often starts again in recycling at later stages (see Table 7.1). It appears in the form of conventional, unstable, or multiple-trial careers and in so-called midcareer crises. We need more studies of the nature and processes of exploration. Jordaan's (1963) essay points the way; Blustein and Strohmer (1987) and Stumpf and Colarelli (1981) are pursuing it.

The construct of vocational maturity, during the 1970s, was operationalized for research and practice largely by Crites's

(1978c) measure (too often only its Attitude Scale) and later by Super and others (1981). It therefore risks being frozen by the instruments that have made it a practical construct useful in counseling. As both Crites and I have pointed out, and as Westbrook (1982), Mitchell (1979b), and others have reiterated, the CPS-derived instruments seek to assess only some of the factors and dimensions that constitute career maturity or that may serve as desired outcomes of career education programs (Hilton, in Super and others, 1963). Attention needs to be given not only to the adequacy of the published measures, singly and in combination, but also to the development of measures or indices of the other components of the construct in the CPS-based Crites and Super models and to new and expanded models that additional theoretical work will suggest and research will support.

Changes in career maturity, as operationally defined by the CPS and by the CMI and CDI, need further study. Crites (1978c) has shown with his CMI that an expected increase in age or grade failed to be confirmed in the last year of high school. In a study of college students, Tilden (1978) found that although CDI scores increased during the first two years of college, they ceased to increase in the junior and senior years. Crites reasoned that a fear of transition (with the approach of leaving school) may lower scores. In college students, it may be that, with planning and exploration provisionally taken care of at the end of the second year by the choice of a major field, there is a letdown in career planning, exploration, and the acquisition and use of career information and skills. This condition may last until the final semester of the final year brings close, and makes real, the transition to work or to graduate school. For many, even graduate school may be a kind of moratorium on occupations and work, as study is prolonged in a familiar field and setting.

The models of vocational maturity have postulated multidimensionality. That Crites's CMI does not fit his multilevel, multifactor model has been documented by Westbrook (1982), who found but one factor in analyses of the CMI. The CDI, however, has been found to be bifactorial (Super and Thompson, 1979; Super and others, 1983), and some of the intercorrelations between the scales that load on these factors are low enough to justify the multidimensional model postulated on the basis of the CPS. *Dimensionality,* as conceived of here, pertains not to factorial purity but to content. For example, planning and exploration are somewhat differing attitudes; decision making, world-of-work information, and knowledge of one's preferred occupational group are different kinds of knowledge (as are biology, physics, psychology, and sociology). Their items make for internal consistency on scales whose intercorrelations are lower than their respective reliabilities. Most of the CDI scales meet all these criteria of dimensionality, and all meet at least the first two. Westbrook's (1982) negative evaluation of the fit of the career maturity data and models, based solely on work with Crites's CMI, is much too sweeping; it is inaccurate and unwarranted, in view of the CPS model and the CDI data.

The model of self-concept formulation of choices, as well as its occupational translation (Super and others, 1963), appear to have considerable validity, both in the freer social system of the United States and in the more rigidly structured United Kingdom. But it has been suggested (Super and others, 1963) that other models of self-and-situation matching may better describe the process in some people, and that other identification and role-casting models may be useful. In a study pursuing this line of thought, Kidd (1982) found that English boys and girls of all classes used the self-concept translation model, whether consciously or not, but that identification and feeling "cast in a role" were more used by some. Studies of these and other possible models of choice need to be made to better describe self-concepts, their determinants, the kinds of youths and adults for whom they are valid, and their comparative outcomes in use.

Until quite recently, the choice process has been neglected, although the need for such studies has been noted from the beginnings of career development theorizing (Super, 1953). Ginzburg, Ginzburg, Axelrad, and Herma (1951) neglected it, even while describing some career stages and dynamics. My own work has perhaps slighted it in focusing on development and its determinants, although it has drawn from decision-making theory in designing a course for career exploration (Super and Bowlsbey, 1979), in making an attempt to synthesize the various segments or elements of life-stage and life-space theory (Super, 1980), and in formulating the translation model of self-concept theory (Super and others, 1963; Super, 1982a). Blau and others (1956) postulate a series of determining influences that culminate in choice, in which choices of individuals encounter choices of employers and are somehow reconciled through compromise or synthesis. Blau and others (1956) provide a formula for this last act in their sequence. Their model, much heralded by the few who know it, has rarely been put to the test, and their formula has gone virtually unnoticed — perhaps for lack of data to put into their equation, and perhaps because, in their equation, development appears to cease with choice and entry.

Decision theory, as applied to career decision making, has led to the development and use of logical or rational models derived from problem-solving theory and research. These models have great appeal for psychologists and teachers, since they lend themselves well to career education and guidance courses, but they assume that people are rational. Research (Arroba, 1978; Harren, 1979a) has shown that there are in fact other decision styles. These styles include the intuitive, the impulsive, and the conforming. The models of Gelatt (1962) and Hilton (1962), which have had special influence on guidance courses, are rational. Card's (1978) model of determinants makes good use of path theory and of methods to identify determinants of choice, but it fails to show how decisions are made. If, as suggested in my use of self-concept or personal-construct theory, the deciding individual is the one who makes the synthesis or compromise of self and situational data, then the key to the problem is available. The process is, for a great many people, the translating or equating of self-concepts according to occupational terms. However, it remains to be described in detail how choices are made when the self-and-occupation matching or translation process is not the one that is used. How and in whom do intuition, impulse, and conformity operate? How, if at all, can their functioning be improved to produce good choices?

Social and occupational changes that result in different career patterns also are in need of more study. The established models may still be valid in an era of increasing ethnic, social, and sexual equality, with rapidly changing technology and changing occupations, but the frequency of transitions and of the differing types of patterns may change. Stable and conventional patterns may become the lot of a small number of highly educated people, and unstable, multiple-trial, and full-time leisure patterns (with the unemployed developing nonwork roles to fill their lives) may become the dominant patterns.

Further research on life stages, career maturity, self-concepts, social learning, decision processes, and career patterns may not lead to major changes in my theoretical formulation as it now exists, but more research will certainly modify, refine, and enrich the career development theory that has come to be known as *developmental self-concept theory*.

Empirical Support

Osipow (1983) summarizes most of the pertinent research and makes the following currently valid evaluation (although he fails to include differential psychology and occupational sociology in his version of my list):

The theory [Super's] is a well-ordered, highly systematic representation of vocational maturation. It has the virtues of building upon aspects of the mainstream of developmental psychology and personality theory and demonstrating how those two streams can come together to clarify behavior in one major realm of human activity. . . . In its current state, the theory has considerable utility for both practice and research in vocational psychology.

Most of the research reported on Super's theory supports his model. The developmental aspects of the theory are well documented, though certain details have been modified as a result of empirical findings such as the specific timing of developmental tasks. . . . The data with respect to . . . self-concept generally agree with the theory. . . . The future prospects for this approach to career psychology appear to be promising. Still needed are better

ways to integrate economic and social factors which influence career decisions in a more direct way than the events
described by the theory currently do, as well as to continue
the development of specific and rigorous formulations about
aspects of career decisions and ways to bring about appropriate behavioral changes which will facilitate [the development of] vocational maturity [Osipow, 1983, pp. 185–
186].

Vondracek, Lerner, and Schulenberg (1986) are now working
along these last lines from a theoretical and methodological
standpoint; it is to be hoped that they and others will soon put
them to empirical tests.

Practical Applications

The application of career development theory to education, assessment, and counseling is the major practical outcome
of the theory. Despite the acknowledged need for developmental guidance, its theories and methods have not developed very
far. Translating developmental theory into a model and methods
of practice is not easy, and those who have studied career development have until recently been too intent on refining and
validating theories to translate them into practice (but see Crites,
1981; Super, 1983a). Curriculum specialists have not been sufficiently familiar with the theories, and counselors, with their
heavy caseloads and other duties, rarely have the time to make
the translation or even to carry on developmental counseling.

Education. Career development theory has in fact provided a theoretical orientation for career education in schools
and colleges. Citing CPS conclusions concerning fostering "planfulness" in the curriculum, Osipow (1983, p. 163) wrote: "In
this statement lie the roots of the Career Education movement."
However, once the notion of stages and tasks of career development had taken hold, most leaders of the movement seem to
have done little more with theory than to borrow and often
distort the meanings of some of its concepts. Career orientation became largely cognitive "awareness" (that is, information)

in the elementary years; "exploration" was to take place only in middle or junior high school and lead to "preparation," beginning with the tenth grade. This lockstep progression is belied by the implications of child psychology and personality development and by the facts on readiness for career decisions, on the importance of attitudes, and on the duration of the exploration process. As we have already seen, unfamiliar with the literature on career development and even with the fact that therein lay their theoretical base, leaders and numerous uninitiated practitioners failed to realize that for many children and youths the development of a sense of internal control, time perspective, self-esteem, and awareness of the world of work, careers, and occupations needs to be cultivated throughout the elementary and high school years and that exploration goes on into the late teens and twenties. They were too much influenced by traditional vocational education, meaning skilled-trade education. *Career,* to many of them, meant occupation and was perhaps used because it sounded nobler and because the term *vocational* had long ago been misappropriated by those concerned with trade, farm, and business training at the secondary level. It was therefore suspect in academic and humanistic circles.

This is no place to attempt to develop the details of a sounder program of career education based on career development theory; Gysbers and Associates (1984), Herr and Cramer (1988), and Hoyt (1975) have done this. Such a program would recognize individual differences in career development and avoid lockstep curricula. In the elementary years, especially, it would seek to foster curiosity and thus exploratory behavior, autonomy, time perspective, and self-esteem. At the same time, it would expose children to a variety of adult role models. Exploration in breadth would normally begin in the middle school, would phase into exploration in depth when the individual appeared ready to focus on one or two groups of occupations (not in lockstep at some predetermined year), and would phase back into exploration in breadth if depth exploration proved unfruitful. Any training would be undertaken with a clear understanding that it is essentially in-depth exploration, and even the first postschool job would be viewed as partly exploratory, although it might well have long-term outcomes. Any job and any occupation, at any age, may prove to be an open door, a hurdle, or a dead end.

Assessment. Career development theory and research, as we have seen, have led to the construction and refinement of measures of career or vocational maturity (Kapes and Mastie, 1982, 1988; Krumboltz and Hamel, 1982; Super, 1974). These measures were viewed at first primarily as means of evaluating programs of career education, but the possibility of using them in counseling was also an application sought by some of their authors (Crites, 1981; Super, 1977; Super and Kidd, 1979; Super and others, 1981). Their use in assessment for counseling was explored and described in an article on a career development assessment and counseling model (Super, 1983a). It is expanded and reproduced in Exhibit 7.1. Given the vocational immaturity of high school students and many college students (immaturity in the sense of lack of planfulness and lack of information about careers and occupations), classical assessment methods are often misused. If a youth knows little about the world of work, scores on interest inventories that use occupational titles or job descriptions may be misleading. If a student or an adult has given little thought to occupational choice or to the unfolding of a career, he or she is not likely to be ready to use aptitude, ability, interest, or value data in planning the next stage or steps in a career.

Exhibit 7.1. A Developmental Assessment Model.

Step   1. Preview
       A. Assembly of data on hand
       B. Intake interview
       C. Preliminary assessment

Step   II. Depth View: Further Testing?
       A. Work salience
          1. Relative importance of diverse roles
             a. Study
             b. Work and career
             c. Home and family
             d. Community service
             e. Leisure activities
          2. Values sought in each role

Exhibit 7.1. A Developmental Assessment Model, Cont'd.

    B. Career maturity
       1. Planfulness
       2. Exploratory attitudes
       3. Decision-making skills
       4. Information
          a. World of work
          b. Preferred occupational group
          c. Other life-career roles
       5. Realism
    C. Self-concepts
       1. Self-esteem
       2. Clarity
       3. Harmony
       4. Cognitive complexity
       5. Realism
       6. Others (Super and others, 1963)
    D. Level of abilities and potential functioning
    E. Field of interest and probable activity

Step III. Assessment of All Data
    A. Review of all data
    B. Matching and prediction
       1. Individual and occupations
       2. Individual and nonoccupational roles
    C. Planning communication with counselee, family, and others
Step IV. Counseling
    A. Joint review and discussion
    B. Revision or acceptance of assessment
    C. Assimilation by the counselee
       1. Understanding the present and next stages
       2. Recognizing one's self-concepts
          a. Accepting the actual
          b. Clarifying the actual and the ideal
          c. Developing harmony among self-concepts
          d. Refining cognitive complexity
          e. Ensuring the realism of self-concepts
          f. Others
       3. Matching self and occupations
       4. Understanding the meaning of life roles
       5. Exploration for maturing
       6. Exploring the breadth for crystallization
       7. Exploration in depth for specification
       8. Choice of preparation, training, or jobs
       9. Searches for outlets for self-realization
    D. Discussion of action implications and planning
       1. Planning
       2. Execution
       3. Follow-up for support and evaluation

Assessment of career maturity thus emerges as an early step in assessment for vocational counseling and for counseling concerning further education in schools, institutes, colleges, or universities. If a counselee scores low on scales that assess planning and exploration, then counseling needs to concentrate on the arousal of interest in careers and in career planning (Super, 1983a). Exploring some field that appears to be of current interest in such a way as to develop more awareness of the need to plan may be more helpful than trying to help the student narrow a choice to one occupational preparation program. If a student is inclined to look ahead, to plan, and to explore but lacks knowledge of the world of work and of how careers unfold, then counseling can focus on wide-ranging exploration (guided by even immature or embryonic interests) to provide better knowledge of the available options. If the student has a good perspective on the world of work but lacks the deeper knowledge of an occupational field that is needed for a wise and confident choice, then counseling can deal with learning more about that field and some of the occupations that are typical of it. Such counseling may be done through preliminary explorations in reading, talking with people, part-time work, or a program of education and training. The latter should be initiated with recognition of the fact that a change of plans may prove desirable and with knowledge of how that program could be used as a step to another type of preparation (rather than perhaps dismissing it as a mistake). The Career Development Inventory makes it possible to assess readiness, as illustrated by the case study of J.C. (Exhibit 7.2) and the related discussion.

It is not sufficient, however, to assume that a measure of career maturity means the same thing in the cases of two different students. As LoCascio (1974) and Richardson (1974) have pointed out, and as role-salience research has demonstrated (Nevill and Super, 1988; Super and Nevill, 1984), the meanings of work are sometimes related to social class or to sex. Work can be seen as drudgery or as liberation, or it may be viewed as unobtainable or irrelevant if one has been raised in dire poverty or with expectations of support without working (for example, substantial inheritance). Furthermore, we now know from role-salience research that the slight relationship between

Exhibit 7.2. Case Study of J.C.

J.C. (Red Ford, Counselor)   Female, 19 years old, first year of college

Parents: small-business owner-managers (hardware store in small regional center). Aspirations of J.C.: B.B.A., then into family business.

J.C.'s aspirations: Journalism at registration, then quick change to social service.

Academic Record: Top-quarter graduate in regional high school. SAT: Verbal, 520; Math, 480.

Strong-Campbell II:	Academic Comfort	22 = very low	
	Introversion	52 = average	

Themes: SEA (65; 47, 46 . . . C37, R37, I35)

Basic Interests:	Very High	Religious activities	68
		Social	68
		Athletic	62
	High	Domestic arts	64
		Adventure	61
	Moderately High	Teaching	59
		Music and drama	61
		Medical service	55
Occupations:	Social		
	Very similar	Special education	60
		LP nurse	55
	Similar	YW director	52
		Recreation leader	47
		Social worker	46
		Guidance counselor	45
		Dental hygienist	50
	Conventional		
	Very similar	Dental assistant	55
	Similar	Food service	50
		Secretary	46

Values Scale (WIS): (Ratings range from 1 = low to 4 = high)

High: Altruism = 4, Social interaction and social relations = 3.8

Middle: Achievement = 3.6, Esthetic = 3, Ability utilization and life-style = 2.6

Low: Advancement = 1, Physical prowess = 1.4, Authority = 1.6, Economic rewards and autonomy = 1.8

Career Development Inventory (CU Form)

Attitudes total:	6th percentile college freshmen
Planning	15th
Exploration	5th
Knowledge total:	49th
Decision making	37th
World of work	71st

Exhibit 7.2. Case Study of J.C., Cont'd.

		Career total:	13th		
		Knowledge preferred occupations (teaching and social service)	55th		

Salience Inventory WIS)		Study	Work	Community Activities	Home and Family	Leisure Activities
(Ratings	Participation	1.5	1.8	2.6	3.2	3.0
range	Commitment	1.8	2.4	4.0	4.0	3.0
from	Value Expec-					
1 = low	tations	2.4	2.4	3.1	3.6	3.1
to 4 =						
high)						

sex and career maturity favors females, rather than males, among contemporary high school and college students. This may be because females generally do better than males on verbal tests of knowledge, not because of career maturity. We do not know. It was shown in these studies, however, that more important than class or sex is work salience — the relative importance of work as one of several major life career roles.

The assessment of the relative importance of the work role to the counselee is thus a second step in career assessment. (It is also shown in Table 7.1.) If the work role is important, then scores on career development and interest inventories mean a great deal; if the work role is not important, then low CDI scores may mean only that occupations and their roles play little part in the counselee's life and that scores on interest inventories have little decision-making value (but may help guide exploration). If circumstances suggest that work roles should be more impor- tant, as today they are for most people, then career arousal is called for; if not, then counseling may appropriately pay more attention to the choice of and preparation for other roles, such as those of leisurite, homemaker, and citizen active in community service. The International Work Importance Study developed the Salience Inventory (Nevill and Super, 1986) as a measure of role (work, student, homemaker, and so on) salience to assist in making such assessments. Its use is shown in Exhibit 7.2.

Self-concepts, including such diverse qualities as self-esteem, self-efficacy, and occupational translations of self-perceived traits, are also important aspects of the person that must be assessed in counseling for career development. What these are has been shown in Table 7.2, and their place in assessment is shown in Exhibit 7.1. Assessing them is important because research (Super, 1982a) has shown that self-esteem (Korman, 1967) and self-efficacy (Betz and Hackett, 1981), for example, affect the role that the translation model plays in formulating occupational preferences and the sense of likelihood of success in an occupation; those who lack self-esteem are less likely to make good matches between self-concept and occupational concept, and those who feel unlikely to succeed avoid the risky choices. Similarly, it is difficult to see how people who have unclear self-concepts can see themselves adequately in any occupational role. A person whose self-concepts are not harmonious — who sees herself or himself, for example, as both gregarious and solitary, or as both friendly and hostile — must also have difficulty making a match to an occupation. One whose self-concepts are unrealistic is likely to make unwise choices, and one whose concept of self is simple (limited to a few dimensions or traits) seems likely to have a less adequate basis for matching than one whose self-concept includes a number of relevant dimensions. Because of the embryonic status of self- and occupational concept measures (Helbing, 1987), their use is not shown in Exhibit 7.2. Self-esteem and efficacy measures do, however, suggest confidence-building treatments.

After assessment, helping clients to recognize how they see their traits does seem basic in the counseling process, as does helping clients accept and clarify their actual and ideal self-concepts, develop harmony among the traits of the personality, refine their self-images, become more realistic in assessing their own traits, and develop feelings of self-efficacy. These are vital steps in the matching of self and occupations for further career development. After that, understanding of the present and next life stages, further exploration, and decision-making activities become possible, meaningful, and likely to be fruitful.

A Sample Case. Exhibit 7.2 illustrates first developmental career assessment and then counseling on the basis of such assessments. J.C. is a first-year university student who decided early in her first term that she did not want to continue with the major she had chosen at first, and she abruptly changed to another. She is clearly unsure of her preferences, having spurned her parents' business and the objective they would like for her, tried out another occupational major at the beginning of her first term, and rejected it immediately. She came for help to the university counseling center, thus demonstrating her continuing uncertainty and a certain limited amount of insight. (Her data could equally well illustrate developmental career counseling at the high school level, but a college-level case was chosen because of the greater freedom there to do in-depth testing and to have some continuity in counseling.)

J.C. is an attractive, outgoing, and rather verbal person. As a high school student, she took a college preparatory course stressing the humanities and social sciences, with some work in music and fine arts. She ranked high in the graduating class of her small-town, regional high school. She took part in sports, without ever starring, but was more prominent in school social activities and in her church youth program, where she was something of a leader. In her parents' hardware store, she was well liked and made many friends. Her SAT scores showed her to be well up in her college freshman group, with a verbal score of 520 and a mathematical score of 480.

J.C.'s vocational interests on the Strong Interest Inventory were very clearly social, without being either extraverted or introverted. Her Academic Comfort score was very low, suggesting that she might not be happy to stay in college for the full four years, despite being well able intellectually to graduate. There is a significant gap between her thematic Social and her Entrepreneurial–Artistic scores and between them and her even lower Conventional–Realistic–Investigative scores. Her interests appear to be largely in the religious activities, social, and athletic fields. Occupationally, her interests are very similar to those of teachers of special education (but like those of no other category of teacher, although she is moderately high on basic interest in teaching). She resembles practical nurses about as much as she does special education teachers. Her interests are similar to those of people in other helping occupations, such as YWCA directors, recreation leaders, social workers, and guidance counselors. Her interests are very similar to those of dental assistants and similar to those of dental hygienists, food service workers, and secretaries. Interested in the helping occupations, she appears to have practical rather than theoretical interests and thus to fit most comfortably into the lower-level professional and subprofessional occupations.

The things that J.C. appears to seek in life, including work, seem attainable in the occupations in which her interests lie; her goals (values) are indeed likely to be attained in the occupational activities that interest her. She scores high, in absolute and ipsative terms, on altruistic and people-oriented values. Achievement, esthetics, ability utilization, and life-style (which to her is a helpful and self-fulfilling way of life) are also of some importance to her. Advancement, power, and material values are not life goals of J.C.

This course-changing first-year college student compares very poorly with other first-year students on attitudes significant in career development, and when these are broken down into planfulness and exploratory approaches to education and work, she is low (15th percentile and 5th percentile) on both dimensions of this factor. Her knowledge of work and careers is average for a freshman, but freshmen typically know little about such things; she has learned less about the principles and determinants of career decision making (37th percentile) but rather more about the career development tasks of students and young adults and about the structure of work and major occupations (71st percentile) than most of her peers. When these scores are combined, her undeveloped attitudes outweigh her knowledge, perhaps showing that the latter is largely accidental and due to working in her parents' store, where she rubbed elbows with people in various lines of work and heard them discuss their working lives and activities. Although fairly knowledgeable for her age and stage, J.C. has not demonstrated an interest in or impetus toward looking ahead at occupations and careers. Her early and seemingly impetuous change of major appears to be a behavioral manifestation of these traits. However, J.C. is as well informed as her peers on her currently preferred occupational group, teaching and social service (a field quite visible to students).

Further light is thrown on these matters by J.C.'s scores on the Salience Inventory, one of the innovative products of the International Work Importance Study. Used ipsatively (that is, to compare J.C.'s scores on any given scale with her scores on other salience scales) the Salience Inventory is helpful for examining both the columns and the rows in her profile. Scanning the rows from left to right, we see that she has been and is still participating more in home and family and in leisure activities than in study or in work, with community activities of a service variety in between. We thus have a picture of a young woman who is not now career-oriented or study-oriented (the latter finding is in keeping with her Academic Comfort score). The five Participation Scales are behavioral. Those for Commitment are affective or attitudinal, and here we see that J.C. is committed to home and family and to community activities but somewhat less to leisure than her participation in leisure activities suggests. The Value Expectations Scales also assess commitment but in a different way, for they reflect what the respondent expects to get from the role in the future, as well as how important it seems now. It may be noteworthy that J.C. seems to expect rather more of work and study than she gets from them now, and that she may expect more from study (perhaps after she finds a major that appeals to her) than she sees in it now.

Reading down the columns instead of across them, we see home and family, community activities, and leisure looming large as roles in J.C.'s life, with study and work (occupational career) less important. (It should be noted that, in making such statements, the significance of the differences between scores must be considered, and that this is a function of the reliability of the scales. Both alpha coefficients and retest reliabilities of this inventory are very high, in the upper .80s and .90s.)

In conclusion, the Strong Interest Inventory has shown that J.C. is a people-oriented person; it suggests that these social interests may be centered more on home and family, community, and leisure than on work or career. The Values Scale can be seen as supporting this interpretation. In addition, J.C.'s Academic Comfort score, her low Career Development Attitudes scores on the CDI, and her Salience Inventory profile support the picture of a young woman who may not prove to be a dedicated student, teacher, or social service worker. As we see her now, in her formative first term in college, it appears that a short-term and easily trainable occupation (such as dental assistant or recreation worker) may be a wise choice. Such an occupation is easily given up when and if full-time homemaking should become her major role, and it is easily resumed later as a supplement to or replacement for a homemaking role, and so she may wish to consider such a field.

But one more major question must still be considered, one that cannot now be answered but that should be faced; that is, will J.C. remain a nonwork, noncareer woman in adulthood? We know that men's interests change some with age (Strong, 1943), but we know nothing about the development of interests in women. The research has not been done, despite Strong's data on women. We do know that in due course many young women without occupational or career aspirations do enter or return to the labor market because of economic reasons or changes in their career development. Will J.C.? Should she be helped to consider the long-term issues, the statistical probabilities? How? To deal with such issues is to become involved in developmental assessment and (much more difficult because less studied, but equally important) with developmental counseling.

Counseling. In considering the implications of career development theory for the practice of counseling, it is essential to be clear first about the objectives of the process and then about the nature of the process itself (Crites, 1981).

The objectives of developmental career counseling are to foster the development of the counselee and of his or her career, so that he or she may find self-fulfillment in it. Here, the term *career* must be without qualifier and must denote the several major roles that constitute a life career, for self-realization was never and is not now likely to be achieved only in the work role, particularly in an increasingly automated economy.

Fostering career development means, in some cases, facilitating it, for sometimes people are self-directing, and merely facilitating with information, a suggestion, or a question that leads to clarification by the counselee is enough. In other cases, it means playing a more directive role in assessment and planning. For this reason, the term *cyclical counseling* (Super, 1947) seems appropriate.

Career development theory makes clear what is to be fostered—occupational self-concept clarification and implementation and handling of the developmental tasks. It is *growth* in autonomy, time perspective, and self-esteem; *exploration* in breadth and then in depth for the crystallization, specification, and implementation of occupational self-concepts, interests, and a vocational preference; *establishment* with trial, stabilization, consolidation, and perhaps advancement; *maintenance* with adaptability, which means at least holding but better still keeping up, innovating, and in some cases transferring; and *decline,* or *disengagement,* and the shifting of role emphases. Assessment instruments, such as those discussed here, can be helpful in determining where the focus should be, and so can interviewing.

The process of counseling for career development may be as complex as career development itself, for development takes place in many contexts, and it may be facilitated or guided in each of these. For example, rehabilitation counseling has helped to enrich the type of counseling done in many university counseling centers, which have been dominated by the nondirective, neoanalytical, and behavior-modification schools, for rehabilitation has recognized better than they that counseling is a multimedia, multiexperiential process. The interview is the experience by means of which the other experiences are used; it is the medium of control. Other growth and exploratory resources, which are sometimes more important and sometimes less important than the interview itself, include pamphlets, books, filmstrips, computerized guidance, talks with school or college officials, talks or demonstrations by members of occupations, exploratory courses, active involvement in an occupationally relevant club or association, observation of someone at work, or part-time or vacation jobs in situations where appropriate work can be observed or even performed. Interviews in a counselor's office have as their vocational guidance function the identification and development of willingness to use experiences that will help the counselee to formulate an occupational objective, understand which experiences may help and how they may help in clarifying that objective, find and arrange for these experiences, evaluate their outcomes, and repeat the process as needed during the exploratory stage. It is the aim of the career development assessment and counseling model and the function of career development counseling to help students and adults anticipate career development tasks, plan how to cope with them, and evaluate the outcomes of coping for planning the next actions.

Counseling interviews may at times be directive and, in effect, provide confrontations with reality. They may be nondirective at other times and help counselees see the meanings or evaluate the results of these confrontations and their implications for action. These various methods are well dealt with in some standard texts (Crites, 1981; Nelson-Jones, 1982). Career development counseling, dealing as it does with development, implies some continuity of contact. It also involves the counselor's being available for counseling when needed, and although it can generally be done through appointments that are based on the timing of exploratory experiences, walk-in counseling opportunities also play an important role. The walk-in, as Rogers and Wallen (1946) are careful to point out, may even take place in a lounge, cafeteria, corridor, or other casual setting.

This definition of the objectives and processes of counseling for career development does not deny or preclude the importance of personal, therapeutic, or family counseling or of other approaches. Personal counseling may be needed in some instances before a client can explore effectively, in which case counseling's function is to facilitate the growth process; therapy may be needed in other cases to help a person understand, cope with, and perhaps accept what is happening in his or her career during the establishment stage, maintenance stage, or stage of decline. Its functions may be to provide support and foster clarification, insight, and self-acceptance. Specialized counselors may provide skills and knowledge that the career development counselor may not have; alternatively, multipotential counseling psychologists may be general development counselors who are able, as needed, to change the focus of counseling and deal with development and adjustment in the various theaters of life. Some of the best counseling is of this type (see the case of John Stasko in Super, 1957).

Certain questions must be faced by the counselor. Can the counselee change in desirable and desired ways? Will he or she change without help? Can the counselor really help, at this stage (the early clarification substage of exploration), with movement into the later stages of exploration? Will role playing or fantasized recycling through the early stages help? Can the counselor help the client (J.C., in this case) plan her study, work, and other life experiences of the next two or three years, so that study and work can become more salient, more important, and better understood by her? In short, can she be helped to mature more constructively and more rapidly than she might have done in the normal course of events?

Interventions that suggest themselves for J.C. include the following:

1. She might be presented with data on the careers of several women (including two or three who were like her when they were college freshmen) who progressed, with varying degrees of speed and difficulty, through the substages through which J.C. seems to need to move, and who coped, with varying degrees of ease and success, with the developmental tasks that she seems likely to encounter. Some dramatized examples of such cases, high school graduates going into the world of work, are provided in the Guided Career Exploration course designed for that group by Super and Bowlsbey (1979). Counseling and career centers usually have such taped and printed materials; interviews with suitably experienced and trained adults can be arranged, and the use of fantasy and role playing can be helpful.

2. Courses might be taken. Some psychology, sociology, education, and family-life departments offer courses in human

development that are intended to facilitate psychological and social growth.

3. Part-time and summer work experience can be used to help develop the needed types of psychological and social understanding (for example, paid or volunteer work in a department of social welfare, in a lawyer's office, in an adult career-counseling center, or in a marriage and family counseling service, especially if the work is guided and evaluated in concurrent counseling or in a seminar). Life can be utilized for counseling purposes!

By way of epilogue, a follow-up telephone conversation with J.C. revealed that in the middle of her final year at the university she had (1) settled on social work as an occupational objective, (2) decided to aim at admission to the graduate school of social work for an M.S.W. degree, and (3) accepted the idea that combining an occupational with a family career might be both very wise and satisfying. It would be informative if, at this stage, she could be readministered the CDI, the Salience Inventory, and the Strong Interest Inventory, to ascertain whether she now appears to be more of a "career woman"; it would also be helpful to review what took place in the final counseling interviews and to learn how she herself now explains her setting of these long-term objectives, which do not seem fully compatible with her inventory scores.

Career Development Programs for Students and Staff. It is too easy to view career development as something that is needed only by students or by employees in positions subordinate to one's own. It is also too easy to think of it as something that is fostered only in individual counseling or only in group programs. The purpose of this final section is not to identify programs in detail but to identify some of the main characteristics of career development programs for students in schools and universities and for staff in business, industry, government, education, or social service. In all these settings, three types of programs are needed: the designing and monitoring of a development- or growth-producing environment, group activities designed to foster career development, and individual counseling.

For students, an environment that fosters career development means a curriculum that facilitates growth, exploration of oneself and the world (particularly the occupational world and the educational world that leads to it), establishment in a field of study leading to a field of work, and maintenance of the role of student (the role of learner or of worker in a learning job). Such an environment requires teachers who are interested in human development, as well as in subject matter. It means a curriculum flexible enough to foster career development and individual counseling. It will contain resources for exploration and for learning that are varied and attractive — libraries, laboratories, shops, and school-community programs (Herr and Cramer, 1988).

Group activities include both self-exploration and occupational exploration projects, which are handled as parts of regular courses (by "infusion," as is often done in elementary schools), as well as special courses in career education for all students (by "addition," as is often done in high schools and colleges). An important objective of these projects, units, or courses — one that is too often missing — is an orientation to careers, in the sense of life stages and developmental tasks. Too often, for reasons given earlier in this chapter, career education deals only with occupations and not with career development; both are needed. The group activities should deal with the person (the individual, as related to occupation and career), with occupations, and with careers. Schedules should be arranged to guide and evaluate career development, with time for monitoring as well as for counseling. *Monitoring* here means reviewing data on counselees, considering their needs, and locating the resources needed for meeting their needs. Some of these functions may be delegated to specialists or to paraprofessionals; for example, resource development, identification, and referral may be done by a resource specialist, as a result of professional assessment and as part of the intervention.

For staff, there is a need for comparable programs, as many companies, agencies, and universities have recognized (Hall and Associates, 1986; London and Stumpf, 1982). The terminology is somewhat different, and some of the specifics of programs are different, but student-oriented programs can learn from staff-oriented programs, and vice versa.

A career development–fostering environment for staff members (whether they are blue-collar, pink-collar, or white-collar workers, and whether they work in production, clerical, managerial, instructional, or social service areas) must (like the educational environment) be one that facilitates and sometimes guides growth. For this to take place, self-esteem is essential, as the famous Hawthorne experiments made clear long ago. Growth may mean advancement (and too often has been construed as just that), but even in the most expansionist of times there are many people who do not seek advancement but instead prefer opportunities for self-expression in or associated with their work. In times of recession, and perhaps in the postindustrial society we seem to be developing, advancement is much more difficult and much less likely, even for the many who seek it. The opportunities that some companies give employees for special community-service projects, the cross-training and job-changing programs that some provide for variety, growth, and job enrichment, are examples of attempts to create and provide growth-fostering environments without advancement.

Exploration has not typically been encouraged by employers, whether they are industrial, governmental, or educational. Employees at any level are expected to concentrate on their jobs and not to digress in order to explore other jobs. Such barriers to exploratory activity are generally functional organizationally, and sometimes they are even necessary, but they can be self-defeating in their failure to develop higher-level or new, specialized talent. They must be overcome if managers capable of coping with broader responsibilities and changing situations are to emerge. Ways have been found of minimizing such barriers, to the benefit of the individual and of the organization.

In many corporations, schools, and colleges, staff members find the maintenance stage a difficult one. Some, frustrated by unrealized hopes or expectations, settle into a rut and merely hold their own at work. In a dynamic field or organization, holding one's own usually means dropping behind, stagnating, or being declared redundant (discharged). If the organization is to remain healthy, the environment must find ways of making refresher training and updating appear not only intrinsically interesting but also rewarding, even when it is not designed to lead to promotion. The environment also needs to be structured so as to make retirement at an appropriate time an acceptable event — perhaps making retirement more of a process than an event. This can mean focusing on specialized tasks, lessened responsibility, modifications in the working day or week, or good retirement programs.

Group programs for staff development have become common. They have long existed for the induction of new employees, who after orientation were often turned loose to shift for themselves, unless insightful supervisors saw their need for help. The focus of group programs has generally been on production, rather than on individual development, but a good career development program for staff members would attend to the continuing growth needs, the exploration and establishment processes, the need to handle the doldrums of the maintenance stage constructively, and the need to face decline and retirement. In recent years, government and industry have led the way in providing comprehensive career development programs, especially for managerial and professional staff members. These programs have not been so easy to conceive or to implement (nor have they been so remunerative) for white-, pink-, and blue-collar workers. College faculties, like top managers, have too often believed themselves immune to career development problems that are actually quite common and quite normal. Independent professionals, such as lawyers and physicians, have, through their associations, provided self-help in keeping up to date, as have the teaching professions; but in their independence, these professions seem to have disregarded their other developmental needs and possibilities.

Counseling for staff members has generally been viewed as psychotherapy or social work. It has therefore typically been seen as a luxury, to be afforded only in special circumstances. Career counseling has too often been viewed as a career development function only when it is linked to the assessment of managerial personnel in whom substantial investment has been and might be made, or as a means of increasing the productivity of white- and blue-collar workers. For understandable reasons, the focus is still on growth, exploration, establishment, maintenance, and decline in the company, rather than in the world at large. But if growth is fostered, then autonomy and curiosity can be expected to lead some staff members to consider outplacement, as well as inplacement. Recognizing this, and providing career counseling that helps the individual to consider all relevant alternatives, may well result in a better self-screened and more contented staff in the long run. There may then be fewer men and women unhappily half-productive while on the plateau of maintenance — fewer men and women fearfully approaching retirement and wondering whether they will be retained long enough to be able to retire, rather than being released before retirement age.

Conclusions

Doing a retrospective on the state of one's art and science and a prospectus of one's work is not an easy task when the past extends over a significant period of time, when the present is crowded with new developments of knowledge and its applications, and when the challenges of the future are partly obscured by complex social, economic, and psychological trends. But it is an interesting endeavor for the writer. It may clarify some current confusions for readers, and if it stimulates theorizing, research and development, and innovative applications in others, it will have been not only a pleasure to the writer but also worth the time of all of those who have been involved in writing, editing, printing, and reading.

Lawrence Hotchkiss
Henry Borow

8

ᴥᴥᴥᴥᴥᴥᴥᴥᴥᴥᴥᴥᴥᴥᴥᴥᴥᴥᴥᴥᴥᴥᴥᴥᴥᴥᴥᴥ

Sociological Perspectives on Work and Career Development

Introduction

Sociologists investigate the characteristics and behavior of people in organized groups. They study humans in their collective roles as members of social institutions, such as family, political, economic, religious, service, and recreational groups. In doing so, sociologists investigate the principles that govern the beliefs and conduct of group members in each of these institutional settings.

One institution that has long commanded the serious attention of sociologists is work. Classical social theorists like Karl Marx, Émile Durkheim, and Max Weber assigned work a central position in their treatises on the organization of society. In sociological parlance, work is the activity performed by individuals to produce goods and services of value to others (Hall, 1986). As Rothman (1987) notes, it is typically performed in a socially structured context and, as such, possesses sets of conventions, both interpersonal and technical, by which the worker is expected to abide.

The sociology of work differs from the psychology of career development in at least three important respects. First, because

262

work, viewed from a social and institutional vantage point, presents a rich variety of facets, its thematic treatment extends considerably beyond the boundaries that hold immediate relevance for counseling theory and practice. Sociologists attend to diverse topics, such as the status hierarchy of the occupational structure, the operation of power and authority in the workplace, work-socialization processes, collegial work groups, labor unions and collective bargaining, work-leisure dynamics, occupational mobility and career patterns, job satisfaction and institutional reward systems (Tausky, 1984), work alienation, sociology of the professions, counterculture work (Miller, 1978), and, of current importance, the operation of the labor market (Montagna, 1977).

Second, psychological theories of career development are generally premised on the notion that individuals potentially have a moderate degree of destiny control in the choice-making process, despite external obstacles and conditions of inequity. Choice making is regarded, at least potentially, as a transitive and reasonably manageable, albeit complex, operation. Sociological theory, by contrast, assigns greater weight to institutional and impersonal market forces that constrain decision making and fulfillment of career decisions.

Third, counseling psychologists, career counselors, and sociologists typically view cause-effect relationships through dissimilar lenses. Psychologists are interested in how constellations of personal attributes, including aspirations, aptitudes, interests, and personality traits, shape subsequent job performance and satisfaction. Sociologists, by contrast, generally are more interested than psychologists are in how such institutional factors as formal rules, informal norms, and supply-and-demand forces shape the settings in which individuals work. Gross (1964, p. 67) observes, for example, that once we know a person's work, "we can broadly estimate the range of his [sic] income, the size of his family, where he lives, where he works, how he spends his leisure time, [and] what clubs he belongs to."

Sociologists have generally viewed paid employment and occupational choice as embedded in a broad system of social stratification, and our review reflects this central theme of the sociological work. Since publication of the first version of this review (Hotchkiss and Borow, 1984), the sociological theory and research related to the stratification of work have shifted even farther from an emphasis on the process of individual career choices and toward a focus on the structural factors that condition those choices and their consequences. Investigation of individual career choices was an important part of the status attainment model, and analysis of structural factors is the focus of the sociology of labor markets.

Such terms as *social structure, structural factors,* and *job structures* are used pervasively in sociological writing about occupations and work. These terms are not given precise operational meanings; rather, they are used as general referents to variables that are defined on units other than individuals. For example, rules of access to highly valued occupations, such as physician or college professor, constitute part of the social structure of those occupations. Formal requirements, such as degrees, and informal rules, which often exclude social minorities from coveted positions, are included in these structural factors.

Students of career development will probably make the connection between status attainment research and their own field more readily than in the case of the sociology of labor markets, because the former emphasizes individual decision making more than the latter does. Nevertheless, the general proposition that structures contained in occupations, industries, and firms could be used to broaden the practice of career guidance beyond its conventional focus on educational and occupational choices warrants attention. An examination of this field of inquiry should help career development psychologists and practicing counselors alike to understand the importance of marketplace realities that lie beyond the limited domain of matching workers' traits to the functional demands of jobs.

The general hypothesis, from the structural approach of interest to career guidance and career development theory, is that many elements of the structure of work influence individuals' sense of well-being in their work. These include the functional requirements of the work but are not limited to them. Other important structural features include whether one is a worker, manager, or employer; chances for advancement; earnings prospects; benefits; job security; supply-and-demand balance; and discrimination. These features of work are partially contained in occupations (for example, some occupations offer more job security and earnings than other occupations do), but these features also are contained in such aspects of work as firms, industries, and geographical location. Large firms, for example, are more likely to provide full benefits packages, chances for promotion, protection against arbitrary firing, and long-term job security than small firms are. But even with firm size and occupation constant, there may be substantial firm-to-firm variation in quality of work setting. Similarly, industries that have been unionized for decades are likely to pay higher wages for given skills than nonunionized industries are. Further, sociologists argue that social structures (such as firm size and unionization) that determine how the fruits of labor are distributed are generally slow to change.

The structural approach was developed partly as a reaction to the status attainment model. Through the 1970s, the status attainment model so dominated empirical research in sociological investigations of work and occupational outcomes that many regarded it as the central paradigm in sociology (Colclough and Horan, 1983). Toward the end of the decade, however, dissatisfaction with status attainment research had begun to appear prominently in the sociological literature (Bibb and Form, 1977; Horan, 1978; Stolzenberg, 1978; Beck, Horan, and Tolbert, 1978). The status attainment model included a focus on educational and occupational choices and, in part, investigated the influence of family background and parents, friends, and relatives on those choices. The status attainment model also considered the influence of career expectations on career attainments.

The subject matter of the sociology of labor markets is much broader and more difficult to study than the subject matter of the status attainment model (narrowly defined). This chapter summarizes both lines of thought (status attainment and the sociology of labor markets), presents findings related to each position, and raises reservations about each.

The sociology of labor markets also developed out of criticisms from economic theory about the connection between schooling and wages, on the one hand, and supply and demand, on the other. Therefore, this chapter summarizes the micro-economic theory of educational decisions and the economic theory of supply and demand as they apply to the labor market. A review of the economic theory is crucial to an understanding of the sociology of work because so much in the sociology of labor markets reacts explicitly to the main theoretical ideas of contemporary economics. Moreover, some understanding of the economic viewpoint is useful to students of career development because the "human capital" school of economics provides a formalized explanation for some important ideas contained in theories of career development.

Status Attainment Theory

Sociologists have paid much attention to occupational mobility. By *occupational mobility,* they generally mean change from one occupation to another occupation at a different socio-economic level. Most of the research has investigated intergenerational mobility — change in occupational standing between one's parents and oneself. Prior to 1967, theoretical speculation about causes of occupational mobility had been confined to somewhat imprecise verbal statements, and measurement of occupational status had been limited primarily to rough classification of occupations into broad socioeconomic status groups, such as blue-collar and white-collar groups.

Publication of *The American Occupational Structure* (Blau and Duncan, 1967) marked a fairly clear line between social-mobility research, which relied on informal theory, imprecise measurement, and analysis of two- or three-variable cross tabulations, and the explicit modeling of status attainments. The chief contribution of Blau and Duncan was to collect the primary elements of the existing theory of individual mobility into a formal model of occupational attainment. A second important contribution was their application of a graded scale to indicate level of occupational status. That scale is commonly called the Socioeconomic Index (SEI) (Duncan, 1961).

In its most parsimonious form, the status attainment model postulates simply that the social status of one's parents affects the level of schooling one achieves, which in turn affects the occupational level that one achieves. An informal path diagram of this idea is given in Figure 8.1 (Duncan, Featherman, and Duncan, 1972). In this view, schooling is seen as a moderator

Figure 8.1. Simplified "Chain Model" of Occupational Attainment.

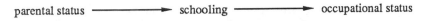

parental status ⟶ schooling ⟶ occupational status

Note: A path diagram is a graph in which variables are connected by arrows, the direction of the arrows indicating the hypothesized direction of effects.

variable between parental status and one's own status. Thus, although education is one of the indicators of status, it also plays a functional role in a process that occurs over time; that is, education is a partial determinant of occupational level. In more complete models of attainments, education also is depicted as a partial determinant of earnings.

A major competitor of the model shown in Figure 8.1 is depicted in the simplified path diagram in Figure 8.2. The distinction between these two models reflects competing world

Figure 8.2. Allocation Model of
Educational and Occupational Attainment.

views about the underlying reasons for the positive relation between the status of one's parents and one's own occupational status. In the first "stylized" view, the only reason for the universally observed positive association between parental status and occupational achievement is that parental status affects one's level of schooling; hence, this viewpoint contains an important element of the proposition that the United States' economic system is a meritocracy, since educational achievement, rather than parental status, is depicted as the direct determinant of the level of occupational attainment. Although educational attainment is partially determined by parental status, it also is due in large measure to individual effort and ability; this proposition is not explicit in Figure 8.1, however. By contrast, the second "stylized" view indicates that the only reason for a positive correlation between schooling and occupational achievement is their common dependence on parental status; that is, family background determines adult status, without regard for merit.

Blau and Duncan's (1967) data analysis is more complex than these two simple path diagrams, but it retains substantial parsimony. The primary model contains two measures of parental status (father's occupation and father's education), number of years of schooling, occupational status at first job, and occupational status at current job. Blau and Duncan's results support a mixed model that contains direct as well as indirect effects of parental status on occupational achievement, but their results show stronger indirect effects than direct effects operating through schooling (Blau and Duncan, 1967).

Two articles appeared soon after publication of *The American Occupational Structure* that substantially expanded the original Blau-Duncan scheme (Sewell, Haller, and Portes, 1969; Sewell, Haller, and Ohlendorf, 1970). The basic idea of what came to be called the Wisconsin model is that social-psychological processes intervene between parental status, on the one hand, and years of schooling and occupational achievement, on the other. In addition, the Wisconsin model added academic performance and standardized test scores to the basic model; the scores were defined as measures of ability. These ideas are depicted graphically in Figure 8.3.

The primary features of the Blau-Duncan model are preserved in the Wisconsin model, but the Wisconsin revision contains substantially more detail. The cognitive variables include a measure of mental ability and academic performance in school. The most important addition to the Blau-Duncan version of the model is contained in the box labeled *social-psychological processes*. This set of variables includes educational and occupational aspirations of youth before leaving high school, parents' encouragement to attend college, teachers' encouragement to attend college, and peers' plans to attend college. Collectively,

Figure 8.3. Simplified Path Diagram of the
Early Wisconsin Model of Status Attainment.

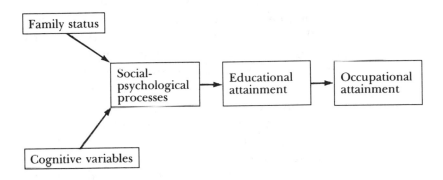

parents' and teachers' encouragement and peers' plans are examples of what are referred to as *significant-other variables*.

Saltiel (1988) reports a study of particular relevance to
the work of career development psychologists and career counselors. In contrast to most work in the status attainment tradition, which attempts to predict the socioeconomic status level
of occupations, rather than the specific occupation that one
selects, Saltiel is interested in predicting the specific job. He uses
several abstract dimensions of occupations, rather than socioeconomic status, to estimate the specific job title, and he concludes, "Given the strong theoretical base, past success with the
Wisconsin model, and the proposed technique for treating discrete choices in a quantitatively precise way, it seems that conditions are favorable for explicating the process by which specific
occupational choices are made" (Saltiel, 1988, p. 353). Saltiel's
work is exploratory, however. Natural extensions include the
adaptation of his technology for use with substantively meaningful dimensions of jobs (rather than use of his abstractions)
and the replication of his basic findings on a sample more representative than a local sample of college students.

The basic theory of the status attainment model can readily
be summarized. The hypothesis is that parents' status affects
the occupational level of their offspring through the following
path of influences: from parents' status to significant others' atti-

tudes about appropriate levels of education and occupation to career plans to schooling to occupational status level. Expanded versions of the model incorporate earnings as the last step in the process (since they depend directly on occupation). However, empirical tests of the model have incorporated other direct paths as well, such as a direct effect of "mental ability" on educational achievement (Sewell and Hauser, 1975). Effects of mental ability tend to operate through a sequence of influences similar to the sequence for parental status.

This relatively simple status attainment model has stimulated an enormous amount of empirical research (Sewell and Hauser, 1975; Alexander and Eckland, 1975; Alexander, Eckland, and Griffin, 1975; Duncan, Featherman, and Duncan, 1972; Featherman and Hauser, 1978; Otto and Haller, 1979; Picou and Carter, 1976; Porter, 1974; Rehberg and Rosenthal, 1978; Hauser, Tsai, and Sewell, 1983; Jencks and others, 1972; Jencks, Crouse, and Mueser, 1983). Each new round of data analysis has generated refinements in the basic model, but no empirical study has challenged the basic results of the model (see, however, Alexander and Pallas, 1984). It is fair to conclude that few models in social research have held up so well under such extensive scrutiny (see Hotchkiss and Borow, 1984, for a more complete summary of the evidence).

Despite strong empirical support for the status attainment model, it has come under heavy criticism for providing only a partial account of status attainments. Few sociologists would argue that the basic elements of the model are wrong, but many do argue that the model is incomplete. According to the critics, the most important omission from the model is an account of how social structures—such as rules of access to jobs, salary schedules, job security, and performance standards—interact with individual characteristics to influence socioeconomic outcomes of individuals. These critiques cannot be fully understood without some familiarity with the economic theory of schooling and competitive markets. We next summarize the pertinent economic theory and then review critiques of both the status attainment theory and economic theory.

Economic Theory of Schooling
and Competitive Markets

Sociologists have aimed as much of their critique at economic theory as they have at the status attainment model (for example, Bibb and Form, 1977; Horan, 1978). The reason is that the economic theory predicts that discrimination in hiring and wage policies of firms will erode over time under competitive pressures. This prediction contrasts with the sociological viewpoint that differences in structural position at work and differences in personal characteristics (for example, race and gender) continue to directly influence such status outcomes as education, occupation, and income.

Two aspects of economic theory have come under particularly heavy fire—human capital theory and theory of competitive markets. We will briefly review these two aspects of economic theory and then summarize why they predict that discrimination will disappear.

Human capital theory is developed around the analogy that individuals invest in their own productivity in a manner similar to the way investments in physical capital are made. Investments include direct outlays for educational costs and foregone earnings during the period of investment (for example, period of college attendance) (Becker, 1975; Mincer, 1974). Individuals differ in preferences and abilities, and each person makes investment decisions so as to maximize discounted lifetime earnings. *Discounted lifetime earnings* is a technical term intended to capture the idea that individuals are interested not only in their current earnings but also in their future earnings. However, people "discount" the value of future earnings because a dollar earned ten years from now (for example) is not worth as much to them as a dollar earned today. More sophisticated versions of the model incorporate job conditions other than earnings as partial determinants of individual investments.

Also, expenditures on noneducational factors, such as health care and migration, are included as human capital investments if they are undertaken to improve earning power.

Individuals incur costs for both health care and migration, and better health and a change of residence both may enhance earnings. Thus, they may be interpreted as investments. However, predominant attention has been paid to education.

An increasingly important aspect of the human capital approach is that individuals make career choices regarding amount of schooling, type of schooling, and occupation that are optimum for themselves (Willis and Rosen, 1979; Heckman and Sedlacek, 1985; Lang and Dickens, 1988); that is, individuals make rational decisions to match their own profiles with features of jobs and occupations. The end result is, in some sense, optimum both for individuals and for society, because it maximizes productivity.

Thus, the human capital model contains much of the basic orientation of career guidance and of career development theory. The primary similarity between them is that both human capital theory and career development theory depend on the postulate that individuals try to match their personal strengths to demands of occupations. The main difference is that human capital theory emphasizes earnings as an indicator of the quality of a job, whereas career development theory pays much more explicit attention to a broad spectrum of job characteristics, particularly job satisfaction and success.

In human capital formulations, wage rates typically increase with labor-market experience, reflecting on-the-job learning. The number of years of labor-market experience has become a standard predictor of earnings; it typically is proxied as a function of age minus years of schooling (Mincer, 1974). The theory appears to depend on the notions that (1) investments in education and other aspects of personal improvement do enhance productivity, and (2) individuals' earnings correspond directly to their productivity. However, it is sometimes argued that most of the empirical predictions of the theory are consistent with the view that investments, such as years of schooling, simply provide statistically accurate "signals" of future productivity that are correlated with but not actually produced by the investment.

In the main formulation of human capital theory, little explicit attention is paid to differences among types of jobs. Labor markets appear to be homogeneous. Lang and Dickens

(1988), however, sketch an explicit human capital model that accounts for heterogeneous labor markets, thus providing an effective response to one of the most frequent criticisms from the structuralist school. More generally, economists have been ingenious in developing incremental refinements to the basic theory that respond to obvious shortcomings in the original formulations, but they leave the fundamental postulates of market mechanisms and individual optimizing behavior intact. For example, Dickens and Lang's model avoids the oversimplified assumption of a single homogeneous labor market but retains the hypothesis that individuals make choices that yield (approximately) the most favorable outcomes for them and the hypothesis that supply and demand interact to determine wage and employment levels. This interplay between structuralist critiques and neoclassical economics appears to have generated an unusually productive intellectual ferment.

Economic theory of competitive markets is based on the assumption that price (wage) adjusts to fluctuations in supply and demand of labor, so that pressures are generated toward an equilibrium in which supply just equals demand. According to the theory, employers are more willing to hire more workers (of a given "quality") if the wage is low than if it is high. Conversely, more workers are willing to work at any given job if the wage is high than if it is low. Whenever the wage is so high that more people are willing to work than employers are willing to hire, there is pressure to lower the wage. The complement to this situation occurs when the wage is so low that there are fewer people willing to work than employers willing to hire. Here, there is pressure to raise the wage. Pressures to change cease only when the wage is at the point where the number of people who want to work just equals the number of workers employers are willing to hire. This is the point where the "demand curve" and the "supply curve" intersect. This is shown in Figure 8.4.

The equilibrium wage thereby guarantees that there will be no unemployment. The persistence of unemployment in the American economy has been an important stimulus to revision of economic theory (see, for example, Bulow and Summers, 1986).

Figure 8.4. Supply and Demand Curves.

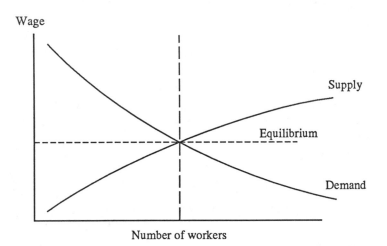

Structuralist Alternatives to Status
Attainment Theory and Economic Theory

Structuralists criticize the status attainment model and human capital theory for overemphasizing the role of individual volition and ability in determining career choices and the distribution of the rewards of work. Several features of the status attainment model are subject to this criticism. These include the postulated effects of (1) "mental ability" on level of educational expectation and on level of educational attainment, (2) level of educational expectation on level of educational attainment, (3) level of occupational expectation on level of occupational attainment, and (4) level of educational attainment on level of occupational attainment and on earnings. All of these postulated effects reflect the idea that ability or personal choices determine outcomes.

By contrast, the status attainment model also postulates and tests for effects of parental status on career attainments. Hence, not all elements of the status attainment model emphasize the importance of individual choice and ability in determining career outcomes.

Human capital theory emphasizes individual choice and merit even more than does the status attainment model. Individuals make "investments" in their productive capacities, and these investments are carried out to achieve a maximum of benefits from one's work life. Moreover, wages are determined by productivity. The end result is one in which aggregate productivity is maximum because each individual has made optimum choices, and one in which individuals are compensated for their work according to their contributions to production. Of course, it is recognized that this is only an approximation to reality, but it is believed to be a useful one.

Structuralists also claim that the interplay of supply and demand does not provide an accurate, or even the most useful, description of how wages are set and how individuals end up in jobs. They claim that institutional arrangements, based on past practices and current beliefs about fair wages, provide a plausible alternative explanation of the process of determining wage and employment levels. Persistent unemployment is evidence that mechanisms other than supply and demand are at work.

The details of the structuralist critiques of status attainment theory and economic theory exhibit considerable variety, but two features appear to characterize most of them. First, it is argued that the degree of individual control over career outcomes is more limited than is implied by the status attainment and human capital models. Second, it is argued that institutional features affecting the quality of individuals' jobs are substantially more complex than the job functions associated with occupations.

The size of the firm or establishment where one works (Stolzenberg, 1978; Baron and Bielby, 1980, 1982, 1984), the industry in which one works (Beck, Horan, and Tolbert, 1978), the degree of job authority (Wright and Perrone, 1977; Parcel and Mueller, 1983), whether one is an employer or an employee (Wright and Perrone, 1977; Parcel and Mueller, 1983), and the geographical location of one's job (Parcel and Mueller, 1983) all influence the quality of work.

Although most of the research attention has been paid to wage or earnings as a measure of the quality of work, the general hypothesis about the importance of institutional settings other than occupation applies to other measures of quality, including job satisfaction, job advancement, job security, "pleasantness" of job tasks, exposure to dangerous or uncomfortable working environments, and opportunities for learning on the job.

Achieving a satisfying career depends more on obtaining a preferred position in these several settings than it does on productivity. Productivity may be higher in positions that carry high rewards, but this is by no means ensured. In any case, measurement of productivity in units that permit valid comparisons between the output of individuals in diverse positions has eluded researchers. Access to desirable positions depends in part on ability to perform job tasks, but it also depends on complex institutionalized rules, both formal and informal. These rules are generated over long periods by processes that entail jockeying for power, norms regarding fair play, and general beliefs about what classes of individuals are suited for specific jobs. These rules are slow to change, even in the face of clear inefficiencies and breach of equity norms. Race and gender are two important criteria determining access to coveted positions.

Kerckhoff (1976) argues that individuals tend to be "allocated" into slots or positions in the work world, rather than encouraged to make well-informed, deliberately planned choices. Although the term *allocation* carries a static connotation, the most persuasive writing about the process of allocation describes a long-term dynamic process. Once he or she is "allocated," it often is difficult for an individual to switch to another "slot."

Rosenbaum's "tournament" model provides a useful metaphor for describing the dynamics of the process (Rosenbaum, 1976, 1981). According to the tournament model, individuals, beginning with the early years of schooling, are gradually eliminated from the most desirable positions over time. For example, a youth who has not taken the toughest courses in junior high school encounters many barriers against taking the high-level math and science courses in high school. College entrance and completion then become only remote possibilities. Similarly, it is difficult if not altogether impossible for a young high school dropout to return to school and eventually become a physician.

In later life, it is difficult for a fifty-five-year-old displaced auto worker to find another job with pay and benefits comparable to those in his or her old job. The processes that determine which individuals win and lose in the tournament of life are composed of a complex interaction of individual actions and "rules of the game." Although the rules are purported to be fair, there is much evidence to suggest that they often are arbitrary and are administered inconsistently.

Dualist Theory of the Economy and the Labor Market

A focal component of the structuralist viewpoint is that command of resources is a central factor in determining the distribution of the rewards of work. In early writings, firms were divided into two categories based on indicators of command over resources, and the labor market was divided into two corresponding segments. Hence, the term *dualist theory* is often applied. The theory is divided into two parts: dual economy theory, which is about firms, and dual labor-market theory, which is about jobs in those firms.

In dual economy theory, firms are classified into two economic sectors—the core and the periphery. Those in the core sector are large, hold monopolistic or oligopolistic market power, apply advanced technology, and participate in national or international markets. Periphery firms are small and exhibit the obverse of the characteristics of core firms. The large firms in the core sector exert control over employees by offering them higher wages, job stability, and opportunity for advancement.

This aspect of the dual economy generates a dual or segmented labor market, with employees in the core-sector firms holding jobs in the primary labor market and employees in periphery firms holding jobs in the secondary labor market. According to the theory, mobility between the two labor markets is highly restricted, but empirical evidence has not borne out this expectation.

Core firms tend to locate themselves in urban centers, are highly unionized, generate demand for highly skilled occupations, and have work forces with high concentrations of white males. Bibb and Form (1977), Hodson and Kaufman (1982), Parcel and Mueller (1983), and Colclough and Horan (1983) provide useful reviews of the dualist conceptions.

The concepts of internal labor markets and job ladders are closely related to segmented labor-market theory. Internal labor markets are characterized by institutionalized ladders of promotion and develop primarily in core firms. Earnings are closely tied to the level of the job, rather than being determined by the interplay of supply and demand, as in a market (Doeringer and Piore, 1971; DiTomaso, 1988; Rosenbaum, 1981). Primary labor markets ("good jobs") are thought to be characterized by internal promotion structures that are associated with job security and high pay. Secondary labor markets ("bad jobs") are described as subject to open competition. From the vantage point of employees, jobs in the secondary labor market are undesirable because wages are determined by supply and demand, and the continuity of such jobs is subject to unpredictable fluctuations in demand. Hence, wages tend to be low, and the risk of unemployment high.

Empirical Evidence of Structural Effects

Numerous quantitative studies have set out to test some of the key predictions of the structuralist orientation. Most of these studies have compared regressions that use independent variables from traditional status attainment and human capital models to regression models in which various indicators of structural position are added.

We believe these results to be pertinent to career development, for two reasons. First, earnings comprise one important (although by no means the only) component of the quality of work life. Earnings not only provide direct purchasing power but also influence other aspects of life satisfaction, including self-esteem and sense of job fulfillment. Second, earnings tend to be positively related to other desirable features of work; hence, hypotheses regarding earnings may also be applied to other outcomes of work (see, for example, Form, Kaufman, Parcel, and Wallace, 1988; Kalleberg and Griffin, 1980). The most useful way for students of career development to view these findings probably is as general hypotheses about the way the world of work operates.

Several early studies relied on dichotomous indicators of membership in either the core or the periphery sector of the economy. We shall review selected studies of this type in a moment, but first a note on terminology, since the postulated parallel existence of a dual economy (composed of firms) and a dual labor market (composed of jobs) presents potential confusion. Most of the studies using dichotomous measures of sector have defined the sectors with variables describing firms, rather than jobs, but both types of indicators have also been used in a single study. In the following discussion, we will use terminology describing the dual economy, rather than try to carefully differentiate between dual economy and dual labor markets. To draw this distinction would unduly complicate the discussion, without adding commensurate clarity.

Studies relying on dichotomous measures of the economic sector have characterized individuals according to the industries in which they work (Bibb and Form, 1977; Beck, Horan, and Tolbert, 1978, 1980; Hodson, 1978) Those working in industries (three-digit census codes) with a predominance of large, capital-intensive, profitable firms were classified as working in the core sector of the economy, and others have been classified as working in the periphery sector. Conclusions from these studies have generally supported the dualist framework. They conclude that (1) those working in the core sector command higher wages than those in the periphery sector, (2) human capital variables, such as education and experience, have a stronger positive impact on wage in the core sector than in the periphery sector, and (3) minorities and women have limited access to jobs in the core sector.

These studies have been subject to strong criticisms. Hauser (1980) reports a reanalysis of the data used by Beck, Horan, and Tolbert (1978), concluding that eliminating zero earners from the data also eliminates their findings. He claims that many of their respondents were erroneously classified as having no earnings because the earnings survey item referred explicitly to earnings in the current job. Thus, those who had recently changed jobs were likely to have been classified in the lowest earnings category and assigned a zero value for the analysis. Although Beck, Horan, and Tolbert (1980) concede nothing in their reply, the criticism seems quite damaging to their case.

Zucker and Rosenstein (1981) report comparisons of the model of Beck, Horan, and Tolbert (1978), using four schemes already in the literature for classifying industries as core or periphery. They find highly inconsistent results among the four classifications, even though each is designed to measure the same construct. They conclude that "the divergent findings which emerge using these four taxonomies demonstrate the need for further comparative examination and clear theoretical specification. Empirical derivation of taxonomies seems unlikely to provide a satisfactory solution, since different investigators report strikingly different relations between key variables. The need for further development of the underlying theoretical models is clear" (Zuker and Rosenstein, 1981, pp. 880–881).

Economists Dickens and Lang (1985a, 1985b) provide interesting evidence of dualism in the process of earnings determination. Rather than relying on an ad hoc classification scheme using industry data (for example, the one used by Beck, Horan, and Tolbert, 1978), they estimate wage equations with an econometric method called "endogenous switching regression with unknown regimes." This method permits identification of two regression lines in a set of data, without a priori separation of the sample into two groups (Dickens and Lang, 1985a). The two groups can be viewed as latent or unmeasured (analogous to factors from a factor analysis). Dickens and Lang report very similar results from two quite different samples. First, they report results from the Panel Study on Income Dynamics (1980 data); second (Dickens and Lang, 1985b), they use the same forty-eight thousand cases from a 1983 population survey. In both instances, analyses were restricted to males, with a dummy variable used to differentiate blacks from whites. Years of schooling and years of experience were both found to have a strong positive effect on wages in the primary labor market and virtually no effect in the secondary labor market, just as predicted by the dualist theory.

In the second paper, Dickens and Lang (1985b) used results of the switching regression to estimate membership in the primary or secondary labor markets for members of the sample. They then compared their results to results from other studies (for example, Beck, Horan, and Tolbert, 1978), using a priori classification schemes based on industry. They found that the a priori schemes that most closely approximated results from the switching regression were also most consistent with dualist theory.

Hodson and Kaufman (1982) provide a systematic review and critique of dualist theory and research. Their strongest criticism is that the framework is descriptive rather than theoretical: "Perhaps the most damning criticism of the dual economy approach is that a systematic model has never been elaborated. . . . Key components of the model (core sector, primary jobs, and so on) have not been clearly defined and the links between these concepts and other components of the full model have not been clearly laid out" (Hodson and Kaufman, 1982, p. 732). Hodson and Kaufman also criticize the dualist conception as unduly simplistic. Rather than a simple dichotomy, many continuous dimensions are needed to characterize structuralist theory of a modern economy. They argue that the primary insight of the dualist framework is that such resources as physical capital and firm size (on the employer's side) and unions (on the employees' side) are important determinants of outcomes for workers—especially earnings.

An important element of the criticism of the early empirical work is that it relied on industry data, whereas data describing firms or establishments would have been preferable. For example, Baron and Bielby (1980) argue that reliance on industries to define structural variables is inadequate. The important determinants of outcomes for workers occur at the firm level, but there is much diversity among firms within any given industry. Form, Kaufman, Parcel, and Wallace (1988) emphasize the importance of establishments and departments within establishments, and they propose a comprehensive data-collection plan for examining the effects of work structures on outcomes for workers. Unlike many other researchers in the sociology of labor markets, Form and his coauthors do not focus on earnings; rather, they propose that workers' skills, autonomy, and job satisfaction are the primary outcomes of interest.

The most interesting empirical studies have not relied on a simple dichotomous measure of economic sector; rather, they have used relatively specific structural variables. For example, Stolzenberg (1978) uses firm size instead of a dichotomy intended to differentiate between the primary and secondary labor markets. He finds clear evidence that the impact of education on earnings is stronger in large firms than in small firms.

Some interesting studies have investigated the effects of one's being an employer, supervisor, or manager on one's earnings. These studies cite Marx's distinction among capitalists (employers and owners), the petite bourgeoisie, and workers, but they broaden the Marxist classification by including additional categories, such as managers. Wright and Perrone (1977) have found that employers, managers, and workers differ with regard to earnings (after controlling for education, occupational status, age, and length of job tenure). They also have found that the effect of education on earnings is strongest for employers, next strongest for managers, and weakest for workers. Kalleberg and Griffin (1980) extend some of the Wright and Perrone (1977) results to a measure of job satisfaction.

Parcel and Mueller (1983) report results of a detailed study of structural effects on earnings. They investigated effects of all the major dimensions of structure identified in the literature, including geographical location, economic segmentation or dualism, occupational differentiation in function, and class or authority. They placed particular emphasis on comparisons among race and gender groups. The most interesting findings reported in this study are associated with the class and authority dimensions. They distinguish among the following fourteen categories of class and authority:

Employers

    Employer, self-employed
    Employer, 1–2 employees

Employer, 3–19 employees
Employer, 20 or more employees

Supervisors

Supervisor—large span of control, large span of responsibility, in firm with low vertical complexity
Supervisor—small span of control, large span of responsibility, in firm with low vertical complexity
Supervisor—large span of control, small span of responsibility, in firm with low vertical complexity
Supervisor—small span of control, small span of responsibility, in firm with low vertical complexity
Supervisor—large span of control, large span of responsibility, in firm with high vertical complexity
Supervisor—small span of control, large span of responsibility, in firm with high vertical complexity
Supervisor—large span of control, small span of responsibility, in firm with high vertical complexity
Supervisor—small span of control, large span of responsibility, in firm with high vertical complexity

Workers

Worker in firm with high vertical complexity
Worker in firm with low vertical complexity

In this classification scheme, *span of control* refers to the number of people supervised; *span of responsibility* refers to the degree of influence a supervisor exercises over promotion and salary increases of those supervised; *vertical complexity* refers to the number of layers of authority (it is high if the respondent's supervisor has a supervisor, and otherwise it is low).

Parcel and Mueller (1983) report very large earnings differences among the class and authority categories after adjusting for human capital variables (for example, education and years of work experience), but these differences are concentrated among white males.

The adjusted mean earnings of white male heads who employed twenty or more employees (8.9 percent of the sample of white male heads) was $30,233 dollars in 1974 dollars (approximately $77,500 in 1989 dollars), compared to $12,827 ($32,877 in 1989 dollars) for workers in industries with high vertical complexity. (The adjustment is simply an alternative way of presenting effects from a regression analysis. The adjusted means are constructed so that their differences equal the corresponding regression coefficients, and their mean equals the overall mean of the dependent variable; see Cohen and Cohen, 1983.) By contrast, in the lowest earnings category of black women (black wives who were supervisors, with no responsibility for employees' raises and large span of control), annual adjusted earnings were $2,601 ($6,667 in 1989 dollars). The primary reason these effects occurred mainly for white males is that no other race-gender grouping had enough cases in the top earnings categories to permit complete classification into all fourteen categories. These results solidify evidence of strong effects of class and authority that earlier were reported in comparatively rudimentary form (Wright and Perrone, 1977; Kalleberg and Griffin, 1980). Parcel and Mueller (1983) demonstrate the degree to which the three-category scheme used in the earlier work masks important differences in annual earnings — for example, between employers of twenty or more employees and self-employed individuals or employers with only a few employees.

Studies of internal labor markets typically have been case studies that lend important insights missing from quantitative studies. For example, in direct observation of work in three establishments, DiTomaso (1988) reports several complexities of jobs and compensation that are never accounted for either in quantitative secondary analyses of large surveys or in theories of vocational choice. She observes that workers in a large manufacturing plant may be assigned to different jobs on different days. In such cases, the wage is either the wage for the permanent job or the wage for the job performed on a given day, whichever is higher. Often workers are assigned to jobs other than their "permanent" jobs for extended periods. In addition, as much as 10 to 20 percent of the workers' annual pay comes from "incentive pay," which is not captured by the product of hours, weeks, and the hourly wage rate. These kinds of arrangements suggest why it is difficult to account for more than a small fraction of the variance in wages or earnings in typical studies based on survey data: the diversity of arrangements for determining workers' pay is simply too high to be expressed in simple regressions.

Rosenbaum (1981) provides a useful description of the operation of an internal labor market. He studied job-advancement mechanisms in one large firm. After examining wage and position records accumulated over a ten-year history, he concluded that his "tournament" model (Rosenbaum, 1976, 1981) describes the process of advancement in the firm. Particular individuals, identified early for advancement, quickly became "stars." Attendance at particular colleges had an important impact on advancement; often, individuals were earmarked for advancement before they had been with the firm long enough to permit sufficient observation of their performance or accurate judgments. Thus, errors in judgments about competence, as well as such extraneous criteria as schools attended, were perpetuated by what amounted to a compounding process.

Kohn (1981) proposes a theoretical viewpoint that explicitly accounts for the feedback between allocation and socialization; thus, his work provides a useful bridge between status attainment and human capital views and structuralist views. He argues that job environment—related to such features as the substantive complexity of work, work autonomy, closeness of supervision, and routinization—affect such personal characteristics as cognitive functioning, attitudes, and conformity.

A substantial body of empirical evidence has accumulated in support of this viewpoint (Kohn and Schooler, 1978, 1982; Miller and others, 1979; Mortimer and Lorence, 1979a, 1979b). Kohn's research on work, intellectual functioning, and other personal characteristics has not been explicitly integrated into the large literature on labor markets, but it clearly is relevant to discussions of internal labor markets and associated promotion criteria. One of the mechanisms that may account for Rosenbaum's (1981) notion of a tournament is the idea that positions may shape incumbents in such a way that they are picked (or are not picked) for the next rung on the job ladder. Of course, the human capital argument in economics could easily accommodate Kohn's results by arguing that they represent on-the-job learning, and thus accumulation of human capital.

Kohn's position, of course, contrasts with (although it does not necessarily contradict) the basic postulate in career guidance: that individuals match their personal characteristics to work environments. For example, Dawis and Lofquist's (1984) theory of work adjustment matches the client's personal traits (vocational needs), as measured by the Minnesota Importance Questionnaire, to features of the job environment (occupational reinforcer patterns) by means of the Minnesota Job Description Questionnaire.

Race and Gender Effects

A substantial and continually expanding literature investigates the effects of race and gender on career outcomes. The key variables in the status attainment model and human capital theory — parental status, education, and years of labor-market experience — are obligatory controls in the study of race and gender effects. Yet neither status attainment theory nor human capital theory provides a good account of the persistent finding that race and gender do exercise direct effects on career outcomes. Moreover, the economic theory of competitive markets predicts that discrimination will evaporate under competitive pressures (Becker, 1957).

Nevertheless, there is empirical evidence of race and gender effects on occupational achievement and earnings, and it is partly in response to these observations that the structuralist framework has been proposed. We summarize the evidence first, and then we review recent theoretical arguments tying the findings to the structuralist framework.

Empirical research clearly demonstrates that minorities are concentrated in low-status occupations and earn substantially less than whites (Porter, 1974; Portes and Wilson, 1976; Stolzenberg, 1975; Tienda and Lii, 1987; Farley and Allen, 1987). In spite of sporadic improvements, women remain heavily concentrated in a narrow band of occupations, and they consistently earn less than men (England and McCreary, 1987; Corcoran and Duncan, 1979; Treiman and Hartman, 1981; England, 1981; England and Farkas, 1986; England and others, 1988; Bielby and Baron, 1986; Bianchi and Spain, 1986). Gender segregation by occupation is more pronounced than racial segregation by occupation. Similarly, earnings differences by gender exceed racial differences. Although educational differences by race and gender account for part of the occupation and income disadvantages of minorities and women, occupational and earnings differences by race and gender persist at every level of education (Stolzenberg, 1975; Suter and Miller, 1973; Treiman and Hartman, 1981; Treiman and Terrell, 1975; Bielby and Baron, 1986; England and others, 1988; Tienda and Lii, 1987).

Recent evidence indicates some decline in the gender segregation of occupations and jobs (England and Farkas, 1986; England, 1981; Bianchi and Spain, 1986). Slight increases in the proportion of women in traditionally male occupations have been registered, and these increases appear to be concentrated among younger women. Bianchi and Spain (1986) report that the rate of convergence between the occupational distributions of men and women has accelerated somewhat in the last two decades, but that nearly 60 percent of men and/or women would have to change occupations (three-digit census codes) to completely equate the occupational distribution of men and women. As England and Farkas (1986) point out, however, it is difficult to project the extent to which these gains will continue in the coming decades.

One of the most compelling analyses in support of gender bias in the workplace is reported by Bielby and Baron (1986). Their data are unique because they contain information about specific firms and specific jobs. It is important to distinguish between *job* segregation and *occupational* segregation. Occupations are collections of similar jobs. It is quite possible for occupations to show a decrease in gender segregation even when jobs within occupations remain almost completely segregated—in a fashion parallel to what happens in desegregated schools in which classrooms remain segregated.

Bielby and Baron (1986) observe that in many cases the degree of job segregation by gender within firms is nearly complete. They find that over 90 percent of men and/or women would have to change specific jobs in order to make the job distributions of men and women equitable (the average index of dissimilarity calculated over firms is 93). Moreover, essentially the same job may be nearly all male in one division of a firm and nearly all female in another division; in these cases, different job titles and pay grades typically are assigned to men and women. Here, since the work that women perform is essentially the same as the work done by men, and since the pay is different, it is difficult to see how even very approximate selection according to individual ability to perform tasks could account for the findings. It seems clear that work structures — that is, the organization of work, not individual productivity — are determining wages in this instance. However, Bielby and Baron's (1986) data are limited to California firms and to the 1960s and 1970s. Good data of the type they report are rare, but a complete picture of the operation of job structures demands additional firm-specific and job-specific data.

There is little doubt that race and gender exercise strong effects on such career outcomes as educational and occupational levels and earnings. Human capital theory suggests that the differences are due to human resource differences — between whites and minorities, and between males and females. Human resource variables include education and on-the-job training. The basic proposition is that if human resource variables are controlled, then race and gender effects diminish to zero. This prediction has not been borne out by empirical research, however (Treiman and Hartman, 1981; Tienda and Lii, 1987; Farley and Allen, 1987; Bianchi and Spain, 1986; England and others, 1988). The fact that income and occupational differences by race and gender cannot be accounted for by human capital variables implies that labor-market discrimination is pervasive, although this conclusion is not firmly grounded in quantitative data because direct measurement of discrimination is rare (the Bielby and Baron findings just cited, however, provide a close approximation). Discrimination is inferred because personal characteristics (such as training and ability) that should be strong indicators of productive capacity do not greatly moderate the effects of race and gender on occupation and earnings.

Human capital variables, such as years of schooling and years of work experience, explain a substantially larger percentage of the gross earnings gap between whites and blacks than they do the gross earnings difference between males and females (Parcel and Mueller, 1983). A primary reason for this result is that the difference in years of schooling completed by males and females is substantially less than the difference between blacks and whites. This fact seems anomalous because blacks report higher educational aspirations than whites do.

One possible explanation for the failure of blacks to realize their educational aspirations is that blacks receive inferior schooling; hence, they do not score as well on standardized tests as whites, and it becomes difficult for them to achieve their aspirations. Standard explanations for low scholastic achievement of blacks include (1) socioeconomic differences between blacks and nonblacks and (2) ability grouping in schools. These explanations have not been fully supported in empirical data, however. Dreeben and Gamoran (1986) report a study that does fully account for racial differences in reading achievement in the first grade. They found that nonblack first graders learn more new words during the school year than black first graders, but the primary reason is that black children are presented fewer words to learn. The major differences in learning opportunities were found between schools, rather than between ability groups, although ability groups were a pervasive feature of the seven Chicago-area schools and the thirteen classes studied. Dreeben and Gamoran's (1986) findings are particularly important, for three reasons. First, they show almost complete elimination of racial differences in learning, after controlling for "educational technology" (that is, number of words presented). Second, their sample consisted of first graders and thus provides information about early school experience, before learning deficits of blacks have had a chance to accumulate. Third, they are based on direct classroom observation; without the classroom observation, the key variables would not have been measured, and the analysis could not have accounted fully for racial differences in learning.

England and others (1988) reviewed economic theory that explains male-female earnings differentials in terms of human capital variables and nonpecuniary compensations. They then synthesized several years of writing in sociology, which ties women's disadvantages in the labor market to women's traditional role as homemakers and child-care providers. In brief, the economic argument is that women prefer jobs that offer relatively high starting wages and that impose small penalties for intermittent work histories. This type of job affords women a better compromise between their work and homemaker roles than do the jobs typically held by males. Jobs typically held by women also provide less pressure and more agreeable working conditions than "male" jobs. Thus, the reason why women hold "women's" jobs is that they prefer them.

By contrast, the sociological argument is that women's preferences for the homemaker role are partly determined by their lack of options in the job market and by the socialization that has grown out of past practices and beliefs. England and others (1988) also question claims that the starting wages of women's jobs are higher and that women are less penalized for intermittent work histories than men are. They report statistical analyses refuting the economic view and supporting the sociological explanation.

One of the most important factors affecting the economic success of both genders is continuity and longevity of employment. Although this is one of the two primary human capital variables, as England and others (1988) argue, the fact that women are out of the labor force much more than men are is intimately tied up with women's traditional gender roles. Of course, the influence of intermittent labor-force participation stretches beyond earnings. Early marriage and childbearing also tend to reduce the labor-force participation of women and to impede their job advancement. By contrast, the evidence suggests that marriage enhances the earnings of men. Thus, a cycle of effects is established that reinforces the relatively low status of women.

An important theoretical connection between race-gender effects and the structuralist view indicates that females and minorities have limited access to preferred jobs. Since the primary labor market's jobs are generally more desirable than the secondary labor market's jobs, and since wages in the primary labor market usually are above wages in the secondary labor market, queues for those jobs are expected. Moreover, since firms make a long-term commitment to workers in the primary labor market, the firms have a special interest in hiring productive workers. Because information about productivity is difficult to obtain, firms tend to rely on such inaccurate but cheap indicators as education, race, and gender.

Social relations on the job that are fostered in internal labor markets may also contribute in myriad ways to job discrimination. Granovetter (1988) cites the case of a black worker in a chemical plant. The worker applied for promotion and was denied but won promotion on appeal. White workers with whom he was going to have to work refused to cooperate with him. Knowing he could not perform his duties without cooperation from his workmates, the black worker withdrew from the higher position. Granovetter interprets this result not only as an instance of discrimination but also as an illustration of how production is the result of social organization and not simply the product of a technical match between person and job. Of course, one anecdotal instance does not substantiate Granovetter's case, but the information needed to build a statistically defensible case would be difficult to obtain by the usual method for gathering quantitative data — a survey. This anecdote is at least suggestive of the type of information that it would be desirable to collect.

Assessment of the Structuralist Framework

In spite of challenging theorizing and interesting data, the conceptual and theoretical underpinnings of the structuralist framework have not been clearly established. The early work, with simple dichotomies to represent primary and secondary labor markets and the location of firms in the core or the periphery, has been largely discredited, although not entirely, if one considers the evidence of Dickens and Lang (1985a, 1985b). Much criticism has been directed against the simplistic dualist notions, however (Zucker and Rosenstein, 1981; Jacobs and Breiger, 1988; Hodson, 1984; Parcel and Mueller, 1983; Hodson and Kaufman, 1982; Kaufman, Hodson, and Fligstein, 1981). More sophisticated empirical work, with variables other than dichotomous measures of economic sector (for example, that of Parcel and Mueller, 1983), gives much stronger evidence of structural effects, particularly for class and authority.

An important shortcoming of much of this work is its reliance on industry-level data, when data describing specific firms or establishments would be much more preferable. For example, the average level of capital investment of the firms in an industry, or the average size of firms in an industry in which one works, probably are not nearly as predictive of earnings as would be direct measures of the capital intensity or size of the specific firm in which one works. Lack of available data is the primary reason for this limitation. Future work is planned to avoid this shortcoming (Form, Kaufman, Parcel, and Wallace, 1988).

Although much progress is in evidence, the structuralist framework remains in flux. There is no general consensus regarding theoretical mechanisms and empirical findings in the sociology of labor markets. The most promising developments currently reside in theoretical work that is attempting to integrate the status attainment model, human capital theory, market theory, and the structuralist framework.

England and Farkas (1986), for example, have proposed an appealing integration of sociological and economic perspectives. They argue that (1) market forces of supply and demand do operate in allocating individuals into jobs, (2) individuals do engage in activities that resemble human capital investments, and (3) employers and prospective employees do tend to match individual characteristics and job demands according to efficiency rules; but these processes are imperfect. First, information is imperfect; many mistakes in matching occur. Once these mistakes are made, they tend to be perpetuated indefinitely. Second, structural factors (such as unions, monopolies, and oligopolies) and norms (especially regarding gender roles at home and work) alter operation of the market to such an extent that inequities between males and females and between minorities and whites persist over extended periods. Although change occurs, it typically occurs sporadically—in a "lumpy" fashion. Internal labor markets are based on "implicit contracts" between employers and employees, and such implicit agreements frequently do not recognize and reward workers' productivity. They also tend to inhibit change.

England and Farkas (1986) argue that it is generally in the interest of employees and employers alike to maintain a fairly long-term relationship—in the interest of employees, for the sake of job security and to avoid the difficulties of finding a new job; in the interest of employers, to gain returns on their investments in developing the skills needed by employees for specific jobs in specific firms. In this employer-employee relationship, employers generally have more power because, if they need to, they can liquidate their capital holdings to cover living expenses. Workers seldom have enough savings or other resources to cover living expenses for long without a job. This imbalance of power, of course, depends greatly on the size of the employer, but in most cases a substantial imbalance exists in favor of the employer because loss of a single employee is of marginal significance to a large firm, but loss of a job usually is of critical importance to the worker.

Although the evidence is not conclusive, a general proposition appears to be consistent with it—that is, much of the process of allocating individuals to positions in school and at work is based on informal practices that derive from social norms and attitudes. In Granovetter's (1988) terms, the economy is "embedded" in a general social structure.

Allocation and socialization operate in concert to produce individuals who can function at least minimally well in their work roles. The connection between this process and production efficiency is indirect and probably far from optimum, but the evidence on this point is very incomplete (see Bishop, 1988). Race and gender stand as the two most visible nonefficiency criteria for allocating individuals into positions. Again, the evidence is incomplete, but institutional barriers encountered by blacks may reside more in the quality of their schooling than in their work settings. For women, the barriers are not so much related to the quantity or quality of schooling as to the type of schooling and the type of work. The types of schooling and work reserved for women lead to lower earnings. By contrast, blacks earn less primarily because they achieve less schooling. It is at least a good hypothesis, supported by limited but good evidence, that poor quality of early schooling is a primary factor in limiting the success of blacks in postsecondary education.

High School Tracking

One of the leading explanations of the influence of family status on years of schooling attained is that schools themselves are stratified into a sequence of tracks, the most prominent tracks being the college preparatory and the vocational. These tracks, and the process of distributing students among them, mirror the stratification system in the larger society (Rosenbaum, 1976). Thus, school structures are thought to play a key role in allocating youth into their adult positions.

The argument is that parental socioeconomic status has an influence on the selection of a pupil's ability group in elementary school. The parents' status and the pupil's ability-group placement influence the student's placement in a track in secondary school. Track placement then influences academic learning and the amount of education one completes. Those in the college-preparatory or academic track are most likely to continue their schooling after high school and least likely to drop out of high school before completion (Vanfossen, Jones, and Spade, 1987; Hotchkiss and Dorsten, 1987).

Rosenbaum (1976) provides the most articulate statement of the theoretical orientation underlying most research into the causes and consequences of tracking. He argues that a tracking system in schools mirrors the larger social system in microcosm, provides an important link between ascribed status and adult achievements, and influences the IQ scores of students in ways that tend to perpetuate the tracking system. His original formulation was based on a case study of a high school in Boston. His evidence regarding tracking's effects on IQ scores was derived from comparisons of changes in test scores among students in different tracks in the high school. Rosenbaum found that relegation to a nonacademic track led to discrimination in at least three forms: repeated insults from teachers, a diluted curriculum, and the application of a weighting system for computing class rank that practically eliminated any student who was not in the top two academic tracks from consideration for admission to college. Rosenbaum characterizes the process of tracking as an approximation to a "tournament." Most individuals start out in the running for higher education and good jobs, but the number of candidates is gradually pared down by a process roughly resembling a tournament. Many other observation-based studies also feature jaundiced descriptions of the operation of tracking, both in the United States and in Britain (Boyer, 1982; Cicourel and Kitsuse, 1963; Schafer and Olexa, 1971; Hargreaves, 1967; Oakes, 1985).

Quantitative studies of tracking have concluded that tracking does play a critical role in the transmission of status from parents to offspring (Alexander and McDill, 1976; Alexander, Cook, and McDill, 1978; Alexander and Cook, 1982; Alexander and Pallas, 1984; Garet and DeLany, 1988; Gamoran, 1987; Gamoran and Mare, 1989; Lee and Bryk, 1988; Vanfossen, Jones, and Spade, 1987). The evidence in these studies generally has not been entirely convincing, however, partly because of their pervasive reliance on students' self-reports of tracking, rather than on transcript data, and partly because of model misspecification. However, Hotchkiss and Dorsten (1987) do report a study based on data from a detailed transcript file, and they confirm the conclusions of many of the earlier studies. A few studies have concluded that tracking is not a very important school mechanism in the transmission of status between generations. These include Rehberg and Rosenthal (1978) and Hauser, Sewell, and Alwin (1976).

On balance, the evidence based on transcript data indicates that curriculum choices in high school probably do play a significant role in linking parents' socioeconomic status to their offspring's adult attainments, and that they often do operate in a substantially less than meritocratic fashion. However, we do not understand all the complex organizational arrangements that have loosely been termed *tracking*. Garet and DeLany (1988) argue that rules vary among schools in ways that cannot be captured by the questioning of students. They demonstrate large effects on enrollments in science and math courses, effects primarily due to differences among schools in graduation requirements. A recent major study of four large urban school systems (in New York, Chicago, Philadelphia, and Boston) concludes that administrative procedures for allocating students into selected high schools, and into specific curricula within high schools, operate to the great disadvantage of all but a select few students (Moore and Davenport, 1988). However, there are no standard labels for different tracks, and students as well as their parents are poorly informed about the nature of different curricula and the consequences of curriculum selections. The Moore and Davenport (1988) study is an important complement to previous work because it examines the role of administrative structures for a large sample. (These school systems contain 12 to 13 percent of the public school students in the nation.) In the past, examination of the impact of administrative procedures on outcomes for students generally has been conducted in the case-study format and in a few schools.

Implications for Career Guidance

As is apparent in the preceding review, sociologists examine work as a social institution. They pay little attention to the development of strategies for facilitating the career decision-making process and occupational adjustment of individuals. Although sociologists have paid some attention to issues related to occupational choice and career patterns (Gross, 1958; Form and Miller, 1962; Sheppard, 1973; Hansen, 1974), only rarely do they directly touch on the question of counseling, and one would be hard pressed to find the literature on career development psychology cited in the sociological literature on stratification and work.

Counselors may be perplexed by sociologists' persistent use of earnings and status as the most significant outcomes of the work experience, and by their commonly held view that the occupations in which people work are as much influenced by socially determined allocation mechanisms as by individual planning and rational choice. Counselors are certain to be skeptical of simplistic dichotomies of labor markets (primary versus secondary) and business firms (core versus periphery) to explain differences in the outcomes of work, but it is useful to view these descriptions as initial sensitizing hypotheses, rather than as definitive formulations. They do suggest the importance of resources in determining who works in what jobs and who receives what compensation, monetary or nonmonetary.

We conclude that—despite shortcomings in the specifics of the sociological work—the thematic content, research methodology, and substantive findings we have reviewed here carry broadly significant, if still largely unexploited, implications for the reconceptualization and practice of career counseling. The insights offered by sociological analysis of such problems as the complexity of the labor market, the role of structures (for example, among industries and firms in the job-sorting process), the influence of significant others (like parents) on career aspirations and decisions, the impact on youth of high school tracking, and the effects of gender and race bias—insights into all these problems carry important implications for the theory and practice of career counseling.

Career development psychologists and counseling practitioners are probably familiar with many of the sociological issues reviewed in this chapter, but it is not clear that they understand how the mechanisms involved operate to condition the thinking, job status, and career histories of individuals. In conceptualizing the career choice-making process as essentially one of rationally matching personal characteristics to the functional requirements of jobs, counselors customarily ignore the powerful influences that labor-market structures exercise over the reward system. Gottfredson's (1981) theory of occupational choice is an exception to the rule. It acknowledges—in fact emphasizes—the significance of gender content and occupational status in choice making, and it reflects the fact that individuals often recognize the importance of these factors in making their decisions.

In capsule form, the implications of sociology for career development theory and practice derive from two primary propositions. First, competition for positions in a stratified hierarchy determines the satisfaction and sense of well-being that people derive from work. The connection between this competition and the efficient matching of individuals to work functions is imprecise. Second, some individuals face structural barriers based on race, gender, and parental status that severely limit their capacity to achieve the most coveted positions. We have concluded that the jury is still out on much of the detailed theorizing in sociology, but there is enough evidence supporting these two broad propositions that they merit serious attention.

What lessons, then, might be learned by those in the career-counseling field from the insights garnered from contemporary sociological thought about work and occupations? Specific implications are limited, for two reasons. First, the sociological literature has not identified well-substantiated propositions that can easily be applied to counseling practice. Second, social factors (for example, gender stereotyping and racial discrimination), identified in the sociological literature as important determinants of the career paths of individuals, often lie outside the purview of counselors. What follows is not a set of specific rules for practice but rather a number of broad and flexible guidelines for reexamining the counseling task and generating strategies that counselees may use to cope with the social environment they encounter.

Informing Clients About the Labor Market. Counselees must be helped to understand something of the complexity of the world of work and the economic order. Success in one's career requires more than making a good person-to-job match. Students are frequently insulated against the work world, and they need help in assessing the difficulties they are likely to encounter in the labor market. A number of instances of how restrictive social conditions, market demands, and the occupational structure may impede occupational choice and career atttainment have been identified in our review. In the proper ways and at the proper times, counselees must be made aware of these structural constraints, and they must know that the world is often not fair. They will need to be provided with coping strategies, including rehearsals, to develop job-search strategies.

Providing Direct Advocacy. The counselor's responsibilities frequently extend beyond individual assessment, interviewing, and advice. Members of bypassed populations, particularly socioeconomically disadvantaged youth, do not know what community resources are available or how to use them. During the War on Poverty's federally sponsored programs of the mid to late 1960s, paraprofessional counselors learned that they could be most effective by interceding actively on behalf of clients with well-intentioned government and business agencies and by guiding their clients through the bureaucratic labyrinth. The recent study by Moore and Davenport (1988) presents evidence that this function of counselors may be a strategic one in nonselective urban schools; Moore and Davenport summarize the extensive paperwork required for admission to schools other than neighborhood schools.

Helping disadvantaged youth to negotiate the college admissions process and applications for financial aid is an additional example of a potentially important function. Students whose parents are well informed about such procedures and help them to complete the necessary applications are more likely to escape the mediocre education they otherwise would be likely to encounter. Counselors should again be encouraged to consider constructive intervention when barriers loom that bewildered clients cannot surmount unaided.

Combating Gender Stereotyping. Deeply rooted socialization processes perpetuate rigid sex-role perceptions that limit career options. This chapter has presented evidence to show that, despite important gains, gender inequities regarding occupational segregation, job segregation, earnings, rank, and job responsibility remain pervasive. Job segregation is particularly extreme. Teachers are often the unwitting purveyors of sex-role stereotypes concerning educational and occupational options; here, counselors can be helpful by familiarizing teachers and other agents of socialization with the trend toward gender-neutral occupations.

Tittle (1982) offers five recommendations for improving the effectiveness of career guidance with women: (1) counter the "hidden curriculum" on sex roles, (2) critically examine traditional gender roles, (3) stress the importance of education to women as strongly as to males, (4) assist youth to develop a realistic understanding of earnings and occupational differences between the sexes, and (5) improve counselors' knowledge of research on gender effects in the labor market. To Tittle's list may be added the planned use of successful feminine role models, a technique that has been shown to be highly effective in emboldening young women to choose career objectives traditionally followed by men. Tangri (1972) published one of the earliest studies showing that mothers' occupations outside the home are instrumental in kindling women's nontraditional career aspirations.

Boys have a more restricted range of acceptable gender-related behaviors than girls do, according to Hayes (1986). Males who choose to enter occupations that are sex-typed for women are more likely to report job dissatisfaction than those who select conventionally male occupations. Although it is obvious that counselors should not discourage the choice of vocational goals that are sexually nontraditional, they must be sure to counsel their clients about the difficulties they are likely to encounter, and they should discuss possible coping strategies.

Reducing Racial and Ethnic Barriers. As we have seen, neither status attainment theory nor human capital theory provides a good accounting of discrimination against minority-group members. Even when parental status and education are controlled for, a disproportionate number of minority workers are seen to be concentrated toward the lower end of the occupational achievement and earnings scale. In contrast to gender inequity, however, the quality of early schooling appears to be an important factor in racial inequity.

Empirical evidence nevertheless clearly favors the conclusion that race, like gender, continues to produce direct effects on status outcomes. An examination of employment data from labor-market structures yields corroborative findings. For example, although no great differences exist between black and white racial representations in either the core or the periphery market, there is a marked disparity favoring whites in positions held (Hall, 1986). We have also seen this effect with respect to class and authority in the data presented by Parcel and Mueller (1983), describing the impacts of authority and business ownership (employer versus worker) on earnings. That family effects are more important than educational effects for the occupational allocation of black males points to the operation of discrimination, according to Featherman and Hauser (1976). However, Featherman and Hauser also found that the combination of family and education effects on the status outcomes of blacks is beginning to resemble that for whites. In general, affirmative action regulations and educational programs have gradually reduced the extent of employment discrimination. Work is carried out chiefly in institutions, however, and since institutions are resistant to rapid change, progress toward equity has been slow (Hall, 1986).

For minority youth, racial and ethnic bias in the job market exerts a two-way adverse influence. It restricts merit-based opportunity for employment and career advancement, and teenagers' awareness of it may also lead them to expect job failure. Although this is certainly not true of all minority youth, many do acquire a perception of the outside world that they will soon enter as essentially unmanageable. They are frequently burdened by negative self-images, feelings of inadequacy as workers-to-be, and disbelief in the efficacy of rational career planning. Unable to accommodate the notion that work may actually be pleasant and psychologically rewarding, they may make, at best, tenuous emotional commitments to their first jobs. Short-term monetary return is frequently the only aim they attach to work.

Evidence is strong that the individual's and society's failure to deal early and effectively with such unrewarding school-to-work transition experiences may lead to protracted work-related difficulties. The early labor-market records of school-leaving teenagers and young adults are often prognostic of the dubious quality of their long-term career histories. For youths whose work entry is a negative and unsettling experience, episodes of chronic joblessness and underemployment are common consequences.

There is, of course, no simple formula for countering the effects of the formidable array of unfavorable conditions identified above, but counselors must at least begin by recognizing their presence and confronting them boldly. A number of general intervention strategies have been tried, with moderate success. Primary among these are inducing youth to remain in school and providing the type of flexible curriculum and reward system that make scholastic persistence possible. Individual and group counseling in building ego strength and in setting realistic goals is often helpful. For racial and minority youth especially, access to teachers, counselors, and successful role models of similar background can be a potent factor in behavioral change. A recreational or community service agency may sometimes be more effective in reaching minority youth on their own terms than a counselor, who may be seen as an unwelcome symbol of school authority. Unfavorable attitudes toward counselors may be particularly acute when counselors are called on to act as enforcers of school rules. Also helpful are guided and monitored job-training experiences like those formerly provided by the Youth Opportunity Centers and currently provided by voluntary agencies like the Opportunities Industrialization Centers.

The long-held view that opportunity for part-time paid work is in itself beneficial to the personal adjustment and career development of in-school youth, including minority youth, is now seriously questioned by some authorities. Summarizing their own studies and those of other researchers, Greenberger and Steinberg (1986, p. 235) conclude that the jobs typically held by today's teenagers "do not generally provide environments conducive to psychological growth and development," nor have they been shown to clarify occupational identity or forge links to full-time career objectives. Work during enrollment in high school does, however, appear to produce a small positive effect on the wages of the jobs obtained right after high school. Nevertheless, we cannot be certain that these unfruitful consequences of part-time work hold true for minority teenagers, since Green-berger and Steinberg's (1986) subjects were mainly middle-class white youths.

Counseling approaches to assisting minority youth with problems of career planning and choice are of three general types: (1) optimizing the chances for completion of schooling, (2) strengthening the work-related attitudes, information, and skills of clients, and (3) aiding clients directly in contacting and using relevant community resources. Given the findings of Dreeben and Gamoran (1986), one important focal point in help-ing blacks to be successful in high school and postsecondary schooling is to improve the quality of their elementary schools. This is a difficult mandate, but it deserves continued attention.

Although occupational sociologists may not quarrel seri-ously with these approaches, they would probably contend that counseling strategies do not directly come to grips with the prin-cipal impediment to satisfactory choice making among racial and ethnic minorities. In the sociological view, institutionalized bias is so pervasive and potent a factor in the assignment of jobs that any real hope for significant change lies much less in in-dividual interventions than in the reform of prevailing employ-ment practices. It is the "gatekeepers," the employers, whose "socially imposed criteria are the basis of actions that allocate people into particular careers" (Rothman, 1987, p. 255).

Raising Educational Aspirations. As this chapter sum-marizes, status attainment research has consistently documented the close relationship between (1) the number of years of school-ing one completes and the status level of one's parents, and (2) the number of years of schooling one completes and one's own success at work. It has become evident that insufficient educa-tional credentials are now pivotal in the exclusion of job seekers from full-time work. Recent surveys reveal that in the United States the unemployment rate among those who lack a high school diploma is more than double that among diploma holders and approximately six times that among college graduates (Bu-reau of the Census, 1987). A recent study of subjects between sixteen and twenty-four years old concludes that, among young

adults without a college degree, job opportunities are shrink-
ing, real earnings are declining, prospects for unemployment
are greater, and marriage is frequently delayed because of financial pressures (Commission on Youth and America's Future,
1988).

It is not clear whether the increasingly heightened educational standards for employment genuinely reflect higher demands for knowledge and skills in a new wave of technologically
sophisticated occupations or whether employers now set more
stringent qualifications because they can choose among a larger
pool of college-trained applicants. Whatever the explanation,
effective career counseling requires counselors to become more
fully aware of the critical importance of formal education to
future job opportunities. It is especially urgent that counselors
convey this message to minority and lower-socioeconomic-status
youth from families that lack tradition of college going and that
may even devalue higher education. A large share of the
estimated twenty million young Americans who do not include
college attendance in their plans are from this disadvantaged
sector of the youth population.

Almost thirty years ago, the sociologist Samuel Stouffer
called attention to the powerful effects of class status on providing educational opportunity for career advancement to some
but not to others. As a means of redressing this inequity, Stouffer
designed and published *Your Educational Plans* (Borow and Super,
1960), a device to assist counselors in identifying such variables
as family background and aspiration level that critically influence
the decision to go to college but that are often slighted in conventional guidance. A variety of similar methods have since been
introduced to raise the educational aims of youth who might
otherwise lag behind in the competition for high-status occupations and high earnings.

That disadvantaged young Americans themselves often
correctly assess the unfavorable odds is suggested by studies that
show a substantially greater gap between the educational expectations and occupational expectations of disadvantaged youth
than observed for other youth. A study by McNair and Brown
(1983) found that among black tenth graders the career maturity
(Attitude Scale of the Career Maturity Inventory) deemed neces-

sary to implement educational and vocational plans was below that of white tenth graders of similar aspiration levels. Most school counselors, of course, are aware of this problem, but they often face obstacles in attempting to alleviate it. The users of school counseling services are predominantly students from middle-class and upper-class families, who have made an early commitment to college planning (Ekstrom and Lee, 1986). Furthermore, the social supports and economic resources of minority and low-socioeconomic-status students are too often not conducive to building and sustaining college aspirations.

Familiarity with such social and economic issues expands the practicing counselor's understanding of how demographic characteristics, restrictive social conditions, and structural properties of the labor market may impede suitable occupational choice and career attainment. The informed counselor is then more readily disposed to venture beyond the conventional personal traits–job requirements model of matching and to prepare clients to deal more appropriately with the realities of the labor market. Counselors should also be encouraged to enlist the assistance of resources beyond the counseling office and the classroom in raising the educational aspirations of students. Repeated analysis of survey data has shown that parents as well as peers influence the educational expectation levels of youth. Accordingly, the counselor's systematic use of social support networks and role models is a recommended strategy. In particular, counselors skilled in family-systems counseling should find this approach helpful to their task.

The dilemma faced by counselors in dealing with the educational plans of blacks is acute. Blacks already have higher educational expectations than whites do, and so it does not seem that raising their expectations even higher would be effective. Their already high expectations need to be combined with improved learning. As we have seen, serious progress in this regard may require attention that begins in the early grades.

Conclusions

The sociological framework for analyzing career paths of individuals considers the interplay between individual choices and the constraints on those choices imposed by the labor market. However, recent sociological work has emphasized the labor-market constraints. In this review, we also have emphasized the importance of structural constraints on individual choice, partly to reflect sociological theory and research and partly to complement the traditional emphasis among career development theorists and practitioners on individual choice processes.

Certainly, the current status of empirical evidence regarding operation of the labor market leaves room for skepticism, but it is important to maintain a balanced perspective in this regard. There are two points here that are important to remember. First, most sociologists probably would contend that one's lifelong sense of achievement and rewards garnered from work depend more on occupational status, earnings, and insulation from employers' arbitrary exercise of power than on such factors as matching of interests, values, and abilities with the functional demands of jobs. In this respect, sociologists are joined by at least one prominent theorist in the career development literature (Gottfredson, 1981). Ultimately, of course, this is an empirical question, and a definitive answer has yet to be achieved.

Second, simplified theories of the labor market introduce parsimony that probably is useful, at least as an initial strategy, for helping to understand how the market works. Typically, early theory in any discipline is excessively simplistic. Improvements are made gradually, in response to criticism and debate. For example, few sociologists today would defend the claim that the labor market and the economy can be divided naturally into two corresponding segments. However, important ideas in dualist theory are retained in the most recent theorizing. These include the basic insight that labor markets are not homogeneous, as well as insights into the absence of perfect competition in setting wages, the influence of resources in the conflict between employers and employees regarding distribution of the income produced from work, and the persistence of institutionalized inequities even in the face of competitive pressures to eliminate them.

Finally, we most emphatically do not want to convey a message of fatalism. The sociological work does not imply that individuals are helpless against overwhelming inequities and rigidities, but only that very real constraints do operate. We believe that the central tenet of the counseling profession — that individuals must act energetically on their own behalf — is fundamental to responsible practice. The sociological perspective does, however, indicate that the content of guidance practice should be broadened beyond the traditional emphasis on functional matching between individuals and positions in the labor market. In addition to assisting youth in formulating their occupational plans, career guidance should actively promote the development of coping strategies in youth for surmounting the barriers that youth are likely to encounter.

Anna Miller-Tiedeman
David V. Tiedeman

9

Career Decision Making: An Individualistic Perspective

Our approach to career decision making is a response to the need we perceive to expand the horizons of previously mapped dimensions of career development and decision-making processes. In past years, career theorists have presented theories of how individuals end up in particular occupations, jobs, or careers. But career theorists have often neglected the essence of the individual's life processes in career development, particularly those of growth, choice, willingness and capacity to adapt and change, and continued self-exploration and self-renewal.

All these essential individual life processes are as much a part of the career development phenomenon as are the occupations themselves in which an individual may work from time to time. Choosing one realm or another depends on what one wants to do. Since our responsibility in this chapter is to deal with career decision making, we will be dealing with those

The late Professor Robert P. O'Hara contributed much to the design of our metaphorical vessel, *Decision Making*. Doctors Lee Joyce Richmond, Betty Bosdell, and Anita Mitchell helped us materially through discussion, suggestion, and editing.

essential individual life processes in the career, not with the chosen occupation itself; other chapters in this book deal with the chosen occupation. Of course, one can deal with both the occupation chosen and the process of decision making in the career. That is what one does when one is interested in generalizing a special-purpose theory and making it a more general-purpose, or unified, theory. That is the purpose to which the Tiedeman and O'Hara (1963) theory of career decision making has led us. Since change in paradigm is a natural development in science, we share some of our voyage on the seas of a unified theory of career development in concluding this chapter.

The occupational slant that dominated career theory in the latter part of the nineteenth century and all of the twentieth century so far proves understandable in relation to the history of natural science in that period. Early career theories emerged during the height of the then-popular Newtonian-Cartesian perspective in psychological life in the late nineteenth and early twentieth centuries, in the industrial era. Those theories tended to be mechanistic and dualistic, not holistic; when viewed as absolute and complete in themselves, they never seriously addressed the role and process of personal choice and decision making in career development.

We do not advocate discarding all previous career theories; instead, we have incorporated into our design of *Decision Making* those models of career development that are available to us today.

We propose that various aspects of the existing career models (such as those in this book) may be used to foster the career development process. These models complement rather than replace each other. This is the premise that led us to conceive of the metaphor of the sailing vessel *Decision Making*. We think of career as part of an exciting journey, rather than as a goal-oriented drudgery that is imposed on individuals by society. In an attempt to foster this attitude in the reader, we have viewed the lifecareer process as analogous to an expedition on open seas. Just as the horizons are seemingly infinite at sea, we view the career process as an ongoing process of growth and change, of evolution that is limitless. Just as a ship's captain can map navigational routes, using the stars, the wind, and sea currents, the individual can make career choices based on nature, social opportunities, and personal inclinations. Just as the sea currents and wind present unforeseen changes so that the captain must make navigational adaptations in the vessel's course, so must individuals adapt to changing natural circumstances and remain flexible. In so doing, the individual acts in the lifecareer process. "And sailing ships unlike bulldozers do no damage to the sea, land or sky while employing the wind-power without any depletion of the vast wealth of universal energy" (Fuller, 1972, p. 56). The individual, therefore, realizes that *lifecareer* is personal power in the renewable resources of life.

The Theory

Super's 1953 self-concept model falls short of being a complete model of personal development. The propositions on which it was based focused on external factors (others, society), rather than the internal characteristics of the individual. Tiedeman and O'Hara gradually noted this absence of individual purpose in Super's 1953 model of career development. They therefore set out to design *Decision Making* to link person to career through the concepts of personality and individual responsibility. They designed the processes of differentiation and integration in decision making into their vessel's hull in *Career Development: Choice and Adjustment* (1963).

While attempting to make the individual the captain of the sailing vessel *Decision Making,* Tiedeman and O'Hara introduced two restraints on career. First, they introduced the following "institutionalized" restraint on the career: "The career affords both opportunity for expression of hope and desire and limitation upon life. In America, we expect that the career is an institutionalized means for exercise of the thrust of personal advantage (comprehensiveness), as modified by acceptance of responsibility for action" (Tiedeman and O'Hara, 1963, p. iv).

Tiedeman and O'Hara imposed this restraint because at that time they accepted the tenets of "other directedness" in Super's 1953 self-concept model of vocational development.

However, they chose Erikson's (1959) psychosocial theory of ego identity as the developmental framework for understanding the many differentiations and reintegrations individuals experience during career development, thereby putting this "other directedness" into a dynamic framework. According to Erikson (1959, p. 102), "It is this identity of something in the individual's core with an essential aspect of a group's inner coherence which is under consideration here: for the young individual must learn to be most himself where he means most to others — those others, to be sure, who have come to mean most to him."

The other, more limiting, restraint Tiedeman and O'Hara placed on careers in their 1963 hull design was that "career development refers to those aspects of the continuous unbroken flow of a person's experience that are of relevance to (personal) fashioning of an identity 'at work.' The term *career development* is a linguistic representation of aspects of experience. The primary terms of this linguistic representation are those of the person developing vocationally. The scientist must fashion an overarching language in order to develop a science of career development" (Tiedeman and O'Hara, 1963, p. 2).

Although deliberately leaving leeway to define *work* as other than paid employment, the above meaning of *career* was still limited to the "vocational" in Tiedeman and O'Hara's design.

The "vocational" does connote "calling" for some persons. Tiedeman and O'Hara did not, however, invoke this somewhat religious and ordinarily other-directed meaning of *vocation* in considering career development. They dealt strictly with the activities with which persons intentionally occupied their time. However, Tiedeman and O'Hara did foresee our present treatment of life being the career developing because they dealt not solely with the *making of a living;* they dealt also with the *making of a life*. But their psychosocial model did not relax either the "institutionalized" emphasis on defining "the group's inner coherence" (group, as in one's different important reference groups) or the "vocational" emphasis in career.

Experience, Cognition, and Language. Language merely represents experience; language is not actual experience. Language thereby imposes its fragmenting nature on movement in our world views (Bohm, 1980). However, in momentarily stopping the continuous flow of experience, language does permit an examination of experience in symbolic reality, which individuals can keep relatively objective if they wish. But the encapsulation of experience in language is like having only a bucketful of brook water to analyze and to evaluate (Weitz, 1961); the bucketful of water is not the brook itself. For this reason, in designing *Decision Making*'s hull, Tiedeman and O'Hara allowed both for events experienced and for the meaning of those events for the person experiencing them.

Differentiation and Reintegration. Tiedeman and O'Hara noted that career development grows out of a continuously differentiating and reintegrating ego identity as it forms and reforms from experience as a self-organizing system. Differentiating is a matter of separating experiences; integrating is a matter of structuring them into a more comprehensive whole. Hierarchical restructuring is what happens when a new and more comprehensive whole is formed from the continuous separating and merging that go on daily and momentarily with each of us. This act of separating and joining together again continually enlarges the wholeness of ourselves. It may be that individuals who fail to experience this separating or the joining experience tend to have less explicit self-contexts simply because they have not had the opportunity to create larger wholes of themselves. If things go well, we have little cause to differentiate. Therefore, reintegration does not occur, and hierarchical restructuring (forming a more comprehensive framework) does not happen. This is especially true when we feel that experiencing uncertainty is too risky or scary. For example, when we have grown accustomed to a certain familiar life pattern (relationship or occupation) that is comfortable or tolerable, then taking a step to make a change in that pattern when the outcome is uncertain may be too risky for the individual who places a high priority on security and stability in constancy and sameness. It is crucial that we take note of the high price paid to maintain this so-called security and stability. Often, we miss opportunities to differentiate and reintegrate within a larger context.

Although differentiation and reintegration may be separated logically, they are not separate in experience. For instance, integration cannot be achieved without prior differentiation. Tiedeman and O'Hara thus presumed that adequate reintegration requires adequate differentiation; differentiation does not invariably result in adequate reintegration.

Tiedeman and O'Hara noted that differentiation originates in various ways. One way is to consider a choice. Experiencing a choice triggers the onset of rational differentiation. The individual becomes aware that his or her present situation is unsatisfactory or is likely to become unsatisfactory.

For example, a counselor experiences job burnout. In addition, she learns that, because of decreasing enrollments, she may not even be employed next year. In either case, the counselor faces a decision, which can be divided into (1) anticipation or preoccupation and (2) implementation or accommodation. Anticipatory behavior may be divided into four steps: (1) exploration (awareness), (2) crystallization (of something), (3) choice (felt being), and (4) clarification (objectification).

During exploration, the counselor may enquire into new job possibilities or consider new ways to create work. The counselor may then talk with people about this, read everything available, check out new possibilities, visit potential workplaces, conduct information interviews, and think about new places to live. In short, the counselor may explore the many aspects of the employment scene. As patterns begin to emerge in the form of alternatives and their consequences, crystallization starts. In crystallization, the counselor would order and consider the information gathered. After the facts crystallize for the counselor, choice becomes easy. The counselor begins to organize and to clarify in preparation for implementation — the counselor is ready to carry out the decision, thereby resolving her burnout.

The second major aspect of the person's decision, the implementation, may involve three steps: (1) induction, (2) reformation, and (3) reintegration. In our burnout example, the counselor would begin to work (induction), feel good about doing it, get proficient in it, and advocate the choice (reformation). For a while, she might believe that everyone needs to be doing what she is doing, but, after a while, the worker gains perspective (reintegration). Each step of the anticipatory and accommodative aspects is further analyzed in the Tiedeman and O'Hara monograph. We illustrate the steps in Figure 9.1 for easy reference.

Each step in this paradigm represents a distinction or change in the person's psychological condition as he or she resolves a career decision. One need not take the steps in ascending order. Some steps may occur simultaneously. In addition, a person may not even be aware of his or her status on the chart at any given time. And, of course, life direction can be changed at any time, so reversibility is taken for granted.

Because each step represents a discrete change in psychological state, the quality of each decision is different at each stage. A change takes place in the person in each step, but the change can be so small that it is not noticed. A person is the whole of all earlier decisions, and each step alters the character of the considerations with regard to a previous step. For instance, as crystallization (focused awareness) occurs, the person can dismiss earlier alternatives and possible considerations.

Tiedeman and O'Hara separated the seven steps in their scheme. The changes they described were neither instantaneous nor irreversible. They represent this two-way or reversible process by double arrows. A person's ability to make a clear, rational choice can move ahead at any point, or the person's wish to change may dissolve. It is also likely that a person's career development may skip around on the scale, but a person's career normally moves forward in comprehensivity, toward unity. Therefore, the advancing arrow is longer and dominant.

This completes our presentation of Tiedeman and O'Hara's decision model concerning the processes of differentiation and reintegration in reaching rational career solutions. They noted that the self initially remains relatively withdrawn from the solution process. The mind — at this beginning point — attempts to introduce awareness into the consciousness by introducing some new visions. Then follow the steps of crystallization (an awareness of something), choice (feeling being), and clarification (objectification).

Figure 9.1. A Paradigm of the Processes of Differentiation and Integration in Deciding.

Time

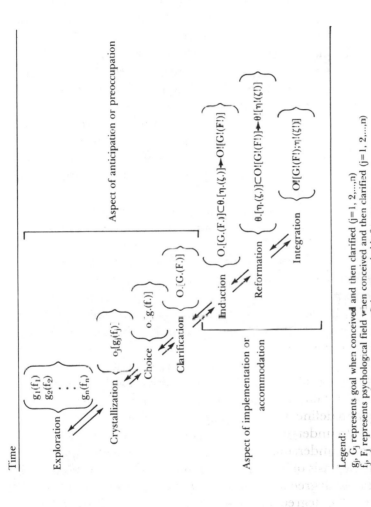

Legend:

g_j, G_j represents goal when conceived and then clarified ($j = 1, 2, ..., n$)

f_j, F_j represents psychological field when conceived and then clarified ($j = 1, 2, ..., n$)

η (the analogue of g) represents goal the group holds for person

ζ (the analogue of F) represents the psychological field defined by the group

o_j, O_j represents organization as conceived and then clarified

θ_j represents the analogue of O_j in the group, that is, the cumulative effect of the O_j's of the group members.

Source: Tiedeman and O'Hara, 1963, p. 40.

The last step in this process is accommodation. In induction, the self first participates in the solution process adaptively. During reformation, we abandon self to our chosen dominant social group's purposes. Finally, in the step of reintegration, the person again attains a certain objectivity about group purpose and self. New awareness then regains primacy for a while. Having mastered the fragmentation of self, the whole of consciousness again takes over, but at this new energy level.

Career development occurs not only within the context of one decision but also as the result of multiple decisions. Crystallization of the first goal leads to an initial organization (for example, a first job). Next, a person can move on toward tentative crystallizations concerning a second goal, a third goal, and so on. In fact, we might consider several decisions about several possible goals.

How an individual makes decisions can influence his or her actions with regard to (1) a particular decision now in progress, (2) earlier decisions whose drama may not yet be played out, and (3) later decisions that are either being considered or are not yet fulfilled. Similarly, experience related to present and prior decisions influences development of later events. Considering one's past experiences and imagining future experiences are most important to the concept of self in the stages of crystallization and reintegration.

The use of Tiedeman and O'Hara's model of differentiation and reintegration can help one to understand the organization of self and environment. This construction helps a person to assess and define his or her career direction. It also helps the individual to understand the basis of this career direction. This basis and its understanding are the career identity. By understanding the basis of how an individual defines her or his career, we locate the degree of openness a person has toward a change of career. The degree of openness is a function of the person's belief system.

Tiedeman and O'Hara held that the aim of vocational counseling is to help persons better understand the dynamic process of career development. This process frees the person to make and act upon a particular decision, as well as to view other possible decisions. With this model, students can see their educational and vocational decisions as a means-end chain; that which is an end at an earlier time may become a means for a later goal. Behavior thereby becomes more understandably general and purposeful; personal evaluations of life actions become more meaningful. A more comprehensive and incisive elaboration of self results. No goal must be so compelling that it destroys judgment in situations of conflicting goals. Any goal can give way to a later, more fulfilling goal.

The evolution of ego identity is a process (1) of a successively more complex differentiation of attitude toward self and environment and (2) of search for integration of experience at more and more comprehensive levels through successive identifications and acceptances. In Erikson's (1959) psychosocial theory of ego development, which Tiedeman and O'Hara adapted to ground their career model, differentiation occurs in relation to persons, things, and ideas, not to perceived wholeness. However, in Tiedeman and O'Hara's theory, reintegrations in personality occur when workable propositions interact to link the continuously differentiated elements of one's experience. Each new whole so emerging in this successive differentiation process cannot be predicted from any part considered separately. Acceptance and reward "fix" these emerging organizations of self and environment.

Because of the commonness of differentiation in their two thought systems, Tiedeman and O'Hara suggested career connections with each of Erikson's eight psychosocial crisis resolutions: trust, autonomy, initiative, industry, identity, intimacy, generativity, and integrity over a life span that includes the stages of infancy, early childhood, play age, school age, adolescence, young adulthood, and the mature age, respectively.

Time and Occupation in the Career. Attitudes and language form in examined experience. Experience results from activity and reflection on one's condition before, during, and after the activity. It takes time to act and to think. It is difficult to consider or undertake two or more things simultaneously because the momentary span of human attention is finite and small. For instance, Simon (1981) claims that the attention-processing part of human memory is capable of processing only four chunks of information simultaneously. These aspects of the human condition require the rational person to fit the personal career into life through the decision process. Decision becomes essential for psychologically manageable limitation of infinite possibilities and thereby makes time important to career development because one's lifetime gradually expires while many possibilities always remain unexplored.

Tiedeman and O'Hara therefore considered quite directly the matter of time limitation of the career. They contended that, to most people, occupation is mere "work" and that the time in which work is practiced in a person's life is boundless. Obviously, neither of these assumptions is a necessary or accurate one. In its root meaning, *occupation* includes thinking, sitting, playing, or myriad activities that may claim attention. Furthermore, the practice of one activity does preclude the practice of another, to some extent at least; the day, the week, the year, the life are each finite. To study the occupancy of time, therefore, is to study the investment or use of time by the main activity of living. With some people, observable allocation of time to activity may be utterly impulsive; such people are largely responsive to the contingencies of living, not to their life intuitions. Other people may treasure time more; for them, time occupancy is to be planned, to have a desired yield. Tiedeman and O'Hara therefore contend that the subject of time occupancy offers a means of organizing the study of wholeness of career development as an analysis of the investment of time.

Obviously, the variety of combinations of activity and awareness that may occupy attention in a particular period of time is extensive. Furthermore, patterns of time occupancy change with age. Physical and mental capacities inflict their mark on the pattern. Intent, plan, and organization of self further individualize time occupancy. Kinds of activities and awareness lend further complexity to the variety of patterns. Tiedeman and O'Hara considered these and other variations in both the biological and the sociocultural realms.

Tiedeman and O'Hara noted that the evolving cognitive

map of relevance for work-career development is further differentiated by the staging of study and work permitted in this country.
The staging of study and work gives rise to a series of choices, and
they in turn imprint vocational development. Tiedeman and
O'Hara referred to the options available in school and work as
positions. They did so because they sought a general word that
permits articulation with the language of sociology without buying
its adaptive insistence on the necessary adoption of roles. In their
lexicon, *position choices* are just another means of further differentiating structures-in-interaction on a personal basis.

Position choices (for example, part-time jobs, courses, initial jobs) in the work career can occur at any instant after attainment of legal working age and prior to retirement from work.
There are times when a work-position choice must occur and
other times when it can occur. In the first case, the situation
is defined externally; in the second, internally. The forces of
relevance to the process of position choice are related to the
discontinuity discussed by Hottel (1955, pp. 4–5, 8, 20, 31).
The vocationally relevant position choices inherent in these
several discontinuities in 1963 included:

1. Selection of part-time employment while in school and
   afterward
2. Selection of subjects to be taken in junior high school
3. Selection of subjects to be taken in high school
4. Selection of a college
5. Selection of a program of study in college
6. Selection of a graduate school
7. Selection of a program of study in graduate school
8. Selection of an armed service
9. Selection of a specialty in an armed service
10. Selection of a first full-time position
11. Selection of subsequent positions when dissatisfaction arises
    over a former position
12. Retirement

The discontinuities and position choices now need updating.

Defining Reality. Miller-Tiedeman and Tiedeman postulated that awareness of one's decision making in the career is
related to the advancement of the career. Furthermore, they contended that how one advances one's career can be seen in the
language one uses; they proposed that the language people use
about their careers mirrors the self, as both a reactor and an
actor, and discloses personal assumptions about the career.

One of the first tasks Miller-Tiedeman and Tiedeman
undertook in considering language in career was to define *reality.*
The phrase "That is not realistic" gets uttered frequently in career
talk. When anyone suggests, "That is not realistic," she or he
is imposing a view on another individual. However, we—each
of us—actually know our own minds and experience better than
anyone else can ever know them. Hence, no one else can know
our minds and experiences enough to comment on them and
call them inaccurate with any high degree of accuracy. "Unreal"
is what one person calls the seemingly impossible thoughts of
another person.

To relieve reality of this potential other-authoritative
burdensomeness, Miller-Tiedeman and Tiedeman (1979) defined
two kinds of reality: personal and common. If people are to advance the development of their careers, each person has to become conscious of the difference between those two realities.
Such consciousness gives individuals a choice of realities to
follow. Making such a choice and keeping straight what is chosen
illuminate life purpose more clearly for the individual.

Personally authoritative reality is defined as an act, thought,
behavior, or direction that the individual feels is right for her
or him, even though someone else may advise that it will never
work. If you *feel* your chosen direction is right for you, then honor
that *feeling.* It will be right for you.

Common reality is what "they" say you should do. For
example, "They say if you don't get a good education, you cannot get a good job." But education never ensures anyone a good
job or any job. And still the "theys" in the world cling to this
myth.

As Miller-Tiedeman brought Tiedeman to appreciate her
major tenet and to realize its absence in his previous works

(Tiedeman and O'Hara, 1963), we (Miller and Tiedeman, 1972) first generalized two models in Tiedeman's heritage — "the language" that Tiedeman and O'Hara had used to describe personal reality in career development, and the "machine" and decision-making development "language" that Ellis and Tiedeman had used in constructing the ISVD (Information System for Vocational Decisions) with others (Tiedeman, 1979a). We generalized the two into a language that holds for individuals when they tackle the problems involved in making their language and action consistent with regard to their career decision making. Comprehension of the "rightness" of one's personal reality arises from the evolution of consistency in one's words and actions. Mastery of this comprehension process gradually enables learners to generalize the content of career decision making in specific career decisions into the process of living a decision-guided life. An individual thereby becomes more proactive instead of reactive. Our experience led us to assume that three basic steps were involved in this comprehension process: (1) problem condition, (2) psychological state, and (3) self-comprehension. For convenience, we arranged the three steps we postulated on each of the three dimensions of a cube (Figure 9.2).

This Miller and Tiedeman cubistic model of decision making schematizes the grammar of the language needed to understand self (primacy of personal reality) in the decision-making process (comprehended common reality). In this grammar, the language of decision making is vicarious while the person is using the decision-making stages as she or he works on a particular problem. The language becomes an object of analysis as the person acts on the final decision. The person goes beyond language to meaning in completing the action. Later, the outcome of the decision may be reviewed for possible different future action.

In considering the objectification of personal reality, remember that the Figure 9.2 model is different from what we ordinarily understand theory to be in psychology. Ours is not a theory that allows another to predict the behavior of a subject (common reality); rather, ours is a value-functioning model that allows a person to put his or her own decision-making activity into perspective for himself or herself (personal reality). The

Figure 9.2. Miller and Tiedeman
Cubistic Model of Decision Making.

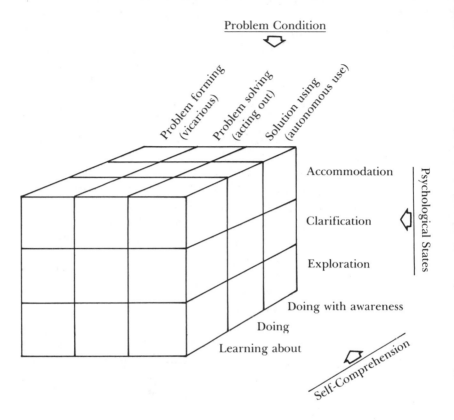

Source: Adapted from Miller and Tiedeman, 1972, p. 10.

model is therefore merely a description of what may be internally experienced during decision making. However, as the individual comes to understand what occurs as he or she thinks,
while acting on information from the common reality, she or
he will have the capacity to be proactive. With this kind of
awareness and confidence, the personal reality will then reign
over the common reality.

As Miller-Tiedeman experimented with the cubistic grammar, it proved to be more complicated than adolescents (the
group on which the cubistic grammar has primarily been tried)

could accommodate, and so she simplified it for use by adolescents by reducing the cube to a pyramid.

She then moved to simplify the cubistic grammar of developed comprehension of decision-making development. Miller-Tiedeman first chose the decision-making strategies derived by Dinklage (1969) as the basis for helping adolescents identify their decision-making habits or strategies. Miller-Tiedeman and Niemi's (1977) adaptation of those styles is noted at upper right of the pyramid in Figure 9.3. Six of the eight styles are essentially deciding-not-to-act styles. Only the Planned and Analytical styles are essentially deciding-to-act styles.

Miller-Tiedeman then designed a number of instructional materials and techniques that she used to help adolescents comprehend their decision-making behavior. They first learned decision-making strategies and then progressed to understanding the different parts of a decision (levels).

The Miller-Tiedeman pyramidal model of decision making presumes that Wilson's (1971) Level 1, Learning About, requires more thought, since it includes the Tiedeman and O'Hara decision-making stages of exploration, crystallization, choice, and clarification. It involves thinking about what might influence or determine the final decision. Wilson's Level 2, Beginning to Act, is that part of the process where action starts on the final decision. A student enters this level with a less thoughtful decision strategy, as well as a more thoughtful one, which might include going through all the Tiedeman and O'Hara stages. At Wilson's Level 3, the individual carries out what she or he has begun in Level 2, whereas Wilson's Level 4 envisages a review, where the individual considers possible redefinition and potential recycling. The broken lines in Figure 9.3 indicate that the Wilson levels are not discrete but flow into each other, as happens in all self-organizing systems.

Empirical and Other Support

Tiedeman and O'Hara designed the hull of *Decision Making* to fulfill an observation that the educational or occupational group chosen proved to be related more to personality than to

Figure 9.3. Miller-Tiedeman Pyramidal
Model of Decision-Making Comprehension.

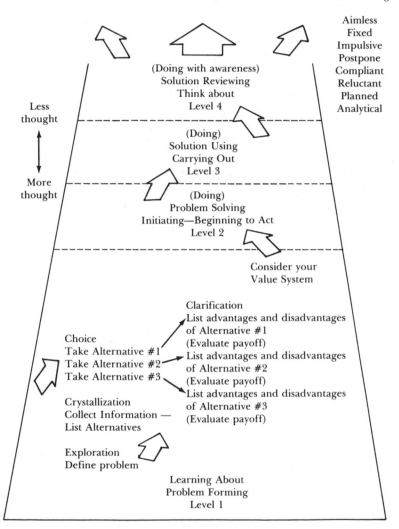

Source: Adapted from Miller-Tiedeman, 1977b, p. 141.

abilities and aptitudes; that is, the research indicated that abilities
and aptitudes did make a difference in how well a person did
in an educational or occupational group, but personality, values,

and interests, more than abilities and aptitudes, influenced what a person actually did (not how well the person did in the elected option).

In 1963, Tiedeman and O'Hara knew that the concepts they had designed into *Decision Making*'s hull were fully intended to deal with the missing personal presence (that is, personality, values, and interests) in educational and occupational decision making. Furthermore, the concepts seemed strong enough to bring the study of educational and career development from the slough into which it had slipped since the lift Roe, Holland, Ginzberg and associates, and Super had earlier given the field in the 1950s. Was the *Decision Making* concept of power sufficient to shift the career development models then in vogue?

Several investigators have sailed on several brief voyages with *Decision Making* since her launching in 1963. Those who sailed her on such trials have been of two kinds: (1) those who took only excursions on her and now use her programmatically, and (2) those who went on expeditions to assess her value for individual action, vocational choices, use, or linguistic structure. We accordingly summarize those trials in the two major categories, Trials of the Excursionists and Trials of the Expeditionists. Space limits us to stating conclusions, in all cases; readers can refer to original studies for details.

Trials of the Excursionists. *Decision Making* has carried a number of passengers who wish to help others learn to make career choices through internalization of language in decision-making processes. Excursionists have included (1) Bernard Dansart (1974), who points to the existentialist nature of *Decision Making;* (2) E. L. Tolbert (1980) and Vernon G. Zunker (1981), who both use *Decision Making* as a fragment of career development theory in introductory texts in career guidance; and (3) Nancy K. Schlossberg, Lillian E. Troll, and Zandy Leibowitz (1978), and Jo-Ann Harris-Bowlsbey and Jack Rayman (1978), who use concepts of *Decision Making* in programs of career guidance.

Trials of the Expeditionists. As *Decision Making* cruised the Seas of Human Career, several other career vessels provisioned from the master vessel and then went on expeditions of their own, using only modified concepts of *Decision Making*. Dansart (1974), Tiedeman (1974), Miller-Tiedeman (1974), Barber (1974), and Peatling (1974) sailed together in the first of the two symposium flotillas. Tiedeman (1979b), Harren (1979c), Schlossberg (1979), Wertheimer (1979), Jepsen (1979), and Mitchell (1979a) sailed in the second of the two symposium flotillas. Together, these symposia attest that *Decision Making* is both robust enough to unite with different models of decision making and heuristic enough to provide leads into new common thought about decision making.

Other travelers have also organized several extensive cruises of their own after provisioning from *Decision Making*. Those expeditions included (1) placing the Tiedeman and O'Hara paradigm into the general literature of work values (Katz, 1959, 1974), career decision making (Jepsen and Dilley, 1974), decision-making styles (Dinklage, 1967), family systems theory (Jorgenson, 1979), and cognitive development (Begin, 1981); (2) instrumentation for both the personal dimensions operating in choice (Begin, 1981; Jepsen, 1974a, 1980; Jepsen and Prediger, 1979; O'Mahoney, 1968) and the decision structure itself (Elenz-Martin and Miller-Tiedeman, 1979; Harren, 1964, 1966; Katz, 1979; Miller-Tiedeman, 1974, 1977a, 1979a, 1979b, 1980; Miller-Tiedeman and Niemi, 1977; Miller and Tiedeman, 1972; Tiedeman, 1979a; Tiedeman and Miller-Tiedeman, 1977, 1979); and (3) studies of the presumed reversibility and staging of decision making (Elenz-Martin, 1977; Harren, 1979b, 1980a, 1980b; Jepsen and Grove, 1981; Levin, 1981).

As noted above, Tiedeman and O'Hara's model, although general, is still explicit enough to work with and robust enough to be used with other models. For instance, investigators found that the model applies linguistically to value clarification, career decision-making models, decision-making styles, family systems models, and cognitive developmental models. In family systems, the model also proves to be a part of the model of career as a multiperson phenomenon, not just as a single-person phenomenon, as now mostly studied. In the cognitive developmental case, the theory proves able to deal with more comprehensive differentiation of the dimension of cognitive — and probably ego — development, which individuals have to integrate in mastering their minds as process.

Decision making suffers from the same affliction as physical phenomena — you can't measure something, not even decision making, without distorting it, and so we must watch potential distortions carefully as we assess investigations of the Tiedeman and O'Hara process model of decision making. Therefore, let us first divide investigations of decision making into three kinds.

At the simple level, the level at which most investigations of career decisions are focused, the decision or choice itself is used as a criterion. Since the Tiedeman and O'Hara model moves from within to without, it is a model of *how* people decide, not of *what* they choose. What most people choose is left to individual interpretation in the Tiedeman and O'Hara model. No one has yet investigated that model in terms of the chosen object.

At the next level, investigators consider the subject's decision state at the time of investigation. Harren's (1980a) Assessment of Career Decision Making (ACDM) has principally been used for investigations of this nature. Since the ACDM is necessarily limited to career decisions at college, the investigations with that instrument are all at that level, except for Jepsen and Grove's (1981) adaptation of the ACDM for high school use.

Harren and Cass (1977, pp. 14–15) state the following general conclusions from their rather extensive work with the ACDM: "Perhaps the overall conclusion to be drawn from these results is that the theoretical propositions generated from the Tiedeman and O'Hara Model, with respect to the other variables in the study, have been borne out. . . . Secondly, the data presented on the reliability and validity of the ACDM suggest that the instrument is an effective measure of the Tiedeman and O'Hara model, and that the decision-making style scales, added to the instrument based on later revisions of the model by Miller and Tiedeman (1972), have considerable promise as a mediating variable in influencing the career decision-making process."

Jepsen and colleagues have devised and studied the adolescent decision-making processes, using their pyramidal model with the Tiedeman and O'Hara model as its base. Furthermore,

Harren and colleagues have studied model-guided decision processes among college students. Various instruments are therefore available for identifying the state of occupational choices from the less visible personal dimensions of deciding. In addition, instruments and programs have been devised and tested that show that clear thinking in decision making points the way to a belief in life-as-career.

At the third level of decision-making studies, particular attention is directed both to what the subject knows about the steps of the decision process in which the subject presently functions and to how that knowledge is generalized into some more comprehensive development scheme.

To collect process-awareness data in adolescent and young adults, Miller-Tiedeman and Elenz-Martin developed the Decision-Making Organizer for high school students (Miller-Tiedeman, 1979b) and for college students (Elenz-Martin and Miller-Tiedeman, 1979). When kept current, it serves as a record of the student's career development process through high school and college.

Analyses of ninth-grade student responses in DeKalb (Illinois) High School to the Decision-Making Organizer reveal three important findings (Miller-Tiedeman, 1977a). First, students in that study did not ordinarily apply the Tiedeman and O'Hara steps in the order that Tiedeman and O'Hara expected from their model of decision making. What may happen (but not in the high school years) is that a learner, after making a first decision and after experiencing its negative consequences, comes back to the crystallization step (collecting and organizing information), uses it more carefully, and then goes on to choose a second time. If this does not work, the learner probably goes back to the crystallization step once again and also goes on to the clarification step before making the final decision. This takes more time and effort. It also slows the decision considerably, but the results may be much more satisfying. This may also happen when the learner gains personal maturity, gets away from peer pressure, and shows more initiative as his or her personal reality changes with the accumulation of more experiences.

Miller-Tiedeman's second finding on career decision making in adolescence was (1) that most of the students in her study were not undecided about plans after high school and (2) that their "decidedness" when they completed the Decision-Making Organizer was valid for them at that moment. Thus, each of the students lived according to his or her personal model of career development. What others thought of their decisions made very little difference in their everyday experience. As far as we know, it may make no difference at all in the long run.

Miller-Tiedeman's third finding concerning ninth-grade decision making was that the personal realities of learners in her study may be far different from the common realities of some professionals in the career development field. These professionals and students "pass like ships in the night," neither having much effect on the other.

Miller-Tiedeman (1979c) also examined evaluation from the point of view of the person. Miller-Tiedeman used herself as an example. In doing so, she used understandings that her summative evaluations had given her. She subsequently revised her program to make self-evaluation the heart of her personal or "I" power process (Miller-Tiedeman, 1977a). What the person feels and intuits matters most.

Directions for "I" empowerment for the adult years have been provided. Tiedeman and Miller-Tiedeman (1976) first outlined a model for adult career education that is considered applicable in higher and continuing education for adults (Tiedeman, 1977a, 1981). Tiedeman (1977b) next applied the model at a mythical university, International Career University (ICU). At ICU, the career education of all professional educational personnel is incorporated throughout the instruction program.

Tiedeman later generalized the application of "I" power still further. He (Tiedeman, 1978) first outlined the self-constructionist alternative to today's develop-or-wither career crisis at midlife. (Self-construction and career making are fashioning life as you want it—seeing yourself as the designer and builder of your life.) In that work, he adds to the potential design of an Information System for Life Decisions treated formally in two books, *Career Development: Designing Our Career Machines* (Tiedeman, 1979a) and *Career Development: Designing Self* (Peatling and Tiedeman, 1977). Tiedeman's (1977a) other work on "I" power discusses discernment of "I" power in the developmental paradigm at midlife. There he specifies conditions for development of "I" power and extends application of the basic tenets to the middle third of life.

David Jepsen has also made numerous expeditions into the area of adolescent career decision making, expeditions that sometimes relied on the design of *Decision Making*. Here, we summarize his particularly powerful statistical investigation of process in career decision making, Jepsen and Grove (1981, p. 248) state the following conclusion concerning stages in the Tiedeman and O'Hara model, as revealed by a high school adaptation of Harren's (1980a) Assessment of Career Decision Making: "Stage order in the Tiedeman-O'Hara paradigm was generally supported by the results. Data on two instruments for three independent samples analyzed by two multidimensional unfolding procedures show remarkably similar stage orders. The results converge on the conclusion that vocational decision-making stages are ordered as Exploration, Crystallization, Clarification, and Choice. The latter two stages are reversed from theoretical order. The finding is difficult to reconcile logically with the theory since the Clarification stage was constructed as a state of postchoice closure and specification separating the feeling of commitment with the act of entering a new position in the implementation phase. Nevertheless, we will offer a possible explanation rather than abandon the theoretical order."

We are currently trying to understand two things about the anticipation aspect of *Decision Making*'s original design. First, when one programs the four steps in computer language, one finds that one can program for only an exploration-crystallization set and a choice-clarification set. This finding has caused us to consider collapsing the four categories into two.

In addition, as noted above, Miller-Tiedeman has found that many adolescents explore and then quickly lock on to choice and just plow ahead into the implementation aspect, without further concern, until trouble arises. Exploration, crystallization, choice, and clarification staging therefore seems to be an ideal progression, not one found in Miller-Tiedeman's (1980) longitudinal study of adolescent decision-making processes.

In summarizing our reaction to the work on *Decision Making*, it seems amazing to us that the Tiedeman and O'Hara paradigm of decision making, which was advanced with so little empirical evidence but with a great deal of rationalization, appears sufficiently robust (1) to be used heuristically and (2) to take practitioners aboard for effective work in decision making. Finally, we marvel that our joint work with it proved the major impetus for Miller-Tiedeman's quantum leap into the lifecareer process theory.

Redesign. Although *Decision Making* has proved to have heuristic and practical value, the more the two of us read about and worked toward empowering people to advance in career decision development (as reported in the next section), the more we became aware of *Decision Making*'s limitations. For instance, it focused mostly on educational and occupational choices within a concept of career that largely unfolded outside the individual. As a result, *Decision Making* did not have a life context, nor did it tend to deal with other life choices that affect an individual's work career as much as or more than educational decisions do.

Decision Making offered the promise of dealing with personal decision making as a process, but it was not originally conceived that way, and not much work has been done on this personal process of deciding. For instance, *Decision Making* was conceived from a theoretician's perspective, not from that of individuals bringing forth and living their own perspectives about life. It was used for study of the work career but had not been applied, in any great measure, to the more general study of career, recognizing that career is the path we leave behind in life, and it includes much more than job or occupation.

For these and other reasons, since 1971 we have been redesigning *Decision Making* to give us an enlarged framework for dealing with the human career (Ulich, 1984). Our enlarged framework is that of Life-is-career.™ In considering Life-is-career, we are talking about (1) the lived-in-the-moment process known only to the individual, (2) more than an individual lifetime, (3) life as it has existed in the universe at large for eons, because we carry that information in our bodies (as Sandage, 1986, p. 2, suggests "every single atom in your body was once inside a star"), and (4) a life lived by inner guidance, which need make sense only to the individual.

Common knowledge in quantum physics now suggests that you have to know what you are looking for in order to see it; otherwise, you act like the Indians in the Caribbean when Columbus's ships first sailed into one of their harbors. The Indians ashore in that harbor are not supposed to have seen the tall ships because tall ships were not yet a part of their experience, and so they did not look for them; they just were not looking for them.

Likewise, the lifecareer is a different ship from the career development that people have been used to seeing. It uses literature outside the career development field. For instance, Miller-Tiedeman builds the concept of the lifecareer on the works of scientists (Bentov, 1977; Bohm, 1980; Capra, 1974, 1982; Swimme, 1984; Young, 1976; Prigogine, 1980) and philosophers (Kuhn, 1970; Ulich, 1984; Wilber, 1979). These works provide tightly reasoned grounds for the following propositions:

1. Consciousness is a concept beyond what we now call unconscious and conscious experiences in humans. (In the writings just mentioned, consciousness is seen as a process in evolution. Humans are a part of that process, with a consciousness both of their part in it and of their own consciousness of it.)
2. Life is a self-organizing system (that is, life is a system that continues to make its own organization, some of which we like and some of which we do not, but life keeps organizing and reorganizing anyway).
3. Objectivity is mostly a subjective experience.

Personal mastery of the above understandings allows humans to experience their own consciousness and to be aware that they are having that experience. Personal mastery and living of the concepts of an open, self-organizing system are crucial to living life fully, to experiencing oneself in development, and to seeing this manifest in the work career. With mastery of such power, humans can live their lives with less stress and more harmony, which will be evident in the work career. However, in order to live the lifecareer, one has to enlarge the ordinary boundaries within which humans think and act. These boundaries are associated with the paradigms (Kuhn, 1970) of the time. One such modern paradigm, which is badly in need of change in career decision making, is from Newtonian-Cartesian thinking to quantum thinking. Further reading on this can be found in Miller-Tiedeman (1988, 1989).

Practical Applications

The authors themselves have used *Decision Making* in many ways, both individually and generally. We will describe individual use in detail shortly. We first provide a summary of general applications of *Decision Making*. Each of the four following general applications provides considerable details on how the authors help persons learn to sail *Decision Making*.

In the general applications, Tiedeman and colleagues at the Harvard Graduate School of Education, the Newton (Massachusetts) School Department, and the New England Educational Data Systems first used *Decision Making* as the core design for a computer-involved Information System for Vocational Decisions (ISVD). In these programs, inquirers could (1) ask questions about educational and vocational opportunities, (2) learn about their decision processes, (3) use the processes in simulated fashion, and (4) gradually assume the simulational structure of the programs, so that they could interact with their vocational reproductions of themselves. This work is reported in Tiedeman (1979a). It represents an initial step in specifying personal use of *Decision Making*.

Next, Dudley and Tiedeman (1977) dealt with the creative process in which hierarchical restructuring occurs. The creative process is at the core of the anticipation aspect of *Decision Making*. The latter phases of the creative process are also a part of the accommodation aspect of *Decision Making* in living the life-career process. In addition to developing a model of hierarchical restructuring during creativity, the volume reports applications of *Decision Making* (1) to the theory of self-conception, (2) to the theory and assessment of guidance as purposeful action, and (3) to designing the Information System for Educational Research Decisions. The 1977 book therefore represented a second step toward specific design of personal use of *Decision Making*.

Peatling and Tiedeman took a third step in applying *Decision Making* with the publication *Career Development: Designing Self.* This volume generalizes the design of the Information System for Vocational Decisions and the Information System for Educational Research Decisions into an Information System for Life Decisions. It also develops a self-constructionist mathematical group model of personality reconstructionism. That model contains our current thought concerning the self-constructionist development that has to occur for one to become a career constructionist who functions with practiced ease. The book therefore represents a needed third element in specifying personal use of *Decision Making.* This needed third element is the model of development in self-constructionism.

We took a fourth general step, which we consider rather valuable to those who want to deal with career as movement during life into living career as perceived wholeness. This was a step beyond the personal use of *Decision Making.* Miller-Tiedeman called it "I" power.

Living the human career in perceived wholeness requires that individuals make the career and the process of career development one in themselves. Miller-Tiedeman has developed a program for helping adolescents progress toward such an objective in their ego development. We describe Miller-Tiedeman's work in some detail at this point to provide an illustration of how one may facilitate "I" power. We personally find no reason to think that one has to use different techniques with different subjects unless cognitive development is not yet at the adolescent level. In the absence of being able to think and talk at a preoperational or formal operational level of cognitive development, one is not likely to advance another step in ego development by Miller-Tiedeman's methods.

Miller-Tiedeman's (1980) curriculum model had three conceptual units: (1) Loevinger, Wessler, and Redmore's (1970) model of ego development, (2) Graves's (1974) values development model, and (3) decision-making strategies (Miller-Tiedeman and Niemi, 1977). Miller-Tiedeman advocated personal harmonization of these three models in the associations noted in Table 9.1.

Table 9.1. Toward Collaboration of Consciousness
Models in Three Areas of Personal Development.

Loevinger, Wessler, and Redmore (1970) Stages in Ego Development	Miller-Tiedeman and Niemi (1977) Decision-Making Strategies	Graves's (1974) Values Level
Integrated	—	Survival for all men, or Existential
Autonomous	Analytical	Personalistic
Individualistic	—	Materialistic
Conscientious	Planned	Religious or Sacrificial
Self-Aware	Reluctant	Manipulative or Exploitive
Conformist	Compliant	Traditionalistic
Self-Protective	Postpone	—
Impulsive	Impulsive	Reactive
—	Fixed	—
—	Aimless	—

The model in Table 9.1 represents only tentative relationships, not direct one-to-one parallels. It is hypothesized that if a learner uses the more thoughtful decision-making strategies (planned and analytical) to guide him or her in selecting experiences that are potentially growth promoting, these experiences should both advance the student in ego development and rearrange priorities in his or her value structure.

Subjects used with this program have included learning disability students, humanities classes, college-preparatory classes, and a career-futures class.

Miller-Tiedeman's learning objectives for her curriculum were based on Romey's (1969) inquiry techniques classified according to the complexity of mental operations, as follows:

- Learning Objective 1: Define the five levels of ego development.
- Learning Objective 2: Define the nine decision-making strategies.
- Learning Objective 3: Identify examples from experience that illustrate the stages of ego development and the decision-making strategies.

- Learning Objective 4: Compare the stages of ego development with the decision-making strategies.
- Learning Objective 5: Discuss the importance of ego development and decision making in life situations.
- Learning Objective 6: Teach another class the ego-development model.
- Learning Objective 7: Help another student with a career-planning unit.

The materials used were contained in Miller-Tiedeman (1976b), Edwards (1953), and Miller-Tiedeman (1975). "Significant diminutions occurred in the number of less thoughtful strategies used in the area of future, education, travel, and work. At the same time, significant advance in the decision-making stages occurred in the education and work areas. These results suggest that the students moved up the decision-making stages in their thought and indicated a smaller number of less thoughtful strategies. Significant drops occurred in reported use of intuitive, delaying, agonizing, and paralytic strategies, while students showed significant gain in critical thinking and all reading test scores as well as in their ego development level. The average gain among all experimental students proved to be about a full level on the ego-development scale" (Miller-Tiedeman, 1980, pp. 180–188).

Helping learners to achieve "I" power requires that you first help them assess their core functioning with regard to ego development, values development, and decision development. In doing so, you give learners a choice. They can decide to live the "I" power idea and go on to unite their ego and values developments through further comprehension of their decision making, or they can discard the idea.

Those people who decide to live "I" power move into the self-aware level of ego development, a level between the Conformist and Conscientious stages of development. They start to realize that we are a species becoming aware of itself being aware. They realize that when you cut loose from the Conformist level, paradigm shifts have a chance to happen. It is a major jump in development because individuals take responsibility for understanding or not understanding ideas being presented. They realize that there are multiple ways of looking at the world, even if they do not, at the moment, understand those ways. That is decidedly different from making a quick judgment and dismissing an idea. Therefore, these people (1) become more conscious of themselves and cooperate with their own evolution or development; (2) ordinarily live more dynamically in the present, as opposed to the past and future; (3) gradually recognize their own planning styles and use them; (4) trust themselves and tolerate anxiety in times of uncertainty; (5) develop sensitivity and concern for others; (6) recognize and discard old ways of thinking from time to time; (7) can more easily separate their personal realities from society's common reality; and (8) follow their own personal realities. These people, therefore, live more holistically (Tiedeman and Miller-Tiedeman, 1977).

To reach the higher level of development, one must let go. Bach (1977) tells the story of creatures at the bottom of a crystal river. They had learned from birth to hold on, but one creature at last said he was tired of clinging (tired of conforming). He said, "Though I cannot see it with my eyes, I trust that the current knows where it is going. I shall trust and see where it goes" (Bach, 1977, p. 15). His friends laughed at him and told him that if he let go, the current would smash him against the rocks, and he would die much more quickly than he would have died of boredom. But he let go, and—sure enough—he was smashed and tossed against the rocks. After a while, he floated free to the surface and found new and wonderful things. Then the creatures at the other end of the river saw him and thought he had come to save them. He told them, "The river delights to lift us free, if only we dare to let go. Our true work is this voyage, this adventure" (Bach, 1977, p. 17).

In letting go of the Conforming stage, we will experience some rocky times; but as we move to the Self-Aware level, we will find that life has not failed us. We will find that the river of development will lift us free, if only we dare let go.

10

Duane Brown

❧❧❧❧❧❧❧❧❧❧❧❧❧❧❧❧❧❧❧❧❧❧❧❧❧❧

Summary, Comparison, and Critique of the Major Theories

In the foregoing chapters, eight major theories of career development have been presented. The aim of the contributors was to
present each theory in its most positive light, although in almost
all instances the contributors pointed out weaknesses in their
various positions. The major purpose of this chapter is to critique the theories systematically.

A number of criteria have been advanced that can be used
to judge the value of theories (Reynolds, 1971; Snow, 1973).
Criteria for evaluating a theory normally include clarity, parsimony, subsumption, lack of triviality, heuristic value, comprehensiveness, allowance for prediction, provision for a sense
of understanding of events, logic, and provision of a basis for
typologies. To this list should be added provision of a guide to
practice. When we consider the relative infancy of career development research — and, therefore, our inability to provide
practitioners with an empirical basis for their functioning — we
must recognize that theory should serve as a guide to practice,
as well as to research. Let us look at the criteria in some detail.

1. *A theory should explain important phenomena.* Patterson
(1980) points out that a theory should have relevance to life

338

events. In the case of career development theory, these events should obviously relate to the career choice-making process. Patterson also points out that importance is difficult to ascertain and therefore must be determined contextually. How often is the theory cited? Does it stimulate work in the field? To what extent does it meet other criteria for good theories? Does the theory stand the test of time? As we have seen in the foregoing chapters, some theories are relatively new. Only in the future will we be able to determine whether these issues have merit. Rejecting a theory on the basis of relevance should be done cautiously.

2. *A theory should explain past and future findings, as well as observations that are already known at the time of its statement.* A theory should be subsumptive. As we shall see, some career development theorists have tried to meet this criterion, although many theories have been derived from other psychological theories and have tried only to be consistent with the data supporting particular perspectives. A much more stringent test of a theory is that it must be able to account for data generated in the future. Few theories in the social sciences have been able to meet this test. Therefore, in judging career development theories, our focus should be on how well they have been able to account for the empirical findings that have appeared since their publication.

3. *A theory should be comprehensive.* Theories of career development should predict and explain the behavior of men and women, majority and minority members, rural and urban dwellers, the rich and the poor, the young and the old. A review of the literature on occupational choice (Brown, 1970) included only a handful of studies with women as participants, and it was not until five years later that career development in women began to be studied extensively. There is still a dearth of research and theory about the career development process of minorities, the rural poor, and other groups that are demographically different from white, middle-class adolescents and young adults, yet the criterion of comprehensiveness demands that the propositions of a theory be as relevant to people at midlife as they are to adolescents.

4. *The terms, constructs, and nature of the interrelationships between and among propositions of a theory should be clearly stated.* At the most simplistic level, terms and constructs included in a theory must be clearly defined. Reynolds (1971) identifies three types of definitions: primitive, derived, and operational. *Primitive definitions* are those on which scientists and practitioners agree; they are more or less commonsense in nature. *Derived definitions* tend to be more prescriptive and comprehensive — for example, "Occupational choice is the process of selecting a single job." A derived definition of occupation might be "the utilization of systematic decision-making processes to evaluate personal and occupational characteristics and to choose a job that optimizes the match between the two." *Operational definitions* simply clarify how primitive and derived terms can be identified in real situations (for example, when occupational choice occurred).

In addition to well-defined terms, a theorist must enumerate causal processes if the theory is to be meaningful. It is not enough to hypothesize that a match between personal attributes and occupational characteristics is essential to job satisfaction; the theorist must also tell why satisfaction is the result of the match.

5. *A theory should be parsimonious.* To be judged positively, a theory must be parsimonious. Einstein's relativity theory, $E = mc^2$, is an elegantly simple statement. Few social science theories can achieve this simplicity. However, theorists have an obligation to define their terms in the most succinct fashion, to limit theorems and postulates to the fewest needed, and to illustrate their ideas in the most straightforward manner.

6. *A theory should be heuristic.* A theory explains a set of complex phenomena that need verification. Verification of some theories comes through clinical observation. However, science generally relies on more empirically based research. Good research depends on our ability to ask good questions, and the time-honored tradition in social science research is to generate questions from existing theory. A theory that does not have good operational definitions and logically related postulates does not lend itself to hypothesis generation and is not likely to be heuristic.

7. *A theory should allow for understanding, prediction, and, eventually, control.* It is important for scientists to understand the phenomena they deal with, to predict when certain events will occur, and, if predictions can be achieved, eventually to control the phenomena. It certainly would be useful for career counselors and psychologists to be able to understand the career-development process so well that they could predict when initial career choice making would begin, what factors lead to midlife career change, and what conditions contribute to a happy retirement. With this knowledge, programs could be designed to deal with emerging career choice, help persons anticipate their life crises, and enable senior citizens to gain greater control over their behavior during retirement years.

8. *A theory should provide a guide to practice.* There are few "facts" in the area of career development and probably no laws. It is a sad commentary on the state of vocational psychology in general and career counseling specifically that Crites (1981) lists six models of career counseling in his definitive book on the process, but very little support for the efficacy of any of these approaches is listed or can be mustered. It is therefore quite likely that career counselors will be forced to continue relying on unsubstantiated theorizing, at least in the near future, as a basis for their work. Therefore, it behooves theorists to take one step beyond an explanation of occupational choice and/or career development — that is, to detail the implications of theory for practice.

Critique

One factor that makes an analysis and evaluation of these theories somewhat difficult is that they were not all developed to explain precisely the same phenomena. Trait and factor theory, Roe's need theory, Bordin's psychoanalytical theory, Holland's typology, and Krumboltz and associates' social learning theory are primarily explanations of the psychological phenomena involved in occupational choice making. Each of these positions contains statements about conditions that may lead to job change; but, even with this in mind, they cannot be viewed as theories of career development. Neither can the sociological perspective presented by Hotchkiss and Borow, since sociologists have concerned themselves primarily with the impact of social status and occupational attainment, rather than with the psychological phenomena associated with occupational choice.

The presentation by Super is on the opposite end of the continuum with regard to the complexity of what it attempts to explain. Super has drafted a statement aimed at explaining the sequence of stages and tasks related to initial and subsequent occupational choices and has attempted to tie these to certain life stages. He has even taken the additional step of explaining how work as a life role meshes with other life roles. He has therefore formulated a comprehensive theory of career development.

The differences among the theories make a critique using a common set of criteria and a single perspective difficult and probably unfair. Nevertheless, that is what is attempted here. Before these critiques are presented, some of the observations of others regarding some of these theories will be presented.

Warnath (1975) wrote a review in which he challenged what he believed to be the basic assumptions underlying career development theory. He questioned the assumption that each person can enter an occupation that will allow the implementation of his or her personality, and that it is logical to expect self-fulfillment from careers in our increasingly technological society. The legitimacy of emphasizing the centrality of work as a life role was also questioned by Warnath, as was the ability of individuals to overcome the constraints of the social system and the demands of our economy and move into rewarding jobs. In summary, he called for career counselors to question the major source of self-fulfillment and suggested that vocational psychologists broaden their theoretical models to general models of human effectiveness. As we have seen, some theorists (for example, Super) have extended their thinking to life development, but many have not. As we have also seen, work is still viewed by most theorists as the major life role, and the assumption for most is that it is possible for most workers to choose, prepare for, and enter careers that are satisfying.

Earlier, Carkhuff, Alexik, and Anderson (1967) had asked a question more akin to the review that follows: How do theories of vocational choice stand up under rigorous scrutiny? They concluded that none of the theories they reviewed, including all those in this volume except trait and factor theory and Krumboltz's theory, measured up to the inductive-deductive model of theory building. It should probably be noted, in fairness to the theorists, that none do lay claim to meeting this rigorous challenge.

Osipow (1975) raised another important question about the relevance of certain career development theories to special groups, such as minorities, women, and the poor. He pointed out the problems of applying the theories that he reviewed (which included those developed by Roe, Super, and Holland) to these groups.

Fitzgerald and Crites (1980) and Perun and Bielby (1981) have also raised questions about the applicability of career development theory to women, but for somewhat different reasons. They point to the rapidly changing nature of women's role in our society and conclude that existing theories have not sufficiently dealt with women's career development. However, they go on to recommend that career counselors be thoroughly grounded in traditional career development theory and in an awareness of the factors that limit their generalizability to women. Perun and Bielby also fault the theories that they critiqued, either because they do not meet their human development criteria (Roe and Holland) or because they have not addressed the unique concerns of the occupational behavior of women (Super). They go on to conclude that new theories of career development that incorporate these unique concerns are needed.

Collin and Young (1986) also reviewed career theory, concluding, first of all, that there is not even agreement regarding the meaning of the term *career*. They also enumerated two related criticisms, which Tiedeman and Miller-Tiedeman (1984, p. 841) noted in the first edition of this book: career theory is concerned primarily with the objective rather than the subjective career, and "career theories have been conceived within the orthodox philosophy of the social sciences."

Collin and Young believe that career theorists have erred by ignoring the subjective experience of the individual, since subjective experience will influence objective experience (that is, the one observed by the scientist). Accepting the subjective experience of the actor would result in changes in our definitions of major career change and work adjustment, since the worker's perceptions and values would be taken into consideration in those definitions. For example, what the observer might classify as a major job change might be perceived as a relatively minor shift by the individual.

Logical positivism has been the underlying philosophy of the social sciences. The underlying assumptions of this philosophy are that the world is orderly and objective and can be investigated, explained, and predicted with traditional scientific method (Collin and Young, 1986). One result of adopting logical positivism as the philosophy that underpins career development theory, according to Collin and Young, has been the assumption that career development is sequential, patterned, and normative, a position that might be quite difficult to maintain if a different philosophy of science had been adopted. The opposite perspective would be that reality is totally subjective and that understanding is a result of the individual's perspective. From this perspective, causal explanations are not possible; thus, the only acceptable approach to research would be to determine the individual's perspective (Collin and Young, 1986).

Clearly, critiques of theories of occupational choice and career development have been less than flattering, whether the focus has been on the assumptions underpinning the theories (Warnath, 1975), the approach to theory building used by the authors (Carkhuff, Alexik, and Anderson, 1967), or the comprehensiveness of the theories (Fitzgerald and Crites, 1980; Osipow, 1975; Perun and Bielby, 1981).

The reviews that follow will echo some of the same criticisms already noted here, although some of the questions that have been raised are also challenged. One point needs to be made first. The architects of the theories presented in this volume are acutely aware of the shortcomings of their work. Some, like Super, believe that comprehensive, integrated theories of career development will emerge as new multivariate research methodologies allow us to test entire models (rather than limited components, as is now the case). Others simply believe that a new generation of theorists will generate better schema. If better theories are formulated, it seems likely that the groundwork can be found not only in the strengths but also in the weaknesses of current theories.

Trait and Factor Theory

The trait and factor model was the first structural theory of occupational choice making to emerge. Others — notably Holland's model — followed, and all possess some common assumptions. Foremost among these is that each individual possesses certain rather stable psychological traits that are inhibited or develop as a result of person-environment interaction. It has also been assumed that certain occupations require more or fewer of these traits for satisfactory performance. Satisfactory performance results in positive feedback and/or need fulfillment. The task of occupational choice making, then, is to match persons to jobs so that individual needs will be met and satisfactory job performance will result. The Dawis, Lofquist, and Weiss (1968a, 1968b) work-adjustment theory goes on to suggest that job change occurs either when the job is being performed unsatisfactorily or when the individual's needs are not being met, and they have provided empirical support for this tenet.

Trait and factor theory can (and has been) criticized on a number of grounds, yet it underlies much of the career counseling that occurs in this country. The basic model has also been applied to personnel selection and placement in industry and to placement in educational settings. The theory does address important phenomena. There is also the suggestion that the theory applies to environments other than work, but these ideas are largely undeveloped (Dawis, Lofquist, and Weiss, 1968a).

It is likely that trait-oriented postulates apply equally well to men and to women, to nonminorities and to minorities, and are therefore comprehensive. However, because in some instances the measurement devices used to assess traits discriminate against minorities and women, the methodology generated by trait psychologists may be of limited use for these groups. If trait and factor ideas are to be used with minorities and women, valid assessment devices must be found.

Trait and factor thinkers have developed relatively sound (if not always mutually agreeable) definitions of traits, occupational choice, occupational change, and so forth. What they have failed to do is adequately consider and define the universe of variables that impinge on the occupational choice-making process and define causal relationships among traits and variables (such as socioeconomic status). Trait-oriented vocational psychologists infer relative freedom of choice but hint that biological, geographical, and sociological factors impinge on the process. These relationships need to be made more explicit. Trait-oriented theorists also need to develop propositions about the interrelationships that exist among traits with regard to occupational choice. What are the relationships among values, needs, aptitudes, and interests as they operate in concert to influence occupational choice making? A large number of multivariate studies could provide the basis for these formulations.

Another concern about trait and factory theory is its failure to deal adequately with the choice-making process itself. There is much current research focused on the complexity of the career decision-making process and on factors related to indecision (for example, Osipow, 1983). Presumably, decision-making ability is related to certain traits (for example, intelligence), and there is a systematic decision-making process that individuals can learn. Both the relationship of traits to career decision making and the process of decision making need explication. (The material contained in Chapter Twelve may serve as a point of departure for this theorizing.)

Dawis, Lofquist, and Weiss (1968a) speculate about satisfaction and satisfactoriness, and their influence on job stability extends the theory beyond its early focus on a single-choice point. However, the developmental process that occurs over the life span is not explained. This serious oversight must be corrected if the theory is to remain viable.

Trait and factor theory gets higher marks on parsimony (but the succinctness of the theory may be related more to oversight than to good theorizing). It also has stimulated hundreds of research studies on traits, provides the rationale for job analysis, has served as the basis for such documents as the *Dictionary of Occupational Titles,* and provides the basis for much predictive work on job performance. Moreover, it has spawned untold numbers of scales, inventories, and tests that are used daily by career counselors. Aspects of trait and factor theorizing have also been integrated into the theories of Super, Roe, and Holland.

In its current state, trait and factor theory cannot stand alone as an explanatory system for occupational choice making and has even less validity as an explanatory system for the career development process. However, the hundreds of studies that suggest a relationship between traits and job success and performance cannot be disregarded; neither can the work-adjustment theory (Dawis, Lofquist, and Weiss, 1968a) or the daily application of the ideas by career counselors.

Holland's Typology

John Holland's structural theory of career choice has proved to be deceptively robust. Holland rather modestly posed his theory as one of occupational choice; but, as Weinrach and Srebalus have pointed out in Chapter Three, the theory has utility in explaining a variety of variables, including occupational choice and satisfaction and the direction of job shifts.

There has been one rather unfortunate aspect connected to Holland's theory that deserves to be put to rest. The Self-Directed Search instrument was developed as a means of measuring personality constructs associated with Holland's theory. This instrument employs raw scores, as opposed to normatively derived scores, and one result is that women fall into the Social and Artistic categories more often than into the Conventional or Realistic ones. There has been a series of attacks on Holland, and he, being a conscientious scientist, has counterattacked. Antagonists have charged that the scale is sexist and that normative scores would result in different profiles for women. Holland's rebuttal is that the results are indicative of the social structure of our society. Both positions have more than a grain of truth. Most young women are socialized differently from young men, and the career counselor should take this into consideration.

However, Holland has done what the good scientist should do. He has developed a theory to explain existing phenomena.

Holland's theory developed from a number of research studies by himself and his colleagues. Constructs have always been carefully defined, and instruments for measuring personality types have been developed. Holland has also rather carefully spelled out the relationships between and among types, the impact of incongruence between personality type and environment, and lack of differentiation and inconsistency in the personality. While some of his propositions have not been fully tested, most have been the focus of major research efforts and have been supported. Holland's theory may well be the best constructed of those presented to date, when one considers parsimony, definition of constructs, and interrelationships among principles.

There are, of course, a number of shortcomings in Holland's theory, a fact he has acknowledged on a number of occasions. Perhaps the major one is that he has failed to provide any real insight into the development of personality, except to suggest that types tend to reproduce themselves. Since personality development has not really been discussed, it is not surprising that Holland has not commented on how problematic personality patterns can be altered. Failure to address the development and change of personality stands as a glaring omission.

As I pointed out in an earlier review (Brown, 1987), and as Holland has acknowledged, some of the basic constructs underpinning the theory are suspect, particularly those of consistency and differentiation. In Holland's reformulation of his theory, he admits to the weakness of these constructs and poses a new one — identity — that is aimed at strengthening the ability of the theory to explain certain aspects of occupational choice and change. Unfortunately, *identity* is poorly defined and is unlikely to correct the inability of consistency and differentiation to account for career behavior.

Holland's best path may well be to reconsider his thinking about differentiation and consistency. For example, *differentiation* is defined as the extent to which a person resembles a single type, and it is operationalized as the difference between the highest and lowest VPI scores. Nevertheless, since personality is actually a constellation of subtypes, why would differentiation, as defined, make any difference in career-related behavior, when that behavior is presumed to be the result of the interaction of the subtypes? The concept of differentiation involves only two aspects of the personality, not the entire personality pattern, and it probably deserves to be dropped.

Consistency — a construct that is related to the infamous hexagon — assumes (erroneously, I believe) that there is something "missing" in the person whose personality profile includes dominant aspects that are great distances from each other in the hexagon. These types are predicted to have lower achievement, less job satisfaction, and less ability to cope with job change. Since all six subtypes represented in the hexagon are presumed to be normal, it may not be logical (or tenable) to assume that a particular personality profile is inconsistent.

Holland also has not addressed the psychological processes involved in choice making, other than to indicate that persons with certain personality types seek environments in which they can implement values and perform tasks that will result in rewards. Some clarification of the decision-making process would make the theory more complete.

Career development per se has also not been of major concern to Holland. He has indicated that when dissatisfaction results from an inappropriate match between environment and personality, career change is likely to occur, but he has not looked at the impact of environmental and economic constraints on this process. He also has not considered the possible validity of the developmental psychologists' positions related to the impact of aging on perceptions of the relative importance of life tasks. This is of particular concern because there is some suggestion in the literature that the role of work may vary as a source of life satisfaction in the middle-aged and older adult (Brown, 1984); thus, Holland's propositions about the importance of personality-environment match may be weakened because individuals gain satisfaction in other ways.

Practitioners have been enriched significantly as a result of Holland's work. Numerous interest inventories based on his ideas have emerged, and the Strong Vocational Interest Blank

(Strong and Campbell, 1981) was revised to incorporate Holland's ideas. Countless self-help books have also been based totally or partly on Holland's work. It is difficult to imagine doing career counseling without using some of Holland's ideas.

There can be little doubt that Holland's ideas will remain viable and perhaps grow in stature in the future. The extent to which his theory holds sway in the long term will probably depend on the degree to which career psychologists begin to concern themselves with life-role saliency (as discussed by Super) and view work as simply one role, eschewing their current preoccupation with the centrality of work in people's lives. Even if this evolution occurs (and I suspect that it will), I also suspect that Holland's ideas, in some expanded form, will prove useful.

Roe's Need Theory

Roe's theory of occupational choice assumes a relationship between certain childhood environments, need development, personality, and, ultimately, job choice. Although her early work focused on rather specific groups, such as artists and scientists, her theory now stands as a general theory. It is primarily a psychological theory in that Roe attempts to account for psychological processes that lead to career choice (although the formulations in this volume indicate that she is aware of the need to integrate environmental and sociodemographic factors into her theory).

Roe posits that each of us is born with certain psychological predispositions and a cluster of physiological and physical strengths and weaknesses. These interact with certain environmental conditions, particularly child-rearing practices, and a need hierarchy develops. Each of us seeks to meet those needs in a particular type of work environment. Roe's (1956) system for classifying occupations stands as a major contribution to occupational psychology. However, her theoretical system is very difficult to research, although a number of attempts have been made. Researchers who have attempted to explore the formulated relationship between child-rearing environment and personality have frequently used retrospective methods and, perhaps not surprisingly, have often (but not invariably) failed to support these ideas. In the absence of longitudinal research that starts with relatively young children, it seems unlikely that an adequate test of Roe's ideas will ever be generated.

Even though Roe has recognized the importance of sociodemographic variables in career choice, she still has not developed an adequate statement about how this interaction occurs, thus encouraging the conclusion that hers is a static theory. In this regard, she is little different from Holland or others; nevertheless, this failure remains as a weakness.

Roe, like many others, has failed to account for the actual decision-making process itself. To be sure, Roe believes that predispositions plus experiences result in preferred ways of expending effort (time), a position that closely parallels Holland's later statements. However, this is a rather mysterious process, since Roe makes no explanatory statements about it. Part of this problem is that Roe's theory focuses on occupational choice, rather than on career development; thus, the steps between personality formation and choice making are not clarified. Roe (or one of her adherents) needs to address these shortcomings in the future.

Even though Roe was trained as a clinical psychologist, she has had little interest in the practical application of her ideas. Others, however, such as Lunneborg, have been interested in applying Roe's theory. The result has been the generation of a number of useful tools for practitioners. Lunneborg, in Chapter Four, points out that five interest inventories are based on Roe's ideas. She points to a number of applications of Roe's ideas in career counseling. With regard to contributing to the enrichment of career counseling, Roe and her disciples get relatively high marks. Nevertheless, one concern is that Roe and her followers have not provided much insight into indecisiveness in career decision making.

The future of Roe's theory seems uncertain at this time. Her reliance on personality theory, and the importance placed on the childhood environment, are not in keeping with psychological thinking in many quarters. Yet there can be no question that a number of practitioners and researchers are still interested in Roe's ideas. There can also be no question that her basic idea — that occupational choice involves an attempt to meet needs — is not out of step with current thinking (although her reliance on Maslow's hierarchy is questionable). It remains to be seen whether Roe's formulations will continue to be clarified and extended. If this does not occur, ideas like her classification system will probably continue to be used, but the theory itself will fall into disuse.

Bordin's Psychodynamic Theory

Bordin's psychodynamic theory is a theory of life development with an emphasis on careers. He posits a relationship between biological needs or drives and family atmosphere, a relationship that results in a certain personality type. These ideas, of course, are similar to those of Roe and Holland, although they grow out of a somewhat different psychological set.

The primary mechanism involved in personality development, at least that portion of it related to the family, is identification with *both* parents, a slight departure from traditional psychoanalytical thinking. The quality of the identification depends on mutuality — the relationship between the parents and the child. When high mutuality exists, external demands are fused with desire to gain satisfaction through play; thus, work can become a happy, playful experience. Without such mutuality, work may be defined as drudgery. The needs that stem from biological drives and identification emerge. Some become prepotent (these vary from time to time) and dictate life-role selection, including the choice of a career.

The definition of terms and interrelationships among constructs has always been a problem in psychoanalytical thinking, and Bordin's ideas suffer similarly. It is easy to understand the idea that biological drives and family atmosphere result in personality development, but just how this happens is not as easily understood. Identification is the primary mechanism, but how does this interact with biological drives to determine a set of needs? Perhaps more important, what determines which needs become prepotent? What is mutuality, and how is it measured?

Bordin's theory is not developmental, in the sense that Super's is. Like Holland and Lofquist and Dawis, he indicates that choice points arise when a job does not meet needs. Bordin, unlike Holland, does not posit that the personality is static; rather, he views the personality as changing, although he does not tell us what causes change. As personality changes, different needs emerge; thus, careers may need to change.

Bordin also helps us to understand the nature of career indecision. Doubts about self, lack of clarity of needs, and a spontaneity-work polarity may cause paralysis in career development. These quite obviously become the targets of our interventions.

Like some other psychological theorists, Bordin almost totally ignores the importance of sociodemographic variables. He implicitly assumes that his theory is a global one, applying generally to males and to females, to various ethnic groups and races, and perhaps also to persons from various socioeconomic groups.

It is of interest to note the evolution of the needs posed by Bordin. In his earlier work, he spoke of manipulative, sensual, anal, genital, and exploratory needs. Now he enumerates needs as being related to curiosity, precision, power, expressiveness, concern with regretted wrongs, and nurturance. It is not a great leap in logic to get from these to Social, Artistic, Conventional, Realistic, Investigative, and Enterprising needs and values.

Psychoanalytical thinking has not contributed as much to career counseling as other theories have, and it has not been as heuristic. However, the theory has been somewhat productive in both areas. Bordin cites a number of interesting studies and outlines a rather comprehensive approach to career counseling. In fairness, it should be pointed out that the psychoanalytical thinkers were the first to recognize the importance of the modeling process, particularly as it relates to parents. It is also to Bordin's credit that he identifies sources of vocational indecision (or, if you prefer, blocks to career development). He also outlines a counseling process that adequately recognizes the complexity of the career development process.

The present status of psychoanalytical thinking is that it has relatively few supporters. Unless this changes, the theory will become of decreasing interest. Three factors may change that situation. First, if clinical psychologists and psychiatrists who have received psychoanalytical training begin to view career counseling as a viable mental health intervention, we can expect a renewed interest in this area. Second, if (as Bordin has begun to do) psychoanalytical thinkers can convert their terminology into more acceptable terms and define them more carefully, more interest in the ideas may occur. Third, if instruments more useful to career counselors are developed, such as needs-assessment devices or interest inventories, wider focus on the theoretical approach may result.

Super's Developmental Theory

Super's theory is the most comprehensive of those presented to date, and therein lie its strengths and its weaknesses. Super has not only attempted to explain career development but has also, in his recent work on role saliency, taken on the broader challenge of theorizing about life roles. It remains to be seen whether these current ideas can be integrated into his work on career development, which is the focus of this critique.

Super owns his roots: differential, developmental, and phenomenological psychology. These give him ties to psychological thinking. They also serve to segment his theory. On one corner of his tripartite model we see the centrality of the self-concept and its evolution and differentiation. On another rest such constructs as developmental tasks and stages and such normative ideas as career maturity. Finally, we see aspects of trait theory (for example, work values) occupying the third corner. It is quite easy to discern how developmental tasks relate to career maturity and to relate those constructs to developmental stage theory. But how does self-concept differentiation relate to these tasks and stages, and what is the relationship of work values and other traits to the other two-thirds of the model? Failure to integrate these aspects into a unified theory has resulted in segments of a metatheory that are not yet unified.

Super readily admits that he has not fully integrated the phenomenological, developmental, and differential aspects of his theory into a cohesive statement. This remains to be done. Similarly, sociodemographic variables need to be more carefully accounted for in his basic propositions. It is true that Super recognized sex, race, and socioeconomic status as variables to be reckoned with in the career development process in his early writings. What he has failed to do, however, is build propositions that, despite people's similarities in career maturity, can account for differences in career patterns observed in persons from lower socioeconomic groups. Propositions regarding the processes that propel women into career patterns similar to and different from men's have also not emerged. Perhaps the place to begin this work is to look at those forces that shape the vocational self-concept. Another obvious variable to include in considerations of the career development of women and minorities is discrimination, regardless of where the process begins. Super has made great strides; however, his fourteen propositions need to be elaborated, so that future research can more systematically explore the efficacy of the theory.

Despite the foregoing criticisms, Super is a good scientist. He has defined his constructs carefully, and in many instances he has also taken the more difficult steps of developing measures of those constructs. He has embarked on numerous research projects to verify his ideas, and his theory and his research have stimulated large numbers of studies, which have resulted in data largely supportive of his ideas.

Practitioners have benefited from Super's work. Super and others (1982) provides a means of assessing certain key elements of career maturity, and his collaborative work with Bowlsbey (Super and Bowlsbey, 1979) resulted in a program for high school students. As he does in this volume, he has commented on the counseling process from time to time and made contributions to career development programs at all educational levels and in business and industry. His newest work on life-role saliency also is being applied to numerous settings. His theory also suggests means of dealing with people who are retarded in the career development process.

The current status of Super's theory of career development is obvious: it occupies stage center, along with Holland's
thinking. There seems to be no reason to doubt that it will continue to be of considerable importance in the future. With his
latest venture into role saliency, it seems quite possible that Super
has again pointed the way for theorizing. However, the lack
of integration of the various aspects of the theory is worrisome
for those who wish to see parsimonious models that account for
the data being generated by researchers and clinicians. The
segmentalization of the theory also needs to be addressed, as
do the decision-making process and the skills required to make
adequate decisions. However, of all available theories, Super's
holds the greatest promise of providing an explanation of the
birth-to-death processes involved in career development.

Krumboltz's Social Learning Theory

Krumboltz has adapted and extended Bandura's (1977b)
social learning theory into an explanatory system of career decision making. He has deviated from Bandura in four regards.
First, he has renamed many of Bandura's constructs; for example, *self-observation generalization* becomes a general construct related to self-efficacy, interests, and so forth. Because Krumboltz
has carefully defined these new labels, he enhances Bandura's
ideas, rather than detracting from them. Second, he has deviated
somewhat from Bandura's ideas by specifying and defining *task
approach skills*. Third, he has generated a set of propositions about
the relative influence of various learning experiences. These propositions are implicit in Bandura's ideas but are not spelled out.
Fourth, he does not appear to assume that certain types of learning are more potent than others. Bandura believes that participants' modeling is a more powerful method of improving
self-efficacy than vicarious modeling. Krumboltz has not made
this distinction, although it may be implicit in his theory.

As already indicated, the constructs are well defined, the
interrelationships among constructs are rather carefully delineated, and the theory is parsimonious. The theory provides a
basis for identifying difficulties in the career decision-making

process, and, because of its relationship to cognitive behaviorism, techniques for remediating deficiencies are identified. To his credit, Krumboltz has integrated economic and social constructs into theoretical constructs, and so his theory is somewhat distinctive in this regard.

Social learning theory is not developmental; thus, it does not really account for job change. This is perhaps the theory's biggest weakness. Whether Krumboltz will take Super's route, defining developmental tasks to be learned, remains to be seen. As the theory now stands, it would be difficult to use it for determining normative behavior or designing career development programs.

Social learning theorists have produced hundreds of studies related to a variety of factors, but few have tested the propositions as they are related to career development. However, those studies are appearing in increasing numbers, and the enunciation of the relationship of career development to social learning theory should stimulate research.

Materials useful for career counselors have been produced but have not yet been incorporated into career counseling and career development programs to the same degree as have those developed by Holland or Super. However, measures of self-efficacy in career decision making (Betz and Hackett, 1981; Taylor and Betz, 1983) are beginning to emerge. Interests, which are a form of self-observation generalization, can be measured with existing inventories, as can career decision-making skills. It remains to be seen what related materials and methods will emerge.

Krumboltz's theory is currently not a major influence (in the sense that Holland's theory is) on either the research regarding career development or the practice of career counseling, but this situation seems likely to change. Because the theory is tightly constructed and because testable hypotheses are provided, researchers should be attracted to projects involving its constructs. Practitioners also seem likely to be increasingly attracted to the theory, particularly if instruments are devised that enable them to measure certain constructs and if clear statements about this approach to career counseling continue to appear in authoritative texts and journals.

Sociological Perspectives on Career Development

Sociologists have added greatly to our understanding of career development by focusing on status barriers to occupational mobility. It now appears that there is some interaction between sociological thinking and the economics-based observation that, given the proper economic conditions, many barriers to career attainment will fall. Nevertheless, both economic and sociological theorizing fail to explain the psychological processes present in the career development process. As Hotchkiss and Borow point out in Chapter Eight, some researchers are trying to correct this oversight, and perhaps we will see a convergence of psychological, economic, and sociological theorizing in the future.

In terms of comprehensiveness, the sociological perspective rates well. Sociologists have not focused exclusively on one particular group, although persons from lower socioeconomic strata may have received greater attention. As Hotchkiss and Borow document, however, sociologists have been concerned with explaining the career development of all groups.

When reading sociological research, one cannot help being impressed with sample sizes and the sophistication of research methodology. Path analysis, a technique employed by a number of sociologists to explore phenomena relevant to career development, has only recently begun to be utilized by psychologists. This procedure may enable sociologists to begin to structure their postulates more carefully and build more systematic theories. Sociological theory is currently open to criticism in this area. This failure to carefully build systematic theories has not deterred research, however, since the status attainment model has been as heuristic as most of the other models presented in this volume.

Hotchkiss and Borow file an appropriate disclaimer at the beginning of their presentation: sociologists are not especially likely to produce data or models that have implications for career counselors. They then belie this position by making a number of astute observations regarding the implications of sociological theory and research for career development practice. Their recommendations support previous recommendations that have grown out of psychological perspectives regarding the importance of parents, job demands, and educational institutions on the career development process.

Hotchkiss and Borow have done an excellent job of critiquing sociological theorizing about career development and of incorporating ideas from economic theory into it. However, future theorizing must integrate psychological variables into sociological thinking, to account for the diverse phenomena related to career development. Further, this integration must take the form of testable propositions.

Miller-Tiedeman and Tiedeman's Individualistic Perspective

In Chapter One, readers were admonished to approach the Miller-Tiedeman and Tiedeman perspective with a different set of expectations. Similarly, it would be inappropriate to critique their work according to the criteria applied to the other theories that were listed at the beginning of this chapter; rather, it is important to consider the philosophical assumptions of their writing, and then try to ascertain their objectives and critique them on these grounds. They would probably reject the idea that their position could be critiqued because such an endeavor implies more order in the universe than they are willing to accept.

Miller-Tiedeman and Tiedeman attempt to set forth a holistic theory that explains how an individual perceives and reacts to life events and how the process creates self and context simultaneously. Self is created as external events come into consciousness and are acted on. One's environment is created through feedback from interaction with the environment.

While self and context develop simultaneously, the impact of the individual on context is neglected in the Miller-Tiedeman position. Perhaps the person-context interaction is neglected by design, but career counselors need more insight into the process. They also need to understand how they can experience the personal realities of clients, so that they can be of assistance in the life career dimension.

The paradigm presented by Miller-Tiedeman and Tiedeman does raise a few questions. For example, if people act
holistically, how can they be proactive and reactive, as is suggested at one point? Ostensibly, we experience and accommodate
our reality. Similarly, how can we objectify reality, when the
objective and subjective blend together in our experience? Also,
given the phenomenologists' use of the metaphor of person-in-
context to explain human existence, should not stages of all types
be ruled out? These smack of the organismic perspective typically
associated with the logical positivist. Dualistic and explanatory
constructs are abhorred by the phenomenologists, and there appear to be some of both in this statement.

In fairness to Miller-Tiedeman and Tiedeman, they are
not suggesting that we discard theories that stem from logical
positivism, but only that we expand them to include the individual's perspective as he or she grows and develops. Therefore,
the position taken in their chapter may not be as incongruent
as it first appears.

Synthesis

Some theories have been more influential than others, in
terms of career development research and counseling practice,
but none have emerged as "finished products." At this time, some
suggestions for future theorizing will be made that involve collapsing current theories into more comprehensive theoretical
statements. This approach is in keeping with the time-honored
tradition of science, and it seems necessary at this juncture.

At the outset, it should be recognized that there is a need
to develop a dual epistemological basis for theories of occupational choice and career development (Collin and Young, 1986;
Sonnenfeld and Kotter, 1982). In one sense, theorists like Super
have begun the process of recognizing the importance of the subjective perspective of the person in the career development process, but his ideas still primarily reflect the tradition of logical
positivism. It is therefore recommended that any future theorizing or synthesis of career development theories give consideration to the Miller-Tiedeman and Tiedeman position, a position
that admittedly is not clearly articulated.

The importance of this statement is that theory building in the future needs to consider both the quantitative and the qualitative aspect of career decision making. The criteria set forth at the beginning of this chapter, which have been advanced to explain theory, will ultimately have to be changed to accommodate the qualitative and "unlawful" aspect of career development.

Five of the theories can be labeled as primarily psychological in nature. Four of the theories — those of Holland, Roe, Bordin, and trait and factor theory — share several ties: (1) the early environment is the major contributing factor to personality development, (2) psychological processes are dominant in the occupational choice-making process, (3) choosing an occupation involves the implementation of one's personality, and (4) development (in the sense that developmental psychologists think of it) is either unimportant or cannot be accounted for by stage theory. Roe and Bordin have focused on the early environment and the identification process and have much more to say about the factors that may be related to personality development than either Holland or the trait and factor theorists, a major weakness in their positions. Because they (particularly Bordin) have focused on the development process, they have more to say about changing personality, another flaw in both Holland's ideas and trait and factor thinking. Holland, however, has developed his personality theory to a relatively high degree and has developed instruments that use an essentially trait and factor model, as well as programs that can be utilized by practitioners. This synthesis would also give legitimacy to other traits.

Several other concerns would require attention in the synthesis. First among these would be differences between the sexes and among the races, and the question of how these differences relate to occupational choice (Fitzgerald and Crites, 1980). More attention also needs to be given to the interaction between the environment and the individual; for example, what is the continuing impact of poverty on personality formation and thus on occupational choice? The decision-making process must be also addressed in the synthesis. As these theories now stand, this is a major oversight. Finally, more insight needs to be provided into the process of personality development and change.

While Bordin does illuminate this process, to some degree, additional clarification would be a welcome addition.

Super's ideas stand alone as the developmental influence on career development practice and research. Certainly, Ginzberg's (1984) ideas have historical value, but they have little to offer contemporary practitioners or researchers. For Super's theory to continue to be viable, he must integrate his segments, which means selecting some central construct and using that as a focal point for reformulating his ideas. Since his idea of self-concept seems to be the most basic of his constructs, it would appear to be a logical point of departure. He needs to show how the subjective perspective of the individual, growing out of self-perception, interacts with normative expectations.

He needs to illustrate how self-concepts develop and to identify forces that result in their change. He now believes that the tenets of social learning theory may account for the development of self-concepts, a position that is not at odds with Krumboltz's position. Hypotheses regarding self-concept development could replace his first three propositions, which now essentially are a restatement of trait and factor theory and are superfluous in the light of his idea that career choice is the implementation of a self-concept.

Super also needs to clarify the interrelationships among self-concepts and to state hypotheses that describe such interaction. His theory currently lacks a motivational source, although (presumably) the self-concepts are the genesis of individual goals. How are goals set for each of the self-concepts? Are they developed around a core of thoughts about self (a "super" self-concept)? What happens when the opportunity structure precludes the implementation of a vocational self-concept? These and other questions must be answered, particularly those regarding the impacts of gender and ethnicity, if Super's segments are to become an integrated whole.

It would also be possible to synthesize Super's developmental theory and the sociological perspective into a position on normal human development, a position deemed desirable by Perun and Bielby (1981) and a task already undertaken, to some degree, by Super.

Finally, Krumboltz's social learning theory is distinctive enough at this time that the only synthesis suggested here is to incorporate more of the sociological perspective into the theory. Krumboltz needs to redraft his hypotheses, taking into consideration status attainment theory and perhaps also some of the ideas growing out of human resource theory.

Krumboltz also needs to extend his thinking on the decision-making process. His current theory lacks a descriptive decision model, although it does contain a prescriptive decision-making model that can be of some use to counselors. Finally, Krumboltz needs to develop some specific statements about the role of ethnicity and gender, self-observation generalizations, and world views on career choice making. Once again, sociological and economic theorizing may serve as guides in this process.

The result of the syntheses suggested here would be more comprehensive but competing theories of career development. They could provide the basis for research and practice and be diverse enough to continue to stimulate thought in the field. Some of the identity of the theorists would be lost in the types of syntheses proposed, but that seems inevitable in the long term anyway.

Conclusions

From a strictly scientific perspective, theories of career development are at a relatively low level of development at this point. From a more pragmatic point of view, the various theories critiqued in this chapter have made tremendous contributions to our thinking, our research, and our practice. The theorists themselves are most aware of the shortcomings of their work. Nevertheless, when we consider that thinking in this area barely spans half a century, we have made significant progress toward understanding what all agree is a complex set of phenomena.

11

Linda Brooks

❧❧❧❧❧❧❧❧❧❧❧❧❧❧❧❧❧❧❧❧❧❧❧❧❧❧❧❧

Recent Developments in Theory Building

Criticism of career development theory has been plentiful and varied. Despite the efforts of some theorists to revise (for example, Super, 1980, 1981a) or clarify (for example, Holland, 1985a) their models or propositions, attacks on theory continue with fervor. Among the most salient of these criticisms are that theories inadequately explain the vocational behavior of special groups, particularly women and racial and ethnic minorities; that theories are too psychologically oriented; that theories are based on limited definitions of human development and have focused on young people, to the neglect of adults; and that theories focus too much on career roles, to the neglect of other life roles. This chapter is intended to capture the most salient responses to these four criticisms.

Women

As I observed in the first edition of this book, a frequent yet very general criticism that is made with regard to theory and its applicability to women is that the "existing theories were formulated primarily to explain the career development of men, and since women's career development is different from men's, the existing theories are inadequate" (Brooks, 1984, p. 355).

This statement leaves unanswered, however, the question of the specific gender differences that theory should be able to explain. For an answer, we turn to the research data on the particular differences between men and women with regard to both the process and the outcomes of vocational behavior. In regard to outcomes, two extensive reviews of the research (Betz and Fitzgerald, 1987; Fitzgerald and Crites, 1980) document that women restrict their occupational choices more than men; that is, they are underrepresented in a variety of fields and professions and, as a group, enter lower-paying, lower-status occupations. Women also underutilize their abilities and talents and are less likely to advance to higher levels in their occupational fields (Betz and Fitzgerald, 1987). The same two reviews conclude that the career development process of women differs from that of men: women's career development, while similar to men's, is more complex (for example, women are more likely to experience conflict between work and family roles), and women's career stages or patterns are different from men's.

Before we consider recent efforts to develop more adequate theory, some mention should be made of early attempts to explain the realities just described. These attempts are only of historical interest at this time, but they are significant in that they point out that the acknowledgment of women's differences and of the importance of trying to explain their life patterns began over thirty years ago. For example, Super (1957) described seven career patterns for women. Zytowski (1969) developed nine postulates to characterize women's occupational participation patterns. Super's ideas were criticized because they gave primacy to the homemaker role; Zytowski's, because of his assumption that homemaking and work roles are mutually exclusive (Vetter, 1973) and his implication that women with high career commitment were deviant or odd (Hansen, 1978).

Since these early statements, efforts to develop theory that more adequately explains women's career development have taken three approaches. One approach, common in theory building, has been to apply a theory from one realm to another. Hackett and Betz's (1981) application of self-efficacy theory to vocational behavior is an example of this approach. A second approach has been to create a new comprehensive theory that is applicable to men as well as to women. Astin's (1984) attempt is an example of this response, as is that of Gottfredson (1981), although, as will be seen, the latter had a broader purpose. A third approach is to suggest ways in which additional concepts can be incorporated into existing theory. Forrest and Mikolaitis's (1986) ideas regarding the need to incorporate the relational component of women's self-identity into career theory is an example of this approach. All of these efforts will be described in some detail in the sections that follow, and, as will become evident, some have apparently been more heuristic for research than others. Brief mention will also be made of two multidimensional models (Farmer, 1985; Fassinger, 1985, 1987).

Hackett and Betz's Self-Efficacy Theory

In developing the application of self-efficacy theory to the career domain, Hackett and Betz (1981) note that while gender differences in vocational behavior are frequently hypothesized to be the result of differential sex-role socialization processes, career development theories have failed to specify the mechanisms through which societal beliefs and expectations affect women's vocational behavior. They propose that differential sex-role socialization prevents women from gaining equal access to information from which self-efficacy expectations are acquired. Thus, Hackett and Betz postulate that women, compared to men, possess lower and weaker career-related efficacy expectations, and that these differences help explain women's vocational behavior (for example, restricted range of options and underutilization of abilities).

As developed by Bandura (1977a), self-efficacy theory is concerned with one's beliefs that a given task or behavior can be successfully performed: "People avoid activities that they believe exceed their coping capabilities, but they undertake and perform assuredly those that they judge themselves capable of managing" (Bandura, 1982, p. 123). As such, self-efficacy expectations are not reducible to one's objective skills; rather, self-efficacy is concerned with one's beliefs about capabilities. Judgments of self-efficacy influence whether behavior will be initiated, the degree of effort that will be expended, and how long the behavior will be maintained in the face of obstacles. Thus, a woman's beliefs about her carpentry skills, for example, would affect the choice of beginning and continuing in a job as a carpenter, as well as the choice of maintaining the job in the face of friends' and colleagues' pressures to find a job more suitable for her gender.

According to Bandura (1977a, 1986), self-efficacy expectations vary on three dimensions: (1) level — that is, the degree of difficulty of the task that an individual feels capable of performing; (2) strength — that is, the confidence the person has in his or her estimates; and (3) generality — that is, the range of situations in which the person feels efficacious.

A variable that interacts with self-efficacy expectations is outcome expectations. The term *outcome expectations* refers to the person's beliefs about the consequences of performance, while self-efficacy expectations refer to beliefs about the ability to perform the behavior. In most everyday situations, Bandura asserts that self-efficacy expectations are not readily distinguishable from outcome expectations, since people perceive outcomes to be contingent on their performance. For example, persons who judge themselves as efficacious in repairing automobiles will envision themselves as successfully completing a tuneup, while those who are less confident might anticipate a jerky ride, with misplaced spark plugs. In this type of situation, outcome expectations will not influence behavior independently of self-efficacy. In other situations, however, outcome expectations are readily distinguishable from efficacy expectations and do have an independent influence on behavior. For example, a woman may believe she has the abilities to perform the role of chief executive officer of a company, but she does not expect that she would be selected for the job if she applied, because company decision makers would prefer a male in the position. Thus, in this example, environmental contingencies are perceived as controlling or influencing the outcome rather than the level or quality of one's behavior. Thus, self-efficacy and outcome expectations need to be differentiated.

Another variable that influences whether behavior will be initiated is incentives. For example, a man may feel efficacious about his abilities to perform the duties of a kindergarten teacher, but he has no incentive to do so because he does not value the outcomes (for example, low salary and status). "Values determine behavior in that prized incentives can motivate activities required to secure them [and] disvalued incentives do not" (Bandura, 1977b, p. 139).

In regard to the development and modification of efficacy beliefs, Bandura (1986) identified four sources of information: performance accomplishments, vicarious experiences (for example, observing others), verbal persuasion or encouragement from others, and physiological or emotional arousal (that is, anxieties). Of the four sources, performance accomplishments and vicarious experiences are thought to be the most powerful influences on self-efficacy expectations.

In applying self-efficacy theory to vocational behavior, Hackett and Betz (1981) state, "If individuals lack expectations of personal efficacy in one or more career-related behavioral domains, behaviors critical to effective and satisfying choices, plans, and achievements are less likely to be initiated and, even if initiated, less likely to be sustained when obstacles or negative experiences are encountered" (Hackett and Betz, 1981, p. 329). While Hackett and Betz recognize that self-efficacy may influence the career behavior of both men and women, as noted earlier, they postulate that the limited position of women in the labor force is due to a lack of strong career-related personal efficacy.

Hackett and Betz (1981) provide an extensive discussion of the ways in which differential sex-role socialization prevents women from gaining access to the four sources of information through which self-efficacy beliefs are acquired. For example, in regard to performance accomplishments, they note that girls are less likely than boys to gain the experiences that will enable them to develop abilities related to male-dominated career areas (for example, mechanical or spatial abilities). In regard to verbal persuasion or support from others, they observe that boys have been found to receive more encouragement for career pursuits than girls and women do.

As noted by Hackett and Betz, the potential utility of self-efficacy theory for understanding and modifying the vocational behavior of women requires empirical investigation of three major questions:

1. To what extent are expectations of self-efficacy related to the individual's perceived range of career options, to effective career decision making, and to effective and persistent pursuit of desired alternatives?
2. To what extent do sex differences in the level, strength, and generality of career-related efficacy expectations contribute to the understanding of sex differences in vocational behavior?
3. Do counseling interventions focused on increasing career-related self-efficacy expectations change vocational behavior, including satisfaction with and success in occupational pursuits? [Hackett and Betz, 1981, p. 334].

To these should be added a fourth question. Does self-efficacy theory add explanatory power to vocational behavior beyond established variables and models (interests and values; locus-of-control models and expectancy theory)? The remainder of this section provides an overview of research relevant to these four questions.

Empirical Support. As Lent and Hackett (1987) note in a review of the research on career self-efficacy, the majority of the empirical work to date has focused on some aspect of the first two questions. In regard to the first question, whether self-efficacy is significantly related to vocational behavior, several studies provide support for this proposition. Lent and Hackett (1987, p. 362) summarize the literature by observing that "research using college students has shown consistently that self-efficacy beliefs are predictive of important indices of career entry behavior, such as college major choices and academic performance in certain fields." In the first empirical study, for example, Betz and Hackett (1981) found that both level and strength of self-efficacy were significantly related to expressed occupational interest for both male and female college students. These results were replicated by Post-Kammer and Smith (1985) with eighth and ninth graders and by Rotberg, Brown, and Ware (1987) with community college students.

The second question, regarding the role of gender differences in career-related self-efficacy expectations and vocational behavior, has also received empirical attention, although the results are not entirely consistent. Betz and Hackett (1981) found, for example, that women's self-efficacy for five of ten traditionally male occupations was lower and weaker than men's. Post-Kammer and Smith's (1985) results were similar, although for fewer of the occupations (two of the ten). By contrast, Ayres (1980), using a different self-efficacy measure (that is, self-efficacy for tasks, rather than for occupations), did not find overall gender differences in the relationship between self-efficacy and occupational considerations. Neither were gender differences found in Lent, Brown, and Larkin's (1984, 1986) research on the relation between self-efficacy and degree of persistence in college students majoring in technical and scientific fields. As Lent and Hackett (1987) point out, the discrepancy between the results of Betz and Hackett (1981), for example, and those of Ayres (1980) and Lent, Brown, and Larkin (1984, 1986) may be due to differences in the level of specificity of the self-efficacy measures (Ayres) and the homogeneity of the sample (Lent, Brown, and Larkin; that is, men and women in science and technical majors may have had more similar efficacy-building experiences than the general population of women and men subjects used by Betz and Hackett).

No published studies are currently available that address the third question, regarding the effects of interventions designed to increase self-efficacy beliefs on vocational behavior.

With regard to the fourth question, whether self-efficacy contributes explanatory power beyond established variables or models, several studies are relevant. Betz and Hackett (1981) completed a regression analysis, using ability (ACT English and math scores), self-efficacy expectation, and sex differences in self-efficacy as independent variables and range of perceived options as the dependent variable. Self-efficacy beliefs were found to be significant predictors, but ability was not. Lent and Hackett (1987) interpret this finding as suggesting that the self-efficacy measure subsumes information contained in the ability measure.

Another established variable of importance is expressed vocational interest. Is occupational self-efficacy substantially different from interests? Several studies bear on this question. For example, Post-Kammer and Smith (1986) found that both interests and self-efficacy were significant predictors of math- and nonmath-related occupational considerations for women, but only interests were predictive for men. In contrast, Lent, Brown, and Larkin (1986) found that vocational interest was not a significant predictor of persistence in a career field, but both self-efficacy and interests added unique variance in predicting occupational consideration. Finally, Rotberg, Brown, and Ware (1987) found mixed support for the hypothesis that self-efficacy would predict range of career options after interests, socioeconomic status, race, gender, and sex-role orientation were partialed out. Self-efficacy was a significant predictor of range of options for male-dominated (but not for female-dominated) occupations. In general, the results of the research on the explanatory power of self-efficacy suggest tentative support for the hypothesis that self-efficacy augments other variables, such as ability and interests. As Lent and Hackett (1987, pp. 362–363) observe, however, "the practical value of self-efficacy's incremental contribution to predictive equations may be questioned."

Three studies have compared the predictive utility of the self-efficacy theory with that of other models. Using college females, Layton (1984) found the self-efficacy model superior to a locus-of-control model in predicting vocational exploration and range of perceived options. Lent, Brown, and Larkin (1987) found that self-efficacy was a more useful predictor of perceived options than person-environment congruence (Holland, 1985a) and the decision-making paradigm of Janis and Mann (1977). Wheeler's (1983) findings, that both self-efficacy expectations and Vroom's (1964) concept of valence contributed significantly to the prediction of occupational preference, led him to recommend that both variables be included. As noted by Lent and Hackett (1987), however, Wheeler used unusual measures of self-efficacy.

Other ways of approaching the question of the explanatory power of self-efficacy are causal modeling and experimental manipulation. Hackett's (1985) study, using path-analytical techniques, showed that gender, gender-role socialization, high school mathematics preparation, and past mathematics achievement influenced math self-efficacy. In turn, math self-efficacy was a significant predictor of math-relatedness of college major choice and math anxiety.

Three experimental studies (Campbell and Hackett, 1986; Hackett and Betz, 1984; Hackett and Campbell, 1988) examined the effects of success or failure in career-related tasks on self-efficacy expectations. Campbell and Hackett (1986), for example, investigated the effects of task success and failure on mathematical and verbal task self-efficacy, task interest, and performance attributions. The results of these three studies are consistent with theoretical predictions regarding the effects of performance accomplishment on career self-efficacy, but methodological limitations of each study suggest that the results should be interpreted cautiously (see Lent and Hackett, 1987).

Evaluation. In general, considerable empirical work supports the predicted relationships between self-efficacy and vocational behavior. Some results, showing that self-efficacy is related to range of perceived options for women but not for men, suggest that women may be more heterogeneous than men with regard to efficacy beliefs about traditional and nontraditional occupations. In other words, the differences among men regarding efficacy about sex-typical and sex-atypical occupations may be small, thus reducing the size of the correlation between self-efficacy expectations and range of perceived options.

Despite this general support for theoretical predictions, as Lent and Hackett (1987) have observed, the results have not always been favorable, and a great deal more work needs to be done to evaluate the potential of self-efficacy theory in explaining and predicting career behavior. In particular, they as well as Betz and Hackett (1986) point to the need to resolve some measurement issues (for example, identifying appropriate levels of specificity), to assess the generalizability to other populations besides students, to examine the relevancy of self-efficacy to other career domains (for example, career adjustment), to continue work on comparing self-efficacy with other theoretical models, to investigate the effectiveness of theory-based interventions, and to use causal modeling procedures. (The interested reader is referred to Betz and Hackett, 1986, and Lent and Hackett, 1987, for elaborations of these ideas, as well as further commentary on conceptual and methodological issues.)

To these ideas should be added two additional ones. First is the need to investigate whether the career domain is one in which outcome expectations and self-efficacy beliefs are joined or disconnected; that is, will outcome expectations add incremental validity over and above self-efficacy? The research thus far has assumed that self-efficacy and outcome expectations are joined in the career domain, since only self-efficacy has been measured. It seems likely, however, that in many career situations individuals would perceive the outcome of their behavior to be dependent not only on their own performance but also on environmental contingencies. This idea has not been subjected to empirical test, however.

The second need is to investigate the influence of incentives on career preferences. It seems intuitively obvious that people may feel quite efficacious with regard to their abilities to perform certain jobs but would not choose to do so because they do not value the expected outcomes that good performance would bring. Although Clement (1987) did not directly study incentives in her study of self-efficacy and occupational preference, she found that men's lesser willingness than women to consider sex-atypical careers was due to their anticipated lack of enjoyment of the occupations, rather than to lack of confidence in their ability to do the work. Although there may be several explanations for this finding, one possibility is that traditional female occupations offer the disincentives of low status and low pay. Incorporating incentives into the self-efficacy research may help explain the mixed results regarding gender differences.

Implications for Counseling. As Hackett and Betz (1981, p. 336) point out in their initial theoretical article, self-efficacy theory has considerable "potential for the broadening of women's options and the facilitation of their pursuit of those options." Presumably, the basis for this statement is partly that Bandura's (1977a, 1986) explication of the four sources of information relevant to the development and/or alteration of self-efficacy beliefs suggests specific targets for interventions. To cite just a few examples, in the area of performance accomplishment the counselor could use a variety of cognitive strategies to help the client view her abilities in a more realistic manner. Reattribution training could enable her to view her successes as due to internal rather than to external causes (Fosterling, 1980). The structuring of incrementally graded success experiences could also be used (Lent and Hackett, 1987). In the area of vicarious learning, the counselor could arrange "shadowing" experiences with successful women in career fields that are of interest. Desensitization procedures could be used to reduce excessive anxiety about career choice or performance.

Clearly, a variety of strategies for increasing efficacy expectations could be devised by the creative counselor. As Goldfried and Robins (1982) point out, however, people's well-developed self-schema can create extreme resistance to counterevidence. In this regard, they provide some very useful cognitive processing strategies that counselors could use to help clients achieve enduring change in efficacy beliefs.

Gottfredson's Model of Occupational Aspirations

Gottfredson's (1981) developmental theory of occupational aspirations is applicable to both men and women. As she notes in a later article (Gottfredson, 1983), she did not set out to explain how aspirations develop; rather, she wanted to explain "how the well-documented differences in aspirations by social group (e.g., race, sex, social class) develop" (Gottfredson, 1983, p. 204). The model contains several basic tenets:

1. People differentiate occupations along dimensions of sex type, level of work, and field of work.
2. People assess the suitability of occupations according to their self-concepts (that is, their images of who they would

like to be) and the amount of effort they are willing to put forth to enter the occupations. Occupations that are compatible with the self-concept will be highly desirable; those that are not will be highly undesirable.

3. Elements of the self-concept that are vocationally relevant are gender, social class, intelligence, interests, values, and abilities. Occupational aspirations are circumscribed according to these elements of the self-concept.

4. Vocationally relevant elements of the self-concept are developed during four stages of cognitive development. In the first stage (Orientation to Size and Power), the child develops the "concept of being an adult" (Gottfredson, 1981, p. 548) (ages 3–5). In the second stage (Orientation to Sex Role), the child develops a gender self-concept (ages 6–8). The third stage (Orientation to Social Evaluation) is concerned with developing abstract concepts of one's social class and intelligence (ages 9–13). The fourth stage (Orientation to Internal Unique Self) involves a refinement of one's distinctive values, traits, attitudes, and interests (age 14 +).

5. As people progress through these four developmental stages, they successively reject occupations as unsuitable on the basis of self-concept. First they reject occupations as unsuitable for their gender, then as inappropriate for their social class and ability level, and, finally, on the basis of personal interests and values. The result is a zone of acceptable alternatives, or a "set or range of occupations that the person considers as acceptable alternatives" (Gottfredson, 1981, p. 548). It is only under unusual circumstances that a person will reconsider an occupation previously rejected as outside this range.

6. People's occupational preferences are the product of job-self compatibility (that is, within the zone) and judgments about the accessibility of jobs. "*Accessibility* refers to obstacles or opportunities in the social or economic environment that affect one's chances of getting into a particular occupation" (Gottfredson, 1981, p. 548). Perceptions of accessibility are based on such factors as availability of a job in the preferred geographical area, perceptions of discrimination or favoritism, and so on.

7. Because the jobs people view as suitable for themselves are not always available, they must compromise. The typical

pattern of compromise is the following: people first sacrifice interests, then prestige level, and finally sex type. In other words, given two choices — one that fits one's interests but not one's sex type, and one that does not fit one's interests but is viewed as sex-appropriate — the latter will be chosen.

Thus, Gottfredson's explanation of why women are in lower-status, lower-level positions is that these occupations are compatible with their self-concepts and views about accessibility.

Empirical Support. Taylor and Pryor (1985) were interested in the compromise tenets of Gottfredson's (1981) model. They explored the relative influence of interests, sex type, and prestige on students' choice of courses. In addition, they investigated the strategies students used when faced with the need to compromise, and they compared the compromises with the original choices in terms of interest, prestige level, and sex type. They interpret their results as providing some support for Gottfredson's basic propositions about the influence of interests, prestige, and sex type on choice but suggest that the process of compromise is more complex than her model suggests.

Holt's (1989) study also investigated the compromise process, using undergraduate social work and engineering majors. Limiting his study to the differential effects of prestige level and interests (omitting gender), he also concludes that the results lend support to Gottfredson's proposition but that the interaction is more complex than proposed. More specifically, his results show Realistic types (engineering majors) to be more concerned with prestige level than with interests, and Social types (social work majors) to be more concerned with interests than with prestige level, suggesting that the compromise process may be a function of Holland types.

Henderson, Hesketh, and Tuffin investigated "whether occupational preferences are narrowed by sex typing before being narrowed by social background and whether this circumscription occurred at the ages suggested by Gottfredson" (Henderson, Hesketh, and Tuffin, 1988, p. 39). In general, the results of their cross-sectional study support the developmental propositions, but the narrowing by sex type occurred at an earlier age (under 6) than that proposed by Gottfredson. Also, girls' sex type for occupations was more flexible than boys', a result also found by Taylor and Pryor (1985) as well as by many others (for example, Frost and Diamond, 1979).

Evaluation. In regard to the strengths of Gottfredson's model, Pryor (1985) notes that it integrates the developmental and decision-making aspect of career behavior in both a descriptive and a potentially predictive way. It includes both psychological and nonpsychological variables and identifies the principles of their interaction, as well as the interplay between development and choice. It explicitly describes the compromise process, takes into account a large body of research, and explains some contradictory findings. In regard to weaknesses, Pryor asserts that the self-concept construct is inadequate because it defines "things in relation to which they stand to other things rather than in terms of their inherent properties," which he terms the "hypostatization" or "reification of relations" philosophical error (Pryor, 1985, p. 155). Conceived in this way, the self-concept lacks explanatory power, thus preventing causal explanations of behavior. Pryor does not view Gottfredson's conceptualization as unique in psychology, however, and he seems to have used her model as a vehicle for making his larger point: that the construct of self-concept should be abandoned in psychological theory. In response, Gottfredson (1985) agrees that the self-concept suffers from inadequate conceptualization and measurement but disagrees that a relational definition prevents causal explanations.

In a separate article, Taylor and Pryor (1985) quarrel with Gottfredson's conceptualization of the compromise process. For example, they question whether the dimensions along which compromise is made (for example, sex type and prestige level) are independent, as the model suggests. It is difficult, they argue, to find low-prestige occupations in Holland's Investigative category, male-typed Conventional fields, and high-prestige female occupations. Thus, it is "unlikely that a person can compromise on vocational interests without also changing the prestige level and sextype of the compromise choice" (Taylor and Pryor, 1985, p. 173). In addition, they question whether the hierarchy of dimensions used in the successive compromise process is universally applicable. They assert, for example, that prestige level may not be as important for some people as maintaining one's interests.

While Pryor's criticisms are confined to comments on the inadequate conceptualization of constructs, Betz and Fitzgerald (1987) object to Gottfredson's model on philosophical grounds. They acknowledge that her concept of a range of acceptable alternatives is not inconsistent with the research data, but they object to the model's deterministic assumptions. They also state that the model is a person-centered explanation and will not account for the increasing numbers of women entering some nontraditional fields. These criticisms seem to be based on a misunderstanding of the theory. Rather than being totally person-centered (that is, social and environmental influences are ignored), Gottfredson's model views self-concept as the consequence of interaction between the social environment and cognitive development, although admittedly Gottfredson is more specific about the mechanisms of the latter than about those of the former. Thus, changes in, say, the patterns of women's occupational choices over time can be accounted for by the interaction of social change (for example, liberalization of sex-role norms) and cognitive development. It is also important to point out that each individual has his or her own zone of acceptable alternatives, shaped partly by the individual's unique social environment. Thus, individuals with a broad sex-type range may consider atypical occupations for their gender, while those with a narrow range will circumscribe their options to those that are more sex-typical.

Two additional weaknesses are that race is subsumed in the model, on the basis of the questionable assumption that racial differences are negligible, and that some of the concepts are difficult to operationalize (for example, zone of acceptable alternatives), making a full test of the model difficult at best (but see Hesketh, Pryor, and Gleitzman, 1989, for one possible solution to the latter problem). Perhaps the measurement issue is responsible for the fact that only three published studies on some aspect of the model could be located.

Implications for Counseling. Gottfredson's theory suggests that clients with indecision problems either do not have clear awareness of their sex types, prestige needs, abilities, interests, and values or are unaware of how these self-concepts match the occupational world. Thus, the counselor would need to help clients clarify their vocational priorities regarding sex type, prestige level, and interests and values. Traditional means of acomplishing these goals, such as interest inventories and ability tests, may be helpful. Vocational card sorts that contain both male- and female-dominated occupations, varying along educational and prestige levels, are one means to help clients clarify prestige level and sex type. (See Brooks, 1988, for a description of how card sorts can be used to clarify and explore range of sex type.)

Clients who may be clear about their self-concepts but unaware of the occupations that fit within their zones of acceptability should be encouraged to explore the world of work through reading occupational information or undertaking volunteer or paid work experience.

The model also suggests that some clients may be dissatisfied because their aspirations are incompatible with their interests or abilities. Examples are the middle- or upper-class student who aspires to a low-level job, in terms of prestige or education, and the lower-class student whose aspirations are unattainable, given his or her abilities or resources. As Gottfredson notes, since conflicting goals are often the issue in these cases, exploration of the standards these clients are trying to fulfill, perhaps ones that have been taken for granted or never questioned, is in order.

Finally, since the vocationally relevant elements of self-concept are proposed to be developed and circumscribed by the time people reach late adolescence, counselors may assume advocacy roles and implement programs with such socialization agents as parents and teachers.

Astin's Need-Based Sociopsychological Model

Astin's (1984) primary intent was to construct a theory that would more adequately describe the career-choice process of women, as well as explain recent changes in women's career aspirations, but the theory is also applicable to men. Her need-based sociopsychological model contains four constructs: motivation, expectations, sex-role socialization, and structure of opportunity. Thus, Astin includes both psychological (motivation, expectations) and sociological (sex-role socialization and opportunity structure) variables in her model.

In regard to motivation, Astin proposes that all humans are motivated to expend energy to satisfy three primary needs: survival, pleasure, and contribution. Survival needs pertain primarily to physiological survival, pleasure needs to intrinsic satisfactions from work, and contribution needs to the need to be useful to society and be recognized for one's contributions. Astin assumes that these three needs are the same for men and women, although they can be satisfied in many different ways.

Expectations are concerned with the individual's perceptions regarding the kind of work that will satisfy needs and the types of work that are accessible and that the person is capable of performing. Expectations differ for men and women because of the sex-role socialization process and the structure of opportunity (for example, distribution of jobs, sex typing of jobs, discrimination). During the sex-role socialization process, the person is rewarded and reinforced for gender-differentiated behavior. The result is that the individual internalizes social norms and values regarding appropriate sex-role behaviors and choices. Interacting with the sex-role socialization process is the opportunity structure, which, while it differs for men and women, is not static; rather, historical events (for example, the women's movement) and scientific and technological advances produce social change. Thus, social changes modify the opportunity structure for women (and men), increasing the options that are available. Such changes in recent years have modified women's expectations, which were initially shaped by the sex-role socialization process and the past opportunity structure. According to Astin, then, the interactive relationship between sex-role socialization and the structure of opportunity is what accounts for the changes in women's aspirations and choices in recent years. "The socialization process probably sets limits to changes in the structure of opportunity, whereas the structure of opportunity ultimately influences the values that are transmitted through the socialization process" (Astin, 1984, p. 122).

Evaluation. Astin's initial theoretical statement was followed by eight commentaries. While many (for example, Gilbert, 1984) were enthusiastic about the potential of Astin's model and lauded her for including such sociological variables as sex-role socialization and the structure of opportunity and for developing a single theory for both genders, others (for example, Harmon, 1984) pointed out that inadequate definitions of terms and the failure to formulate specific hypotheses make it extremely difficult if not impossible to test the model empirically. Still others pointed out that the model fails to recognize that the "male model" of the structure of work, which is based on the assumption that work is the central life role, poses barriers to the integration of career and families (Gilbert, 1984). Also, since "family work" is identified as a means of meeting needs (and, therefore, as a "career choice"), the distinction between unpaid housework and paid work is eliminated, which is objectionable on several grounds (see Betz and Fitzgerald, 1987, pp. 89–90, for further discussion of this point). Finally, Fitzgerald and Betz (1984) judged that the model had no redeeming value, since it failed to meet any of the criteria for evaluating a theory's adequacy. These problems perhaps account, in part, for the fact that no research on the model has been published to date. Despite its shortcomings, the model does contain some intuitively valid ideas for both research and practice, such as exploring the influence on career choice of people's perceptions of the opportunity structure.

Implications for Counseling. Astin's model is silent on the counseling process, although it does suggest some general diagnostic directions that can be pursued by counselors. For example, the model implies that the reason why a woman (or a man) may experience problems in making a career choice is that she (or he) is unclear about which of the three needs is the most important to satisfy or about which occupations would satisfy these needs, given expectations regarding capabilities and the types of jobs that are accessible. In addition, a person may feel a conflict between internalized views of sex-role–appropriate oc-cupations and changes in the opportunity structure. One woman, for example, may perceive that the opportunity structure places limits on her options, while another may feel that the changing opportunity structure is placing pressure on her to expand her view of sex-role–appropriate occupations.

Career-adjustment problems may result when there is an imbalance among the three primary needs. Astin cites the ex-ample of a business person who overemphasizes survival needs, to the neglect of leisure and contribution.

Relational Identity

Forrest and Mikolaitis (1986) note that while most theories contain the constructs of identity or self-concept, the usual orien-tation is more to the male perspective of the separate and ob-jective self than to the female perspective of the connected and attached self. More specifically, drawing on the work of Chod-orow (1974, 1978), Gilligan (1977, 1979, 1982), and Lyons (1983), they note that "in describing themselves, many women reflect their sense of identity primarily in terms of their con-nection to others. . . . Self is perceived in the context of con-nection with and responsiveness to others" (Forrest and Miko-laitis, 1986, p. 80). Men, in contrast, describe themselves with words that convey their sense of separateness: "Their sense of self is created by differentiating themselves from others in terms of abilities and attributes" (Forrest and Mikolaitis, 1986, p. 80). Maturity, however, requires a convergence of these two perspec-tives. Therefore, career development theories need to include a more complex concept of identity, which recognizes that the relational component of identity is central to both genders.

Forrest and Mikolaitis (1986) suggest that this perspec-tive can be integrated into existing career theories, and they provide several examples of how it can be incorporated into Hol-land's theory in particular: "Women or men whose self-descrip-tions and real-life moral conflicts express a predominantly connected self (or separate self) identity would be more likely to prefer work environments where this component of their iden-tity could be expressed and valued" (Forrest and Mikolaitis,

1986, p. 83). Among the implications for practice that they identify is the need for the counselor to assess the client's orientation toward these two identity perspectives and to assess how they may influence career decisions.

Farmer's and Fassinger's Multidimensional Models

In this section, brief mention will be made of two recent models that seem promising because of their multidimensionality and causal frameworks.

Farmer's (1985) social learning–oriented model proposes that the career motivation of adolescents develops through three interacting influences: background variables (gender, race, social status, school location, age), personal psychological variables (academic self-esteem, success attributions, intrinsic values, homemaking commitment), and environmental variables (support from teachers and parents, support for women working). She identifies three aspects of career motivation: level of occupation chosen (aspiration), motivation to achieve a short range of challenging tasks (mastery), and degree of commitment to long-range prospects of the career (career).

Fassinger's (1985, 1987) covariance structural modeling of career-choice realism and career choice (traditionality, prestige, and science-relatedness) is based on Betz and Fitzgerald's (1987) review of the research on women's vocational behavior. The model of career-choice realism incorporates a set of variables similar to Farmer's: background variables (previous work experience, academic success), environmental variables (role-model influence, perceived encouragement), and psychological variables (attitudes toward work, sex-role attitudes). The model of career choice hypothesizes that ability, instrumentality, feminist orientation, and family orientation influence career orientation and mathematics orientation, and the latter two variables in turn influence career choice. Ability and family orientation are also hypothesized to have a direct influence on career choice. The advantage of covariance structural modeling is that causal inferences can be made from nonexperimental data, and so such a model is more powerful than most traditional experimental designs (Betz and Fitzgerald, 1987).

Racial and Ethnic Minorities

While a variety of criticisms have been made with regard to the inadequacy of theory to explain the career development of racial and ethnic minorities, three themes are recurrent: the theories are based on erroneous assumptions, particular theoretical concepts are not applicable, and important career determinants are omitted from the theories. One erroneous assumption, for example, is that people have an array of choices open to them; that is, they are free to choose among alternatives that are close to their interests, values, and abilities. Thus, the restrictions imposed by the sociopolitical environment are ignored (Osipow, 1975; Smith, 1983). Also, the theories are viewed as exaggerating the role of personality characteristics (Osipow, 1983; Warnath, 1975; W. S. Williams, 1972), a criticism that sociologists label the *psychological bias* of theories.

The complaint that the theories were developed to explain middle-class white males — a group viewed as having the advantage of psychological and economic resources that ensure optimal career development — calls attention to aspects of specific theories that are inapplicable to racial and ethnic minorities. For example, Super's model of developmental stages, which proposes that career development is a sequential and continuous process, has been challenged as inapplicable to poor black males, who, rather than having the luxury of the exploration stage, instead must find jobs in their early teens and must then take a series of unrelated jobs interspersed by unemployment (Osipow, 1975). Additional developmental tasks may be encountered as well, such as "coming to terms with the issue of race and what this means for . . . career development in American society" (Smith, 1983, pp. 189–190). A final example is that the higher-level occupational environments (for example, Enterprising, in Holland's model) may not be equally available to ethnic minorities and the white male middle class.

The complaint that theories omit variables that are important career determinants for racial and ethnic minorities most frequently focuses on the constraining factors of mainstream America's sociopolitical system, particularly racism and the effects of the differential opportunity system (Griffith, 1980; Smith, 1983).

Underlying all these criticisms, of course, is the notion that racial and ethnic minorities' career development process and outcomes are different from those of other Americans. Do data support this claim? If so, what are the specific differences (put another way, what empirical realities must career theory explain)? It would seem a simple matter, at this point, to summarize the research on the special needs of ethnic minorities. Unfortunately, at least two specific problems with the research in this area preclude such an approach.

First, much of the research has been conducted with a "psychology of race differences" approach. This paradigm assumes that the "proper approach to the study of minority people is to compare them to whites" (Korchin, 1980, p. 263). More often than not, the variables are conceptualized and measured from a white middle-class perspective. The difficulty with this approach is that we may learn little about the ethnic group, except that its members are unlike white Americans in certain respects. In addition, the causes of any differences found are implicitly if not explicitly attributed to race. The underlying message is that racial differences are the result of inherent and unchangeable determinants (Korchin, 1980).

A second problem with the research is that race has often been confounded with social class (Osipow, 1975; Smith, 1975). For example, it is frequently noted that blacks are less vocationally mature than whites. A closer look at the research reveals that the consistent finding is that lower-class blacks are less vocationally mature than white middle-class youth. To determine whether the differences are due to race or class, Smith (1975) points out that lower-class blacks need to be compared with middle-class blacks.

The point of this discussion is not that research on race differences is irrelevant. As Korchin (1980, p. 264) observes, the investigation of ethnic differences "is a first step toward the development of theory and research methods appropriate to the understanding of cultural diversity." Rather, the point is that such research should be done from a cross-cultural or multi-cultural perspective. The intent of cross-cultural research is "to understand the functioning of particular behaviors as they make sense within a particular culture" (p. 264). Racist thinking or "cultural disadvantage" assumptions that align differences "along an inferior–superior axis and ascribe them to unchangeable determinants" are to be avoided (p. 265).

The research on special career development problems of ethnic groups must be interpreted cautiously, both because of the confounding of race, class, ethnic, and economic variables and because of cultural-disadvantage assumptions. Smith's review of the career literature on blacks is a case in point. She notes that "the profile of the black individual in the research . . . is a portrait of a vocationally handicapped person" (Smith, 1975, p. 55). Among other characteristics, the literature suggests that blacks lack positive work-role models, are not committed to careers, are alienated from work, are vocationally immature, have negative self-images, have limited occupational mobility, have restricted interests and low career expectations, and are more interested in job security than in self-fulfillment. "The extent to which this profile is accurate or inaccurate is still open to debate and research verification, for there are many notable exceptions to it" (Smith, 1975, p. 55). Smith cites the research of Hauser (1971), which takes an "internal frame of reference" approach (one that is closer to a cross-cultural perspective), as one example of research that contradicts the assertion that work is less important to black youths in comparison with white youths. It is not so much that work is less important as it is that blacks are frustrated and disappointed with the "sociocultural predicaments" they face (for example, limited job opportunities). Smith's conclusion reiterates a previous point that bears repeating: "Studies have indicated that racism and its deleterious effects should be taken into consideration when analyzing the minority person's career development" (Smith, 1975, p. 48).

In spite of these difficulties with the research, certain observations about the current status of ethnic minorities strongly support the following observations about the career development of minority groups.

First, it seems evident that racial and ethnic minorities are overrepresented in certain occupational environments and underrepresented in others. Black males, for example, are over-represented in Realistic jobs and underrepresented in Enterprising jobs (Gottfredson, 1978), while Asian-Americans dispro-portionately pursue scientific, mathematical, and technologically oriented fields (Smith, 1983).

Second, some racial and ethnic minorities — specifically, blacks, Hispanics, and Native Americans — have higher unem-ployment rates and lower incomes than majority Americans do (Smith, 1983).

Third, while the specifics are not well documented, it seems safe to assume that the career development process involves some differences. Smith (1983) reviews several studies that provide sup-port for the idea that racial and ethnic minority youth, particular-ly black Americans, Hispanics, and Native Americans, have less occupational information than majority Americans have. One obvious implication of this finding is that the career choice-making process for minorities may be restricted.

There have been numerous criticisms concerning the in-adequacy of career development theory in regard to racial and ethnic minorities; nevertheless, no effort to develop new theory or adapt old theory could be located in the literature. In fact, it seems clear that work in this area has decreased in recent years. As Greenhaus and Parasuraman (1986, p. 127) have observed, "research on the career development of black Americans seems to be at a virtual standstill . . . there is a critical need for theory building and empirical research on the career development of diverse cultural groups." Recent theoretical developments in regard to women do seem to incorporate some of the important concepts relevant to minorities — for example, the components of the structure of opportunity in Astin's (1984) model, and the effects of self-efficacy on career behavior (Hackett and Betz, 1981) — but the fact remains that a model to specifically explain and predict the career development of racial and ethnic minor-ities has not been developed. To be sure, some authors have identified the variables that should be included (for example, Smith, 1983), but no explicit proposition about the specific mechanisms through which these variables affect minorities has been formulated. For example, it is widely assumed that racism, discrimination, and stereotyping are constraining factors; but, as Gottfredson (1986, p. 139) observes, these are "ill-defined, all-embracing terms that are more emotionally evocative than scientifically descriptive." She further observes that, in an effort to get away from the "deficiency" model, the literature on racial and ethnic minorities has focused on documenting cultural differences. Unfortunately, she notes, these efforts have produced mixed effects. First, in some instances they have, ironically, perpetuated the stereotypes they sought to eradicate. Second, they have focused too much on problems and have neglected strengths. Third, culture, as an explanatory construct, has been inconsistently applied. For example, Gottfredson notes that the higher than average achievements of the so-called model ethnic minority — Asian-Americans — are attributed to the group's cultural values, but the lower than average attainments of other groups (for example, Native Americans) are explained by barriers imposed by the majority culture.

In an attempt to deal with some of these problems, Gottfredson (1986) proposes that the barriers faced by special populations (including but not limited to racial and ethnic minorities) can be conceptualized in an "at risk" framework. Although this is intended as a framework for counseling and assessment, rather than for theory, the model may also be heuristic for theory development. In essence, Gottfredson's premise is that special groups face varying degrees of risk that creates career-choice problems. "Risk factors are attributes of the person or of the person's relation to the environment that are associated with a higher-than-average probability of experiencing the types of problems under consideration" (Gottfredson, 1986, p. 143). A poor education, for example, decreases the probability of success. She postulates three categories of risk: factors that cause people to be different from the general population (for example, low intelligence, poverty, cultural segregation, low self-esteem), factors involving differences within one's own social group (for example, having nontraditional interests for one's gender, social class, or racial or ethnic group), and factors involving family responsibilities (for example, being a primary caregiver or primary economic provider). Then, on the basis of either a review of the literature or her own estimates (in the absence of literature), she identifies the degree to which each category of risk is faced by five racial and ethnic groups (for example, Hispanics, blacks), males and females, and six handicapped groups (for example, hearing-impaired and mentally retarded persons). Blacks, for example, are at risk in all categories of difference from the general population (for example, coming from a poor family, being culturally isolated or segregated) and black females (but not black males) are at higher than average risk with respect to caregiving and economic providing. It is important to note that this "at risk" framework is essentially intended to identify the barriers to free career choice. Thus, the Hispanic male is estimated to be at risk regarding family responsibilities (with respect to fulfilling the role of economic provider), which means, for example, that he is less free to seek self-fulfillment in other roles that do not produce income.

One advantage of this framework is that it avoids the "different is deficient" implication that emerges when analysis is confined to the problems of racial and ethnic groups. All groups (even white males) are at risk in some areas; the risks are simply different.

Gottfredson's framework is not a theoretical statement on racial and ethnic minorities, but it does suggest some directions for future theorizing. In particular, it recognizes that all groups have problems, although the problems of white males have typically gone unrecognized. It also recognizes, implicitly if not explicitly, that the variables that have been forgotten in relation to racial and ethnic minorities, if incorporated at a level of specificity necessary for hypothesis testing, will probably be found to better explain the career behavior of all groups, although the specific weight given to each variable may differ. At the risk of oversimplification, if career development theory is to be adequately comprehensive, it seems that what is needed is a framework that gives sufficient attention to the reciprocal determinism of sociological variables (such as racism and the differential opportunity structure), established psychological variables (such as interests, values, abilities), and nonestablished psychological variables (such as racial-identity development).

Some mention should be made here of the potential theoretical relevance of models of racial-identity development in

American society (for example, Sue and Sue, 1971; Helms, 1984). Helms (1984), for example, has proposed a stages model of racial consciousness for both blacks and whites. Although her models are not intended to explain career development (in fact, they were developed to explain the effects of race on counseling), it seems clear that features of the models could be incorporated into future or existing theory. For example, as blacks progress through the stages that Helms proposes, how they wish to interact with or withdraw from American society may certainly influence their perceptions of career alternatives that are desirable and accessible. In the Preencounter stage, for example, blacks perceive their characteristics as negative, but they idealize white characteristics. One result is low self-esteem. A career-related hypothesis would be that at the Preencounter stage of black racial consciousness, individuals perceive their options as restricted to occupations that require only a low level of ability or that fit social stereotypes regarding appropriate choices for blacks. In contrast, in the Immersion/Emersion stage, where blacks are idealized and whites are rejected, the model proposes that blacks may dwell on their blackness, as well as on forms of racial discrimination. Blacks' occupational preferences at this stage, then, may be influenced by the need to avoid whites and "prove that they have not 'sold out' to the white world" (Helms, 1984, p. 155).

Helms's proposed stages of white racial consciousness suggest that whites vary in the degree to which they can tolerate racially discriminatory practices. For example, in the Reintegration stage, whites are overtly and covertly antiblack and act on stereotyped views. Presumably, then, whites at this stage would be quite tolerant of racial discrimination (for example, in employment situations) and would favor occupational segregation. In the Autonomy stage, however, cultural diversity is valued. Individuals at this stage presumably would be more proactive about reducing the barriers to full employment of blacks (at least on the individual level, if not the group level).

Life-Span/Life-Role Approaches

While Super's developmental-stage model and his recent work on life-role salience are notable, a frequent complaint about career development theory has been that it neglects adult development and the interaction of one's career with one's other important life roles. Three responses to these criticisms will be briefly outlined here.

Life-Cycle Approaches. Sonnenfeld and Kotter (1982) note in their critique of career development theory that a recent emerging perspective is that of the life cycle. According to these authors, the life-cycle approach, sparked by the life-stage approaches of Gould (1972), Levinson and others (1978), Sheehy (1974), and Vaillant (1977), includes factors associated with work, family, and the individual. In essence, the life-cycle approach "focuses on the dynamic evolution of people, their families, and their careers over a life time" (Sonnenfeld and Kotter, 1982, p. 33). This line of inquiry suggests that in order to understand career outcomes one needs to focus on adult development, family, and life-style, as well as on career stages. Noting that the life-cycle approach does not incorporate important concepts from sociological and trait and factor theory, Sonnenfeld and Kotter propose that what is needed for the maturation of career development theory is an integration of the various approaches. Their two-dimensional model includes time, on the horizontal axis (from birth on), and life space, on the vertical axis (nonwork/family space, individual/personal space, and work/occupational space). Nine major sets of variables within the model show the interactions among occupational, personal, and family factors. For example, the adult family/nonwork history interacts with adult developmental history and work history.

Vondracek, Lerner, and Schulenberg (1983, 1986) developed their life-span developmental approach partly to ameliorate what they saw as three problems in career development theory: lack of a rigorous and adequate definition of human development, failure to include a contextual perspective, and omission of the relational aspect (that is, the dynamic relation between individuals and their changing contexts). In essence, their "developmental-contextual, life-span view leads to the idea that people, by interacting with their changing context, provide a basis of their own development" (Vondracek, Lerner, and Schulenberg, 1986, p. 77). Their oval-shaped model provides a picture of their dynamic interactionist perspective and includes eight contextual variables in the outer circle (for example, social/educational policy, organizational context) and four inner circles that depict the interactions of the contexts of the family of origin and the family of procreation and the adult and child extra-familial networks. They view their model as able to accommodate two important, changing targets: the individual and his or her context. They acknowledge that their model makes the study of career development a very complex task.

Applying this model to practice, they propose that interventions be developmental, defined as "any effort that involves a planned, deliberate, and programmatic intrusion into the development of individuals or groups of individuals" (Vondracek, Lerner, and Schulenberg, 1983, p. 191). Given the relationships between individuals and their context, the target of the intervention is not confined to the individual but may also focus on the family or on the community, in order to affect the individual. The model also suggests a focus on optimization and prevention as outcomes and on attention to events, processes, and life periods that are antecedents of career decisions. As they note, a careful developmental assessment is a necessary prerequisite of intervention. Finally, intervention should be viewed as a succession of procedures designed to help the individual to adapt his or her vocational functioning to his or her changing status and changing context. As they acknowledge, one of the difficulties here is the values question underlying the goals of the intervention; for example, what is optimal development? Another difficulty not mentioned is the question of the extent to which interventions can influence development.

Brown's Life-Role Development. Brown (1988) asserts, as do others, that career development theory is inadequate because of its individualistic, nonenvironmental focus and its failure to attend to the role of psychological deficits in career problems. Brown calls attention to the need to integrate systems theory with the individualistic psychological perspectives usually taken by career development theory. He proposes an approach that would view people more holistically and recognize the interrelationships of subsystems (for example, family and work), and he suggests an approach called *life-role development*. He argues that life roles (for example, student, worker, citizen) are interdependent, and that to understand individuals as workers we must consider the other components of their lives (for example, the family). To do so means that we must also recognize that the interdependency perspective on systems theory means that a change in one part of the system will influence other parts; because of this, a variety of interventions, sometimes targeting seemingly unrelated subsystems, may be effective (for example, intervening in the family role to affect the work role). His model is based on the assumptions (1) that life roles are interdependent (they can be complementary, compensatory, or conflicting); (2) that individuals strive for dynamic homeostasis among life roles; (3) that values are the most influential of the cognitive structures and, given unrestricted choice, individuals will act on values; (4) that career-related problems stem from lack of cognitive clarity, interrole and intrarole conflict, and barriers in the opportunity structure; (5) that each role provides the opportunity for satisfaction and dissatisfaction; (6) that change occurs as a result of conflict in the system; and (7) that interventions into life roles should consider the cognitive clarity of the individual, particularly as this relates to decision making and to how well values are clearly differentiated and integrated.

Brown outlines the specific steps involved in using this approach for practice. For example, in the assessment stage, it is necessary to identify the cognitive clarity of the client, as well as intrarole and interrole congruence. According to findings in the assessment stage, a variety of strategies can be used, such as cognitive techniques (countering, logical analysis) and interventions frequently employed by systems theorists (paradox, reframing).

Conclusions

This chapter has attempted to describe and summarize some recent directions in career development theory, with particular emphasis on women and racial and ethnic minorities. While new developments are disappointingly sparse in some areas, one conclusion that seems to be emerging is that if career development theory is to be comprehensive, it must incorporate some variables that have been omitted in past theory. Some areas of omission involve the interaction of sociocultural variables (such as the opportunity structure and sex-role socialization) with psychological variables (such as sex role and racial identity and the influence of other life roles on vocational choice and adjustment). On the one hand, comprehensiveness is a seemingly worthwhile goal for theory; on the other hand, the ultimate payoff may be slim, since all-encompassing theories pose barriers to research. Gottfredson (1983, p. 206), for example, notes that breadth of coverage can be a drawback: "Some philosophers of science point out [that] the pursuit of such grand theory shows much ambition but little promise — developing and integrating middle-range theories proves more productive."

12

Duane Brown

۞۞۞۞۞۞۞۞۞۞۞۞۞۞۞۞۞۞۞۞۞۞۞۞۞۞۞۞۞

Models of Career Decision Making

Earlier chapters in this volume have focused on the major theories of career development and occupational choice. As Jepsen and Dilley (1974) noted a decade and a half ago, the two most prominent theories, those of Super and Holland, are not actually theories of decision making. This is true because neither theorist has incorporated a model of decision making into his work. For the most part, the observation that theories of career development and occupational choice are not decision-making theories also extends to the other theories presented. Certainly, there is no hint in Bordin's work, or in the sociological theory set forth by Hotchkiss and Borow, of how decision makers arrive at their choices. Krumboltz's theory, as described by Mitchell and Krumboltz, does provide some insight into the complex decision-making process, but because it is discussed elsewhere, it will not be included in this chapter. Krumboltz's theory, as a decision-making theory, is discussed in more detail in an earlier publication (Mitchell and Krumboltz, 1984). Similarly, Miller-Tiedeman and Tiedeman have presented the influential decision-making model developed earlier by Tiedeman and O'Hara (1963); thus, it will not be discussed in this chapter.

With the exceptions just noted, some of the major career decision-making models will be presented in this chapter. The term *model* has been chosen because it has more limited connotations than the term *theory*. As Vroom (1964), Jepsen and Dilley (1974), and others have pointed out, decision-making models grow out of more comprehensive psychological theories, such as those set forth by Tolman (1959), Rotter (1954), Atkinson (1964), Edwards (1954), and others. For a fuller discussion of these antecedents, Vroom's (1964) work can be consulted.

Two types of models of decision making have evolved: prescriptive and descriptive (Jepsen and Dilley, 1974; Mitchell and Beach, 1976; Wright, 1984). Prescriptive decision-making models describe how decisions ought to be made, and descriptive models look at how people actually make decisions. Both types of models will be discussed in this presentation.

One quandary that arose in the development of this chapter was which models of career decision making would be addressed. Jepsen and Dilley (1974) chose four descriptive models (Fletcher, 1966; Hilton, 1962; Hsu, 1970; Vroom, 1964) and three prescriptive models (Gelatt, 1962; Katz, 1963; Kaldor and Zytowski, 1969). As Jepsen (1984) noted, career decision-making models have also been presented by Mitchell (1975), Janis and Mann (1977), Harren (1979b), and others. These contributions, with the exception of Janis and Mann's, have primarily reconceptualized or embellished existing models. Of the original eight models reviewed by Jepsen and Dilley, only those advanced by Tiedeman and O'Hara and by Vroom have stimulated research, although Katz's model provided the basis for a major computerized decision-making system, SIGI (Katz, 1974), which has been researched extensively. Vroom's (1964) model, which is by most estimates the most influential of the decision-making models (see Wanous, Keon, and Latack, 1983), will be discussed here as one representative of descriptive decision-making models. The descriptive conflict model of decision making delineated by Janis and Mann (1977) will also be discussed. The prescriptive Subjective Expected Utility model (Wright, 1984) will also be presented because it has stimulated a fair amount of research in the social sciences and has utility for practitioners interested in helping clients improve their career decision making. Other prescriptive models elaborated by Mitchell (1975) and Tversky

(1972) have also been included because of their potential utility to career counselors. These six models will first be described and then examined in terms of their empirical support. Finally, implications for practitioners will be drawn.

Background

Career decision-making models have been developed to explain the actual process of choosing an occupation. The concept of choice needs to be delineated from that of preference for an occupation. As Mitchell and Beach (1976) have noted, occupational preferences may be quite different from actual choices that are made. For example, an individual may prefer engineering over business but, for a variety of reasons, choose the latter field. Earlier, Vroom (1964) pointed out that we also need to distinguish between occupational choice and occupational attainment. Once a person chooses an occupation, he or she may have difficulty entering it because of training requirements, economic conditions, and so forth, and may not attain his or her choice. However, the individual who chooses a career that he or she cannot enter may have undergone a faulty decision-making process, although the failure to attain entry into a career once a choice has been made may be due to a variety of factors. The models discussed in this chapter focus on occupational choice, not on preferences for occupations or occupational attainment.

Harren (1979b, p. 119) defines a career decision-making model as "a description of a psychological process in which one organizes information, deliberates among alternatives, and makes a commitment to a course of action." Jepsen and Dilley (1974) indicate that the choice-making process involves several elements, including a decision maker and a decision situation in which two or more alternatives exist. The alternatives available to the career decision maker carry with them potential outcomes (for example, probability of attaining the choice) to which some probability or likelihood of occurrence can be assigned. Therefore, models of career decision making are predicated on the assumption that the outcomes of the career decision-making process can be predicted clearly enough that the decision maker can assign values to them. Conversely, it should be obvious that if there is only one solution to a problem, no decision-making process is required. It should also be clear that if two alternatives have equal probability of occurring and are equivalent with regard to attractiveness or value, a decision-making process is required, but the outcome is not critical in that no loss or gain will result from the decision.

The decision maker is the key variable in the decision-making process, and the influence of such factors as age, gender, personality traits, risk taking, and socioeconomic status on decision making has been studied extensively. That literature will not be reviewed here because the primary purpose of this chapter is to examine basic career decision-making models. However, career counselors, faced with clients in the real world, need to be acutely aware of the influence of the characteristics of their clients on the decision-making process.

Descriptive Models of Career Decision Making

Vroom's Expectancy Model

According to Vroom (1964), the plan for the book that presented his model and the research related to it evolved in 1959, and he decided to draft a 150-page monograph during the summer of 1961. This monograph grew to a 325-page book, which was published three years later. His intent was to appraise and integrate existing knowledge about work and motivation, in order to promote future advances in the field.

In setting forth his work, Vroom elected to focus on individuals, as opposed to groups; to deal only with work behaviors; to focus on the explanation of work-related behavior; to assume that human behavior is motivated from within; and to restrict the sources of data that he would consider valid to those that had arisen from objective observations. Since he believed that *work* is an ambiguous term, he adopted instead the concept of *work role,* which he defined as "a set of functions to be performed by a role occupant" (Vroom, 1964, p. 6). He went on to note that no two work roles are identical. *Motivation*, the second important concept in Vroom's theory, was defined as the processes that regulate voluntary activity.

Two constructs are crucial to an understanding of Vroom's theory: valence and expectancy. *Valence* is defined as an "affective orientation toward particular outcomes" (Vroom, 1964, p. 15) and is used synonymously with *preference*. Outcomes may have positive, negative, or neutral valences. Motives are associated with valence; that is, a person may have a positive, neutral, or negative motive that implies his or her wish to move toward or away from or to make no movement toward a particular outcome. Vroom does not equate the valence of an outcome with the value that the end has to the decision maker. For Vroom, the valence of an outcome is not based on the actual satisfaction provided, which is its value; rather, it is based on the satisfaction that the individual anticipates deriving from the outcome. The strength of the valence of an outcome is based on the degree of anticipated satisfaction that will be derived from a particular outcome. With regard to valence, Vroom proposes that the choice of an occupation allows those choosing it to attain certain goals or ends, such as security, status, or income. The valence of an occupation will be directly related to the sum of the valences of the goals that the individual perceives will be attained if that occupation is chosen. The results of a choice are not simply related to the decision making of the individual; external forces also affect the decision maker. Each decision maker has some idea about the impact of these external events upon his or her decision making. Therefore, a decision maker makes decisions that are partly based on preferences for outcomes and, to some degree, on expectancies, which Vroom defines as beliefs that choices can be realized. These expectancies are subjective, since no decision maker can be fully apprised of the actual probability of the attainment of a career choice.

Vroom borrowed Lewin's (1951) concept of force to specify how valences and expectancies interact to determine career choice. According to this construct, behavior, including decision making, takes place in a field of conflicting forces, which move the person toward or away from certain alternatives. Vroom accounts for force by viewing it as a result of valences and expectations. The force on the decision maker to choose a particular career, Vroom proposes, is directly related to the sum of the valences of all outcomes and the strength of his or her expectancies that the choice of a given career will result in the attainment of the desired outcomes.

Vroom elaborates on this second proposition by discussing the nature of the interacting expectancy and valence. For example, he indicates that high expectancy of attainment of a career choice will have little impact on force to choose a career if the valence of that choice is zero or very low. Similarly, a high valence will not increase force to make a choice if expectancy of entering that career is low. However, the two together combine to predict the forces on an individual to exert effort. If the valence of a particular career choice is high and the expectancy for attainment of that choice is high, it will be predicted that an individual will expend substantial effort in pursuing that career choice. Vroom's theory does not predict performance, only effort (Mitchell, 1974).

Empirical Support. Vroom's (1964) career decision-making model has proved quite heuristic. A number of literature reviews have examined empirical investigations based on Vroom's model (Mitchell, 1974; Mitchell and Beach, 1976; Wanous, Keon, and Latack, 1983). The Wanous, Keon, and Latack (1983) review focuses on the results of sixteen studies based on Vroom's model and presents a seventeenth study. They conclude that samples limited the generalizability of the results to the well-educated, and that some of the designs used in the research were inappropriate, but that the overall results are supportive of the model: "The empirical results using expectancy theory as a model of occupational/organizational choice process are supportive of the theory" (Wanous, Keon, and Latack, 1983, p. 82). They that suggest longitudinal research is needed to test the model more fully, that more diverse subject groups need to be studied, and that some methodological improvements will be needed in future research.

Implications for Practitioners. Vroom's model of career decision making has a number of implications for practitioners. First, counselors need to understand that career choice is a means to a variety of ends, not an end in itself. This means that the choice of a career puts the individual on the threshold of a vast array of outcomes, some of which are primarily related directly to the career itself and some of which are secondary to it. Primary outcomes of a career choice are related to geographical location of the workplace, working conditions, amount of time and energy expended on the job, and the degree to which work values are reinforced. Secondary outcomes of career choice are related to status, impact on family relationships, social obligations, and so on. Vroom's career decision-making model suggests that individuals need to consider carefully both the primary and the secondary outcomes of career choice, since these determine valence or affective orientation toward a particular career.

As noted in the foregoing section, expectancies are based on subjective estimates of outcomes. To a certain extent, these estimates can be improved by such information as job descriptions and data on the availability of jobs and future trends. However, expectancies are formed by the individual and are shaped by the interaction of the knowledge base with the individual's perception of the information. Career counselors must help individuals acquire information that will help them shape their expectancies and identify any of their own characteristics that may be influencing expectancies.

Force is also a useful concept for career counselors. If either expectancies or valences are low, effort will be negligible. Career counselors need to work on both sides of the equation, helping clients to identify positive and negative factors about careers and to develop realistic expectancies about entering those careers.

Janis and Mann's Conflict Model

Janis and Mann (1977) posit that conflicts arise whenever an individual has a decision to make that is of personal consequence. This conflict occurs because within each individual who is faced with a personally relevant decision are "simultaneous opposing tendencies to accept and reject a given course of action" (Janis and Mann, 1977, p. 46). The results of these conflicting forces are feelings of uncertainty, hesitancy to act, and even emotional distress.

The conflict that arises from the need to make personally relevant decisions gives rise to stress, which is defined as "a high degree of unpleasant emotion (such as anxiety, guilt, or shame) that affects normal patterns of information processing" (Janis and Mann, 1977, p. 50). Janis and Mann set forth the relationship between stress and decisional conflict in four basic assumptions, which are paraphrased here:

1. The amount of stress arising from a decisional conflict is related to the goals of the individual, the needs associated with those goals, and the expectation that certain needs will be unmet as a result of the decision. The greater the expectation that needs will be unmet, the greater the stress.

2. Threats and/or opportunities precipitate decision making. Decisional stress is related to the degree to which the decision maker is committed to his or her present course of action whenever threats or opportunities arise.

3. When all viable alternatives to the problem and threat are perceived as serious risks, there is loss of hope that a desirable alternative can be located, and defensive avoidance occurs. Defensive avoidance is characterized by exaggeration of the gains or minimization of the losses that will result from the alternatives, by procrastination, by dependence on others, and by selective attention to data.

4. When a moderate degree of stress is induced by a decisional conflict, a vigilant effort is made to identify or evaluate an available alternative, so long as there is hope that a reasonable alternative can be found.

The decision-making process begins with some type of threat to the decision maker; thus, she or he feels compelled to act on a situation that is perceived as an opportunity to advance toward her or his goals. Janis and Mann believe that decision makers ask themselves a series of questions when they are faced with decision-making opportunities. The first of these is "Are there risks involved if I do not change?" If the answer to this question is no, then no stress is generated, and the result is unconflicted adherence. In other words, the person simply changes to meet the demands of the situation because there appears to be no reason not to do so. An analogous situation in career decision making may occur when a person is transferred to a lateral position that makes very little difference to her work life or out-of-work life. It is unlikely that there will be stress or conflict in this situation.

The second question is "Are the risks serious if I do change?" Janis and Mann believe that if the answer to this question is negative, unconflicted change results. However, because stress is minimal, the decision maker may use a "Band-Aid" approach and not seriously consider all alternatives or even the information about obvious alternatives. The high school senior who simply moves into the family business after graduation because some of his salient alternatives appear to hold some minimal risks is engaged in unconflicted change if those alternatives were higher choices initially. The senior who joins the family business also demonstrates a decided lack of commitment to other career choices, another prerequisite of unconflicted change, since commitment to a course of action will produce stress and increase vigilance.

If decisional conflict is great, the third question confronting the decision maker is "Can I hope to find a viable solution to the problem?" If the answer to this question is no, defensive avoidance may occur. If the answer is maybe or yes, a fourth question arises: "Is there sufficient time to search for viable alternatives?" If the answer to this question is no, hypervigilance is the result. If the answer to the question about available time is yes, vigilance is the result. A hypervigilant approach to decision making occurs in emergency situations, where individuals are faced with real time limitations. In this situation, it is impossible to consider all alternatives or information about the alternatives. Vigilance, which is obviously the preferred decision-making state, is characterized by careful attention to the generation of data, collection of information about alternatives, and objective weighing of information about the decision.

As noted earlier, persons who engage in defensive avoidance may procrastinate, become dependent on others, or fail to consider objectively the positive and negative consequences of various alternatives. This latter approach, which Janis and Mann call *bolstering,* involves rationalization of a particular choice. Rationalization occurs through minimizing risks or losses and/or exaggerating gains. The fifty-five-year-old career decision maker who has lost a middle-management position that pays $50,000 per year may adopt an approach of defensive avoidance toward decision making. He may also become hypervigilant if he has financial concerns that are immediate and overwhelming. The result of either approach is likely to be a decision that is less than optimal.

One final aspect of Janis and Mann's model is worth noting. They posit that pursuing a vigilant approach to decision making tends to immunize decision makers against postdecisional stress. They believe that if one carefully considers all alternatives, one is better able to handle problems that may arise out of the decision, having done one's best in arriving at the decision. They have also developed a balance-sheet approach to decision making that represents the vigilant approach.

Empirical Support. Janis and Mann's model of decision making has stimulated a few research studies regarding career decision making. It was used by Harren (1979b) in his development of a model of career decision making for college students. Much of the research growing out of the Janis and Mann model has focused on the use of a balance-sheet procedure to improve decision making because, as Mann (1972, p. 291) puts it, "Conflict theory assumes that sound decision making involves careful scanning of all the relevant types of considerations that enter into a decisional 'balance sheet.'" Mann also notes that when individuals develop decisional balance sheets, avoiding errors is important to well-being. Avoiding errors entails carefully delineating the positive and negative outcomes of various alternatives. If these outcomes are identified accurately, the decision maker is inoculated against experiencing negative affect, even if he or she makes decisions that have negative outcomes.

Mann (1972), building on prior research by Janis (1968), engaged high school students in constructing their own decisional balance sheets regarding the choice of a college. Students in this study were asked to generate a list of colleges that they were considering, describe the positive and negative features of their top alternatives, and construct a balance sheet that listed gains and losses to themselves regarding each alternative, gains and losses to others, approval and disapproval of others that would occur as a result of each alternative, and self-approval or self-disapproval that would occur as a result of each choice. Mann concluded that students exposed to this type of procedure appeared to demonstrate greater decisional stability than students in a control group. He also found that the experimental group demonstrated lower postdecisional conflict and regret. His findings support those found previously by Janis (1968). Later, Janis and Mann (1977) looked at the number of errors in the balance sheets developed by subjects and concluded that the fewer errors made in the identification of utilities and sources of approval and disapproval, the greater the likelihood of satisfaction with a decision. Janis and Mann also present a number of case studies and empirical studies that support their propositions. Few of these studies deal directly with career decision making, however. Similarly, studies by Hoyt and Janis (1975) and by Colten and Janis (1982) focus on the use of the balance sheet in decision making but are unrelated to career decision making.

Implications for Practitioners. Two implications for practitioners grow out of Janis and Mann's career decision-making model. The most obvious of these involves the concept of the balance-sheet approach to making career decisions. There are sixteen steps in preparing a balance sheet such as the one shown in Exhibit 12.1:

1. Generate career alternatives.
2. Assign importance ratings to these alternatives (+ 5 to
    − 5).

Exhibit 12.1. The Balance Sheet.

	Alternative Courses of Action					
	Alternative 1		Alternative 2		Alternative 3	
	+	−	+	−	+	−
A. Utilitarian gains or losses for self						
1. Personal income						
2. Interest value of work						
3. Opportunity to live in preferred city						
4. Social status						
5. Educational opportunities						
6. Leisure opportunities						
7. Other						
B. Utilitarian gains or losses for significant other						
1. Personal income						
2. Interest value of work						
3. Opportunity to live in preferred city						
4. Social status						
5. Educational opportunities						
6. Leisure opportunities						
7. Other						
C. Self-approval or -disapproval						
1. Moral or legal consideration						
2. Serving others						
3. Self-image (e.g., variable)						
4. Other						
D. Social approval or disapproval						
1. From wife/husband						
2. From close friends						
3. From colleagues						
4. Other						

Source: Reprinted with permission of The Free Press, a Division of Macmillan, Inc., from *Decision Making: A Psychological Analysis of Conflict, Choice, and Commitment,* by Irving L. Janis and Leon Mann. Copyright © 1977 by The Free Press.

3.   List utilitarian gains for oneself for each alternative.
4.   Assign importance ratings to these alternatives (+ 5 to − 5).
5.   List utilitarian gains for others.
6.   Assign importance ratings to these gains (+ 5 to − 5).
7.   Repeat steps 3–6 for utilitarian losses.
8.   List sources of social approval for each alternative.
9.   Assign importance ratings to such approval (+ 5 to − 5).
10. List sources of social disapproval for each alternative.
11. Assign importance ratings to such disapproval (+ 5 to − 5).
12. List types and sources of self-approval for each alternative.
13. Assign importance ratings to such self-approval (+ 5 to − 5).
14. List sources and types of self-disapproval for each alternative.
15. Assign importance ratings to such self-disapproval (+ 5 to − 5).
16. Compute the value of each alternative by summing positive and negative weights.

A shortcoming of this approach is that there is no safeguard against the premature elimination of careers. It may be wiser for the decision maker to employ the Elimination by Aspects (EBA) model (Gati, 1986) to reduce the number of alternatives and then use the balance-sheet approach. The EBA model, described later in this chapter, requires the decision maker to focus on critical features of the alternatives as a major factor in decision making.

The second implication of this model of decision making involves the fact that Janis and Mann identify maladaptive decision-making styles. In a sense, so do the other models discussed in this chapter: if one is not following the models as laid out, the results are likely to be poor career decisions. However, Janis and Mann's constructs of acquiescence, hypervigilance, and defensive avoidance can be useful to career counselors who are interested in diagnosing maladaptive approaches to career decision making.

Prescriptive Career Decision-Making Models

Restle's Reconceptualized Choice Model (RCM)

Mitchell (1975) has reconceptualized Restle's (1961) choice model to fit the special case of career decision making. Restle's original model posited that the decision maker compares the implications of a decision situation with an ideal situation in his or her mind. The resulting decision is predicted to be the one that most closely approximates the ideal situation or outcome.

Mitchell suggests that one problem in applying Restle's model to career decision making is that many career decision makers may have no ideal alternatives in their minds; instead, the career decision maker may have a "set of . . . preferences for certain characteristics and priorities" (Mitchell, 1975, p. 316). In the consideration of a number of career alternatives, the preferences may be present in some, all, or none of them. Obviously, the goal is to choose from among the alternatives. To make a choice, the decision maker must make explicit distinctions among the valued aspects of career alternatives.

The elements of the preferences can be categorized in the following way:

1. *Absolute constraints:* These characteristics of a career must be present or absent for an alternative to be viable. Those that must be present are called *positive absolutes,* and those that must be absent are labeled *negative absolutes.*
2. *Negative characteristics:* These are undesirable aspects of a career choice. However, the degree of their undesirability varies.
3. *Positive characteristics:* These are desirable aspects of a career choice. The degree of desirability of these aspects also varies.
4. *Neutral characteristics:* These elements are irrelevant to the choice at hand.

These characteristics are represented as follows: K = negative absolutes, K' = positive absolutes, C = negative characteristics, P = positive characteristics, and N = irrelevant characteristics.

Mitchell (1975) has developed certain axioms regarding career choice. The most obvious of these is that if a given career alternative does not satisfy the absolute alternatives, the probability of its being chosen will be zero. Perhaps just as obvious is the second axiom, which is that if a given alternative has a positive characteristic that corresponds to the positive elements that the decision maker associates with a career choice, the probability of that career's being chosen is greater than zero, by comparison with a second alternative that does not have that positive characteristic. The converse of this statement would be true if career A possessed a negative characteristic and career B did not; that is, the likelihood of choosing career B is greater than zero, by comparison with career A.

Mitchell (1975) suggests that the career decision maker may actually make decisions in a number of ways:

1.   He or she may compare only the positive characteristics of the alternatives.
2.   He or she may consider one alternative at a time, weighing positive characteristics against negative characteristics.
3.   He or she may choose an alternative not so much because of its merits but because of its negative characteristics. The choice in this situation is, in a sense, avoidance behavior.
4.   He or she may view the alternatives as having only negative characteristics. In this case, the decision maker minimizes the negative impact of the choice.
5.   He or she may see the alternatives as having both positive and negative characteristics, and these aspects are considered simultaneously.
6.   He or she may view some alternatives as having only positive characteristics, others as having only negative characteristics, and still others as having both types of characteristics.

Predictions can be made from this model only if one knows the magnitude of the weights attached by the decision maker to various characteristics of the available alternatives. Obviously, when absolute constraints are lacking (positive) or present (negative), an alternative will be eliminated. However, if the decision maker focuses only on the positive characteristics of an alternative, we can only predict that the choice will be related to the magnitude of the coefficients attached to the aspects of that alternative. Since these weights are idiosyncratic, they must be elicited from the individual. Mitchell suggests that this can be done with either interviews or paper-and-pencil measures.

Empirical Support. No empirical support for Mitchell's (1975) revision of Restle's (1961) model was found, nor, unfortunately, was any research found on Restle's model of decision making that would be useful in evaluating it as a basis for the career decision-making process.

Implications for Practitioners. Mitchell's revision of Restle's decision making model has some interesting implications for practitioners. Chief among these is the idea that there are absolute constraints, of both a positive and a negative nature. Determining these at the outset of the career exploration process may be a useful way to begin. Another useful idea is that career decision makers may look at careers in different ways at different times, focusing variously on positive and negative characteristics or perhaps on some combination of the two. One useful exercise may be to determine what characteristics of a career are being considered. Mitchell (1975) makes no mention of the maturity of career decision makers; nevertheless, a decision maker who is less mature probably would consider only some of the data regarding a particular alternative. It would also be interesting to know whether a decision maker may focus to such a large extent on certain positive and negative characteristics that he or she overlooks a vast amount of information about a career (or, as Janis and Mann, 1977, suggest, a decision maker may exaggerate the favorable consequences of one action and minimize the negative consequences of another).

Subjective Expected Utility (SEU) Model

Prescriptive models of decision making have been developed to show people how they should make decisions. The subjective expected utility (SEU) model of decision making, derived from certain mathematical principles, purportedly will help decision makers maximize the likelihood of attaining desirable outcomes. This principle is called the *maximization of expectancies,* which simply means that when a decision maker is faced with a number of outcomes, the value or utility of each outcome, along with the probability of its occurrence, should dictate the action to be performed (Mitchell and Beach, 1976; Wright, 1984). In some instances, actual values and probabilities can be attached to outcomes; in the area of career decision making, however, subjective values and probabilities must be assigned.

The subjective expected utility of a particular career alternative can be illustrated as follows (Mitchell and Beach, 1976, p. 237):

$SEU = (P_k \times U_k) + (1 - P_k) (-U_k)$

P_k = Probability that outcome k will occur if particular career decision is made $(0 - 1)$

U_k = Utility of receiving k $(1 - 10)$

$1 - P_k$ = Probability that outcome k will not occur if that same career decision is made

$-U_k$ = Disutility of not receiving k $(1 - 10$ values$)$

When a college student is faced with the choice of a major, the following situation may evolve:

Art History versus Business

Expected outcome (k) = Employment in field at time of graduation with B.A.

SEU (Art History) $= (.1 \times 10) + (1 - .9) (-4)$

                       $= 1 + (-.4)$

                       $= .6$

                       $(P_k \times U_k) + 1 - P_k) - U_k$

                       $= (.1 \times 10) + (1 \times .9) (-4)$

                       $= 1 + -.36$

                       $= .64$

SEU (Business) $= (.6 \times 10) + (1 - .6) (-4)$

                       $6 + -2.4$

                       $= 3.6$

Please note that students assign all weights according to their own subjective estimates of the importance of different variables. In this case, business would be the choice dictated by the model. As we shall see in the next section, this formula changes and simplifies whenever there is likelihood that all desired outcomes will occur to some degree, given the range of decisions.

The subjective expected utility of a particular career choice is obtained first by multiplying the subjective values associated with that career and the probabilities that the desired outcomes will be attained if that career is chosen ($P_k \times U_k$). To this number is added the product that the desired outcome will not occur, even if that choice is made, and the disutility of not receiving that outcome $[(1 - P_k)(-U_k)]$. As seen in the equation, what is actually being added is a negative coefficient. In this model, the career decision maker must compute a subjective expected utility for each career option. The option with the highest coefficient is the one that should be chosen (Mitchell and Beach, 1976).

Wright (1984) suggests a simpler algebraic approach to determining the correct decision. In the example of the college student who was considering art history versus business, the disutility of not getting a job related to his training was built in as a negative factor. However, in the examples that follow, two career choice makers are confronted with choice situations, the first of which involves all positive utilities. The second example illustrates how negative utilities can be plugged in to the formula in a somewhat less confusing manner than the one suggested by Mitchell and Beach (1976). Our first career decision maker is faced with choosing between teaching mathematics and becoming an engineer. She desires certain kinds of outcomes as a result of this choice. These are:

Utilities (1–10)	Probability of Achieving If (0 to 1)	
	Teacher	*Engineer*
Job security (9)	1.0	.8
High salary (10)	.1	1.0
Status (6)	.2	.6

Geographic mobility (6)	1.0	.9
Challenging job (7)	.4	.8
Time for leisure (4)	1.0	.4
Time for family (7)	1.0	.4

SEU (teacher) = 9 + .1 + 1.2 + .6 + 2.8 + 4 + 7 = 24.7
SEU (engineer) = 7.2 + 10 + 3.6 + 5.4 + 5.6 + 1.6 + 2.8 = 36.2

From the SEU decision-model perspective, this person should become an engineer.

In the foregoing example, the utilities (the values associated with certain outcomes related to a job choice) were all positive, but they could have been negative (Mitchell and Beach, 1976). For example, working in a dangerous environment may be assigned a value of -8, or commuting into a major city may be assigned a weight of -10 by some career decision makers. When negative values are assigned, the computation of subjective expected utility of two career choices may appear as follows:

Utilities (− 10 to + 10)	*Probability of Achieving If (0 to 1)*	
	Salesperson	*Accountant*
High income (8)	.9	.9
Autonomy on the job (10)	.8	.2
Security (4)	.3	.8
Free time (8)	.9	.3
Commuting long distances (− 8)	.9	.5
Opportunity for spousal employment (7)	.8	.7

SEU (salesperson) = 7.2 + 8.0 + 1.2 + 7.2 − 7.2 + 5.6 = 22.0
SEU (accountant) = 7.2 + 2.0 + 3.2 + 2.4 − 4.0 + 4.9 = 15.7

The model dictates that becoming a salesperson is the preferable choice.

Empirical Support. In a review of the empirical literature related to the SEU model of career decision making, Mitchell and Beach (1976) critiqued half a dozen studies and concluded that they were generally supportive of the model. However, two subsequent reviews were somewhat more critical. Pitz and Harren (1980) indicate that the SEU approach shows promise as an aid to career decision making, but that there are problems in its usage because of its inability to handle dynamic value systems and problems in decision analysis. These authors did conclude that "regardless of the problems confronting those who wish to use EU theory [SEU], it still appears to be the most defensible approach to decision making, especially if it is supplemented with the techniques of the counselor in completing the structure of the problem" (Pitz and Harren, 1980, pp. 340–341). Interestingly, Wright (1984), who reviewed the general research literature on decision making, including that related to risk taking through gambling, concludes, "The general conclusion from this research is that SEU does not describe choice between gambles and, by generalization, will not describe decision making under uncertainty in the more complex real world" (Wright, 1984, pp. 65–66).

Implications for Practitioners. Good career decision makers must be able to identify viable alternatives that will lead to hoped-for outcomes. As Pitz and Harren (1980) have noted, one of the counselor's roles is to help clients analyze their career choices and frame them in a manner that will allow the types of analyses described in the foregoing sections.

Establishing the subjective values of the various outcomes of a career decision is critical to ensuring that the final decision is the best one. There are psychometric instruments available that may be utilized to help clients clarify values and thus enhance their ability to assess the worth of certain outcomes of career choices. However, engaging clients in work-values clarification exercises, such as asking them what they enjoy (value) about their current jobs, may be a more useful way of facilitating this process.

Probabilities that certain choices will lead to certain outcomes can be discerned, to some degree, through access to various sources of occupational information. To be sure, there are questions about the extent to which persons retain any type of information, just as there are difficulties in finding the information needed. For career information to be retained and utilized, it must have personal relevance (Katz, Norris, and Pears, 1978; Pitz and Harren, 1980). Information, to be helpful in establishing probabilities, must provide data about all the relevant outcomes sought by the decision maker (Slovic and Mac Phillamy, 1974).

To help individuals maximize their retention and usage of occupational information, certain variables appear to be important. First, if Katz, Norris, and Pears (1978) are correct, each individual must have a well-developed view of self, particularly her or his own values, so that material can be interpreted in light of this personal frame of reference. Second, information must provide data that relate to the expected outcomes of a particular choice. Third, information should be presented in a fashion that will inform all the possible alternatives, not simply the one that seems most feasible. Pitz and Harren (1980) point out that decision makers often ignore information related to less probable but feasible occupations. Finally, as Pitz and Harren (1980) and Wright (1984) suggest, the SEU model can be used as a decision-making aid in a variety of situations, including career decision making.

Elimination by Aspects (EBA) Model

The SEU model, just discussed, requires that all of the outcomes relating to a choice be identified, scaled, and weighted. The alternative chosen is the one with the greatest weight across attributes. This model of career decision making, while it shows promise, appears to have limitations whenever there is uncertainty about either the values associated with choices or the probability of attaining the desired outcomes. Tversky (1972), along with a number of others, has developed a model of decision making that is perhaps more useful under conditions of uncertainty. The Elimination by Aspects (EBA) model focuses on all choices simultaneously. Each choice has numerous characteristics or aspects. For example, one career offers a desirable beginning salary range, certain work conditions, a particular geographical location, and certain opportunities for the future, while another career offers other characteristics or aspects. According to Tversky, at each stage in any decision-making process a particular aspect or characteristic of a job is considered. For example, once a list of potential career choices is selected, decision makers may look at salaries and eliminate alternatives that are not likely to meet their minimum expectations. Tversky (1972, p. 298) warns that the "major flaw in the principle of elimination lies in its failure to ensure that the alternatives retained are, in fact, superior to those which are eliminated."

Gati (1986), adapting Tversky's model to what he terms a *sequential elimination approach,* contrasts it with the SEU model. He suggests that while the EBA model may appear incompatible with career-development theories, this is not the case. Career decisions are made sequentially; at various choice points, certain options are eliminated. He goes on to suggest that the whole developmental process associated with career decision making can be conceptualized as increasing the specification of career choices as different aspects of various occupations are considered. He outlines the career decision-making process as follows:

1. Identify the relevant aspects or characteristics of the careers to be considered. This identification process can be considered either as an ongoing process or as a single event that may occur within the context of career counseling.
2. Rank aspects by importance. This process should include rankings based on subjective measures (such as values), objective constraints (such as physical requirements and aptitudes), and the nature of the job itself (including work environment, salary, prestige, and so on).
3. Identify the acceptable range of the most important (highest-ranked) aspect.
4. Eliminate careers that do not provide an acceptable range of the aspect being considered.
5. Keep repeating steps 3 and 4 until the list of careers being considered is acceptably short.
6. Do further exploration of the occupations that remain.

Presumably, as exploration continues, more knowledge about the aspects of a job will be acquired, and sequential elimination will occur until a single choice remains. Gati (1986) observes that Gottfredson's theory of occupational decision making appears to follow the framework of the EBA model.

Empirical Support. To date, no studies have tested the use of the EBA model of career decision making, probably because it has only recently been adapted to the career decision-making process.

Implications for Practitioners. Gati (1986) believes that the EBA model of career decision making may be more useful than the SEU model, since the latter approach does not correspond to the cognitive structure of decision making and some of its assumptions are rejected by many. He believes that the SEU model may be useful only if the decision maker is faced with a small number of alternatives — perhaps five or fewer. The EBA model may have its greatest utility in reducing a large number of career options to a few, which can be studied in detail.

The EBA model requires the individual to identify the positive and negative aspects of particular career choices, to rank them, and to establish acceptable ranges of each aspect. Then, one aspect at a time, choices are eliminated. This process accommodates people's cognitive limitations (Gati, 1986) and allows them to make decisions under conditions of uncertainty. But, as Tversky (1972) himself has warned, nothing in the model ensures that the decision maker will not eliminate alternatives that would potentially satisfy the criteria that he or she has established. However, a career counselor can work with a client to identify acceptable characteristics of a job and to secure information about jobs that will help the career decision maker form judgments to maximize the probability that the chosen career will meet the criteria.

Evaluating the Models

Five models of career decision making have been presented in the foregoing pages. Two of these are descriptive models; that is, they were developed by the model builders to represent the normal decision-making process. Three of the models were developed as prescriptive models. In a sense, evaluating these two types of career decision-making models is like distinguishing between the proverbial apples and oranges. Descriptive models can be evaluated only with regard to a single criterion: How well do they actually describe the decision-making process that is engaged in by the typical person faced with career decisions? Prescriptive models of decision making should be evaluated only on the basis of the extent to which they improve decision making once they are taught to decision makers. As noted earlier, the model developed by Vroom (1964) has been empirically supported, while Restle's reconceptualized model has not (Mitchell, 1975). The SEU model has also been supported by empirical research, although not under conditions of uncertainty, and the EBA model has not been widely researched.

Another approach to evaluating these models concerns the extent to which application of a model produces the best career decision. Not all of the five models presented here were designed as *optimizing* models; that is, not all were designed to produce the *best* career decision. Rather, some models were designed to produce *satisfactory* career decisions. These models are termed *satisficing models*. These two types of models are illustrated in Figure 12.1.

Optimizing career decision-making models were developed with the intent of identifying the alternative that would produce the best decision. This particular approach to decision making requires that every viable alternative and all information about that alternative be considered (Janis and Mann, 1977). However, as Simon (1967), Wright (1984), and others have noted, the typical person is unable to process the amount of information related to most decisions, at least not without the aid of a computer.

If one considers the initial career decision-making process as a case in point, it is literally impossible for a single individual to consider all of his or her traits, the demands of the job, job-trend data, information about the impact of the job on his or her personal life and leisure activities, and other pertinent data simultaneously. Vroom's model and the SEU model are optimizing approaches to decision making. However, with regard to Vroom's model, it is also important to note that what it actually predicts is effort to achieve a goal, not the attainment of the goal itself.

It is also important to reiterate one criticism of the SEU

Figure 12.1. Schematics of Optimizing and
Satisficing Models of Decision Making.[a]

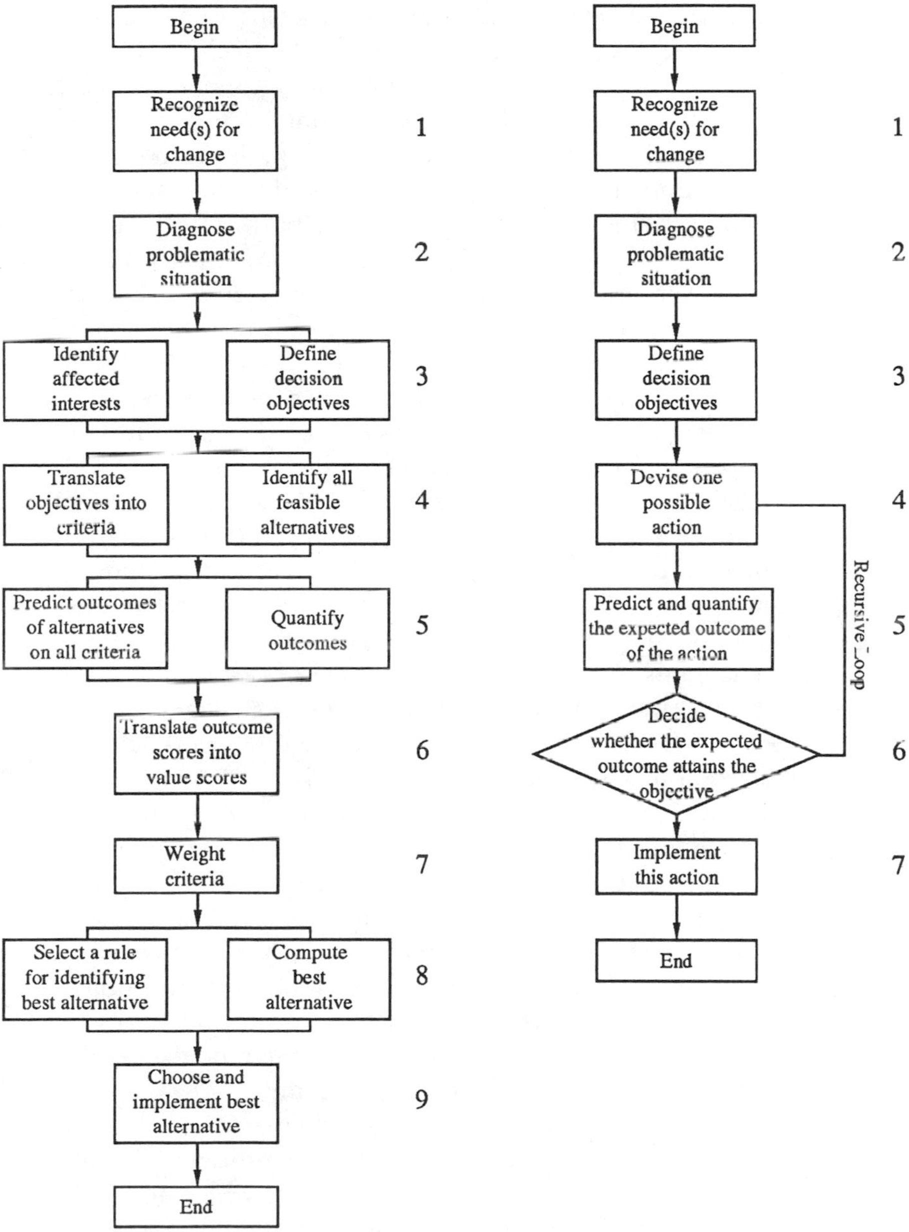

[a]The satisficing decision model is the less complex one on the right. The optimizing decision model is the one on the left, which becomes more complex from the third step through to the end of the process.

Source: Easton, A. (1976). *Decision Making: A Short Course for Professionals: Book I — An Overview.* New York: John Wiley & Sons, Inc., p. 7. Reprinted with permission.

model: it does not seem to work well under conditions of risk or uncertainty, perhaps because, as Janis and Mann (1977) have observed, there are conflicting forces at work whenever the decision to be made is personally relevant to the decision maker. The SEU approach does not consider conflict, stress, or possible mental health problems, and this may account for its deficiencies.

In satisficing models of decision making, decision makers establish minimal requirements for jobs and then seek solutions that meets these requirements (Janis and Mann, 1977). In this approach, as typified by either Restle's model or the EBA model, decision makers establish a few ground rules or criteria that, if applied to the decisions at hand, will result in the choice of the best alternative (for example, a career must provide high status, allow me to live in the South, and be commensurate with my interests). It is possible to meet all of these criteria and yet arrive at a very unsatisfactory career choice. The problem in the satisficing approach to decision making is to identify a small but salient set of criteria by which alternatives can be judged. Regardless of the list chosen, there are no assurances that the decision reached will be as satisfactory as the one selected according to all possible criteria.

The Janis and Mann (1977) model of decision making was not set forth as either an optimizing or a satisficing model, for the authors of the model believed that either approach was likely to result in a less than satisfactory decision, for the reasons already stated. Rather, they hoped to identify the conditions under which vigilant decision making occurs, a prerequisite of the optimizing approach to decision making. Ultimately, with the development of their balance-sheet approach to decision making, Janis and Mann did set forth an optimizing approach to career decision making (and are perhaps inadvertently subject to their own criticisms). Restle's (1961) original model, as well as Mitchell's (1975) reconceptualization of the model, are also optimizing models of career decision making.

Both the optimizing and the satisficing approaches to career decision making appear to have shortcomings. The obvious question that must be raised concerns which model(s) should be adopted. Since there seems to be no definitive answer, the safest response seems to be to use some combination of the models. Gati (1986) has suggested that career counselors adopt both the SEU model and the EBA model and adapt them to the needs of particular clients or use them sequentially with a single client (to extend Gati's recommendation). Career counselors may actually wish to draw on all the models suggested here as they work with career decision makers.

As Gati has suggested, career decision makers can be helped to establish gross criteria and to use a satisficing approach, such as the EBA model, to narrow their choices to a manageable number. Next, an optimizing model, such as the SEU model, can be employed to facilitate choosing from this short list. Other combinations are also possible.

Restle's or Janis and Mann's models may help career counselors either to discern which characteristics of careers are the focus of the search or to identify nonvigilant decision-making strategies. Vroom's decision-making model may be a useful tool for predicting the motivational level of a client and, thus, the effort that he or she will expend in pursuing a career goal. Certainly, Vroom's idea that career choices lead to certain valued outcomes (such as status and income) is an important concept. In a related vein, Vroom's construct of expectancy is certainly useful for career counselors when it is coupled with the construct of valence. Just because a career is valued does not mean that it will be pursued, if the client's expectancy of actually entering that career is low. The factors that influence both valence and expectancy must be examined in the career decision-making process.

Conclusions

For the most part, those who have built theories of career development and occupational choice have all but ignored the crucial decision-making processes. Including these models in this chapter may stimulate career development theorists to consider career decision making more carefully as they revise their thinking. This chapter should also provide career counselors with some approaches to help their clients as they struggle with the career decision-making process, although none of the models presented here has enough logical and/or empirical support to justify its wholesale adoption by career counselors.

13

Douglas T. Hall

৸৵ ৸৵

Career Development Theory in Organizations

Career development does not take place in a vacuum. It takes place in a social or institutional context, whether in a large organization like IBM (for an engineer or manager who works there) or in a smaller setting (say, for the customers and colleagues of an independently employed plumber). It will be the purpose of this chapter to discuss what difference the organizational context makes.

I have defined the term *career* as the sequence of work-related experiences and attitudes that occur over the span of the person's work life (Hall, 1976). One of the early differences to appear between the organizational approach to careers and the vocational psychology approach was in the time span considered: the former approach dealt with lifelong work experiences, while the latter focused more on the initial occupational choices of high school and college students. This has changed, to some extent, as such vocational researchers as Super have looked at mid- and late-career issues. Phillips, Cairo, Blustein, and Myers (1988) provide an excellent review of specific organizational influences that affect vocational behavior. However, there is still a general tendency for vocational psychologists to look more at students and young workers, while organizational career researchers focus more on people in their adult working lives.

422

Perhaps a more fundamental difference between the two approaches is that vocational psychology is more concerned with basic individual processes, such as decision making (Tiedeman and O'Hara, 1963; Tiedeman and Miller-Tiedeman, 1984) and person-occupation fit (Holland, 1973a), which lead to good adjustment of the individual in the career role. Organizational career theorists, in contrast, look more at situational influences in the organizational career environment that affect a wide range of outcomes beyond adjustment (for example, performance, job mobility, organizational commitment, changes in values and identity, and work-family interactions).

With that overly brief summary of the differences between the two fields, I will start this chapter by providing some historical background on the study of careers in organizational contexts and will move on to an overview of major models and theories. Next I will present some of my thoughts in relation to these models. I will also comment on contemporary issues in organizational career development (such as midcareer change and alternative career patterns) and consider why the work of vocational psychologists and organizational career development scholars has taken such different paths over the years.

Background

The study of careers in organizations began with early writings in the social science disciplines on human behavior in work settings. In social psychology, Kurt Lewin and his associates at the Massachusetts Institute of Technology's Center for Research on Group Dynamics examined the notion of the individual's *life space,* which involves the interactions between the person and the social environment. In sociology, what is now known as the Chicago school looked at institutions, the roles of their members, and how these influences affected the members over time; for example, see Becker, Geer, Hughes, and Strauss's (1957) classic study of the socialization of medical students. In political science, the focus was on organizational structures and norms, and their effect on the integration of the individual into the organization. An example here would be Kaufman's (1960) study of how rangers in the U.S. Forest Service were socialized to act independently but in accordance with the Forest Service's policies. Finally, in labor relations and organizational behavior, the psychological contract — that is, the mutual set of expectations between the individual and the employing organization — was viewed as a long-term career process. Let us review each of these historical approaches to organizational careers in turn.

Lewin's Field Theory. Kurt Lewin, a German psychologist, was one of the first to apply psychological principles and research to the problems of social change. He was concerned with social attitudes and prejudice, and he had a normative agenda for improving relations between various types of groups, such as Jews and gentiles and blacks and whites. Much of this concern grew out of the social tensions that became manifest around World War II.

Lewin and his colleagues created a center for the study of group dynamics at MIT and later moved to the University of Michigan. Lewin believed that the best social research made a difference or led to change. He also thought that the best way to test a theory was through action (that is, to see if it produced the predicted results). One of his best-known quotations is "There is nothing so practical as good theory," which captures this notion (Marrow, 1969). This change-oriented view of research has come to be called *action research.*

One institutional result of Lewin's program of research was the National Training Laboratories, which started with training groups (or T-groups) for instructing participants in the basic skills of group interaction. Out of this work grew the field of organizational development. Such current applied behavioral science activities as participative management, cooperative labor-management quality-of-work-life (QWL) experiments, and organization and job redesign can be traced to Lewinian origins.

For our purposes, perhaps the most powerful concept from Lewin's work is the idea that a person's behavior (B) is a product of both the person (P) and the environment (E). He expressed this mathematically as $B = f(P,E)$ (Lewin, 1951). This was a drastic departure from the then prevailing notion in psychology (primarily from Freud and the early, biologically oriented psychologists) that inborn or early socialized individual differences were largely responsible for most human behavior. Lewin's contribution was to get people looking at the social environment as a source of influence, in interaction with individual differences.

In particular, Lewin used the concept of the person's life space — the view of the world from the individual's perspective. He felt that each person constructed his or her own view of the world and then behaved in response to that view (or life space). In the life space are the various facets, roles, and key involvements that collectively represent the person's total life. Various boundaries separate the different areas of one's life, and a boundary separates the person from each sphere of life. Within this life space, the person's life can be viewed as a series of transactions with various key individuals and institutions over time.

The concept of the life space gave us an early sense of organizational career, in two important senses. First, it was one of the first holistic models (that is, it dealt with the whole person). This was in contrast to other early work in psychology, which dealt primarily with particular slices of life, such as early childhood experiences. The second career-relevant notion was that of time. Lewin's was one of the first approaches to look at adult behavior over time in institutional settings. He was concerned with how people changed in response to their experiences in groups and organizations. This work spanned the 1930s, the 1940s, and the 1950s. It showed up later primarily in the field of organizational behavior, which I will discuss in more detail later.

The Chicago School of Sociology. The University of Chicago was the first American university to establish a department of sociology. Underlying much of the work in the department was the idea that one could not develop formal theory until one understood the details of everyday social life. Thus, much of the work of the Chicago sociologists was focused on the rich variety of social settings found in Chicago in the 1920s and later. Various forms of social deviance were frequently studied, in areas of the city with high rates of prostitution, jazz music, marijuana use, and homelessness. W. I. Thomas and his colleagues developed the use of life histories to study the chain of social events that led people to move into certain social roles, such as the role of juvenile delinquent (Thomas, 1923). Like Lewin, Thomas's stress was on the researcher's ability to understand how members of a social group perceive their own lives, how they construct reality. One of his most often quoted statements is "If men define situations as real, they are real in their consequences" (Thomas and Thomas, 1928, p. 572). The difference between Thomas and Lewin was that Thomas and the other sociologists were focusing on the social role and on how the person entered and operated within it; for Lewin, the focus was on the person and on how the environment affected the person.

The first scholar of the Chicago school to make explicit use of the term *career* in relation to formal institutions was Everett C. Hughes (1958). Under Hughes's guidance, people in a wide variety of occupations were studied: medical students, nurses, school teachers, lawyers, airline pilots, taxi drivers, and many others (Barley, 1989). In contrast to other researchers, who used *career* to mean something more like *profession,* Hughes and his colleagues used it more generally to apply to any social role or facet of a person's life. Thus, for example, Erving Goffman (1961) wrote a famous essay titled "The Moral Career of the Mental Patient."

Hughes (1937) pointed out that a career has two facets. The *objective* career is the series of positions or offices ("statuses") that the person holds. This is the way the person's career looks to external observers. The *subjective* career is the individual's view of his or her career experiences, "the moving perspective in which the person sees his life as a whole and interprets the meaning of his various attributes, actions, and the things that happen to him" (Hughes, 1937, p. 403). This dual focus, on both the internal and the external, provided a powerful way of looking at the links between individuals and organizations. Out of the Chicago school developed a rich understanding of the various roles and stages through which people are recruited by, enter, move through, and move out of organizations. Various forms of socialization, rites of passage, and transition points were identified for a variety of careers, and the effects of institutions and social roles on the self were made clear through this work.

Political Science. In contrast to the psychological approach of Lewin and his colleagues, where the prime focus was the individual, and to the sociological work of the Chicago school, where the prime focus was the social role and institution, the early work of certain political scientists focused on administrative practices in the organization, which controlled the careers of the individual. This provided a finer-grained, specific view of the operations of particular organizations as they affected individuals over time.

Barnard (1938) and Simon (1957) detail specific operations of management procedures that affect individual decision making and behavior over time. Although they do not specifically use the term *career*, the organizational concepts they introduce provide extremely valuable tools for analyzing career processes.

Similarly, Kaufman (1960) examines the seeming paradox of how an individual (in this case, a district ranger in the U.S. Forest Service) can possess a high degree of autonomy yet make critical land-use decisions in accord with the official policies of the organization. The answer to the paradox, which Kaufman uncovered in his research, is a sophisticated process of organizational socialization by which the individual ranger comes to internalize personal values congruent with the organization's goals, thus becoming a dependable yet independent agent of the organization's mission.

Organizational Behavior. Influenced by all these approaches was a field that began to emerge in the 1950s: the study of human behavior in organizations, called *organizational behavior* for short. Some of the earliest books in this field were March and Simon's (1958) *Organizations,* Argyris's (1957) *Personality and Organization,* and McGregor's (1960) *The Human Side of Enterprise.* A major issue that these works address is how the needs of psychologically healthy individuals and the goals of complex organizations can be successfully integrated.

The most detailed analysis of how an individual is affected by an organization over time is provided by Argyris (1957). He posits a set of needs posssessed by the healthy individual (autonomy, challenge) and a set of requirements of formal organizations (control). Then he goes on to show how the organization, in pursuit of its goals, tends to suppress the need fulfillment of the individual. In response, the individual reacts by resisting or becoming apathetic, which results in further organizational controls. This results in more adaptive behavior by employees, and a vicious cycle ensues. McGregor (1960) takes a more positive view, showing how such practices as participative management and mutual goal setting can lead to individual-organization congruence. Neither of these works explicitly uses the term *career* to a great extent, but in fact, with their long-term, holistic view of people and organizations, they are both talking about organizational impacts on career experience.

Another career strand in early organizational behavior work is Schein's (1973) research on organizational socialization. His interest in this area started with his studies of brainwashing and attitude change by the Chinese during the Korean War, and he later applied these concepts to related topics, such as management development (Schein, 1968). What Schein found was that many of the processes by which groups influence the attitudes of the individual can also be applied to the process by which organizations socialize their members. Thus, he brought some of the ideas that had originated with Lewin and the study of group dynamics into the forefront of organizational careers.

Now that these four streams of scholarly work that feed into the study of careers in organizations have been identified, let us get on to the business at hand: contemporary theories of organizational careers.

Overview of Major Organizational Career Theories

As we have said, the distinctive feature of the organizational approaches to career development has been their focus on adults in organizational work settings. The previous section examined early work that had a career-like perspective. Now we will consider theories which explicitly addressed issues of careers in organizational settings.

Hall: Psychological Success

My own work has centered on issues of identity and psychological success and how they are related over time in the career. My early research studied young managers in the first five to eight years of their careers (Berlew and Hall, 1966; Hall and Nougaim, 1968). (This work was part of Doug Bray's management progress study at AT&T.) This research found that the first year in an organization is a critical period for learning; that is, the more challenging the person's initial job assignment is, the more successful (in terms of salary and promotions) the person will be five to eight years later.

One possible explanation for this finding is that there may have been a visibility factor operating, so that people in very challenging initial assignments may have received more attention from their superiors than people in less challenging roles, and this visibility may have been responsible for their higher salary increases and rates of promotion. However, further analysis revealed that performance was a critical intervening variable; only if the person performed well in a challenging role did he or she experience success. Thus, visibility alone does not explain the impact of early challenge (Berlew and Hall, 1966).

Subsequent research (Hall and Nougaim, 1968) led to the discovery of a psychological success cycle, which works in the following manner (Hall, 1971). If a person sets a challenging goal, he or she is likely to exert a high level of effort directed toward that goal, more than if there were no goal. Generally speaking, we know from expectancy theory (Vroom, 1964) that if a person has the necessary ability, then the more effort that the person exerts, the more likely he or she is to attain that goal (that is, to perform well). Strong performance on a valued, stretching, or difficult goal will produce a feeling of psychological success (pride, intrinsic satisfaction), which will enhance the person's self-esteem and lead him or her to have a more competent identity. All of these intrinsic rewards will increase the person's involvement in that area of career work and will raise his or her level of aspiration regarding future goals. This psychological success model is summarized in Figure 13.1.

**Figure 13.1. The Psychological Success Model
of Organizational Career Development.**

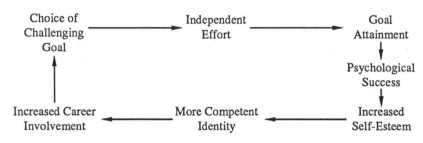

Source: Hall, 1976.

At the heart of this model is the concept of *identity:* the person's conception of who he or she is in relation to the various significant others in the social environment. The driving force is self-esteem; people are motivated to do things that enhance self-esteem, and they tend to avoid things that diminish self-esteem. Thus, the psychological success model explains how task success can promote self-esteem, which promotes involvement, which in turn promotes higher goals and greater task success. Thus, success breeds success.

More specific examination of career experiences can be made through the components of identity, or subidentities. Each subidentity represents an aspect of the person that is engaged when he or she is behaving in a particular social role. Each social role (for example, employee, parent) represents the expectations of other people involved in that role (for example, superiors and co-workers for the employee role, children and spouse for the parent role). The corresponding subidentity for each role represents the individual's perception of himself or herself as he or she behaves in relation to these expectations. Identities can be visualized, as in Figure 13.2, which shows the identities of two hypothetical people with high and low career involvement. Hall

Figure 13.2. Sample Subidenties.

Low Career-Involved Person

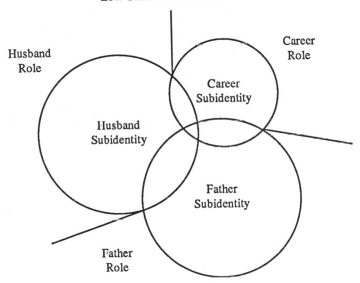

High Career-Involved Person

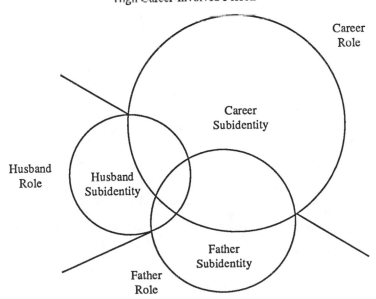

Source: Hall, 1976.

(1971) develops a number of propositions related to the development of career subidentities in organizational settings.

Organizations impose various constraints, as well as opportunities, which affect the way the stages of careers develop. Hall (1976) integrates the work of Super (1957), Levinson (1978), and Erikson (1963) to create a model of organizational career stages, illustrated in Figure 13.3. The Super concepts are indicated on the graph line, and the Levinson categories are the abbreviations. GIAW means "getting in the adult world," SD means "settling down," and BOOM means "becoming one's own man" (or, of course, one's own woman). What we are currently finding is that with flatter, delayered organizations, the establishment stage is ending earlier and maintenance is starting earlier, often in the early thirties. In many cases, people recycle into second or third careers, a phenomenon that is being accentuated by the current rash of early-retirement programs, which are part of corporate downsizing efforts.

Figure 13.3. An Integrative Model of
Organizational Career Stages.

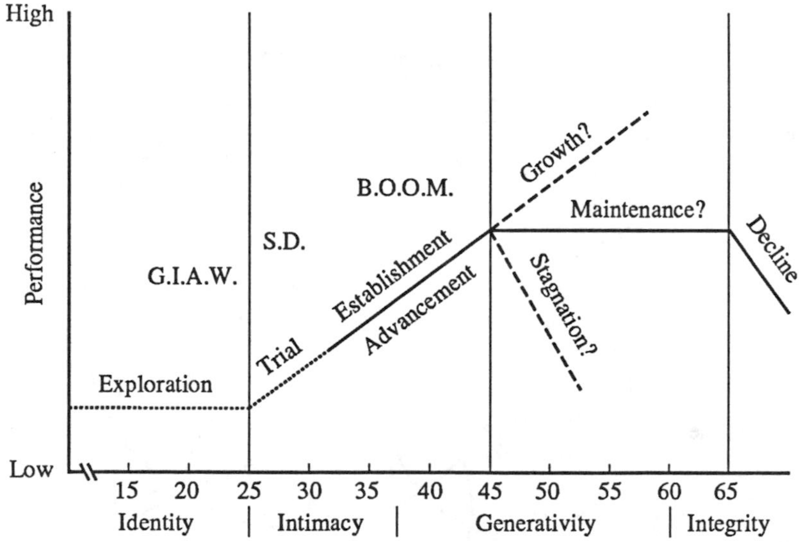

Source: Hall, 1976.

Triggering Midcareer Change. Hall's later work (Hall and Associates, 1986) has focused on midcareer and the factors that trigger midcareer change. He identifies a variety of influences in the person, in the work environment, and in the organization, which tend to disrupt the career routine (that is, the cycle of routine behavior) that gets created during the establishment stage just described. Once the career routine is broken, an exploratory process is initiated. It leads to a new phase of trial activity, which, if successful, is adopted. This midcareer "routine-busting" process is shown in Figure 13.4.

As Figure 13.4 indicates, the central problem in midcareer change is the career routine, which develops through earlier experiences of psychological success. Thus, success not only breeds success but can also lead to failure, in the long run, by stifling exploration and change. The career routine is shown as a large block in the figure, to illustrate the barrier that this habitual, noncognitive behavior represents to future career growth. Various triggers in the organization or society, in the work role, and in the person can disrupt a career routine and lead to new exploratory behavior. Under the proper conditions, such exploration can lead to trial activity in new areas, identity changes, increased adaptability, and a heightened sense of self as agent (in charge of one's own career).

Organizational or environmental triggers may be new technologies that render one's craft or job obsolete, or economic recession and corporate restructuring that eliminate jobs. If the organization has human resource policies that value job rotation and reward managers for developing subordinates, then there can be a growth environment and rewards for change, which facilitate midcareer growth. (An example here would be Digital Equipment Corporation, as described by Kochan, MacDuffie, and Osterman, 1988.) The more the organization takes a short-term perspective and stresses current performance, however, the less likely people are to take risks with innovative behavior because they do not want to risk failure on current tasks.

In the work role, the more the job demands change, such as is the case with project work (Hall, 1985), the more adapt-

Figure 13.4. A Model of Midcareer Subidentity Development.

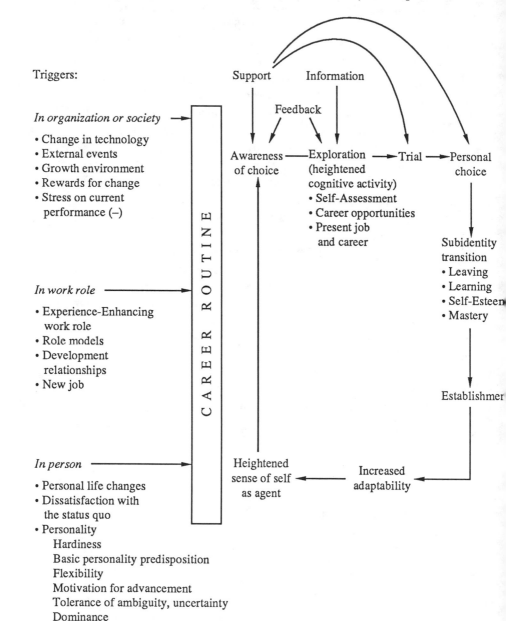

Source: Hall and Associates, 1986.

ability is required, and innovation is simply built in to everyday work. Role models of adaptive midcareer people, conditions favoring developmental relationships, and periodic job rotation are all work-based factors that can promote midcareer change.

Research tells us that personal life changes can also trigger important career change (Osherson, 1980). Major changes in family relationships, health, age, and so on can all cause the person to reexamine career priorities. Similarly, if the person becomes dissatisfied with the status quo, either through a change in needs or values or through greater personal awareness, this can suddenly exceed some trigger level and become a strong frustration that causes a change. We also know that certain personality qualities, identified as "hardiness" by Kobasa (1982), can give a person a more proactive approach to change. Howard (1984), in a twenty-year longitudinal study of AT&T managers, found a set of personality constructs that correlated with midcareer organizational success and adaptability: flexibility, motivation for advancement, tolerance of ambiguity, dominance, and independence.

Learning in the Career. Another way to think about this contemporary change of focus is that it is a shift in the type of learning being examined. Elsewhere (Hall and Associates, 1986), I have discussed four different learning outcomes that may be associated with career growth. These four types of learning can be analyzed in terms of the time span they represent (short term versus long term) and the focus or target of learning (task versus self). The result is the 2 × 2 table shown in Table 13.1.

Two primary points can be made about the types of learning represented in Table 13.1. First, most learning in formal organizational career-development activities has a short-term focus, rather than a long-term focus. The concern is usually with immediate or near-term future development. As the designer of a high-level executive career development program for a progressive company put it recently, "We want people to take something away from this program that they can use immediately over the next few months. We are not concerned with development over something like a five-year time frame."

Table 13.1. Task and Personal Learning Dimensions.

	Task Learning	Personal Learning
Short term	Improving *performance*-related knowledge, skills, and abilities	Resolving issues regarding *attitudes* toward career and personal life
Long term	Improving *adaptability*	Developing and extending *identity*

Source: Hall and Associates, 1986.

Second, most learning in formal organizational training and development is aimed at task learning, rather than at personal learning. The concern is usually with work-related knowledge, skills, and abilities that the participant will need in the present job or in the next job.

When we put these two ideals together, we can see that most so-called development activity in organizational settings is aimed at current performance. There is less concern for (future) adaptability on the task side and even less concern for self-related outcomes, such as attitudes and self-reflection. The very least possible amount of attention is usually devoted to identity learning. If one thinks about the typical corporate career or executive-development program, either within a company or in a university setting (such as Harvard's Advanced Management Program), perhaps it becomes more apparent that the cases, simulations, and even action-learning projects that they employ all are aimed at skills and knowledge to aid performance and perhaps adaptability. There is little personal learning, however.

Nevertheless, I would argue that it is precisely more personal learning that is required if truly effective task learning is to occur. Put another way, personal learning is the limiting factor in task learning. There are two important reasons for this.

First, for people who have become established in a career, the very task success that they have experienced thus far, together with its resulting psychological success, leads to very high involvement in these same task activities. The psychological success model (presented earlier, in Figure 13.1) illustrates the way this process of channelling into a particular task area operates. However, since the person's identity has become associated with the present area of work, it becomes threatening for the person to think about moving into new, untried task areas. The person would rather continue playing to his or her strengths than risk developing new qualities, which may currently be weak but developable points.

Second, if the person has negative attitudes toward a new area of activity or does not see himself or herself as the type of person who would be comfortable doing that kind of work, no amount of task training will overcome these attitudinal or identity barriers. Until the person is helped to see himself or herself as a different kind of person and to feel good about that area, these personal qualities — the affective side of the person — will effectively block the new learning. If the person does personal learning first, however, and comes to see himself or herself as a proactive, self-directed learner, then the enhanced self-esteem from this learning will build in a powerful personal catalyst for change. The person will then seek out change opportunities in a variety of settings — on the job, in relationships, and in formal training situations.

Research Support. The original empirical support for the psychological success model came from studies at AT&T by Berlew and Hall (1966) and by Hall and Nougaim (1968), which established the relationship between job-related expectations, personal needs, performance, success, and involvement. Subsequent research with a larger number of AT&T companies also found support for this success cycle (Bray, Campbell, and Grant, 1974).

In a study of Roman Catholic priests, Hall and Schneider (1973) empirically tested the model and found support for it. This support was especially strong for priests whose work provided challenge, autonomy, and support, which are necessary ingredients for stretching goals and independent effort. Further experimental support was provided by Hall and Foster (1977), who found increases over time in involvement and self-esteem following task success. A review of the job-involvement literature (Rabinowitz and Hall, 1977) found a number of other studies whose findings suggest that involvement may be linked to task success and self-esteem. In an unpublished field experiment, Goodale, Hall, and Rabinowitz (1982) found further support for the model, using three waves of data.

In a study designed to provide an explicit test of the Hall theory, Stumpf (1981) tested for the existence of the success cycle across three separate career roles (using the subidentity role model shown in Figure 13.2) in a sample of business school faculty. The three roles were researcher, teacher, and administrator/committee member. Using a combination of partial correlation analysis (to fine-tune the variables to be included) and path analysis (to test the empirical model), as well as an analysis of implied indirect effects, Stumpf found moderate support for the psychological success model for each role. Stumpf also tested competing models and concluded, "Given that other models were examined . . . which did not exhibit even moderate relationships across the three roles, the simple linkage proposed by Hall was supported" (Stumpf, 1981, pp. 110, 111). Consistent with the idea that the identity is made up of several subidentities, Stumpf also found that one's "feelings of role-related success were generally additive across roles. This suggests that feelings of success in each role may contribute to one's overall feeling of career success" (Stumpf, 1981, p. 111). Stumpf concluded by calling for future research on a heterogeneous sample, to extend the generalizability of the model.

Research on the newer midcareer change model has not yet been conducted, but there are studies that are relevant. Latack (1984), for example, found that major career transitions are associated with important transitions in one's personal life. Mihal, Sorce, and Comte (1984) reviewed several studies indicating that career surprises or unmet expectations can lead to exploration and the creation of new roles. In a similar vein, Bailyn and Lynch (1983) found that midcareer engineers who had made some sort of job or project change in recent years were more satisfied than those whose jobs had been unchanged. In a study of the effects of career-planning workshops for midcareer employees at Monsanto, Christiansen (1983) found that participants were more open to nontraditional job moves, had better information on their strengths and weaknesses and promotion prospects, and had clearer career information and career goals after the workshops than before. While not specifically directed at midcareer processes, the work of Louis (1980) shows that major transitions create surprise, which leads to heightened cognitive activity and exploration.

Looking at midcareer in the opposite way, what of people who do not make a major change? As mentioned earlier, the psychological success model would predict that success will reinforce paths established in early career. In a study of midcareer AT&T executives, Howard (1984) found evidence of a "hardening" of personality for managers in the predivestiture era (that is, these were people whose careers had been generally stable). The more successful people were, the more strongly set their behavior patterns seemed to be.

Schein: Individual-Organization Interaction

If the Hall approach is more of a psychological view, the work of Edgar Schein leans more toward the sociological. Schein's early work was on socialization and brainwashing processes, and his basic approach to careers is to examine the way the person is changed as he or she moves through various parts of an organization. Schein (1971) views the organization as a three-dimensional space like a cone, whose external boundary is round and whose core region exists in the center (see Figure 13.5). Given these three dimensions, there are three directions in which a person can move in the career: vertically (up or down through the ranks), radially (becoming more of an insider or more of an outsider in the social system), and circumferentially (moving laterally to a different function, business, division, or other unit). Schein goes on to present a number of hypotheses about how socialization and innovation occur over the span of the career (in socialization, the organization influences the person; in innovation, the person influences the organization). Basically, Schein argues that socialization is most likely to occur early in the career and early in one's tenure within an assignment, while innovation is more likely to occur in the middle of one's tenure in an assignment.

Figure 13.5. Schein's Three-Dimensional
Model of an Organization.

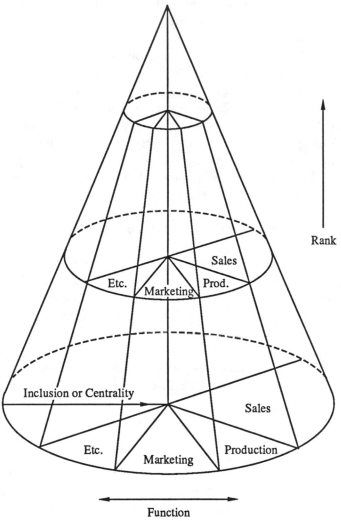

Source: From Edgar H. Schein, "The Individual, the Organization, and the Career: A Conceptual Scheme," *Journal of Applied Behavioral Science,* 7 (1971). Reprinted with permission.

Career Anchors. A critical part of the individual-organization interaction upon which Schein focuses is the development of career anchors (Schein, 1978). *Career anchor* is the term Schein uses to describe the occupational self-concept. It has three components: (1) self-perceived talents and abilities (derived from work successes), (2) self-perceived motives and needs (identified from self-diagnosis in work situations and from feedback from others), and (3) self-perceived attitudes and values (based on various interactions between self and the culture of the organization). Schein finds that career anchors can be discovered only after a number of years in the early career, since they manifest themselves only in actual work experiences. The critical feature of the career anchor is that it "serves to guide, constrain, stabilize, and integrate the person's career" (Schein, 1978, p. 127). It functions in the person's life as a way to organize experience, to clarify the best-fit areas of one's work over the long run, and to establish criteria for one's own personal definition of success.

In Schein's panel study of MIT graduates, he found five basic types of anchors. One was *autonomy,* which led individuals to conclude that they could not work in large organizations. A second was *creativity,* which usually led to some sort of entrepreneurial activity — a new product, company, or service. *Technical or functional competence* was a third type, which led people to make career decisions that would keep them in their areas of professional specialization (as opposed to moving up into management positions, for example). A fourth group was oriented toward *security,* preferring to work in stable, established organizational settings. The final group was concerned with moving up the corporate ladder, into *general management.*

Schein (1978) presents several case examples to illustrate how the career concerns of established employees are strongly influenced by their particular career anchors. When employees make career and job changes, these moves are generally in the direction of a better fit with their career anchors.

Research Support. Studies of the extent of socialization or innovation within assignments have been generally supportive of Schein's theory. Katz (1978) did a detailed study of the length of time that people spent in given jobs and concluded that there are three stages: *socialization,* when the person is especially sensitive to feedback; *innovation,* when the person is feeling fully motivated and energized by the full potential of the job; and *adaptation,* when the person is relatively unaffected by the job and its challenge. Presumably other (extrinsic) factors are important to the person at the third stage. Stage one covers approximately the first six months on the job, stage two lasts six months to five years, and stage three spans the period beyond five years. The first two stages fit with Schein's hypotheses, and these would fit with the experiences of the large number of people who do not stay in any one assignment for more than five years.

A recent study by Gabarro (1987) traced the learning and impact of seventeen general managers and functional managers at different points in time as they moved into and through assignments. Gabarro found that the managers had three general stages of change in their assignments: a *taking-hold* period (three to six months) of learning and corrective action; a later *reshaping* period (the maximum-change stage, between fifteen and twenty months), and a less significant *consolidation* period (twenty-seven to thirty months). Again, the first two critical stages fit with Schein's (and Katz's) socialization and innovation stages, and consolidation seems consistent with Katz's adaptation, although consolidation comes earlier. The fact that Gabarro's sample contained high-level managers, while Katz's consisted of lower-level professionals, may be a factor; the executives may have felt a need (and the power) to innovate and settle in faster.

The second major area of research based on Schein's theory deals with career anchors. Data from Schein's panel study of MIT's Sloan School graduates provide evidence of the existence and utility of the basic concept (Schein, 1978). A method for identifying anchors is included at the end of Schein's (1978) book, and a commercial instrument for assessing anchors is also available. De Long (1985) has done further instrumentation work, finding through factor analysis the existence of two factors: a management-autonomy cluster, and a security-technical cluster.

Whereas Schein's career anchors deal with the person's orientation toward the organization, a somewhat different approach is provided by Derr (1986), who identifies five success orientations, basic ways of relating to one's career, not just to the specific work or organization: (1) getting ahead (moving up in one's field or organization), (2) getting high (experiencing challenge and self-fulfillment through stimulating, exciting work), (3) getting secure (achieving a safe, secure place in which to work), (4) getting free (achieving independence and self-direction in one's work), and (5) getting balanced (achieving a good balance between work involvement and involvement in home or personal pursuits). Derr has developed a questionnaire called the Career Success Map to help people assess these different orientations. He argues that this particular configuration of styles is most descriptive of contemporary careerists, whose needs, talents, and values he examines in detail. He also looks at these individuals from the organization's point of view and proposes incentives and human resource management policies that would best motivate each type. Derr's main thesis is that today's work force is highly diverse, and that these five success orientations provide important clues about how best to manage it.

Van Maanen: Organizational Socialization

On the basis of work by Brim and Wheeler (1966), Van Maanen has discussed the major strategies that organizations use to induct new members (Van Maanen, 1978; Van Maanen and Schein, 1979).

Six Strategies. There may also be others, but Van Maanen has identified the following six strategies as quite common.

1. *Collective versus individual processes.* The first organizational strategy is to socialize people in groups (or cohorts, or "classes"). Military boot camp, the pledging system in fraternities, group training for new sales employees, and most university graduate programs would be examples of collective processes. The opposite is the individual approach, in which recruits are processed singly and in isolation from one another; apprenticeships, on-the-job training, and internships would be examples here. Collective processes usually produce more homogeneous change; but, by definition, they require larger numbers of re-

cruits and more careful planning. Individual socialization can be adapted more easily to more complex roles because one can tailor training to each individual's learning needs. Mentoring would be an example of such a one-to-one (individual) socialization process.

2. *Formal versus informal processes.* In a formal process, the newcomer is isolated from other members and placed in a special role, which conveys a "learner" status. Police academies, internships, management training programs, and apprenticeships would be examples of formal programs. In informal methods, there is no attempt to distinguish the newcomer's role, and he or she is usually placed directly into an operational unit and role. Since no formal training is provided, this forces the person to learn on the job. Formal methods may be more necessary if there is little transfer of previously learned skills or attitudes to the new role. In informal methods, the individual must take more responsibility for his or her own learning.

3. *Sequential versus random steps in the process.* In the sequential process, there is a clearly prescribed series of steps in the learning process that lead to the target role. Most occupational training programs are designed in this way. However, more complex roles, such as general manager, may have any number of paths that lead to them. The more hierarchical and formally structured an organization is, the more likely it is to have a sequential socialization process. An example here would be the military, with its many levels and functions and clear training processes provided as people prepare for new ranks and job functions.

4. *Fixed versus variable processes.* In a fixed process, there is a predetermined time requirement. If the individual performs satisfactorily during that period, full membership is conferred. In a variable process, the person may have few cues about how long the socialization process will continue. Political prisoners and psychiatric patients would be examples of people who do not know just how long their roles will continue (that is, when they will be deemed to have "learned the truth" or been "cured," respectively). In industry, some companies have special six-month job-rotation training programs for college graduates (a

fixed process), while others simply assign graduates to assignments for high-potential candidates and observe their progress over many years (a variable process).

5. *Serial versus disjunctive processes.* In a serial process, experienced members of the organization coach and serve as role models for new members. In a disjunctive process, there are no role models, and the path of a newcomer is quite different from that of his or her predecessors. Examples of a serial process would be military training programs and career-advancement systems, where large numbers of people have already moved through the positions occupied by the recruit. An example of a disjunctive process would concern a person hired to fill a newly created role or a person who is the first of his or her type to occupy an established role (for example, the first black vice-president or the first woman partner in a law firm). Peer socialization and networking often become more critical in disjunctive processes, since few role models are available, and people have to turn to others who have been in similar situations for help in coping with problems when no precedents exist.

6. *Investiture versus divestiture processes.* The issue here is whether the organization is attempting to confirm or disconfirm the identity of the new recruit. In investiture processes, the organization is valuing and accepting the recruit's qualities and is attempting to build on them. In divestiture processes, the organization is attempting to deny or strip away certain qualities. Many management-development programs are designed to enhance the self-image of the incumbents, stressing the honor and select quality of the high-potential group (investiture). Examples of divestiture processes would be the first year of medical school, the novitiate period in religious orders, Outward Bound–type programs, and U.S. Marines boot camp. Part of the strategy here is to challenge the recruits to discover for themselves that they have skills and strengths that they were not aware of previously. Divestiture may also be more effective if drastic attitude change, as opposed to skills training, is the objective.

Van Maanen (1978) presents propositions about the conditions under which various socialization approaches would be most common and most effective. His thesis is that these people-processing strategies are often unconscious and unexamined; thus, to increase role innovation and organizational renewal, it is important to pay more attention to the way organizations attempt to integrate new members.

Research Support. To the best of my knowledge, no research has tested for the existence of these socialization methods. Various writers have employed these constructs to explain various career processes (for example, Hall and Associates, 1986, in a discussion of midcareer as a shift from collective to individual socialization experiences), but my sense is that the strategies have been invoked more than tested. Wanous's (1980) work on organizational entry and Louis's (1980) and Nicholson and West's (1989) research on early-career transitions provide examples of how the socialization concepts are useful for understanding the processes of status passage, but the studies are not intended to test socialization theory. This does seem to indicate a gap in the literature; it would be useful to see studies that explicitly attempt to test for the existence of these socialization strategies, as well as to probe their causes and consequences.

Driver: Career Concepts

An earlier way of looking at the individual's orientation to the career was provided by Driver (1980), a cognitive psychologist. The basic premise of Driver's work is that "people develop relatively stable cognitive structures concerning their careers" (Driver, 1980, p. 9). These structures are how people see or make sense of their careers. People differ in how they view their careers with respect to how permanent they see their career choices as being, the directions of career movement that represent success, and the points in life that they see as appropriate for making career choices. Let me be more specific by discussing each of Driver's career concepts below.

Four Concepts. Driver identified four basic career concepts. The first involves a *transitory* style, in which choices are made frequently, perhaps over one- to four-year intervals, with major changes in direction. Most of the changes are lateral. External observers may view these changes as representing instability, but to the individual this style represents a consistent cognitive system that can guide his or her whole life. When linked to certain motives, this style manifests itself in socially desirable ways (for example, a mobile manager, an entrepreneur). At the other extreme, the transitory style can show up in a person who is unable to hold down a steady job and constantly moves in and out of unemployment. The central motives for the transitory style are identity, challenge, and variety.

The second concept involves a *steady-state* style, in which the individual makes an early commitment to a career field and holds it for life. There may be minor moves, representing professional development, but there are no major shifts. The steady-state style is usually associated with the professions and the skilled trades, where one's specialized work role is one's career. For example, as Hall and Schneider (1973) found for Roman Catholic clergy, the priest role is the career, and the thought of moving up the hierarchy is foreign to most priests. The main motives here are security and competence.

The third concept, and the one most popularly associated with the term *career*, involves the *linear* style, which reflects the idea that the career is a progression of upward moves within a field or organization. There may be some moves across organizations or fields, but the main idea is that there is steady advancement, or upward mobility (as it is more popularly known). This concept is common in managerial careers, as well as in political and in some professional careers. The central motives here are achievement and power.

The fourth concept, perhaps the most currently relevant, involves the *spiral* style. Here, the career is seen as a cyclical process, with major changes every seven to ten years. The person becomes established in one area, becomes bored, explores other areas, and then moves on. Then a new cycle of establishment, mastery, and restlessness begins. Spiral patterns are quite common in the arts and are becoming more common in business as the rate of organizational change increases. The driving motive here is growth.

Research Support. Empirical studies have generally supported the existence and utility of these career concepts. In a
sample of professionals and administrators, Driver and Coombs
(1983) found good representation for each of the four concepts.
They also found that people whose career concepts fit with the
prevailing culture of their organizations showed higher productivity and satisfaction with work and with life in general. Furthermore, younger workers were more likely to be transitory,
middle-aged workers tended to be steady-state and linear, and
older employees were more likely to be spiral. These findings
would also fit with career-stage concepts, since the transitory
style implies exploration, the steady-state style implies establishment (for professionals), and the linear style represents advancement (for administrators). The later career stages do not
necessarily fit with the spiral style, but this does seem functional
as a way of producing late-career change.

In another vein, Prince (1984) examined attitudinal correlates of the four concepts. Work centrality was highest for the
linears and lowest for the steady-staters and the transitories.
Organizational commitment was higher for linears and steady-
staters than for transitories. These relationships seem consistent with the nature of these concepts and can be viewed as a
type of construct validation.

Using data on actual job moves to assess these four career
concepts, Latack and D'Amico (1985) found that steady-state
youths entered high-status occupations with moderate aspirations. Linears had high aspirations but did not necessarily choose
high-status occupations. Transitories had low aspirations and
entered low-status occupations. In this study, 70 percent of the
sample was linear, 15 percent was steady-state, and 4 percent
was transitory (again, these figures are based on job moves, not
on questionnaire measures of the career concepts).

In a study of engineers, McKinnon (1987) found two types
of linears: managerial linears and technical linears. He also
found technical steady-staters, accounting for 50 percent of his
sample. The technical steady-staters were older and less educated
than the linears, and they were not interested in advancement;
what was most important to them was new and challenging proj-

ects that would enhance their influence over their jobs (Driver, 1988). The two linear types both wanted to move up a ladder (presumably on different sides of the dual technical-managerial ladder). The cognitive style of the technical linears was more detailed and complex than that of the managerial linears.

In his review of this literature, Driver points out a lack of strong evidence for the spiral concept: "It may be noted that despite calls for 'Spiral' career approaches by organization behavior analysts, this concept has emerged least clearly in current concept research" (Driver, 1988, p. 249). Driver examines other studies, not designed explicitly to study the career concepts, and reports mixed data on whether we are currently seeing a linear (financially driven) or a spiral (related to quality of life) trend in contemporary society. He concludes that there was a decline of linear-type motives in the 1960s and early 1970s, which was reversed around 1975 for college freshmen and around 1980 for MBA graduates. What seems more important to me is that within any contemporary organization there is a diversity of career concepts, and the organization needs to provide a comparable diversity of career opportunities if it is to tap the full potential and commitment of its members.

Implications for Practitioners

Alternative Career Patterns. As a result of this growing diversity of midcareer orientations in contemporary society, the models of career stages and career concepts discussed in this chapter do not seem to cover adequately the complexity of modern organizational careers. Some of the variations on these traditional patterns are shown in Figure 13.6. In the design of career programs in organizations, these different patterns will have to be taken into account.

For purposes of comparison, the traditional (linear) pattern is shown in simplified form in graph 1 of Figure 13.6. A fast-track version of the traditional model is shown in graph 2 (the "American Dream," also variously associated with terms like *waterwalker, crown prince, crown princess, jet job,* and so on). Many people have internalized this model as their personal

Figure 13.6. Alternative Career-Path Models.

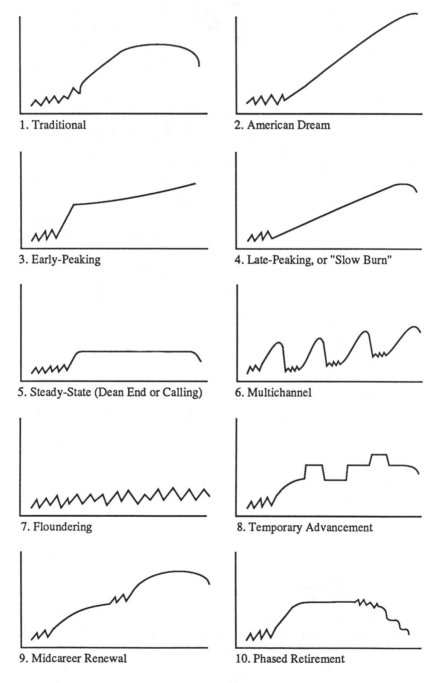

1. Traditional

2. American Dream

3. Early-Peaking

4. Late-Peaking, or "Slow Burn"

5. Steady-State (Dean End or Calling)

6. Multichannel

7. Floundering

8. Temporary Advancement

9. Midcareer Renewal

10. Phased Retirement

definition of success, but it represents so few people that it almost ensures that the majority of people will feel like comparative failures. One growing problem with the fast track is that, as a result of corporate delayering, many people hit an early peak (graph 3) and then plateau. Many people now plateau in their thirties, as opposed to their forties or fifties. Special programs for plateaued employees, especially for members of the "baby boom" cohort, are being created in many organizations (Hall and Richter, 1989; Hall and Associates, 1986; Hall and Louis, 1988).

An alternative to the fast track is the slow-burn or late-peaking path (graph 4), often favored by the Japanese. The development strategy here is to use lateral movement and leave people in positions longer, so that they really master their work and develop social networks and the capacity to be adaptable. If everyone moves up at this slower rate, no one will feel like a failure. In fact, this slower "churn rate," as it is often called, is appearing in many organizations. More open communication of this fact is necessary, so that employees' expectations will become more realistic.

Another career path that is becoming more popular reflects the steady-state style, as described by Driver (1980). Here, the person stays in one role, usually a craft or professional position, for most of the career (graph 5). The attempt is to change the view of this, from dead end to vocation or calling. Dual-ladder reward structures are being developed in many organizations to support this model. Some organizations even have triple ladders, with project management serving as a bridge between the technical and managerial ladders (Hall, 1985).

The multichannel model (graph 6) represents the idea of periodic shifts in the career, as in Driver's spiral style. In the future, with rapid organizational change becoming the norm, the spiral style should be fostered in organizational career programs. A less positive view of frequent change is shown in graph 7 ("Floundering"); the person cannot seem to find a good fit. The temporary-advancement model (graph 8) is found in some organizations that appoint people to managerial positions for fixed periods (say, three or five years), with the understanding that these people will rotate back to specialist work later. This removes the "ratchet effect" from promotions (that is, the situation in which people can move only one way — up, but not down).

Midcareer renewal (graph 9) is what happens when a person experiences some sort of trigger to change in midcareer. Practical interventions for helping people break midcareer routines are described in Hall and Associates (1986). Phased retirement (graph 10) is becoming more common as organizations show more flexibility in retirement planning — letting older workers stay on as part-timers or consultants, giving them longer vacations, or doing something else to enable a more gradual move from work to retirement. It is becoming clear that retirement from an organization should be thought of as a transition to a later life and/or career stage rather than seen as the end of work.

It is difficult to identify a brief list of recommendations for practitioners, since much of the field of organizational careers deals with organizational influences and practices that affect careers. For example, a major portion of the Schein (1978) book covers a model for a human resource management system to promote effective career management. Hall (1976) and Hall and Associates (1986) also deal largely with career interventions; Hall and Associates (1986), in particular, discusses specific companies' career programs. Detailed accounts of particular organizational programs are also found in Gutteridge (1986). For people designing and managing career programs, a particularly useful work, based on solid theory and research, is Leibowitz, Farren, and Kaye (1986).

Contemporary career development in organizations, in my view, consists of managing around a dilemma. I call it the dilemma of learning systems. The dilemma is caused by the massive environmental turbulence facing most organizations (due to business and demographic changes, new values and cultures, and constantly altered structures). To deal with this change, the organization must become more adaptive; it must become more of a learning organization. To achieve adaptability, the organization will come to depend more on its employees to learn and adapt. The dilemma comes in the fact that the individual learning that is necessary to the organizational objectives must be self-directed, but it must also be managed or coordinated by the organization in some way. Thus, to produce organizational transformations, we need to find new ways of integrating individual career growth and human resource planning.

Integrating Vocational and Organizational Approaches. Why are the concepts that we have discussed in this chapter so different from those typically found in the work of vocational psychologists? Probably a major factor involves the settings in which the two different kinds of scholar typically operate. Vocational psychology has been associated with the educational system, and its stress has been on helping prepare young people to enter the world of work. Thus, the term *career*, for vocational researchers, has been related to occupations, and *career development* has been used to describe the process by which a person forms an initial occupational choice (Holland, 1973a; Super, 1957).

For people in the organizational behavior field who study careers, the focus has been more on the employing organizations. From the organizational perspective, the central criterion is job performance, and so students of organizational careers tend to be interested in what will predict adjustment and success in work roles. This is also why there is so much interest in such processes as socialization and mobility, which describe the organization as much as they describe the individual.

However, as organizations are downsizing and delayering, we are seeing more individuals hitting career plateaus and becoming more immobile. My prediction is that with more individuals facing steady-state careers (or at least longer steady-state periods within their careers), we may see growing interest among organizational researchers in vocational concepts of decision making and person-work fit. Already, for example, we have seen the work of Holland being used in corporate career-planning programs and in studies of midcareer change (Hall and Associates, 1986). In organizational psychology, there is growing interest in identity and self-attitudes (see, for example,

Brockner, 1988), both as research topics and as targets of personal learning in corporate career self-assessment workshops (Peters, 1986). Furthermore, volumes like this one, as well as the one by Arthur, Hall, and Lawrence (1989), contain works in both fields, reflecting an integration of the vocational and organizational realms. More attention to the integration of the vocational and organizational approaches to careers could be an important step toward effective management of the dilemma of learning systems.

14

Linda Brooks

༄༅ ༄༅

Career Counseling Methods and Practice

All counselors operate according to some theoretical system or value laden model of behavior, whether implicitly or explicitly. Counselors use models or theories to help them define a client's problem, provide services to a client, formulate goals of counseling, and assess results. The preceding chapters on theory discussed the implications of theory for career counseling in terms of diagnosis, the process of counseling, goals or expected outcomes of counseling, and the use of occupational information. This chapter is meant to be a critique and synthesis of the theories on these four aspects of individual career counseling.

Diagnosis

One of the first challenges facing the counselor is to make some determination of the source of the client's problem. Why is the student having difficulty deciding on a college major? Why is the CPA unhappy about his or her work situation? Answering diagnostic questions will partly determine the kind of intervention that will help the client resolve the problem or correct the situation. The underlying assumption of diagnosis is that different problems require different treatments. Since no theory of career counseling can be judged to be fully adequate at this time, the counselor who is able to conceptualize career problems from diverse theoretical systems may be better able to develop different treatments.

The primary intent of this section is to compare how the theories explain career choice and adjustment problems. Issues of assessment of clients' interests, values, and skills for purposes of collecting information for decision making will be discussed in the next section.

Since the theories differ in their explanations of career choice, they also lead the practitioner to different diagnoses. Despite these differences, some convergence is apparent in that theories tend to explain career problems in one of four ways. Difficulties are caused by (1) problems of matching one's interests, needs, or skills with the appropriate occupation (trait and factor theory, Holland, Bordin, Roe), (2) problems of development or vocational immaturity (Super), (3) problems in the decision-making process (Tiedeman and Miller-Tiedeman, Krumboltz), or (4) problems with barriers or obstacles posed by the social environment (sociological perspective). Of those theories that view career indecision as primarily a matching problem, trait and factor theory is perhaps the most straightforward in terms of diagnosing the client's difficulty. As Brown has mentioned, the trait and factor counselor would first categorize the client's problem into one of four types — no choice, unwise choice, uncertain choice, or discrepancy between interests and aptitudes. This is a useful beginning, but a further step toward identifying the underlying problem must be taken. Why is the client, for example, experiencing no choice or an uncertain choice? The traditional trait and factor approach suggests that the decision problem is due to lack of information or insight into one's traits, the world of work, or how the two go together. Career or job dissatisfaction is explained as an error in initial choice, presumably due to errors in tests or occupational information or inaccurate information about oneself. The work-adjustment theory, however, suggests that the counselor consider additional sources of the problem for the dissatisfied worker. Have the person's needs changed, or have the demands of the job changed? If so, satisfaction may not be possible in the current situation.

A strict interpretation of Holland's theory, like the trait

and factor approach, suggests that career indecision is due to lack of information about those variables that are to be matched. Rather than individual traits and specific job requirements, however, the client lacks information or understanding about personality type or compatible work environments. For the dissatisfied employed person, the theory asserts that incongruence between type and environment is the cause of the problem.

Weinrach and Srebalus have extended the diagnostic implications of Holland's theory with their observation that undifferentiated persons (that is, persons whose type is not well defined) may have a poor sense of identity or be depressed. Similarly, Holland (1979, p. 30) notes that flat profiles may indicate a confused and disorganized person, and low flat profiles "may go with lack of involvement in the culture, self-deprecation, and a diffused sense of identity." Holland, Daiger, and Power (1980) explicitly recognize additional factors that may underlie career decision problems. More specifically, three possible sources of indecision are (1) inadequate vocational identity (for example, uncertainty about strengths and weaknesses), (2) lack of information about jobs or training, and (3) environmental or personal barriers (for example, lack of financial resources, or influential person does not approve of the choice).

In contrast to Holland and trait and factor theory, Bordin's matching theory posits psychologically based constructs as explanations for career decision problems. Bordin does not provide a specific discussion of diagnosis in this volume, but his presentation indicates that he views career difficulties as caused by (1) identity problems, (2) gratification conflicts, (3) lack of clarity regarding one's "intrinsic motivators," or personality needs, or (4) lack of information regarding what occupations would provide fulfillment of one's needs. Presumably, Bordin would also explore the possibility that more severe personality problems are causing the career problem.

Like Bordin, Roe gives prominence to personality needs. Thus, possible sources of the client's problem, in Roe's approach, may be a lack of awareness of career-relevant needs, lack of knowledge about what occupations would fulfill needs, or unfilled or unsatisfied needs in the current occupation.

The theories discussed thus far concentrate on explaining career choice and preference. In contrast, Super is more concerned with explaining the career development process. His model posits developmental concepts as explanations for career problems. Super makes it clear in this volume that he would determine the focus of counseling by first assessing the career maturity of the client. The Career Development Inventory (CDI) (Super and others, 1981) will tell the counselor which of five areas are problematic—career planning, career exploration, decision-making skills, world-of-work information, or knowledge of preferred occupational group. Super's recent concentration on work importance has led him to suggest that career maturity scores need to be interpreted in terms of motivation to work. If work importance is a low value to the client, then career maturity scores may mean very little. Career maturity scores also need to be interpreted in terms of issues that are relevant to the life stage of the client. In the maintenance stage, for example, career choice may be less the issue than career adjustment in the face of younger competition.

The career development process is ignored or deemphasized in the theories of Krumboltz and Tiedeman and Miller-Tiedeman, both of which focus on decision-making difficulties. Mitchell and Krumboltz are quite explicit about how the social learning theory views the client's problem: indecision is caused by dysfunctional or inaccurate self-observation generalizations or world-view generalizations, lack or failure to use task approach skills, or inadequate entry behaviors. Mitchell and Krumboltz suggest several techniques for identifying dysfunctional self-observation generalizations (for example, thought listing, thinking aloud during imagery) and task approach skills (interest inventories, career maturity indices, Vocational Exploration Inventory, decision simulations). They omit discussion of ways to assess entry behavior problems, although presumably the counselor could rely on similar techniques.

As with social learning theory, Tiedeman and O'Hara and Tiedeman and Miller-Tiedeman focus on barriers to decision making as the source of the client's problem. Unlike social learning theory, their theory incorporates developmental concepts in terms of ego identity. According to Miller-Tiedeman and Tiedeman, then, the client's problem would be one of the following: (1) lack of awareness regarding one's "personal reality"; (2) one's personal reality is overwhelmed by the "common reality"; (3) one's decision-making style is ineffective; (4) one's ego identity is not fully developed, particularly in the sense of autonomy and the acceptance of responsibility for directing one's own life ("I" power); or (5) lack of awareness of, or skill in, using the decision-making process. Presumably, any or all of these could leave one stuck in a decision-making stage (for example, exploration). Counselors working with college students could use Harren's (1980a) Assessment of Career Decision Making to identify client stage and style of decision making (rational, intuitive, or dependent).

As might be expected, the sociological perspective presented by Hotchkiss and Borow provides fewer guidelines for diagnosis. Nevertheless, status attainment theory is conceptually useful with clients whose preferences show a discrepancy between their abilities or attainments and the options that are accessible or acceptable for their social class or gender. Gottfredson (1981) has described two examples that illustrate this inconsistency: the high-ability lower-class client with low aspirations, and the low-ability higher-class client with high aspirations. Similar examples could be constructed that illustrate the discrepancy between gender and ability. Status attainment theory suggests that the sources of these discrepancies may be traced to obstacles inherent in the sociopolitical system, such as job discrimination, or to the attitudes and beliefs of the client's reference group, including significant others. In regard to explaining career-adjustment problems, structuralist theory suggests that characteristics of institutions and organizations (for example, the degree of job authority, size of the firm, and so on) affect the quality of work for an individual.

A synthesis of all of these approaches (except for the sociological perspective) is evident in the three-pronged diagnostic system proposed by Crites (1978a, 1981). Briefly, *differential* diagnosis asks, "What is the client's problem — indecision or unrealism?" *Dynamic* diagnosis asks why the client is experienc-

ing the problem: is it "simple indecision or pervasive indecisiveness" (Crites, 1981, p. 175)? *Decisional* diagnosis asks about problems with the process of career choice (for example, career
immaturity). Unfortunately, Crites's system omits attention to
barriers in the social system and thus is subject to the criticism
that counseling models are intrapsychically biased.

Process of Counseling

It is clear from the previous section that diagnosis of
clients' career problems will differ, depending on the counselor's
theoretical framework. Career indecision could be viewed as
primarily an information problem, a developmental problem,
or a decision-making problem by counselors following Holland,
Super, or Tiedeman, respectively. Thus, a counselor operating
under one theoretical framework may approach the counseling
process differently from a counselor using another theoretical
framework.

This discussion will compare, contrast, and critique issues
related to the focus of the counseling and the methods and techniques suggested by the theories. The same four categories of
theories used in the previous section on diagnosis will be used
as a point of departure for this discussion.

The primary focus of counseling in the trait and factor
and Holland matching models is on helping the client to gather
sufficient information to make a choice. Self-knowledge and occupational knowledge are assumed to be of equal importance.
Both approaches rely heavily on standardized assessment devices
(tests and inventories) as the primary method of collecting information about the client's traits or personality. Occupational
information is primarily obtained through reading or various
exploration endeavors, such as volunteer work or interviewing
workers.

In traditional trait and factor counseling, the counselor
takes an active role, usually by determining the data-collection
methods or assessment devices to be used and by reviewing and
interpreting the data to the client, often in terms of making
predictions. In Williamson's (1939) view, both the counselor and

the tests are the authority. Holland's emphasis on self-directed methods and the provision of materials (for example, the SDS and the VEIK) to implement this approach represents a departure from Williamson in that clients make their own interpretations.

In essence, both of these approaches focus on objective information gathering. As Brown notes in Chapter Two, the trait and factor approach assumes that career choice is a straightforward cognitive process that simply involves matching persons and their traits to job requirements. The only difficulties involved are possible errors in information and invalidity of tests. Although Williamson recognized the possibility of emotional instability, it was to be handled by helping the client to clarify thinking through the information-matching process. Holland, too, views the process as rather straightforward. Although he recognizes that some clients need more help or are more confused than others (in fact, the VEIK was developed for this kind of client), he would keep the focus of counseling on occupational choice. Holland has little to offer the client who is unable to make decisions because of psychological dysfunction. Holland would not object to this observation, however, for he has been a strong critic of practitioners who make the counseling process overly complex and who insist on individual counseling when it is clearly not necessary for the majority of people who need assistance (Holland, 1974b, 1978a, 1978b).

Both the trait and factor and Holland approaches have made valuable contributions to counseling in the form of various standardized assessment inventories. Holland's personality types and work-environments model enable the counselor and client to organize the data in a parsimonious system. As Weinrach and Srebalus observe, Holland's system is easy to understand and explain to the client. The relationships between personality types and occupations are clear. However, the decision-making process is rather obscure, and few guidelines are provided for helping clients with severe problems.

Clearly, Holland and trait and factor theories have the most to offer clients with career-choice problems. Neither approach offers much help to counselors working with clients whose problems are more complex. Holland's MVS recognizes that clients may have other problems (vocational identity, barriers from significant others), but so far he has not provided either theoretical or practical guidelines for helping these clients. Moreover, since it cannot be presumed that all career problems of adults are the results of inappropriate choice, the approaches are of limited value with many adult clients. The Lofquist and Dawis model is of some help when the problem is one of work dissatisfaction caused by changes in needs or job demands. In these cases, before exploring new choices, the counselor could focus on helping the client to develop strategies to change the demands of the environment.

Some of these same criticisms can be made about the matching approaches of Roe and Bordin (for example, the lack of a decision-making model). Nevertheless, these two approaches recognize that the focus of counseling will at times necessarily be broader than information gathering. Moreover, both give more prominence to the relationship of psychological needs to career choice.

Theoretically, counselors who use Roe's theory would help the client to clarify important needs, as well as interests, and then relate them to occupations. However, the needs aspects of Roe's theory have not been translated into specific counseling techniques or assessment devices that measure needs. Lunneborg's review of assessment devices and programs based on Roe's theory makes it clear that applications of the theory have been concerned with the classification system of occupations. This system does show the relationship of interests to two need dimensions: orientation toward people versus the natural environment, and orientation toward purposeful communication versus resource utilization. Thus, these needs could be clarified by first identifying the client's occupational interests through one of the assessment devices described by Lunneborg and then classifying them according to Roe's system. Roe's most valuable contribution to counseling has been her classification system, a particularly useful tool when the client is ready to match. Unfortunately, this system has been underutilized.

Bordin takes Roe's theory a step further in his suggestion that needs must be clarified and that psychological problems may interfere with and interact with career dilemmas. Thus, if the client is experiencing identity problems, Bordin would approach that difficulty within the context of career choice. For example, clients may have conflicting senses of their needs or "intrinsic motivators" because of a failure to fully differentiate themselves from their parents; or, perhaps because of parental influence, a client may view work as compulsion and effort, rather than as the opportunity to integrate work and play. These issues would need to be resolved before the client would be free to explore career alternatives that would fulfill his or her needs. The stereotype of the psychodynamic career counselor is that the client would be engaged not only in a long-term process to resolve these problems but also directed to a focus on the personal problem rather than the vocational problem. Bordin makes it explicit elsewhere (1968) and implicit in this volume that it is inappropriate to seduce the client into psychotherapy. It may be a surprise to some readers that Bordin views one-interview counseling as satisfactory, in many cases. A particular strength of Bordin's ideas is that they recognize the psychological complexity of career problems and thus are as useful with young clients as with older clients.

At this time, the full application of Bordin's ideas is limited by the failure to classify the full range of occupations according to the needs identified by the theory. In addition, no specific assessment devices have been developed to help clients clarify needs. Bordin makes it clear that certain personality inventories may be helpful in this regard, but he does not specify how they would be used.

In contrast to matching theories, which focus on career-choice issues, Super's model directs the counselor to foster the career development process. Super contends that the focus of counseling depends in part on the career maturity of the client. If the client is vocationally mature (and motivated for work), then the counselor can focus on one of the matching models (Super, 1983a). If the client is vocationally immature, then the counselor must focus on developing the client's readiness for career planning.

Since a sense of autonomy, time perspective, and self-esteem are thought to be determinants of planfulness (Super,

1983a), techniques to foster these characteristics would be important. Making the client aware of future developmental tasks is one technique Super suggests to help the client recognize the need to engage in career exploration. The same technique could be used to foster time perspective. The counselor must keep in mind, however, that certain developmental tasks are age-related, so that a sense of autonomy and the needed time perspective necessary for career decision making may not be possible to achieve to a high degree with younger clients. Counseling with these clients would be focused not so much on choosing as on exploring. One purpose of the exploration, for the less mature and less motivated client, would be to discover possible life options. Exploration for more mature clients, who are better acquainted with the world of work, would be to help them to deepen their understanding of those specific occupations that interest them.

The focus of counseling with adults depends on the developmental stage of life and career. For example, the client in the decline stage may need help with ways to reduce work demands so that other valued pursuits and role fulfillment are possible.

Given Super's emphasis on exploration as necessary at all stages, it is not surprising that he believes that one role of the counselor is to help clients to identify and arrange exploratory experiences. He urges counselors to broaden their views about the context and the methods of counseling. All counseling need not occur in the office. Counselors should reduce their excessive reliance on interview techniques and use multimedia approaches.

Two strengths of Super's ideas are attention to developmental stages and the interaction of career roles with other life roles. He provides a model for life planning that would reduce the false dichotomy between work and other aspects of one's life. In addition, the model recognizes that adults change and that each stage brings forth new tasks to be mastered. Adult problems are not confined to career-choice issues.

The outline of developmental stages and tasks and the graphic representation of the Life Rainbow provide counselors with some very useful counseling tools. Both of these can be shared with clients as a means of gaining perspective about upcoming developmental tasks and the place of work in one's changing life.

Super laments the fact that developmental counseling has not been fully explicated, meaning that differential techniques for the problems and tasks of each stage have not yet been specified. This is necessary before Super's ideas can be used to their fullest. Nevertheless, Super has written extensively about the application of his theory to counseling, and the interested reader would profit from consulting some of these earlier publications (for example, Super, 1954, 1955a, 1956, 1960).

The models of Krumboltz and Tiedeman focus on the process of decision making, rather than on career development. Krumboltz recognizes the need at times to focus the counseling first on correcting myths and misconceptions about work and careers to clear the way for the decision-making process. Mitchell and Krumboltz suggest the use of cognitive restructuring techniques in this regard, although presumably other techniques derived from social learning theory could be used (for example, stress-inoculation training). Once interfering misconceptions are removed or corrected, the client can be guided toward and reinforced for developing and using task approach skills, particularly those involved in career decision making. As is characteristic of other behavioral approaches to counseling, the process of the counseling is quite explicit, as are the techniques to facilitate clients' progress. Krumboltz's work is particularly strong in providing techniques to motivate clients to engage in information seeking, such as the Job Experience Kits and exposure to reinforced role models.

The focus of counseling, according to Miller-Tiedeman and Tiedeman, is primarily on teaching the decision-making process. Presumably, problems of ineffective decision-making styles, inadequate ego identity, and lack of awareness of personal reality are corrected through teaching the decision-making process.

The sociological perspective (Hotchkiss and Borow) implies that the counselor would focus on removing barriers or obstacles to career choice or advancement. Possible issues of concern are deterrent attitudes of significant others; the limiting effects of class, race, or sex; discrimination in the workplace; and other barriers posed by the social, political, and economic system. The theory suggests that counselors need to educate their clients about these marketplace realities and to teach them strategies to overcome or cope with them.

It is obvious that each of the approaches has shortcomings with regard to counseling. To deal with all possible problems that clients may present, some combination of theories seems necessary. Super, for example, presents a rather complete model of career development stages. Although different techniques for each stage are not now available, a counselor could identify appropriate methods without much difficulty. Super does not, as he acknowledges, provide us with a model for decision making; however, the work of Miller-Tiedeman and Tiedeman may provide the conceptual framework, and the techniques of Krumboltz's social learning theory could foster learning and use of skills. Holland has provided self-directed devices that have proved helpful for persons with high vocational identity, but he has had little to say about the process of individual counseling. Other approaches, such as Bordin's, could be used when the problem is more severe.

Outcomes

The specific counseling outcomes suggested by the various models are related to their approaches to diagnosis and the counseling process. In general, the goal for all models is for the client to make some choice or decision that will bring satisfaction or fulfillment. As noted previously, however, the models vary as to whether they place primary emphasis on process (that is, facilitating development or building skills in decision making) or on content (that is, facilitating career choices).

Counselors using either trait and factor theory or Holland's model would focus on helping the client to make specific career choices. Super's model directs the counselor to concentrate more on fostering career development; the particular choice is less important. Neither career choice nor career development is of primary interest to Krumboltz and Miller-Tiedeman and

Tiedeman, as they are more interested in facilitating the decision-making process. According to Krumboltz's social learning theory, outcomes should be improved self-observation skills, task approach skills (including decision making), and entry behavior skills. Miller-Tiedeman and Tiedeman focus on the decision-making process, so that clients will be able to take charge of influencing their future ("I" power).

One would expect the goals of counseling based on Roe's need theory to be to help the client make choices that best satisfy needs. Lunneborg's analysis of various approaches that have used Roe's occupational classification system, however, reveals the additional goals of increased knowledge of one's preferences for work activities and the world of work, increased occupational exploration, and greater understanding of the concept of career development.

Bordin's theory, like trait and factor theory, Holland, and Roe, suggests that the goal is the selection of satisfying choices. In this volume, however, Bordin makes it clear that he is less concerned with making specific choices than he is with helping the client to identify and reduce barriers that prevent commitment to truly gratifying goals.

It seems that the three goals of facilitating development, building decision-making skills, and making career-related choices could be achieved with each individual client. Whether or not the counselor should focus on all three goals, however, is another matter. Goals are determined not only by the model from which one operates but also in accordance with the objectives of the client. Holland (1978a, p. 131) believes that the majority of clients want "most of all to arrive at or confirm one or more vocational alternatives they can feel good about." He suggests that any other goals are those of the professional, not the client, and that it is the highly skilled counselor who can effectively work toward all three goals.

This brief overview of the expected outcomes of career counseling points once again to the observation that theories have tried to explain occupational preference and selection, to the neglect of work adjustment, or adaptation. Since it is only recently that career development research and practice have begun to give attention to adults, it is not surprising that these theorists have been more concerned with the choices of adolescents and young adults.

Uses of Occupational Information

Presumably, decisions made with accurate information are better than those based on misconceptions or ignorance, and so all models, in one way or another, give prominence to occupational information. Trait and factor theory views occupational information as equal in importance to self-knowledge if clients are to make realistic career choices. Super includes occupational information as one dimension of career maturity. Social learning theory identifies seeking and using occupational information as an important task approach skill.

Despite the central importance attributed to occupational information, Holcomb and Anderson (1977) found it to be the least researched area in vocational guidance. In addition to noting the lack of research, authors have noted that it is inadequately used (Frederickson, 1982), dull (Magoon, 1964), inaccessible (Magoon, 1964), poorly organized (Srebalus, Marinelli, and Messing, 1982), and unrealistic, since it usually presents only positive and neutral information. Moreover, Crites (1981) believes it to be the aspect of career counseling that is most neglected. He cites an unpublished study that shows that most counselors simply referred clients to an occupational file and that only 5 percent of the clients actually used it. Counseling apparently often stops when it is time to seek information. Thus, one issue concerning occupational information is how to make the most effective use of it in assisting clients with career choice.

Few specific suggestions have been made along these lines, other than that occupational information is a necessary part of the choice process. Crites (1978a, 1981) has suggested that counselors integrate occupational information into the counseling process by reinforcing clients for gathering information outside the interview. He does not specify how he would implement this specifically, other than verbally rewarding the client. It does seem clear that before counselors can reinforce clients for seeking information, they must conceive of the counseling process as going beyond the "referral to the file" stage.

Of the theorists represented in this book, Krumboltz and his colleagues have given the most attention to the occupational information-seeking process. They, too, would suggest reinforcing the client for seeking occupational information, and they have made efforts to make the process itself reinforcing. The Job Experience Kits, for example, are designed to provide clients with success experiences, as well as information. Apparently, the computerized information systems are also reinforcing, since one study cited by Mitchell and Krumboltz found that students learned more from this mode than they did from the counselors. Mitchell and Krumboltz's review of the research showing that films that included problem-solving tasks produced more learning suggests that counselors work with clients to help them identify the kinds of information or questions they want answered through information, rather than simply sending them off to do random reading. For example, clients who have a clear picture of their work-related values or preferred activities would seek information about which occupations would satisfy particular needs.

A second issue in regard to occupational information is what kind of information is needed by the client. Most printed occupational information gives a rather standard account of education and training requirements, worker characteristics, job activities, future demand, and so on. Four models suggest that additional kinds of information are needed if clients are to identify those jobs most likely to be satisfying. The developmental model of Super suggests that clients would find career-pattern information most helpful. Bordin and Roe would see the client as best served by information about which personality needs can be satisfied by which occupations. Holland would provide a client with information on working environments that are compatible with personality types. The sociological perspective points to the need for information on the complexity of the world of work, on the difficulties individuals are likely to encounter due to structural constraints, and on community resources that can provide assistance. Unfortunately, the most commonly used sources of information on occupations (for example, the *Occupational Outlook Handbook*) do not meet the requirements of these models. It is common for occupational information files to be organized according to Holland's six types, rather than according to the *Dictionary of Occupational Titles* (DOT) system. Roe's classification system could be used in a similar way to enable clients to identify those occupations that are relevant to their interests and their major orientations — that is, interpersonal relations versus natural phenomena, and purposeful communication versus resource utilization. Files could also be organized according to the needs suggested by Bordin. As Brown, Super, Mitchell and Krumboltz, and Weinrach and Srebalus observe, however, printed materials are not the only source of occupational information and perhaps not the best one. Interviewing workers in the field, volunteer experience, and "shadowing" workers are only a few of the many possibilities.

A third issue in regard to occupational information is the question of purpose, or function. According to Brown, Williamson (1965) believed that, in addition to providing information about options, occupational information could provide reality testing and stimulate continued exploration. Mitchell and Krumboltz imply that the purpose of occupational information is to assess options. Miller-Tiedeman and Tiedeman's model of decision making suggests that occupational information can help to suggest alternatives. They expect occupational information to facilitate decision making.

According to Super, however, career choice involves a series of minidecisions, and so the purpose or function of information varies with the career maturity of the client. If the client knows little about the world of work, seeking information through broad exploration will help the client understand possible options. Better-informed clients may need detailed information on specific occupations.

Super's views are related to a fourth issue: namely, when should occupational information be presented? Frederickson (1982) says it should be timely. Similarly, Brown states that it depends on the stage of counseling and the readiness of the client. Only Super speaks specifically to the readiness issue when he notes that clients will not become involved in career decision

making until they have sufficient career maturity and motivation to work. Since occupational information seems aimed at
assisting clients with decision making, perhaps it will have no
significant effect until the client is ready to receive it. A study
by M. F. Miller (1982), showing a positive relationship between
information seeking and self-esteem, suggests that clients may
not be ready until feelings of self-worth are sufficiently high.

It is unfortunate that so little research has been completed
on the effects of occupational information on clients. We do know
from Mitchell and Krumboltz that certain methods of dissemination increase both learning and information seeking. We also
know that information changes perceptions about occupations
(Osipow, 1962; Remenyi and Fraser, 1977). We do not know,
however, how clients process the information or even if it leads
to better decisions. One study, in fact, found little support for
the assumption that occupational information affects career indecision (Barak, Carney, and Archibald, 1975).

Conclusions

If a survey were taken of practicing career counselors,
we would undoubtedly find that some of the models presented
here enjoy widespread use, whereas others receive merely a nod
of recognition. Brown observes in Chapter Two, for example,
that the trait and factor model underlies much career counseling. Similarly, Srebalus, Marinelli, and Messing (1982, p. 55)
believe that the dominant approach is likely a "trait-factor approach matured through developmental contributions." They
believe it is particularly chosen "when the problem is clearly a
career-decision dilemma."

Holland has asserted that if a theory is valuable, people
will use it; if not, they will not. Clearly, counselors will find
some models more useful than others. One determinant of the
extent to which a model is used is the amount of effort that has
been devoted to translating the theory into practical methods
for the counselor.

In utilitarian terms, Holland's work is outstanding. He
and his colleagues have developed several assessment devices
that are directly connected to his model (VPI, SDS, VEIK),

as well as specific materials on the occupational classification system (Occupations Finder) that clearly link types and environments. Moreover, his extensive research, as well as other writings (Holland, 1974b, 1985c; Holland and Gottfredson, 1976), have provided many additional suggestions to counselors. In this volume, Weinrach and Srebalus provide even more specific techniques and make the valid observation that one valuable aspect of Holland's model is that it is easy to understand. It bears reiteration, however, that although Holland's work has provided many pragmatic tools for the counselor, his efforts have been directed primarily at noncounselor interventions.

Super is another theorist who has written extensively about counseling applications. Moreover, his work has been the stimulus for the development of several instruments in the area of career maturity (Crites, 1979; Gribbons and Lohnes, 1975; Super and others, 1981). The recent development of the Work Importance Scale (Super, 1982b) is an important addition. Similarly, many useful assessment devices have been developed from the trait and factor model. Williamson, in particular, wrote rather extensively about counseling techniques. Krumboltz has been quite explicit about the ways social learning theory can be applied, and the presentation by Mitchell and Krumboltz in this volume is the most comprehensive statement to date.

Other theories rate less well on their efforts toward application. In some instances, this is related directly to the inclinations of the theorist. Roe, for example, has been less interested in counseling than other theorists have been. Lunneborg's contribution in this volume has remedied this neglect by reviewing several assessment inventories and programmatic approaches that use Roe's occupational classification system. Those involved in the sociological perspective on career development have not been interested in counseling, for obvious reasons.

Many of the suggestions for counseling in this volume need to be subjected to research validation. By far the most research on counseling interventions has been completed by Holland and Krumboltz and their associates. Despite the recent increase in research on career interventions, much remains to be learned about which models may be most effective with particular types of career difficulties.

Duane Brown

Linda Brooks

15

൧ൟ ൧ൟ

The Case of K:
Theory into
Career Counseling Practice

In previous chapters, authors of the major theories of career development and occupational choice discussed the general application of theory to career counseling. In addition to asking the authors to write generally about the practical utility of their theories, we also asked them to react to one set of case materials regarding K, a young female client. The case material, along with the reactions from various theorists, makes up the majority of this chapter.

The reactions to K are assembled in this chapter so that the reader can make a more direct comparison of the theories of career development and occupational choice, as they relate to career counseling. Each theorist responded to the following questions:

1. What additional assessment information do you need about K before proceeding with career counseling?
2. What observations would you care to make regarding K's current status and career plans?
3. What would be your immediate and long-term concerns as you engaged in career counseling with K?

4. What strategies would you employ in your career counseling with K?

After having read the case of K and the responses to the foregoing questions, the reader should try to answer the following questions:

1. Is the diagnostic process consistent with the theorist's stated position?
2. What counseling process is implicit or explicit in the author's statement?
3. What are the expected outcomes of the counseling process?
4. How is information about careers utilized in the process?

To answer these questions, the reader may wish to construct a diagram, such as the one shown in Table 15.1.

Table 15.1. Comparison of Counseling Theorists.

	Theories						
	Trait and Factor	*Holland*	*Roe/ Lunneborg*	*Bordin*	*Krumboltz*	*Super*	*Miller- Tiedeman and Tiedeman*
1. Diagnosis consistent with theory.							
2. What are expected outcomes?							
3. Identify apparent process.							
4. How is occupational information utilized?							

Besides using the guidelines in Table 15.1 for comparing the theorists' responses to K, readers may also wish to identify the unique aspects of each theorist's approach. Then, after analyzing each of the reactions to the case of K, readers may themselves wish to answer the questions posed to the theorists. One way of answering these questions is to revisit the data placed in Table 15.1 and estimate the extent of agreement or disagreement with the various authors. Readers may also want to write out answers to each of the questions, just as the theorists did.

The Case of K

K is a twenty-four-year-old white female who is currently employed as assistant business manager and assistant to the director of development of an exclusive private preparatory school in a large eastern city. This is her first full-time job, although she held numerous part-time jobs in the admissions and alumni offices of the small liberal arts school where she did her undergraduate work. Her undergraduate major was English, and her overall cumulative GPA was 3.3.

K has had a number of career goals, including being an author, a public health administrator, and, more recently, an accountant. This latter interest developed during her senior year in college, when she took an accounting course and "loved it." She is currently applying to major accounting firms, hoping to get a traineeship, but she realizes that this is a long shot. She is also applying to master's degree programs in accounting and business because she feels that she will need training later to get the type of job she desires.

K's parents divorced when she was quite young, and she lived with her mother, who trained to be a medical technologist and now serves as a consultant to a number of firms that produce equipment and supplies for hospitals. Her relationship with her mother has always been good except for some rocky times during K's rebellious early-adolescent period. She has also maintained a good relationship with her father but admits that she has some difficulty in her relationship with men. Raised as a Protestant, she converted to Roman Catholicism during her adolescence.

K describes her leisure interests as "partying," which involves going to social gatherings that range from singles' bars to any festive occasion that looks like fun. She also swims religiously, loves to sunbathe, plays golf once or twice a year, reads, and goes to the opera (another of her "loves").

K hopes to get married and have children at some point in her life, a goal that she does not see as incompatible with her career goals. Currently, there are no serious marital prospects in her life, and even if there were, she would continue to pursue a career.

K is an ESTJ (extraverted, sensory, thinking, judgmental) type on the Myers-Briggs Type Inventory (Myers, 1962) and loves to be with people. She tends to set goals with time limits and to pursue them vigorously once they are established. She also responds well to challenges. When told that her writing was substandard, she worked diligently to improve her skills, to the point where she received considerable praise for her written work.

On the Strong Vocational Interest Blank (SVIB) (Strong, Hansen, and Campbell, 1985), K was similar to bankers and restaurant managers and very dissimilar or dissimilar to a number of Artistic, Investigative, and Realistic occupations. She was moderately similar to public administrators, investment managers, chamber of commerce executives, purchasing agents, funeral directors, accountants, IRS agents, credit managers, and nursing home administrators. Her only moderately high General Occupational Theme on the SVIB was in the conventional area. However, on Basic Interest Scales, she had a number of moderately high (one high) scores, including those on military activities, mathematics, medical science, writing, religious activities, law/politics, and business management. Her Academic Comfort score was 55, and her I/E score was 51.

K describes herself as hardworking, conservative (politically), goal-oriented, neat (although not fastidious), playful, trustworthy, and oriented toward money and success.

K has a great deal of confidence in her ability to achieve her goals once they are established and is seeking confirmation of her current career goal of being an accountant. She admits to not balancing her checkbook very well but points out that she is responsible for computerized and manual systems of accounts payable and receivable, as well as for payroll where she now works. She has also developed a record-keeping procedure for the development office.

The Case of K: A Trait and Factor Perspective
Duane Brown

Analysis: K has already completed a number of inventories, and she has reported her grade point average. However, since she has expressed an interest in a quantitative field, it would be of interest to know her grades in college math and how she fared on the quantitative section of the GMAT or the GRE. I would also administer the SDS as one way to confirm her interests.

I would also determine how much K knows about the day-to-day functioning of an entry-level accountant, what kind of salary expectations she has, and whether she understands the career ladders for accountants. I would also want to help K explore jobs related to accounting.

Synthesis/Prognosis: Assuming that K has the needed quantitative ability to compete in the mathematical components of accounting, she can probably do very well in a training program. She has interests that are similar or moderately similar to a number of workers who employ accounting skills, including accountants. Her Academic Comfort scores on the SVIB also indicate that she has interests that should enable her to complete advanced-level graduate training.

K's undergraduate work in English and liberal arts generally may not provide the best preparation for training in accounting, and in many ways she is probably more similar to the typical MBA student than she is to an accounting major. Some encouragement to consider an MBA program with an emphasis on accounting may be in order.

K seems to be more extraverted than one would expect the typical accountant to be, a trait that may be more in line with an orientation to management. Some of her other self-descriptions (goal-oriented, oriented toward money and success) also suggest that K may be an Entrepreneurial type (an SDS would confirm this).

Diagnosis/Counseling: There appear to be no major barriers to counseling K. Her goals seem to be largely aligned with her ability, interest, and personality. The counseling process should focus on fine-tuning what appear to be some tentative statements about goals. It is suspected that the discrepancies that exist are the result of inadequate exploration of the occupational opportunities open to K.

K would be given information, such as the *Occupational Outlook Handbook,* to use in the exploration of career options available to her. She would also be asked to conduct interviews with workers, such as accountants and managers (for example, investment managers, public administrators), and perhaps to do some job "shadowing." One homework assignment for K would be to construct some potential career ladders based on the job paths her interviewees had taken.

After K had collected data about a wide range of occupations, she would be asked to compare her own interests, work values, and specific goals (for example, earnings) to the data base she had assembled. She would be also encouraged to consider her personal goals (marriage and family, leisure) as she narrowed her career choices. K would be encouraged to refine her educational goal beyond its present, rather vague state. Finally, K would be helped to identify suitable training programs that would correspond to her training goals, and she would be encouraged to make applications.

The Case of K from a "Holland" Perspective
David J. Srebalus

The case of K, like any brief case study, is difficult to analyze because of sketchy descriptions and missing information. However, Holland's theory can add considerable definition to the vague description provided for K.

To begin, let us review the data and begin identifying where on Holland's hexagonal model K's different vocational

Stephen Weinrach, coauthor of Chapter Three, declined to comment on the case of K.

activities fit. This can help us see how well her career progress and plans have been differentiated and how consistent they may be. We can begin to consolidate our understanding of her via Holland types and subtypes; at the minimum, we can begin to rule out some of those types.

The data have been converted into the job titles that follow, found in the *Dictionary of Occupational Titles* (in brackets), with Holland codes (in parentheses). The Holland codes can be found in Gottfredson, Holland, and Ogawa (1982).

K's undergraduate major: English (AIS).

K's expressed occupational daydreams: Author [Writer] (ASI); Public Health Administrator [Public Health Service Officer] (IES); Accountant [Accountant] (RCS).

K's master's degree interests: Accountant [Accountant] (RCS); Business [Business Manager] (ESC).

K's full- and part-time employment: Assistant Business Manager [Business Manager, College or University] (ESR); Assistant to the Director of Development [Director of Fundraising] (ESA); Admissions Office [Director of Admissions] (ESA); Alumni Office [Alumni Secretary] (ESA).

Because of the case study's brevity, this list probably is incomplete. For example, if K were being interviewed, the list of occupational daydreams could be much longer and thus more descriptive of her.

Let us take this information to illustrate how Holland's occupational classification system can organize a work history. A summary Holland code can be computed, as described in Holland (1987a). With more complete information from K, more confidence could be placed in the summary code.

Below is a summary code that has been based on weighting the ten three-letter codes for the information supplied. Here is the presentation of that method:

College English major (A = 3) (I = 2) (S = 1)
Writer (A = 3) (S = 2) (I = 1)
Public health service officer (I = 3) (E = 2) (S = 1)
Accountant (R = 3) (C = 2) (S = 1)
Accountant (R = 3) (C = 2) (S = 1)

Business manager (E = 3) (S = 2) (C = 1)
Business manager, college or university (E = 3) (S = 2)
   (R = 1)
Director of fund raising (E = 3) (S = 2) (A = 1)
Director of admissions (E = 3) (S = 2) (A = 1)
Alumni secretary (E = 3) (S = 2) (A = 1)
Totals: R = 7 I = 6 A = 9 S = 16 E = 17 C = 5
Summary Code = ESA

The information provided on the SVIB is easiest to convert into a Holland code if the General Occupational Theme scores are used. This information is converted into a summary code of CA/S (C = 58, A = 53, S = 53). SCII information, however, is not unambiguous; "moderately similar" and "similar" Occupational Scales scores are clustered in the Enterprising and Conventional areas of the profile.

Holland assisted Campbell in improving the interpretability of the Strong Vocational Interest Blank, but the Holland codes resulting from the use of the SVIB have little empirical validity when used with the Holland codes (see Gottfredson, Holland, and Ogawa, 1982, p. xii).

To summarize some important information provided in the converted Holland codes, we get the following:

Undergraduate major (AIS)
Summary code from combined information (ESA)
SCII General Theme scores (CA/S)
Graduate major (RSC or ESC)

It seems that several observations can be made on the basis of this information. K seems to be a person with a strong Social and a strong Artistic theme in her personality. She has sought outlets for them in managerial employment with considerable social contact, as well as through her avocations. It is no wonder that she enjoys social gatherings and the opera so much. The Conventional theme, identified by the SVIB, is a deviation from this. It adds some inconsistency to the picture we can draw of K.

Does this mean that there is a tug or conflict between the C and A themes, which seeks resolution in the E and S combination (see hexagon) that shows up in much of the summary information? In any case, K does not get an unqualified "go ahead" from this evidence for a redirection of her career — away from managing people and toward intense involvement in ledgers and computer-driven accounting models.

In counseling K, it would be important to explore how an accounting degree would fit with her ongoing life experience, which to date seems satisfying to her but different from what she seems to be planning for the future, at least as far as employment is concerned.

Nevertheless, we might remember Holland's "rule of intra-occupational variability," which he views as important in interpreting interest inventories (Holland, 1985c, p. 13). He reminds us that different occupations and fields of study include a variety of people. This means that all general accountants, working in large accounting firms, are not RCS subtypes; data suggest that 75 percent of the workers have high-point codes headed by any one of the three letters in an occupational code. Thus, K's SVIB code (CA/S) fits that rule for accounting as an occupation. However, a considerable amount of information does not support her tentative choice of accounting but is more supportive of business management. Using Holland codes in connection with the sketchy information supplied on K reveals that she is far from being a "pure" Holland type. Thus, there is all the more pressure on her and her career counselor to actively examine how she can use the information supplied by the theory to confirm or disconfirm her tentative choices.

1. *What additional assessment information do you need about K before proceeding with career counseling?* In the case of K's expressed career need, only a Self-Directed Search would be needed. A Vocational Preference Inventory would also be an acceptable choice, if she were to work closely with a career counselor. She probably would not need to complete both. At times, however, the SDS does benefit from support by VPI results; then both would be used.

2. *What observations would you care to make regarding K's current status and career plans?* Her current status and career plans have been addressed in the reply.

3. *What would be your immediate and long-term concerns as you engaged in career counseling with K?* There are no immediate or long-term concerns in working with K. She seems quite in control of her own career development, with a series of successes and effective choices to date. Her request for confirmation of a choice of master's degree would be taken at face value, with no effort to prescribe more treatment than she requested.

4. *What strategies would you employ in your career counseling with K?* The use of the Self-Directed Search, along with brief career counseling, appears to be sufficient to assist K. Holland (1985c, p. 29) recommends the following:

1. Provide as much information on vocational development and occupations as the person requests.
2. Provide clear and simple instructional materials about decision-making, self-assessment, job hunting, and employment outlook.
3. Encourage exploration of alternatives for information and experience.
4. Act more like a consultant than a therapist.

A Roe Career Counselor Considers the Case of K
Patricia W. Lunneborg

What are your *needs,* K? That is, what are your interests? Your work values? What personality traits are crucial to your sense of identity?

If you decide to see me for career counseling, what we are going to do, first and foremost, is work at your having a clear understanding of what your needs are, where they came from, how they can be satisfied by different occupations, and how you can change those needs yourself, if you wish to.

You will be involved in four activities: (1) *assessment*— taking and considering the results of tests and inventories; (2) *information gathering*—finding out more about the occupations that appear to satisfy your needs; (3) *informational interviewing*—finding out more about the occupations that appear to meet your needs from people who are trying to do the same thing; and (4) *con-*

structing your plan of action — laying out a course of activities and experiences directed at fulfilling your needs in the immediate and the far future.

Anne Roe has not specified how a career counselor could work with her theory. She never prescribed a precise procedure because, as she has said, she is not a counselor, and her theory was not devised with the counseling situation in mind. What she did do for practitioners, however, may be more important than highly specified techniques: she underscored the importance of occupations for meeting higher-order, self-actualizing needs.

If we just keep our eyes on that goal — What are this person's needs, and how can she or he satisfy them through work? — we may be able to do the best possible job for clients because we are free to use any resource we can think of to help clients implement need satisfaction through career choice. Which are better, in the last analysis — explicit procedures tied to one theoretical perspective, or the full armament of counseling strategies in the hands of a thinking practitioner?

First, let us analyze K's case from Roe's theoretical point of view. I would use my analysis of the background information provided by K (her Strong Vocational Interest Blank and Myers-Briggs Type Inventory scores) in our first discussion together as part of step 1, *assessment:* "If the main reason for your seeing me is to confirm your choice of being an accountant, K, then we can see from the SVIB that your interests are moderately similar to those of accountants and a number of people in administrative occupations that also involve money management. Further, there is a lot of consistency here between how you describe yourself and the general theme you scored highest on, Conventional. Conventional folks like to organize — data, people, and things. They see themselves as orderly and conscientious, persistent and efficient. They value business and economic achievement. This is just how you describe yourself, right?

"You've also given me other bits of support for a career in accounting or business management. You've taken an accounting course and liked it. All your work experience has been in management and administration. And your accomplishments are Conventional — handling payroll and accounts payable, and devising a better record-keeping procedure. These facts support the idea that studying for a master's degree in business administration or accounting would be compatible with your needs as expressed through the SVIB."

I can provide an environment in which clients at least go through the appearance of considering other alternatives.

What would be the strategies for career counseling with K? There would be the four-step process delineated earlier: assessment, information gathering, informational interviewing, and plan of action. She would also be offered group counseling in a small, all-woman group, with meetings lasting two hours and held weekly over a two-month period. There would be heavy reliance on independent readings, exercises, and activities outside the counseling sessions. Clients are expected to work at generating and gathering self-knowledge and knowledge of the world of work for at least ten hours a week, in addition to attending group meetings. There would also be lots of discussion about upbringing, the mother's needs and her career, identification with the mother, family values, family expectations for sons and daughters, and how skills and abilities have been shaped by family experience.

There would be informational interviewing with women in the careers being considered. K would interview an accountant and a public administrator (one in her thirties, the other in her forties or older), and I would also suggest interviewing a broker and a restaurant manager. Delineating the daily satisfactions and frustrations of these highly related but different jobs is important to K's choice of a graduate program. Should she get the broader MBA degree or the narrower accounting degree? The highlights of these informational interviews are shared with the group; in that way, everyone learns about alternatives that they may not even have heard about before.

Group work (for example, exercises with the *Dictionary of Occupational Titles*) would be devoted to understanding how occupations satisfy needs, interests, traits, and values. In K's case, what are people like who are very satisfied with account-

ing? What kinds of people do not make it as investment managers? Would K thrive or wither as an IRS agent? Would she
rather socialize with bankers or restaurant patrons?

"What needs would you like to change?" The group would
work on this topic in pairs. Each pair would then share with
the group how the partner would like to change, and the group
would suggest how to do it: change of geography, different living arrangement, specialized education, new friends, expanded
recreation. The following week, each person would report on
steps she had taken to change a need, in a direction freely chosen.

At the last group meeting, each member would lay out
a plan of action for meeting her career and life goals. A five-
year plan is the minimum — ideally, at least, a hazy sketch of
how the client would handle the long-term crisis of generativity
versus stagnation and ego integrity versus ego despair.

Finally, I would wrap things up by passing out a list:

1. Very few decisions are totally wrong.
2. Very few decisions are irrevocable.
3. Every decision involves a leap of faith.
4. Indecision is a decision not to decide.
5. When it comes to a career decision, you are not choosing
   for a lifetime. Your needs will change, and so you can and
   will change your career.

Now, with a plan of action drawn up and decisions made,
the next step is to start implementing.

Comments on the Case of K
Edward S. Bordin

My initial interview with K would consist of a series of
probes aimed at a fuller understanding of her dilemma: what
is motivating the search for change, and how this search for
change fits into her larger life plan and life-style. My probes
are listed in the likely order of pursuit, but I would expect to
modify the order so as to follow up her own connections of these
issues — for example, her response to satisfactions in her pres-

ent job may lead her into talking about her mother's occupational experience and why she moved from medical technology to consulting with related business. If it seems important, I would at that time follow this connection to her mother, seeking to get a clearer picture of the ways in which she sees herself as similar and how accepted and integrated that sense of herself is.

The following set of probes occurs to me:

1. *What parts of her present job satisfied her?* From what I can see of her present job, I anticipate that it is a fund-raising position that requires the preparation of written materials to promote giving, the staging of events, and a great number of personal contacts. It may tap into some levels and varieties of educational interests. The test results suggest that she could express satisfaction with the social and promotional aspects of her work.

2. *What parts was she frustrated by or dissatisfied with?* This question would be important as a source of understanding why she is thinking about change. To what extent is she trying to get away from a dissatisfying occupation or being drawn to another occupation that promises satisfaction of unfulfilled wishes? Again, on the basis of tests, we may wonder whether she dislikes the pressure for developing new, creative campaigns or whether it is the need to sell herself that she dislikes.

3. *What attracts her about the occupation of accounting?* Here I am interested in whether and how she reacts to the opportunities to be precise and systematic, accounting's involvement with the details of the financial aspects of business, and the opportunity for a form of analytical thinking. She may speak of her feeling that she likes to associate with persons who are precise, careful, and analytical. In connection with her thoughts about checking the realism of accounting and an MBA, I would be interested in her undergraduate level of performance and her performance on college aptitude tests.

4. *What seems to make it difficult to decide?* This probe is designed to investigate to what extent the problem resides in the difficulty of reconciling disparate personal needs and styles — for example, a soaring form of personal and social expressiveness with a fear of ambiguity and making errors. Of course, it could turn out that extrinsic considerations (level of pay or income)

are a major consideration and that seeking counseling is connected with her style of basing decisions on a careful examination of the facts.

5. *What about her father and her family?* We already know about her mother, her entry training or occupation, and her current field of work. But what about her father, his work history, and his character? I look for ways in which she may see herself as similar to him. Naturally, I am interested in how old she was at the time of the divorce. Does the phrase "quite young" refer to ages under two, six, thirteen, or even older? The impact of the divorce could be very different, according to age. The place of her father in her sense of self and in identity formation may vary considerably as a function of contact prior to the divorce and of how she was used by the parents in their conflict with each other (for example, forcing her to choose sides). There is no mention of siblings. Does this mean that she was the only child of that marriage? Does the lack of mention mean that neither parent remarried? All of these questions are in the service of getting a clearer idea of the marriage in which her identity development is embedded.

6. *What about her sense of herself regarding numbers and management of people?* Here I would be investigating the fact that her sense of herself, particularly as revealed in the SVIB, suggests considerable interest in managing money, as well as people. Her approach to managing people seems to represent concern with building a logical system, rather than great attention to or empathy for individuality.

As can be seen by the foregoing probes, I feel that there would be a great deal more to learn about her before I would have a solid sense of where she is regarding her current career status and her life plans. In advance, I see no evidence that clearly marks her as a person blocked from making decisions, either by unresolved conflicting wishes or by standards or habits that block or interfere with pursuing important wishes. I would have the suspicion that, even more than accounting or the management of money (say, as a broker or investment banker), the technical management of people would turn out to be a satisfying work role.

As reflected in my series of questions, my concerns about K are directed toward certain potential tensions in the picture. One of these would be a concern about whether her seeming avoidance of attention to her own inner life and that of others reflects an unresolved tension. If this is in fact the case, is it reflected in superficial relationships? While she speaks of marriage and children, it is put off until the future. What are her relationships with men like? How difficult or easy is it for her to keep them superficial? How about her relationships with women? Does her interest in money and success reflect a similar externalization of her personal investments and experience? To what extent does her pattern of recreation reflect an effort to escape a feeling of loneliness?

For the most part, these questions, while having some bearing on her vocational decisions, are more centered on her life plans as a whole and her satisfactions in them.

My strategy would give priority to the vocational decisions she brings. If our process uncovers very important tensions around the more general ways in which she is approaching and living her life, I would explore with her how much she wanted to enter into a change alliance and the nature of a meaningful change goal. Finally, we would consider the proper place and time for such an effort, and with whom it should be attempted. This could result in our continuing beyond her vocational decision, or in my referring her, or in her deciding to postpone closure on the decision until completion of a change effort.

The Case of K Viewed Developmentally
Donald E. Super

K is in some ways a classic case in that, as she approaches the age of twenty-five, she is still exploring but appears to be about ready to settle on what might be a "life work." Working in an educational setting, much of what she does in the business office is related to accounting, and she is considering how to improve her qualifications for accounting and how to get established in that field. She is perhaps classic, too, in that while aiming at eventual marriage and child rearing, she wants to pursue a career in the world of work. In this sense, she is a contemporary classic.

In thinking about next steps in career development assessment and counseling, it seems important to understand rather better her present stage of development. She has changed goals three times so far, beginning with the literary field ("author"), then the social ("public health administrator"), and now the conventional ("accountant"). How likely is she to stay with this preference? Is this, in the real sense of the word, her choice? Will it still be her choice three or five years from now, when she may, with some combination of classroom and on-the-job training, be qualified as an accountant? I would want to pursue these questions in interviewing, and I might ask her to complete a career-development inventory such as those by Crites (1978c) and Super and others (1982, 1985). The latter group's CDI would be my choice for assessing how mature her exploratory attitudes are, how much she knows about career decision making, and what she knows about careers and occupations, including the business-analytical field.

It is also important to know more about the relative importance to her of the work and homemaking roles that she has in mind. Will both remain important to her? In a world in which most adult women, especially university women, work for some combination of material, ability-utilization, interest-expression, and social-affiliation objectives and marry for conjugal and parental reasons, K is, in this respect, probably realistic. But if she embarks on a two-year, full-time MBA program, serves a three-year apprenticeship in an accounting firm, and spends three to five more years getting established in her field, she will be thirty-two or thirty-four years old by the time she can consider herself established. And if, as is not unlikely, the first regular job or two do not turn out to suit her, she will be close to the point of no return for childbearing . . . and still perhaps not have a husband! Has she thought this through? This is, of course, the pessimistic scenario, but it is one that is not infrequently seen in adult counseling centers and more often still in everyday life. K needs to understand all this, and an interview, supplemented by an instrument such as the Salience Inventory (Nevill and Super, 1986), would help her to focus on and clarify these questions.

What does K actually want from life? Self-fulfillment, evidently. But what does that mean, in her case? Material wealth? Friends? A better world? We do have some data bearing on this, at least by inference. But more interviewing, with questions such as these and a good measure of values, would help focus her thoughts and help the counselor's assessment.

Finally, two experience-assessment questions, one of which may be irrelevant but may add to an understanding of K's values: Why did she change from Protestantism to Catholicism — for philosophical, social, emotional, or other reasons? What did the users of the record-keeping system she devised think of it and the way in which it was introduced, and how did her superiors evaluate the project? The answers may throw light on her prospects and on her need to learn in accountancy and human relations.

About K's status: her goals have changed from literary to social to conventional, and she is now seeking to implement this last preference. The methods she is considering seem well thought out. But does she know the difference between an accountant and a CPA? Her leisure interests are social and esthetic, her occupational interests are conventional (a term not as illuminating as *business analytical*); is this a conflicting or a complementary interest? The Strong may help to answer this question. The Myers-Briggs may also throw some light on it, and so may a values inventory. The asking of these questions may appear to suggest more doubts than are intended, but they are asked for definitive diagnostic purposes only.

Short-term and long-term concerns have been covered in the first two sections, but I have one concern about my own assessment and counseling hunches (conclusions?) at this point. Confirmation of K's goals, and of her two alternative plans for attaining them, appears to be warranted on the basis of what is now known about her, as shown in the psychometric data and in the writeup. The case seems to be an easy one. But is it too easy? In what ways can the emerging confirmation of K's plans be tested? The answer would seem to lie in further probing through interviewing and testing, as outlined, and in helping her to view the planning that is done, the early pursuit of plans, and her training and posttraining work experience as further exploration (what in the developmental model is called *trial with commitment*). It may lead to accounting; it may lead to something as different as city planning or the secret service. Gribbons and Lohnes (1968) apply to adolescence a term that I like to apply also to young adulthood: *emerging careers*. Careers can be allowed to emerge, and they can be helped to emerge.

Intervention comes up next, a term that, like *strategies*, seems much too directive but need not be so. (Incidentally, the faddist term *strategy* does not actually have the meaning intended by its pedagogue users, and it should not be used in describing counselor-client relations. It means getting the other party into the position and condition in which one wants him or her to be. It denotes manipulating rather than helping the client to develop once he or she has assumed the role of counselee.) I would resume the assessment and counseling process by explaining to K that I would like her to talk some more about her experiences to date, and perhaps I would ask her to complete two or three more inventories that get at things not covered by those she has taken so far. I would ask her to tell me about her changes of objectives, from author to health administrator to accountant. Once discussion is launched, my tactics would be nondirective, keeping her on track with an occasional "I see," "Uh-huh," or "You do have some feeling about that." I would seek to understand whether her changes became increasingly experience- and data-based as she got older. In this manner, her career development—her maturing—could be assessed.

In order better to understand K's career maturity and to help her understand her present life stage in perspective, I would at some point steer the conversation, if she did not do so herself, to the subject of marriage, family, and childbearing. This would serve both an assessment and a counseling purpose. I would ascertain how well she understands the possible impact that launching a career, requiring considerable investment of time, money, and affect, normally has on founding a family and a home. In the process, we would consider how these dual goals could be attained and whether she is willing to seek them under those conditions.

Somewhere during these activities I would want K to complete the Career Development Inventory (College and University Form). I would explain that some of the items, being designed for students still in college or graduate school, may seem a bit inappropriate for her, but I would ask her to put herself in a student's position and answer them as well as she could. The reasons for this and the other instruments have been explained in the first section of this writeup. I would ask her to take the Salience Inventory for more light on the work-and-family question. I would be interested especially in the somewhat future-oriented Value Expectations Scales. If time and motivation permitted, I would ask her to fill out either the Values Scale (Nevill and Super, 1986) or the Work Values Inventory (Super, 1970) — probably the former, for its focus on life in general, as well as on work.

With K's test results organized, I would go over her profiles with her. After whatever explanation of their meanings is needed for her to be able to react, I would leave it to her to tell me what they mean to her, and to explain to herself and to me why they are what they are and what their implications are for her career plans. If I saw interpretations that she did not mention, I would tentatively suggest them to her. We would discuss any differences in our interpretations and see if these differences could be resolved . . . without my conveying the idea that they had to be resolved then and there; rather, they could in due course be clarified by experience. Then, after she had assimilated the results, and after I had modified my own interpretations in light of our discussion, we would take up their implications for her now (presumably) to-be-confirmed goal of accounting and for the choice of a means of preparation and entry into that field. There could also be other alternatives we would want to look into as a result of the review of choice-related data.

At this point, the focus would probably be on the question of the MBA program, with perhaps part-time work in that field while she was a full-time student, so as not to delay entry and establishment any longer than necessary. I would also want to get her to consider the question of eventual marriage and perhaps that of how to put herself in the way of finding a suitable mate without investing too much time or ego in that effort. One of a career counselor's functions is to help to make happy accidents happen. How to get her to think about this question that she recognizes but does not place high on her agenda? I would remind her of the relevant statistics. That done, the ball would be in her court. And how would she be helped to see how to bring about this "happy accident"? I would ask her how some of her married friends met, and with what results. If she lacked data, we could plan discreet inquiries. I could even share some of the stories I know about, after she has cited some stories of her acquaintances, and we could try to evaluate the outcomes of the workings of the marriage market.

Finally, in terminating counseling after a number of interviews (which cannot, at this point, be estimated with any accuracy), but perhaps after only one more contact, I would not, to borrow a phrase and a concept from Frank Fletcher, "kiss the client good-bye at the door" — not without keeping the door open, for development does not stop at the doorstep. The welcome mat must be out. A note a few months later might ask her how things were going.

The Case of K in Social Learning Theory
John D. Krumboltz, Linda K. Mitchell

The social learning theory of career decision making (SLTCDM) represents career decision making as a product of a lifelong sequence of learning experiences, planned and unplanned, which occur during complex interactions between the decider and the environment. Let us see how the theory applies to the case of K and then consider the implications for counseling.

Learning Experiences. K has had a variety of career goals: author, public health administrator, and accountant. How did she acquire each of these occupational goals? What led her to drop one goal and formulate another? The case study does not enable us to delve into K's previous learning experiences, but the SLTCDM would postulate that K had experienced a series of instrumental and/or associative learning experiences, which taught her skills and generalizations that she combined to form and change her goals.

What were these learning experiences? What is the origin of her desire to become an accountant? The only information we are given is that in her senior year in college she took an accounting course and "loved it." Why did she love it? Was the instructor particularly enthusiastic and charismatic? Was the material explained particularly well? Did she get higher grades in accounting than she did in any of her other courses? We cannot answer these questions from the case-study material; but, as career counselors, we would want to explore some of the experiences that led her to her current goal in order to determine how solidly they were grounded.

The SLTCDM posits that career goals may arise from instrumental learning experiences — for example, the positive reinforcement of an A grade on an accounting quiz. Interest may also be generated by associative learning experiences — for example, K may have been impressed with the integrity and logic of her accounting instructor. K may have met an accountant whom she admired (the principle of modeling). If her past learning experiences with accounting had been skimpy, a career counselor could help her design ways of learning more.

Genetic and Environmental Background. Obviously, K could not have been successful on an accounting quiz if she had not had prior learning experiences that taught her the necessary skills and work habits. Each skill was built onto previous skills, in a long sequence of learning experiences going back to infancy. The extent to which K's genetic makeup may have predisposed her to develop certain abilities and talents remains a mystery of the type that psychologists still debate.

The fact that K had the learning experiences that she did is to a large extent dependent on the particular culture in which she developed. We do not know about her early family and schooling experiences, but clearly she grew up in the United States in an urban environment. Had she grown up in Japan, or Singapore, or Saudi Arabia, her learning experiences would have been markedly different, and she might or might not have developed an interest in accounting as it is practiced in those cultures. The SLTCDM clearly specifies that environmental influences play a major role in shaping the nature and extent of the learning experiences that each individual encounters.

K's parents were divorced when she was quite young, and this event probably influenced the nature of many of her learning experiences. It seems likely that her mother became a strong role model for her. The fact that marriage is a goal that she does not see as incompatible with her career goals may be a result of modeling by her medical-technologist mother, as well as of K's following the norm for her own generation. She desires marriage but admits to some difficulty in her relationships with men. What does that mean—the normal ups and downs of romantic relationships, or difficulties with men that could have important implications for her career? Interpersonal and emotional problems are intertwined with career problems. A career counselor cannot afford to separate them.

Self-Observation Generalizations. As a result of all of the genetic factors, environmental influences, and an infinitely complex series of learning experiences, K has now reached the point where she comes to a counselor, seeking confirmation about her desire to become an accountant. How did she get to this point?

Her previous learning experiences enabled her to form a number of self-observation generalizations—her conceptions of her own abilities, traits, and qualities. For example, on the Myers-Briggs Type Inventory she is identified from her own self-reports as extraverted, sensory, thinking, and judgmental. She says she loves to be with people.

She also likes to "party," sunbathe, play golf, read, and attend the opera. She has generalized from watching herself enjoy these experiences, and she can therefore describe them as some of her current leisure interests.

On the Strong Vocational Interest Blank, K responded to the items about what she liked and disliked in ways similar to bankers and restaurant managers, for example. These self-reported interests are, in the language of the SLTCDM, another form of self-observation generalization.

As K encountered the various learning experiences throughout life, she formed additional self-observation generalizations about her own personality. She sees herself as hardworking, for example. How did she arrive at the conclusion that she is hardworking? Indeed, how hardworking is she? Presumably, she judged her efforts on various school and work tasks as more extensive than those of others around her; if she had been in a different environment with people who worked harder than she, she might have described herself as lazy. The self-descriptions are a function of the particular environment in which she grew up and of the specific learning experiences she encountered there. A skilled career counselor might want to explore the background of her most salient self-observation generalizations if they seemed to inhibit her planning.

Task Approach Skills. Another outcome of her long series of learning experiences are task approach skills — her abilities for coping with the environment. She says that she cannot balance her own checkbook very well. Does that mean that she does not know how to balance her checkbook? Or does it mean that she trusts the bank and prefers not to engage in the labor of reconciling her account? She apparently has some ability in the accounting field in that she is currently responsible for several accounting tasks and has developed a record-keeping procedure.

Other task approach skills are her ability to set goals with time limits and pursue them vigorously and her ability to respond to challenges. For example, she improved her writing skills when she was told that they were substandard, and then she received praise (positive reinforcement) for subsequent written work. Is this the only instance in which she responded well to a challenge? Are there other incidents in which she did not respond well to challenges? A career counselor would want to help her examine the skills she has learned and the enthusiasm she has felt as she has performed these tasks.

1. *What additional assessment information is needed?* K has come to the counselor to seek confirmation of her accountant

goal. Since any goal is the product of a long series of learning experiences, a counselor would want to inquire a little bit about the origin of that goal. What experiences has K had with accounting activities? What is it about accounting that she likes? What is it about accounting that she does not like?

At the moment, K believes she wants to become an accountant but wants some assurance from the counselor that she is going in the right direction. Certainly, there is nothing on the Strong Vocational Interest Blank that would be counter to her professed interest. But what is the basis of her beliefs? Might she have some beliefs about herself or about the occupation of accounting that are inaccurate? Has she been challenged to think through the basis of her goals?

The Career Beliefs Inventory (CBI) could be a useful device to help her identify her assumptions. She basically wants to think through the option she is considering and apparently would welcome a challenge. The CBI would give her an opportunity to examine, for example, whether her accounting goal is based on a fear of changing her current career direction or whether it is based on more fundamental interest in the activity itself. She could get feedback on her willingness to consider other job options and to be influenced by others. She could assess with a counselor her willingness to assume responsibility for her own choices, to work hard to overcome obstacles, and to risk failure. She could be challenged to examine whether she is intrinsically interested in accounting or more interested in the perks and extrinsic satisfactions. The purpose of the CBI would be to reveal her beliefs about herself so that, with the help of a counselor, she could examine the implications of her own beliefs.

2. *What is the status of K's career plans?* If K were absolutely certain that she wanted to be an accountant, she might not be coming to see a counselor. How much does K actually know about the profession of accounting? In the language of the SLTCDM, she needs to test some of her world-view generalizations. It could be helpful for her to do some networking with currently employed accountants, to find out more about the responsibilities, opportunities, problems, and satisfactions associated with their work.

Many people enter an occupation with only the scantiest of notions about the responsibilities and opportunities of that occupation. A great deal of occupational dissatisfaction can be traced to the process by which people initially get into the occupation itself. Since K clearly requests this kind of help, a career counselor would want to encourage her to investigate the accounting profession by reading, study, and personal contact. The counselor would also encourage her to explore some other fields for comparison purposes.

Now is the time for K to invest some time and energy in exploring alternatives. The evidence suggests no fundamental reason why accounting is the wrong choice for her; but, of course, only she can determine what is right for her. An informed choice is the best choice. The job of the counselor is to help her engage in a process of informing herself about herself and about the alternatives available to her.

3. *What are the immediate and long-term concerns?* The most immediate concern is helping K engage in a set of learning experiences that will either confirm or disconfirm her interest in accounting.

Another immediate concern would be to defuse the urgency with which she might be viewing her current career situation. One of the subscales on the CBI, for example, deals with the client's willingness to see choices without urgency. While she wants to take steps that will enable her to make a satisfying choice now, she needs to see it as a choice that could be modified later. Perhaps K does eventually decide to enter the accounting field and gains admission to a master's degree program in accounting. Perhaps after a semester there she decides that accounting is not the field for her. If the counselor has done a good job of helping her view career shifts as normal adjustments to changing circumstances, she may well decide to switch to some other field, without suffering the psychological anguish of labeling herself a quitter.

For the longer term, K needs to see her career as a lifelong journey of adventure. The counselor could encourage her to avoid viewing decisions as life-or-death struggles and see them instead as forks in the road that bear careful investigation. Many paths could lead to instructive and delightful adventures. Should they not prove as satisfactory as K desires, she can alter her course again.

4. *What strategies should be employed in career counseling with K?* The first strategy is to find out who K is, from K's point of view. What is her perception of the problem? How did she get to be where she is now? What is her reason for seeking counseling at this point? What fears and hopes does she have? The first job of the counselor is to build a trusting relationship with K. All of K's thoughts, feelings, emotional concerns, and interpersonal problems may impinge on her career plans.

The second strategy is to assess the basis of K's beliefs about herself and her place in the world of work. The results of the CBI need to be discussed with a sensitive counselor. Challenges to one's beliefs are not always easy to accept. Only in an atmosphere of warmth and trust can one reveal and consider alternative beliefs. The counselor needs to use gentle confrontation from time to time, to help K test her current beliefs.

The third strategy is to structure exploratory experiences. K's learning experiences have brought her to where she is now, but the counselor can empower her to construct further learning experiences of her own. These new experiences will help K determine whether she is launched on a path she desires or whether some other alternative might be more agreeable to her.

The fourth strategy is to help K integrate what she finds from her explorations with what she has learned about herself. She needs to think a plan of action through that will move her toward her goal. It is not sufficient to leave her with "Accounting is my goal" as the end product of her decision making. If accounting is her goal, how is she going to get there? What is the best path to take? Should she get a master's degree in accounting? If so, which school should she attend? What happens to typical graduates of that particular school? How did currently employed accountants get trained? What career paths did they follow? How has the accounting profession changed recently? How have training and working conditions changed for accountants in recent years? What stereotypical notions about accountants may be influencing her? A counselor could refer her to such articles as those by Johnson and Dierks (1982), Brown (1981), and Bedeian, Mossholder, Touliatos, and Barkman (1986). No counselor is expected to be conversant with all the career paths available for every occupation, but with the thousands of reference materials available in career libraries and the convenience of computer searches, each client can be helped to find the needed information.

Finally, the counselor would engage in some cognitive restructuring, to help K see the journey ahead of her as an exciting adventure to be filled with both problems and satisfactions. The counselor would reinforce her belief that she can overcome difficult challenges. K would see that the process by which she made a decision and constructed a plan of action this time will be a handy task approach skill that she can use again. K should expect to make many more career decisions in the years ahead. A good career counselor will have taught her the decision-making skills that she will need.

The Case of K from an Individualist Perspective
Anna Miller-Tiedeman and David V. Tiedeman

Like the little boy who refused to indulge the emperor's advisers and notables concerning his nonexistent new clothes as the emperor rode nude to show his supposed new duds to his subjects, we have to immediately exclaim upon reading the case of K, "K wears no lifecareer clothes!"

Sorry, readers, but we simply have to tell it like it is from our lifecareer perspective, in this case. Career development has been undertaken too long as a fundamental trait and factor matter, not as a fundamental life matter. It is therefore time to write of career as it is—a consciousness phenomenon in life (not as it has been, only occupationally scientized).

For instance, look at the case history. Out of about 630 words in the case history, practically all of them are trait and factor words—that is, the words of our occupational scientism of seventy years or so. A mere 3 percent of the words are in any possible way K's personal words about herself. Finally, not even any of those personal words are of the spirit of life—that is, of the grounds of what we call *lifecareer*. In fact, to the extent that one can judge from the scientism of the case, rather than just from its words, K's dominant lifecareer content is probably fright or, at the least, personal doubt.

Bennis (Bennis and Nanus, 1985) spearheaded a recent study of leaders in American businesses. One of his many interesting conclusions is that managers do things right and leaders do right things. Bennis's distinction between leadership and management frames our general lifecareer implication concerning the case of K. She seemingly seeks confirmation of her current career goal of being an accountant. In Bennis's scheme, she is therefore still trying to "do things right." She has not matured to that leadership level of personal responsibility in her lifecareer understanding in which she "does right things." If she would learn to read her inner wisdom, she would be empowered to advance her present rabbitlike lifecareer into a lionlike lifecareer, in which she takes responsibility for what she is doing, be its outcome "right" or "left." Only she knows that kind of difference.

As noted in introduction, the case of K provides a telling example of how the field of career development currently deals with a very small part of an individual's lifecareer potential — namely, the personality-occupation interaction, at which personality is occupation, and vice versa (as both the Roe and Holland theories presume). In both of those theories, an individual is seemingly just what she or he does, and vice versa. But there is no room in either the Roe or the Holland theories for the participation of personal consciousness in personality-occupation relationships. In those theories, a personality is an occupation, or the reverse; that is all there is to career in either of these basic "wheels" of theory. In both theories, it is all scientism; there is nothing of personal understanding and action.

Furthermore, the presence of K's type in the case, as revealed by the Myers-Briggs Type Inventory, does nothing to challenge our conclusion that the career counselor presenting the case of K is dealing with only one-seventh of the lifecareer deck. Yes, the Myers-Briggs may very well indicate that K is an ESTJ type. Furthermore, the characteristics noted for an

ESTJ type may very well be statistically somewhat discriminative of occupational livelihoods, as noted. However, this does not change the fact that the information is still at the bottom of consciousness — the point where there are restraints on consciousness, and where no degree of freedom exists for the flow of lifecareer consciousness in the individual.

If career counselors were to deal with Myers's typology as Myers conceived it, the discriminative part of the Myers-Briggs Type Inventory would have to be used by K, not by the counselor. In short, Myers's purpose in isolating types was to let a person know the divisiveness of his or her use of life potential, so that he or she could work toward the integration of those facets, rather than stay in one slot and use that position to occupational advantage, as defined by someone else. In short, to use the Myers-Briggs as career counselors now do is to freeze the person in development. It is to use the off-centeredness of consciousness for society's purposes, rather than using society for the purposes of personal mirroring and development.

What, then, does the case of K reflect of a lifecareer kind? Practically nothing, as we have noted. Furthermore, the life-career implication is just that K still has to venture into personal meaning and responsibility. She will not have much consciousness of her lifecareer before then. Both personal meaning and responsibility are conditions essential to the advance of individuals into living lifecareer to the fullness of its potential. First, a career counselor has to reassure K that each of us has a career, and that its kind does not make as much difference to success in work as do personal conviction and understanding concerning its being the "right thing" for the individual.

The case of K fares little differently when viewed in relation to the more circumscribed career decision-making theory of Tiedeman and O'Hara. In order to apply the career decision-making theory, one has to order the career decision tree through which the individual has passed. K is twenty-four years old and employed. She also went to college and worked as she studied. Something is also told of her parents' occupations. However, none of this is really put together: first, in a time frame; then, in a frame denoting the bases of her decisions and the progress she made in the potential development ladder of personal responsibility in each of her major decision points. Her career identity is therefore effectively absent from public view. For these reasons, even the 3 percent of the case history's words having any self-reference cannot be put together for use in a developmental framework.

In conclusion, then, we reiterate our major point: namely, K wears no lifecareer clothes. Considering the currently short history of lifecareer theory, that absence is possibly excusable. However, considering the fact that career development theory has been around for at least forty years, its similar absence in consideration of K's career fortunes suggests that she is getting the short end of today's quite extensive career stick.

It appears, then, that career decision making has miles to go before it will take on the individualistic, evolutionary perspective now so necessary in today's work arena. And that is a pity, when lifecareer is all here now; it only remains for individuals to put lifecareer into living action. That is a purpose that should warm holistic counselors' hearts.

Summarizing the Case of K

It is obvious that each of the contributors to this volume who wrote about K relished the challenge presented in the case. To be sure, Miller-Tiedeman and Tiedeman declined to make any actual observations because the material was too "scientized." It is interesting to note that in their efforts to criticize not only this case but also others, they likewise declined to comment on even the most rudimentary aspects of what they would want to do with K. It is clear that each of the contributors wants to empower K as she searches for meaning in her life.

It is also clear that each author identifies unique approaches to career counseling with K, while all converge on some aspects of the process and strategies. Not unexpectedly, Super places the greatest emphasis on integrating career and life planning, while Lunneborg and Bordin emphasize the importance of early development. In fairness to Krumboltz and Mitchell, it should be noted that they also emphasize the importance of early modeling but seem more willing to look at learning as a process that continues over the life span.

Certainly, career counseling seems more of a circumscribed activity for some of the contributors than for others. Srebalus, in representing a Holland-based perspective, sticks exclusively to the career area. Brown (trait and factor theory), Lunneborg (Roe), and Krumboltz and Mitchell (SLTCDM) also focus on the career area almost entirely. As already mentioned, Super takes a broader, more holistic perspective, as does Bordin. Not unexpectedly, some of Bordin's questions seem to be directed not so much at role integration (as are Super's) as at underlying psychological problems.

It is interesting to note that a trait and factor theme runs through all the positions taken (except that of Miller-Tiedeman and Tiedeman). Certainly, Krumboltz talks about learning experiences as the basis for self-observation generalizations, and Lunneborg and Bordin look to early experiences as the genesis of these variables. Not unexpectedly, neither Srebalus nor Brown speaks to the origin of traits or the importance of diagnosing problems that may have occurred in their development. As expected, both emphasize the importance of matching traits to occupations.

Crites (1981, p. 49) once noted that the trait and factor approach had gone "into incipient decline" and "has devolved into what has been caricatured as 'three inventories and a cloud of dust.'" As stated earlier, trait and factor theory is still very much alive and well among career counselors, primarily because few substitutes have arisen to challenge it. To some degree, it seems that the approaches of Lunneborg, Bordin, Krumboltz and Mitchell, and, of course, Holland are derivations of trait and factor thinking. While Super relies on trait analysis as an essential part of his diagnostic process, he seems to go far beyond the caricature described by Crites. Whether others will follow his lead remains to be seen, but the idea of looking at the totality of the individual's functioning seems to be a trend of the future among career counselors.

Finally, it can be observed that while the philosophical position taken by Miller-Tiedeman and Tiedeman (phenomenology) offers a clear alternative to the logical positivism underpinning the other theories of career development and occupational choice, their comments on career counseling also "wear no clothes." It is not sufficient to criticize others and the construction of the case itself. We need viable alternatives — new metaphors, if you will — that will help us understand K and how to assist her. Perhaps by the time this volume goes into a third edition, substantive new approaches to career counseling will evolve from Miller-Tiedeman and Tiedeman, as well as from others.

16

Issues and Trends in Career Development: Theory and Practice

The foregoing chapters attempted to present current theories and practices of career development. Implicit in the various presentations are a number of unresolved issues and trends that will shape future thinking, research, and practice. This chapter will be devoted to a discussion of these issues and trends.

Issues

1. *Do we need separate career development theories for women and minorities?* On the positive side of this issue, it can be asserted that separate theories are needed because the results of the unique socialization due to race and sex have never been adequately considered in the present theories, which were developed to explain the career development and occupational choice making of white males. As Brooks notes in Chapter Eleven, a number of theoretical statements have been set forth that focus on women, but no separate statements have yet surfaced regarding minorities. It seems to be only a matter of time before a theory regarding the career development of minorities is presented.

506

There are some powerful arguments favoring theoretical statements for women and minorities, including the charge that major theories contain a bias toward white males. Also, as Holland and Super have both argued, it is premature to attempt global theories of career choice and development. Perhaps the most salient argument for separate theories of career choice and development for various subgroups is the likelihood that greater numbers of research studies will be focused on these groups as a result. This has certainly been the result of the Hackett and Betz (1981) statement, as Brooks has carefully documented.

Despite the already mentioned criticisms of current theories of career development and well-reasoned statements by Osipow (1975) and Fitzgerald and Crites (1980), several arguments can be mounted to counter the position that separate theories are needed for women and minorities. First, while sex role and race do influence socialization, and thus the career development process, it may be more feasible to revise current theories, as Super (1957, 1984) attempted to do, so that differences can be accommodated within more global theories. Current theories should not be discarded in favor of piecemeal theories. To discard them would result in throwing out years of research and thinking, which have some degree of validity, since many of the psychological, sociological, and economic variables influence men, women, and minorities in a similar manner. Second, there is no compelling evidence that the current theories predict any less well for women and minorities than they do for white males, although Roe's observation — that certain aspects of the career development of women (for example, being a housewife) are not accounted for — is an apt one. There is also controversy about the use of some of the devices that have been developed to measure theoretical constructs (see Weinrach and Srebalus, Chapter Three), but it may be the instruments, not the theories, that are at fault. A third counterargument to the need for separate theories is that the building of good science requires comprehensive theories, and minitheories may fragment scientists' efforts to explore and explain the complex phenomena associated with career choice and development.

2. *Is work the most salient life role?* Warnath (1975) criticizes career development theorists for according work central status in human functioning. As we have already seen, most theorists now at least acknowledge the importance of other life roles, and some, like Super (1982b), have suggested that role saliency shifts as individuals move through the life span. But, as we saw in his chapter, his paradigm suggests that work is the most salient role during what we have traditionally viewed as the working years.

Some, including Warnath, would posit that we must discontinue our perseveration about the centrality of work simply because the needs of many individuals cannot be met in the workplace, and thus we may be fostering an unreal expectation about the potential rewards of working. Although it is not a certainty at this point, it appears likely that a portion of our population will be unemployed for periods of time during their lives, and that a greater proportion will be underemployed, perhaps for the majority of their lives (U.S. Department of Labor, 1982). To perpetuate the idea of the centrality of work is to tie self-worth to finding fulfilling work, with the result that alienation and lowered self-esteem will increase among certain groups of workers.

In emphasizing that work should be the most salient life role, several counterpoints can be made. Among these is the often cited decline in both productivity rate and quality of products in America, which for some are related to the decline in the work ethic. We must, according to this school of thought, reinforce the importance of work if we are to be competitive with countries that have maintained this point of view. Most Americans are going to spend a great proportion of their lives in a work role. The shorter work week and the growing importance of leisure, alluded to by such articles as the one by Winters and Hansen (1976), have simply not materialized. Workers need to accept this reality and attempt to maximize their performance, regardless of the jobs in which they find themselves.

3. *What is the role of tests in career counseling?* In both Brown's chapter on trait and factor theory and Weinrach and Srebalus's exposition of Holland's ideas, issues were raised regarding the

use of tests. This controversy has a number of dimensions and seems likely to continue.

Prediger (1980, p. 304) analyzed the marriage between tests and career counseling and concluded that it was sound, "although there are some problems over 'sex,'" by which he meant sex bias in interest inventories. As we have seen in earlier chapters, others, particularly those aligned with the trait and factor point of view, agree. They posit that tests are efficient ways of collecting data about our clients, can provide valid self-explanation activities, particularly when used in conjunction with other activities (Prediger, 1980), and can provide objective data that can help students assign probabilities to certain career options. They also argue that in the hands of a skilled clinician the biases pointed to so vociferously by detractors of testing can be eliminated and a positive experience can result.

Those who attack tests point quickly to the racial and gender biases inherent in many tests and express concern that many test users are either unaware of these discriminating features or unconcerned about their impact. They also express concern that test and inventory developers have not responded quickly and aggressively to these obvious weaknesses. Detractors also point to the fact that stated interests predict job choice as well as inventoried interests, and data about aptitudes and work values can be gained by a skillful career counselor without the need to introduce the mental set that may result from a low test score or an interest profile that suggests a stereotypical occupational group. Tests can become a substitute for skillfully conducted interviews — an inferior substitute, at that.

4. *What is the role of self-directed career development approaches?* As Weinrach and Srebalus pointed out earlier, Holland has long advocated that self-directed approaches may be as effective as and, in the same instances, preferable to traditional career counseling as means of identifying career options. Bolles (1988) has also suggested that self-directed procedures (namely, his own job-hunting manual) can be more effective than traditional career counseling and placement in developing job-hunting skills.

Brown (1981) takes exception to some of the underlying assumptions of the self-help procedures — namely, that career decision making is a process uncomplicated by mental health concerns and inadequate decision-making skills, and that the developer of the self-directed procedures can anticipate all of the self and occupational information needed by the person using them. But, one could quickly rejoin, the literature in this area is at best equivocal and at worst (depending on one's point of view) supportive of self-help procedures (see Holland, Magoon, and Spokane, 1981). Touché! But research designs have been weak, and the true tests of self-help versus career counseling approaches remain in the future.

Trends in Career Development

1. *Technology will both compound and provide assistance with the career development problems of workers.* Most of us have become increasingly aware of the impact of technology on workers, both through our professional reading and through the mass media, which depict devices ranging from skilled robots in a Toyota manufacturing plant to computers that handle data at unparalleled speeds. We also see advertisements for teleconferences that reduce the need for business meetings, and we are aware that communications devices grow more sophisticated daily. The results are displaced semiskilled workers in the automobile industry, reduced person-to-person communication in some industries (Hahn, 1980), information overload that results in increased stress (Hald, 1981), and increased requirements that the worker engage in lifelong learning in order to keep abreast of the onslaught of changes (Herr, 1982). Hoyt (1987) suggests that the major challenge to career counselors that grows out of technological change is to assist workers in maintaining their commitment to work.

Cianni-Surridge (1983) suggests that while career counselors need to be aware of the negative impact of technology, they also should be prepared to deal with the results of using the new technological advances. Specifically, she recommends that microcomputers be used to provide assistance in the decision-making process, that computerized files of occupational information be established, and that telematics be used in the placement process to facilitate the interview process by allowing out-of-work people to be interviewed in their own homes or in a placement office. This latter technique could do much to eliminate geographical barriers to employment that now exist, and the others could greatly facilitate career counseling.

2. *The impact of employment and unemployment on mental health will be of increasing concern.* The attention of psychologists is increasingly turning to the relationship between certain employment conditions and mental health concerns, as well as to the psychological implications of unemployment.

In 1984, in the first edition of this volume, I pointed out that there is substantial evidence to support the idea that job dissatisfaction is related to the degree of match between personality type and work environment. Osipow (1983) has suggested that an interaction between interests, personality characteristics, and variables in the work setting (for example, stress) may result in certain mental health problems. Smith (1989) has also called attention to this problem.

Similarly, articles by Fisher and Cunningham (1983) and Turkington (1983) have reviewed findings that loss of employment may produce certain adjustment problems. Fisher and Cunningham point out that the data are by no means clear on this point, but they also note that findings of immediate depression and loss of self-esteem (for example, Perfetti and Bingham, 1983) are common. Cunningham (1983) also suggests that stress related to unemployment may create problems for the families of workers.

In the immediate years ahead, vocational psychologists will be called on to explore factors involved in the worker–work environment interaction that create or worsen mental health problems, and to explore the short- and long-term impact of unemployment on adjustment.

Brown (1984, 1985) and Brown and Brooks (1985) have noted that career counselors will need to broaden the base of career counseling to consider mental health concerns and become more aware of the relationship between them and employment conditions. It may well be that this broader base will include anticipating mental health problems that may arise on the job in the career choice-making process (Smith, 1989) and (just as would be the case with other employability skills) helping the client develop means of avoiding these problems. When counseling the unemployed, we may also need to discard the traditional assumption that career counseling proceeds only after mental health is established (Crites, 1981) and to view the relationship between career and mental health counseling as a dynamic one.

3. *Career development programs will be increasingly available in a greater variety of settings and from a wider range of personnel.* Earlier in this volume, Hall (Chapter Thirteen) discussed specific theories of organizational career development. The spread of career development services into business and industry has been well chronicled (see Keller and Piotrowski, 1987). Herr (1982) has observed that career development programs are available in prisons, hospitals, and shopping centers. There can be little doubt that the microcomputer revolution, accompanied by interactive career exploration programs, will soon be available for home use as well.

With the growth of career development programs will come a change in groups interested in providing these services. Traditionally, counseling psychologists, college counselors, rehabilitation counselors, employment counselors, and school counselors have provided career development services. It is hoped that those groups who have traditionally been less interested in this area, such as clinical psychologists, mental health counselors, and social workers, will be increasingly interested in career development programs and their delivery. It can be stated with some certainty that human resource development specialists, industrial psychologists, and others involved with the workplace will be increasingly concerned with the career development process.

This burgeoning interest in career development poses a problem for a variety of professions — namely, establishing standards for the practice of career counseling. The reaction to this problem points to another trend.

4. *There will be increased interest in credentialing career counselors.* Licensing and certification of mental health workers is commonplace. All fifty states have licensing laws for psychologists,

and many of the states have licensing laws for counselors and social workers. In 1982, the National Career Development Association (then the National Vocational Guidance Association) launched an effort to develop a credentialing process for career counselors. This effort has culminated in a certification process for career counselors. Currently, there are only a few nationally certified career counselors, but the number is growing. As the public becomes more aware of the need to seek qualified assistance with career planning and adjustment, the demand for credentialing will grow.

5. *An increased recognition of the complexity of career counseling will occur.* Throughout this volume, there have been references to the stereotype that career counseling is a rather straightforward process that requires little skill to conduct. One need look no further than Brooks's discussion of the diagnosis, focus, process, and outcomes of career counseling to realize that this stereotype is incorrect. When one considers the growing realization of the impact of work on mental health, the need to deal with racial and sexual stereotypes in the counseling process, the knowledge required to use tests and other types of data correctly, the number of sources and the complexity of occupational information, and so forth, the error in this view is even more obvious. Therefore, Myers's (1982) view — that there will be an increasing recognition of the complexities of career counseling and a parallel effort to provide better training in this area — seems appropriate.

6. *There will be an increasing emphasis on the postmidlife period of career development, including retirement planning.* As Brown (1984) indicates, interest in midlife career change has accelerated during the last half-century. This interest can be expected to continue and to be extended into the late adult years to include retirement planning and the retirement years (Sinick, 1976). Wiggins's (1982) study of retired teachers appears to be the forerunner of many research efforts in that it points not only to the validity of Holland's theory but also to potential directions for helping retirees make important life decisions. Super's (1982b) role-saliency research and theorizing should also provide helpful ways of conceptualizing counseling and career development activities with older workers.

7. *A greater concern for the career development and career counseling of special subgroups will emerge.* Recent reports highlighting the future importance of women and minorities in the work force (see National Alliance of Business, 1988) have already stimulated efforts to enhance the career development of these groups. Legislative efforts can be expected to produce new programs that will continue and extend these efforts. Whether this national focus on women and minorities will produce the desired result — full integration of these groups into every level of the work force in the near term — remains doubtful.

With regard to research, it can be expected that women's career development will increasingly be the focus of investigation. As Brooks has noted, the career development of minorities is not receiving the attention it deserves, and it seems unlikely that this will occur unless the professional groups concerned with career development attract large numbers of members from the ranks of minorities.

Categories of special students, such as gifted students (Wilson, 1982), handicapped students (Dahl, 1982; Humes, 1982), and disadvantaged students (J. V. Miller, 1982), will receive additional consideration from legislators, as well as from researchers and practitioners. The passage of P.L. 94-142 was the signal that our society is committed to providing the least restrictive educational and vocational opportunities for handicapped persons. These individuals can no longer be ignored by our educational institutions. Efforts are also under way to provide better educational and counseling services to gifted and disadvantaged students in many locales. These efforts seem unlikely to decline and will probably accelerate. Some of the tools and techniques applicable to these groups have been developed by rehabilitation counselors and need to be adopted by career counselors. In other instances (career counseling for ethnic minorities), established techniques and procedures have not evolved; therefore, career counselors must proceed cautiously. Perhaps the only sound advice that can be offered is that career counselors should not assume that those procedures developed for white middle-class clients can be generalized directly to these other groups.

8. *There will be a greater emphasis on work-adjustment factors,*

particularly as they relate to productivity and quality. In the April 1983 issue of *American Psychologist,* seven articles were concerned with the relationship of psychological factors and economic productivity. In the first of these, Perloff and Nelson (1983) provide an overview of the problem. Two of the articles (Quale, 1983; Nathan, 1983) discuss the negative impact of alcoholism and drug abuse on productivity. Two deal with psychological approaches to improving productivity (Hunter and Schmidt, 1983; Katzell and Guzzo, 1983). Two others issue challenges to psychologists (Alluisi and Meigs, 1983; Tuttle, 1983). Notably absent was any discussion of these issues by a vocational psychologist. It seems likely that vocational psychologists will increasingly focus their attention on this area of national concern.

As the focus on productivity develops, two things should result. First, research regarding career development will be extended to the workplace in an attempt to identify personal factors related to productivity and to tie these to career development. Lofquist and Dawis's (1969) theorizing about work satisfaction and satisfactoriness can be viewed as the forerunner of this type of effort. Chapter Thirteen of this volume contains the best of the current thinking about organizational career development. Second, career counselors, particularly in business and industry, will be increasingly asked to deal with unproductive workers. In the past, the focus of employee assistance programs has been on drug and alcohol abuse, marital problems, and similar concerns because these were viewed as causal factors in unsatisfactory job performance. In the future, the relationship between the worker and his or her match with the occupation will be of greater concern.

9. *There will be an increasing emphasis in research and practice on factors related to the decision-making process.* Ultimately, most theories of career choice were designed to explain why people choose certain types of occupations. Career development programs and career counseling are pursued to develop the skills, information bases, and personal insights that will result in good choices at the appropriate times. To be sure, the appropriate time may be either in the immediate present or at some distant point, but the purpose is the same: making a satisfactory career choice.

Super recommends incorporating career decision-making models into theories of career development in his chapter, and Mitchell and Krumboltz recognize that decision making is an important task approach skill. None of the other theorists incorporates an actual model of decision making into his or her position, although it is presumed that none would doubt the importance of decision making in the career development process. In the years that follow, it can be expected that increasing emphasis will be placed on the decision-making area.

10. *There will be an increasing focus on the relationship of literacy to career development.* The popular press has focused on the weaknesses of our public educational system for more than half a decade. The National Alliance of Business (1988) has linked literacy and economic well-being. In short, there has been a rude awakening in our society: without a literate population, the United States is in danger of becoming a second-class economic power.

It seems likely that we will see a flurry of programs in both the public and private sectors aimed at identifying the educational skills needed by various types of workers and at promoting the development of these skills. It also appears certain that career development programs and literacy programs will be linked, particularly in public schools. The General Accounting Office (1987), in response to a request from Congress, attempted to identify successful dropout-prevention programs. In almost every case, these programs combined some form of life or career planning and literacy improvement. At this writing, the U.S. Office of Education is considering funding fifteen to twenty exemplary dropout-prevention efforts. Many of these programs are likely to include basic education, vocational education, and career development components. These programs, once funded, will be carefully evaluated. These efforts appear to be the forerunners of many programs in a variety of settings.

11. *Theories and research in career development will increasingly reflect the phenomenological philosophical perspective.* At the end of Chapter One, Brooks and I inserted a discussion of one of the current issues in the social sciences: logical positivism versus phenomenology as the basis for theory and research. Since the

turn of the twentieth century, thinking about career development and occupational choice has been influenced by logical
positivism. While this position will probably remain at center
stage in the near future, it seems likely that more and more
theories will be articulated that either reflect some of the assumptions of phenomenology or are based solely on these assumptions. These perspectives will lead to an emphasis on qualitative
methods of looking at career choice, career development, and
the interrelationship among life roles. As Collin and Young
(1986) note, some research in the qualitative tradition has already
begun to surface; the few studies that have been published por-
tend a flood of qualitative research efforts.

References

Abe, C., and Holland, J. L. *A Description of College Freshmen: I. Students with Different Choices of Major Field*. ACT Research Report no. 3. Iowa City, Iowa: American College Testing Program, 1965.

Aldis, O. *Play Fighting*. Orlando, Fla.: Academic Press, 1975.

Alexander, K., and Eckland, B. K. "Basic Attainment Process: A Replication and Extension." *Sociology of Education*, 1975, *48*, 457–495.

Alexander, K., Eckland, B. K., and Griffin, L. J. "The Wisconsin Model of Socioeconomic Achievement: A Replication." *American Journal of Sociology*, 1975, *81*, 324–342.

Alexander, L., and Cook, M. A. "Curricula and Coursework: A Surprise Ending to a Familiar Story." *American Sociological Review*, 1982, *47*, 626–640.

Alexander, L., Cook, M. A., and McDill, E. L. "Curriculum Tracking and Educational Stratification: Some Further Evidence." *American Sociological Review*, 1978, *43*, 47–66.

Alexander, L., and McDill, E. L. "Selection and Allocation Within Schools: Some Causes and Consequences of Curriculum Placement." *American Sociological Review*, 1976, *41*, 963–980.

Alexander, L., and Pallas, M. "Curriculum Reform and School Performance: An Evaluation of the 'New Basics.'" *American Journal of Education*, 1984, *92*, 391–420.

Allport, G. W., Vernon, P. E., and Lindzey, G. *Study of Values.* Boston: Houghton Mifflin, 1970.

Alluisi, E. A., and Meigs, D. K., Jr. "Potentials for Productivity Enhancement from Psychological Research and Development." *American Psychologist,* 1983, *38,* 487–493.

Almquist, E. M. "Sex Stereotypes in Occupational Choice: The Case for College Women." *Journal of Vocational Behavior,* 1974, *5* (1), 13–21.

Anastasi, A. *Psychological Testing.* (5th ed.) New York: Macmillan, 1982.

Anastasi, A. "Evolving Trait Concepts." *American Psychologist,* 1983, *38,* 175–184.

Ansell, E. M. "An Assessment of Vocational Maturity of Lower-Class Caucasians, Lower-Class Negroes, and Middle-Class Caucasians in Grades Eight Through Twelve." Unpublished doctoral dissertation, Department of Counseling and Human Services, State University of New York, Buffalo, 1970.

Argyris, C. *Personality and Organization.* New York: Harper & Row, 1957.

Aronfreed, J. *Conduct and Conscience: The Socialization of Internalized Control over Behavior.* Orlando, Fla.: Academic Press, 1968.

Arroba, T. "Styles of Decision Making and Their Use." *British Journal of Guidance and Counseling,* 1978, *5,* 149–158.

Arthur, M. B., Hall, D. T., Lawrence, B. S. (eds.). *Handbook of Career Theory.* New York: Cambridge University Press, 1989.

Astin, A. W. "Effects of Different College Environments on the Vocational Choices of High-Aptitude Students." *Journal of Counseling Psychology,* 1965, *12* (1), 28–34.

Astin, H. S. "The Meaning of Work in Women's Lives: A Sociopsychological Model of Career Choice and Work Behavior." *Counseling Psychologist,* 1984, *12* (4), 117–126.

Astin, H. S., and Bisconti, A. S. *Career Plans of College Graduates of 1965 and 1970.* Bethlehem, Pa.: CPC Foundation, 1973.

Atkinson, J. W. *An Introduction to Motivation.* New York: D. Van Nostrand, 1964.

Ayres, A. L. "Self-Efficacy Theory: Implications for the Career Development of Women." Unpublished doctoral dissertation, Ohio State University, 1980.

Bach, R. *Illusions: The Adventures of a Reluctant Messiah.* New York: Dell, 1977.

Bachtold, L. M. "Personality Characteristics of Women of Distinction." *Psychology of Women Quarterly,* 1976, *1,* 70–78.

Bailyn, L., and Lynch, J. T. "Engineering as a Lifelong Career: Its Meaning, Its Satisfactions, Its Difficulties." *Journal of Occupational Behavior,* 1983, *4,* 263–283.

Baird, L. L. "The Relation of Vocational Interests to Life Goals, Self-Ratings and Ability and Personality Traits, and Potential for Achievement." *Journal of Counseling Psychology,* 1970, *17,* 233–239.

Baird, L. L. "Cooling Out and Warming Up in the Junior College." *Measurement and Evaluation in Guidance,* 1971, *4* (3), 160–171.

Bandura, A. *Principles of Behavior Modification.* New York: Holt, Rinehart & Winston, 1969.

Bandura, A. *Aggression: A Social Learning Analysis.* Englewood Cliffs, N.J.: Prentice-Hall, 1973.

Bandura, A. "Self-Efficacy: Toward a Unifying Theory of Behavioral Change." *Psychological Review,* 1977a, *84,* 191–215.

Bandura, A. *Social Learning Theory.* Englewood Cliffs, N.J.: Prentice-Hall, 1977b.

Bandura, A. "Self-Efficacy Theory in Human Agency." *American Psychologist,* 1982, *37,* 122–147.

Bandura, A. *Social Foundations of Thought and Action: A Social-Cognitive Theory.* Englewood Cliffs, N.J.: Prentice-Hall, 1986.

Barak, A., Carney, C. G., and Archibald, R. D. "The Relationship Between Vocational Information Seeking and Educational and Vocational Decidedness." *Journal of Vocational Behavior,* 1975, *7,* 149–159.

Barak, A., and Rabbi, B. "Predicting Persistence, Stability, and Achievement in College by Major-Choice Consistency: A Test of Holland's Consistency Hypothesis." *Journal of Vocational Behavior,* 1982, *20,* 235–243.

Barber, L. W. "The Counselor as General Contractor: Implications for Curriculum." *Character Potential: A Record of Research,* 1974, *7,* 22–27.

Barley, S. R. "Careers, Identities, and Institutions: The Legacy of the Chicago School of Sociology." In M. B. Arthur, D. T. Hall, and B. S. Lawrence (eds.), *Handbook of Career Theory.* New York: Cambridge University Press, 1989.

Barnard, C. I. *The Functions of the Executive.* Cambridge, Mass.: Harvard University Press, 1938.

Baron, J. N., and Bielby, T. "Workers and Machines: Dimensions and Determinants of Technical Relations in the Workplace." *American Sociological Review,* 1980, *45,* 737–765.

Baron, J. N., and Bielby, T. "Workers and Machines: Dimensions and Determinants of Technical Relations in the Workplace." *American Sociological Review,* 1982, *47,* 175–188.

Baron, J. N., and Bielby, T. "The Organization of Work in a Segmented Economy." *American Sociological Review,* 1984, *49,* 454–473.

Barry, W. A., and Bordin, E. S. "Personality Development and the Vocational Choice of the Ministry." *Journal of Counseling Psychology,* 1967, *14,* 395–402.

Beall, L., and Bordin, E. S. "The Development and Personality of Engineers." *Personnel and Guidance Journal,* 1964, *48,* 23–32.

Beck, A. T. *Cognitive Therapy and Emotional Disorders.* New York: International Universities Press, 1976.

Beck, A. T., and others. *Cognitive Therapy of Depression: A Treatment Manual.* New York: Guilford Press, 1979.

Beck, E. M., Horan, P. M., and Tolbert, C. M. II. "Stratification in a Dual Economy." *American Sociological Review,* 1978, *43,* 704–739.

Beck, E. M., Horan, P. M., and Tolbert, C. M. II. "Social Stratification in Industrial Society: Further Evidence for a Structural Alternative (Reply to Hauser)." *American Sociological Review,* 1980, *45,* 712–719.

Becker, G. S. *The Economics of Discrimination.* Chicago: University of Chicago Press, 1957.

Becker, G. S. *Human Capital: A Theoretical and Empirical Analysis with Special Reference to Education.* (2nd ed.) New York: Columbia University Press, 1975.

Becker, H., Geer, B., Hughes, E. C., and Strauss, A. *Boys in White.* Chicago: University of Chicago Press, 1957.

Bedeian, A. G., Mossholder, K. W., Touliatos, J., and Barkman, A. I. "The Accountant's Stereotype: An Update for Vocational Counselors." *Career Development Quarterly,* 1986, *35,* 113–122.

Begin, L. *To Help or Not to Help: A Cognitive-Developmental View.* Ottawa, Ont.: Canada Department of Manpower and Immigration, 1981.

Belz, H. F., and Geary, D. C. "Father's Occupation and Social Background: Relation to SAT Scores." *American Educational Research Journal,* 1984, *21,* 473–478.

Bennett, G. K., Seashore, G., and Wesman, A. G. *Differential Aptitude Test Technical Manual.* New York: Psychological Corporation, 1974.

Bennis, W., and Nanus, B. *Leaders: Strategies for Taking Charge.* New York: Harper & Row, 1985.

Bentov, I. *Stalking the Wild Pendulum.* New York: Dutton, 1977.

Berg, I. (ed.). *Human Resources and Economic Welfare: Essays in Honor of Eli Ginzberg.* New York: Columbia University Press, 1972.

Bergland, B. "Career Planning: The Use of Sequential Evaluated Experience." In E. L. Herr (ed.), *Vocational Guidance and Human Development.* Boston: Houghton Mifflin, 1974.

Berlew, D. E., and Hall, D. T. "The Socialization of Managers: Effects of Expectations on Experience." *Administrative Science Quarterly,* 1966, *11,* 207–223.

Berlyne, D. E. *Conflict, Arousal, and Curiosity.* New York: McGraw-Hill, 1960.

Betz, E. L. "A Study of Career Patterns of Women College Graduates." *Journal of Vocational Behavior,* 1984, *24,* 249–263.

Betz, N. E., and Fitzgerald, L. F. *The Career Psychology of Women.* Orlando, Fla.: Academic Press, 1987.

Betz, N. E., and Hackett, G. "The Relationship of Career-Related Self-Efficacy Expectations to Perceived Career Options in College Men and Women." *Journal of Counseling Psychology,* 1981, *27,* 44–62.

Betz, N. E., and Hackett, G. "Applications of Self-Efficacy Theory to Understanding Career-Choice Behavior." *Journal of Social and Clinical Psychology,* 1986, *4,* 279–289.

Bianchi, S. M., and Spain, D. *American Women in Transition.* New York: Russell Sage Foundation, 1986.

Bibb, R., and Form, W. H. "The Effects of Industrial, Occupational, and Sex Stratification on Wages in Blue-Collar Markets." *Social Forces,* 1977, *55,* 974–996.

Bielby, T., and Baron, N. "Men and Women at Work: Sex Segregation and Statistical Discrimination." *American Journal of Sociology,* 1986, *91,* 759–799.

Biggs, D. A., and Keller, K. E. "A Cognitive Approach to Using Tests in Counseling." *Personnel and Guidance Journal,* 1982, *60,* 528–532.

Birnbaum, J. L. "Life Patterns, Personality, Style, and Self-Esteem in Gifted Family-Oriented and Career-Committed Women." Unpublished doctoral dissertation, Department of Psychology, University of Michigan, 1971.

Bishop, J. *The Productivity Consequences of What Is Learned in High School.* Working Paper no. 88-18. Center for Advanced Human Resource Studies, School of Industrial and Labor Relations, Cornell University, 1988.

Blau, P. M., and Duncan, O. D. *The American Occupational Structure.* New York: Wiley, 1967.

Blau, P. M., and others. "Occupational Choice: A Conceptual Framework." *Industrial Labor Relations Review,* 1956, *9,* 531–543.

Blauner, R. *Alienation and Freedom.* Chicago: University of Chicago Press, 1964.

Blustein, D. L., and Strohmer, D. C. "Vocational Hypothesis Testing in Career Decision Making." *Journal of Vocational Behavior,* 1987, *31,* 45–62.

Bohm, D. *Wholeness and the Implicate Order.* Boston: Routledge & Kegan Paul, 1980.

Bolles, R. N. *What Color Is Your Parachute? A Practical Manual for Job Hunters and Career Changers.* (6th ed.) Berkeley, Calif.: Ten Speed Press, 1988.

Bolton, B. "Discriminant Analysis of Holland's Occupational Types Using the Sixteen Personality Factor Questionnaire." *Journal of Vocational Behavior,* 1985, *27,* 210–217.

Boocock, S. S. "The Life Career Game." *Personnel and Guidance Journal,* 1967, *45,* 8–17.

Bordin, E. S. "A Theory of Vocational Interests as Dynamic Phenomena." *Educational and Psychological Measurement,* 1943, *3,* 49–66.

Bordin, E. S. "Diagnosis in Counseling and Psychotherapy." *Educational and Psychological Measurement,* 1946, *6,* 169–184.

Bordin, E. S. *Psychological Counseling.* (2nd ed.) East Norwalk, Conn.: Appleton-Century-Crofts, 1968.

Bordin, E. S. "Fusing Work and Play: A Challenge to Theory and Research." *Academic Psychology Bulletin,* 1979, *1,* 5-9.

Bordin, E. S., Nachmann, B., and Segal, S. J. "An Articulated Framework for Vocational Development." *Journal of Counseling Psychology,* 1963, *10,* 107-116.

Bordin, E. S., and Wilson, E. H. "Change of Interest as a Function of Shift in Curricular Orientation." *Educational and Psychological Measurement,* 1953, *13,* 297-307.

Borgatta, E. F., and Lambert, W. W. (eds.). *Handbook of Personality Theory and Research.* Skokie, Ill.: Rand-McNally, 1968.

Borgen, F. H., and Weiss, D. J. *Supervisor Perceptions of Occupational Environments and Roe's Classification of Occupations.* Research Report no. 13. Minneapolis: Work-Adjustment Project, University of Minnesota, 1968.

Borow, H. "Career Development Theory and Instrumental Outcomes of Career Education: A Critique." In J. D. Krumboltz and D. A. Hamel (eds.), *Assessing Career Development.* Mountain View, Calif.: Mayfield, 1982.

Borow, H., and Super, D. E. "Review of Your Educational Plans." *Personnel and Guidance Journal,* 1960, *28,* 754-758.

Bowlesbey, J. H. "The Computer as a Tool in Career Guidance Programs." In N. C. Gysbers and Associates, *Designing Careers.* San Francisco: Jossey-Bass, 1984.

Boyer, E. L. *High School: A Report on Secondary Education in America.* New York: Harper & Row, 1982.

Bray, D. W., Campbell, R. J., and Grant, D. E. *Formative Years in Business.* New York: Wiley, 1974.

Brewer, J. M. *History of Vocational Guidance.* New York: Harper & Row, 1942.

Brim, O. G., and Wheeler, S. G. *Socialization After Childhood.* New York: Wiley, 1966.

Brockner, J. *Self-Esteem at Work: Research, Theory, and Practice.* Lexington, Mass.: Lexington Books, 1988.

Brooks, L. "Counseling Special Groups." In D. Brown, L. Brooks, and Associates, *Career Choice and Development: Applying Contemporary Theories to Practice.* San Francisco: Jossey-Bass, 1984.

Brooks, L. "Encouraging Women's Motivation for Nontraditional Career and Life-Style Options: A Model for Assessment and Intervention." *Journal of Career Development,* 1988, *14,* 223–241.

Brooks, L., and Haigler, J. "Contract Career Counseling: An Option for Some Help Seekers." *Vocational Guidance Quarterly,* 1984, *33,* 178–182.

Brown, D. *Students' Vocational Choices: A Review and Critique.* Guidance Monograph Series, no. 4. Boston: Houghton Mifflin, 1970.

Brown, D. "Emerging Models of Career Development Groups for Persons at Midlife." *Vocational Guidance Quarterly,* 1981, *29,* 332–340.

Brown, D. "Mid-Life Career Change." In D. Brown, L. Brooks, and Associates, *Career Choice and Development: Applying Contemporary Theories to Practice.* San Francisco: Jossey-Bass, 1984.

Brown, D. "Career Counseling: Before, After, or Instead of Personal Counseling." *Vocational Guidance Quarterly,* 1985, *33* (3), 197–201.

Brown, D. "The Status of Holland's Theory of Vocational Choice." *Career Development Quarterly,* 1987, *36,* 13–23.

Brown, D. "Life-Role Development and Counseling." Paper presented at the meeting of the National Career Development Association, Orlando, Fla., 1988.

Brown, D., and Brooks, L. "Career Counseling as a Mental Health Intervention." *Professional Psychology: Research and Practice,* 1985, *16,* 860–867.

Brown, J. R. "Women Auditors—A Quiet Invasion into the Male World." *Government Accountants Journal,* 1981, *31* (1), 24–27.

Brown, J. S., Grant, C. W., and Patton, M. J. "A CPI Comparison of Engineers and Managers." *Journal of Vocational Behavior,* 1981, *18,* 255–264.

Brown, S. D., and Lent, R. W. (eds.). *Handbook of Counseling Psychology.* New York: Wiley, 1984.

Bruch, M. A., and Gilligan, J. F. "Extension of Holland's Theory to Assessment of Marital and Family Interactions."

American Mental Health Counselors Association Journal, 1980, *2* (2), 71–82.

Brunkan, R. J. "Perceived Parental Attitudes and Parental Identification in Relation to Field and Vocational Choice." *Journal of Counseling Psychology,* 1965, *12,* 39–47.

Buehler, C. *Der menschliche Lebenslauf als psychologisches Problem* [The Human Life Course as a Psychological Subject]. Leipzig: Hirzel, 1933.

Bulow, I., and Summers, H. "A Theory of Dual Labor Markets with Application to Industrial Policy, Discrimination, and Keynesian Unemployment." *Journal of Labor Economics,* 1986, *4* (3), pt. 1.

Bureau of the Census. *Statistical Abstract of the United States, 1988, 108th Edition.* Washington, D.C.: U.S. Government Printing Office, 1987.

Byers, A. P., Forrest, G. G., and Zaccaria, J. S. "Recalled Early Parent-Child Relations, Adult Needs, and Occupational Choice: A Test of Roe's Theory." *Journal of Counseling Psychology,* 1968, *15,* 324–328.

Cacioppo, J. T., Glass, C. R., and Merluzzi, T. V. "Self-Statements and Self-Evaluations: Cognitive-Response Analysis of Heterosexual Social Anxiety." *Cognitive Therapy and Research,* 1979, *3,* 249–262.

Cairo, P. C. "Measured Interests Versus Expressed Interests as Predictors of Long-Term Occupational Membership." *Journal of Vocational Behavior,* 1982, *20,* 343–353.

Campbell, A. A., Converse, P. E., and Rogers, W. L. *The Quality of American Life.* New York: Russell Sage Foundation, 1976.

Campbell, D. P. *Strong-Campbell Interest Inventory Manual.* Stanford, Calif.: Stanford University Press, 1985.

Campbell, N. K., and Hackett, G. "The Effects of Mathematics Task Performance on Math Self-Efficacy and Task Interest." *Journal of Vocational Behavior,* 1986, *28,* 149–162.

Campbell, R. E., and Parsons, J. L. "Readiness for Vocational Planning in Junior High School: A Socioeconomic and Geographic Comparison." *Journal of Vocational Behavior,* 1972, *2,* 401–417.

Capra, F. *The Tao of Physics: An Explanation of the Parallels Be-*

tween Modern Physics and Eastern Mysticism. New York: Bantam, 1974.

Capra, F. *The Turning Point: Science, Society, and the Rising Culture.* New York: Simon & Schuster, 1982.

Card, J. J. "Career Commitment Processes in the Young Adult Years." *Journal of Vocational Behavior,* 1978, *12,* 53–75.

Carkhuff, R. R., Alexik, M., and Anderson, S. "Do We Have a Theory of Vocational Choice?" *Personnel and Guidance Journal,* 1967, *46,* 335–345.

Cattell, R. B., Eber, H. W., and Tatsuoka, M. M. *Handbook of the Sixteen Personality Factor Questionnaire.* Champaign, Ill.: Institute for Personality and Ability Testing, 1970.

Centers, R. *The Psychology of Social Classes.* Princeton, N.J.: Princeton University Press, 1949.

Centers, R. S., and Bugental, D. S. "Intrinsic and Extrinsic Job Motivation of the Working Population." *Journal of Applied Psychology,* 1966, *50,* 193–197.

Champoux, J. E. "A Sociological Perspective on Work Involvement." *International Review of Applied Psychology,* 1981, *30,* 65–86.

Chodorow, N. "Family Structure and Feminine Personality." In M. Rosaldo and L. Maphere (eds.), *Women, Culture, and Society.* Stanford, Calif.: Stanford University Press, 1974.

Chodorow, N. *The Reproduction of Mothering.* Berkeley: University of California Press, 1978.

Christiansen, K. C. "Case Study of a Career Management System." Workshop presented at annual meeting of the American Psychological Association, Anaheim, Calif., 1983.

Chusmir, L. H. "Characteristics and Predictive Dimensions of Women Who Make Nontraditional Vocational Choices." *Personnel and Guidance Journal,* 1983, *62,* 43–47.

Cianni-Surridge, M. "Technology and Work: Future Issues for Career Guidance." *Personnel and Guidance Journal,* 1983, *61,* 413–422.

Cicourel, A., and Kitsuse, J. *The Educational Decision-Makers.* Indianapolis, Ind.: Bobbs-Merrill, 1963.

Clarke, R., Gelatt, H. B., and Levine, L. "A Decision-Making Paradigm for Local Guidance Research." *Personnel and Guidance Journal,* 1965, *44,* 40–51.

Clement, S. "The Self-Efficacy Expectations and Occupational Preferences of Females and Males." *Journal of Occupational Psychology*, 1987, *60*, 257–265.

Cohen, J., and Cohen, P. *Applied Multiple-Regression/Correlation Analysis for the Behavioral Sciences.* (2nd ed.) Hillsdale, N.J.: Erlbaum, 1983.

Colclough, G., and Horan, P. "The Status Attainment Paradigm: An Application of a Kuhnian Perspective." *Sociological Quarterly*, 1983, *24*, 25–42.

Cole, N. S., and Hanson, G. R. "An Analysis of the Structure of Vocational Interest." *Journal of Consulting Psychology*, 1971, *18*, 478–486.

Collin, A., and Young, R. A. "New Directions for Theories of Career." *Human Relations*, 1986, *39*, 837–853.

Colten, M. E., and Janis, I. L. "Effects of Self-Disclosure and the Decisional Balance Sheet Procedure in a Weight-Loss Clinic." In I. Janis (ed.), *Counseling on Personal Decision Theory and Field Research in Helping Relationships.* New Haven, Conn.: Yale University Press, 1982.

Commission on Youth and America's Future. "Noncollege Graduates Are Treated as Failures, Study Says." *Minneapolis Star Tribune*, Nov. 18, 1988, p. 13A.

Corcoran, M. E., and Duncan, G. J. "Work History, Labor-Force Attachment, and Earnings Differences Between the Races and Sexes." *Journal of Human Resources*, 1979, *14*, 3–20.

Corsini, R. *Encyclopedia of Psychology.* New York: Wiley, 1984.

Corsini, R. *Concise Encyclopedia of Psychology.* New York: Wiley, 1987.

Costa, P. T., Jr., McCrae, R. R., and Holland, J. L. "Personality and Vocational Interests in an Adult Sample." *Journal of Applied Psychology*, 1984, *69*, 390–400.

Cox, S. H. "Intrafamily Comparison of Loving–Rejecting Child-Rearing Practices." *Child Development*, 1970, *41*, 437–448.

Crabbs, M. A., and Black, K. U. "Job Change Following a Natural Disaster." *Vocational Guidance Quarterly*, 1984, *32*, 232–239.

Crabtree, P. D. "A Test of Holland's Hexagonal Model of Occupational Classification Using a Rural High School Population." Unpublished doctoral dissertation, Ohio University, 1971.

Crites, J. O. "Parental Identification in Relation to Vocational Interest Development." *Journal of Educational Psychology,* 1962, *53,* 262–270.

Crites, J. O. *Vocational Psychology.* New York: McGraw-Hill, 1969.

Crites, J. O. "Career Counseling: A Comprehensive Approach." In J. M. Whiteley and A. Resnikoff (eds.), *Career Counseling.* Pacific Grove, Calif.: Brooks/Cole, 1978a.

Crites, J. O. "Career Counseling: A Review of Major Approaches." In J. M. Whiteley and A. Resnikoff (eds.), *Career Counseling.* Pacific Grove, Calif.: Brooks/Cole, 1978b.

Crites, J. O. *Career Maturity Inventory.* Monterey, Calif.: CTB/McGraw-Hill, 1978c.

Crites, J. O. *Career Adjustment and Development Inventory.* College Park, Md.: Gumpert, 1979.

Crites, J. O. *Career Counseling: Models, Methods, and Materials.* New York: McGraw-Hill, 1981.

Crites, J. O. "Testing for Career Adjustment and Development." *Training & Development,* 1982, *36* (2), 20, 22–28.

Cunningham, S. "Shock of Layoff Felt Deep Inside Family Circle." *APA Monitor,* 1983, *14,* 10–11.

Cutts, C. C. "Test Review — First Review." *Measurement and Evaluation in Guidance,* 1977, *10* (2), 117–120.

Dahl, P. R. "Maximizing Vocational Opportunities for Handicapped Clients." *Vocational Guidance Quarterly,* 1982, *31,* 43–52.

Dalton, G. W., and Thompson, P. H. "Are R&D Organizations Obsolete?" *Harvard Business Review,* 1976, *54,* 105–116.

Dansart, B. "Existentialism in the Thought of David V. Tiedeman." *Character Potential: A Record of Research,* 1974, *7,* 1–8.

Darley, J. G. *Clinical Aspects and Interpretation of the Strong Vocational Interest Blank.* New York: Psychological Corporation, 1941.

Darley, J. G., and Hagenah, T. *Vocational Interest Measurement.* Minneapolis: University of Minnesota Press, 1955.

Davidson, P. E., and Anderson, H. D. *Occupational Mobility in an American Community.* Stanford, Calif.: Stanford University Press, 1937.

Davis, L. E., and Cherns, A. B. (eds.). *The Quality of Working Life.* New York: Free Press, 1975.

Dawis, R. V., England, G. W., and Lofquist, L. H. "A Theory of Work Adjustment." *Minnesota Studies in Vocational Rehabilitation,* no. 15. Minneapolis: University of Minnesota Industrial Relations Center, 1964.

Dawis, R. V., and Lofquist, L. H. "Personality Style and the Process of Work Adjustment." *Journal of Counseling Psychology,* 1976, *23,* 55–59.

Dawis, R. V., and Lofquist, L. H. *A Psychological Theory of Work Adjustment.* Minneapolis: University of Minnesota Press, 1984.

Dawis, R. V., Lofquist, L. H., and Weiss, D. J. "A Theory of Work Adjustment." *Minnesota Studies in Vocational Rehabilitation,* no. 23. Minneapolis: University of Minnesota Industrial Relations Center, 1968a.

Dawis, R. V., Lofquist, L. H., and Weiss, D. J. "A Theory of Work Adjustment: A Revision." *Minnesota Studies in Vocational Rehabilitation,* no. 49. Minneapolis: University of Minnesota Industrial Relations Center, 1968b.

De Long, T. "Comparing Rural and Urban Educators, Using the Variable of Career Orientation." Unpublished paper, Harvard Business School, 1985.

Dege, D., Perreault, G., Mills-Novoa, B., and Hansen, S. L. *Video Viewers' Guide No. 3: Women: Choices and Changes.* Washington, D.C.: U.S. Office of Education, 1980.

Derr, C. B. *Managing the New Careerists: The Diverse Career Success Orientations of Today's Workers.* San Francisco: Jossey-Bass, 1986.

Dickens, W. T., and Lang, K. "A Test of Dual Labor Market Theory." *American Economic Review,* 1985a, *75,* 792–805.

Dickens, W. T., and Lang, K. "Testing Dual Labor Market Theory: A Reconsideration of the Evidence." National Bureau of Economic Research Working Paper no. 1670, 1985b.

Dinklage, L. B. *Adolescent Choice and Decision Making: A Review of Decision-Making Models and Issues in Relation to Some Developmental Stage Tests of Adolescence.* Monograph 2A. Cambridge, Mass.: Graduate School of Education, Harvard University, 1967.

Dinklage, L. B. "Decision Strategies of Adolescents." Unpublished doctoral dissertation, Graduate School of Education, Harvard University, 1968.

Dinklage, L. B. *Student Decision-Making Studies of Adolescents in the Secondary Schools.* Report no. 6. Cambridge, Mass.: Graduate School of Education, Harvard University, 1969.

DiTomaso, N. "Income Determination in Three Internal Labor Markets." In G. Farkas and P. England (eds.), *Industries, Firms, and Jobs: Sociological and Economic Approaches.* New York: Plenum, 1988.

Doeringer, P. B., and Piore, M. J. *Internal Labor Markets and Manpower Analysis.* Lexington, Mass.: Heath, 1971.

Dorn, F. J. "Career Development in Business and Industry." *Journal of Counseling and Development,* 1986, *64,* 653–654.

Doyle, R. E. "Career Patterns of Male College Graduates." *Personnel and Guidance Journal,* 1965, *44,* 410–415.

Dreeben, R., and Gamoran, A. "Race, Instruction, and Learning." *American Sociological Review,* 1986, *51,* 660–669.

Drever, J. *Dictionary of Psychology.* New York: Penguin, 1952.

Driver, M. J. "Career Concepts and Organizational Change." In C. B. Derr (ed.), *Work, Family, and the Career: New Frontiers in Theory and Research.* New York: Praeger, 1980.

Driver, M. J. "Careers: A Review of Personal and Organizational Research." In C. L. Cooper and I. Robertson (eds.), *International Review of Industrial and Organizational Psychology.* New York: Wiley, 1988.

Driver, M. J., and Coombs, M. "Fit Between Career Concepts, Corporate Culture, and Engineering Productivity and Morale." *Proceedings, IEEE Careers Conference.* New York: Institute for Electrical and Electronic Engineering, 1983.

Dudley, G. A., and Tiedeman, D. V. *Career Development: Exploration and Commitment.* Muncie, Ind.: Accelerated Development, 1977.

Duncan, O. D. "A Socioeconomic Index for All Occupations." In A. J. Reiss, Jr. (ed.), *Occupations and Social Status.* New York: Free Press, 1961.

Duncan, O. D., Featherman, D. L., and Duncan, B. *Socioeconomic Background and Achievement.* New York: Seminar Press, 1972.

Easton, A. *Decision Making: An Overview*. New York: Wiley, 1976.

Edwards, A. L. *Edwards Personal Preference Schedule*. New York: Psychological Corporation, 1953.

Edwards, W. "The Theory of Decision Making." *Psychological Bulletin*, 1954, *51*, 380–417.

Eibl-Eibesfeldt, I. "Concepts of Ethology and Their Significance in the Study of Human Behavior." In H. W. Stevenson, E. H. Hess, and H. L. Rheingold (eds.), *Early Behavior*. New York: Wiley, 1967.

Ekstrom, B., and Lee, E. *Student Access to Guidance Counseling in High School*. Princeton, N.J.: Educational Testing Service, 1986.

Elenz-Martin, P. "A Study of Preoccupational Effects of the Resident Assistant Experience on Career Decision Making During the College Years." Unpublished doctoral dissertation, Department of Leadership and Educational Policy Studies, Northern Illinois University, 1977.

Elenz-Martin, P., and Miller-Tiedeman, A. *Decision-Making Organizer: College*. Bensenville, Ill.: Scholastic Testing Service, 1979.

Elliott, T. R., and Byrd, E. K. "Scoring Accuracy of the Self-Directed Search with Ninth-Grade Students." *Vocational Guidance Quarterly*, 1985, *34*, 85–90.

Ellis, A. *The Essence of Rational Psychotherapy: A Comprehensive Approach to Treatment*. New York: Institute for Rational Living, 1970.

Elton, C. F. "Male Career Role and Vocational Choice: Their Prediction with Personality and Aptitude Variables." *Journal of Counseling Psychology*, 1967, *14*, 99–105.

Elton, C. F., and Rose, H. A. "Significance of Personality in the Vocational Choice of Women." *Journal of Counseling Psychology*, 1967, *14*, 293–298.

Elton, C. F., and Rose, H. A. "Male Occupational Consistency and Change: Its Prediction According to Holland's Theory." *Journal of Counseling Psychology*, 1970, *17* (6), pt. 2 (entire issue).

Emery, A. O. "The Effectiveness of a Career-Exploration Program." Unpublished doctoral dissertation, Department of Educational Administration, Temple University, 1978.

England, P. "Assessing Trends in Occupational Sex Segregation, 1988–1976." In I. Berg (ed.), *Sociological Perspectives on Labor Markets.* Orlando, Fla.: Academic Press, 1981.

England, P., and Farkas, G. *Households, Employment, and Gender: A Social, Economic, and Demographic View.* New York: Aldine De Gruyter, 1986.

England, P., and McCreary, L. "Gender Inequality in Paid Employment." In B. B. Hess and M. M. Ferree (eds.), *Analyzing Gender: A Handbook of Social Science Research.* Newbury Park, Calif.: Sage, 1987.

England, P., and others. "Explaining Occupational Sex Segregation and Wages: Findings from a Model with Fixed Effects." *American Sociological Review,* 1988, *53* (4), 544–558.

Englander, M. E. "A Psychological Analysis of Vocational Choice: Teaching." *Journal of Counseling Psychology,* 1960, *7,* 257–264.

English, H. B., and English, A. C. *A Comprehensive Dictionary of Psychological and Psychoanalytic Terms.* New York: Longmans, Green, 1958.

Erb, T. O., and Smith, W. S. "Validation of the Attitude Toward Women in Science Scale for Early Adolescents." *Journal of Research in Science Teaching,* 1984, *21,* 391–397.

Erikson, E. H. "Identity and the Life Cycle." *Psychological Issues,* 1959, *1* (entire issue).

Erikson, E. H. *Childhood and Society.* (2nd ed.) New York: Norton, 1963.

Farley, R., and Allen, W. R. *The Color Line and the Quality of Life in America.* New York: Russell Sage Foundation, 1987.

Farmer, H. S. "Model of Career and Achievement Motivation for Women and Men." *Journal of Counseling Psychology,* 1985, *32,* 363–390.

Fassinger, R. E. "A Causal Model of Career Choice in College Women." *Journal of Vocational Behavior,* 1985, *27,* 123–153.

Fassinger, R. E. *The Testing of a Model of Career Choice in Two Populations of College Women.* Unpublished doctoral dissertation, Ohio State University, 1987.

Featherman, D. L., and Hauser, R. M. "Prestige or Socioeconomic Scales in the Study of Occupational Achievement." *Sociological Methods and Research,* 1976, *4,* 403–422.

Featherman, D. L., and Hauser, R. M. *Opportunity and Change.* Orlando, Fla.: Academic Press, 1978.

Ferster, C. B., and Skinner, B. F. *Schedules of Reinforcement.* East Norwalk, Conn.: Appleton-Century-Crofts, 1957.

Fisher, I. "Midlife Change." Unpublished doctoral dissertation, Teachers College, Columbia University, 1989.

Fisher, K., and Cunningham, S. "The Dilemma: Problem Grows, Support Shrinks." *APA Monitor,* 1983, *14,* 2.

Fisher, S., and Fisher, R. L. *Pretend the World Is Funny and Forever.* Hillsdale, N.J.: Erlbaum, 1981.

Fisher, T. J., Reardon, R. C., and Burck, H. D. "Increasing Information-Seeking Behavior with a Model-Reinforced Videotape." *Journal of Counseling Psychology,* 1976, *23,* 234–238.

Fitzgerald, L. F., and Betz, N. E. "Astin's Model in Theory and Practice: A Technical and Philosophical Critique." *Counseling Psychologist,* 1984, *12* (4), 135–138.

Fitzgerald, L. F., and Crites, J. O. "Toward a Career Psychology of Women: What Do We Know? What Do We Need to Know?" *Journal of Counseling Psychology,* 1980, *27,* 44–62.

Flanagan, J. C. *Project TALENT: Five Years After High School.* Pittsburgh: American Institutes for Research, 1971.

Fletcher, F. M. "Concepts, Curiosity, and Careers." *Journal of Counseling Psychology,* 1966, *13,* 131–138.

Ford, R. N. *Motivation Through the World Itself.* New York: American Management Association, 1969.

Form, W., Kaufman, R. L., Parcel, T. L., and Wallace, M. "The Impact of Technology on Work Organization and Work Outcomes: A Conceptual Framework and Research Agenda." In G. Farkas and P. England (eds.), *Industries, Firms, and Jobs: Sociological and Economic Approaches.* New York: Plenum, 1988.

Form, W. H., and Miller, D. C. "Occupational Career Pattern as a Sociological Instrument." In S. Nosow and W. H. Form (eds.), *Man, Work, and Society.* New York: Basic Books, 1962.

Forrest, L., and Mikolaitis, N. "The Relational Component of Identity: An Expansion of Career Development Theory." *Career Development Quarterly,* 1986, *35,* 76–88.

Foss, C., and Slaney, R. "Increasing Nontraditional Career Choices in Women: Relation of Attitudes Toward Women and Responses to a Career Intervention." *Journal of Vocational Behavior,* 1986, *28,* 191–202.

Fosterling, F. "Attributional Aspects of Cognitive Behavior Modification: A Theoretical Approach and Suggestions for Techniques." *Cognitive Therapy and Research,* 1980, *24,* 27–37.

Frederickson, R. H. *Career Information.* Englewood Cliffs, N.J.: Prentice-Hall, 1982.

Frost, F., and Diamond, E. "Ethnic and Sex Differences in Occupational Stereotyping by Elementary School Children." *Journal of Vocational Behavior,* 1979, *15,* 43–45.

Fuller, R. *Intuition.* New York: Doubleday, 1972.

Gabarro, J. J. *The Dynamics of Taking Charge.* Boston: Harvard Business School Press, 1987.

Gade, E. M., Fuqua, D., and Hurlburt, G. "The Relationship of Holland's Personality Types to Education Satisfaction with a Native American High School Population." *Journal of Counseling Psychology,* 1988, *35,* 183–186.

Galinsky, M. D. "Personality Development and Vocational Choice of Clinical Psychologists and Physicists." *Journal of Counseling Psychology,* 1962, *9,* 299–305.

Galinsky, M. D., and Fast, I. "Vocational Choices as a Focus of the Identity Search." *Journal of Counseling Psychology,* 1966, *13,* 89–92.

Gamoran, A. "The Stratification of High School Learning Opportunities." *Sociology of Education,* 1987, *60,* 135–155.

Gamoran, A., and Mare, R. D. "Secondary School Tracking and Educational Inequality: Compensation, Reinforcement, or Neutrality?" *American Journal of Sociology,* 1989, *94,* 1146–1183.

Gardner, J. G. *No Easy Task.* New York: Harper & Row, 1968.

Garet, M. S., and DeLany, B. "Students, Courses, and Stratification." *Sociology of Education,* 1988, *61,* 61–77.

Garfinkle, M. "The Relationship Between General Self-Concept, Role Self-Concept, and Role Behavior in High School." Unpublished doctoral dissertation, Department of Psychology, Teachers College, Columbia University, 1958.

Gati, I. "A Hierarchical Model for the Structure of Vocational Interests." *Journal of Vocational Behavior*, 1979, *15*, 90–106.

Gati, I. "On the Perceived Structure of Occupations." *Journal of Vocational Behavior*, 1984, *25*, 1–29.

Gati, I. "Making Career Decisions—A Sequential Elimination Approach." *Journal of Counseling Psychology*, 1986, *33*, 408–417.

Gati, I., and Meir, E. I. "Congruence and Consistence Derived from the Circular and the Hierarchical Models as Predictors of Occupational Choice Satisfaction." *Journal of Vocational Behavior*, 1982, *20*, 354–365.

Gault, F. M., and Meyers, H. H. "A Comparison of Two Career-Planning Inventories." *Career Development Quarterly*, 1987, *35*, 332–336.

Gelatt, H. B. "Decision Making: A Conceptual Frame of Reference for Counseling." *Journal of Counseling Psychology*, 1962, *9*, 240–245.

Gelatt, H. B. "Positive Uncertainty: A Strategy for Making Decisions in Modern Times." *CACD Journal*, 1987, *8*, 49–55.

General Accounting Office. *School Dropouts: Survey of Local Programs*. Washington, D.C.: General Accounting Office, 1987.

Gerstein, M., Lichtman, M., and Barokas, J. U. "Occupational Plans of Adolescent Women Compared to Men: A Cross-Sectional Examination." *Career Development Quarterly*, 1988, *36*, 222–230.

Ghiselli, E. E. "The Validity of Aptitude Tests in Personnel Selection." *Personnel Psychology*, 1973, *26*, 461–477.

Gibson, D. L., Weiss, D. J., Dawis, R. V., and Lofquist, L. H. "Manual for the Minnesota Satisfactoriness Scales." *Minnesota Studies in Vocational Rehabilitation*, no. 27. Minneapolis: University of Minnesota Labor Relations Center, 1970.

Gilbert, L. A. "Comments on the Meaning of Work in Women's Lives." *Counseling Psychologist*, 1984, *12* (4), 129–130.

Gilligan, C. "In a Different Voice: Women's Conceptions of Self and Morality." *Harvard Educational Review*, 1977, *47*, 481–517.

Gilligan, C. "Woman's Place in Man's Life Cycle." *Harvard Educational Review*, 1979, *49*, 431–445.

Gilligan, C. *In a Different Voice*. Cambridge, Mass.: Harvard University Press, 1982.

Ginzberg, E. "Toward a Theory of Occupational Choice: A Restatement." *Vocational Guidance Quarterly,* 1972, *20* (3), 169–176.

Ginzberg, E. "Career Development." In D. Brown, L. Brooks, and Associates, *Career Choice and Development: Applying Contemporary Theories to Practice.* San Francisco: Jossey-Bass, 1984.

Ginzberg, E., Ginzburg, S. W., Axelrad, S., and Herma, J. L. *Occupational Choice: An Approach to a General Theory.* New York: Columbia University Press, 1951.

Ginzberg, E., and others. *Life-Styles of Educated Women.* New York: Columbia University Press, 1966.

Glass, C. R. "Advances and Issues in Cognitive Assessment." Paper presented at annual meeting of American Psychological Association, Montreal, Canada, Sept. 1980.

Goffman, E. "The Moral Career of the Mental Patient." In E. Goffman (ed.), *Asylums.* New York: Anchor, 1961.

Goldfried, M. R., and Robins, C. "On the Facilitation of Self-Efficacy." *Cognitive Therapy and Research,* 1982, *6,* 361–380.

Goldin, P. C. "A Review of Children's Reports of Parent Behaviors." *Psychological Bulletin,* 1969, *71,* 222–236.

Goldschmidt, M. L. "Prediction of College Majors by Personality Tests." *Journal of Counseling Psychology,* 1967, *14,* 302–308.

Goodale, J. G., Hall, D. T., and Rabinowitz, S. "A Longitudinal Test of a Psychological Success Model of Job Involvement." Unpublished manuscript, Boston University, 1982.

Gordon, R. A., and Arvey, R. D. "Perceived and Actual Ages of Workers." *Journal of Vocational Behavior,* 1986, *28,* 21–28.

Gottfredson, G. D. "Career Stability and Redirection in Adulthood." *Journal of Applied Psychology,* 1977, *62,* 436–445.

Gottfredson, G. D., and Holland, J. L. "Vocational Choices of Men and Women: A Comparison of Predictors from the Self-Directed Search." *Journal of Counseling Psychology,* 1975, *22,* 28–34.

Gottfredson, G. D., and Holland, J. L. "Toward Beneficial Resolution of the Interest Inventory Controversy." In C. K. Tittle and D. G. Zytowski (eds.), *Sex-Fair Interest Measurement: Research and Implications.* Washington, D.C.: National Institute of Education, 1978.

Gottfredson, G. D., Holland, J. L., and Ogawa, D. K. *Dic-*

tionary of Holland Occupational Codes. Palo Alto, Calif.: Consulting Psychologists Press, 1982.

Gottfredson, L. S. "Providing Black Youth More Access to Enterprising Work." *Vocational Guidance Quarterly,* 1978, *27,* 114–123.

Gottfredson, L. S. "Circumscription and Compromise: A Developmental Theory of Occupational Aspirations." *Journal of Counseling Psychology Monograph,* 1981, *28,* 545–579.

Gottfredson, L. S. "Creating and Criticizing Theory." *Journal of Vocational Behavior,* 1983, *23,* 203–212.

Gottfredson, L. S. "Role of Self-Concept in Vocational Theory." *Journal of Counseling Psychology,* 1985, *32,* 159–162.

Gottfredson, L. S. "Special Groups and the Beneficial Use of Vocational Interest Inventories." In W. B. Walsh and S. H. Osipow (eds.), *Advances in Vocational Psychology.* Vol. 1. *Assessment of Interests.* Hillsdale, N.J.: Erlbaum, 1986.

Gould, R. "The Phases of Adult Life: A Study in Developmental Psychology." *American Journal of Psychiatry,* 1972, *129,* 521–531.

Granovetter, M. "The Sociological and Economic Approaches to Labor-Market Analysis: A Social Structural View." In G. Farkas and P. England (eds.), *Industries, Firms, and Jobs: Sociological and Economic Approaches.* New York: Plenum, 1988.

Graves, C. W. "Human Nature Prepares for a Momentous Leap." *Futurist,* 1974, *8,* 72–85.

Green, L. B., and Parker, N. J. "Parental Influence Upon Adolescents' Occupational Choice: A Test of an Aspect of Roe's Theory." *Journal of Counseling Psychology,* 1965, *12,* 379–383.

Greenberger, E., and Steinberg, L. *When Teenagers Work.* New York: Basic Books, 1986.

Greenhaus, J. H., and Parasuraman, S. "Vocational and Organizational Behavior: A Review." *Journal of Vocational Behavior,* 1986, *24,* 115–176.

Greenlee, S. P., Damarin, F. L., and Walsh, W. B. "Congruence and Differentiation Among Black and White Males in Two Non-College-Degreed Occupations." *Journal of Vocational Behavior,* 1988, *32,* 298–306.

Greenwald, B. S. "The Effects of Early Childhood Experience on Vocational Choice." Unpublished doctoral dissertation, Department of Psychology, University of Michigan, 1963.

Gribbons, W. D., and Lohnes, P. R. *Emerging Careers*. New York: Teachers College Press, 1968.

Gribbons, W. D., and Lohnes, P. R. *Readiness for Career Planning*. (Rev. ed.) Buffalo: Department of Educational Psychology, State University of New York, 1975.

Gribbons, W. D., and Lohnes, P. R. *Careers in Theory and Experience*. Albany: State University of New York Press, 1982.

Griffith, A. R. "A Survey of Career Development in Corporations." *Personnel and Guidance Journal*, 1980, *58*, 537–543.

Grigg, A. E. "Childhood Experience with Parental Attitudes: A Test of Roe's Hypothesis." *Journal of Counseling Psychology*, 1959, *6*, 153–155.

Gross, E. *Work and Society*. New York: Crowell, 1958.

Gross, E. "The Worker and Society." In H. Borow (ed.), *Man in a World at Work*. Boston: Houghton Mifflin, 1964.

Grotevant, H. D., and Thorbecke, W. L. "Sex Differences in Styles of Occupational Identity Formation." *Developmental Psychology*, 1982, *18*, 396–405.

Guilford, J. P., and others. "A Factor-Analysis Study of Human Interests." *Psychological Monographs*, 1954, *68* (4), entire issue.

Guthrie, W. R., and Herman, A. "Vocational Maturity and Its Relationship to Holland's Theory of Vocational Choice." *Journal of Vocational Behavior*, 1982, *21*, 196–205.

Gutteridge, T. G. "Organizational Career-Development Systems: The State of the Practice." In D. T. Hall and Associates, *Career Development in Organizations*. San Francisco: Jossey-Bass, 1986.

Gysbers, N. C., and Associates. *Designing Careers: Counseling to Enhance Education, Work, and Leisure*. San Francisco: Jossey-Bass, 1984.

Gysbers, N. C., Johnston, J. A., and Gust, T. "Characteristics of Homemaker and Career-Oriented Women." *Journal of Counseling Psychology*, 1968, *15*, 541–546.

Hackett, G. "The Role of Mathematics Self-Efficacy in the Choice of Math-Related Majors of College Women and Men:

A Path Analysis." *Journal of Counseling Psychology,* 1985, *32,* 47–56.

Hackett, G., and Betz, N. "A Self-Efficacy Approach to the Career Development of Women." *Journal of Vocational Behavior,* 1981, *18,* 326–339.

Hackett, G., and Betz, N. E. "Gender Differences in the Effects of Relevant and Irrelevant Task Failure on Mathematics Self-Efficacy Expectations." Paper presented at the annual meeting of the American Educational Research Association, New Orleans, 1984.

Hackett, G., and Campbell, N. K. "Task Self-Efficacy and Task Interest as a Function of Performance on a Gender-Neutral Task." *Journal of Vocational Behavior,* 1988, *30,* 203–215.

Hagen, D. "Careers and Family Atmospheres: An Empirical Test of Roe's Theory." *Journal of Counseling Psychology,* 1960, *7,* 251–256.

Hahn, W. A. "The Postindustrial Boom in Communications." In C. S. Sheppard and D. C. Carroll (eds.), *Working in the Twenty-First Century.* New York: Wiley, 1980.

Hald, R. D. "Toward the Information-Rich Society." *Futurist,* 1981, *15,* 25–30.

Hall, D. T. "A Theoretical Model of Career Subidentity Development in Organizational Settings." *Organizational Behavior and Human Performance,* 1971, *6,* 50–76.

Hall, D. T. *Careers in Organizations.* Santa Monica, Calif.: Goodyear, 1976.

Hall, D. T. "Project Work as an Antidote to Career Plateauing in a Declining Engineering Organization." *Human Resource Management,* 1985, *24,* 271–292.

Hall, D. T., and Associates. *Career Development in Organizations.* San Francisco: Jossey-Bass, 1986.

Hall, D. T., and Foster, L. W. "A Psychological Success Cycle and Goal Setting: Goals, Performance, and Attitudes." *Academy of Management Journal,* 1977, *20,* 282–290.

Hall, D. T., and Louis, M. R. "When Careers Plateau." *Research and Technology Management,* 1988, *31,* 41–45.

Hall, D. T., and Nougaim, K. "An Examination of Maslow's

Need Hierarchy in an Organizational Setting." *Organizational Behavior and Human Performance,* 1968, *3,* 12–35.

Hall, D. T., and Richter, J. "Managing the Baby-Boom Generation." Unpublished paper, Boston University, 1989.

Hall, D. T., and Schneider, B. *Organizational Climates and Careers: The Work Lives of Priests.* Orlando, Fla.: Academic Press, 1973.

Hall, L. G., and Tarrier, R. B. *Hall Occupational Orientation Inventory Counselor's Manual.* (3rd ed.) Bensenville, Ill.: Scholastic Testing Service, 1976.

Hall, R. H. *Dimensions of Work.* Newbury Park, Calif.: Sage, 1986.

Handley, H. M., and Hickson, J. F. "Background and Career Orientations of Women with Mathematical Aptitude." *Journal of Vocational Behavior,* 1978, *13,* 255–262.

Hansen, D. A. "Social Change and Humanistic Confusion: Considerations for a Politics of Counseling." In E. L. Herr (ed.), *Vocational Guidance and Human Development.* Boston: Houghton Mifflin, 1974.

Hansen, J.-I. C., and Campbell, D. P. *Manual of the SVIB-SCII.* Palo Alto, Calif.: Consulting Psychologists Press, 1985.

Hansen, L. S. "Promoting Female Growth Through a Career Development Curriculum." In L. S. Hansen and R. S. Rapoza (eds.), *Career Development and Counseling of Women.* Springfield, Ill.: Thomas, 1978.

Harder, D. F. "Differentiation of Curricular Groups Based on Response to Unique Items of MMPI." *Journal of Counseling Psychology,* 1959, *6,* 28–34.

Hargreaves, D. H. *Social Relations in a Secondary School.* London: Tinling, 1967.

Harmon, L. W. "What's New? A Response to Astin." *Counseling Psychologist,* 1984, *12* (4), 127–128.

Harren, V. A. "A Study of the Vocational Decision-Making Process Among College Males." Unpublished doctoral dissertation, Department of Educational Psychology, University of Texas, 1964.

Harren, V. A. "The Vocational Decision-Making Process Among College Males." *Journal of Counseling Psychology,* 1966, *13,* 271–277.

Harren, V. A. "A Career Decision-Making Model." Paper presented at the convention of the American Personnel and Guidance Association, Las Vegas, 1979a.

Harren, V. A. "A Model of Career Decision Making for College Students." *Journal of Vocational Behavior,* 1979b, *14,* 119–133.

Harren, V. A. "Research with the Assessment of Career Decision Making." *Character Potential: A Record of Research,* 1979c, *9,* 63–69.

Harren, V. A. *Assessment of Career Decision Making (ACDM): Preliminary Manual.* Carbondale: Department of Psychology, Southern Illinois University, 1980a.

Harren, V. A. *Career Decision Making: A Comprehensive Model for Assessment and Counseling.* Carbondale: Department of Psychology, Southern Illinois University, 1980b.

Harren, V. A., and Cass, R. A. *The Measurement and Correlates of Career Decision Making.* Carbondale: Department of Psychology, Southern Illinois University, 1977. (Mimeographed.)

Harris, J. A. "The Computerization of Vocational Information." *Vocational Guidance Quarterly,* 1968, *17,* 12–20.

Harris-Bowlsbey, J., and Rayman, J. R. *DISCOVER: The Career Guidance System: System Description and Counselor Guide.* Baltimore, Md.: IBM Corporation, 1978.

Hartmann, H. *Essays on Ego Psychology.* New York: International Universities Press, 1964.

Hauser, R. M. "On 'Stratification in a Dual Economy' (Comment on Beck, et al., *ASR,* October, 1978)." *American Sociological Review,* 1980, *45,* 702–712.

Hauser, R. M., Sewell, W. H., and Alwin, D. F. "High School Effects on Achievement." In W. H. Sewell, R. M. Hauser, and D. Featherman (eds.), *Schooling and Achievement in American Society.* Orlando, Fla.: Academic Press, 1976.

Hauser, R. M., Tsai, S., and Sewell, H. "A Model of Stratification with Response Error in Social and Psychological Variables." *Sociology of Education,* 1983, *56* (1), 20–46.

Hauser, S. T. *Black and White Identity Formation: Studies in the Psychosocial Development of Lower-Socioeconomic-Class Adolescent Boys.* New York: Wiley-Interscience, 1971.

Havighurst, R. J. *Human Development and Education.* New York: Longman, 1953.

Havighurst, R. J. "Youth in Exploration and Man Emergent." In H. Borow (ed.), *Man in a World at Work.* Boston: Houghton Mifflin, 1964.

Hawley, P. "Perceptions of Male Models of Femininity Related to Career Choice." *Journal of Counseling Psychology,* 1972, *19* (4), 308–313.

Hayes, R. "Men's Decisions to Enter or Avoid Nontraditional Occupations." *Career Development Quarterly,* 1986, *35,* 89–101.

Healy, C. C. "Relation of Occupational Choice to the Similarity Between Self-Ratings and Occupational Ratings." *Journal of Counseling Psychology,* 1968, *15,* 317–323.

Heckman, J., and Sedlacek, G. "Heterogeneity, Aggregation, and Market Wage Functions: An Empirical Model of Self-Selection in the Labor Market." *Journal of Political Economy,* 1985, *93* (6), 1077–1125.

Heilbrun, A. B., Jr. "Parental Identification and the Patterns of Vocational Interests in College Males and Females." *Journal of Counseling Psychology,* 1969, *16,* 342–347.

Heitzmann, D., Schmidt, A. D., and Hurley, F. W. "Career Encounters: Career Decision Making Through On-Site Visits." *Journal of Counseling and Development,* 1986, *65,* 209–210.

Helbing, H. *The Self-Concept in Career Development.* Amsterdam: The Psychological Laboratory, University of Amsterdam, 1987.

Helms, J. E. "Toward a Theoretical Explanation of the Effects of Race on Counseling: A Black-and-White Model." *Counseling Psychologist,* 1984, *12* (4), 153–165.

Helms, S. T. "Practical Applications of the Holland Occupational Classification in Counseling." *Communique,* 1973, *2,* 69–71.

Helson, R. "Women Mathematicians and the Creative Personality." *Journal of Consulting and Clinical Psychology,* 1970, *36,* 210–220.

Henderson, S., Hesketh, B., and Tuffin, K. "A Test of Gottfredson's Theory of Circumscription." *Journal of Vocational Behavior,* 1988, *32,* 37–48.

Henry, W. E., Sims, J. H., and Spray, S. L. *The Fifth Profes-*

sion: Becoming a Psychotherapist. San Francisco: Jossey-Bass, 1971.

Herr, E. L. "Comprehensive Career Guidance. A Look to the Future." *Vocational Guidance Quarterly,* 1982, *30,* 367–376.

Herr, E. L., and Cramer, S. H. *Career Guidance Through the Life Span.* Boston: Little, Brown, 1979.

Herr, E. L., and Cramer, S. H. *Career Guidance and Counseling Through the Life Span.* Glenview, Ill.: Scott, Foresman, 1988.

Hesketh, B., Pryor, R., and Gleitzman, M. "Fuzzy Logic: Toward Measuring Gottfredson's Concept of Occupational Space." *Journal of Counseling Psychology,* 1989, *36,* 103–109.

Hill, R. E. "Interpersonal Needs and Functional Area of Management." *Journal of Vocational Behavior,* 1974, *4,* 15–24.

Hill, R. E. *Interpersonal Needs and Vocational Specialization Among Female Business Students.* Ann Arbor: Graduate School of Business, University of Michigan, 1980.

Hilton, T. L. "Career Decision Making." *Journal of Counseling Psychology,* 1962, *9,* 291–298.

Hind, R. R., and Wirth, T. E. "The Effect of University Experience on Occupational Choice Among Undergraduates." *Sociology of Education,* 1969, *42* (1), 50–70.

Hodgkinson, G. P. "A Note Concerning the Comparability of the Standard and Automated Versions of the Vocational Preference Inventory." *Journal of Occupational Psychology,* 1986, *3,* 337–339.

Hodson, R. "Labor in the Monopoly, Competitive, and State Sectors of Production." *Politics & Society,* 1978, *3–4,* 429–480.

Hodson, R. "Companies, Industries, and the Measurement of Economic Segmentation." *American Sociological Review,* 1984, *49,* 335–348.

Hodson, R., and Kaufman, R. L. "Economic Dualism: A Critical Review." *American Sociological Review,* 1982, *47,* 727–739.

Hoffman, M. L. "Developmental Synthesis of Affect and Cognition and Its Implications for Altruistic Motivation." *Developmental Psychology,* 1975, *11,* 607–622.

Hogan, R., DeSoto, C. B., and Solano, C. "Traits, Tests, and Personality Research." *American Psychologist,* 1977, *32,* 255–264.

Hogan, R., and Nicholson, R. A. "The Meaning of Personality Tests." *American Psychologist,* 1988, *43,* 621–626.

Holcomb, W. R., and Anderson, W. P. "Vocational Guidance Research: A Five-Year Overview." *Journal of Vocational Behavior,* 1977, *10,* 341–346.

Holland, J. L. "A Theory of Vocational Choice." *Journal of Counseling Psychology,* 1959, *6, 35*–45.

Holland, J. L. "Some Explorations of a Theory of Vocational Choice: I. One- and Two-Year Longitudinal Studies." *Psychological Monographs,* 1962, *76* (26), entire issue.

Holland, J. L. "Explorations of a Theory of Vocational Choice and Achievement: II. A Four-Year Prediction Study." *Psychological Reports,* 1963a, *12,* 537–594.

Holland, J. L. "Explorations of a Theory of Vocational Choice: I. Vocational Images and Choice." *Vocational Guidance Quarterly,* 1963b, *11,* 232–240.

Holland, J. L. "Explorations of a Theory of Vocational Choice: II. Self-Descriptions and Vocational Preferences." *Vocational Guidance Quarterly,* 1963c, *12,* 17–21.

Holland, J. L. "Explorations of a Theory of Vocational Choice: III. Coping Behavior, Competencies, and Vocational Preferences." *Vocational Guidance Quarterly,* 1963d, *12,* 21–24.

Holland, J. L. "Explorations of a Theory of Vocational Choice: IV. Vocational Daydreams." *Vocational Guidance Quarterly,* 1963–64, *12,* 93–97.

Holland, J. L. "Explorations of a Theory of Vocational Choice: V. A One Year Prediction Study." Moravia, N.Y.: Chronicle Guidance Professional Services, 1964.

Holland, J. L. *The Psychology of Vocational Choice.* Waltham, Mass.: Blaisdell, 1966.

Holland, J. L. "Explorations of a Theory of Vocational Choice: VI. A Longitudinal Study Using a Sample of Typical College Students." *Journal of Applied Psychology,* 1968, *52* (1), entire issue.

Holland, J. L. "A Critical Analysis." *Counseling Psychologist,* 1969, *1,* 15–16.

Holland, J. L. *Professional Manual for the Self-Directed Search: A Guide to Educational and Vocational Planning.* Palo Alto, Calif.: Consulting Psychologists Press, 1972.

Holland, J. L. *Making Vocational Choices: A Theory of Careers.* Englewood Cliffs, N.J.: Prentice-Hall, 1973a.

Holland, J. L. *Sexism, Personal Development, and the Self-Directed Search.* Unpublished manuscript, Center for Social Organization of Schools, Johns Hopkins University, 1973b.

Holland, J. L. *Some Practical Remedies for Providing Vocational Guidance for Everyone.* Baltimore, Md.: Center for Social Organization of Schools, Johns Hopkins University, 1973c.

Holland, J. L. "Some Guidelines for Reducing Systematic Biases in the Delivery of Vocational Services." *Measurement and Evaluation in Guidance,* 1974a, *6* (4), 210–218.

Holland, J. L. "Vocational Guidance for Everyone." *Educational Research,* 1974b, *3,* 9–15.

Holland, J. L. "The Use and Evaluation of Interest Inventories and Simulations." In E. E. Diamond (ed.), *Issues of Sex Bias and Sex Fairness in Career Interest Measurement.* Washington, D.C.: National Institute of Education, 1975.

Holland, J. L. *The Self-Directed Search.* Palo Alto, Calif.: Consulting Psychologists Press, 1977.

Holland, J. L. "A New Synthesis for an Old Method and a New Analysis of Some Old Phenomena." In J. M. Whiteley and A. Resnikoff (eds.), *Career Counseling.* Pacific Grove, Calif.: Brooks/Cole, 1978a.

Holland, J. L. "Career Counseling: Then, Now, and What's Next?" In J. M. Whiteley and A. Resnikoff (eds.), *Career Counseling.* Pacific Grove, Calif.: Brooks/Cole, 1978b.

Holland, J. L. *The Self-Directed Search Professional Manual.* Palo Alto, Calif.: Consulting Psychologists Press, 1979.

Holland, J. L. "Some Implications of Career Theory for Adult Development and Aging." Paper presented at American Psychological Association convention, Washington, D.C., 1982a.

Holland, J. L. "The SDS Helps Both Females and Males: A Comment." *Vocational Guidance Quarterly,* 1982b, *30* (3), 195–197.

Holland, J. L. "A Theory of Careers: Some New Developments and Revisions." Paper presented at the American Psychological Association convention, Toronto, Ont., 1984.

Holland, J. L. *Making Vocational Choices: A Theory of Vocational Personalities and Work Environments.* (2nd ed.) Englewood Cliffs, N.J.: Prentice-Hall, 1985a.

Holland, J. L. *Manual for the Vocational Preference Inventory.* Odessa, Fla.: Psychological Assessment Resources, Inc., 1985b.

Holland, J. L. *Professional Manual Self-Directed Search.* Odessa, Fla.: Psychological Assessment Resources, Inc., 1985c.

Holland, J. L. *The Occupations Finder.* Odessa, Fla.: Psychological Assessment Resources, Inc., 1985d.

Holland, J. L. *You and Your Career.* Odessa, Fla.: Psychological Assessment Resources, Inc., 1985e.

Holland, J. L. "Alphabetized Occupations Finder." In J. L. Holland, *1987 Manual Supplement for the Self-Directed Search.* Odessa, Fla.: Psychological Assessment Resources, Inc., 1987a.

Holland, J. L. "Current Status of Holland's Theory of Careers: Another Perspective." *Career Development Quarterly,* 1987b, *36,* 31–44.

Holland, J. L., Daiger, D. C., and Power, P. G. *My Vocational Situation.* Palo Alto, Calif.: Consulting Psychologists Press, 1980.

Holland, J. L., and Gottfredson, G. D. "Using a Typology of Persons and Environments to Explain Careers: Some Extensions and Clarifications." *Counseling Psychologist,* 1976, *6* (3), 20–29.

Holland, J. L., Gottfredson, G. D., and Nafziger, D. H. "Testing the Validity of Some Theoretical Signs of Vocational Decision-Making Ability." *Journal of Counseling Psychology,* 1975, *22,* 411–422.

Holland, J. L., Gottfredson, G. D., and Power, P. G. "Some Diagnostic Scales for Research in Decision Making and Personality: Identity, Information, and Barriers." *Journal of Personality and Social Psychology,* 1980, *39,* 1191–1200.

Holland, J. L., Magoon, T. M., and Spokane, A. R. "Counseling Psychology: Career Interventions, Research, and Theory." *Annual Review of Psychology,* 1981, *32,* 279–305.

Holland, J. L., and Nichols, R. C. "Explorations of a Theory of Vocational Choice: III. A Longitudinal Study of Change in Major Field of Study." *Personnel and Guidance Journal,* 1964, *43,* 235–242.

Holland, J. L., and Whitney, D. R. "Changes in the Vocational Plans of College Students: Orderly or Random?" ACT Research Report no. 25. Iowa City, Iowa: American College Testing Program, 1968.

Holland, J. L., and others. *Counselor's Guide to the Vocational Exploration and Insight Kit (VEIK)*. Palo Alto, Calif.: Consulting Psychologists Press, 1980a.

Holland, J. L., and others. *The Vocational Exploration and Insight Kit (VEIK)*. Palo Alto, Calif.: Consulting Psychologists Press, 1980b.

Hollingshead, A. B. *Elmtown's Youth*. New York: Wiley, 1949.

Hollon, S. D., and Kendall, D. C. "Assessment Techniques for Cognitive-Behavioral Processes." In D. C. Kendall and S. D. Hollon (eds.), *Assessment Strategies for Cognitive Behavioral Interventions*. Orlando, Fla.: Academic Press, 1981.

Holt, P. A. "Differential Effects of Status and Interest in the Process of Compromise." *Journal of Counseling Psychology*, 1989, *36*, 42–47.

Horan, P. "Is Status-Attainment Research Atheoretical?" *American Sociological Review*, 1978, *43*, 534–540.

Horner, J. T., Buterbaugh, J. G., and Carefoot, J. J. *Factors Relating to Occupational and Educational Decision Making of Rural Youth*. Lincoln: College of Agriculture, University of Nebraska, 1967.

Horrocks, J. E., and Jackson, D. W. *Self and Role*. Boston: Houghton Mifflin, 1972.

Hoshmand, L. "Alternate Research Paradigms." *Counseling Psychologist*, 1989, *17*, 3–80.

Hotchkiss, L., and Borow, H. "Sociological Perspectives on Career Development and Attainment." In D. Brown, L. Brooks, and Associates, *Career Choice and Development: Applying Contemporary Theories to Practice*. San Francisco: Jossey-Bass, 1984.

Hotchkiss, L., and Dorsten, L. E. "Curriculum Effects on Early Post–High School Outcomes." *Research in the Sociology of Education and Socialization*, 1987, *7*, 191–219.

Hottel, A. K. *How Fare Women? A Report of the Commission on the Education of Women of the American Council of Education*. Washington, D.C.: American Council on Education, 1955.

Howard, A. "Cool at the Top: Personality Characteristics of

Successful Executives." Presentation at the annual convention of the American Psychological Association, Toronto, Ont., 1984.

Hoyt, K. B. *Career Education*. Salt Lake City, Utah: Olympus, 1975.

Hoyt, K. B. "The Impact of Technology on Occupational Change: Implications for Career Guidance." *Career Development Quarterly*, 1987, *35*, 269–278.

Hoyt, M. F., and Janis, I. L. "Increasing Adherence to a Stressful Decision via a Motivational Balance Sheet Procedure: A Field Experiment." *Journal of Personality and Social Psychology*, 1975, *31*, 833–839.

Hsu, C. C. "A Conceptual Model of Vocational Decision-Making." *Experimental Publication System*, 1970, *8*, 270–276.

Hughes, E. C. "Institutional Office and the Person." *American Journal of Sociology*, 1937, *43*, 21–25.

Hughes, E. C. *Men and Their Work*. New York: Free Press, 1958.

Hughes, H. M. "Vocational Choice, Level, and Consistency: An Investigation of Holland's Theory on an Employed Sample." *Journal of Vocational Behavior*, 1972, *2*, 377–388.

Huizinga, J. *Homo Ludens: A Study of the Play Elements in Culture*. Boston: Beacon Press, 1955.

Humes, C. W. II. "Career Guidance for the Handicapped: A Comprehensive Approach." *Vocational Guidance Quarterly*, 1982, *30*, 353–358.

Hunter, J. E., and Schmidt, F. H. "Quantifying the Effects of Psychological Interventions on Employee Job Performance and Work-Force Productivity." *American Psychologist*, 1983, *38*, 473–478.

Iachan, R. "A Measure of Agreement for Use with the Holland Classification System." *Journal of Vocational Behavior*, 1984, *24*, 133–141.

Inaba, L. A. "A Longitudinal Study of Hawaii's F-Test Data and the Development of the Fukuyama Profile." In *Final Report of the Third International Conference on Vocational Guidance*. Hyogo, Japan: Ashiya University, 1982.

Inaba, L. A. "The New Computer Version of the Fukuyama Profile." In *Final Report of the Fifth International Conference on Vocational Guidance*. Hyogo, Japan: Ashiya University, 1987.

Jacobs, J. A., and Breiger, R. L. "Careers, Industries, and Occupations: Industrial Segmentation Reconsidered." In G. Farkas and P. England (eds.), *Industries, Firms, and Jobs: Sociological and Economic Approaches.* New York: Plenum, 1988.

Janis, I. "Stages in the Decision-Making Process." In R. P. Abelson (ed.), *Theories of Cognitive Consistency.* Skokie, Ill.: Rand-McNally, 1968.

Janis, I. L., and Mann, L. *Decision Making: A Psychological Analysis of Conflict, Choice, and Commitment.* New York: Free Press, 1977.

Jencks, C., Crouse, J., and Muescr, P. "The Wisconsin Model of Status Attainment: A National Replication with Improved Measures of Ability and Aspiration." *Sociology of Education,* 1983, *56* (1), 3–19.

Jencks, C., and others. *Inequality: A Reassessment of the Effect of Family and Schooling in America.* New York: Basic Books, 1972.

Jepsen, D. A. "The Stage Construct in Career Development." *Counseling and Values,* 1974a, *18,* 124–131.

Jepsen, D. A. "Vocational Decision-Making Strategy Types." *Vocational Guidance Quarterly,* 1974b, *23,* 17–23.

Jepsen, D. A. "Comment on Symposium." *Character Potential: A Record of Research,* 1979, *9,* 93–94.

Jepsen, D. A. "Data-Seeking Activity and Cognitive Career Decision Making." Unpublished manuscript, University of Iowa, 1980.

Jepsen, D. A. "Career Decision Making." In L. W. Hamm (ed.), *The Individual's Use of Information in Career Development.* Columbus: National Center for Research in Vocational Education, Ohio State University, 1984.

Jepsen, D. A., and Dilley, J. S. "Vocational Decision-Making Models: A Review and Comparative Analysis." *Review of Educational Research,* 1974, *44,* 331–349.

Jepsen, D. A., and Grove, W. M. "Stage Order and Dominance in Adolescent Decision-Making Processes: An Empirical Test of the Tiedeman–O'Hara Paradigm." *Journal of Vocational Behavior,* 1981, *18,* 237–251.

Jepsen, D. A., and Prediger, D. J. "Dimensions of Adolescent Career Development: A Multiinstrument Analysis." Unpublished manuscript, University of Iowa, 1979.

Johnson, J. A., and Hogan, R. "Vocational Interests and Effective Police Performance." *Personnel Psychology,* 1981, *34,* 49–52.

Johnson, P. L., and Dierks, P. A. "What Are Women Accountants Really Like?" *Management Accounting,* 1982, *33,* 436–439.

Jones, G. B., and Krumboltz, J. D. "Stimulating Occupational Exploration Through Film-Mediated Problems." *Journal of Counseling Psychology,* 1970, *17,* 107–114.

Jones, K. J. "Occupational Preference and Social Orientation." *Personnel and Guidance Journal,* 1965, *43,* 574–579.

Jordaan, J. P. "Exploratory Behavior: The Formation of Self- and Occupational Concepts." In D. E. Super and others (eds.), *Career Development: Self-Concept Theory.* New York: College Entrance Examination Board, 1963.

Jordaan, J. P., and Heyde, M. B. *Vocational Maturity During the High School Years.* New York: Teachers College Press, 1979.

Jorgenson, J. "Research Methodology and Theoretical Perspective in Dual Work-Career Construction." Unpublished doctoral dissertation, Department of Leadership and Educational Policy Studies, Northern Illinois University, 1979.

Juni, S. "Career Choice and Quality." *Journal of Vocational Behavior,* 1981, *19,* 78–83.

Kahn, R. L. *Work and Health.* New York: Wiley, 1981.

Kaldor, D. R., and Zytowski, D. G. "A Maximizing Model of Career Decision Making." *Personnel and Guidance Journal,* 1969, *47,* 781–788.

Kalleberg, A. L., and Griffin, J. "Class, Occupation, and Inequality in Job Rewards." *American Journal of Sociology,* 1980, *85* (4), 731–768.

Kanchier, C. J., and Unruh, W. R. "Frequency and Direction of Managerial Occupational Change." *Career Development Quarterly,* 1987, *35,* 304–315.

Kapes, J. T., and Mastie, M. M. (eds.). *A Counselor's Guide to Vocational Guidance Instruments.* Falls Church, Va.: National Vocational Guidance Association, 1982.

Kapes, J. T., and Mastie, M. M. (eds.). *A Counselor's Guide to Career Assessment Instruments.* (2nd ed.) Falls Church, Va.: National Career Development Association, 1988.

Kaplan, D. M., and Brown, D. "The Role of Anxiety in Career

Indecisiveness." *Career Development Quarterly*, 1987, *36*, 148–162.

Katz, M. R. *You: Today and Tomorrow.* (3rd ed.) Princeton, N.J.: Educational Testing Service, 1959.

Katz, M. R. *Decisions and Values.* New York: College Entrance Examination Board, 1963.

Katz, M. R. "A Model of Guidance for Career Decision Making." *Vocational Guidance Quarterly*, 1966, *15*, 2–10.

Katz, M. R. "Career Decision Making: A Computer-Based System of Interactive Guidance and Information (SIGI)." In Educational Testing Service (ed.), *Proceedings of the 1973 Invitational Conference on Testing Problems.* Princeton, N.J.: Educational Testing Service, 1974.

Katz, M. R. *SIGI: A Computer Based System for Interactive Guidance and Information.* Princeton, N.J.: Educational Testing Service, 1975.

Katz, M. R. "Job Longevity as a Situational Factor in Job Satisfaction." *Administrative Science Quarterly*, 1978, *23*, 204–223.

Katz, M. R. "Assessment of Career Decision Making: Process and Outcome." In A. M. Mitchell, G. B. Jones, and J. D. Krumboltz (eds.), *Social Learning and Career Decision Making.* Cranston, R.I.: Carroll Press, 1979.

Katz, M. R., Norris, L., and Pears, L. "Simulated Occupational Choice: A Diagnostic Measure of Competencies in Career Decision Making." *Measurement and Evaluation in Guidance*, 1978, *10*, 222–232.

Katz, R. "Job Enrichment: Some Career Considerations." In J. Van Maanen (ed.), *Organizational Careers: Some New Perspectives.* New York: Wiley, 1977.

Katzell, R. A., and Guzzo, R. A. "Psychological Approaches to Productivity Improvement." *American Psychologist*, 1983, *38*, 468–472.

Kaufman, H. *The Forest Ranger.* Baltimore, Md.: Johns Hopkins Press, 1960.

Kaufman, R. L., Hodson, R., and Fligstein, N. P. "Defrocking Dualism: A New Approach to Defining Industrial Sectors." *Social Science Research*, 1981, *10*, 1–31.

Kegan, R. G. "The Evolving Self: A Process Conception for Ego Psychology." *Counseling Psychologist*, 1979, *8*, 5–34.

Keller, J., and Piotrowski, C. "Career Development Programs in Fortune 500 Companies." *Psychological Reports,* 1987, *61,* 920–922.

Keller, K. E., Biggs, D. A., and Gysbers, N. C. "Career Counseling from a Cognitive Perspective." *Personnel and Guidance Journal,* 1982, *60,* 367–370.

Kelly, G. A. *The Psychology of Personal Constructs.* New York: Norton, 1955.

Kelly, G. F. "Guided Fantasy as a Counseling Technique with Youth." *Journal of Counseling Psychology,* 1972, *19,* 355–361.

Kelso, D. F. "A Study of Occupational Stereotypes Reflected in the Strong Interest Test." Unpublished thesis, Department of Psychology, State College of Washington, 1948.

Kerckhoff, A. C. "The Status-Attainment Process: Socialization or Allocation?" *Social Forces,* 1976, *55,* 368–381.

Kerr, B. A., and Ghrist-Priebe, S. L. "Intervention for Multipotentiality: Effects of a Career Counseling Laboratory for Gifted High School Students." *Journal of Counseling and Development,* 1988, *66,* 366–369.

Kidd, J. M. "Self- and Occupational Concepts in Occupational Preferences and Entry into Work." Unpublished doctoral dissertation, National Institute for Careers Education and Counseling, Cambridge, England, and the Hatfield Polytechnic, Hertfordshire, England, 1982.

Kidd, J. M. "The Relationship of Self- and Occupational Concepts to the Occupational Preferences of Adolescents." *Journal of Vocational Behavior,* 1984, *24,* 48–65.

Kipnis, D., Lane, G., and Berger, L. "Character Structure, Vocational Interest, and Achievement." *Journal of Counseling Psychology,* 1969, *16,* 335–341.

Klein, K. L., and Wiener, Y. "Interest Congruency as a Moderator of the Relationship Between Job Tenure and Job Satisfaction and Mental Health." *Journal of Vocational Behavior,* 1977, *10,* 91–98.

Kleinberg, J. L. "Adolescent Correlates of Occupational Stability and Change." *Journal of Vocational Behavior,* 1976, *9,* 219–232.

Knapp, R. R. "Classification of Occupational Interests into Groups and Levels." Paper presented to the Society of Multivariate Experimental Psychology, Berkeley, 1967.

Knapp, R. R., and Knapp, L. "Interest Changes and the Classification of Occupations." Unpublished manuscript, 1977.

Knapp, R. R., and Knapp, L. *COPS Interest Inventory Technical Manual.* San Diego, Calif.: EdITS, 1984.

Knapp, R. R., and Knapp, L. *California Occupational Preference System: Self-Interpretation Profile and Guide.* San Diego, Calif.: EdITS, 1985.

Knapp, R. R., Knapp, L., and Knapp-Lee, L. "Occupational Interest Measurement and Subsequent Career Decisions: A Predictive Follow-Up Study of the COPSystem Interest Inventory." *Journal of Counseling Psychology,* 1985, *32,* 348–354.

Kobasa, S. "The Hardy Personality: Toward a Social Psychology of Stress and Health." In G. S. Sanders and J. Suls (eds.), *Social Psychology of Health and Illness.* Hillsdale, N.J.: Erlbaum, 1982.

Kochan, T. A., MacDuffie, J. P., and Osterman, P. "Employment Security at DEC: Sustaining Values amid Environmental Change." *Human Resource Management,* 1988, *27,* 121–143.

Kohn, M. L. "Personality, Occupation, and Social Stratification: A Frame of Reference." In D. J. Treiman and R. V. Robinson (eds.), *Research in Social Stratification: A Research Annual.* Vol. 1. Greenwich, Conn.: JAI Press, 1981.

Kohn, M. L., and Schooler, C. "The Reciprocal Effects of the Substantive Complexity of Work and Intellectual Flexibility: A Longitudinal Assessment." *American Journal of Sociology,* 1978, *84,* 24–52.

Kohn, M. L., and Schooler, C. "Reciprocal Effects of Job Conditions and Personality." *American Journal of Sociology,* 1982, *87,* 1257–1286.

Korchin, S. J. "Clinical Psychology and Minority Problems." *American Psychologist,* 1980, *35,* 262–269.

Korman, A. K. "Self-Esteem as a Moderator of the Relationship Between Self-Perceived Abilities and Vocational Choice." *Journal of Applied Psychology,* 1967, *51,* 65–67.

Korn, H. A. "Differences Between Majors in Engineering and Physical Sciences in CPI and SVIB Scores." *Journal of Counseling Psychology,* 1962, *9,* 306–312.

Krebs, D. L. "Altruism: An Examination of a Concept and a Review of the Literature." *Psychological Bulletin,* 1970, *73,* 258–302.

Krieshok, T. S. "Review of the Self-Directed Search." *Journal of Counseling and Development,* 1987, *65,* 512–514.

Krumboltz, J. D. (ed.). *Job Experience Kits.* Chicago: Science Research Associates, 1970.

Krumboltz, J. D. "A Social Learning Theory of Career Decision Making." In A. M. Mitchell, G. B. Jones, and J. D. Krumboltz (eds.), *Social Learning and Career Decision Making.* Cranston, R.I.: Carroll Press, 1979.

Krumboltz, J. D. *Private Rules in Career Decision Making.* Columbus: National Center for Research in Vocational Education, Ohio State University, 1983.

Krumboltz, J. D. *Career Beliefs Inventory.* Palo Alto, Calif.: Consulting Psychologists Press, 1988a.

Krumboltz, J. D. "The Key to Achievement: Learning to Love Learning." In G. Walz (ed.), *Building Strong School Guidance Programs.* Alexandria, Va.: American Association for Counseling and Development, 1988b.

Krumboltz, J. D., and Baker, R. D. "Behavioral Counseling for Vocational Decisions." In H. Borow (ed.), *Career Guidance for a New Age.* Boston: Houghton Mifflin, 1973.

Krumboltz, J. D., Baker, D., and Johnson, R. G. *Vocational Problem-Solving Experiences for Stimulating Career Exploration and Interest: Phase II.* Washington, D.C.: U.S. Office of Education, 1968.

Krumboltz, J. D., and Hamel, D. A. (eds.). *Assessing Career Development.* Mountain View, Calif.: Mayfield, 1982.

Krumboltz, J. D., Mitchell, A. M., and Jones, G. B. "A Social Learning Theory of Career Selection." *Counseling Psychologist,* 1976, *6* (1), 71–81.

Krumboltz, J. D., and Rude, S. "Behavioral Approaches to Career Counseling." *Behavioral Counseling Quarterly,* 1981, *1,* 108–120.

Krumboltz, J. D., and Schroeder, W. W. "Promoting Career Exploration Through Reinforcement." *Personnel and Guidance Journal,* 1965, *44,* 19–26.

Krumboltz, J. D., and Thoresen, C. E. "The Effects of Behavioral Counseling in Group and Individual Settings on Information-Seeking Behavior." *Journal of Counseling Psychology,* 1964, *11,* 324–333.

Krumboltz, J. D., Varenhorst, B. B., and Thoresen, C. E. "Nonverbal Factors in the Effectiveness of Models in Counseling." *Journal of Counseling Psychology,* 1967, *14* (5), 412–418.

Krumboltz, J. D., and others. *Vocational Problem-Solving Experiences for Stimulating Career Exploration and Interest.* Washington, D.C.: U.S. Office of Education, 1967.

Kuder, F. *Manual to the Kuder Preference Record.* Chicago: Science Research Associates, 1946.

Kuder, F. *Kuder Occupational Interest Survey, Form DD (KOIS).* Chicago: Science Research Associates, 1985.

Kuhn, T. S. *The Structure of Scientific Revolutions.* (2nd ed.) Chicago: University of Chicago Press, 1970.

Kwak, J. C., and Pulvino, C. J. "A Mathematical Model for Comparing Holland's Personality and Environmental Codes." *Journal of Vocational Behavior,* 1982, *21* (2), 231–241.

Lang, K., and Dickens, W. T. "Neoclassical and Sociological Perspectives on Segmented Labor Markets." In G. Farkas and P. England (eds.), *Industries, Firms, and Jobs: Sociological and Economic Approaches.* New York: Plenum, 1988.

Laramore, D. "Jobs on Film." *Vocational Guidance Quarterly,* 1968, *17,* 87–90.

Laramore, D. "Counselors Make Occupational Information Packages." *Vocational Guidance Quarterly,* 1971, *19,* 220–224.

Latack, J. C. "Career Transitions Within Organizations: An Exploratory Study of Work, Nonwork, and Coping Strategies." *Organizational Behavior and Human Performance,* 1984, *34,* 296–322.

Latack, J. C., and D'Amico, R. "Career Mobility Among Young Men." In S. Hills and others (eds.), *The Changing Market.* Columbus: Center for Human Resources Research, Ohio State University, 1985.

Lawler, E. E. "Strategies for Improving the Quality of Work Life." *American Psychologist,* 1982, *37* (5), 486–493.

Layton, P. L. *Self-Efficacy, Locus of Control, Career Salience, and Women's Career Choice.* Unpublished doctoral dissertation, University of Minnesota, 1984.

Lee, V. E., and Bryk, A. S. "Curriculum Tracking as Mediating the Social Distribution of High School Achievement." *Sociology of Education,* 1988, *61,* 78–94.

Leiberman, J. N. *Playfulness*. Orlando, Fla.: Academic Press, 1977.

Leibowitz, Z. B., Farren, C., and Kaye, B. L. *Designing Career Development Systems*. San Francisco: Jossey-Bass, 1986.

Lent, R. W., Brown, S. D., and Larkin, K. C. "Relation of Self-Efficacy Expectations to Academic Achievement and Persistence." *Journal of Counseling Psychology*, 1984, *31*, 356–363.

Lent, R. W., Brown, S. D., and Larkin, K. C. "Self-Efficacy in the Prediction of Academic Performance and Perceived Career Options." *Journal of Counseling Psychology*, 1986, *33*, 265–299.

Lent, R. W., Brown, S. D., and Larkin, K. C. "Comparison of Three Theoretically Derived Variables in Predicting Career and Academic Behavior: Self-Efficacy, Interest Congruence, and Consequential Thinking." *Journal of Counseling Psychology*, 1987, *34*, 293–297.

Lent, R. W., and Hackett, G. "Career Self-Efficacy: Empirical Status and Future Directions." *Journal of Vocational Behavior*, 1987, *30*, 347–382.

Lent, R. W., Larkin, K. C., and Hasegawa, C. S. "Effects of a 'Focused Interest' Career Course Approach for College Students." *Vocational Guidance Quarterly*, 1986, *34*, 151–159.

Levin, J. S. "A Study of Recycling in the Career Decision-Making Process During an Undergraduate Internship." Unpublished doctoral dissertation, Department of Education, Washington University, 1981.

Levinson, D. J., and others. *The Seasons of a Man's Life*. New York: Knopf, 1978.

Levinson, E. M. "Incorporating a Vocational Component into a School Psychological Evaluation: A Case Example." *Psychology in the Schools*, 1987, *24*, 254–264.

Lewin, K. *Field Theory in Social Science*. New York: Harper & Row, 1951.

Linton, R. *The Cultural Background of Personality*. East Norwalk, Conn.: Appleton-Century-Crofts, 1945.

Lister, J. L., and McKenzie, D. H. "A Framework for the Improvement of Test Interpretation in Counseling." *Personnel and Guidance Journal*, 1966, *45*, 61–66.

Little, D. M., and Roach, A. J. "Videotape Modeling of Interest in Nontraditional Occupations for Women." *Journal of Vocational Behavior*, 1974, *5*, 133–138.

LoCascio, R. "Continuity and Discontinuity in Vocational Development Theory." *Personnel and Guidance Journal*, 1967, *46*, 32–46.

LoCascio, R. "The Vocational Maturity of Diverse Groups." In D. E. Super (ed.), *Measuring Vocational Maturity for Counseling and Evaluation*. Washington, D.C.: American Personnel and Guidance Association, 1974.

Loevinger, J., Wessler, R., and Redmore, C. *Measuring Ego Development*. 2 vols. San Francisco: Jossey-Bass, 1970.

Lofquist, L. H., and Dawis, R. V. *Adjustment to Work*. East Norwalk, Conn.: Appleton-Century-Crofts, 1969.

Lofquist, L. H., and Dawis, R. V. "Application of the Theory of Work Adjustment to Rehabilitation and Counseling." *Minnesota Studies in Vocational Rehabilitation*, no. 48. Minneapolis: University of Minnesota Industrial Relations Center, 1972.

Lofquist, L. H., and Dawis, R. V. "Values as Secondary to Needs in the Theory of Work Adjustment." *Journal of Vocational Behavior*, 1978, *12*, 12–19.

Lokan, J. J., and Taylor, K. F. (eds.). *Holland in Australia: A Vocational Choice Theory in Research and Practice*. Hawthorn, Victoria, Australia: Australian Council for Educational Research, 1986.

London, M., and Stumpf, S. *Managing Careers*. Reading, Mass.: Addison-Wesley, 1982.

London, P. "The Rescuers: Motivational Hypotheses About Christians Who Saved Jews from the Nazis." In J. Macaulay and L. Berkowitz (eds.), *Altruism and Helping Behavior*. Orlando, Fla.: Academic Press, 1970.

Longstaff, H. P. "Fakability of the Strong Interest Blank and Kuder Preference Record." *Journal of Applied Psychology*, 1948, *32*, 360–369.

Lopez, F. M., Kesselman, G. A., and Lopez, F. E. "An Empirical Test of a Trait-Oriented Job Analysis Technique." *Personnel Psychology*, 1981, *34*, 479–501.

Loughary, J. W., and Ripley, T. M. *"This Isn't Quite What I Had in Mind": A Career Planning Program for College Students*. Chicago: Follett, 1978.

Louis, M. R. "Surprise and Sense Making: What Newcomers Experience in Entering Unfamiliar Organizational Settings." *Administrative Science Quarterly,* 1980, *25,* 226–251.

Lowenthal, M. F., and others. *Four Stages of Life: A Comparative Study of Women and Men Facing Transitions.* San Francisco: Jossey-Bass, 1975.

Lunneborg, C. E., and Lunneborg, P. W. "Is There Room for a Third Dimension in Vocational Interest Differentiation?" *Journal of Vocational Behavior,* 1977, *11,* 120–127.

Lunneborg, P. W. *The Vocational Interest Inventory (VII) Manual.* Los Angeles: Western Psychological Services, 1981.

Lunneborg, P. W., and Lunneborg, C. E. "Roe's Classification of Occupations in Predicting Academic Achievement." *Journal of Counseling Psychology,* 1968, *15,* 8–16.

Lunneborg, P. W., and Wilson, V. M. *To Work: A Guide for Women College Graduates.* Englewood Cliffs, N.J.: Prentice-Hall, 1982.

Lynch, K. R. "Vocational Planning with the Reluctant Veteran." *Vocational Guidance Quarterly,* 1979, *27,* 259–263.

Lyons, N. P. "Two Perspectives: On Self, Relationships, and Morality." *Harvard Educational Review,* 1983, *53,* 125–145.

Macaulay, J., and Berkowitz, L. (eds.). *Altruism and Helping Behavior.* Orlando, Fla.: Academic Press, 1970.

McClelland, D. C., and others. *The Achievement Motive.* East Norwalk, Conn.: Appleton-Century-Crofts, 1953.

McGowan, A. S. "The Predictive Efficiency of Holland's SDS Summary Codes in Terms of Career Choice: A Four-Year Follow-Up." *Journal of Vocational Behavior,* 1982, *20,* 294–303.

McGregor, D. *The Human Side of Enterprise.* New York: McGraw-Hill, 1960.

McKinnon, P. "Steady-State People: A Third Career Orientation." *Research Management,* 1987, *30,* 26–32.

McLaughlin, D. H., and Tiedeman, D. V. "Eleven-Year Career Stability and Change as Reflected in Project Talent Data Through the Flanagan, Holland, and Roe Occupational Classification Systems." *Journal of Vocational Behavior,* 1974, *5,* 177–196.

McNair, D., and Brown, D. "Predicting the Occupational Aspirations, Occupational Expectations and Career Maturity of Black and White Male and Female Tenth Graders." *Vocational Guidance Quarterly*, 1983, *32*, 29–36.

Maddux, C. D., and Cummings, R. E. "Alternate Form Reliability of the Self-Directed Search — Form E." *Career Development Quarterly*, 1986, *35*, 136–140.

Magoon, T. "Innovations in Counseling." *Journal of Counseling Psychology*, 1964, *11*, 342–347.

Mahoney, M., and Arnhoff, D. "Cognitive and Self-Control Therapies." In S. Garfield and E. Bergin (eds.), *Handbook of Psychotherapy and Behavior Change*. (2nd ed.) New York: Wiley, 1978.

Mann, L. "Use of a Balance-Sheet Procedure to Improve the Quality of Personal Decision Making: A Field Experiment with College Applicants." *Journal of Vocational Behavior*, 1972, *2*, 291–300.

Mansfield, R. "Self-Esteem, Self-Perceived Abilities, and Vocational Choice." *Journal of Vocational Behavior*, 1973, *3*, 433–441.

Maola, J., and Kane, G. "Comparison of Computer-Based Versus Counselor-Based Occupational Information Systems with Disadvantaged Vocational Students." *Journal of Counseling Psychology*, 1976, *23*, 163–165.

March, J. G., and Simon, H. A. *Organizations*. New York: Wiley, 1958.

Marrow, A. *The Practical Theorist: The Life and Work of Kurt Lewin*. New York: Basic Books, 1969.

Maslow, A. H. *Motivation and Personality*. New York: Harper & Row, 1954.

Medvene, A. M. "Occupational Choice of Graduate Students in Psychology as a Function of Early Parent-Child Interactions." *Journal of Counseling Psychology*, 1969, *16*, 385–389.

Medvene, A. M., and Shueman, S. A. "Perceived Parental Attitudes and Choice of Vocational Specialty Area Among Male Engineering Students." *Journal of Vocational Behavior*, 1978, *12*, 208–216.

Meehl, P. E. *Clinical Versus Statistical Prediction*. Minneapolis: University of Minnesota Press, 1954.

Meichenbaum, D. *Cognitive Behavior Modification*. Morristown, N.J.: General Learning Press, 1977.

Meir, E. I. "Empirical Test of Roe's Structure of Occupations and an Alternative Structure." *Journal of Counseling Psychology*, 1970, *17*, 41–48.

Meir, E. I. "The Structure of Occupations by Interests — A Smallest-Space Analysis." *Journal of Vocational Behavior*, 1973, *3*, 21–31.

Meir, E. I. *Manual for the Ramak and Courses Interest Inventories.* Tel Aviv: Department of Psychology, Tel Aviv University, 1975.

Meir, E. I. "A Test of the Independence of Fields and Levels in Roe's Occupational Classification." *Vocational Guidance Quarterly*, 1978, *27*, 124–128.

Meir, E. I., Keinan, G., and Segal, Z. "Group Importance as Mediator Between Personality-Environment Congruence and Satisfaction." *Journal of Vocational Behavior*, 1986, *28*, 60–69.

Meir, E. I., and Shiran, D. "The Occupational Cylinder as a Means for Vocational Maturity Enhancement." *Journal of Vocational Behavior*, 1979, *14*, 279–283.

Mendonca, J. D. "Effectiveness of Problem-Solving and Anxiety-Management Training in Modifying Vocational Indecision." Unpublished doctoral dissertation, Department of Psychology, University of Western Ontario, 1974.

Mendonca, J. D., and Siess, T. F. "Counseling for Indecisiveness: Problem-Solving and Anxiety-Management Training." *Journal of Counseling Psychology*, 1976, *23*, 339–347.

Merwin, J. C., and DiVesta, F. J. "A Study of Need Theory and Career Choice." *Journal of Counseling Psychology*, 1959, *6*, 302–308.

Mihal, W., Sorce, P., and Comte, T. "A Process Model of Individual Career Decision Making." *Academy of Management Review*, 1984, *9*, 95–103.

Millar, S. *The Psychology of Play.* New York: Penguin, 1968.

Miller, A. L., and Tiedeman, D. V. "Decision Making for the '70s: The Cubing of the Tiedeman Paradigm and Its Application in Career Education." *Focus on Guidance*, 1972, *5* (1), 1–15.

Miller, C. H. "Vocational Guidance in the Perspective of Cultural Change." In H. Borow (ed.), *Man in a World at Work.* Boston: Houghton Mifflin, 1964.

Miller, D. C., and Form, W. H. *Industrial Sociology.* New York: Harper & Row, 1951.

Miller, G. *Odd Jobs: The World of Deviant Work.* Englewood Cliffs, N.J.: Prentice-Hall, 1978.

Miller, I. W., and Haller, A. O. "A Measure of Level of Occupational Aspiration." *Personnel and Guidance Journal,* 1964, *42,* 448–455.

Miller, J., and others. "Women and Work: The Psychological Effects of Occupational Conditions." *American Journal of Sociology,* 1979, *85,* 156–166.

Miller, J. V. "Lifelong Career Development for Disadvantaged Youth and Adults." *Vocational Guidance Quarterly,* 1982, *30,* 359–366.

Miller, M. F. "Interest Pattern Structure and Personality Characteristics of Clients Who Seek Career Information." *Vocational Guidance Quarterly,* 1982, *31,* 28–35.

Miller, M. J. "Usefulness of Gati's Hierarchical Model of Vocational Interests for Career Counselors." *Journal of Employment Counseling,* 1986, *23,* 57–65.

Miller, S., Jr. "Relationship of Personality and Occupation, Setting, and Function." *Journal of Counseling Psychology,* 1962, *9,* 115–121.

Miller-Tiedeman, A. L. "Deliberate Decision-Making Education: A Self-Centering Approach." *Character Potential: A Record of Research,* 1974, *7,* 12–21.

Miller-Tiedeman, A. L. *Individual Career Exploration Inventory (ICE).* Bensenville, Ill.: Scholastic Testing Service, 1975.

Miller-Tiedeman, A. L. *Individual Career Exploration: Manual of Directions.* Bensenville, Ill.: Scholastic Testing Service, 1976a.

Miller-Tiedeman, A. L. *Our Career: A Career Planning Unit Delivered by Students to Students.* Los Angeles: National Institute for the Advancement of Career Education, University of Southern California, 1976b.

Miller-Tiedeman, A. L. "Structuring Responsibility in Adolescents: Actualizing 'I' Power Through Curriculum." In G. D. Miller (ed.), *Developmental Theory and Its Application in Guidance Programs: Systematic Efforts to Promote Personal Growth.* Minneapolis: Minnesota Department of Education, 1977a.

Miller-Tiedeman, A. L. *Individual Career Exploration, Picture Form: Manual of Directions.* Bensenville, Ill.: Scholastic Testing Service, 1977b.

Miller-Tiedeman, A. L. "Creating the 'I' Power Potential of Decision Making During Secondary School Education." *Character Potential: A Record of Research,* 1979a, *9,* 83–92.

Miller-Tiedeman, A. L. *Decision-Making Organizer.* Bensenville, Ill.: Scholastic Testing Service, 1979b.

Miller-Tiedeman, A. L. "Student Decision Making and Its Evaluation." *Journal of Career Education,* 1979c, *5,* 250–261.

Miller-Tiedeman, A. L. "Explorations of Decision Making in the Expansion of Adolescent Personal Development." In V. L. Erickson and J. M. Whiteley (eds.), *Developmental Counseling and Teaching.* Pacific Grove, Calif.: Brooks/Cole, 1980.

Miller-Tiedeman, A. L. *LIFECAREER: The Quantum Leap into a Process of Career.* Vista, Calif.: Lifecareer Foundation, 1988.

Miller-Tiedeman, A. L. *How to NOT Make It . . . and Succeed: The Truth About Your LIFECAREER.* Vista, Calif.: Lifecareer Foundation, 1989.

Miller-Tiedeman, A. L., and Niemi, M. "An 'I' Power Primer: Part Two. Structuring Another's Responsibility into His or Her Action." *Focus on Guidance,* 1977, *9* (8), 1–20.

Miller-Tiedeman, A. L., and Tiedeman, D. V. "Personal and Common Realities in Careers: A Position Exemplified in the Young Adolescent Period." Los Angeles: National Institute for the Advancement of Career Education, University of Southern California, 1979.

Mincer, J. *Schooling, Experience, and Earnings.* New York: National Bureau of Economic Research, 1974.

Mischel, W. *Personality and Assessment.* New York: Wiley, 1968.

Mitchell, A. M. "From My Window." *Character Potential: A Record of Research,* 1979a, *9,* 95–100.

Mitchell, A. M. "Relevant Evidence." In A. M. Mitchell, G. B. Jones, and J. D. Krumboltz (eds.), *Social Learning and Career Decision Making.* Cranston, R.I.: Carroll Press, 1979b.

Mitchell, L. K., and Krumboltz, J. D. "Research on Human Decision Making: Implications for Career Decision Making and Counseling." In S. D. Brown and R. W. Lent (eds.), *Handbook of Counseling Psychology.* New York: Wiley, 1984.

Mitchell, L. K., and Krumboltz, J. D. "The Effects of Cognitive Restructuring and Decision Making Training on Career Indecision." *Journal of Counseling and Development,* 1987, *66,* 171–174.

Mitchell, T. R. "Expectancy Models of Job Satisfaction, Occupational Reference, and Effort." *Psychological Bulletin,* 1974, *81,* 1053–1077.

Mitchell, T. R., and Beach, L. R. "A Review of Occupational Preference and Choice Research Theory." *Journal of Occupational Psychology,* 1976, *49,* 231–248.

Mitchell, W. D. "Restle's Choice Model: A Reconceptualization for a Special Case." *Journal of Vocational Behavior,* 1975, *6,* 315–330.

Mohney, C., and Anderson, W. "The Effect of Life Events and Relationships on Adult Women's Decisions to Enroll in College." *Journal of Counseling and Development,* 1988, *66,* 271–274.

Monahan, C. J. "Construct Validation of a Modified Differentiation Index." *Journal of Vocational Behavior,* 1987, *30,* 217–226.

Montagna, P. D. *Occupations and Society: Toward a Sociology of the Labor Market.* New York: Wiley, 1977.

Montross, D. H., and Shinkman, C. J. (eds.). *Career Development in the 1980s: Theory and Practice.* Springfield, Ill.: Thomas, 1981.

Moore, R., and Davenport, S. *The New Improved Sorting Machine.* Madison: National Center on Effective Secondary Schools, University of Wisconsin, 1988.

Morrison, R. F. "Career Adaptivity: The Effective Adaptation of Managers to Changing Role Demands." *Journal of Applied Psychology,* 1977, *62,* 549–558.

Mortimer, J., and Lorence, J. "Occupational Experience and the Self-Concept: A Longitudinal Study." *Social Psychology Quarterly,* 1979a, *42,* 307–323.

Mortimer, J., and Lorence, J. "Work Experience and Occupational Value Socialization: A Longitudinal Study." *American Journal of Sociology,* 1979b, *84,* 1361–1385.

Moss, C., and Bradley, R. W. "Response to the Publican, Using the Perspective Provided by Anne Roe." *Career Development Quarterly,* 1988, *36,* 208–210.

Mulvey, M. C. "Psychological and Sociological Factors in Prediction of Career Patterns of Women." *Genetic Psychology Monographs,* 1963, *68* (2), 309–386.

Murray, H. A. *Explorations in Personality*. New York: Oxford University Press, 1938.

Musgrave, P. W. "Toward a Sociological Theory of Occupational Choice." *Sociological Review*, 1967, *15*, 33–45.

Myers, I. B. *The Myers-Briggs Type Indicator*. Palo Alto, Calif.: Consulting Psychologists Press, 1962.

Myers, R. A. "Education and Training—The Next Decade." *The Counseling Psychologist*, 1982, *10*, 39–44.

Myers, R. A., and others. *The Educational and Career Exploration System: Report of a Two-Year Field Trial*. New York: Department of Psychology, Teachers College, Columbia University, 1972.

Nachmann, B. "Childhood Experiences and Vocational Choice in Law, Dentistry, and Social Work." *Journal of Counseling Psychology*, 1960, *7*, 243–250.

Nachmann, B. "Cross Currents in the Occupational Evolution of Religious Careers." In W. E. Bartlett (ed.), *Evolving Religious Careers*. Washington, D.C.: Center for Applied Research in the Apostolate, 1970.

Nathan, P. E. "Failures in Prevention—Why We Can't Prevent the Devastating Effect of Alcoholism and Drug Abuse." *American Psychologist*, 1983, *38*, 459–467.

National Alliance of Business. *Employment Policies: Looking to Year 2000*. Washington, D.C.: National Alliance of Business, 1988.

Nauss, A. H. "The Ministerial Personality: On Avoiding a Stereotype Trap." *Journal of Counseling Psychology*, 1968, *15*, 581–582.

Nelson-Jones, R. *Theory and Practice of Counseling Psychology*. New York: Holt, Rinehart & Winston, 1982.

Nevill, D. D., and Super, D. E. *Manual for Salience Inventory: Theory, Application, and Research*. Palo Alto, Calif.: Consulting Psychologists Press, 1986.

Nevill, D. D., and Super, D. E. "Career Maturity and Commitment to Work in University Students." *Journal of Vocational Behavior*, 1988, *32*, 139–151.

Nicholson, N., and West, M. "Transitions, Work Histories, and Careers." In M. B. Arthur, D. T. Hall, and B. S. Lawrence (eds.), *Handbook of Career Theory*. New York: Cambridge University Press, 1989.

Nishida, Y. "The Development of Junior High School Student Ability in Occupational Selection — Retention and Alteration of Vocational Choice at Large- and Small-Scale Schools." In *Final Report of the Fifth International Conference on Vocational Guidance.* Hyogo, Japan: Ashiya University, 1987.

Noeth, R. J., Engen, H. B., and Noeth, P. E. "Making Career Decisions: A Self-Report of Factors That Help High School Students." *Vocational Guidance Quarterly,* 1984, *32,* 240–248.

Nord, C. "Personality Types of Undecided Students." Unpublished doctoral dissertation, Florida State University, 1976.

Norman, R. D., and Redlo, M. "MMPI Personality Patterns for Various College Major Groups." *Journal of Applied Psychology,* 1952, *36,* 404–409.

Notz, W. W. "Work Motivation and the Negative Effects of Extrinsic Rewards." *American Psychologist,* 1975, *30,* 889–891.

Oakes, J. *Keeping Track: How Schools Structure Inequality.* New Haven, Conn.: Yale University Press, 1985.

Obleton, N. B. "Career Counseling Black Women in a Predominantly White Coeducational University." *Personnel and Guidance Journal,* 1984, *62,* 365–368.

O'Hare, M. M. "Career Decision-Making Models: Espoused Theory Versus Theory-in-Use." *Journal of Counseling and Development,* 1987, *65,* 301–303.

Oliver, L. W. "The Relationship of Parental Attitudes and Parent Identification to Career and Homemaking Orientation in College Women." *Journal of Vocational Behavior,* 1975, *7,* 1–12.

Olson, S. K. "Validity of My Vocational Situation for Homemakers and Displaced Homemakers." *Measurement and Evaluation in Counseling and Development,* 1985, *18,* 17–25.

O'Mahoney, T. J. *Self-Development Processes: A Model and an Heuristic Procedure for Investigating Aspects of These Processes.* 2 vols. Unpublished doctoral dissertation, University of Leeds, England, 1968.

Osherson, S. D. *Holding On or Letting Go.* New York: Free Press, 1980.

Osipow, S. H. "Perceptions of Occupations as a Function of Titles and Descriptions." *Journal of Counseling Psychology,* 1962, *9,* 106–109.

Osipow, S. H. "Consistency of Occupational Choices and Roe's Classification of Occupations." *Vocational Guidance Quarterly,* 1966, *14,* 285–286.

Osipow, S. H. "Cognitive Style and Educational-Vocational Preference and Selection." *Journal of Counseling Psychology,* 1969, *16,* 534–546.

Osipow, S. H. "Success and Preference: A Replication and Extension." *Journal of Applied Psychology,* 1972, *56,* 179–180.

Osipow, S. H. *Theories of Career Development.* (2nd ed.) Englewood Cliffs, N.J.: Prentice-Hall, 1973.

Osipow, S. H. "The Relevance of Theories of Career Development to Special Groups: Problems, Needed Data and Implications." In J. S. Picou and R. E. Campbell (eds.), *Career Behavior of Special Groups.* Westerville, Ohio: Merrill, 1975.

Osipow, S. H. *Theories of Career Development* (3rd ed.) Englewood Cliffs, N.J.: Prentice-Hall, 1983.

Osipow, S. H., and others. *The Career Decision Scale.* (3rd ed.) Columbus, Ohio: Marathon Consulting and Press, 1976.

Otto, L. B., and Haller, A. O. "Evidence for a Social Psychological View of the Status-Attainment Process: Four Studies Compared." *Social Forces,* 1979, *57,* 887–914.

Pallas, A. M., Dahmann, J. S., Gucer, P. W., and Holland, J. L. "Test-Taker Evaluations of the Self-Directed Search and Other Psychological Tests." *Psychological Documents,* 1983, *13,* 11.

Pallas, A. M., and others. "Test-Taker Evaluations of the Self-Directed Search and Other Psychological Tests." Unpublished manuscript, Johns Hopkins University, n.d.

Pallone, N. J., Rickard, F. S., and Hurley, R. B. "Key Influences of Occupational Preference Among Black Youth." *Journal of Counseling Psychology,* 1970, *17* (6), 498–501.

Pappas, J. P., and Crites, J. "Pioneers in Guidance—Donald Super." *Personnel and Guidance Journal,* 1978, *56,* 585–592.

Parcel, L., and Mueller, W. *Ascription and Labor Markets: Race and Sex Differences in Earnings.* Orlando, Fla.: Academic Press, 1983.

Parker, H. J., and others. *Parent–Child Relations Research Status, Measurement, and Predictive Value.* Studies in the Assessment of Parent-Child Relationships, monograph 1. Oklahoma City: University of Oklahoma Medical Center, 1967.

Parsons, F. *Choosing a Vocation*. Boston: Houghton Mifflin, 1909.

Passmore, J. "Logical Positivism." In P. Edwards (ed.), *The Encyclopedia of Philosophy*. Vol. 5. New York: Macmillan, 1967.

Paterson, D. G., and others. *Minnesota Occupational Rating Scales and Counseling Profile*. Chicago: Science Research Associates, 1941.

Patterson, C. H. *Theories of Counseling and Psychotherapy*. (3rd ed.) New York: Harper & Row, 1980.

Peatling, J. H. "The Architecture for Self as Its Own Builder." *Character Potential: A Record of Research*, 1974, *7*, 28–36.

Peatling, J. H., and Tiedeman, D. V. *Career Development: Designing Self*. Muncie, Ind.: Accelerated Development, 1977.

Peraino, J. M., and Willerman, L. "Personality Correlates of Occupational Status According to Holland Types." *Journal of Vocational Behavior*, 1983, *22*, 268–277.

Perfetti, L. J., and Bingham, W. C. "Unemployment and Self-Esteem in Metal Refinery Workers." *Vocational Guidance Quarterly*, 1983, *31*, 195–202.

Perloff, R., and Nelson, S. D. "Economic Productivity and the Behavioral Sciences." *American Psychologist*, 1983, *38*, 451–453.

Perun, P. J., and Bielby, D.D.V. "Towards a Model of Female Occupational Behavior: A Human Development Approach." *Psychology of Women Quarterly*, 1981, *6*, 234–252.

Peters, D. L. *Skills Awareness Workshop*. Indianapolis, Ind.: Eli Lilly & Co., 1986.

Phillips, S. D., Cairo, P. C., Blustein, D. L., and Myers, R. A. "Career Development and Vocational Behavior, 1987: A Review." *Journal of Vocational Behavior*, 1988, *33*, 119–184.

Piaget, J., and Inhelder, B. *The Psychology of the Child*. London: Routledge & Kegan Paul, 1969.

Pickering, J. W. "A Comparison of Three Methods of Career Planning for Liberal Arts Majors." *Career Development Quarterly*, 1986, *35*, 102–112.

Pickering, J. W., and Vacc, N. A. "Effectiveness of Career Development Interventions for College Students: A Review of Published Research." *Vocational Guidance Quarterly*, 1984, *32*, 149–159.

Picou, J. S., and Carter, M. T. "Significant-Other Influence and Aspirations." *Sociology of Education*, 1976, *49*, 12–22.

Pirnot, K., and Dustin, R. "A New Look at Value Priorities for Homemakers and Career Women." *Journal of Counseling and Development,* 1986, *64,* 432–436.

Pittman, T. S., Emery, J., and Boggiano, A. K. "Intrinsic and Extrinsic Motivational Orientations: Reward-Induced Changes in Preference for Complexity." *Journal of Personality and Social Psychology,* 1982, *42,* 789–797.

Pitz, G. F., and Harren, V. A. "An Analysis of Career Decision Making from the Point of View of Information Processing and Decision Theory." *Journal of Vocational Behavior,* 1980, *16,* 320–346.

Porter, J. N. "Race, Socialization, and Mobility in Educational and Early Occupational Attainment." *American Sociological Review,* 1974, *39,* 303–316.

Portes, A., and Wilson, K. L. "Black-White Differences in Educational Attainment." *American Sociological Review,* 1976, *41,* 414–431.

Post-Kammer, P., and Smith, P. L. "Sex Differences in Career Self-Efficacy, Consideration, and Interests of Eighth and Ninth Graders." *Journal of Counseling Psychology,* 1985, *32,* 551–559.

Post-Kammer, P., and Smith, P. L. "Sex Differences in Math and Science Career Self-Efficacy Among Disadvantaged Students." *Journal of Vocational Behavior,* 1986, *29,* 89–101.

Potter, B. A. *Preventing Job Burnout.* Los Altos, Calif.: Crisp Publications, 1987.

Prediger, D. J. "Data Information Conversion in Test Interpretation." *Journal of Counseling Psychology,* 1971, *18,* 308–313.

Prediger, D. J. "The Role of Assessment in Career Guidance." In E. L. Herr (ed.), *Vocational Guidance and Human Development.* Boston: Houghton Mifflin, 1974.

Prediger, D. J. "The Marriage Between Tests and Career Counseling: An Intimate Report." *Vocational Guidance Quarterly,* 1980, *28,* 297–305.

Prigogine, I. *From Being to Becoming: Time and Complexity in the Physical Sciences.* New York: W. H. Freeman, 1980.

Prince, B. "Allocative and Opportunity Structures and Their Interaction with Career Orientation." Unpublished doctoral dissertation, University of Southern California, 1984.

Pritchard, D. H. "The Occupational Exploration Process — Some Operational Implications." *Personnel and Guidance Journal,* 1962, *40,* 674–680.

Pryor, R.G.L. "Toward Exorcising the Self-Concept from Psychology: Some Comments on Gottfredson's Circumscription/Compromise Theory." *Journal of Counseling Psychology,* 1985, *32,* 154–158.

Quale, D. "American Productivity — The Devastating Effect of Alcoholism and Drug Abuse." *American Psychologist,* 1983, *38,* 454–458.

Quinn, F., and Staines, G. *The 1977 Quality of Employment Survey.* Ann Arbor: Institute for Social Research, University of Michigan, 1979.

Rabinowitz, S., and Hall, D. T. "Organizational Research on Job Involvement." *Psychological Bulletin,* 1977, *84,* 265–288.

Rangel, M. "Recent Developments in the Educational System." In *Final Report on the Fifth International Conference on Vocational Guidance.* Hyogo, Japan: Ashiya University, 1987.

Reardon, R., Psychological Assessment Resources, Inc., and Holland, J. L. *Self-Directed Search: Computer Version.* Odessa, Fla.: Psychological Assessment Resources, Inc., 1985.

Reardon, R. C. "Development of the Computer Version of the Self-Directed Search." *Measurement and Evaluation in Counseling and Development,* 1987, *20,* 62–67.

Reardon, R. C., and Loughead, T. "A Comparison of Paper-and-Pencil and Computer Versions of the Self-Directed Search." *Journal of Counseling and Development,* 1988, *67,* 249–252.

Rehberg, R. A., and Rosenthal, E. R. *Class and Merit in the American High School.* New York: Longman, 1978.

Rehberg, R. A., and Sinclair, J. "Adolescent Achievement Behavior, Family Authority Structure, and Parents' Socialization Processes." *American Journal of Sociology,* 1970, *75* (6), 1012–1034.

Reissman, L. "Levels of Aspiration and Social Class." *American Sociological Review,* 1953, *18,* 233–242.

Remenyi, A. G., and Fraser, B. J. "Effects of Occupational Information on Occupational Perceptions." *Journal of Vocational Behavior,* 1977, *10,* 53–68.

Restle, F. *Psychology of Judgment and Choice.* New York: Wiley, 1961.

Reynolds, P. D. *A Primer in Theory Construction.* Indianapolis, Ind.: Bobbs-Merrill, 1971.

Richardson, M. S. "Vocational Maturity in Counseling Girls and Women." In D. E. Super (ed.), *Measuring Vocational Maturity for Counseling and Evaluation.* Washington, D.C.: American Personnel and Guidance Association, 1974.

Roberts, K. "The Social Conditions, Consequences, and Limitations of Career Guidance." *British Journal of Guidance and Counseling,* 1977, *5,* 1-9.

Roberts, K. "The Sociology of Work Entry and Occupational Choice." In A. G. Watts, D. E. Super, and J. M. Kidd (eds.), *Career Development in Britain.* Cambridge, England: Hobson's Press, 1981.

Roe, A. *The Psychology of Occupations.* New York: Wiley, 1956.

Roe, A. "Early Determinants of Vocational Choice." *Journal of Counseling Psychology,* 1957, *4,* 212-217.

Roe, A. "Cross-Classification of Occupations." Unpublished manuscript, 1966.

Roe, A. *Classification of Occupations by Group and Level.* Bensenville, Ill.: Scholastic Testing Service, 1976.

Roe, A., and Baruch, R. "Occupational Changes in the Adult Years." *Personnel Administration,* 1967, *30* (4), 26-32.

Roe, A., and Klos, D. "Classification of Occupations." In J. M. Whiteley and A. Resnikoff (eds.), *Perspectives on Vocational Development.* Washington, D.C.: American Personnel and Guidance Association, 1972.

Roe, A., and Siegelman, M. "A Parent–Child Relations Questionnaire." *Child Development,* 1963, *34,* 355-369.

Roe, A., and Siegelman, M. *The Origin of Interests.* APGA Inquiry Studies, no. 1. Washington, D.C.: American Personnel and Guidance Association, 1964.

Roe, A., and others. "Studies of Occupational History. Part 1: Job Changes and the Classification of Occupations." *Journal of Counseling Psychology,* 1966, *13,* 387-393.

Rogers, C. R. *Client-Centered Therapy.* Boston: Houghton Mifflin, 1951.

Rogers, C. R., and Wallen, J. L. *Counseling with Returned Service Men.* New York: McGraw-Hill, 1946.

Romey, W. D. *Inquiry Techniques for Teaching Science.* Englewood Cliffs, N.J.: Prentice-Hall, 1969.

Rose, H. A., and Elton, C. F. "Sex and Occupational Choice." *Journal of Counseling Psychology,* 1971, *18,* 456–461.

Rose, H. A., and Elton, C. F. "The Relation of Congruence, Differentiation, and Consistency to Interest and Aptitude Scores in Women with Stable and Unstable Vocational Choices." *Journal of Vocational Behavior,* 1982, *20,* 162–174.

Rosen, D., Holmberg, M. S., and Holland, J. L. *The College Majors Finder.* Odessa, Fla.: Psychological Assessment Resources, Inc., 1987.

Rosen, S. D., and others. "Occupational Reinforced Patterns, Second Volume." *Minnesota Studies in Vocational Rehabilitation,* no. 59. Minneapolis: University of Minnesota Industrial Relations Center, 1972.

Rosenbaum, J. E. *Making Inequality: The Hidden Curriculum of High School Tracking.* New York: Wiley, 1976.

Rosenbaum, J. E. "Careers in a Corporate Hierarchy: A Longitudinal Analysis of Earnings and Level Attainments." In D. J. Treiman and R. V. Robinson (eds.), *Research in Social Stratification and Mobility: A Research Annual.* Vol. 1. Greenwich, Conn.: JAI, 1981.

Rotberg, H. L., Brown, D., and Ware, W. B. "Career Self-Efficacy Expectations and Perceived Range of Career Options in Community College Students." *Journal of Counseling Psychology,* 1987, *34,* 164–170.

Rothman, R. A. *Working: Sociological Perspectives.* Englewood Cliffs, N.J.: Prentice-Hall, 1987.

Rotter, J. B. *Social Learning and Clinical Psychology.* Englewood Cliffs, N.J.: Prentice-Hall, 1954.

Rubinton, N. "Career Exploration for Middle School Youth: A University–School Cooperative." *Vocational Guidance Quarterly,* 1985, *33,* 249–255.

Salomone, P. R., and Daughton, S. "Assessing Work Environments for Career Counseling." *Vocational Guidance Quarterly,* 1984, *33,* 45–54.

Salomone, P. R., and Slaney, R. B. "The Applicability of Holland's Theory to Nonprofessional Workers." *Journal of Vocational Behavior,* 1978, *13,* 63–74.

Saltiel, J. "The Wisconsin Model of Status Attainment and the Occupational Choice Process: Applying a Continuous-Choice Model to a Discrete-Choice Situation." *Work and Occupations,* 1988, *15,* 334–355.

Sandage, A. *Creation of the Universe — Notes on Physics.* Kent, Ohio: PTV Publications, 1986.

Savickas, M. L., Passen, A. J., and Jarjoura, D. G. "Career Concerns and Coping as Indicators of Adult Vocational Development." *Journal of Vocational Behavior,* 1988, *33,* 82–98.

Schaefer, E. S. "Converging Conceptual Models for Maternal Behavior and for Child Behavior." In J. C. Glidewell (ed.), *Parental Attitudes and Child Behavior.* Springfield, Ill.: Thomas, 1961.

Schaefer, E. S. "A Configurational Analysis of Children's Reports of Parent Behavior." *Journal of Consulting Psychology,* 1965, *29,* 552–557.

Schafer, W. E., and Olexa, C. *Tracking and Opportunity: The Locking-Out Process and Beyond.* Scranton, Pa.: Chandler, 1971.

Schein, E. H. "Organizational Socialization and the Profession of Management." *Industrial Management Review,* 1968, *9,* 1–15.

Schein, E. H. "The Individual, the Organization, and the Career: A Conceptual Scheme." *Journal of Applied Behavioral Science,* 1971, *7,* 401–426.

Schein, E. H. "Personal Change Through Interpersonal Relationships." In W. G. Bennis, D. E. Berlew, E. H. Schein, and F. I. Steele (eds.), *Interpersonal Dynamics.* (3rd ed.) Homewood, Ill.: Dorsey Press, 1973.

Schein, E. H. *Career Dynamics: Matching Individual and Organizational Needs.* Reading, Mass.: Addison-Wesley, 1978.

Schein, E. H. "Increasing Organizational Effectiveness Through Better Human Resource Planning and Development." In R. Katz (ed.), *Career Issues in Human Resource Management.* Englewood Cliffs, N.J.: Prentice-Hall, 1982.

Schlesinger, V. J. "Anal Personality Traits and Occupational Choice: A Study of Accountants, Chemical Engineers, and

Educational Psychologists." Unpublished doctoral dissertation, Department of Psychology, University of Michigan, 1963.

Schlossberg, N. K. "An Interview Model for Career Counseling." *Character Potential: A Record of Research,* 1979, *9,* 71–76.

Schlossberg, N. K., Troll, L. E., and Leibowitz, Z. *Perspectives on Counseling Adults: Issues and Skills.* Pacific Grove, Calif.: Brooks/Cole, 1978.

Schneidman, E. "The Indian Summer of Life." *American Psychologist,* 1989, *44,* 684–694.

Schwartz, R. H., Andiappan, P., and Nelson, M. "Reconsidering the Support for Holland's Congruence-Achievement Hypothesis." *Journal of Counseling Psychology,* 1986, *33,* 425–428.

Scott, N. A., and Sedlacek, W. E. "Personality Differentiation and Prediction of Persistence in Physical Science and Engineering." *Journal of Vocational Behavior,* 1975, *6,* 205–216.

Segal, S. J. "A Psychoanalytic Analysis of Personality Factors in Vocational Choice." *Journal of Counseling Psychology,* 1961, *8,* 202–210.

Segal, S. J., and Szabo, R. "Identification in Two Vocations: Accountants and Creative Writers." *Personnel and Guidance Journal,* 1964, *43,* 252–255.

Seligman, R. "Test Reviews." *Measurement and Evaluation in Guidance,* 1974, *7* (2), 138–140.

Sewell, W. H., Haller, A. O., and Ohlendorf, G. "The Educational and Early Occupational Attainment Process: Replications and Revisions." *American Sociological Review,* 1970, *35,* 1014–1027.

Sewell, W. H., Haller, A. O., and Portes, A. "The Educational and Early Occupational Attainment Process." *American Sociological Review,* 1969, *34,* 89–92.

Sewell, W. H., Haller, A. O., and Strauss, M. A. "Social Status and Educational and Occupational Aspiration." *American Sociological Review,* 1957, *22,* 67–73.

Sewell, W. H., and Hauser, R. M. *Education, Occupation, and Earnings: Achievement in the Early Career.* Orlando, Fla.: Academic Press, 1975.

Sharf, R. S. "Vocational Information-Seeking Behavior: Another View." *Vocational Guidance Quarterly,* 1984, *33,* 120–129.

Sheehy, G. *Passages: Predictable Crises of Adult Life.* New York: Dutton, 1974.

Sheffey, M. A., Bingham, R. P., and Walsh, W. B. "Concurrent Validity of Holland's Theory for College-Educated Black Men." *Journal of Multicultural Counseling and Development,* 1986, *14,* 149–156.

Sheppard, H. L. "Youth Discontent and the Nature of Work." In D. Gottlieb (ed.), *Youth in Contemporary Society.* Newbury Park, Calif.: Sage, 1973.

Shubsachs, A. P., Rounds, J. B., Jr., Dawis, R. V., and Lofquist, L. H. "Perceptions of Work Reinforcer Systems: Factor Structure." *Journal of Vocational Behavior,* 1978, *13,* 54–62.

Siegelman, M., and Roe, A. *Manual, the Parent–Child Relations Questionnaire II.* Tucson, Ariz.: Simroe Foundation, 1979.

Simon, H. A. *Administrative Behavior.* New York: Macmillan, 1957.

Simon, H. A. "Motivational and Emotional Controls of Cognition." *Psychological Review,* 1967, *74,* 29–39.

Simon, H. A. "Studying Human Intelligence by Creating Artificial Intelligence." *American Scientist,* 1981, *69,* 300–309.

Sinick, D. "Counseling Older Persons: Career Change and Retirement." *Vocational Guidance Quarterly,* 1976, *25,* 18–25.

Slaney, R. B., and Dickson, R. D. "Relation of Career Indecision to Career Exploration with Reentry Women: A Treatment and Follow-Up Study." *Journal of Counseling Psychology,* 1985, *32,* 355–362.

Slovic, P., and Mac Phillamy. "Dimensional Commensurability and Cue Utilization in Comparative Judgment." *Organizational Behavior and Human Performance,* 1974, *11,* 172–194.

Smart, J. C., Elton, C. F., and McLaughlin, G. W. "Person-Environment Congruence and Job Satisfaction." *Journal of Vocational Behavior,* 1986, *29,* 216–225.

Smith, E. J. "Profile of the Black Individual in Vocational Literature." *Journal of Vocational Behavior,* 1975, *6,* 41–59.

Smith, E. J. "Issues in Racial Minorities' Career Behavior." In W. B. Walsh and S. H. Osipow (eds.), *Handbook of Vocational Psychology. Vol. 1. Foundations.* Hillsdale, N.J.: Erlbaum, 1983.

Smith, R. "Mental Health Issues in the Workplace." In D. Brown and C. W. Minor (eds.), *Working in America: A Status*

Report on Planning and Problems. Alexandria, Va.: National Career Development Association, 1989.

Snow, R. E. "Theory Construction for Research and Testing." In R. W. Traves (ed.), *Second Handbook of Research on Teaching.* Skokie, Ill.: Rand McNally, 1973.

Snygg, D., and Combs, A. W. *Individual Behavior.* New York: Harper & Row, 1949.

Sonnenfeld, J., and Kotter, J. P. "The Maturation of Career Theory." *Human Relations,* 1982, *35,* 19–46.

Spokane, A. R. "A Review of Research on Person-Environment Congruence in Holland's Theory of Careers." *Journal of Vocational Behavior,* 1985, *28,* 306–343.

Srebalus, D. J., Marinelli, R. P., and Messing, J. K. *Career Development: Concepts and Procedures.* Pacific Grove, Calif.: Brooks/Cole, 1982.

Steimal, R. J., and Suziedelis, A. "Perceived Parental Influence and Inventories Interest." *Journal of Counseling Psychology,* 1963, *10,* 289–295.

Stephens, W. R. *Social Reforms and the Origins of Vocational Guidance.* Washington, D.C.: National Vocational Guidance Association, 1970.

Stewart, D., and Nejedlo, R. J. "Pyramid Power in Career Development." *Personnel and Guidance Journal,* 1980, *58,* 531–534.

Stewart, L. H. "Mother-Son Identification and Vocational Interest." *Genetic Psychology Monographs,* 1959, *60,* 31–63.

Stolzenberg, M. "Bringing the Boss Back In: Employer Size, Employee Schooling, and Socioeconomic Achievement." *American Sociological Review,* 1978, *43,* 813–828.

Stolzenberg, R. M. "Education, Occupation, and Wage Differences Between White and Black Men." *American Journal of Sociology,* 1975, *81,* 299–323.

Stone, C. P. "The Play of Little Children." In R. E. Herron and B. Sutton-Smith (eds.), *Child's Play.* New York: Wiley, 1971.

Stotland, E., and others. *Empathy, Fantasy and Helping.* Newbury Park, Calif.: Sage, 1978.

Strahan, R. F. "Measures of Consistency for Holland-Type Codes." *Journal of Vocational Behavior,* 1987, *31,* 37–44.

Strong, E. K., Jr. *Vocational Interests of Men and Women.* Stanford, Calif.: Stanford University Press, 1943.

Strong, E. K., Jr. *Vocational Interests Eighteen Years After College.* Minneapolis: University of Minnesota Press, 1955.

Strong, E. K., Jr., and Campbell, D. P. *Strong-Campbell Interest Inventory.* Stanford, Calif.: Stanford University Press, 1981.

Strong, E. K., Jr., Hansen, J. C., and Campbell, D. P. *Strong Vocational Interest Blank Form T325, Revised Edition.* Palo Alto, Calif.: Consulting Psychologists Press, 1985.

Stumpf, S. A. "Career Roles, Psychological Success, and Job Attitudes." *Journal of Vocational Behavior,* 1981, *19,* 98–112.

Stumpf, S. A., and Colarelli, S. M. "The Effect of Career Education on Exploratory Behavior and Job Search Outcomes." *Academy of Management Proceedings,* 1981, *41,* 76–90.

Stumpf, S. A., and Hartman, K. "Individual Exploration to Organizational Commitment or Withdrawal." *Academy of Management Journal,* 1984, *27,* 308–329.

Sue, D. W. "Asian-Americans: Social-Psychological Forces Affecting Their Life-Styles." In J. S. Picou and R. E. Campbell (eds.), *Career Behavior of Special Groups.* Westerville, Ohio: Merrill, 1975.

Sue, D. W. "Counseling the Culturally Different: A Conceptual Analysis." *Personnel and Guidance Journal,* 1977, *55,* 422–425.

Sue, D. W., and others. "Position Paper: Cross-Cultural Counseling Competencies." *Counseling Psychologist,* 1982, *10,* 45–52.

Sue, S., and Sue, D. W. "Chinese-American Personality and Mental Health." *Amerasia Journal,* 1971, *1,* 36–49.

Super, D. E. "Occupational Level and Job Satisfaction." *Journal of Applied Psychology,* 1939, *23,* 547–564.

Super, D. E. *Avocational Interest Patterns: A Study in the Psychology of Avocations.* Stanford, Calif.: Stanford University Press, 1940.

Super, D. E. *The Dynamics of Vocational Adjustment.* New York: Harper & Row, 1942.

Super, D. E. "The Cyclical Use of Directive and Nondirective Techniques." *Counseling,* 1947, *5,* 2–5.

Super, D. E. *Appraising Vocational Fitness.* New York: Harper & Row, 1949.

Super, D. E. "Vocational Adjustment: Implementing a Self-Concept." *Occupations,* 1951, *30,* 88–92.

Super, D. E. "A Theory of Vocational Development." *American Psychologist,* 1953, *8,* 185–190.

Super, D. E. "Career Patterns as a Basis for Vocational Counseling." *Journal of Counseling Psychology,* 1954, *1,* 12–20.

Super, D. E. "Personality Integration Through Vocational Counseling." *Journal of Counseling Psychology,* 1955a, *2,* 217–226.

Super, D. E. "The Dimensions and Measurement of Vocational Maturity." *Teachers College Record,* 1955b, *57,* 151–163.

Super, D. E. "Getting Out of an Occupation." *Personnel and Guidance Journal,* 1956, *34,* 491–493.

Super, D. E. *The Psychology of Careers.* New York: Harper & Row, 1957.

Super, D. E. "The Critical Ninth Grade: Vocational Choice or Vocational Exploration." *Personnel and Guidance Journal,* 1960, *39,* 106–109.

Super, D. E. "Self-Concepts in Vocational Development." In D. E. Super and others (eds.), *Career Development: Self-Concept Theory.* New York: College Entrance Examination Board, 1963.

Super, D. E. "Vocational Development Theory." *Counseling Psychologist,* 1969, *1,* 2–30.

Super, D. E. *Work Values Inventory.* Boston: Houghton Mifflin, 1970.

Super, D. E. "Vocational Development Theory: Persons, Positions, Processes." In J. M. Whiteley and A. Resnikoff (eds.), *Perspectives on Vocational Guidance.* Washington, D.C.: American Personnel and Guidance Association, 1972.

Super, D. E. (ed.). *Measuring Vocational Maturity for Counseling and Evaluation.* Washington, D.C.: American Personnel and Guidance Association, 1974.

Super, D. E. "Vocational Maturity in Midcareer." *Vocational Guidance Quarterly,* 1977, *25,* 294–302.

Super, D. E. "A Life-Span, Life-Space Approach to Career Development." *Journal of Vocational Behavior,* 1980, *16,* 282–298.

Super, D. E. "A Developmental Theory: Implementing a Self-Concept." In D. H. Montross and C. J. Shinkman (eds.), *Career*

Development in the 1980s: Theory and Practice. Springfield, Ill.: Thomas, 1981a.

Super, D. E. "Approaches to Occupational Choice and Career Development." In A. G. Watts, D. E. Super, and J. M. Kidd (eds.), *Career Development in Britain.* Cambridge, England: Hobson's Press, 1981b.

Super, D. E. "Self-Concepts in Career Development: Theory and Findings After Thirty Years." Paper presented to the International Association for Applied Psychology, Edinburgh, Scotland, 1982a.

Super, D. E. "The Relative Importance of Work: Models and Measures for Meaningful Data." *Counseling Psychologist,* 1982b, *10,* 95–104.

Super, D. E. "Assessment in Career Guidance: Toward Truly Developmental Counseling." *Personnel and Guidance Journal,* 1983a, *61,* 555–562.

Super, D. E. "History and Development of Vocational Psychology: A Personal Perspective." In W. B. Walsh and S. H. Osipow (eds.), *Handbook of Vocational Psychology.* Hillsdale, N.J.: Erlbaum, 1983b.

Super, D. E. "Career and Life Development." In D. Brown, L. Brooks, and Associates, *Career Choice and Development: Applying Contemporary Theories to Practice.* San Francisco: Jossey-Bass, 1984.

Super, D. E. "Review of Holland's Making Vocational Choices (Second Edition)." *Contemporary Psychology,* 1985, *30,* 771.

Super, D. E., and Bachrach, P. *Scientific Careers and Vocational Development Theory.* New York: Teachers College Press, 1957.

Super, D. E., and Bohn, M. *Occupational Psychology.* Pacific Grove, Calif.: Brooks/Cole, 1970.

Super, D. E., and Bowlsbey, J. A. *Guided Career Exploration.* New York: Psychological Corporation, 1979.

Super, D. E., and Kidd, J. M. "Vocational Maturity in Adulthood: Toward Turning a Model into a Measure." *Journal of Vocational Behavior,* 1979, *14,* 255–270.

Super, D. E., and Knasel, E. G. *Specifications for a Measure of Career Adaptability in Young Adults.* Cambridge and Hertford, England: National Institute for Careers Education and Counseling, 1979.

Super, D. E., Kowalski, R. S., and Gotkin, E. H. *Floundering and Trial After High School.* New York: Teachers College, Columbia University, 1967.

Super, D. E., and Nevill, D. D. "Work-Role Salience as a Determinant of Career Maturity in High School Students." *Journal of Vocational Behavior,* 1984, *25,* 30–44.

Super, D. E., and Overstreet, P. L. *The Vocational Maturity of Ninth-Grade Boys.* New York: Teachers College Press, 1960.

Super, D. E., and Thompson, A. S. "A Six-Scale, Two-Factor Measure of Adolescent Career or Vocational Maturity." *Vocational Guidance Quarterly,* 1979, *28,* 6–15.

Super, D. E., and Thompson, A. S. *The Adult Career Concerns Inventory.* New York: Teachers College, Columbia University, 1981.

Super, D. E., Thompson, A. S., and Lindeman, R. H. *The Adult Career Concerns Inventory.* Palo Alto, Calif.: Consulting Psychologists Press, 1988.

Super, D. E., and others. *Vocational Development: A Framework for Research.* New York: Bureau of Publications, Teachers College, Columbia University, 1957.

Super, D. E., and others (eds.). *Career Development: Self-Concept Theory.* New York: College Entrance Examination Board, 1963.

Super, D. E., and others. *Career Development Inventory.* Palo Alto, Calif.: Consulting Psychologists Press, 1981.

Super, D. E., and others. *Career Development Inventory.* Palo Alto, Calif.: Consulting Psychologists Press, 1982.

Super, D. E., and others. *Career Development Inventory.* Palo Alto, Calif.: Consulting Psychologists Press, 1983.

Super, D. E., and others. *Adult Career Concerns Inventory.* Palo Alto, Calif.: Consulting Psychologists Press, 1985.

Super, D. E., and others. *Adult Career Concerns Inventory.* Palo Alto, Calif.: Consulting Psychologists Press, 1988.

Suter, L., and Miller, A. "Income Differences Between Men and Career Women." *American Journal of Sociology,* 1973, *78,* 962–974.

Swimme, B. *The Universe Is a Green Dragon.* Santa Fe, N.Mex.: Bear & Co., 1984.

Switzger, D. K., and others. "Early Experiences and Occupational Choice: A Test of Roe's Hypothesis." *Journal of Counseling Psychology,* 1962, *9,* 45–48.

Tangri, S. S. "Determinants of Occupational Role Innovation Among College Women." *Journal of Social Issues,* 1972, *28,* 177–199.

Tausky, C. *Work and Society: An Introduction to Industrial Sociology.* Itasca, Ill.: Peacock, 1984.

Taylor, K. F., Kelso, G. I., Longthorp, N. E., and Pattison, P. E. "Differentiation as a Construct in Vocational Theory and a Diagnostic Sign in Practice." *Melbourne Psychology Reports,* 1980, *68,* entire issue.

Taylor, K. M., and Betz, N. "Applications of Self-Efficacy Theory to the Understanding and Treatment of Career Indecision." *Journal of Vocational Behavior,* 1983, *22,* 63–81.

Taylor, N. B., and Pryor, R.G.L. "Exploring the Process of Compromise in Career Decision Making." *Journal of Vocational Behavior,* 1985, *27,* 171–190.

Terkel, S. *Working.* New York: Pantheon, 1972.

Thomas, W. I. *The Unadjusted Girl: With Cases and Standpoint for Behavior Analysis.* Boston: Little, Brown, 1923.

Thomas, W. I., and Thomas, D. S. *The Child in America: Behavior Problems and Programs.* New York: Knopf, 1928.

Thompson, A. S., and others. *Career Development Inventory.* Vol. 1. *User's Manual.* Palo Alto, Calif.: Consulting Psychologists Press, 1981.

Thompson, A. S., and others. *Career Development Inventory, College and University Form: Supplement to User's Manual.* Palo Alto, Calif.: Consulting Psychologists Press, 1982.

Thompson, A. S., and others. *Career Development Inventory.* Vol. 2. *Technical Manual.* Palo Alto, Calif.: Consulting Psychologists Press, 1984.

Thoresen, C. E., Hosford, R. E., and Krumboltz, J. D. "Determining Effective Models for Counseling Clients of Varying Competencies." *Journal of Counseling Psychology,* 1970, *17,* 369–375.

Thoresen, C. E., and Krumboltz, J. D. "Similarity of Social Models and Clients in Behavioral Counseling: Two Experimental Studies." *Journal of Counseling Psychology,* 1968, *15* (5), 393–401.

Thurstone, L. L. "A Multiple-Factor Study of Vocational Interests." *Personnel Journal,* 1931, *10,* 198–205.

Tiboni, V.B.A. "The Bearing of Certain Aspects of the Mother–Son Relationship upon the Son's Tendency Toward Narcotics Addiction." Unpublished doctoral dissertation, School of Education, Catholic University of America, 1976.

Tiedeman, D. V. "Putting the Backbone in Self: Overview of a Symposium." *Character Potential: A Record of Research,* 1974, *7,* 9–11.

Tiedeman, D. V. "A Person's-Eye View of Career Development Education and Enactment." *Illinois Career Education Journal,* 1977a, *34* (2), 13–17.

Tiedeman, D. V. *Towards the Career Education of All Educational Personnel in Illinois.* Springfield: Illinois State Board of Education, 1977b.

Tiedeman, D. V. "The Self-Constructionist Alternative to Today's Develop-or-Wither Career Crisis at Midlife." *Character Potential: A Record of Research,* 1978, *8,* 131–139.

Tiedeman, D. V. *Career Development: Designing Our Career Machines.* Schenectady, N.Y.: Character Research Press, 1979a.

Tiedeman, D. V. "Converting Tiedeman and O'Hara's Decision Making Paradigm into 'I' Power: A Symposium." *Character Potential: A Record of Research,* 1979b, *9,* 61–62.

Tiedeman, D. V. "Graduate Education: A Career Education Thrust." *Thresholds in Secondary Education,* 1981, *7* (4), 22–26.

Tiedeman, D. V., and Miller-Tiedeman, A. "Adult Career Education Model." *Thresholds in Secondary Education,* 1976, *2* (1), 20–22.

Tiedeman, D. V., and Miller-Tiedeman, A. "An 'I' Power Primer. Part One: Structure and Its Enablement of Intuition." *Focus on Guidance,* 1977, *9* (7), 1–16.

Tiedeman, D. V., and Miller-Tiedeman, A. "Choice and Decision Processes and Career Revisited." In A. M. Mitchell, G. B. Jones, and J. D. Krumboltz (eds.), *Social Learning and Career Decision Making.* Cranston, R.I.: Carroll Press, 1979.

Tiedeman, D. V., and Miller-Tiedeman, A. "Career Decision Making: An Individualistic Perspective." In D. Brown, L. Brooks, and Associates, *Career Choice and Development: Applying Contemporary Theories to Practice.* San Francisco: Jossey-Bass, 1984.

Tiedeman, D. V., and O'Hara, R. P. *Career Development: Choice and Adjustment.* New York: College Entrance Examination Board, 1963.

Tiedeman, D. V., Rulon, P. J., and Bryan, J. G. "The Multiple-Discriminant Function — A Symposium." *Harvard Educational Review,* 1951, *21,* 71–95.

Tienda, M., and Lii, D.-T. "Minority Concentration and Earnings Inequality: Blacks, Hispanics, and Asians Compared." *American Journal of Sociology,* 1987, *93,* 141–165.

Tilden, A. J. "Is There a Monotonic Criterion for Measures of Vocational Maturity in College Students?" *Journal of Vocational Behavior,* 1978, *12,* 43–52.

Tittle, C. K. "Sex Bias in Educational Measurement: Fact or Fiction?" *Measurement and Evaluation in Guidance,* 1973, *6,* 219–226.

Tittle, C. K. "Career Counseling in Contemporary U.S. High Schools: An Addendum to Rehberg and Hotchkiss." *Educational Researcher,* 1982, *11,* 12–18.

Tittle, C. K., and Zytowski, D. G. (eds.). *Sex-Fair Interest Measurement: Research and Implications.* Washington, D.C.: National Institute of Education, 1978.

Toffler, A. *The Third Wave.* New York: Morrow, 1980.

Tolbert, E. L. *Counseling for Career Development.* (2nd ed.) Boston: Houghton Mifflin, 1980.

Tolman, E. C. "Principles of Purposive Behavior." In S. Koch (ed.), *Psychology: A Study of Science.* Vol. 2. New York: McGraw-Hill, 1959.

Touchton, J. G., and Magoon, T. M. "Occupational Daydreams as Predictors of Vocational Plans of College Women." *Journal of Vocational Behavior,* 1977, *10,* 156–166.

Treiman, D. J., and Hartman, H. I. (eds.). *Women, Work, and Wages: Equal Pay for Jobs of Equal Value.* Washington, D.C.: National Research Council, National Academy of Sciences, 1981.

Treiman, D. J., and Terrell, K. "Sex and the Process of Status Attainment: A Comparison of Working Women and Men." *American Sociological Review,* 1975, *40,* 174–200.

Trent, J. W., and Medsker, L. L. *Beyond High School: A Psychosociological Study of 10,000 High School Graduates.* San Francisco: Jossey-Bass, 1968.

Tryon, W. W. "The Test-Trait Fallacy." *American Psychologist,* 1979, *34,* 402–406.

Turkington, C. "Losing Job Means Shattered Dreams, Broken Traditions." *APA Monitor,* 1983, *14,* 8.

Tuttle, T. C. "Organizational Productivity. A Challenge for Psychologists." *American Psychologist,* 1983, *38,* 479–486.

Tversky, A. "Elimination by Aspects: A Theory of Choice." *Psychological Review,* 1972, *79,* 281–299.

Ulich, R. *The Human Career.* New York: Harper & Row, 1984.

Unruh, W. R. "Career Decision Making: Theory Construction and Evaluation." In A. M. Mitchell, G. B. Jones, and J. D. Krumboltz (eds.), *Social Learning and Career Decision Making.* Cranston, R.I.: Carroll Press, 1979.

U.S. Department of Defense. *Armed Services Vocational Aptitude Battery.* Washington, D.C.: U.S. Department of Defense, 1976.

U.S. Department of Labor. *Dictionary of Occupational Titles.* (4th ed.) Washington, D.C.: U.S. Government Printing Office, 1977.

U.S. Department of Labor. *Guide to the Use of the General Aptitude Test Battery. Section II: Norms: Occupational Aptitude Pattern Structure.* Washington, D.C.: U.S. Government Printing Office, 1979a.

U.S. Department of Labor. *Guide to the Use of the General Aptitude Test Battery. Section III: Development.* Washington, D.C.: U.S. Government Printing Office, 1979b.

U.S. Department of Labor, Bureau of Labor Statistics. *Occupational Outlook Handbook.* Washington, D.C.: U.S. Government Printing Office, 1982.

U.S. Employment Service. *General Aptitude Test Battery Technical Manual.* Washington, D.C.: U.S. Department of Labor, 1970.

U.S. Employment Service. *Dictionary of Occupational Titles.* (4th ed.) Washington, D.C.: U.S. Government Printing Office, 1977.

Utton, A. C. "Recalled Parent–Child Relations as Determinants of Vocational Choice." *Vocational Rehabilitation and Education,* 1960, *3* and *4,* 20.

Vaillant, G. E. *Adaptation to Life.* Boston: Little, Brown, 1977.

Vandergoot, D., and Engelkes, J. R. "An Application of the

Theory of Work Adjustment to Vocational Counseling." *Vocational Guidance Quarterly,* 1977, *26,* 45–53.

Vanfossen, E., Jones, D., and Spade, J. S. "Curriculum Tracking and Status Maintenance." *Sociology of Education,* 1987, *60,* 104–122.

Van Maanen, J. "People Processing: Major Strategies of Organizational Socialization and Their Consequences." In J. Paap (ed.), *New Directions in Human Resource Management.* Englewood Cliffs, N.J.: Prentice-Hall, 1978.

Van Maanen, J., and Schein, E. H. "Toward a Theory of Organizational Socialization." *Research in Organizational Behavior,* 1979, *1,* 209–264.

Vernon, P. E. "Classifying High-Grade Occupational Interests." *Journal of Abnormal and Social Psychology,* 1949, *44,* 85–96.

Vetter, L. "Career Counseling for Women." *Counseling Psychologist,* 1973, *4,* 54–67.

Viteles, M. S. *Industrial Psychology.* New York: Norton, 1932.

Vondracek, F. W., Lerner, R. M., and Schulenberg, J. E. "The Concept of Development in Vocational Theory and Intervention." *Journal of Vocational Behavior,* 1983, *23,* 179–202.

Vondracek, F. W., Lerner, R. M., and Schulenberg, J. E. *Career Development: A Life-Span Developmental Approach.* Hillsdale, N.J.: Erlbaum, 1986.

Vroom, V. H. *Work and Motivation.* New York: Wiley, 1964.

Wakefield, J. A., Jr., and Cunningham, C. H. "Relationships Between the Vocational Preference Inventory and the Edwards Personal Preference Schedule." *Journal of Vocational Behavior,* 1975, *6,* 373–377.

Walsh, W. B., Hildebrand, J. O., Ward, C. M., and Matthews, D. F. "Holland's Theory and Non-College-Degreed Working Black and White Women." *Journal of Vocational Behavior,* 1983, *22,* 182–190.

Walsh, W. B., Woods, W. J., and Ward, C. M. "Holland's Theory and Working Black and White Women." *Journal of Multicultural Counseling and Development,* 1986, *14,* 116–123.

Wanous, J. P. *Organizational Entry.* Reading, Mass.: Addison-Wesley, 1980.

Wanous, J. P., Keon, T. L., and Latack, J. C. "Expectancy

Theory and Occupational Choices: A Review and Test." *Organizational Behavior and Human Performances,* 1983, *32,* 66–86.

Ward, G. R., Cunningham, C. H., and Wakefield, J. A., Jr. "Relationships Between Holland's VPI and Catell's 16 PF." *Journal of Vocational Behavior,* 1976, *8,* 307–312.

Warnath, C. F. "Vocational Theories: Direction to Nowhere." *Personnel and Guidance Journal,* 1975, *53,* 422–428.

Warner, S. G., and Jepsen, D. A. "Differential Effects of Conceptual Level and Group Counseling Format on Adolescent Career Decision-Making Process." *Journal of Counseling Psychology,* 1979, *26,* 496–501.

Warner, W. L., Meeker, M., and Eells, K. *Social Class in America.* Chicago: Science Research Associates, 1949.

Washington Precollege Program. *Student Career Planning and Interpretation Guide, 1988–89.* Seattle: Washington Precollege Program, 1988.

Watts, A. G., Super, D. E., and Kidd, J. M. (eds.). *Career Development in Britain.* Cambridge, England: Hobson's Press, 1981.

Weingart, M. "Implementation of the F-Test, the Fukuyama Profile, in New York City, October 1985." In *Final Report of the Fifth Annual International Conference on Vocational Guidance.* Hyogo, Japan: Ashiya University, 1987.

Weinrach, S. G. (ed.). *Career Counseling: Theoretical and Practical Perspectives.* New York: McGraw-Hill, 1979a.

Weinrach, S. G. "Trait-and-Factor Counseling: Yesterday and Today." In S. G. Weinrach (ed.), *Career Counseling: Theoretical and Practical Perspectives.* New York: McGraw-Hill, 1979b.

Weinrach, S. G. "Have Hexagon Will Travel: An Interview with John Holland." *Personnel and Guidance Journal,* 1980a, *58* (6), 406–414.

Weinrach, S. G. "Discrepancy Identification: A Model for the Interpretation of the Kuder DD and Other Interest Inventories." *Vocational Guidance Quarterly,* 1980b, *29,* 42–52.

Weiss, D. J., England, M. E., Dawis, R. V., and Lofquist, L. H. "Manual for the Minnesota Satisfaction Questionnaire." *Minnesota Studies in Vocational Rehabilitation,* no. 46. Minneapolis: University of Minnesota Industrial Relations Center, 1967.

Weitz, H. "Guidance as Behavior Change." *Personnel and Guidance Journal,* 1961, *39,* 550–560.

Weller, L., and Nadler, A. "Authoritarianism and Job Preferences." *Journal of Vocational Behavior,* 1975, *6,* 9–14.

Wertheimer, L. C. "An Integrated Approach to Career Counseling Based on the Work of Tiedeman and O'Hara and Knefelkamp and Slepitza." *Character Potential: A Record of Research,* 1979, *9,* 77–82.

Westbrook, B. W. "The Construct Validation of Career Maturity Measures." In J. D. Krumboltz and D. A. Hamel (eds.), *Assessing Career Development.* Mountain View, Calif.: Mayfield, 1982.

Westbrook, B. W., and Parry-Hill, J. W., Jr. *Cognitive Vocational Maturity Inventory.* Raleigh, N.C.: Center for Occupational Education, North Carolina State University, 1973.

Wheeler, K. G. "Comparisons of Self-Efficacy and Expectancy Models of Occupational Preferences for College Males and Females." *Journal of Occupational Psychology,* 1983, *56,* 73–78.

White, B. J. "The Relationship of Self-Concept and Parental Identification in Women's Vocational Interests." *Journal of Counseling Psychology,* 1959, *6,* 202–206.

White, J. C. "Cleanliness and Successful Bank Clerical Personnel — A Brief." *Journal of Counseling Psychology,* 1963, *10,* 192.

Whitlock, G. E. "Passivity of Personality and Role Concepts in Vocational Choice." *Journal of Counseling Psychology,* 1962, *9,* 88–90.

Whitney, D. R. "Predicting from Expressed Choice. A Review." *Personnel and Guidance Journal,* 1969, *48,* 279–286.

Wiggington, J. H. "The Applicability of Holland's Typology to Clients." *Journal of Vocational Behavior,* 1983, *23,* 286–293.

Wiggins, J. D. "Holland's Theory and Retired Teachers." *Vocational Guidance Quarterly,* 1982, *30,* 236–242.

Wiggins, J. D. "Personality–Environmental Factors Related to Job Satisfaction of School Counselors." *Vocational Guidance Quarterly,* 1984, *33,* 169–177.

Wiggins, J. D. "Effective Career Exploration Programs Revisited." *Career Development Quarterly,* 1987, *35,* 297–303.

Wiggins, J. D., and Moody, A. *Compatibility Index Description.* Dover, Del.: Training Associates, Inc., 1981.

Wiggins, J. D., and Moody, A. "Identifying Effective Counselors Through Client–Supervisor Ratings and Personality–Environmental Variables." *Vocational Guidance Quarterly,* 1983, *31,* 259–269.

Wiggins, J. D., and Weslander, D. L. "Tested Personality Typologies and Marital Compatibility." *American Mental Health Counselors Association Journal,* 1979, *1* (1), 44–52.

Wilber, K. *No Boundary.* Boulder: Shambhala, 1979.

Wilber, K. "Let's Nuke These Transpersonalists: A Response to Ellis." *Journal of Counseling and Development,* 1989, *67,* 332–335.

Wiley, M. O., and Magoon, T. M. "Holland High-Point Social Types: Is Consistency Related to Persistence and Achievement?" *Journal of Vocational Behavior,* 1982, *20,* 14–21.

Williams, C. M. "Occupational Choice of Male Graduate Students as Related to Values and Personality: A Test of Holland's Theory." *Journal of Vocational Behavior,* 1972, *2,* 39–46.

Williams, W. S. "Black Economic and Cultural Development: A Prerequisite to Vocational Choice." In R. L. Jones (ed.), *Black Psychology.* New York: Harper & Row, 1972.

Williamson, E. G. *How to Counsel Students.* New York: McGraw-Hill, 1939.

Williamson, E. G. "An Historical Perspective on the Vocational Guidance Movement." *Personnel and Guidance Journal,* 1964, *42,* 854–859.

Williamson, E. G. *Vocational Counseling.* New York: McGraw-Hill, 1965.

Williamson, E. G. "Trait-and-Factor Theory and Individual Differences." In B. Stefflre and W. H. Grant (eds.), *Theories of Counseling.* New York: McGraw-Hill, 1972.

Williamson, E. G., and Hahn, M. E. *Introduction to High School Counseling.* New York: McGraw-Hill, 1940.

Willis, R. J., and Rosen, S. "Education and Self-Selection." *Journal of Political Economy,* 1979, *87,* S7–S36.

Wilson, E. H. "The Development and Potential Testing of a System for the Teaching of Decision Making." Unpublished doctoral dissertation, Graduate School of Education, Harvard University, 1971.

Wilson, S. "A New Decade: The Gifted and Career Choice." *Vocational Guidance Quarterly,* 1982, *31,* 53–59.

Winer, J. L., Wilson, D. O., and Pierce, R. A. "Using the Self-Directed Search—Form E with High School Remedial Reading Students." *Vocational Guidance Quarterly*, 1983, *32*, 130–135.

Winters, R. A., and Hansen, J. "Toward an Understanding of Work–Leisure Relationships." *Vocational Guidance Quarterly*, 1976, *24*, 228–243.

Wright, E. O., and Perrone, L. "Marxist Class Categories and Income Inequality." *American Sociological Review*, 1977, *42*, 32–55.

Wright, G. *Behavioral Decision Theory*. Newbury Park, Calif.: Sage, 1984.

Wylie, R. C. *The Self-Concept*. (Rev. ed.) Lincoln: University of Nebraska Press, 1974, 1979. (2 vols.)

Young, A. *The Reflexive Universe*. Novato, Calif.: Robert Briggs Associates, 1976.

Young, R. A. "Counseling the Unemployed: Attributional Issues." *Journal of Counseling and Development*, 1986, *64*, 374–378.

Zener, T. B., and Schnuelle, L. *An Evaluation of the Self-Directed Search*. Center for Social Organization of Schools, Report no. 124. Baltimore, Md.: Johns Hopkins University, 1972.

Zenke, K. G. "F-Test for Appraising the Ability to Choose Methodically Among Occupations—Fukuyama Profile." In *Final Report of the Fifth International Conference on Vocational Guidance*. Hyogo, Japan: Ashiya University, 1987.

Ziegler, D. J. "Distinctive Self- and Occupational Member Concepts in Different Occupational Preference Groups." *Journal of Vocational Behavior*, 1973, *3*, 53–60.

Zucker, G., and Rosenstein, C. "Taxonomies of Institutional Structure: Dual Economy Reconsidered." *American Sociological Review*, 1981, *46*, 869–884.

Zunker, V. G. *Career Counseling: Applied Concepts of Life Planning*. Pacific Grove, Calif.: Brooks/Cole, 1981.

Zytowski, D. G. "Toward a Theory of Career Development for Women." *Personnel and Guidance Journal*, 1969, *47*, 660–664.

Zytowski, D. G. "Comparison of Roe's and Holland's Occupational Classifications: Diverse Ways of Knowing." *Journal of Counseling Psychology*, 1986, *33*, 479–481.

Name Index

Subject Index

605